Economics

Theory & Practice

Fourth Edition

Also available from The Dryden Press for use with *Economics: Theory & Practice*, Fourth Edition:

Study Guide

by Patrick J. Welch and Gerry F. Welch
ISBN 0-03-055247-8

This supplement provides reviews of key concepts and additional problems that are tied specifically to those in the text.

If your bookstore does not have the *Study Guide* in stock, please ask the bookstore manager to order copies for you and your fellow classmates.

Economics
Theory & Practice

Fourth Edition

Patrick J. Welch
St. Louis University

Gerry F. Welch
St. Louis Community College at Meramec

The Dryden Press
A Harcourt Brace Jovanovich College Publisher

Fort Worth   Philadelphia   San Diego   New York   Orlando   Austin   San Antonio
Toronto   Montreal   London   Sydney   Tokyo

Acquisitions Editor: Jan Richardson
Developmental Editor: Rita West
Project Editor: Teresa Chartos
Art and Design Manager: Alan Wendt
Production Manager: Bob Lange
Permissions Editor: Cindy Lombardo
Director of Editing, Design, and Production: Jane Perkins

Text and Cover Designer: Rebecca Lemna
Copy Editor: Cheryl Wilms
Indexer: Leoni McVey
Compositor: Graphic World
Text Type: 10/12 Palatino

Library of Congress Cataloging-in-Publication Data

Welch, Patrick J.
    Economics, theory and practice / Patrick J. Welch, Gerry F. Welch.
  —4th ed.
      p.   cm.
    Includes bibliographical references and index.
    ISBN 0-03-055238-9
    1. Economics   I. Welch, Gerry F.   II. Title.
HB171.5.W3935 1992
320—dc20

Printed in the United States of America   91–9657
  23-039-98765432   CIP
Copyright © 1992, 1989, 1986, 1982 by The Dryden Press.

Requests for permission to make copies of any part of the work should be mailed to:
Permissions Department, Harcourt Brace Jovanovich, Publishers, 8th Floor, Orlando, FL, 32887.

Address orders:
The Dryden Press
Orlando, FL 32887

Address editorial correspondence:
The Dryden Press
301 Commerce Street, Suite 3700
Fort Worth, TX 76102

The Dryden Press
Harcourt Brace Jovanovich

Cover: Painting by Paul Klee, "Polyphonie," 1932. Emanuel Hoffman-Foundation, Kunstmuseum Basel and COSMOPRESS.

The Dryden Press Series in Economics

Preface

Our lives are affected daily by economic decision making. Some of these decisions are major: world leaders establish policies, often rooted in economics, that determine how peacefully we live; government programs affecting people's standards of living are initiated and cancelled; businesses choose technologies that decide the types of jobs available for a work force; and individuals make career plans that direct their lives for years into the future. There are also many other daily economic decisions that are personal to each of us and involve choices about spending money, recycling waste, working overtime, and whether to smoke.

Since economics touches everyone's life in so many different ways, a course that focuses on fundamental economic concepts and institutions is a valuable part of a person's education. *Economics: Theory & Practice*, Fourth Edition, is written for students who want such a foundation in economics. This book is designed as a primary text for a one-term introduction to economics or a survey of economics course, and offers a balanced presentation of macroeconomics and microeconomics.

Objective of the Book

The overall objective of this textbook is to introduce and survey basic economic concepts and institutions in a way that provides students with a solid *understanding* of key economic relationships and terms. This book should also give students a foundation that will enable them to use economic *thinking* in their educational pursuits, to apply economics to their own decision making, and to critically evaluate opinions, news reports, and other sources of economic information. We also hope that by using this text students will enjoy economics enough to become interested in reading further or pursuing other aspects of the field.

Economic Concepts

In introducing and surveying economic concepts, *Economics: Theory & Practice*, Fourth Edition, includes a broad and selective overview of what economists label the "principles of macroeconomics and microeconomics." In covering these areas, the text presents basic concepts including (but not limited to) supply and demand, spending and business fluctuations, money creation, alternative viewpoints on macroeconomic policy, cost-benefit analysis, the behavior of firms in different market settings, and comparative advantage. These concepts are explained and applied in a manner that aims at providing a clear understanding of a number of key relationships, rather than an in-depth analysis of the details of a few selected relationships. Although a detailed explanation of theoretical tools is essential for the student who continues in economics, the same may not be true for the nonmajor whose potential application of economics will rest on a simpler conceptual and institutional foundation. We also understand that instructors of introductory economics courses typically establish that foundation by developing a basic understanding of a broad range of concepts.

Economic Institutions

In addition to surveying basic economic concepts, the text introduces key institutions with which students should be familiar if they are to understand the operation of the economy. These institutions range from the Federal Reserve System and the European Economic Community to the method for gathering unemployment statistics, antitrust laws, foreign exchange markets, and others. Institutional considerations are important in an introductory economics text for two reasons. First, institutions link the real world to the conceptual world of basic economic principles and provide a vehicle through which students can relate to those principles. Second, institutional considerations have economic, social, political, and other dimensions that allow economics to be viewed in a broader perspective, thereby permitting students who do not major in economics to better tie economics to other areas of study.

Features of the Book

There are several important features of *Economics: Theory & Practice* that contribute to the successful teaching and learning of introductory economics. These include the balance and flexibility of the text; the range of topics covered; the applications, critical thinking cases, learning aids, and organizers in each chapter; and the ancillary materials for both the instructor and the student. Underlying these features is a text that has been cited by students through three editions as highly readable, understandable, and enjoyable.

Balance and Flexibility of the Text

Economics: Theory & Practice offers a balanced presentation of macroeconomic and microeconomic topics. The book is divided into four parts: a three-chapter introduction covering basic concepts and definitions, economic systems, and supply and demand; six chapters on macroeconomics; six chapters on microeconomics; and a fourth part containing two chapters on international economics. Thus, there is a roughly equal distribution between macroeconomic and microeconomic coverage.

Economics: Theory & Practice is also written and arranged in a way that permits flexibility. The text is easily adapted to an instructor's preference for the sequencing of topics, the breadth of coverage, and the inclusion of outside assignments.

First, topics are arranged so that the book can be used in a *macroeconomic-microeconomic* sequence, by going directly through the text, or in a *microeconomic-macroeconomic* sequence, by reversing the order of Parts Two and Three. Because basic tools and definitions, such as opportunity cost, graphing, and supply and demand, are presented in the introductory part of the text, the macroeconomic and microeconomic parts of the text are independent of each other. Since some instructors prefer a *microeconomic-macroeconomic* sequence, we have been extremely careful in developing this text to ensure that Parts Two and Three can stand alone *after* the introductory material has been covered. An alternative course outline for a micro-economic–macroeconomic sequence is presented on page xv, following this preface.

Second, a course could be shortened by eliminating whole chapters, such as Chapter 14, "Government and the Markets," or Chapters 16 and 17 on international trade and international finance. Coverage could also be reduced by eliminating various chapter subtopics. For example, the historical development of the U.S. economy could be eliminated from Chapter 2, the calculation of the output multiplier from Chapter 5, or unionism and collective bargaining from Chapter 15.

Third, those wishing to add to the content of a course could do so by including the various chapter appendixes. These include the appendix to Chapter 5 on the determination of aggregate equilibrium and to Chapter 13 on profit-maximizing behavior. A course could also be expanded by assigning the discussion questions or the critical thinking case at the end of each chapter, or the computational exercises from the text's *Study Guide*. The annotated suggested readings at the end of each chapter provide another method for expanding a course. These readings range from Adam Smith to current economists, and from science fiction on scarcity to a short story on inflation in Germany by Thomas Mann.

Range of Topics

A broad and up-to-date range of topics is presented throughout the book. For example, in addition to the traditional core topics, Part Two (on the macroeconomy) includes material on classical economics and rational expectations, productivity, the natural rate of unemployment, the relationship between the federal budget and monetary policy, changes in the financial depository institutions system, and the savings and loan crisis. On the microeconomic side, in addition to the traditional basic subject matter, are such topics as cost-benefit analysis, public choice, externalities, mergers and acquisitions, production and technological change, and antitrust, regulation, and deregulation.

Applications and Critical Thinking Cases

The range of the text is further broadened by the applications in each chapter that provide additional and in-depth real-world examples, background information, and opinions concerning topics introduced in the chapter, or highlight some policy problems and issues for students to consider. Many applications are excerpted from nontraditional sources of economic literature, such as *American Demographics*, *The Futurist*, *Mother Jones*, and *The Atlantic*. Others are from more conventional sources, such as *The Wall Street Journal*, *The New York Times*, the *Monthly Labor Review*, *The Economist*, and the Federal Reserve Bank of New York. Topics covered in applications include the demand for vanity license plates, coping with inflation, Fed watching, costs created by uninsured motorists, the disappearance of phonograph records, leading antitrust decisions, and the external debt crisis.

Similar to the applications are the critical thinking cases at the end of each chapter. Each case focuses on a real-world problem or issue and includes questions designed to help students develop critical thinking skills. The critical thinking cases range from the containment of medical costs to the sale of human organs, illegal drug markets, the budget deficit, the environmental degradation of the Aral Sea, price fixing of college tuition, and the fear of Fortress Europe.

Chapter Learning Aids and Organizers

There are several learning aids and organizers in every chapter. Each chapter begins with a listing of *chapter objectives* that identifies the major topics that will be covered. Important terms and concepts are highlighted in the text and defined in the margins. This *running glossary* is an excellent aid for student review. An alphabetical *cumulative glossary* follows at the back of the text. Each figure and table includes a full *legend* that describes or adds to the information presented. Every chapter has a *"Test Your Understanding"* exercise so students can check their progress. Finally, each chapter ends with a *summary*, a list of that chapter's *key terms and concepts*, *discussion questions*, *review questions*, a *critical thinking case*, and *annotated suggested readings*.

Ancillary Materials

Three separate ancillary volumes supplement *Economics: Theory & Practice*: a *Study Guide*, *Test Bank*, and *Instructor's Manual*. The student *Study Guide* includes, for each chapter, a listing of chapter objectives and terms from the text, a study organizer identifying important concepts, a chapter review self-test, computational exercises, and practice examination questions.

Answers to the exercises and sample questions are included at the end of the *Study Guide*.

The *Test Bank* contains more than 2,400 multiple-choice, true/false, and short essay questions, many requiring students to make computations. All questions for this edition are new or have been revised or updated. A *Computerized Test Bank* containing all test questions from the printed test bank is available for IBM and Apple personal computers.

An *Instructor's Manual* provides an overview for teaching a one-term introductory course, which is particularly useful for the new instructor. It also includes a sample syllabus that provides information about timing of topic coverage, assignments, examinations, and such. The *Instructor's Manual* also includes, for each chapter, a restatement of chapter objectives, teaching suggestions, and recommendations on incorporating the discussion and review questions, critical thinking cases, and suggested readings into a course. *Transparency Masters* for many of the illustrations in the text, and other illustrations that supplement those in the text, are also included with the *Instructor's Manual*. A set of full-color *transparency acetates* contains graphs, diagrams, and tables that supplement text content.

New to the Fourth Edition

The fourth edition of *Economics: Theory & Practice* retains the essential features of the earlier editions, such as the balance between macroeconomics and microeconomics and the flexibility of topic coverage, and is updated in terms of data, applications, and state-of-the-art concepts and topics.

All data in figures, tables, and the text reflect the latest available at the time of publication. Applications have been updated to introduce recent real-world problems and developments and to explore important policy issues. Exercises that test student understanding of concepts and computations have also been updated.

Most changes in this edition result from the inclusion of new terms, concepts, and topics in order to keep the text current, and from improved methods of presentation that have been developed because of our own experiences teaching the one-term course over the years. Highlights of these changes include the following:

- Coverage of new topics: changing economic systems, particularly in Eastern Europe (Chapter 2); the effect of GNP on the environment (Chapter 4); the effects of changes in tax policy on automatic stabilization (Chapter 6); problems with the deregulation of financial depository institutions and the savings and loan crisis (Chapter 7); the costs of economic growth (Chapter 9); leveraged buyouts and junk bonds (Chapter 14); and the European Economic Community (Chapter 17).

- Introduction of new terms and concepts: Glasnost and Perestroika (Chapter 2); the natural rate of unemployment (Chapter 4); money market deposit accounts and the Resolution Trust Corporation (Chapter 7); infrastructure (Chapter 9); price searchers (Chapter 13); joint ventures, leveraged buyouts, and junk bonds (Chapter 14); and the European Community (Chapter 16).

- Revised treatment of topics that appeared in the third edition: updated examples of supply and demand (Chapter 3); structural unemployment, the composition of jobs, and the natural rate of unemployment (Chapter 4); Phillips curve analysis (Chapter 9); deregulation and the performance of regulation (Chapter 14); the pattern of U.S. international trade (Chapter 16); and the external debt crisis in less-developed countries (Chapter 17).

- "Test Your Understanding" exercises in the text of each chapter, including exercises on changes in supply and demand (Chapter 3); calculating price indexes and GNP (Chapter 4); determining a small business's demand for labor (Chapter 15); and the effects of changes in the supply and demand of currencies on foreign exchange rates (Chapter 17).

- A critical thinking case at the end of each chapter. Each case highlights certain critical thinking skills and economic concepts and applies those skills and concepts to a specific topic through a series of questions. Critical thinking cases involve topics such as using statistics in decision making (Chapter 4); evaluating the federal budget deficit (Chapter 6); closing a manufacturing plant (Chapter 12); exploring the anomaly of competition causing higher prices (Chapter 13); and intervening in U.S. foreign exchange markets (Chapter 17).

- Expanded number of end-of-chapter discussion and review questions; over 50 applications, 60 percent of which are new; and updated end-of-chapter annotated readings.

Acknowledgments

There are many people who have contributed to this project and to whom we owe our gratitude. We have been fortunate to receive valuable, constructive reviewers' comments in earlier editions from Frederick Arnold, *Madison Area Technical College*; William Askwig, *University of Southern Colorado*; Mark Berger, *University of Kentucky*; Ronald Brandolini, *Valencia Community College*; G.E. Breger, *University of South Carolina*; William Brown, *California State University, Northridge*; Lee Button, *Fox Valley Technical Institute*; Gerald Carlino, *The Federal Reserve Bank of Philadelphia*; Kristin Carrico, *Umpqua Community College*; Ronald Dulaney, *University of Montana*; Donald Fell, *Ohio State University*; Mary Ann Ferber, *University of Illinois*; Arthur Friedberg, *Mohawk Valley Community College*; David Green, *Tidewater Community College*; Roberta Greene, *Central Piedmont Community College*;

Chris Greveson, *DeVry Technical Institute*; Laura Johnson, *University of Akron*; Sol Kaufler, *Los Angeles Pierce College*; Stephen King, *Midstate Technical Institute*; John Lafky, *California State University, Fullerton*; Charles Lave, *University of California, Irvine*; Carole Lundeberg, *Hartford State Technical College*; Beth Matta, *New Mexico State University*; Bernard McCarney, *Illinois State University*; Kenneth McKnight, *Spokane Community College*; Phillip Moery, *Shephard College*; Terry Riddle, *Central Virginia Community College*; Roger Riefler, *University of Nebraska*; Hushang Shahidi, *Wright State University*; William Small, *Spokane Community College*; and Sidney Wilson, *Rockland Community College*.

The fourth edition has benefited from the reviews of Joe Atallah, *DeVry Institute of Technology, Los Angeles*; Gordon Blake, *Kearney State College*; James Clark, *Wichita State University*; Gail Hawks, *Miami-Dade Community College*; Hong Nguyen, *University of Scranton*; Roger Riefler, *University of Nebraska*; Louis Sage, *University of Akron*; Ted Scheinman, *Mt. Hood Community College*, and Richard Watson, *University of California, Santa Barbara*.

In addition, the *Test Bank* was reviewed by Knowles Parker, *Wake Technical Community College*, and David Cooper, *DeVry Institute of Technology, Los Angeles*.

There are also many other people to thank for their input into and support of this textbook. Gerry's Meramec colleagues, especially Dan Cobb, Claude Cox, and George Wasson, have provided countless excellent suggestions for changing examples or developing topics. Many of our students at St. Louis University and Meramec have given helpful recommendations for text, study guide, and application material. Bill Kuba has our thanks for some photo suggestions. We have also received enthusiastic encouragement from Russ Boersma, the Dryden/HBJ sales representative in the St. Louis area, for each edition of this text. We are grateful for Russ's advice, support, and good humor.

During the development of this edition, we have benefited from the talent and support of Jan Richardson, the acquisitions editor at the Dryden Press, Rita West, the extremely pleasant and well-organized developmental editor with whom we worked, Teresa Chartos, project editor, Alan Wendt and Jane Perkins in design and production, and Cindy Lombardo and Doris Milligan, who managed to track down permissions for applications and photos. Our thanks also go to Cheryl Wilms, copy editor, and to Patricia Feldmann who typed our ancillaries.

It has been a decade since the first edition of *Economics: Theory & Practice* was published. In this time we have developed many professional and personal relationships with the staff at The Dryden Press. Because The Dryden Press is relocating from Hinsdale, Illinois, to Fort Worth, Texas, we will no longer be working with some people for whom we have great affection and respect. While we look forward to new relationships with the staff at Fort Worth, it is with fondness that we say good-by to Alan Wendt, Rita West, Jane Perkins, Cindy Lombardo, Doris Milligan, and Jan Richardson. To each of you go our gratitude and best wishes.

Pat Welch
Gerry Welch

November 1991

Alternative Course Outline

Economics: Theory & Practice is written to permit an instructor to teach in either a macro-micro sequence of topics or a micro-macro sequence. Since Parts Two and Three are independent of each other, either can follow Part One, the introductory section. Instructors who choose the micro-macro sequence should consider the following.

Contents in Brief

Contents

Part One

Introduction to Economics

Chapter One

Introduction to Economics

The debate over whether to harvest more of the forests of the Northwest for lumber or to protect the spotted owl illustrates the basic lesson of the study of economics: choices are imposed on individuals, businesses, and society because of the scarcity of resources.

Source: © 1990 Brian Lanker/Lanker Inc.

Chapter Objectives

1. To define economics and introduce the scarcity problem, which underlies economics.

2. To understand the relationship between scarcity and choice.

3. To define opportunity cost.

4. To explore how efficiency and equity are related to the problem of scarcity.

5. To identify the four factors of production and the income return to each type of factor.

6. To differentiate between economic theory and economic policy.

7. To introduce the tools economists use to express theories and policies.

8. To show through a production possibilities example how the tools of economics can be used to illustrate and explain the basic problem of scarcity.

9. To differentiate between macroeconomics and microeconomics.

10. To explain (in an appendix) how to construct a graph and interpret the illustrated relationship.

What Is Economics?

Economics

The study of how scarce, or limited, resources are used to satisfy unlimited material wants and needs.

Economics is the study of how scarce, or limited, resources are used to satisfy people's unlimited material wants and needs. Broadly, economics is concerned with material things and how people make decisions about these things. It is concerned with having and not having, with shoes, food, cars, hamburgers, bridges, bombers, medical services, entertainment, and the like. Happiness, sorrow, beauty, virtue, and sin are not direct concerns of the discipline of economics (although economic principles have been used by some to explain them). Rather, the focus is on the standard of living of individuals and societies as defined in terms of material goods and services.

The field of economics is extensive and it is always growing. Economists are willing to examine almost anything that affects the material aspects of life. Most often economists voice concern over unemployment, inflation, interest rates, labor problems, poverty, government regulation, energy, the environment, and international trade. But this just scratches the surface. The list of what interests economists goes on and on. This text will introduce you to some of the major areas of study in economics, some key institutions and relationships, and some controversial policy issues. A quick glance through the table of contents will give you an idea of the breadth of topics included in the discipline of economics.

Why study economics? What can it do for you? A course in economics provides information that enables you to think smarter. On one level, economics deals with the concepts that explain the operation of the economy as a whole. Understanding these overall relationships allows you to appreciate why the budgetary decisions of Congress are so closely watched, to participate in debates over the impact of the public debt, to interpret news reports concerning the value of the dollar in foreign exchange markets and the nation's trade balance, and, in general, to better evaluate national and international policy decisions. On another level, economics explores the ways in which people, businesses, and societies in general use cost–benefit analysis to make decisions, and the environments in which those decisions are made. As a consequence of this understanding you should be better able to evaluate your own decisions about how you spend your money and your time, as well as the decisions that businesses make regarding pricing, product differentiation, wage payments, and related matters. In addition to the benefits of making you a better informed citizen and decision maker, understanding economics is important for success in many career areas: communications, journalism, law, education, business, health, and others.

Economics and Scarcity

Scarcity
The result of not enough goods and services to satisfy the wants and needs of all individuals, households, and societies.

Scarcity is the framework within which economics exists. Put another way, without scarcity there would be no reason to study economics. This scarcity framework means that there are not enough, nor can there ever be enough, goods and services to satisfy the wants and needs of all individuals, families, and societies. An examination of your own situation makes this obvious. Do you own the car you would most enjoy? Do you have enough financial resources for the tapes, dates, concerts, textbooks, and boots you want? Does your family ever remark that the recent automobile repair bill means hamburgers, beans, and franks this month? Societies face the same scarcity problem on a larger scale. Money spent for roads is money not available for hospitals. Resources devoted to defense are not available for schools or welfare. Gasoline and oil used now for automobiles will not be available in the future.

The root of the scarcity problem lies in the definition of economics—that people have limited resources to satisfy their unlimited material wants and needs. Material wants are satisfied by the items that people would like to have, such as compact disc players, skateboards, public parks, or a fifth pair of shoes; material needs are satisfied by the goods and services required by people, such as food, medical care, and shelter. Whether a good or service is wanted or needed is sometimes hard to determine, and what is more, we often confuse our own wants and needs. You may think you need a compact disc player when, in fact, you may only have an intense want for it; the officials of a mid-size city might believe that the city needs a convention center when, in fact, the officials just want one.

For either wants or needs, however, people appear to have the psychological ability to continually require more goods and services and to become dissatisfied with what they possess. When this drive for more is considered for all members of society, wants and needs become so great in number that they can be viewed as virtually unlimited. For example, you could devote one class period to listing everything everyone in the class desired both for themselves and for society in general. By the next class period, and in all later periods, the list would increase as students would add goods and services originally forgotten or introduced to them throughout the semester. The list would never be completed! One might recall that ten years ago the average American did not "need" microwave food, a personal computer, sunscreen, a minivan, the services of a fitness center, premium ice cream, antilock brakes, or public libraries with computerized card catalogues.

People's unlimited material wants and needs are satisfied by using the limited resources available to produce goods and services. These resources include all of the people, materials, machinery, and other items that contribute to the production of goods and services. For example, to create fast, delivered pizzas, a franchise needs cheese and other food products, cooks, order takers, electricity, water, ovens, refrigerators, trucks, cars, managers, boxes, engineers, buildings, and so on. Every resource available for production is limited in amount; there is not an infinite supply of labor, energy, or any other resource.

The problem of limited resources also occurs for individuals. People never seem to control enough resources to earn the money required to purchase everything they want and need, and never have enough time to accomplish everything they want to do. Limited resources keep many students from taking a trip over spring break, upgrading an audio system, or buying a new car instead of repairing an old one. Many students would also like to produce a high grade point average, work at a part-time job, and enjoy an active social life, but cannot achieve all of these due to time constraints.

Scarcity and Choice

Scarcity forces individuals and societies to make choices or decisions. In fact, an alternative definition of economics could be that it is the study of decision making in a world of scarcity. Since it is impossible to satisfy all wants and needs, decisions must be made about which wants and needs to fulfill and how to use limited resources. A student, for example, who is pressed by the demands of a job and the need to study for an examination must make a decision about how to use his or her limited available time.

Tradeoff

Giving up one thing for something else.

The choices imposed by scarcity involve **tradeoffs** and necessitate an awareness of the consequences of those tradeoffs. Suppose that a student has $45 (a limited sum) and has narrowed the uses of that money to two alternatives—a textbook or a date. The date becomes the tradeoff for the textbook, and the textbook is the tradeoff for the date. In choosing between these alternatives, the student will evaluate the consequences of each alternative. The textbook purchase might result in a good grade in a course (as well as an increase in the knowledge of a subject), and the date might mean an evening of fun.

In making a choice, the decision maker's value judgment plays an important role. A **value judgment** is the relative importance that a person assigns to various actions or alternatives. If the student faced with the choice of a date or a book decides that a good grade is more important than a good time, the book will be purchased with the $45; if a good time is valued more than a good grade, the student will choose the date.

If someone in your family were to win $10,000 in a lottery, the same problem of choice would arise. The $10,000 is a limited sum; it buys only so much. Your family would have to consider alternatives, or tradeoffs, for spending the $10,000. Ultimately, the decision as to how the money would be used would be based on the value judgments of some members of the family.

Society faces the same scarcity-related tradeoff problem. In some communities, the public school conditions, both physical and intellectual, are appalling. This may be a reflection of the value judgments of the community. On a ballot, individuals face the choice of increasing or not increasing tax dollars for their schools. The tradeoff is whether to use household income for schools or for additional shoes, food, furniture, or other preferences of the family. On the national level, if a society chooses to go to war, it must give up some consumer goods (like jeans and convertibles) for defense goods (like uniforms and missiles). If society chooses to increase its population, there will be less space and fewer resources for each person. Each of these tradeoffs is necessary because we cannot have everything. And each tradeoff reflects the value judgments of the decision makers.

Opportunity Cost   In making decisions, individuals and societies evaluate both the benefits and the costs of their choices. Because of scarcity, every decision to acquire a particular good or service or to spend time or money in a certain way has a cost attached to it. Economists call these costs **opportunity costs.** An opportunity cost is the cost of a purchase or a decision measured in terms of a forgone alternative; that is, what was given up to attain the purchase or carry out the decision. Once time or money is devoted to one thing, the opportunity to use that time or money for other things is lost. There is nothing that anyone can purchase or do that does not have an opportunity cost attached to it. If a student spends $45 to acquire a textbook, the opportunity cost of that text is what was given up to obtain it—perhaps a date. What was the opportunity cost of the last purchase you made? What is the cost of cutting a class in this course?

The opportunity cost to parents of choosing to acquire more shoes or food, rather than supporting an increase in a school tax, might be an inferior

Value judgment
The relative importance one assigns to various actions or alternatives.

Opportunity cost
The cost of a purchase or decision measured in terms of a forgone alternative; what was given up to attain a purchase or carry out a decision.

education for their children. The opportunity cost of going to war would include the jeans and convertibles that are not produced in order to obtain more uniforms and missiles. Because of scarcity, individuals, families, and societies must make tradeoffs — choices based on both the benefits and the opportunity costs of their decisions.

Application 1.1, "Americans Say They Will Sacrifice to Save the Environment," deals with some choices and costs facing Americans with regard to the environment. With problems such as toxic waste, pesticide run-off, scarce landfills, air and water pollution, and the greenhouse effect becoming more apparent, the question of how much money and time people are willing to give for a healthier environment becomes increasingly important.

Efficiency and Equity

In dealing with the basic problem of scarcity — not enough goods and services to satisfy everyone's wants and needs — there are two important concepts to consider: efficiency, which is concerned with how effectively limited resources are used in producing goods and services, and equity, which involves the distribution of those goods and services among the members of a society.

Efficiency is concerned with producing the largest attainable output of a desired quality from a given set of resources or, put another way, with using resources to their fullest. **Efficiency** occurs when goods and services are produced at the lowest possible cost. If all goods and services were produced efficiently, society would experience the greatest possible lessening of the scarcity problem. Producing efficiently does not eliminate scarcity, but it does allow for the production of the maximum amount of goods and services to satisfy unlimited material wants and needs. This is an important consideration in a world of scarcity, and is generally regarded as a major economic goal.

Efficiency

Producing the largest attainable output of a desired quality with a given set of resources; producing at the lowest possible cost.

When is a student efficient? Is the student who studies 70 hours a week more efficient than the student who studies just 40 hours? If a student's goal is to learn enough of a course to earn a high grade, then the student is efficient when this is accomplished in the least amount of time possible. This could result from effective notetaking, good study habits, comprehensive reading skills, and the like. Students who study efficiently have more time for other activities or get the most from their limited resource of time, just as a society gets the most from its limited resources when effective techniques of production allow those resources to be used to the fullest. Inefficient students waste their time, and an inefficient use of a society's limited resources wastes those resources.

Equity

Justice or fairness in the distribution of goods and services.

In a world of scarcity, where there are not enough goods and services to satisfy everyone's wants and needs, the issue of what is a fair, just, or equitable distribution of goods and services is important. **Equity**, or justice and fairness, raises two basic questions: should a fair distribution of goods

Application 1.1

Americans Say They Will Sacrifice to Save the Environment

There is every indication that the decade of the nineties will focus on environmental concerns. A *Wall Street Journal*/NBC News poll taken shortly before Earth Day 1990 found that Americans are increasingly willing to make substantial tradeoffs in order to protect the environment. Pollsters conducting the study said, "Every indicator in this survey suggests that voters care about the environment, that they are personally making efforts to protect the environment and that they are willing to change their behavior and purchasing habits in order to ensure that we have a cleaner world."[a]

The accompanying table lists some of the opportunity costs people in this survey indicated that they were willing to absorb in order to protect the environment. Most of the respondents were willing to separate their garbage and recycle, give up foam food containers, keep the emissions levels from autos down, and ban disposable diapers. There was

a slightly less enthusiastic response to requiring the use of public transportation one day a week, limiting the number of large cars, and requiring cleaner, but more expensive, gasoline.

Where the opportunity cost of a cleaner environment meant the loss of jobs, Americans had a different opinion. Most of the survey respondents thought that this cost was too high. Even though 76 percent of those sampled indicated that environmental concerns have altered the products they buy and that they conserve energy, and two-thirds thought that the environment is in worse shape now than it was 20 years ago, job loss was not an acceptable cost for protecting the environment.

[a]See source below, page 1.
Source: Barbara Rosewicz, "Americans Are Willing to Sacrifice to Reduce Pollution, They Say," *The Wall Street Journal*, April 20, 1990, pp. A1, A12.

What Americans Will Do—And Won't—For the Environment

	Favor	Oppose		Favor	Oppose
Require people to separate garbage and solid waste for recycling	93%	6%	In metropolitan areas, require people who drive to work to take public transportation one day a week	57%	41%
Ban foam containers used by fast-food chains and other packaging that adds to the solid waste problem	84%	14%	Enforce stricter air quality regulations increasing utility bills $10.00 per month	57%	40%
Require testing and repairs of your car each year for air pollution emissions	80%	19%	Limit the number of large cars that could be produced	51%	44%
Ban disposable diapers reducing the amount of solid waste in landfills	74%	23%	A 20-cent per gallon increase in the price of gasoline for cleaner fuels	48%	50%
Require pollution control equipment that would add $600 to the cost of a new car	68%	28%	Close pollution-producing factories, resulting in loss of jobs	33%	59%

and services be an economic goal for a society, and if it is, how is a fair distribution defined and achieved?

The concept of what constitutes an equitable distribution of goods and services is controversial because it is based on people's value judgments. To some people, equity occurs when goods and services are divided equally: every person receives as much as every other person. To others, the distribution of goods and services should be made according to people's needs: for example, people who are ill or have large families should receive the goods and services they need. And to some, equity in the distribution of goods and services results when people are rewarded according to what they contribute to production: those who contribute more or better re-sources should receive more. This last view—that what a person receives should depend upon what that person contributes to producing goods and services—is the philosophical basis of a market system. Market and other systems will be discussed in the next chapter.

The issue of how to define and achieve equity is not easily resolved since there are so many diverse viewpoints. In the United States, for example, there is a continuing political debate over whether the government should aid those who are in need but not working, or whether there should be a work requirement attached to this aid.

Factors of Production

**Resources
(factors of production)**
Persons and things used to produce goods and services; limited in amount; categorized as land, labor, capital, and entrepreneurship.

Labor
All physical and mental human effort used to produce goods and services.

Capital
All made-made items, such as machinery and equipment, used in the production of goods and services.

Land
All productive inputs that originate in nature, such as coal and fertile soil.

Entrepreneurship
The function of organizing resources for production and taking the risk of success or failure in a productive enterprise.

Thousands upon thousands of different types of **resources,** or **factors of production,** are used to produce goods and services. To bring order and manageability to any discussion about these resources, economists have found it helpful to classify them into four groups: labor, capital, land, and entrepreneurship.

Labor includes all human effort, both physical and mental, going into the production of goods and services. It encompasses the efforts of everyone from physicians to drill press operators to lifeguards—all who work to produce goods and services.

Capital includes warehouses, machinery and equipment, computers, paper clips, and all other goods that are used in the production of other goods and services and that are not used for final consumption.

Land includes all inputs into production that originate in nature and are not man-made—for example, oil, iron ore, and fertile soil.

Any resource could be classified into one of these three groups. To say that something is direct human effort, is man-made, or originates in nature covers all possibilities. Yet economists speak of the four, not three, factors of production. The final factor of production, **entrepreneurship,** is the perfor-mance of a number of critical tasks that must be carried out in all productive processes. Without the performance of these tasks, no economic activity would occur. First, entrepreneurship involves the organization, or the bringing together, of labor, land, and capital to produce a good or service.

Figure 1.1   Relationship between Resources and Material Wants and Needs

Producers transform factors of production into goods and services to satisfy society's material wants and needs.

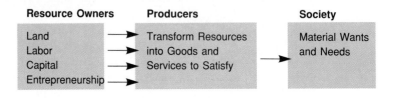

A small business owner may do this alone, while large corporations hire managers and engineers to perform this function. Second, entrepreneurship involves bearing risk. If a business is successful, someone makes a profit; if it is a failure or does poorly, someone takes a loss. In a small business, the risk taker is the proprietor; in a large corporation, risk is taken by the stockholders. The proprietor or stockholder receives the residual, or what is left over, after all contractual obligations have been met. Entrepreneurship, in essence, is the function of organizing and risk taking.

The relationship between productive resources and society's material wants and needs is summarized in Figure 1.1.

Factors and Income

No resource will be contributed to the production of a good or service unless the owner of the resource expects some personal gain from the effort. The gain may take the form of simple personal satisfaction, or the feeling of belonging to a group such as a family, sorority, or lodge. But most often, the personal gain takes the form of money income. Although money is money, and $100 received by a worker is no different from $100 received by the owner of a machine, it is helpful to give different names to the income received by the different types of resources. Thus, we have

Wages
Income return to labor.

Interest
Income return to owners of capital.

Rent
Income return to owners of land resources.

Profit
Income return to those performing the entrepreneurial function.

- **wages,** the income received by the suppliers of labor;

- **interest,** the income received by owners of capital;

- **rent,** the income received by owners of land resources; and

- **profit,** the income received by those who carry out the entrepreneurial function.

It might appear trivial to give a separate name to the income received by each of the different groups of resources. Yet, the distinction can be significant. For example, various legislative and public policy initiatives are

Table 1.1   Availabilities of Selected Resources in the U.S. Economy

While there is a large number of resources in the U.S. economy, there are not enough to satisfy all material wants and needs.

Resource	Amount in 1988
Total civilian labor force	123 million people
Total farm land	995 million acres
Petroleum pipelines	168 thousand miles
Commercial buildings	4.2 million buildings
Personal computers in use	45 million computers

Source: U.S. Bureau of the Census, *Statistical Abstract of the United States: 1990*, 110th ed. (Washington, D.C.: U.S. Government Printing Office, 1990), pp. 378, 617, 638, 729, 759. The commercial building figure is for 1986.

aimed at particular income groups. This occurs, for example, with the Social Security program. Payments into this program come from wages and the income or profit earned by the individual entrepreneur. Rent, interest, and corporate profit are incomes that do not fall within the jurisdiction of the Social Security system. Thus, under this program certain income groups are affected, and others are not. The classification of people into different earning groups is also important for social reasons. As the economist Robert Heilbroner put it, "It is not just Labor on the one hand and Land or Capital on the other; it is the Bronx on the one hand and Park Avenue on the other."[1] In addition, Marxian theory, which is the most persistent and powerful critique of capitalism, is based on the premise that there is a conflict between wage and profit earners that is inherent in, and ultimately fatal to, capitalistic systems.

Scarce Resources

As previously noted, part of the economic problem is that resources, or factors of production, are scarce, or limited. How scarce are resources? A look at Table 1.1 suggests that there is an abundance of people and things with which to produce goods and services. In the U.S. economy alone, there are over one hundred and twenty million people working or looking for work, millions of commercial buildings, almost a billion acres of farm land, and tens of thousands of miles of petroleum pipelines. The list of available resources goes on and on. Yet, we say resources are scarce. The problem is that while large numbers of resources may be available in an *absolute* sense, they are still

[1] R. L. Heilbroner, *The Limits of American Capitalism,* Harper Torchbook ed. (New York: Harper and Row, 1967), p. 71.

limited. Furthermore, resources are scarce compared to the goods and services they would have to produce in order to satisfy our unlimited material wants and needs. That is, they are scarce *relative* to the wants and needs their use attempts to satisfy. Even if there were no destruction of oil facilities as happened in Kuwait during the war with Iraq, no crop-destroying floods or droughts, and no production-stopping strikes, people's wants would continue to outrun the economy's ability to satisfy them.

If we cannot solve the scarcity problem, can we at least ease it? Over the last few decades, there has been debate over whether the scarcity problem has become better or worse. On the positive side, we seem to have made progress on some goals: life expectancies have increased because of the availability of improved medical techniques; technological changes in transportation allow us to travel rapidly from one place to another; fashionable clothing is available to buyers of all income levels; and we can prepare food faster than ever before. In addition, the amount of material items owned by the average person has increased.

But there is evidence to suggest that, in some respects, the scarcity problem has worsened. At one time economics students learned about gifts of nature, or free goods, such as air and water, available for everyone's use at no cost. Since then we have discovered that although air and water are free, clean air and water are not free. The opportunity cost of freely using these resources has been a general decline in air and water quality and specific problems such as acid rain, a slow deterioration of our forests, and destruction of the ozone layer. Thus, while we have come a long way in satisfying people's desires for material goods and services, we have not broken free from the specter of scarcity. Indeed, some people argue that we are more acutely aware of the limits of our productive capability than ever before.

Economic Theory and Policy

Since scarcity keeps people from having all that they want, households, businesses, and governments are forced to make millions of choices as they conduct their economic activities in an effort to satisfy their wants and needs. In order to make intelligent choices that will maximize our satisfaction, we need to know about production and how to get the most from our resources; about employment and how to put all available resources to work; about consumer behavior; about a money system; about government in the market; and so on. In short, we need to bring order to the complexity in which the decisions are made and to gain a clear concept of some of the basic relationships in the economy. This is the task of economic theory.

In any economic situation there are several different courses of action that could be followed, each leading to a different result. For example, a city budget could be analyzed and the decision reached to build hospitals rather than prisons, or parking lots instead of playgrounds. When a decision maker follows a specific course of action, he or she is said to be following a policy. Thus, when people speak of different policies for dealing with rising prices or unemployment, they are referring to different ways of dealing with these problems. Ideally, theories and policies are related. Before becoming committed to a particular course of action, a person should make an effort to order and understand the basic relationships with which he or she is dealing.

Economic Theory

Economic theory

A formal explanation of the relationship between economic variables.

An **economic theory** is a formal explanation of the relationship between economic conditions, or variables.[2] Very simply, a theory gives a reason why something happens, or offers a cause-and-effect interpretation for a set of events. There are economic theories to explain unemployment, inflation, price increases in the hog market, wage rates paid to teenagers, urban decay, and almost any other economic condition. For example, one simple economic theory deals with the relationship between the price of an item, say coffee, and the quantity of that item demanded by a consumer. According to this theory, if other circumstances do not change (for example, if there is no newly published health report extolling the virtues of coffee drinking or no shift in people's taste toward tea), as the price rises, consumers will decrease the amount of coffee they demand. This theory then offers one explanation for a drop in coffee sales.

The economist defends economic theories by showing that the relationships under consideration are mathematically or logically valid, or by using statistics to show that the real world behaves as the theories say it should. The federal government and private sources provide valuable information and extensive data on many facets of economic life, and the computer has made possible speedier and more sophisticated testing of ideas. As a result, **econometrics,** which is the use of statistical techniques to describe the relationships between economic variables, has become an important part of economic analysis.

Econometrics

The use of statistical techniques to describe the relationships between economic variables.

In economics, as in the other social sciences, theories are much more open to dispute than they are in the natural sciences. One reason for this is that the variables in the social sciences are not identical in each instance. In chemistry, for example, one learns that two molecules of hydrogen and one of oxygen form H_2O, or water. This is always true because molecules of hydrogen and oxygen are all the same. In applying an economic theory to coffee consumption, however, the economist must consider that buyers of coffee have different tastes, incomes, and so on. By controlling for these differences in tastes and such, the economist can statistically and mathe-

---

[2] A dictionary definition of a theory is: "Systematically organized knowledge applicable in a relatively wide variety of circumstances; especially, a system of assumptions, accepted principles, and rules of procedure devised to analyze, predict, or otherwise explain the nature or behavior of a specified set of phenomena." From *The American Heritage Dictionary of the English Language,* ed. William Morris (New York: American Heritage Publishing Co., Inc., 1973), p. 1335.

matically show that consumers will decrease the quantity of coffee demanded as the price rises. But this conclusion is a generalization. There are always buyers who do not fit the economist's pattern. For example, some few individuals may still buy the same amount of coffee regardless of its price.

A second reason that theoretical disputes are likely in economics is that a variety of factors can be considered in analyzing an economic problem, and in constructing a theory an economist may choose to explore the relationship between an event and only one or a few of the many variables affecting that event. For example, if an unusually large number of students were to receive high grades on the first exam in this course, one could theorize as to why this happened by considering any of several factors: the caliber of the instruction, the excellence of the textbook, the students' IQs, hours studied, suggested readings completed, amount of sleep and food intake before the exam, and so on. Suppose your instructor statistically examined the relationship between hours studied, study guide exercises completed, and the test scores. At the same time one of the students explored the relationship between sleep and food intake and the grades. Assume your instructor found that the class studied and read for many long hours, hence the high grades. The student discovered that each classmate took the exam thoroughly rested and after a nutritious breakfast, hence the high grades. In reading the results the department chairperson claimed that both studies were unreliable because neither considered IQ or quality of instruction. Enter controversy! Who is correct? In each of these instances, a clear relationship was established: several reasons for the high grades were identified.

Assumptions

Conditions held to be true; form the framework in which a particular theory is explained.

Economic theories are also often disputed because of the assumptions that are made in presenting a theory. **Assumptions** are conditions held to be true that form the framework in which a particular theory is explained. For example, if one were to develop an economic theory about the impact of raising property taxes on a community's revenue, assumptions could be made about the rate of population growth in the community, expected changes in the price of housing and homeowners' incomes, the reaction of businesses to the tax increase, and so on.

Whether an assumption is true does not matter within the context of a theory. For purposes of developing the theory, it is assumed to be true. For example, in examining the effect of a rise in property taxes in a community, one could assume an annual population growth rate of 0 percent, 3 percent, 12 percent, or any other rate. Whatever rate was assumed would be held constant while the theory was presented.

It is important to understand, however, that different assumptions can cause theoretical relationships and study conclusions to vary, and that the assumptions that form the setting for a theory must be valid in the real world if the conclusions drawn from the theory are to be relevant. Assuming rapidly increasing property values in a crime-ridden area, a substantial amount of competition for a business that is a monopoly, or that the economy is expanding when it is in a recession could lead to theoretical conclusions that are not meaningful in reality.

There has always been serious controversy among economists concerning their theories. Scholarly publications sometimes devote many pages to running disputes between practitioners in the field. Questions arise as to the assumptions underlying a theory, the significance and appropriateness of the variables studied, the importance of the overall problem, and the possibility that a more influential factor has not yet been tested. This questioning, of course, gives rise to the continuing development of economics.

 In summary, economic theories explain the relationships between economic variables. By focusing on one or a few key relationships, they simplify reality so that it can be better understood. But since economic conditions are always changing, the assumptions that underlie theories must be carefully evaluated to be sure that they lead to conclusions that are meaningful in the real world.

Economic Policy

Economic policy

An action taken to change an economic condition.

An **economic policy** is an action taken to change an economic condition. A tax decrease to speed up the economy, mandatory anti-pollution measures, and quotas on foreign-produced items are all examples of economic policies.

Economic policy is the result of a decision by a policy maker such as a business manager, state or local legislature, the Congress, voters, the president, or the Board of Governors of the Federal Reserve.[3] In most instances of economic policy creation, several courses of action are available. For example, a state's legislature could choose to either increase, decrease, or leave unchanged its sales tax; there are several alternative methods for fighting inflation; and there are many options for easing a foreign trade problem.

It is important when selecting a policy to remember that each alternative carries consequences that may be further reaching than the problem itself. Take the problem of job loss in the auto industry due to imports of foreign-produced cars. A policy could be designed to discourage Americans from buying foreign cars by increasing the tariff (tax) imposed on vehicles as they enter the United States (thereby increasing their price), or by putting quotas, or limits, on the number of imported autos that may enter the United States. The result of this policy to slow down sales of foreign cars could be an improvement in American car sales and in employment for auto workers. But what about the other consequences? Foreign nations could retaliate by taxing products the United States exports, thus decreasing employment in

---

[3] The Federal Reserve System is the central banking system in the United States and oversees the money supply. The Federal Reserve System and its operations are explained in Chapter Seven.

a different industry. Tariffs or quotas could reduce an important source of competition with U.S. auto makers, or lead to price increases on foreign cars that could worsen an inflation problem as the consumer is forced to pay more. The policy maker must select a course of action not only on the basis of the problem to be solved, but also on the basis of the consequences resulting from the chosen policy.

A policy decision is based on the value judgment of the policy maker. In the case of foreign-produced automobiles, if the policy maker values jobs in the domestic auto industry as the most important consideration, an effort will be made to enact job-saving legislation. If the main concern is with inflation and the consumer, the policy maker will not favor tariffs and quotas. The question of granting tax credits for college tuition is another example of policy-making and value judgments. Families facing financial difficulties in sending their children to college may favor this type of tax break. People who think that existing programs for granting aid to college students are sufficient may find this policy unimportant and oppose it.

Since economic theory explains how economic variables interact, and since economic policy involves the manipulation of those economic variables, it is crucial that policy makers have some knowledge of these theories and their complexities. If policy makers do not understand basic economic principles, the consequences of their policy decisions could be disastrous. One benefit of a course in economics is that it enables you to evaluate better the consequences of policies and to judge how well or how poorly policy makers are informed.

Application 1.2, "Airline Deregulation and Its Impact on Fares," illustrates different conclusions from a number of studies measuring the effects of the 1979 government policy to deregulate air travel and allow airlines to set fares without government approval. Many of the conclusions of these studies differ because of differences in the variables used and the time frames considered. How might some of the problems leading to theoretical disputes that were introduced in the preceding pages explain differences in these study conclusions? How might the results of these studies affect a policy maker's position on future airline legislation?

Tools of the Economist

Words, Graphs, and Mathematical Equations

There are several ways that economic theories and policies can be expressed. The first and most basic method used by the economist is a verbal presentation, or descriptive statement. Earlier we noted that the quantity of coffee demanded will fall as its price increases. This is a simple verbal statement about buyer demand. The advantage of using this method to express a theory is the ease with which concepts can be conveyed.

But the advantage hides a weakness: verbal descriptions tend to be imprecise. In the above example, we have merely stated that a relationship

Application 1.2

Airline Deregulation and Its Impact on Fares

Ask a dozen researchers about the effects of airline deregulation on fares, and you'll probably get a dozen different answers.

Since free enterprise in the skies entered its second decade last year, at least 12 studies have tried to measure its impact on fares. Though they may reach similar conclusions on narrow points, the studies often clash on broad issues: some researchers pronounce deregulation a smashing success, while others say consumer savings are grossly exaggerated or nonexistent.

That's because the studies give different weight to different factors. How one views deregulation may depend on the following considerations.

The Time Frame   A Bureau of Labor Statistics study in April 1990 concluded that airline fares were 10.3 percent higher in March than a year earlier. A February 1990 Transportation Department study concluded that fares adjusted for inflation were 15 percent lower in 1988 than in 1984. "Up," says an American Express study. "Down," says an Air Transport Association study. Generally the direction of the change in airfares depends on the years used for the study.

National Averages vs. Specific Cities   Following deregulation some cities were left with just one or two dominant carriers. One study concluded that rate changes were different in cities served by several competing airlines than in cities dominated by one or two airlines.

Capacity Constraints   In cities where the airports have reached capacity limits, there could be upward pressure on airfares regardless of deregulation.

Business vs. Vacation Travelers   One study has indicated that business travelers have fared worse than vacation travelers with deregulation.

Customer Value   Studies have overlooked the difference in the product that consumers now purchase. Such factors as nonrefundable tickets and corner-cutting on meals are hard to measure but important to consider.

Source: Asra Q. Nomani, "One Sure Result of Airline Deregulation: Controversy About Its Impact on Fares," *The Wall Street Journal*, April 19, 1990, pp. B1, B10.

Graph

An illustration showing the relationship between two variables that are measured on the vertical and horizontal axes.

exists between coffee prices and the quantity of coffee demanded, without saying anything about the strength of that relationship. We do not know if consumers will be prepared to buy 10 percent less coffee when the price increases from, say, $2 to $4 a pound, or 75 percent less coffee when the price increases from $2 to $4 a pound, or just what numbers are involved. Unfortunately, when one tries to be numerically precise, verbal explanations become very clumsy.

The second method for expressing theories and policies, graphs, allows a more precise statement about the relationships between economic variables. A **graph** is a picture illustrating the relationship between two variables, one shown on the horizontal axis and the other on the vertical axis. For instance, returning to our coffee example, the graph in Figure 1.2 shows a relationship between the price of a pound of coffee and the number of pounds of coffee demanded by consumers over a certain period of time.

The major advantage to using graphs is that numbers can easily be incorporated, allowing relationships to be presented more specifically. For

Figure 1.2　　　Relationship between Coffee Prices and the Amount of Coffee Demanded

The downward-sloping line in this graph illustrates the various amounts of coffee demanded at different coffee prices.

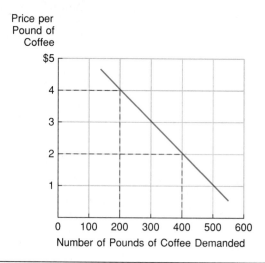

Number of Pounds of Coffee Demanded

example, the graph in Figure 1.2 tells us that at a price of $4 per pound 200 pounds of coffee are demanded, and at a price of $2 the quantity demanded increases to 400 pounds. Or, if the price is $4 and you lower it by 50 percent, you will increase the quantity of coffee demanded by 100 percent. Or, if you are interested in selling 300 pounds of coffee, the price will need to be $3 per pound. In addition, once you have had some practice in reading graphs, you will discover that a line or curve illustrates at a glance whether the relationship between the variables graphed is **direct** (the variables move in the same direction) or **inverse** (the variables move in opposite directions), as well as the strength of the relationship. If you are uncomfortable working with graphs you should stop at this point and read the appendix to this chapter. In it, direct and inverse relationships and other information on constructing and interpreting graphs are presented.

The third method used by economists to express theories and policies is mathematical equations. A major drawback with equations is that many people lack confidence in using mathematics. But equations have an important advantage: they are very specific about how economic variables are related. Let us return to our coffee example.

Suppose we found that the relationship between the price of coffee and the amount demanded is shown by the equation

$$Qc = 600 - 100 \ Pc.$$

Direct relationship

Two variables move in the same direction: when one increases, so does the other; graphs as an upward-sloping line.

Inverse relationship

Two variables move in opposite directions: when one increases, the other decreases; graphs as a downward-sloping line.

Green guilt or gracious living? New environmentalism gets personal

By David Foster
Associated Press

SEATTLE — In a city known for environmental righteousness, Carl and Anya Woestwin are among the most righteous of all.

Anya hoards plastic produce bags, washing and re-using them until they fall apart. Carl urinates into a milk carton, then uses it to fertilize their organic garden. What's more, Carl and Anya insist, they enjoy every minute of their low-impact lifestyle.

"This is not privation," Anya said. "The basic goal is to use as few external resource inputs as possible, produce as much as possible — and have a really good time."

Good time? Environmentalism? Not many people would mention those ideas in the same breath.

Environmental responsibility, once a comfortable enough notion when the villains were corporate polluters with belching smokestacks, has become more personal. Pollution control increasingly focuses not on the likes of Acme Slag & Sludge but on small excesses committed daily by ordinary citizens.

Do you know anybody, like maybe yourself, who can't be bothered to sort trash into recycling bins? Or who uses a smoke-billowing lawn mower that's been kicking around the garage since the 1960s? Or who, when nobody's looking, dumps the black ick from an oil change in the back yard?

Such penny-ante polluters have become the environmental scoundrels of the 1990s, judging from all the new rules cracking down on them:

■ The federal Environmental Protection Agency last spring proposed new air-pollution standards for lawn mowers, then followed up in October by clamping down on recreational motorboats.

■ Last winter in Denver, residents were ordered

not to use fireplaces or woodstoves 132 times, or nearly half the days that anyone would want a fire, in an effort to clear up the city's air.

■ More than 6,600 communities nationwide now have curbside recycling programs, up from about 1,000 just five years ago. Many are mandatory, requiring households to use separate bins for glass, cans, and paper.

■ Smog-control officials in the San Francisco area urged residents in September not to use aerosol deodorants, barbecue lighter fluid or even alcohol-based perfumes, all in the name of reducing gases that create smog.

"As we have gotten the biggies under control, the smaller sources of pollution become more important," said Jerry Martin, spokesman for the California Air Resources Board.

"We cracked down on industry, and the cheap and easy things have been done," agreed Carol Piening, an air-quality planner with the Washington state Department of Ecology. "If we want the air to continue to get cleaner, it's time for people to take personal responsibility."

How to promote that responsibility, and how much responsibility is really necessary, are matters of fierce debate — a debate that's sure to continue as the new Republican-controlled Congress takes a hard look at the proliferation of environmental regulations.

Should government mandate environmental consciousness, with stiff fines for violators? Should it try to shame people into less-polluting lifestyles with education campaigns?

Either way, some conservatives say, environmentalists and their allies in government are threatening the economy by forcing an excuse-me-for-living mentality on Americans.

Here Qc represents the quantity of coffee demanded, and Pc represents the price of coffee. By putting different prices in place of the Pc term, you can see how much coffee buyers would want. For example, if the price were \$4 per pound, buyers would want 200 pounds of coffee [200 = 600 − 100(4)]. If the price fell to \$2, they would want 400 pounds [400 = 600 − 100(2)]. If coffee were given away, people would want 600 pounds; and if coffee were \$6 per pound, people would stop buying it.

Scarcity, Model Building, and Graphs

Since economists frequently illustrate concepts and theories through graphs, we will use this tool to explore scarcity in greater detail.

Modeling Scarcity

Model

The setting within which an economic theory is presented.

Economists often build a formal model to illustrate an economic theory. A **model** is the setting within which a relationship is explained or a problem is analyzed. For example, model railroaders usually construct settings, or displays, in which to operate trains; architects create scale models, or replicas, of buildings before they are constructed; and students, perhaps subconsciously, establish mental models of their lifestyles (work schedules, sleeping habits, carpooling arrangements, and so on) before selecting a semester's class schedule.

In developing a model, both facts and assumptions need to be defined. Facts serve as boundaries to set some limits on the model. For example, a common boundary-setting fact in economic model building is a time period. In the coffee example, the time period tells us whether we are looking at coffee demand for a day, a week, or a year. It would be difficult to determine how much of a product was demanded without knowing what time period to consider.

Assumptions are the conditions held to be true that are assigned to a model. Most often these assumptions are kept constant; that is, they do not change through the course of the model unless the reader is warned. For example, in building a model to plan study time during a semester, a student could assume that a certain number of hours per week would be devoted to a part-time job and that classes would be regularly held as scheduled.

In the example that follows, a model of a hypothetical economy viewed over a short period of time is developed using the following assumptions.

1. All resources, or factors of production, are held constant. This means that there are no increases or decreases in the available amounts of the economy's labor, machinery, trucks, and so on.

2. All resources are fully employed. Everyone who wants a job has one, and all other resources (such as factories and tractors) available for

Table 1.2   Possible Combinations of VCRs and Minivans

This production possibilities table illustrates various combinations of VCRs and minivans that a hypothetical economy could produce with full employment and fixed resources and technology.

VCRs (Millions)	Minivans (Hundreds of Thousands)
25	0
24	2
20	4
15	6
9	8
0	10

use are being used. There is no involuntary unemployment of resources.

3. The existing technology is held fixed; no new inventions or innovations occur.

Although this model economy, like any economy, has the potential for producing a large assortment of goods and services, all of its resources will be diverted to the production of only two items: video cassette recorders (VCRs) and minivans. Table 1.2 lists some possible combinations of VCRs and minivans that could be produced in our model economy given our assumptions. Notice from this table that if all resources are fully employed in the production of VCRs, then 25 million VCRs can be made, but no minivans. If some minivans are manufactured (for example, 200,000), then some resources employed in the production of VCRs must be diverted to minivans and fewer VCRs will be produced. If all factors are used in the manufacture of minivans, no VCRs can be made.

The **production possibilities table** in Table 1.2 can be graphed to illustrate the same relationship. In Figure 1.3 the different minivan and VCR combinations from the table are plotted on a graph and the points are connected with a line to form a **production possibilities curve**.

Production possibilities table (or curve)

An illustration of the various amounts of two goods that an economy can produce with full employment and fixed resources and technology.

Interpreting the Model

The basic conclusion of the production possibilities model is a restatement of the scarcity problem: even with full employment, limited resources allow limited production of goods and services. In our hypothetical economy, it would be impossible to produce 35 million VCRs in the time

Figure 1.3   Possible Combinations of VCRs and Minivans

The production possibilities curve illustrates graphically the various combinations of two goods that an economy could produce with full employment and fixed resources and technology. Under these conditions, more of one good can be produced only by producing less of the other.

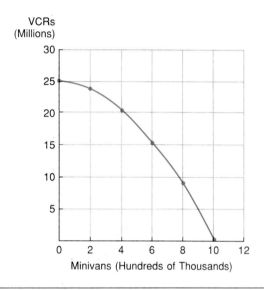

VCRs
(Millions)

Minivans (Hundreds of Thousands)

allowed, even if desired, because there are not enough factors of production to do so. In a sense, scarcity imposes a boundary, or limit, on an economy that is illustrated by a production possibilities curve. Our hypothetical economy cannot produce beyond (to the right of) the curve in Figure 1.3.

The production possibilities model also emphasizes the concepts of tradeoff and opportunity cost. When an economy operates at full employment, more of one good can be produced only by giving up some amount of another good. If this economy were producing 20 million VCRs and 400,000 minivans, and households demanded 600,000 minivans, then households could have the additional minivans only by giving up some VCRs. This tradeoff concept is a restatement of the principle of opportunity cost, which was introduced earlier: the cost of additional minivans can be measured by the number of VCRs given up, and vice versa. The opportunity cost of going from 400,000 to 600,000 minivans is 5 million VCRs. What is the opportunity cost of going from 800,000 to 1,000,000 minivans?

Several other economic concepts can be illustrated with the production possibilities model by altering the model's assumptions. If the assumption of full employment is dropped and it is assumed that some resources available for production are not used, or there is **unemployment,** then the economy

Unemployment

Resources available for production are not being used.

Figure 1.4   Unemployment in a Production Possibilities Model

With unemployment, an economy is unable to reach the combinations of goods and services that it could produce if resources were fully employed. Point A represents production with unemployment.

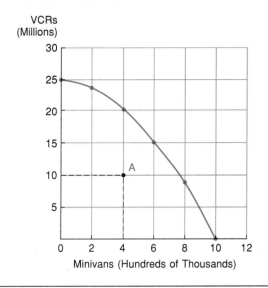

VCRs
(Millions)

Minivans (Hundreds of Thousands)

---

cannot produce as much as it did under the condition of full employment. With full employment, one production combination was that of 15 million VCRs and 600,000 minivans. If some labor, machinery, or other resource is idle, then less will be produced — perhaps only 10 million VCRs and 400,000 minivans. The condition resulting from unemployment is illustrated graphically by a point inside, or to the left of, the production possibilities curve, such as point A in Figure 1.4.

Economic growth

An increase in an economy's full employment level of output over time.

A nation's **economic growth** can be explained if the assumptions of fixed resources and fixed technology are dropped. With more labor, machinery, and/or better methods of production (technology), the economy would effectively have more resources with which to produce goods and services. For example, more labor would allow an increase in VCR and minivan production. The same effect could be accomplished with a newly automated process for the production of either good. This economic growth can be illustrated graphically by a shift of the production possibilities curve to the right as shown in Figure 1.5. Point B, which was unattainable under the old condition, is now within reach of the economy.

"Test Your Understanding: Production Possibilities" provides an opportunity to examine your command of the concepts illustrated by the production possibilities model. Here the model is used to evaluate the choices

Figure 1.5   Economic Growth in a Production Possibilities Model

An increase in the number of available resources or an improvement in technology allows the production of goods and services to increase, and the economy's production possibilities curve shifts to the right.

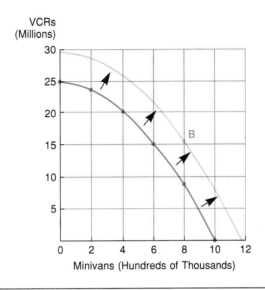

Capital goods

Goods, such as machinery and equipment, that are used to produce other goods and services.

Consumer goods

Goods, such as food and household furniture, that are produced for final buyers.

Macroeconomics

The study of the operation of the economy as a whole.

Microeconomics

The study of individual decision-making units and markets within the economy.

an economy must make between producing **capital goods,** such as machinery and equipment, which are used to produce other goods and services, and **consumer goods,** such as food and household furniture, which are produced for final buyers.

Macroeconomics and Microeconomics

There are two basic approaches for analyzing economic activity: macroeconomics and microeconomics. Much of economics is organized under these two major headings.

Macroeconomics concerns the operation of the economy as a whole and the interactions of the major groups (called the household, business, government, and foreign sectors) in the economy. It includes such topics as inflation, unemployment, taxes and government spending, and money. Part Two of the text, titled "The Macroeconomy," deals with the major sectors in the economy, levels of total output and employment, prices, money and banking, and related matters.

Microeconomics focuses on the behavior of individual businesses and households and on specific product and resource markets. It includes such topics as consumer behavior, cost-benefit analysis, the determination of

Test Your Understanding

Production Possibilities[a]

[a]Answers can be found at the back of the book.

All economies are subject to a tradeoff between the production of capital goods, which are used to produce other goods and services, and consumer goods, which are produced for final buyers. Assume that in a hypothetical economy with full employment and fixed resources and technology, the following amounts of consumer and capital goods can be produced.

Consumer Goods (Millions of Units)	Capital Goods (Millions of Units)
0	45
10	40
20	32
30	20
40	0

Illustrate these production possibilities in the accompanying graph, and answer the following questions.

1. What is the opportunity cost of increasing the production of consumer goods from 20 to 30 million units? What is the opportunity cost of increasing the production of capital goods from 40 to 45 million units?

2. On the accompanying graph, illustrate the effect of a small amount of unemployment with a point labeled A, and a large amount of unemployment with a point labeled B.

3. Where, in your opinion, is the ideal point on the production possibilities curve for the United States to operate? Label this as point C. On what value judgment about the importance of capital goods and consumer goods did you base your location of point C? What would cause another student to locate point C elsewhere on the production possibilities curve?

4. What would happen to the economy if it produced only consumer goods? What would happen if it produced only capital goods?

5. Demonstrate graphically what would happen if new technology were created for producing both capital goods and consumer goods.

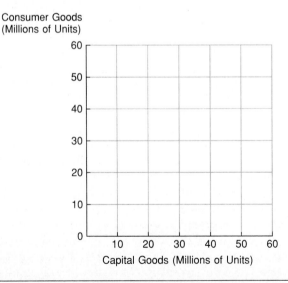

business profits, and the determination of prices in specific markets. Part Three of the text, titled "The Microeconomy," is concerned with understanding the behavior of these individual decision-making units in the economy.

Summary

Economics is the study of how limited resources are used to satisfy unlimited material wants and needs. The basis of economics is a scarcity of goods and services caused by people's insatiable desire for material things coupled with a limited amount of resources to produce them. Since individuals and societies cannot have everything they want, they must make choices, or tradeoffs. These tradeoffs are influenced by the decision maker's value judgments. Tradeoffs carry an opportunity cost, which measures the cost of a decision or purchase in terms of a forgone alternative.

In dealing with the problem of scarcity, efficiency and equity are important considerations. Efficiency results when a good or service is produced at the lowest resource cost, and its effect is the greatest attainable lessening of scarcity since resources are used to their fullest. Equity refers to fairness in the distribution of goods and services, and the determination of equity differs with people's value judgments.

Resources, or factors of production, are those items used in the production of goods and services. All resources are scarce, or limited, in amount. Economists classify these limited factors into four categories: land, labor, capital, and entrepreneurship. When sold, these generate incomes termed, respectively: rent, wages, interest, and profit.

In studying economics, it is necessary to know the distinction between economic theory and policy. Economic theory explains why an event occurs, or gives a generalized interpretation of the relationship between economic variables. Assumptions, which are conditions held to be true, form the framework for the development of a theory. Economic policy is an action taken to change an economic condition. Value judgments are important in the selection of economic policies. In expressing theories and policies, the economist uses the tools of verbal statements, graphs, and mathematical equations, with each tool having some advantages and disadvantages. An upward-sloping line in a graph illustrates a direct relationship between variables, and a downward-sloping line indicates an inverse relationship.

A production possibilities table and curve can be used to illustrate scarcity. These show that, with assumptions of full employment and constant resources and technology, more of one good can be obtained only by giving up some of another good, making tradeoffs necessary. The effect of unemployment, which causes an economy to produce fewer goods and services than with full employment, is shown by a point inside, or to the left of, the production possibilities curve. Increases in technology and/or resources allow for economic growth, permitting a shift of the curve to the right.

Macroeconomics is concerned with the operation of the economy as a whole and with the interactions of its major sectors. Microeconomics deals with individual operating units and markets within the economy.

Key Terms and Concepts

Economics	Economic theory
Scarcity	Econometrics
Tradeoff	Assumptions
Value judgment	Economic policy
Opportunity cost	Graph
Efficiency	Direct relationship
Equity	Inverse relationship
Resources (factors of production)	Model
Labor	Production possibilities table (or curve)
Capital	Unemployment
Land	Economic growth
Entrepreneurship	Capital goods
Wages	Consumer goods
Interest	Macroeconomics
Rent	Microeconomics
Profit	

Review Questions

1. Classify each of the following factors of production into one of the four resource categories used in economics and identify the income return to each.
   a. The scanner used to check out groceries in a supermarket
   b. The instructor of this course
   c. A pasture used for grazing a herd of cattle
   d. A coffee urn used by a catering service
   e. The owner/manager of a lawn service company
   f. The manager of a discount store that is part of a national chain

2. What is meant by a direct and an inverse relationship between economic variables? Illustrate each of the following relationships using the graphs on the next page, and indicate whether each relationship is direct or inverse.
   a. Inches of rain and sales of umbrellas
   b. Tuition and students demanding to enroll in a university
   c. Consumers purchasing the same amount of gasoline regardless of its price
   d. Salaries and years of education

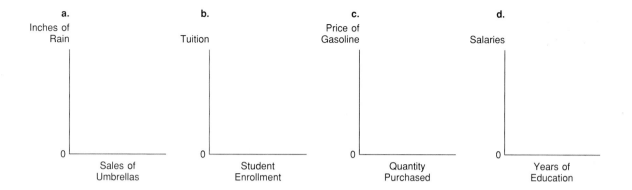

3. Distinguish between economic theory and economic policy. Discuss some of the reasons for economic theory controversies and economic policy controversies. Give some recent examples of economic policy actions.

4. How does a production possibilities curve illustrate the tradeoffs, or choices, that must be made when an economy is operating at full employment? Explain how a production possibilities curve appears, and how unemployment and economic growth can be shown on this graph.

5. What is a capital good and what is a consumer good? How does an economy's choice about how many of its resources to devote to capital goods production as compared to consumer goods production affect its current standard of living and its future standard of living?

6. The following production possibilities table gives the various combinations of hours that can be worked and grade point averages that can be earned by a college student who holds a job and takes 12 credit-hours of courses a semester. Plot this table on the graph provided and answer the following questions.
   a. What is the opportunity cost for this student if he or she increases the hours worked per week from 10 to 20?
   b. What factors could cause this curve to shift to the right?
   c. What factors could cause this student to operate inside, or to the left, of this production possibilities curve?
   d. What would determine the student's best location on this curve?
   e. Are there any similarities between the choices that this student makes concerning hours worked and GPA and the choices an economy makes between the production of capital goods and consumer goods?

Hours Worked per Week	GPA
50	0.00
40	1.00
30	1.90
20	2.60
10	3.25
0	3.75

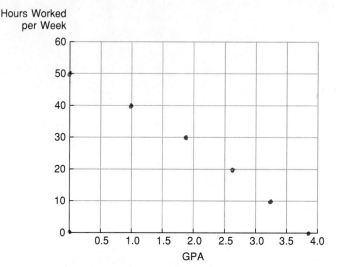

7. Based on the information in the appendix to this chapter, explain how the relationship between driving at higher speeds and the likelihood of injury in an automobile accident can be illustrated in one graph to make it appear that the likelihood of injury increases relatively little at higher speeds, and in another graph to make it appear that the likelihood of injury increases dramatically at higher speeds. What warning does this sound about basing a decision on a quick scan of the appearance of a line in a graph?

8. Distinguish between macroeconomics and microeconomics and identify some topics relevant to each.

Discussion Questions

1. If resources are scarce and if people are always wanting more than the economy can provide, how is it possible that we would ever have unemployment?

2. Suppose that you are an advisor to a health team working in a less developed country. In that country, 20 percent of the children die of a particular disease. If the health team were to inoculate the population, the disease would cease to be a problem. However, with more people surviving, the country's food supply would become grossly inadequate, and it is estimated that about 20 percent of the children would die of starvation. Which policy would you follow: inoculation or no inoculation? What are the tradeoffs with each policy? Why would you follow your policy choice, and how are your values important in reaching a decision?

3. Why do economists devote so much time to the concepts of tradeoffs, choices, and opportunity costs? With this in mind, is there anything in this world that is free?

4. Is there a tradeoff between efficiency and equity, or are these two goals mutually compatible for an economy?

5. In your opinion, what would be an equitable distribution of goods and services in a society? Why would this be an equitable distribution and what value judgments underlie your opinion? How and why does your opinion differ from some of the other major views identified in the text?

6. Should national defense–related goods, such as submarines and nuclear weapons, be classified as capital goods or consumer goods? Why?

7. Individuals and societies evaluate both the benefits and costs of their choices when making decisions. Can you think of recent decisions you made where you weighed the benefits and costs of possible courses of action? Can you think of a decision where you did not weigh the benefits and costs—but wish now that you had?

Critical Thinking Case 1

■ Rethinking Medical Care[a]

Critical Thinking Skills | Defining a problem
Determining criteria for selecting possible solutions to a problem
Identifying reasonable solutions to a problem

Economic Concepts | Scarcity
Choice

Americans are rapidly moving toward a major problem that affects life itself: soaring costs of medical care. Hospitals charge from $900 to $3,000 for a day in a cardiac-care unit, the monthly payment for medical insurance for a family can be over $500, and a heart or liver transplant may cost over $100,000.[b] The technology that enables people to live longer, the increasing incidence of expensive diseases such as cancer and AIDS, and the aging of the population have contributed to this escalation in cost. Can we—either individually or collectively—continue to absorb these rising costs?

The philosophy in the United States has always been to pursue all medical procedures necessary to prolong life; this includes organ transplants and life support equipment. But some of these procedures have pushed the overall cost of medical care so high that people are forgoing preventive care, including routine medical exams, x-rays, or blood tests. While this saves money in the short run, it can become very costly in the long run when more expensive treatment is necessary because of lack of early detection. This will eventually further complicate the problem of escalating costs.

Are scarce resources and increasing costs now forcing Americans to reevaluate their thinking about medical care? Officials in Oregon have ranked 1,600 medical procedures in terms of costs and benefits in order to choose what ailments and injuries will be covered by the limited funds available for health care through the Medicaid program. For example, in terms of benefits per dollar of health care expended, the detection and prevention of AIDS is high on the list, but treatment when a patient is close to death is near the bottom. To quote Richard Lamm, former Governor of Colorado: "The miracle of medicine has outstripped our ability to pay for it. Somebody has to have the guts to say what policy brings the most good to the most people. Oregon is the first state to face up to it."[c] In addition to Oregon's policy proposal, Americans are now seeing controversial books and articles on the costs and benefits of some types of care that would have been unthinkable twenty years ago.

Do Americans need to make some hard choices about health care, or can we continue to operate as we have? What are these choices?

Questions

1. What is the basic problem presented in this case?

2. There are many solutions to this problem, but not all are reasonable or appropriate. What criteria, or factors, should be considered in deciding which solutions are acceptable? Should these criteria be solely economic, or should they include ethical and legal considerations?

3. What reasonable solutions are available for alleviating the problem given in the case? Why are they reasonable?

[a]At the end of each chapter a **Critical Thinking Case** will be presented. These cases have two objectives: the development of critical thinking skills and the application of economic concepts. As shown in **Case 1,** the specific critical thinking skills and economic concepts associated with each case will be specified. A few suggested questions for dealing with each case are also included. If your instructor makes no specific assignment regarding a case, you may want to try answering the questions on your own.

[b]"The Money Trail," *The Wall Street Journal Reports: Medicine & Health,* May 11, 1990, p. R20; Memo on Enrollment in Insurance Plans, St. Louis Community College Human Resource Development Department, April 26, 1990, p. 3.

[c]Quote and other material concerning the Oregon proposal is taken from "Oregon Lists Illnesses by Priority to See Who Gets Medicaid Care," *The New York Times,* May 3, 1990, pp. A1, A10.

Suggested Readings

Rachel Carson, **"A Fable for Tomorrow,"** and **"The Obligation to Endure,"** *Silent Spring* (Greenwich, Conn.: Fawcett Publications, Inc., 1962), pp. 13–23.
A discussion of the opportunity costs that could accompany our efforts to control nature, from the classic book that introduced many to environmental concerns.

Robert Frost, **"The Road Not Taken,"** *Robert Frost Poetry and Prose,* eds. E. C. Lathem and L. Thompson (New York: Holt, Rinehart and Winston, 1972), p. 51.
A poem about opportunity cost by the well-known poet.

Nancy Gibbs, "How America Has Run Out of Time," *Time,* April 24, 1989, pp. 58–67.
An account of the scarcity of time and the opportunity cost of the way we live.

D. H. Meadows, D. L. Meadows, J. Randers, and W. W. Behrens III, *The Limits to Growth* (New York: Universe Books, 1974).
A pessimistic view of the future of humanity that gained wide attention when published.

Arthur M. Okun, *Equality and Efficiency, The Big Tradeoff* (Washington, D.C.: The Brookings Institution, 1975).
A discussion of the value of equality and efficiency, the tradeoff between them, and some measures to achieve both goals.

I. Papps and W. Henderson, *Models and Economic Theory* (Philadelphia: W. B. Saunders Co., 1977).
An introduction to modeling and problems of modeling in economics.

F. Pohl, "The Midas Plague," *Spectrum: A Science Fiction Anthology,* eds. K. Amis and R. Conquest (New York: Harcourt, Brace and World, Inc., 1962), pp. 13–67.
Science fiction about life in a world without scarcity.

"Statistics Brief: Playing with Numbers," *The Economist,* May 31, 1986, pp. 78–79.
A concise synopsis of some ways in which statistics can be manipulated.

Andrew Tanzer, "How Do You Shut the Darn Thing Off?" *Forbes,* November 13, 1989, pp. 38–40.
A description of Japan's emphasis on capital goods expenditures and their effect on its competitiveness and economic growth.

John Tierney, "Betting the Planet," *The New York Times Magazine,* December 2, 1990, pp. 52–53, 74–81.
A story surrounding a wager, made in 1980 and paid in 1990, between an ecologist and an economist on the future of the world.

Appendix to Chapter 1

Graphing

A graph is a picture illustrating the relationship between two variables. These variables are given on the vertical and horizontal axes of the graph. For example, the relationship between the price of tennis racquets and the number of tennis racquets demanded is given in Figure 1A.1.

The numbers along the axes of a graph are important for proper interpretation of the graph. In assigning numbers to a graph, several rules need to be remembered: (1) always use zero at the origin (the point where the horizontal and vertical axes meet); (2) work up the number scale as you go out on each axis;[1] and (3) when moving along an axis, use equal spaces for

---

[1]For those students who are familiar with graphing techniques, we might point out that only the first, or northeast, quadrant of a graph is used in most examples in this text.

Figure 1A.1

The Relationship between the Price of Tennis Racquets and the Number Demanded

Points A, B, and C match different prices of tennis racquets with the number of racquets demanded at each price.

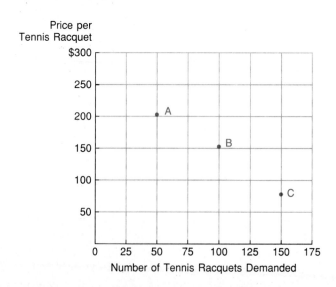

Table 1A.1   Hourly Wage Rates and Numbers of Applications for a Job

This table illustrates a relationship between hourly wage rates and the numbers of teenagers applying for a job.

Hourly Wage Rate	Number of Teenagers Applying for a Job
$1.50	50
2.25	100
3.00	150
3.75	200
4.50	250
5.25	300
6.00	350

equal amounts. Notice the application of these rules in Figure 1A.1. Zero is used at the origin, numbers along each axis move up the number scale, the vertical axis is labeled in equal series of $50, and the horizontal axis is labeled in equal series of 25 units.

A point on a graph indicates a specific combination of the two variables compared in the graph. For example, point A in Figure 1A.1 indicates that at a price of $200, 50 tennis racquets are demanded. This can be read by putting a real or imaginary line from point A to the vertical axis, and from point A to the horizontal axis. Point B says that at a price of $150, 100 racquets are demanded. What does point C designate? Where would point D be located if it indicates that at $250 per tennis racquet, no racquets are demanded?

A line on a graph is nothing more than a series of connected points. For example, Table 1A.1 lists the numbers of teenagers applying for a job at various hourly wage rates. Each of these wage rate–application combinations from this table is plotted as a point on Figure 1A.2a. These points are then connected to form the line given in Figure 1A.2b. (Notice that in Figure 1A.2, 75¢ is included on the vertical axis of both graphs although this was not given as a wage rate in the table. Why is this done?)

Earlier in the chapter, it was pointed out that the slope of a line in a graph indicates whether there is a direct or an inverse relationship between the variables. A direct relationship exists when both variables move in the same direction; that is, as one gets larger or smaller, so does the other. For example, if you observed how many hot fudge sundaes an ice cream store would like to sell at different prices, you would probably find a direct relationship. Graphically, a direct relationship is illustrated by a line that slopes upward like that in Figure 1A.3a. At a price of $3.00, hot fudge sundae sellers would

Figure 1A.2   Hourly Wage Rates and Numbers of Applications for a Job

A line in a graph is a series of connected points; each point represents a
particular combination of two variables.

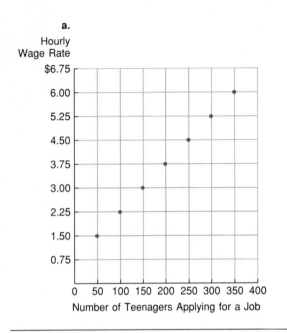

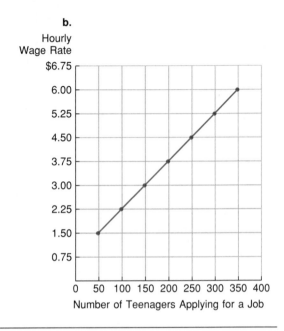

like to sell 2,000 a day; when the price falls to $1.00 they would like to sell
only 500 (preferring instead to devote their attention to more profitable
items).

An inverse relationship exists when the variables move in opposite
directions; that is, as one becomes larger, the other becomes smaller, and
vice versa. For example, when sugar prices increase, the amount demanded for purchase falls. Graphically, an inverse relationship is illustrated by a line that slopes downward such as that in Figure 1A.3b. Note
in Figure 1A.3b that when the price per pound of sugar is 40¢, consumers
would like to purchase 5 tons per day, and when the price drops to 30¢
per pound, the quantity demanded per day increases to 6 tons. What do
the lines in Figure 1A.4 say about the relationships in those graphs? Be
specific in your answers.

It should be noted at this point that students often have trouble reading
a graph when there are no numbers given on the axes. If this is the case with
you, just put a few hypothetical numbers along each axis and try reading it
again. (Remember the rules for numbering when you do this.) After you
have some practice in reading graphs, this problem should disappear.

Figure 1A.3   Direct and Inverse Relationships

A direct relationship is illustrated by an upward-sloping line in a graph, and an inverse relationship is illustrated by a downward-sloping line.

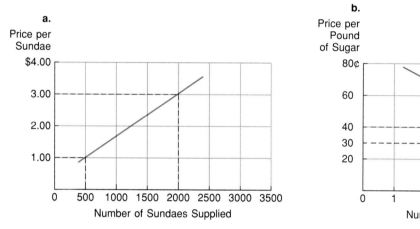

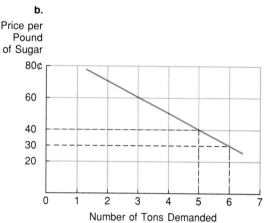

In interpreting information given in graphs, one should be aware that graphs can be used to present a point of view in a way that is often not apparent to the reader. For example, the two graphs in Figure 1A.5 give exactly the same information, yet they do not look the same. What is the difference between them? Why would someone choose to use a figure such

Figure 1A.4   Examples of Direct and Inverse Relationships

What type of relationship (direct or inverse) is illustrated in each of these graphs?

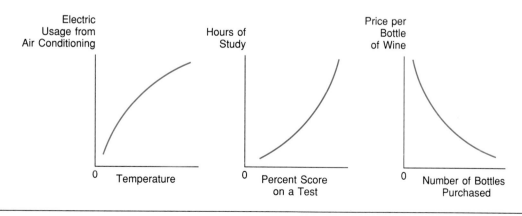

Figure 1A.5   Numbers of Homes with Smoke Alarms[a]

The appearance of data in a graph and the impression created for the reader can be affected by how the axes of the graph are numbered.

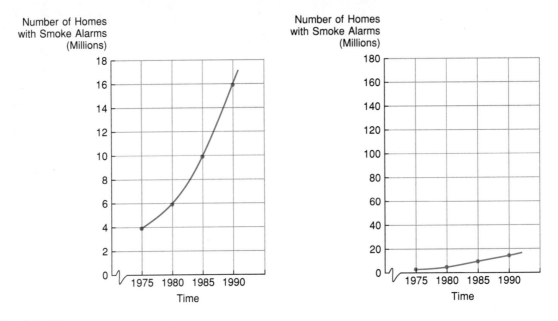

[a]Hypothetical data.

as the one to the left rather than the one to the right?[2] For information about manipulating statistics to present a point of view, see "Statistics Brief: Playing with Numbers," which is cited in the Suggested Readings at the end of this chapter.

[2]The difference between the two graphs in Figure 1A.5 is the spacing used for the numbers on the vertical axis. The graph to the left uses each vertical mark to represent 2 million homes, and the graph to the right uses each vertical mark to represent 20 million homes. When the unit of measure of the variable on the vertical axis is given a wider space, it results in a line that appears to be more steeply sloped than the line that would result if a narrower space were given to the unit of measure. If one wanted to create the impression of a dramatic increase or decrease in the variable measured on the vertical axis, then one would use more exaggerated spacing. To create the impression of a relatively small increase or decrease, narrower spacing would be used.

Chapter Two

Economic Decision Making and Economic Systems

The collapse of the Berlin Wall in 1989 symbolized dramatic political and economic changes that swept across Europe and the USSR and opened the way for transforming their economic systems.

Source: © Carol Guzy/The Washington Post.

Chapter Objectives

1. To introduce the basic economic choices that must be made in every society because of scarcity.

2. To differentiate between a market and a planned economy, and to introduce the manner in which the basic economic choices are made in different economic systems.

3. To explain the structure and operation of a market economy.

4. To explain why, where, and how government intervenes in decision making in a mixed economy.

5. To distinguish among capitalism, mixed capitalism, and socialism, and to discuss recent changes that have taken place in the economies of the Soviet Union and Eastern Europe.

6. To explore the British foundations and the historical highlights of the development of the U.S. economy.

Chapter One makes clear that the study of economics is based on the scarcity of material things. No economy can provide enough automobiles, magazines, welding machines, parks, medical care, and other goods and services to satisfy everyone. Because of this, people in every economy must make decisions about what goods and services will be produced and who will receive them. In this chapter we focus on those decisions and how they are made in different economies.

Scarcity and Society's Basic Economic Decisions

Each year every economy produces some combination of goods and services. In a recent year approximately $4.5 trillion worth of goods and services, including 196 million barrels of beer, over 300 million pairs of jeans, and over 1 million houses were produced in the United States.[1] Unfortunately, this voluminous output served only to satisfy some of the wants and needs of some of the people; the economy was incapable of satisfying all the wants and needs of all of its citizens.

How do we decide which wants and needs to satisfy for which people? How does an economy arrive at its particular product mix? Why do some

---

[1] U.S. Bureau of the Census, *Statistical Abstract of the United States: 1990*, 110th ed. (Washington, D.C.: U.S. Government Printing Office, 1990), pp. 426, 715, 751, 754.

people acquire a new Mazda while others do not, and why do some households eat steak while others eat hamburger? The economic predicament is similar to that faced by Santa Claus—millions of cherubic boys and girls dreaming of endless toys but only one workshop, a few elves, and just one sleigh to carry the goodies. What does Santa put in the bag on Christmas Eve?

Basic economic decisions

The choices that must be made in any economy regarding what to produce, how to produce, and to whom production is distributed.

In every economy, regardless of its wealth and power, certain choices concerning production and distribution have to be made. Specifically, there are three **basic economic decisions** that must be made in every economy: (1) what goods and services are to be produced and in what quantities; (2) how these goods and services are to be produced; and (3) to whom these goods and services are to be distributed.

The first economic question, what is to be produced, refers to the fact that every society must decide on the types and quantities of goods and services that it will produce. For example, if motor vehicles are to be manufactured, a decision or choice to do so must first be made. Decisions must also be made as to what types of motor vehicles to produce (passenger cars, buses, pickup trucks, recreational vehicles, and so forth), and how many of each type of vehicle to produce.

The second economic question, how goods and services are to be produced, refers to the fact that any good or service can be produced in several different ways, so that choices must be made about which scarce resources to use, and how they will be used. For example, running shoes can be constructed by machinery or by hand, and the material can be vinyl, cotton, or another appropriate fabric. Electricity can be produced by firing generators with water, coal, oil, or nuclear power.

The third question, to whom do the produced goods and services go, refers to distribution. It must be decided which members of society will receive what share of the limited goods and services that have been produced. To whom will the motor vehicles, running shoes, medical services, homes, and frozen dinners go?

Economic Systems

The Basic Economic Choices and Economic Systems

Economic system

The way in which an economy is organized; defined by the method chosen to make the basic economic choices.

The manner in which a society makes the three basic economic choices depends upon its **economic system.** An economic system is a particular way of organizing the relationships among businesses, households, and the government to make basic choices about what goods and services to produce, how to produce them, and to whom they will go. For purposes of classification, it is helpful to define three types of economic systems: a market economy, a planned economy, and a mixed economy.

In a market economy, the basic economic decisions are made through the interactions of individual buyers and sellers in the marketplace. In a planned economy, the decisions are made by planners who are either associated with

Figure 2.1

Scarcity, the Basic Economic Choices, and Economic Systems

Scarcity imposes three basic economic choices on a society. The manner in which these choices are made depends upon a society's economic system.

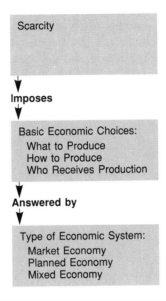

the government or are in some other way representative of the members of the society. A mixed economy is one that combines elements of planning and individual decision making. It may range from a basic market economy with some degree of government intervention, to a basic planned economy with some dependence on individual decisions made in markets. The relationship between scarcity, the basic economic choices, and economic systems is summarized in Figure 2.1.

A Market Economy

A **market economy** is one in which the basic economic choices are made by individual buyers and sellers interacting in markets.[2] A market system is also termed a **price system** because price is the language through which buyers and sellers communicate their intentions. For example, McDonald's expresses its intention to sell Big Macs by making them available at a particular price, and a student tells McDonald's that he or she wants a Big Mac by

Market economy
An economy in which the basic economic decisions are made through the interaction of individual buyers and sellers in markets using the language of price.

Price system
A market system; one in which buyers and sellers communicate their intentions through prices in markets.

[2] A market is defined as a place or situation in which the buyers and sellers of a product interact for the purpose of exchange. Markets are discussed in detail in the next chapter.

paying the price asked. The exchange of the burger is made because the price is suitable to both buyer and seller.

A pure market system, where all economic decisions are made by individual buyers and sellers with no government intervention, is virtually nonexistent in the world today, although it is the philosophical basis for economies such as that of the United States. Historically, the U.S. economy has been closer to a pure market system than it is now. Over the years, while still keeping the market tradition, the United States has become more of a mixed economy as the role and importance of government have increased.

It is noteworthy that markets have existed in different types of economies throughout the history of the world. In some instances markets have served simply as allocation mechanisms to aid in answering one of the basic economic questions. For example, there was intensive trading activity in ancient Greece at the time of Aristotle, despite the fact that the economy had not progressed to the point where it would be described as a market economy.[3] What we are concerned with here, however, is not the operation of a market as an allocation mechanism, but rather with the study of an entire economic system in which all decisions are made solely through the interaction of individual buyers and sellers in markets.

Circular flow model

A diagram showing the real and money flows between households and businesses and the relationships between households and businesses in output, or product, markets and input, or resource, markets.

Output markets (product markets)

Markets in which businesses are sellers and households are buyers; consumer goods and services are exchanged.

The Operation of a Market Economy   The operation of a market economy can be illustrated by a **circular flow model,** such as that in Figure 2.2, which shows how businesses and households relate to one another as buyers and sellers. In one part of this relationship, businesses are the sellers of goods and services and households are the buyers. Shown in the lower half of Figure 2.2, this part of the relationship involves a "real flow" of goods and services from businesses to households, and a "money flow" of dollars from households to businesses. For example, autos, t-shirts, televisions, fajitas, and furniture flow to households, which give businesses dollars for these items. Transactions of this type, where businesses are the sellers of goods and services and households are the buyers, occur in **output,** or **product, markets.** In these markets a buyer and seller may deal with one another face to face, as in an automobile showroom or restaurant, or their dealings might be more impersonal, as in the case of a buyer ordering from a catalogue or using a vending machine.

In the second part of the market household-business relationship, businesses are the buyers and households are the sellers. In order for businesses to produce goods and services they need resources, or factors of production, which belong to households. In the upper half of Figure 2.2, a real flow of labor, capital, land, and entrepreneurship goes from households (the sellers) to businesses (the buyers). In return for these resources, businesses send a money flow of wages, interest, rents, and profits to households. For example, in order to produce a car, auto workers are needed. They sell their services

[3]Karl Polanyi, "Aristotle Discovers the Economy," in *Primitive, Archaic and Modern Economies,* ed. George Dalton (Garden City, N.J.: Doubleday & Co., Inc., 1968), p. 80.

Figure 2.2

The Circular Flow of Economic Activity

Households sell factors of production to businesses in input markets, and businesses sell goods and services to households in output markets.

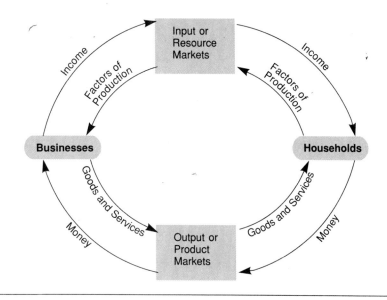

Input markets (resource markets)

Markets in which the factors of production are bought and sold; households are sellers and businesses are buyers.

to the car manufacturers for an income. These transactions involving the exchange of factors of production occur in **input, or resource, markets.**

The basic structure of a market economy can be fully explained by focusing on the two buyer-seller relationships of businesses and households at the same time, or on Figure 2.2 as a whole. Businesses and households relate to one another through input markets and output markets. Households sell labor, capital, land, and entrepreneurship to businesses in return for income in input markets. That income is then used to buy goods and services from businesses in output markets.

Economic Decisions in a Market Economy   How are the critical economic choices of what, how, and to whom made in a market system? The first question, what and how much to produce, is the result of millions of independent decisions by individual households and businesses in the marketplace. An item will be produced if a business perceives that enough households will purchase the item at a price that will make its production profitable. If a business determines that individuals do not want a good or service, or will not pay a profitable price, the business will eventually stop producing that item. This type of decision making accounts for the continued appearance of pocket calculators and the Ford Mustang, and the disappearance of particular clothing styles and the slide rule from the market. Also, the emergence of such items as camcorders and CD players resulted from household demand for these products and the ability of businesses to produce and sell them at a profit.

Is it believable that individual buyers can force large sellers like auto manufacturers or soft drink producers to change their products? The balance of power between a single person and a single business is obviously weighted in favor of the business. Yet individuals do influence businesses. While one buyer acting alone may be virtually powerless against a business, the situation changes when many buyers share the same opinion. Without talking to one another, individual buyers decide for or against a product by the way they spend their money. The dollars consumers spend for businesses' products are tallied in the same way that electoral votes are tallied for a political candidate. Those businesses that do not get enough dollar votes may be forced to change their products or leave the market completely.[4] Application 2.1, "Missing the Market," describes three cases where consumers decided against a product.

The second critical question, how goods and services will be produced, is answered by businesses in a market economy through their choices of particular methods of production. Any good or service can be produced in more than one way, and a business must decide which of the available techniques it will use for production. For example, suppose that the engineers at a company manufacturing stereo receivers identify three different production methods for assembling the identical product: by machine, by hand, or by a combination of labor and machinery. The cost for each of the three methods is given in Table 2.1. Which method of production will the company choose in a market economy?

It would be in the best interest of the company's owners to choose the second method, which uses both machinery and labor, because it is the **least-cost method of production,** or the most **efficient** method. Since an owner's profit on an item is the difference between the product's price and its cost, the lower the cost, the greater the profit. For example, if the stereo receivers can be sold for $300 each, profit will be $50 per unit with method 1, $70 with method 2, and $40 with method 3.

What is true for this company selling in a market economy is also true for other sellers in a market economy: that is, in the interest of profit, businesses seek the lowest cost of production in providing goods and services. Which method of production is cheapest depends on the prices a business must pay for its factors of production and how those factors are used. In the United States, for example, agriculture has become highly mechanized with a

Least-cost (efficient) method of production

The method of production that allows a good or service to be produced at the lowest cost.

---

[4] An important question must be raised: to what extent are individuals' decisions influenced by businesses' advertising and other promotional activities? If businesses exert a strong influence on people's attitudes and tastes, do the dollars consumers spend reflect their independent choices, or do they represent something else? Put differently, do businesses respond to consumers' preferences, do they shape those preferences, or is there some mixture of the two? The independence of consumers' economic decision making is a very controversial issue. What is your position on this question?

Table 2.1   Costs of Stereo Receiver Assembly Using Different Production Methods
Method 2 illustrates the least-cost method of producing stereo receivers.

Methods of Assembly	Cost to Company per Unit
1. All machine-assembled	$250.00
2. Hand-and-machine-assembled	230.00
3. All hand-assembled	260.00

dependence on sophisticated machinery for planting and harvesting. In many other countries crops are grown by persons using only shovels and hoes. Given the cost of farm machinery and labor and the way each is used, it is cheaper for U.S. farmers to mechanize than to try to grow and harvest the same output using mainly labor. The same is not true for producers in other parts of the world where abundant labor and cheaper labor costs (relative to machinery costs) result in a greater dependence on human effort.

How the third economic question, who receives the produced goods and services, is answered in a market economy can be illustrated through a circular flow model, such as that in Figure 2.2. In output markets, a flow of goods and services going to households from businesses is matched by a flow of dollars going the other way. In a market economy a person will receive an item only if he or she can pay for it. In other words, in a market economy goods and services are distributed to those who can afford them.

A household's ability to afford goods and services depends on the value and amount of the factors of production it has to sell in resource markets. People lacking marketable skills are not paid well in resource markets, causing them to fare poorly in acquiring goods and services. People commanding many resources, or resources that are highly valued, may enjoy a substantial income from input markets, enabling them to buy the items they want in output markets. In other words, if you own a successful corporation, oil wells, and are the president of a bank, you may well afford a Ferrari, a country home, an original Matisse, and a cellar of French wine.

In summary, in a market economy the basic economic choices are made by individual buyers and sellers. Businesses produce the goods and services that buyers indicate they want by their spending patterns in the markets. These goods and services are produced using the least-cost method of production, since this method allows the owners of businesses to maximize their profits. Finally, it is the individual household's ability to sell its own resources in input markets that determines its ability to acquire the goods and services of its choice in output markets.

Application 2.1

Missing the Market

There's more than one way to miss a market. That's what many businesses discovered in the 1980s. During a decade when knowing the consumer became increasingly important, many companies—and even whole industries—failed to understand their markets. Some companies neglected core consumers in favor of the fringe; others ignored important market shifts. Many failed to recognize when a market had peaked; some launched products with no target in sight. Others knew their market but failed to reach it. [Below are three examples of marketing mishaps.]

Coke's Classic Mistake

Coca-Cola blundered by tampering with success, changing the formula of the world's most popular soft drink. Coke replaced its original soft-drink formula with a sweeter concoction in April 1985. Though the company claimed it had found a better-tasting syrup, its strategy aimed to compete with Pepsi's campaigns for teenaged and overseas markets.

On paper, there was good cause for Coca-Cola to pursue America's teens: people aged 15 to 18 consume more soft drinks per capita than older people, and Pepsi was capturing these consumers. . . . But Coke forgot about the giant generation that controls much of American business—the baby boom.

At the time, the baby boomers were aged 21 to 39, no longer teenagers but still attached to the drink that symbolized their free-spirited generation. Within three months of the introduction of the new-formula Coke, adult fans forced the company to bring back the original Coke. . . .

Too Many Cabbages in One Patch

In 1985, Cabbage Patch Kids were the rage, and Coleco Industries was at the top of the heap in the toy world. The dolls' popularity peaked that year,

with $600 million in sales. But sales plummeted to $230 million in 1986, and the toy company suffered major losses. [In 1989] Coleco sold most of its assets to a chief competitor, Hasbro Industries.

Profits in the toy world, even among the giants, are dependent on the passing whims of children. Success means producing a variety of toys so that a company is not at the mercy of fads. Cabbage Patch dolls were a fad, and in 1985 they accounted for fully 85 percent of Coleco's profits.

Home Banking Went for Broke

One of the decade's most popular myths was that Americans were returning to home and hearth. . . . Fear of crime would make people stay home. Overworked dual-earner couples would escape to their electronic cottages. If Domino's Pizza could profit from home delivery, why not more sophisticated services like home banking?

During the 1980s, 75 banks offered home banking. Householders could transfer funds, review accounts, and pay bills through their personal computers or special television hookups. But home banking soured by the late 1980s. . . .

One household in five owns a computer, according to the Electronic Industries Association. But those who own computers are not clamoring for banking services. Eighty-one percent of computer owners want to use their machine for word processing. . . .

Seventy-eight percent are interested in using it as an educational tool for their children, and 72 percent want to play video games on it. Barely half of computer owners are interested in home banking.

Source: Excerpted from "Missing the Market," *American Demographics*, December 1989, pp. 16–21. Copyright © 1989 American Demographics, excerpted with permission.

Evaluating Market Economies   A market economy has both strengths and weaknesses. On the plus side, market economies are efficient because of the operation of incentives. The profit incentive causes businesses to produce in an efficient manner, and income rewards provide an incentive for households to use their resources effectively or to improve them. Many students, for example, invest in an education to become more productive in input markets and obtain a higher salary. Market systems are also efficient in that the information required for decisions on production and distribution passes directly between buyers and sellers rather than through a central clearing house or authority as in a planned economy. The market, rather than a planner, coordinates business and household actions. An additional strength of a market economy is that production and distribution decisions reflect the value judgments of buyers and sellers in the market rather than the value judgments of planners.

One of the weaknesses of a market system is that it offers no protection for people lacking adequate knowledge to make informed market decisions. For example, the effects of chemicals used in certain foods and medications or the inner workings of an automobile or appliance may not be fully understood by the average consumer. In a market system, there is no organized effort to ensure that products will be safe for use by the uninformed consumer. There is also nothing in the market mechanism to ensure that households lacking adequate resources will be able to acquire enough goods and services to maintain themselves. Put another way, a market does not have a morality of its own. Also, the ability of consumers to influence the quantities, quality, and prices of products in a market system may be weakened if individual markets become dominated by small groups of firms: it is easier for consumers to influence the quality of a product when there are one hundred competing producers than when there are two. Finally, the incentive to produce at the least cost could cause businesses to make production decisions that have a detrimental effect on the environment.

A Planned Economy

Planned economy (command economy)

An economy in which the basic economic decisions are made by planners rather than by private individuals and businesses.

A **planned economy**, also termed **command economy**, is one where the basic economic choices are made by a planning authority rather than by individual buyers and sellers in markets. The planning authority may be a government agency, bureau, commission, or the like. If the economy is purely planned, allowing no market activity, an extensive bureaucracy may be necessary to make millions of detailed economic decisions and to deal with the vast numbers of problems that invariably arise. A planned economy usually operates according to a blueprint (termed a "plan") that establishes stated general objectives to be accomplished in some specified period of time. There may be an overall long-range plan (perhaps for ten or twenty years) with several short-range plans (perhaps for two or five years) and some yearly or quarterly plans. For example, the Soviet Union, which was considered to be a planned economy until important changes occurred in 1989, operated under a series of five-year plans.

Although the objectives of most plans are primarily economic, noneconomic considerations such as political, social, and military goals can be important as well. For example, a plan may call for the development of a steel industry, the buildup of a powerful navy, the elimination of unemployment, or any other objective.

Economic Decisions in a Planned Economy   In a planned economy, the first economic question, what should be produced, is decided by the planning authority. The types, as well as the amounts, of goods and services to be produced are decided by administrative command in order to accomplish the stated objectives of the plan. Planners, through their value judgments, determine whether and how many cars, buses, stoves, submarines, dry-cleaning plants, shoes, and other items are to be produced. For example, if the planning authority feels that resources that could be used for assembling television sets are needed for computers, then fewer television sets are produced, regardless of how much they are in demand. If the planners determine that every household should have a television set, then forces will be set into motion to accomplish that objective.[5]

The second economic question, how goods and services are to be produced, is again decided by the planning authority, although the authority's influence is less direct than it is for the first question. Imagine the difficulty in instructing every enterprise about how to produce a particular type of good or service. Because of this complexity, pure planning to resolve this economic question becomes cumbersome and may force the planning authority to depend on salary incentives, bonuses, and other inducements to accomplish its objectives.

The main influence planners have over how goods and services will be produced comes through determining which factors of production and processes will be made available to producers. For example, in printing, type can be set by a staff of keyboard operators or automatically by sophisticated electronic equipment. If planners wish to keep keyboard typesetters employed, they will simply not permit or "plan for" the production of electronic typesetting machinery. Printers will then use what is available — the keyboard typesetter. In a purely planned economy, a producer cannot order a machine, part, or piece of equipment if the authority has not permitted it to be produced.

To whom the produced goods and services go, the third economic question, is again decided by the planners. A rationing system for the distribu-

---

[5] Be careful to note the difference between a plan and an accomplished objective. A planner's determination of what and how much an economy should produce can be vastly different from what it actually produces. Many events beyond a planner's control may occur to alter a plan: poor weather conditions for crops, international crises, political unrest, and unforeseen bottlenecks in production, to name a few.

tion of goods and services could be instituted where individuals are allotted specific items (for example, two pairs of shoes per year or one coat). An alternative distribution method would be to permit individuals to freely purchase what has been produced through the plan. If individuals are allowed to choose goods and services for themselves, then planners face the additional problem of income determination. That is, they must decide how much the various factors of production should be paid for their services.

Evaluating a Planned Economy   Several problems can emerge in a planned economy. First, the goods and services that planners consider to be important may not be valued by the consumers for whom they are intended, or the elapsed time from the beginning to the end of a plan may cause products that were once desirable to lose their importance. Either of these problems could result in the overproduction of some items and the underproduction of others. Second, the complexity of planning the allocation of resources and the choice of allowable processes could lead to bottlenecks, shortages, and stoppages in the production of goods and services. Third, inferior quality products could result from a lack of producer incentives, from the fact that it is easier to mandate the quantity than the quality of outputs, or from a planning apparatus that has become so large and cumbersome that it adversely affects the flow of commands and information to and from producing units. Finally, the planning process, especially one where decision makers are removed from production locations, could result in long-term environmental damage. As has been seen in Eastern Europe, serious air and water pollution has been a consequence of the failure of planners to consider the environment in many of their decisions.

What advantages of the planning mechanism offset these weaknesses? First, certain goals of society may be achieved faster in a planned economy than in a less formally organized economy. For example, the development of a "high-tech" industry or the buildup of the agricultural sector might be accomplished more rapidly when efforts are coordinated by a central authority. Second, it should be easier to eliminate unemployment when producers can simply be ordered to use more labor in their production processes. Finally, the ability to control the distribution of goods and services can be a benefit when there is a question about the equity, or fairness, of people's shares in the output of the economy. For example, it would be a simple matter for the planning authority to remedy a situation where elderly poor people were not getting enough heating fuel. Table 2.2 summarizes and compares the strengths and weaknesses of market and planned economies.

Mixed economy
An economy in which the basic economic decisions are made through a combination of market and centralized decision making.

A Mixed Economy

The third type of economic system is a **mixed economy.** In this system the three basic questions are answered by some combination of market and centralized decision making. Technically, all economies are mixed. Pure market and pure planned economies are polar cases that help us order our

Table 2.2

Strengths and Weaknesses of Market and Planned Economies

Strengths and weaknesses can be identified for both market and planned economies.

Market Economy	Planned Economy
Strengths	
Incentives for businesses and households to act efficiently	Ability to accomplish noneconomic goals quickly
Direct communication of information between buyers and sellers	Reduction of unemployment by planning more labor into production processes
Composition of goods and services reflects buyers' and sellers' value judgments	Modification of the distribution of goods and services to correct inequities in output shares
Weaknesses	
No protection for people lacking adequate knowledge to make informed market decisions	Overproduction of some goods and underproduction of others
Nothing to ensure people an adequate amount of goods and services	Production bottlenecks, shortages, and stoppages
Buyers may face a small number of sellers in a market	Inferior product quality due to a lack of incentives and other problems
Few incentives to protect the environment	Few incentives to protect the environment

thinking but have no real world counterparts. Thus, an important factor giving different economies their unique styles is the manner and degree to which individual and planned decision making are combined.

Why would the participants in a market economy seek some centralized decision making, and why would the authorities in a planned economy allow some decision making by private individuals in markets? The answer is found in the bottom half of Table 2.2: neither pure market nor pure planned economies are perfect. When a market system creates a problem for a society or fails to achieve a society's goals, **market failure** occurs; and when a problem arises or a goal cannot be reached in a command economy, **planning failure** results. The response to market or planning failure gives rise to mixed economies.

Although all economies are mixed, the term "mixed economy" has come to be most closely associated with systems, such as that of the United States, that depend primarily on markets, but have some government intervention into private decision making. For this reason, we will examine sources of market failure that give rise to government intervention, and where and how government typically participates in a market economy.

Market failure

A market system creates a problem for a society or fails to achieve a society's goals. .

Planning failure

Centralized planning creates a problem for a society or fails to achieve a society's goals.

Types of Market Failure   Several types of market failure could lead to government intervention in a market economy. First, as noted earlier, markets may fail to operate in a socially desirable way when they become dominated, or monopolized, by one or a few sellers. In this case, the interaction between buyers and sellers becomes "lopsided," with undesirable consequences for buyers. For example, a person who purchases a soft drink and a sandwich at an airport or stadium that has just one food concessionaire will likely pay a high price for those items.

Market failure may also occur when the information needed to make good buying or selling decisions is too expensive to obtain or too technical to understand. For example, consumers could be injured by the products they purchase if they do not possess adequate knowledge about the products' contents, uses, and the like. Firms producing at the lowest possible cost might also generate market failure if their cost-minimizing efforts lead to pollution or other problems that must be dealt with by society.

Age, race, or sex discrimination that results in unequal treatment for some workers may be viewed as market failure since it destroys the incentive to use labor resources efficiently and undermines the social goal of equal treatment for equal work. Finally, a market system fails to provide goods and services for those who cannot contribute to production. This means that some children, elderly, and disabled persons have no means to support themselves.

Government Intervention in a Market Economy   Where and some examples of how government can intervene in a market economy in response to market failure are illustrated in Figure 2.3. Despite the apparent complexity of a mixed economy, government intervention can occur in only four places: (1) the business sector, (2) the household sector, (3) output markets, and (4) input markets. Since the circular flow of activity in a market system centers around these four components, government intervention is automatically limited to these areas if the basic market system is to be preserved.

How government intervenes in economic affairs is more complicated to explain than where intervention occurs. We can identify several general ways in which government influences decision making: establishing the rules of the game, regulating specific industries, regulating certain aspects of business or production, protecting workers and wages, taxing and spending, and maintaining income support programs. Within these and other broad categories,[6] any number or type of laws can be enacted, their specifics differing from economy to economy. We can further understand how government intervenes in basic market decision making by examining the experience of the United States in each of these areas.

---

[6] Government intervention in a market economy is not limited to the categories identified here.

Figure 2.3   Government Intervention in a Market Economy

Government can intervene in four basic areas of a market economy in specific ways, as the examples illustrate.

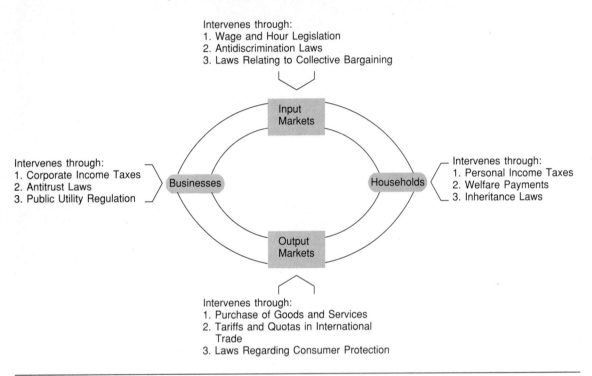

Intervenes through:
1. Wage and Hour Legislation
2. Antidiscrimination Laws
3. Laws Relating to Collective Bargaining

Intervenes through:
1. Corporate Income Taxes
2. Antitrust Laws
3. Public Utility Regulation

Intervenes through:
1. Personal Income Taxes
2. Welfare Payments
3. Inheritance Laws

Intervenes through:
1. Purchase of Goods and Services
2. Tariffs and Quotas in International Trade
3. Laws Regarding Consumer Protection

Establishing the rules of the game refers to the government's role in setting the legal framework within which businesses and households must operate when dealing with one another. This framework extends to all four areas of the circular flow and involves such items as the definition of property rights, contracts, and court procedures. Also included in this category in the United States are the antitrust laws, which were passed in order to preserve and maintain competition and prohibit certain business practices that could ruin competition.

With regulation of specific industries, business ownership remains in private hands but a government commission oversees and becomes involved in many managerial decisions. These decisions range from considerations about pricing and profit to the availability of service. In the United States, the communications, natural gas, water, electric utility, and other industries are subject to widespread regulation.

Government regulation of certain aspects of business or production focuses on the business sector and output markets. This type of regulation is directed toward specific problems, such as pollution caused by production, or activities, such as the manufacture of food or pharmaceuticals for human consumption, and may have an impact on many different kinds of businesses.

Worker and wage protection is an example of government intervention into production as well as into input, or resource, markets. In the United States most industries are required to pay workers a minimum wage. The government has also passed laws relating to collective bargaining, union activities, safety and health conditions for workers, and other labor-related issues.

Government taxing and spending policies can influence economic activity in two ways. First, because of its sheer size, government spending can significantly affect certain industries and markets. Second, government can tax and spend in a manner that can improve or worsen the employment or inflation conditions in the economy. That is, government taxing and spending policies can expand or contract the economy. For example, Congress has several times cut the personal income tax to stimulate a sluggish economy.

The final example of government intervention is through income support programs. These can take the form of outright grants of money or goods and services to individuals to provide for their maintenance, or they can involve special programs to improve a person's earning potential. Examples of this intervention include welfare checks, Social Security payments, and job training programs that enable a person to learn marketable skills. These and other examples of how government intervenes in the flow of economic activity in the United States are illustrated in Figure 2.3.

"Test Your Understanding: Economic Decision Making and the Circular Flow" allows you to practice distinguishing among the different economic systems, and to review the key relationships in a market economy.

Capitalism vs. Socialism

Up to now we have been classifying economies on the basis of whether the fundamental economic choices are made in markets by households and businesses, or according to a plan or command. A second, perhaps more popular, way of grouping economies is based on the ownership of resources, or factors of production. Using this approach, economic systems can be classified as capitalism, mixed capitalism, and socialism.

Capitalism describes an economic system in which the factors of production are privately owned and business is operated on a free enterprise basis. Essential to capitalism are **property rights** that give individuals the freedom to possess and dispose of goods, services, and resources as they choose. **Free enterprise** refers to the ability of businesses to function with a profit motive and to make their own decisions about price, quality, and other product-related matters. In pure capitalism there is little room for government interference in economic decision making. Because of its characteristics, a capitalist system is associated with economic decision making in a market environment.

Capitalism

An economic system with private property rights and free enterprise; economic decision making occurs in a market environment.

Property rights

Rights to possess and dispose of goods, services, and resources; in capitalism these rights are privately held by individuals.

Free enterprise

The right of a business to make its own decisions and to operate with a profit motive.

Economic Decision Making and the Circular Flow[a]

[a]Answers can be found at the back of the book.

1. Indicate for each of the following situations whether it would most likely occur in a pure market economy, a pure planned economy, or a mixed economy.
   a. Businesses in a particular industry are constantly on the lookout for new cost-reducing production techniques since every dollar saved in cost is an extra dollar of profit.
   b. An economics instructor in a particular country does not bother to explain the circular flow model because it has no relevance to how the basic economic questions are answered in that country.
   c. Union and management representatives submit a deadlocked labor contract negotiation to the government for mediation.
   d. Workers who have lost their jobs and incomes cut back their spending because there is no alternative source of emergency financial support once their savings run out.
   e. Consumers are unable to obtain carburetors and windshield wiper motors for their cars because they are not being produced, yet accordians, which are plentiful and not in demand, continue to be produced.
   f. A catering business goes bankrupt, but its employees receive unemployment compensation while they look for other jobs.

2. Suppose that, because of uncertainty about future jobs and incomes, households decide to increase their savings and reduce their current purchases of goods and services from businesses. With the aid of the circular flow diagram below, answer each of the following questions.
   a. Identify the flows on the bottom half of the circular flow model and explain what impact this decision will have on each of those flows.
   b. Identify the flows on the upper half of the circular flow model and explain what impact the actions taken on the bottom half of the model will have on the flows on the upper half.
   c. As households save more and spend less, trace the order in which the four flows on the circular flow model are affected.

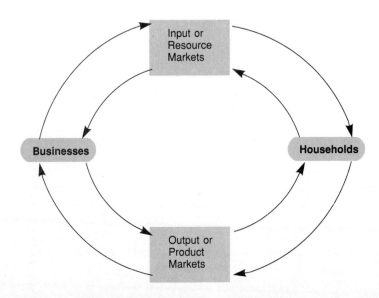

Mixed capitalism

An economic system with the basic features of capitalism but with some degree of government intervention in economic decision making.

Socialism

An economic system in which many of the factors of production are collectively owned and there is an attempt to equalize the distribution of income.

Mixed capitalism is a system that retains the essential features of capitalism, including private ownership of resources and a dependence on the market for decision making, but incorporates some degree of government intervention in decisions and markets.

A **socialist** system is one in which many of the factors of production are owned by the society itself and where there is an attempt to make the distribution of income more equal. A socialist system may depend heavily on planning, or may, as in the case of market socialism, employ some planning but also rely heavily on markets.[7]

Why classify economies as market or planned systems when the ideas of capitalism and socialism are available? There are several advantages to the market/planning approach. First, this approach focuses on the basic economic problem by highlighting how societies deal with scarcity and the critical economic decisions caused by scarcity. It also helps to define the roles of households and businesses and points out whether they solve the scarcity problem by acting independently using individual value judgments in markets or through group planning.

A second reason for using this approach is that the notions of markets and planning are more ideologically neutral than those of capitalism and socialism. For many people, "capitalism" and "socialism" have taken on important political and philosophical meanings beyond their simple economic definitions. For example, some people believe that capitalism represents an economic system that allows freedom, independence, and an opportunity to accumulate and control property. Others feel that it is a system where certain members of society are exploited by other members. To some, socialism represents a system where people share wealth and income, while to others it represents the suppression of individualism and self-initiative. As a result of these ideological overtones, this classification system may lead people to view economies as either capitalistic or socialistic, with nothing in between.

A third advantage in classifying economies as market or planned is that this approach allows us to sort economies according to the degree to which they depend on individual or collective decision making in answering the basic economic questions. For example, we might view different economies as falling along a continuum, such as that in Figure 2.4. At one end are the pure market economies (of which there are none in the real world), and at the other end are the pure planned economies (of which there are also none in the real world). In between are the world's economies, which differ from one another in the degree to which they employ markets or planning to answer the basic economic questions. The United States, which depends

---

[7] In market socialism some goods and services (such as those used by households) are allocated through markets while others (such as machinery and equipment used by businesses) are allocated by the planners. See Oskar Lange, "On the Economic Theory of Socialism," *Comparative Economic Systems: Models and Cases*, 5th ed., ed. Morris Bornstein (Homewood, Ill.: R. D. Irwin, Inc., 1985), pp. 118–126.

Figure 2.4

Continuum of Economic Decision Making

Economies can be classified according to their dependence on planned versus market decision making.

Pure Planned — U.S.S.R. — England — U.S. — Pure Market

heavily on the market system, tends toward the pure market side, and the USSR, which depended primarily on planning until the late 1980s, and which still uses planning in an important way, tends toward the other end. An economy such as England's might fall somewhere in the middle.

Changing Economic Systems

Beginning in the mid-1980s, dramatic changes occurred in many of the world's planned economies. The Soviet Union, the People's Republic of China, Poland, Hungary, and others began moving quickly toward greater use of free markets and individual decision making. Described in terms of Figure 2.4, these and other planned economies shifted to the right along the continuum of economic systems. In many, but not all, of these countries, the economic reforms have been accompanied by greater political freedom: for example, the election of non-Communist Party candidates to top positions in several of the Soviet republics and to many important local positions, the election of a non-Communist president in Poland, and the reunification of East and West Germany.

Central to the reforms in the Soviet Union and Eastern Europe were economic and political changes initiated by Soviet President Mikhail Gorbachev. Two significant departures from traditional procedures that occurred under his leadership were **Glasnost,** a policy of openness designed to lead to greater freedoms of speech and in elections, as well as other freedoms, and **Perestroika,** a program of economic reforms designed to lead the country to greater dependence on markets and individual initiative.

One lesson learned in the last few years is that economic reform on such a large scale does not occur smoothly or quickly. While the commitment to change may be professed quickly, the change itself comes slowly since the social, economic, and political institutions in these countries are the result of generations of living under a nonmarket ideology. Planned economies are deeply rooted in a philosophy of collectivism, and the transition to a philosophy of individualism takes time. People are accustomed to direction from government officials and the rewarding of individual initiative is not part of their experience. Also, those with a vested interest in the planned system may be threatened by, and opposed to, the proposed changes.

Glasnost

A policy of openness designed to allow greater freedoms in the USSR.

Perestroika

A program of economic reforms designed to lead the USSR to greater dependence on markets and individual initiative.

There are also shortages of readily available professionals to help put such changes into effect. Business experts who are taken for granted in Western economies, such as lawyers familiar with the writing of contracts, entrepreneurs who know how to organize new ventures, and accountants, are simply not available in adequate numbers within planned economies.

Another problem of transition is that property rights must be redefined and clarified to allow private ownership so that individuals can buy and sell factors of production and business can be carried out through markets rather than through state-run enterprises. The conversion to private property can be complicated. For example, from whom would an entrepreneur wanting to start a business in what was East Germany purchase land — the state or the persons from whom the land was confiscated decades ago?

The transition to a market economy may also be accompanied by inflation if prices for goods and services are suddenly market determined. Producers may seek to raise prices if they find it hard to cover their costs at pre-transition prices, especially when state subsidies to their operations are removed. A surge in buyers' demands may increase prices as well. Application 2.2, "Economic Change in Hungary," describes some of the obstacles that this country faces in its transition from a planned to a market economy. This application is excerpted from an article that chronicles the experience of some U.S. businesspeople trying to open a copy shop in Budapest.

The success of the changes in these planned economies, how long they will last, and the final forms they will take are far from clear and yet to be seen.

The U.S. Economic System

The U.S. economy has been described as a mixed economic system, basically dependent on markets and individual decision making with a lesser but important role played by government. The evolution of the U.S. economy into its present form can be understood by focusing on two important sets of developments: the first occurred in England and Scotland in the eighteenth and nineteenth centuries, and the second involved major historical events in the United States.

The British Foundations of the U.S. Economy

Three factors helped to transform England and Scotland into industrial, market economies that served as a model, in both practical and philosophical terms, for the U.S. economy. These factors were the decline of mercantilism, the rise of an intellectual justification for a system of economic individualism, and the British Industrial Revolution.

The Decline of Mercantilism   An economic system in which the interests of the national state are of overriding importance is referred to as

Application 2.2

Economic Change in Hungary

Hungary is the Eastern European country that most people singled out as most likely to succeed in a free market. Well before revolution swept over Eastern Europe a year ago, Hungary had moved away from central planning and allowed a measure of free enterprise and foreign investment. The result is something called Goulash Communism. Westerners, however, often fail to note that Hungary still needed time to develop the constellation of habits that drive a capitalist economy. The country lacked accounting principles, a rational legal structure, clear-cut property laws.

. . . Moneymaking is still suspect in some quarters in Eastern Europe. [I]t is associated with greed, tawdriness and unfairness. As a consequence, some of the most visible new entrepreneurs in Eastern Europe have operated at the margins of acceptability—money-changers and black marketeers. You cannot make money without cheating someone, a Romanian told me. Property is theft. . . .

Privatizing with the right mix of efficiency and justice is only one of the problems facing Hungarians today. The average family income is $200 a month; the standard of living is extremely low. Prices are rising. The assumption that everyone will be taken care of, fostered by years of socialism, will be hard to change. So will the corollary assumption: that everything belongs to everyone. On one of my early trips to Budapest, I bought a book from the Museum of Fine Arts in German because the museum store had run out of the English version. A Hungarian friend told me to take the book to any bookstore downtown and exchange it for the English version. I was skeptical that any store would exchange a used book bought elsewhere for a new one. But he was right: with no questions asked, a clerk exchanged the German for the English book. My friend explained: "They don't care. It's not their book. In a way, they do not feel entitled to withhold the book from you." . . .

Paradoxically, the larger the deal, the easier the negotiation. You are dealing with the very top of the power structure. . . . A Communist system is perfect for approving deals from the top; what it does not encourage or comfortably tolerate is individuals who come forward with an idea of their own to start an enterprise of their own.

The Hungarian system is no longer Communist; but it's not a free market yet, either. It's in transition, and because of that it is harder to do even the big deals today than it was a year ago. . . .

Source: Excerpted from Fred Martin, "Heard the One About the Copy Shop in Budapest?" *The New York Times Magazine,* December 16, 1990, pp. 42–48. Copyright © 1990 by The New York Times Company. Excerpted by permission.

Mercantilism

An economic system or philosophy in which the interests of the nation are of greatest importance; individual interests are subservient to those of the nation.

mercantilism. Fundamental to mercantilism is the idea that the state, rather than the individual, is the best judge of what is good for the economy. Historically, the system coincided with the rise of strong national states in England and France during the seventeenth and eighteenth centuries. Under mercantilism the purpose of economic activity was to increase the power of one's own nation relative to that of other nations. For example, a country could achieve this end by exporting goods and services in return for gold and silver, which would then be available for building the king's war chest; or a nation could increase its economic power by colonizing another country or newly discovered territory. Much of the early colonization of North America coincided with the mercantilist period.

By the end of the eighteenth century, mercantilism was challenged by a rising spirit of individualism among the people of Britain. Wesley C. Mitchell, a noted economist, observed that some of this rising spirit was expressed in business ventures spontaneously organized without the aid of government. Along with a growth in new businesses was the development of individual initiative in the arts, exploration, religion, and other areas.[8] In short, the directing role of government was being challenged and the foundations of mercantilism as an economic philosophy were crumbling in the face of growing individual achievement.

The Rise of an Intellectual Justification for a System of Economic Individualism   In 1776 a Scottish philosophy professor named Adam Smith (1723–1790) published a book, entitled *The Wealth of Nations,* that was to have a profound impact on economic thinking not only in his generation but in future generations as well. Smith's main contribution was not so much the novelty of his ideas as it was the forcefulness and systematic nature of his arguments in favor of free enterprise. His thesis, put simply, was that the best way of increasing the wealth of a nation is through individual decision making with minimal government interference, a system that has come to be called **laissez-faire capitalism.** Smith, incidentally, is still considered a champion of capitalist economies and is often quoted in that regard.

Central to Smith's argument for an economic system based on individual decision making was the **invisible hand doctrine.** According to this doctrine, it is foolish to expect people to base their business dealings with others on benevolence, or the best interests of the other person. Rather, people carry on their business in a way that serves their own best interests. In a system of free and open competition, it is in the producer's or seller's best interest to try to give the buyer what he or she wants on terms that are acceptable to both parties. In this way, Smith believed, by pursuing one's own best interest, one is guided "as if by an invisible hand" to advance the interests of all society. There is no need for government to oversee the operation of the economy since people working for their personal gain will achieve the most desired results. Thus, Smith's arguments and concepts provided an intellectual justification for an economic system based on individualism.

The British Industrial Revolution   From roughly 1750 to 1850, at the same time as the decline of mercantilism and the rise of the free enterprise philosophy, significant technological and social changes were occurring that would ultimately transform England and Scotland into modern industrial economies. These changes are known today as the British **Industrial Revolution.** The British experience with industrialization served as a model for other countries that had their own industrial revolutions at later dates, and it is important for understanding the development of the U.S. economy.

Prior to the mid-1700s, economic activity in Britain was primarily agricultural, and manufacturing was carried on in simple cottage or home

Laissez-faire capitalism
Capitalism with little or no government interference.

Invisible hand doctrine
Adam Smith's concept that producers acting in their own self-interest will provide buyers with what they want and thus advance the interests of society.

Industrial Revolution
A time period during which an economy becomes industrialized; characterized by social and technological changes such as the growth and development of factories.

[8]W. C. Mitchell, *Types of Economic Theory,* vol. I, ed. J. Dorfman (New York: Augustus M. Kelley, 1967), pp. 67–76.

industries. Then a series of inventions and innovations began in the textile industry and spread to other industries, changing the emphasis of economic activity from agriculture and home production to a system fostering the growth of factories.

With industrialization came the introduction of many new and different products, such as the steam engine, as well as new production techniques, such as mass production and the factory system, that increased overall output. It was a time when great strides were made in providing goods and services.

Industrialization, however, had its dark side. People who worked in the factories often experienced poor working conditions, low pay, and long hours. A reliance grew upon the labor of women and children, who were easier to control than men and would work for less. It may be no coincidence that in 1818 Mary W. Shelley wrote about the relationship between people and science in a work entitled *Frankenstein*. The poem, "The Factory Girl's Last Day," also written in the early 1800s and excerpted in Application 2.3, makes a strong statement about the factory system. What can you learn from the poem about the girl's age and her living and working conditions?

In summary, the British contribution to the U.S. economy was twofold. First, a philosophical and intellectual defense of individualism and free enterprise was introduced and adopted. Second, significant economic changes occurred in Britain that illustrated both the benefits of capitalism and the problems that this system could create.

Historical Highlights in the Development of the U.S. Economy

In the early history of the United States, the economy was closer to a pure market system than it is today. It was considered to be laissez-faire capitalism, the system advocated by Adam Smith. Over the years, however, the U.S. economy has developed into one that, although still essentially market in nature, has extensive amounts of government regulation, control, and influence. Several key historical periods and events can be viewed as milestones in the movement of the U.S. economy from laissez-faire to its current status. These include the U.S. industrial boom, the New Deal, the World War II era, and the regulatory and deregulatory waves of recent decades.

The Industrial Boom   Prior to the Civil War, the U.S. economy was primarily agricultural, with production taking place in homes or small workshops and with trade carried on in local markets. In this environment laissez-faire was the prevailing system. But after the Civil War, through the late 1800s and into the early 1900s, substantial and significant changes occurred in American economic and social life. These changes were similar to those the British had undergone a century before in their industrial revolution. Growth in transportation and communications, primarily the

Application 2.3

The Factory Girl's Last Day

The art and poetry of a particular time period often re-
flect some of the social attitudes of the day. Several
poems were written during the British Industrial Rev-
olution to make strong statements about the poor
working conditions in factories. Given below is an ex-
cerpt from "The Factory Girl's Last Day," written
in the early 1800s and attributed to various authors.

" 'Twas on a winter morning,
    The weather wet and mild,
Two hours before the dawning
    The father roused his child:
Her daily morsel bringing,
    The darksome room he paced,
And cried: 'The bell is ringing;
    My hapless darling, haste!'

" 'Dear father, I'm so weary!
    I scarce can reach the door;
And long the way and dreary:
    O, carry me once more!'
Her wasted form seems nothing;
    The load is on his heart:
He soothes the little sufferer,
    Till at the mill they part.

"The overlooker met her
    As to her frame she crept;
And with his thong he beat her,
    And cursed her when she wept.
It seemed, as she grew weaker,
    The threads the oftener broke;

The rapid wheels ran quicker,
    And heavier fell the stroke.

"She thought how her dead mother
    Blessed her with latest breath,
And of her little brother,
    Worked down, like her, to death:
Then told a tiny neighbor
    A half-penny she'd pay
To take her last hour's labor,
    While by her frame she lay.

"The sun had long descended
    Ere she sought that repose:
Her day began and ended
    As cruel tyrants chose.
Then home! but oft she tarried;
    She fell and rose no more;
By pitying comrades carried,
    She reached her father's door.

"At night, with tortured feeling,
    He watched his sleepless child:
Though close beside her kneeling,
    She knew him not, nor smiled.
Again the factory's ringing
    Her last perceptions tried:
Up from her straw bed springing,
    'It's time!' she shrieked, and died!'"

Source: Robert Dale Owen, *Threading My Way* (New York: Augustus M. Kelley, 1967), pp. 129–130. Original publication, 1874.

railroads and telephone, opened new marketplaces, and the exploitation of
energy sources such as oil and electricity permitted mass production and the
growth of a factory system. Great numbers of inventions introduced many
new goods such as typewriters, light bulbs, automobiles, bicycles, and more
efficient farm machinery. At the same time people began to move from the
farm to the city seeking work and greater opportunities.

Two changes were occurring in the midst of this industrial boom that
would bring about government intervention. First, some businesses were
becoming large and powerful corporations capable of monopolizing an
entire industry (as Standard Oil did), and others were joining together with
competitors to form trusts (as in the sugar and tobacco industries). Second,

the living and working conditions of some Americans were becoming inordinately harsh. Many labored long hours for low wages in often intolerable and dangerous conditions; child labor was permitted; city slums flourished; and attempts to form unions were often met with violence. As a result of these two major changes in the U.S. economy, significant legislation was passed that would alter the laissez-faire tradition.

With regard to the monopoly problem, in 1890 Congress made its first attempt to preserve a competitive landscape in America by passing the Sherman Antitrust Act. This act prohibits businesses from working together to restrain trade and from monopolizing or attempting to monopolize a market. The Sherman Act was followed, in 1914, by the Clayton Act, which prohibits certain specific business practices that have anticompetitive effects. Also in 1914 the Federal Trade Commission (FTC) was established, with the charge, among other things, of prohibiting unfair methods of competition.

The living and working conditions experienced by many American laborers were not changed by a single sweeping law; rather, improvement resulted from bits and pieces of federal and state legislation that began in the early 1900s. Some of this legislation resulted from the writings and other publications of muckrakers, a group of authors, journalists, photographers, and others who stirred the nation through their exposés of the seamy and unsanitary side of life. For example, Jacob Riis, in *How the Other Half Lives*, wrote about and photographed working conditions and tenement poverty in New York.[9] Upton Sinclair, probably the best-known muckraker, wrote of conditions in the meat packing industry in *The Jungle*. The following excerpt shows the sensationalist manner in which Sinclair and other muckrakers wrote. It is no wonder that one response to this book was the Meat Inspection Act of 1907.

> . . . *This is no fairy story and no joke; the meat would be shovelled into carts, and the man who did the shoveling would not trouble to lift out a rat even when he saw one—there were things that went into the sausage in comparison with which a poisoned rat was a tidbit. There was no place for the men to wash their hands before they ate their dinner, and so they made a practice of washing them in the water that was to be ladled into the sausage. There were the butt-ends of smoked meat, and the scraps of corned beef, and all the odds and ends of the waste of the plants, that would be dumped into old barrels in the cellar and left there. Under the system of rigid economy which the packers enforced, there were some jobs that it only paid to do once in a long time, and among these was the cleaning out of the waste barrels. Every spring they did it; and in the barrels would be dirt and rust and old nails and stale water—and cart load after cart load of it would be taken up and dumped into the hoppers with fresh meat, and sent out to the public's breakfast. Some of it they would make into "smoked" sausage—but as the smoking took time, and was therefore expensive, they would*

---

[9] See the Suggested Readings at the end of this chapter.

call upon their chemistry department, and preserve it with borax and color it with gelatine to make it brown. . . .[10]

Other legislation of this period included a Food and Drug Act in 1906 that has since been amended several times; state legislation limiting the hours and ages of working children; laws setting maximum hours and minimum wages for women; state workmen's compensation insurance for injury on the job; and many other laws affecting matters that ranged from fire regulations to mandatory schooling.

Because of the antitrust legislation and some consumer and worker regulations, by 1920 the government had established precedence for intervening in economic activity, and the U.S. economy had moved away from laissez-faire capitalism.

The New Deal   A second and massive wave of government intervention came in the 1930s. The stock market crash of 1929 and the following Great Depression were met with a series of programs and legislative reforms instituted during the presidential administration of Franklin D. Roosevelt and termed the **New Deal.**

New Deal

A series of programs and legislative reforms instituted during the administration of Franklin D. Roosevelt in the Great Depression of the 1930s.

These programs had various objectives. Some were designed to give substantial government aid to specific sectors of the economy. For example, in an attempt to raise agricultural prices, farmers for the first time were paid not to grow crops. Farmers could also look to the government for help in refinancing when they could not meet farm mortgage payments. To ease the hardships of the unemployed, agencies such as the Works Progress Administration (WPA) and the Civilian Conservation Corps (CCC) were organized to provide jobs building bridges, roads, schools, and the like, as well as some forestry and park work. Also, the Social Security Act was passed in 1935 to provide income for the aged, blind, and others.

Other programs were designed to regulate or bolster business activity. The Securities and Exchange Commission was created to prevent fraudulent practices in the sale of securities and to establish some safeguards in securities markets. Banking was affected by the creation of several programs, such as the Federal Deposit Insurance Corporation (FDIC), and agencies such as the Federal Communications Commission (FCC) and Civil Aeronautics Board (CAB) were established. Also, in 1935 the National Labor Relations Act gave workers the right to bargain collectively.

One other economic event from this period that should be noted is that the government began to run deficit budgets on a regular basis; that is, it typically spent more than it received from taxes and other revenues. This practice was a break from the past and began a type of government budget policy previously not considered.

---

[10] Upton Sinclair, *The Jungle* (New York: Signet Classics, The New American Library), pp. 136–137. Original publication, 1906.

By the end of the 1930s, government intervention in economic activity was part of U.S. capitalism, and many programs begun in that era are firmly entrenched in the economy today.

The World War II Era   Because of the extent and magnitude of World War II, many government agencies were instituted at that time to control production, manpower, wages, prices, and such. Although most of these agencies were dismantled after the war, they did create a precedent for future reestablishment. For example, controls on wages and prices were instituted again in 1951 and in the early 1970s.

Employment Act of 1946

Legislation giving the federal government the right and responsibility to provide an environment for the achievement of full employment, full production, and stable prices.

Following World War II, one of the most significant steps toward more government involvement in economic activity occurred with the passage of the **Employment Act of 1946.** This act gave the federal government the right and responsibility to provide an environment in which full employment, full production, and stable prices could be achieved. Under this act Congress could now manipulate taxes and government spending and run deficit budgets in an effort to bring the economy to a desired level of activity. This meant that rather than influencing some specific part of the circular flow model (such as the input or output markets), government could influence the entire model by blowing it up or deflating it like a balloon. Such a powerful influence had never been legislated before this period.

The Regulatory and Deregulatory Waves   Government intervention in the economy increased with a wave of regulatory action that resulted in the creation of numerous federal agencies in the 1960s and 1970s. From 1964 through 1977, 24 such agencies were established, compared to only 10 during the 1930s.[11] These agencies include the Environmental Protection Agency, the Equal Employment Opportunity Commission, the Consumer Product Safety Commission, and the Occupational Safety and Health Administration.

The regulatory wave of the 1960s and early 1970s was reversed, however, in the late 1970s and 1980s as the economy went through a wave of deregulation during the Carter and Reagan presidential administrations. Regulatory authority in various industries, such as commercial aviation, trucking, and natural gas, was reduced, and the number of full-time positions in federal regulatory agencies began to decline in the early 1980s. Thus, in one sense, the role of government in economic activity was decreasing during this latter period, and the economy was moving back toward laissez-faire.

Recent Developments   At the same time that regulatory activity was rolled back in the 1980s, the federal debt, or the amount owed by the federal government, grew dramatically — almost tripling through the Reagan years

---

[11]See Table 14.2 for a full chronological listing of federal government regulatory agencies.

from $908.5 billion in 1980 to $2.6 trillion in 1988. By 1991 the debt had reached $3.6 trillion.[12] In addition, total government expenditures as a percentage of the economy's output also increased during the 1980s.[13] Viewed from this perspective, the government's impact on the economy did not diminish over the decade of the 1980s. Also, it appears that the deregulatory trend of the Carter and Reagan administrations was reversed by the Bush administration. Hiring and budgetary support for federal regulatory agencies were increased, as was the number of business mergers that were challenged by antitrust enforcement agencies for potential anticompetitive effects.

Thus, although generally speaking the economy has moved toward more government intervention, the events of recent years demonstrate that the movement has not been smooth and continuous.

Summary

Scarcity is a problem common to all economies in the world; no economy can completely satisfy all of its members' wants and needs for goods and services. For this reason, every society must answer three basic economic questions: what goods and services will be produced and in what quantities; how will those goods and services be produced; and who will receive those goods and services.

The way in which a society answers these three basic economic questions depends on its economic system. Economic systems can be classified as market, planned, or mixed.

In a market economy the three basic decisions are made by individual buyers and sellers communicating through prices in markets. Goods and services are produced in a market economy if buyers demand them at a price that allows sellers to produce them at a profit. In this type of economy, production is carried out by businesses seeking the least-cost method of production so that they can reap greater profits from what is sold in the market, and goods and services go to those who can pay for them. How much an individual can afford to buy depends largely on the value of his or her resources sold in input markets. In a planned economy the basic economic decisions are made by planners associated with the government or otherwise representative of the members of a society. In a mixed economic system the basic economic questions are answered by a combination of market and centralized decision making. Mixed economies arise in response to planning or market failures that create problems for a society or keep a society from meeting a goal.

---

[12]U.S., *Economic Report of the President* (Washington, D.C.: U.S. Government Printing Office, 1991), p. 375. The 1991 figure is estimated.

[13]See Table 6.1.

The strengths of a market economy include incentives to produce and use resources efficiently, direct communication of information between buyers and sellers, and a reflection of the value judgments of individuals in production and distribution choices. Planned economies allow noneconomic goals to be achieved more easily, can limit the unemployment of labor, and can provide for a more equal distribution of goods and services if that is a goal of society. Market failures include a lack of protection for the uninformed, no provision of goods and services to those unable to contribute to production, and the possible growth of monopolized markets. Weaknesses of a planned economy include poor product quality, production stoppages, and difficulties in coordinating production with consumer choices. Neither type of economy has an incentive to protect the environment.

The basic structure of a market economy can be illustrated by a circular flow model. This model shows how businesses and households relate to one another as buyers and sellers in output and input markets. The circular flow model also identifies where government can intervene in the market mechanism in mixed economic systems.

A second method for classifying economies is according to whether they are capitalistic, mixed capitalistic, or socialistic. In capitalism the means of production are privately owned, and businesses operate on a free enterprise basis. In socialism some of the means of production are collectively owned by the members of society. In mixed capitalism resource ownership is basically private, but the government has important decision-making power over how the privately owned resources will be used. In the late 1980s and early 1990s, the Soviet economy and other planned economies moved in the direction of greater dependence on markets and individual decision making.

The evolution of the U.S. economy can be better understood by examining key developments in eighteenth- and nineteenth-century British history and nineteenth- and twentieth-century U.S. history. The British developments include the decline of mercantilism, the rise of a philosophy of individualism, and the Industrial Revolution. It was in this time period that Adam Smith wrote *The Wealth of Nations,* which was to become a cornerstone in the philosophy of U.S. capitalism. Important events in U.S. history that helped to shape the U.S. economy include the industrial boom following the Civil War, the Great Depression and the New Deal, the World War II era, the regulatory and deregulatory waves of recent decades, and other developments.

Key Terms and Concepts

Basic economic decisions	Price system
Economic system	Circular flow model
Market economy	Output, or product, markets

Input, or resource, markets	Socialism
Least-cost, or efficient, method of production	Glasnost
	Perestroika
Planned, or command, economy	Mercantilism
Mixed economy	Laissez-faire capitalism
Market failure	Invisible hand doctrine
Planning failure	Industrial Revolution
Capitalism	New Deal
Property rights	Employment Act of 1946
Free enterprise	
Mixed capitalism	

Review Questions

1. What are the three basic economic questions and why must they be answered in every economy?

2. Explain how the three basic economic questions are answered in a market, a planned, and a mixed economy. Use a circular flow diagram to illustrate how these questions are answered in a market economy and where and how government can intervene in a mixed economy.

3. Below are listed six activities. Indicate for each whether it is (a) a real flow through a product market; (b) a money flow through a product market; (c) a real flow through a resource market; or (d) a money flow through a resource market.
    a. Receiving a paycheck at the end of each month
    b. Delivering a specially ordered automobile to a buyer
    c. A physician caring for patients
    d. Using a credit card to buy a meal in a restaurant
    e. Two college students earning profit over the summer from their own ice cream stand
    f. Obtaining college credits

4. Identify three strengths and three weaknesses for a market economy and for a planned economy. How are market failure and planning failure similar, and how do they differ? What are some examples of market failure?

5. Define capitalism, mixed capitalism, and socialism. What are some advantages of distinguishing economies on the basis of the extent to which they depend on markets or planning, rather than by whether they are capitalist or socialist?

6. Explain the invisible hand doctrine and why it is important for laissez-faire capitalism. How was the British Industrial Revolution important to the development of the U.S. economic system?

7. Indicate whether, and explain why, each of the following moved the U.S. economy closer to, or further from, laissez-faire capitalism.

a. The Food and Drug Act of 1906 and the Meat Inspection Act of 1907
b. The New Deal programs of the Roosevelt administration in the 1930s
c. The regulatory reforms of the Carter and Reagan administrations
d. The federal budgetary developments during the 1980s

Discussion Questions

1. Suppose that you have been chosen to be on a blue-ribbon panel of experts to determine how well or poorly each of the economies of the world is operating. Your task is to come up with a checklist of five factors by which the different economies of the world could be judged. Which five factors would you pick to judge these different economies, and why?

2. What considerations might cause one nation to choose to operate as a market economy and another to choose to operate as a planned economy?

3. Several years ago a scandal erupted on Wall Street involving "insider trading," or the buying and selling of a company's stock on the basis of secret information—known only to a few key people—that could affect the stock's price in the future. Is insider trading an example of a market system using information efficiently, or is it an example of market failure? Who is helped and who is hurt by insider trading, and should it be controlled by the government?

4. The historical overview of the U.S. economy, the reading on Hungary in Application 2.2, and developments in the People's Republic of China and elsewhere illustrate that economic systems are not static: they change over time. What are some forces that would lead to the evolution of an economic system, and how would these forces cause an economy to change?

5. It was noted in the text that the movement from a planned economy to a market economy has not been smooth or fast for the Eastern European nations. What, in your opinion, is the biggest obstacle to this change?

6. Would mercantilism, the economic system that was important in Europe in the seventeenth and eighteenth centuries, be most consistent with a market economy, a planned economy, or a mixed economy? Why? Do you know of any economic activity occurring at the present time that could be described as mercantilistic? What?

7. Based on your general knowledge of U.S. history, in your opinion what event was most significant in ensuring that the United States would not return to laissez-faire capitalism?

8. As discussed in Chapter One, efficiency and equity are important considerations affecting economic decisions. For each of the three basic economic questions, discuss whether the answer should be based primarily on efficiency, or primarily on equity.

Critical Thinking Case 2

◼ Will Capitalism Survive?

Critical Thinking Skills | Identifying central issues
| Recognizing stereotypes and clichés

Economic Concepts | Capitalism and socialism
| The transformation of economic systems

Over fifty years ago, Joseph Schumpeter, the eminent—and conservative—economist wrote the following.

> *Can capitalism survive? No. I do not think it can. But this opinion of mine, like that of every other economist who has pronounced upon the subject, is in itself completely uninteresting. What counts in any attempt at social prognosis is not the Yes or No that sums up the facts and arguments which lead up to it but those facts and arguments themselves. . . .*
>
> *. . . The thesis I shall endeavor to establish is that . . . the capitalist system . . . [is not] breaking down under the weight of economic failure, but that its very success undermines the social institutions which protect it, and "inevitably" creates conditions in which it will not be able to live and which strongly point to socialism as the heir apparent. My final conclusion therefore does not differ . . . from that of most socialist writers and in particular from that of all Marxists. But in order to accept it one does not need to be a socialist. . . . One may hate socialism or at least look upon it with cool criticism, and yet foresee its advent. Many conservatives did and do.*[a]

Contrary to Schumpeter's prediction, many people would say that, based on developments in Russia, Eastern Europe, and elsewhere, the late 1980s and early 1990s have been capitalism's finest hour.

Questions

1. What are the key elements of a capitalist system? Could they be undermined by the system's success? If so, how, and if not, why?

2. Develop arguments to support either the position that capitalism will survive and prosper or the position that it will fail. Critically evaluate the key points in your arguments to see if they are based on verifiable facts and good logic, or on unsupported beliefs and unreasoned declarations.

---

[a]Joseph A. Schumpeter, *Capitalism, Socialism, and Democracy,* (New York: Harper and Brothers Publishers, 1942), p. 61.

Suggested Readings

Friedrich Engels, "Working-Class Manchester," *The Marx-Engels Reader,* ed. Robert C. Tucker (New York: W. W. Norton & Co., Inc., 1972), pp. 429–435.
A description of living conditions in the worker district of an English city during the Industrial Revolution, extracted from Engels's *The Condition of the Working Class in England in 1844.*

Esther B. Fein, "Daily Routine in Moscow: Waiting, Always Waiting," *The New York Times,* June 19, 1990, pp. 1, 6.
A chronicle of life in Moscow during the period of economic reform.

Milton Friedman and Rose Friedman, *Free to Choose* (New York: Harcourt Brace Jovanovich, 1980).
A critical view of the proper role of government in the economic process.

Friedrich A. Hayek, "The Price System as a Mechanism for Using Knowledge," *Comparative Economic Systems: Models and Cases,* 5th ed., ed. Morris Bornstein (Homewood, Ill.: R. D. Irwin, Inc., 1985), pp. 29–40.
An argument for the superiority of market forces over central planning in using knowledge to make economic decisions.

Geoffrey A. Hosking, "The Paradox of Perestroika," *The Atlantic,* February 1990, pp. 20–24.
An essay on problems confronting economic reforms in the USSR.

F. D. Klingender, *Art and the Industrial Revolution,* ed. and rev. Arthur Elton (New York: Schocken Books, 1970).
Text and art on the Industrial Revolution in Britain.

Antonin Kratochvil and Marlise Simons, "Eastern Europe, the Polluted Lands," *The New York Times Magazine,* April 29, 1990, pp. 30–35.
A photo essay on the serious and recently revealed pollution problems in Eastern Europe.

Philip Revzin, "Progress in Work," *The Wall Street Journal,* April 5, 1990, pp. 1, A18.
On Western investment in transforming production conditions in a planned economy.

U.S., "Ch 6: Economies in Transition Around the World," *Economic Report of the President* (Washington, D.C.: U.S. Government Printing Office, 1991), pp. 193–232.
A discussion of changes in nations' economies around the world—but primarily in Eastern Europe and Latin America; covers principles of reform, the implementation of reform, and other topics.

Two muckraker classics are:
Jacob A. Riis, *How the Other Half Lives,* Dover ed. (New York: Dover Publications, 1971).
The unabridged republication of Riis's 1901 edition, with added photographs. Portrays life in the tenements of New York and evoked enough controversy to lead to some tenement reforms.

Upton Sinclair, *The Jungle* (New York: Signet Classics, The New American Library). Original publication, 1906.
Depicts the life of a working class family in Chicago in the early twentieth century. Focuses on the meat-packing industry.

Chapter Three

Demand, Supply, and the Determination of Price

The people in this shopping mall are participants in a market economy where buyers and sellers interact to determine prices and the types and amounts of products sold.

Source: © 1987 Lewis Portnoy/Spectra-Action, Inc.

Chapter Objectives

1. To define demand, Law of Demand, supply, and Law of Supply.

2. To explain demand and supply through schedules and graphs.

3. To show how price is determined in a market through the interaction of demand and supply.

4. To define and illustrate equilibrium price, equilibrium quantity, and shortages and surpluses in a market.

5. To explain the reasons for a change in demand or a change in supply.

6. To distinguish between a change in demand or supply, and a change in quantity demanded or quantity supplied.

7. To explain how changes in demand and changes in supply affect equilibrium price and quantity in a market.

8. To illustrate how government-imposed price ceilings and price floors influence market conditions.

9. To introduce the concept and calculation of price elasticity, which measures buyers' and sellers' sensitivities to price changes.

In Chapter Two it was shown that a society can answer the basic economic questions through individuals coming together as buyers and sellers in markets. This market decision making is a cornerstone in the operation of many economies, especially economies such as that of the United States. For this reason, two basic tools of economics, demand and supply, are designed to study the behavior of buyers and sellers. Together, these tools help us understand the forces at work in a market economy. In this chapter demand and supply will be explored in detail, along with the manner in which they interact to determine the prices of goods and services.

Demand and Supply

Demand

Demand refers to the buyer's side of the market, or to a buyer's plans concerning the purchase of a good or service. For example, you might have a demand for an airplane ticket to Hawaii, tennis lessons, or a chemistry lab book. A business might have a demand for workers, raw materials, machinery, or any other factor of production. Many considerations go into deter-

Table 3.1   John's Weekly Demand for Fresh-Baked Chocolate Chip Cookies

This demand schedule lists different amounts of cookies that would be demanded per week at various prices, and illustrates the Law of Demand: there is an inverse relationship between price and quantity demanded.

Price per Cookie	Number of Cookies Demanded Weekly
$0.15	15
0.30	12
0.45	10
0.60	8
0.75	6
0.90	4
1.05	2
1.20	1

mining the demand for a good or service. These include the product's price as well as nonprice factors such as the buyer's income and attitude toward the item, and available substitute products.

Demand

The different amounts of a product that a buyer would purchase at different prices in a defined time period when all nonprice factors are held constant.

In formal terms, a buyer's **demand** for a good or service is defined as the different amounts of a good or service that a buyer would purchase at different prices in a given time period when all nonprice factors affecting the buyer's plans for the product are held constant. Therefore, when we speak of a buyer's demand for coffee, gasoline, or whatever, we are speaking of the different amounts of these items that the buyer would purchase at different prices over some period of time, such as a day, a week, or a year, with all nonprice factors unchanged. It should be emphasized that, in determining demand, only the product's price is allowed to change: all nonprice factors, such as the buyer's income, are held constant in order to highlight the relationship between the product's price and the amount of the product a person would buy.

Demand schedule

A list of the amounts of a product that a buyer would purchase at different prices in a defined time period when all nonprice factors are held constant.

The relationship between the amount of a product that a consumer would buy and the product's price can be illustrated through the use of a **demand schedule.** Table 3.1, showing John's weekly demand for fresh-baked chocolate chip cookies, illustrates such a demand schedule.[1] Note the relationship between the price per cookie and the number of cookies demanded by John. As the price per cookie goes up from $0.15 to $0.30, the number of cookies John would buy falls from 15 to 12; as the price increases from $0.30 to $0.45, the amount demanded falls from 12 to 10; and each additional $0.15

[1] All of the examples used in this chapter are hypothetical.

increment further reduces the number of cookies John would buy. In other words, as the price increases, John would buy fewer fresh-baked chocolate chip cookies. Restaurant meals, television sets, clothes, or just about any other good or service, and any other consumer, could have been used for the example in Table 3.1 with the same result: the quantity demanded would have fallen as the price rose, and the quantity demanded would have risen as the price fell.

Thus, the behavior illustrated in Table 3.1 is typical of any buyer's plan to purchase a good or service, and it shows a relationship between price and quantity demanded that we know to be generally true. This relationship is called the **Law of Demand.** It states that, holding all nonprice factors constant, as a product's price increases, the quantity of the product demanded decreases, and as a product's price decreases, the quantity demanded increases. In other words, the Law of Demand says that there is an inverse relationship between a product's price and the quantity of that product demanded.

Why do consumers react this way to changes in price? The reason for the Law of Demand goes back to the fundamental problem of economics: scarcity and choice. A consumer purchasing goods and services faces a scarcity problem in the form of a limited income. The consumer can buy only so much. This means that as the price of an item goes up, he or she may not be able to afford as much as was afforded at the lower price. On the other hand, when the price of a good or service falls, the consumer can purchase more of the item for the money and enjoy an opportunity to increase his or her material possessions.

Likewise, choice influences demand because alternative, or substitute, products can be purchased. As the price of fresh-baked chocolate chip cookies increases, John can choose to eat other foods — donuts, ice cream, or fruit, to name a few — in place of cookies. As the price of cookies decreases, he may choose to eat more of them and less of other items.

Typically in economics, demand is displayed in graphs rather than in schedules. Figure 3.1 illustrates John's demand for chocolate chip cookies as shown in the demand schedule in Table 3.1. On this graph, price is measured on the vertical axis and the quantity demanded on the horizontal axis. Observe that when each price-quantity combination in the demand schedule in Table 3.1 is plotted and connected by a line, the line — called a **demand curve** — slopes downward. As indicated in Chapter One, downward-sloping lines such as that in Figure 3.1 represent inverse relationships. Because the Law of Demand states that an inverse relationship exists between price and quantity demanded, we can generalize that demand curves slope downward to show that more is demanded at lower prices and less is demanded at higher prices.

Economists frequently use the Law of Demand to explain people's behavior. Application 3.1, "The Demand for Vanity Plates," cites a study undertaken by some economists to confirm their hunch that price is an underlying determinant of the number of vanity license plates found on cars

Law of Demand

There is an inverse relationship between the price of a product and the quantity demanded.

Demand curve

A line on a graph that illustrates a demand schedule; slopes downward because of the inverse relationship between price and quantity demanded.

Figure 3.1   John's Weekly Demand for Fresh-Baked Chocolate Chip Cookies

The downward-sloping demand curve illustrates the Law of Demand by showing that less is demanded at higher prices and more is demanded at lower prices.

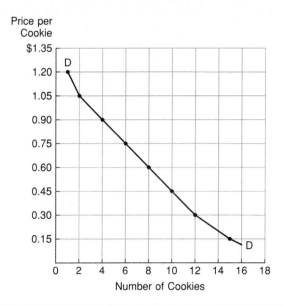

in different states. This study also found several nonprice factors that were important in explaining the demand for vanity plates.[2]

Supply

A seller's plan to make a good or service available in the market is referred to as supply. Like demand, supply is affected by the product's price as well as by nonprice factors that influence the seller, such as the cost of producing the product and the seller's expectation of future market conditions. Specifically, **supply** is defined as the different amounts of a good or service that a seller would make available for sale at different prices in a given time period when all nonprice factors affecting the seller's plans for the product are held constant. In other words, supply indicates how many hot fudge sundaes, haircuts, tires, or any other product a supplier would be willing to sell at different prices during, say, a week, a month, or a year, with all

Supply

The different amounts of a product that a seller would make available for sale at different prices in a defined time period when all nonprice factors are held constant.

[2] The economists found that income, the range of choices in letter and number spaces and symbols, whether front and rear or just rear plates were issued, the age distribution of the population, and the amount of time the program had been in effect influenced the demand for vanity plates.

Application 3.1

The Demand for Vanity Plates

"I saw a lot of 'vanity' license plates when I was in Virginia. There were a lot more than I'd seen in Boston, and I wondered about it," recalls Neil Alper, an economist at Boston's Northeastern University.

Mr. Alper was taking a sabbatical at the College of William and Mary when he made his observation. "[Two colleagues] and I got to talking about it at lunch one day, and we decided it might be interesting to investigate why."

A quick look in the faculty parking lot seemed to confirm Mr. Alper's observation. . . .

Since the three are economists, their natural supposition was that price might have something to do with the apparent proliferation of Virginia vanity.

The numbers confirmed their suspicion. The economists compared average annual [prices] of having personalized instead of ordinary plates over a five year period. Virginia charges an extra $10 per year for the plates. Mr. Alper's home state of Massachusetts charges almost $30. As a percentage of all license plates issued, vanity plates are more than four times as common in Virginia as in Massachusetts.

This is the sort of finding that stirs an economist's soul. The trio decided to embark on a full-fledged study of the demand for personalized plates.

The results were surprising. While nearly all states permit drivers the option of buying personalized plates, the fees charged vary tremendously—from $2 a year in Georgia to $60 in Ohio.

Source: "The Demand for Vanity," *The Margin*, October 1987, p. 11. Reprinted with permission.

nonprice factors unchanged. As with demand, all nonprice factors affecting supply are held constant to highlight the relationship between a product's price and the quantity of the product supplied.

The relationship between the amount of a product a seller would make available for sale and the product's price can be illustrated in a **supply schedule** such as that in Table 3.2, which shows the numbers of chocolate chip cookies of a particular size and quality that the Country Bakery Shop is willing to sell at different prices on a weekly basis. Observe the direct relationship between price and the quantity supplied in Table 3.2. At a low price the bakery would offer no or few cookies for sale; but it is willing to offer more for sale as the price increases. If the supply of any other good or service were chosen as an example, the same relationship would appear: the quantity supplied would increase as the price increased, and the quantity supplied would decrease as the price decreased. This relationship illustrates the **Law of Supply**, which states that, holding nonprice factors constant, there is a direct relationship between price and quantity supplied.

Why does the bakery react in this manner? The basic reason for the bakery's or any other supplier's behavior, and for the Law of Supply, is a seller's ability to cover costs and earn a profit. At very low prices a seller may not be able to cover costs and would, therefore, not be particularly interested in supplying the product. But as prices increase, costs could be

Supply schedule

A list of the amounts of a product that a seller would offer for sale at different prices in a defined time period when all nonprice factors are held constant.

Law of Supply

There is an direct relationship between the price of a product and the quantity supplied.

Table 3.2   Country Bakery's Weekly Supply of Chocolate Chip Cookies

The Law of Supply is illustrated in this supply schedule, which shows that more cookies are supplied at higher prices.

Price per Cookie	Quantity Supplied per Week
$0.15	0
0.30	0
0.45	50
0.60	300
0.75	500
0.90	650
1.05	750
1.20	800

covered and a small profit could be earned. If a seller were producing many products, as is the case with a bakery, the seller might choose to produce some of the product for a small profit, but might also concentrate on producing other items with a more favorable return. At higher prices, the quantity supplied would be further increased as additional costs from producing more could be covered and greater profits could be made.[3] The bakery, for example, might be willing to decrease its production of birthday cakes, danish, eclairs, and other products in order to increase its production of chocolate chip cookies if the price and profit on the cookies were extremely high.

Supply, like demand, is typically illustrated graphically, with price measured on the vertical axis and the quantity supplied on the horizontal axis. Each of the price-quantity combinations from the supply schedule in Table 3.2 is plotted in Figure 3.2, and a **supply curve** is drawn by connecting each of the points. Note that the supply curve slopes upward, showing that higher prices are associated with larger quantities supplied. Because the Law of Supply states that there is a direct relationship between price and quantity supplied, and because direct relationships are graphed as upward-sloping lines, it can be generalized that supply curves slope upward.

Supply curve

A line on a graph that illustrates a supply schedule; slopes upward because of the direct relationship between price and quantity supplied.

[3] Is it valid to assume that the cost per cookie might increase as the bakery produces more cookies? Yes. For example, the owner might incur extra expenses from additional repairs on equipment because it is used more often, or producing more cookies might require that the bakery's employees work overtime at a higher wage rate. See Chapter Twelve for details on rising costs associated with increased production.

Figure 3.2

Country Bakery's Weekly Supply of Chocolate Chip Cookies

The upward-sloping supply curve illustrates the Law of Supply by showing that more is supplied at higher prices and less is supplied at lower prices.

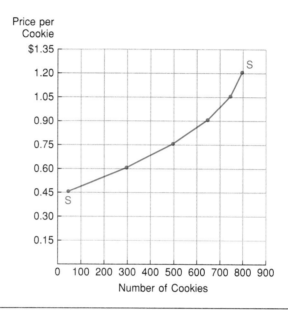

Market Demand, Market Supply, Equilibrium Price, and Equilibrium Quantity

Market Demand and Market Supply

Market

A place or situation in which the buyers and sellers of a product interact for the purpose of exchange.

Market demand and market supply

The demand of all buyers and supply of all sellers in a market for a particular good or service; is found by adding together all individual demand or supply curves or schedules.

When buyers and sellers come together for the purpose of exchanging a good or service, a **market** is formed. This can take place anywhere—at a store, showroom, used car lot, stock exchange, or vending machine, for example. **Market demand** and **market supply** are, respectively, the sum of all the individual quantities demanded and supplied of a product at each price in a market. For example, the market demand for an Academy Award–winning motion picture is made up of all of the individual demands to see the film. In a market, it is the demand and supply of all buyers and sellers, rather than individual demand and supply, that is important.

Markets and the Setting of Prices

Markets perform a critical function when economic decisions are made by businesses and households, because it is in markets that the prices for goods and services are determined through the interaction of buyers and sellers.

Table 3.3

Weekly Market Demand and Supply of Fresh-Baked Chocolate Chip Cookies

Market demand and market supply illustrate the different amounts of a product that all buyers in a market would demand and all sellers in a market would supply at various prices.

Price per Cookie	Quantity Demanded	Quantity Supplied
$0.15	30,000	2,000
0.30	24,000	8,000
0.45	20,000	12,000
0.60	16,000	16,000
0.75	12,000	20,000
0.90	8,000	24,000
1.05	4,000	28,000
1.20	2,000	30,000

In order to understand the operation of a market, particularly with regard to the determination of prices, let us return to the chocolate chip cookie example, where we analyzed John's individual demand and Country Bakery's individual supply, and observe the behavior of market demand and market supply for this product. Table 3.3 shows market demand and market supply schedules for fresh-baked chocolate chip cookies. Market demand is found by adding up the amount of cookies that John and all other buyers in this market would purchase at each price, and market supply is found by adding up the quantity of cookies that Country Bakery and all other sellers in this market would make available at each price. In the analysis of this market and those that follow, it is assumed that a high degree of competition exists among buyers and sellers. No buyer or seller exerts any unusual or undue influence, and no price-controlling government regulation occurs.[4]

In the market in Table 3.3, the price for a fresh-baked chocolate chip cookie ranges from $0.15 through $1.20. What would happen in this market if the price were $0.15 per cookie? At $0.15, buyers would demand 30,000 cookies, and sellers would offer only 2,000 for sale. Thus, at a price of $0.15 the quantity supplied would fall short of the quantity demanded by 28,000 cookies, or there would be a **shortage** on the market of 28,000 cookies. As a reaction to this shortage, sellers who observe the number of buyers left

Shortage

Occurs in a market when the quantity demanded is greater than the quantity supplied, or when the product's price is below the equilibrium price.

---

[4] A more technical definition of a market is presented in Chapter Thirteen. At this point it is useful to know that a particular market is made up of a group of sellers that compete with each other for the same group of buyers. In other words, because of geography, there are many separate markets for fresh-baked chocolate chip cookies in the United States. For instance, the market in Houston is not the same as the market in Seattle because each is composed of different buyers and sellers.

unsatisfied in the market would raise the price. In response to this price rise, the quantity supplied would increase (because of the Law of Supply), the quantity demanded would fall (because of the Law of Demand), and the shortage would be reduced.

What would happen if the price were $0.30 per cookie? At $0.30, the quantity demanded would be 24,000 cookies, and the quantity supplied would be 8,000 cookies. The market would again experience a shortage, but of only 16,000 cookies (24,000 quantity demanded minus 8,000 quantity supplied). Again, the market reaction would be a price rise above $0.30, the quantity demanded by buyers would decrease, the quantity supplied by sellers would increase, and the shortage would shrink.

Surplus

Occurs in a market when the quantity demanded is less than the quantity supplied, or when the product's price is above the equilibrium price.

What would happen if the sellers charged $1.20 per cookie? At $1.20, consumers would want to buy only 2,000 cookies, but sellers would offer 30,000 cookies for sale. As a result, the quantity demanded would fall short of the quantity supplied by 28,000 cookies, or there would be a **surplus** of 28,000 cookies on the market. Sellers would react like any other seller with excess merchandise at a price consumers will not pay: they would lower their price. As the price fell, the Law of Demand would go into operation, and some buyers who would not purchase cookies at $1.20 each would do so at the lower price. At the same time, because of the Law of Supply, the lower price would lead to a reduction in quantity supplied, and the surplus would diminish. If the price charged were $1.05, a surplus of 24,000 cookies would develop, sellers would again lower their price, and the surplus would again shrink.

Equilibrium Price and Equilibrium Quantity

Equilibrium price and equilibrium quantity

The price and quantity at which demand equals supply; the price and quantity toward which a free market automatically moves.

The market in Table 3.3 appears to be moving automatically toward a price of $0.60, where the quantity demanded and quantity supplied are both 16,000 cookies. If sellers charge $0.60 per cookie, there will be no surpluses or shortages and no tendency to raise or lower price. The price that sets buyers' plans equal to sellers' plans, $0.60, is termed the **equilibrium price.** The quantity at which those plans are equal, 16,000 cookies, is termed the **equilibrium quantity.** Thus, equilibrium price and equilibrium quantity are the price and quantity toward which a market will automatically move. At the equilibrium price, quantity demanded equals quantity supplied, and there is no tendency to change the price.[5]

If the price of a good or service is below its equilibrium level, a shortage will develop, causing the price to automatically increase toward equilibrium. If the price is above equilibrium, a surplus will develop, causing the price to decrease toward equilibrium.

---

[5] The equilibrium price is sometimes referred to as the "market clearing price," since at this price the amount demanded by buyers is equal to the amount supplied by sellers, thereby "clearing" the market of the good or service.

Figure 3.3   Weekly Market Demand and Supply of Fresh-Baked Chocolate Chip Cookies

The equilibrium price and quantity in a market occur at the intersection of the market demand and supply curves. At equilibrium, the quantity demanded in a market equals the quantity supplied.

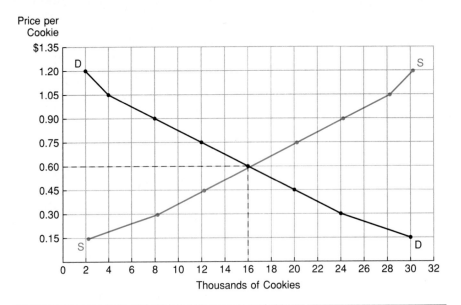

The cookie market shown in Table 3.3 is graphed in Figure 3.3. The demand curve is derived from the "Price per Cookie" and "Quantity Demanded" columns, and the supply curve is drawn from the "Price per Cookie" and "Quantity Supplied" columns. From the graph it is easy to see that the equilibrium price and quantity occur at the intersection of the supply and demand curves, in this case at a price of $0.60 per cookie and a quantity of 16,000 cookies.

It is also possible to illustrate shortages and surpluses graphically. Figure 3.4a shows that at a price of $0.90 the quantity demanded is 8,000 cookies and the quantity supplied is 24,000 cookies: there is a surplus of 16,000 cookies. The difference between the demand and supply curves at $0.90 is equal to the amount of the surplus. Notice that as the price comes closer to the equilibrium level, the distance between the demand and supply curves narrows, and the surplus becomes smaller. Figure 3.4b measures the shortage of 8,000 cookies that would occur at a price of $0.45. Can you determine the shortage at a price of $0.30 per cookie?[6]

[6] There would be a shortage of 16,000 cookies.

Figure 3.4   Measuring Shortages and Surpluses on Demand and Supply Curves

The surplus or shortage at a particular price is equal to the difference between the quantity demanded and the quantity supplied at that price.

a. Measuring the Surplus at a Price of $0.90

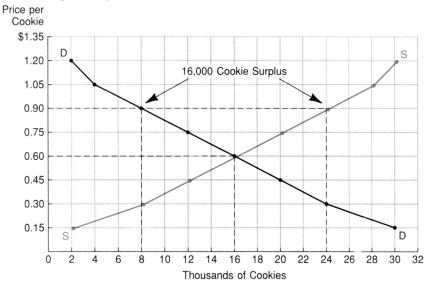

b. Measuring the Shortage at a Price of $0.45

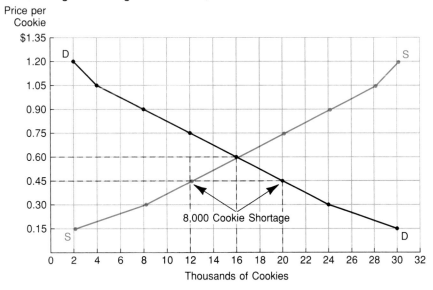

*Changes in Quantity Demanded
and Quantity Supplied*

When the price of cookies changed in Table 3.3 and Figure 3.3, the amount
that buyers would have purchased also changed. For example, as the price
rose from $0.15 to $0.30, the amount buyers demanded fell from 30,000 to
24,000 cookies. When a change in a product's *price* causes a change in the
amount that would be purchased, a **change in quantity demanded** occurs.
A change in quantity demanded is shown by a movement *along* a demand
curve from one price-quantity point to another, such as from the point
representing $0.15 and 30,000 cookies to the point representing $0.30 and
24,000 cookies on the demand curve in Figure 3.3.

Likewise, the amount of cookies that the sellers in Table 3.3 and Figure
3.3 were prepared to sell changed as the price changed. As the price fell from
$1.20 to $1.05, the amount supplied fell from 30,000 to 28,000. When a change
in a product's *price* causes a change in the amount of the product that a seller
would supply, a **change in quantity supplied** occurs. A change in quantity
supplied is illustrated graphically by a movement *along* a supply curve from
one price-quantity point to another, such as from the point representing
$1.20 and 30,000 cookies to the point representing $1.05 and 28,000 cookies
on the supply curve in Figure 3.3.

Changes in Demand and Supply

In introducing demand and supply, it was emphasized that the buyers and
sellers of a product are affected both by the product's price and by nonprice
considerations. It was also noted that these nonprice factors are held constant when developing demand and supply schedules and curves in order to
explain how changes in a product's price affect buyers' and sellers' behavior.
For example, if you were deriving a demand schedule to illustrate the different amounts of a particular brand of cola a person would be willing to purchase at different prices, only the cola's price would be allowed to change: all
nonprice factors, such as the buyer's income and taste for cola, the popularity
of cola, and the degree of substitutability between this brand and other colas,
or between colas and other beverages, would be held constant.

For any product, hundreds of nonprice factors may influence demand
and supply. To better understand how they affect buyers, sellers, and markets, these factors can be placed into several categories. Some major **nonprice factors influencing demand** are (1) income; (2) expectations concerning future income, prices, or availabilities; (3) taste, fashion, and popularity;
(4) the prices of related goods; and, when considering market demand, (5)
the number of buyers. Some major **nonprice factors influencing supply** are
(1) the cost of producing the item;[7] (2) expectations of future market

---

[7]Care must be taken to distinguish between the terms *price* and *cost*. Price is the amount for
which an item can be sold. Cost is the expenditure required to produce the item.

**Change in quantity
demanded and
quantity supplied**
A change in the amount
of a product demanded
or supplied that is caused
by a change in its price;
represented by a
movement along a
demand or supply curve
from one price-quantity
point to another.

**Nonprice factors
influencing demand**
Factors such as income,
taste, and expectations
that help to formulate the
demand for a product.

**Nonprice factors
influencing supply**
Factors such as the cost of
production and the
number of sellers that
help to formulate the
supply of a product.

Table 3.4

Gwen's Weekly Demand Schedule for 12-Ounce Cans of Cola Before and After an Increase in Her Income

A change in a nonprice factor causes a change in the amount of an item demanded at each price. After an increase in income, the number of cans of cola demanded by Gwen each week increases at every price.

Before		After	
Price per Can	Number of Cans Demanded Weekly	Price per Can	Number of Cans Demanded Weekly
10¢	20	10¢	26
20	17	20	23
30	14	30	20
40	12	40	18
50	10	50	16
60	8	60	14
70	6	70	12
80	4	80	10
90	3	90	9

conditions; (3) the prices of other items the producer does or could sell; and, when dealing with market supply, (4) the number of sellers.

The reason nonprice factors are held constant when deriving demand and supply schedules and curves is that *changes in the nonprice factors that influence demand and supply cause demand and supply schedules and curves to change.* These changes are referred to as "changes in demand" and "changes in supply."

Changes in Demand

Change in demand

A change in the demand schedule and curve for a product caused by a change in one or more nonprice factors influencing the product's demand; the demand curve shifts to the right or left.

The expression **change in demand** refers to a change in the demand schedule and curve for a product that is caused by a change in one or more nonprice factors influencing that demand. The old schedule and curve no longer hold as the buyer develops a new set of plans. For example, a person's weekly demand for a particular brand of cola could change because of a change in a nonprice factor influencing that demand. For instance, an increase in income could change demand by permitting a person to buy more cola at each price than was previously afforded. This type of change is illustrated in Table 3.4, which shows Gwen's demand for cola before and after a change in income. Notice, for example, that the number of cans demanded weekly at $0.50 increases from 10 to 16 following the increase in her income.

Figure 3.5   Increase in Gwen's Weekly Demand for 12-Ounce Cans of Cola

An increase in Gwen's demand for cola causes the demand curve to shift to the right from D1 to D2, indicating that a larger quantity is now demanded at each price.

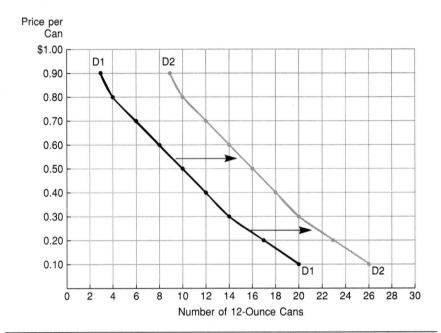

Increase in demand

A change in one or more nonprice influences on demand causes more of a product to be demanded at each price; the demand curve shifts to the right.

A change in demand may be designated as either an increase in demand or a decrease in demand. An **increase in demand** means that a change in one or more nonprice factors has caused a buyer to want to purchase more of a product at every price. Some factors that could bring about an increase in the demand for a product are an increase in buyers' incomes, an increase in the popularity of the good or service, an increase in the price of a substitute good or service that makes the product demanded look relatively cheaper to buyers, expectations of a price increase or of non-availability of the item in the future that make consumers want to purchase more of the product now, and an increase in the number of buyers in the market.

Graphically, an increase in demand causes the demand curve for a good or service to *shift* to the right. This shift is shown in Figure 3.5, which graphically illustrates Gwen's demand schedules for cola in Table 3.4. Gwen's original demand for cola before her income changes is shown by D1 in Figure 3.5. When Gwen's income increases, and she wants to purchase more cola, her demand schedule changes. When this new schedule is graphed in Figure 3.5, the demand curve shifts to the right, to D2. Observe on the graph that at $0.80 she is now willing to buy 10 rather than 4 cans,

Figure 3.6   Decrease in a Homeowner's Demand for Plastic Lawn and Leaf Bags

A decrease in a homeowner's demand for lawn bags causes the demand curve to shift to the left from D1 to D2, indicating that a smaller quantity is now demanded at each price.

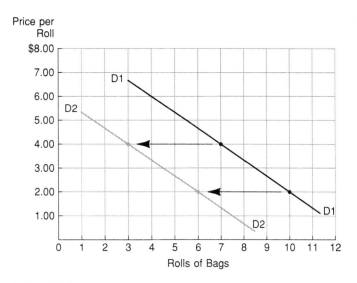

Decrease in demand

A change in one or more nonprice influences on demand causes less of a product to be demanded at each price; the demand curve shifts to the left.

and at $0.50 she is now willing to buy 16 rather than 10 cans. Clearly, she demands more at each price, or has experienced an increase in demand.

A **decrease in demand** means that a change in one or more nonprice factors has caused a buyer to want to purchase less of a product at every price. Graphically, a decrease in demand causes the demand curve to *shift* to the left. For example, a homeowner who stops collecting grass clippings because of concern over landfill shortages will want to buy fewer rolls of plastic lawn and leaf bags at each possible price. This is illustrated in Figure 3.6, where D1 is the homeowner's original demand curve for lawn bags. Before she was concerned about the environment, the homeowner would have purchased ten rolls per year at $2.00 each, or seven at $4.00 each. The new demand curve, D2, illustrates demand after the decision to stop bagging grass. The homeowner will now buy only six rolls at $2.00 each, or three at $4.00 each. A decrease in demand has clearly occurred.

Other factors that could cause a decrease in the demand for a good or service are a decrease in the number of buyers in the market, a decrease in buyers' incomes, expectations of future price or income decreases that would make consumers want to purchase less of the product now, and a decrease in the price of a substitute good or service that would make the product demanded appear to be relatively more expensive.

Figure 3.7

Increase in the Supply of Video Games

An increase in the supply of video games causes the supply curve to shift to the right from S1 to S2, indicating that a larger quantity is supplied at each price.

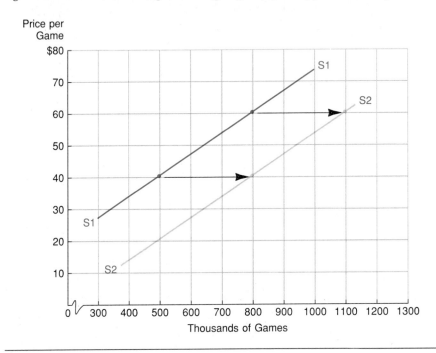

In summary, an increase in demand means that more of a product is demanded at each price and the demand curve shifts to the right. A decrease in demand means that less is demanded at each price and the demand curve shifts to the left.

Changes in Supply

Change in supply

A change in the supply schedule and curve for a product caused by a change in one or more nonprice factors influencing the product's supply; the supply curve shifts to the right or left.

Increase in supply

A change in one or more nonprice influences on supply causes more of a product to be supplied at each price; the supply curve shifts to the right.

A **change in supply** results from a change in one or more nonprice factors affecting the supply of a product. The nonprice changes cause either an increase or a decrease in supply.

An **increase in supply** means that a seller is willing to offer more of a good or service for sale at each price, and that the supply curve for the good or service *shifts* to the right. In Figure 3.7, assume that S1 is the original supply curve indicating that a seller of video games was willing to sell 500,000 games at $40 each or 800,000 at $60 each. After an increase in supply, which causes the supply curve to shift to S2, the seller is willing to offer more games at each price: for example, 800,000 at $40 and 1,100,000 at $60.

Figure 3.8

Decrease in the Supply of Health Club Memberships

A decrease in the supply of health club memberships causes the supply curve to shift to the left from S1 to S2, indicating that a smaller quantity is supplied at each price.

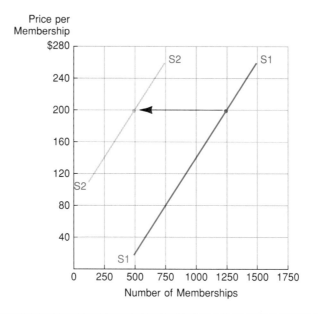

What could cause an increase in supply? A seller could experience a decrease in the cost of production, which would allow the seller to make more of the product available at the same dollar outlay. Perhaps an input used in producing the item becomes available at a lower cost, or perhaps the seller can adopt some new technology for producing the item for less. An increase in supply could also occur because a seller is trying to increase its sales now for fear of a weakening market in the future, or because it is ceasing production of a less profitable item and concentrating more of its resources on a more profitable product. Finally, in dealing with market supply, new sellers could enter the market, thus shifting the supply curve to the right.

Decrease in supply

A change in one or more nonprice influences on supply causes less of a product to be supplied at each price; the supply curve shifts to the left.

A **decrease in supply** means that a change in one or more nonprice factors has made a seller willing to offer less of a product for sale at each price, causing the supply curve to *shift* to the left. In Figure 3.8, a health club's original supply curve for memberships, S1, indicates that it was willing to sell 1,250 at a price of $200 each. A decrease in supply, which is represented by a shift of the supply curve to S2, reveals that the club is now willing to sell less at each price—for example, only 500 at $200 each.

Rain Alone Will Not Rescue the West

The plentiful and cheap water that made the West rich, powerful and populous has now turned scarce and ever more costly to find.

A fourth straight year of drought has descended on California and the Southwest. It has brought not only painful shortages and restrictions on water use but also profound questions about the region's capacity to grow the way it has and preserve its comfortable style of life without devastating environmental consequences and bitter divisions.

But by contrast with previous droughts, shortages will endure even if rain and snowfall return to normal next winter, officials say. Enormous population growth, environmental concerns, contamination of underground water and court rulings have all combined to make it harder and harder to keep up with demand. . . .

This week, officials of the San Francisco Water Department are expected to recommend mandatory rationing for that city, [whose sole source of water was down to 27 percent of capacity]. . . .

Rationing has been a fact of life for some time on the central coast of California, the hardest-hit area. In Monterey, each household must cut back by 20 percent from normal use or face stiff fines. Farther south, in the seaside city of Santa Barbara, . . . people find themselves reduced to watering lawns with buckets. . . .

The drought also means that California for the first time will feel the effects of a 1964 Supreme Court decision that limited the state's right to Colorado River water in dry years. California officials say increased demand by Arizona will likely mean that the water to be diverted this year to Southern California will be cut by a quarter.

Against this backdrop of shrinking resources, population continues to grow. California grew by an estimated 5.2 million people during the 1980s and . . . Southern California has been growing by about 300,000 people a year.

In the past, the water barons of the West easily and eagerly coped with such demand. . . .

But [water] projects are not so easily built today. Major elements of the State Water Project, which diverts water from the Sacramento River delta, remain unfinished, bogged down in environmental and legal battles. Concerns about San Francisco Bay, [lawsuits and agreements about the eastern slope of the Sierras, and endangered salmon have delayed the movement of water].

Source: Excerpted from Robert Reinhold, "Rain Alone Won't Ease Latest Drought in West," *The New York Times*, April 16, 1990, p. A11. Copyright © 1990 by The New York Times Company. Excerpted by permission.

A decrease in the supply of a product can result from increased costs of production due to such factors as higher wages, equipment costs, or costs of borrowing money. Other possible causes of a decrease in supply include a switch in production to another item that is more profitable; an expectation that conditions will improve for sellers at a future date; and, in the case of market supply, the exit of some sellers from the market.

In summary, an increase in supply means that a larger quantity of a product is made available for sale at each price, causing the supply curve to shift to the right. A decrease in supply means that a smaller quantity is made available for sale at each price, causing the supply curve to shift to the left.

Nonprice factors play a significant role in determining the demand and supply of a product. Application 3.2, "Rain Alone Will Not Rescue the West," discusses some specific problems affecting the market for water in California. As you read this application, try to identify the particular nonprice factors that have increased or decreased demand or supply, and think of how each factor would be graphically illustrated. To give you a start, the drought is a nonprice factor affecting the supply of water, and mandatory rationing is a nonprice factor affecting the demand for water.

Warning: Changes in Quantity Demanded and Quantity Supplied vs. Changes in Demand and Supply

A frequent source of confusion for students of economics stems from the difficulty in maintaining a clear distinction between changes in quantity demanded and quantity supplied, and changes in demand and supply. Although the terms are similar, they refer to completely different concepts. Because this distinction is so important, it is worthwhile to review it one more time.

Changes in quantity demanded and quantity supplied are caused *only* by a change in a product's price, and are illustrated by a movement *along* a fixed demand or supply curve from one price-quantity combination to another. For example, the movement along the demand curve in Figure 3.9a from $20 and 100 units to $10 and 150 units illustrates an increase in quantity demanded: more is demanded as the price falls. The movement along the supply curve in Figure 3.9b from $20 and 100 units to $10 and 50 units illustrates a decrease in quantity supplied: less is supplied as the price falls.

Changes in demand and supply are *not* caused by a change in a product's price; they are the result of changes in the nonprice determinants of demand and supply, and are portrayed by a *shift* of the demand or supply curve to the right or left. An increase in demand is illustrated by the shift of the demand curve in Figure 3.9c to the right from D1 to D2. Without the price changing from $20, the amount demanded increases from 100 to 150 units because of a change in one or more of the nonprice factors affecting the demand for the product. The shift of the supply curve in Figure 3.9d from S1 to S2 illustrates a decrease in supply: less is supplied at $20 and at every other price because of a change in one or more of the nonprice factors affecting the supply of the product.

You will find it easier to understand the behavior of buyers and sellers in markets, and how they react to various price and nonprice considerations, if you remember these distinctions.

Changes in Equilibrium Price and Equilibrium Quantity

We have seen that a change in a nonprice factor affecting demand or supply will cause a demand or supply curve to shift, and that the equilibrium price and quantity of a good or service are shown by the intersection of its demand and supply curves. Therefore, whenever a product's demand or supply curve shifts, its equilibrium price and quantity will change as well.

Figure 3.9   Changes in Quantity Demanded and Quantity Supplied
                                   Versus Changes in Demand and Supply

Changes in quantity demanded or quantity supplied are shown by movements along a fixed demand or supply curve, but with changes in demand or supply, the entire curve shifts.

Change in Quantity Demanded and Quantity Supplied

a. Increase in Quantity Demanded

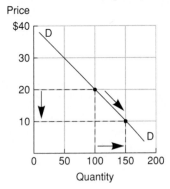

b. Decrease in Quantity Supplied

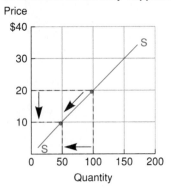

Change in Demand and Supply

c. Increase in Demand

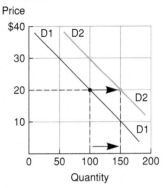

d. Decrease in Supply

It is useful to be able to predict and analyze how changes in buyer and seller behavior can alter both the equilibrium price of a product and the quantity bought and sold. To order our thinking about these changes in market conditions, we will consider separately the effects on equilibrium price and quantity of an increase in demand, a decrease in demand, an increase in supply, and a decrease in supply.

Figure 3.10

Effect of an Increase in Demand

An increase in the demand for a product, such as volleyball nets, causes an increase in the product's equilibrium price and equilibrium quantity.

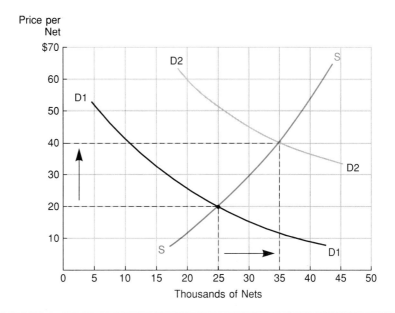

Effect of an Increase in Demand

What effect does an increase in demand have on the equilibrium price and quantity of a product? Consider an item that becomes a fad. Suppose that volleyball is the "in" sport, and that all over the country people are searching for volleyball nets to put in their yards and take to parks and beaches. Common-sense analysis of the volleyball net market suggests that such an increase in demand would push the price of nets up, and that even at this increased price more nets would be sold. Let us examine the graphic analysis in Figure 3.10 to determine whether our common-sense analysis is correct.

S is the monthly market supply curve for volleyball nets, and D1 shows the monthly demand for volleyball nets before the sport becomes a fad. With supply curve S and demand curve D1, the equilibrium price is $20 per net, and the equilibrium quantity is 25,000 nets. As the game becomes fashionable, the demand for volleyball nets increases, and the demand curve shifts to the right to D2. At the new equilibrium of S and D2, 35,000 nets are sold to buyers at a price of $40 each. Thus, an increase in the demand for a product causes both its equilibrium price and equilibrium quantity to increase.

Figure 3.11   Effect of a Decrease in Demand

A decrease in the demand for a product, such as turntables, causes a decrease in the product's equilibrium price and equilibrium quantity.

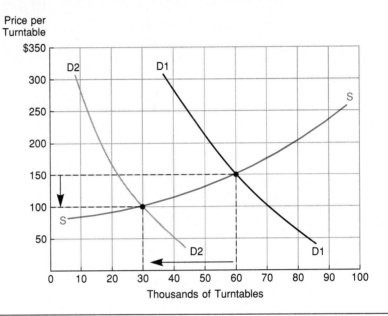

Effect of a Decrease in Demand

What effect does a decrease in demand have on the equilibrium price and quantity of a product? Consider the market for phonograph record turntables. Assume that there is no change in supply, but that the demand falls as people switch to cassette tape decks and compact disc players. The market situation is shown in Figure 3.11. Here, S is the monthly supply curve for turntables, and D1 shows the monthly demand before people start shifting to other products. With S and D1, the equilibrium price is $150 a unit, and the equilibrium quantity is 60,000 units. But after people become interested in tape decks and disc players, the demand for turntables falls, and the demand curve shifts to the left to D2. As a result of the decrease in demand, the equilibrium price falls to $100 a unit, and the equilibrium quantity falls to 30,000 turntables. Thus, a decrease in the demand for a product causes both its equilibrium price and equilibrium quantity to fall. Consider the passing of any recent fad. Is that not what happened to the price and the quantity sold as the product became less popular?

Figure 3.12

Effect of an Increase in Supply

An increase in the supply of a product, such as pocket calculators, causes a decrease in the product's equilibrium price and an increase in its equilibrium quantity.

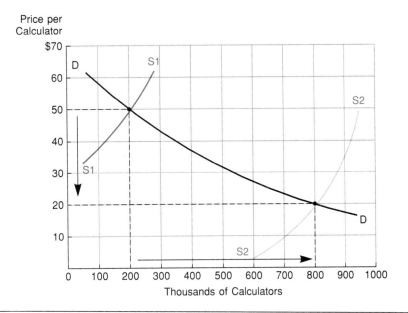

Effect of an Increase in Supply

What effect does an increase in supply have on the equilibrium price and quantity of a product? An immediate response to this question might be that an increase in the supply of a product means that the price will fall and the amount sold will increase. Let us test this response. Over the years several products, such as pocket calculators, have increased significantly in supply because technology has made production cheaper, and because new companies have entered the market. In Figure 3.12, S1 and D are the original supply and demand curves for pocket calculators. With this supply and demand, the equilibrium price is $50 a unit, and the equilibrium quantity is 200,000 units. Later, as new technologies and new manufacturers make their impacts felt on the market, the supply curve shifts to S2. Following this increase in supply, the new equilibrium price is $20 per unit, and the equilibrium quantity is 800,000 units. Thus, with an increase in supply, the equilibrium quantity increases, but the equilibrium price falls.

Figure 3.13   Effect of a Decrease in Supply

A decrease in the supply of a product, such as gasoline, causes an increase in the product's equilibrium price and a decrease in its equilibrium quantity.

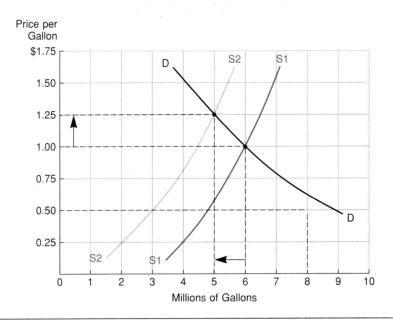

Effect of a Decrease in Supply

What effect does a decrease in supply have on the equilibrium price and quantity of a product? Assume that the supply of gasoline decreases, but not the demand. D and S1 in Figure 3.13 are the demand and supply curves for gasoline before the available amounts are reduced. With D and S1 the equilibrium price is $1.00 per gallon, and the equilibrium quantity is 6 million gallons. Suppose now that there is a cutback in the amount of gasoline brought to the market, causing the supply curve to shift to the left to S2. With this decrease in supply, the new equilibrium price is $1.25 per gallon, and the equilibrium quantity is 5 million gallons. Thus, a decrease in supply leads to an increase in the equilibrium price and a decrease in the equilibrium quantity.

"Test Your Understanding: Changes in Supply and Demand" lets you evaluate your skill at analyzing the factors causing supply and demand curves to shift, and the effects of those shifts on equilibrium price and quantity.

Test Your Understanding

Changes in Supply and Demand[a]

[a]Answers can be found at the back of the book.

Complete the table by determining which of the following each example represents.
a. An increase in demand
b. A decrease in demand
c. An increase in supply
d. A decrease in supply
e. No change in either demand or supply

Example	Result	Graphic Change	Change in Equilibrium Price	Change in Equilibrium Quantity
1. Some sellers drop out of the car wash market.	d.	supply curve shifts to the left	increase	decrease
2. A clothing retailer increases the effectiveness of its advertising campaign without increasing its advertising costs.				
3. A local water company finds its costs increasing because of environmental regulations.				
4. The price of autos goes up.				
5. Buyers in the sailboat market experience a decline in their incomes.				
6. Fans become more supportive of a local football team because it has a winning season.				
7. A technological advance makes it cheaper to produce cellular telephones.				
8. Buyers decide that a product that has been a fad is out of style.				
9. Buyers expect that antifreeze will be unavailable or in short supply in the future.				
10. Sellers of landfill space raise their prices.				
11. The number of buyers in the farm implements market decreases.				
12. Several new stores renting videotaped movies open in town.				
13. The price of rollerblades goes down.				
14. A seller of a popular soft drink shifts more resources toward that product after discontinuing production of a less successful beverage.				

Effect of Changes in Both Demand and Supply

In each of the preceding examples of how equilibrium price and quantity are affected by changes in demand or supply, only one side of the market was changed, while the other side was held constant. In reality, simultaneous changes might occur. For example, both demand and supply might increase at the same time. Although such simultaneous changes are not illustrated here, your graphing skills should enable you to arrive at some conclusions about them.[8]

Limiting the Movement of Prices

Up to this point we have dealt with free market conditions, where buyers and sellers interact independent of any other force, such as the government, in determining prices. Government, however, has on occasion stepped into certain markets and interfered with free pricing by setting upper or lower limits beyond which a price cannot go. Several types of goods and services, including some farm products, electricity, and long-distance phone service, and some types of labor, have had their prices limited in this way to prevent them from becoming too high or too low. Supply and demand analysis can be used to explain how this type of government intervention affects market conditions.

Price Ceilings or Upper Price Limits

Price ceiling (upper price limit)

A government-set maximum price that can be charged for a particular good or service; if the equilibrium price is above the price ceiling, a shortage will develop.

Legally imposed upper price limits, called **price ceilings,** keep prices from rising above certain levels. They have at times been placed on such items as natural gas shipped in interstate commerce, rental apartments,

---

[8] If you try graphing simultaneous changes in demand and supply you should get the following results.

Change	Equilibrium Price Will:	Equilibrium Quantity Will:
Demand and supply both increase	Increase, decrease, or stay the same	Increase
Demand and supply both decrease	Increase, decrease, or stay the same	Decrease
Demand increases and supply decreases	Increase	Increase, decrease, or stay the same
Demand decreases and supply increases	Decrease	Increase, decrease, or stay the same

In the cases where equilibrium price or quantity can increase, decrease, or stay the same, the actual change depends on the size of the change in supply and demand. For example, an increase in demand that is larger than an increase in supply will result in an increase in price, whereas an increase in demand that is smaller than an increase in supply will result in a decrease in price.

Figure 3.14   Effect of a Price Ceiling on a Market

When the equilibrium price for a product is below its legal upper limit, the price ceiling has no effect on the market; but when the equilibrium price is above its legal upper limit, the price ceiling takes effect and a shortage develops.

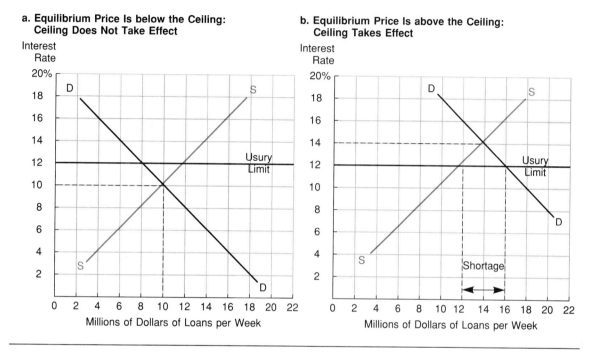

a. Equilibrium Price Is below the Ceiling: Ceiling Does Not Take Effect

b. Equilibrium Price Is above the Ceiling: Ceiling Takes Effect

and the interest rates people pay for borrowed money. If the equilibrium price for a good or service is below its government-established upper legal limit, or ceiling, the limit will have no impact on buyers and sellers since it will not take effect. But if the equilibrium price for a good or service is above its upper legal limit, the price ceiling will take effect and a shortage will occur.

For example, suppose that a law sets the maximum interest rate to be charged on some types of loans at 12 percent. Such maximum interest rate laws are called "usury laws" and have been adopted in the past by several state governments to apply to some loans, such as those for home mortgages. Figure 3.14a gives the demand for and the supply of loans where the ceiling on interest rates has no impact. Here borrowers' and lenders' wishes are equalized at an interest rate of 10 percent, and $10 million is loaned each week. The government-imposed ceiling on interest rates has not been reached in the market.

Suppose, however, that an increase in the demand for borrowed money occurs, causing the demand curve to shift to the right. This new situation is shown in Figure 3.14b. If the market were free to go to equilibrium after this increase in demand, the new interest rate would be 14 percent. However, the upper legal limit is 12 percent, so lenders may charge no more. Rather than increasing from 10 percent to 14 percent, the interest rate can rise only to the legal limit of 12 percent. At the 12 percent rate, borrowers would like to have $16 million in loans, but lenders would provide only $12 million in funds. At the 12 percent usury limit, there would be a $4 million shortage of funds for borrowing. Thus, when the free market equilibrium price is above the government-imposed upper limit, or ceiling, a shortage develops.

Price Floors or Lower Price Limits

Price floor (lower price limit)

A government-set minimum price that can be charged for a particular good or service; if the equilibrium price is below the price floor, a surplus will develop.

Legally imposed lower price limits, called **price floors,** prevent prices from falling below certain levels. Examples of lower price limits include the minimum wage law, which sets the minimum hourly payment that many workers can earn, and government-guaranteed farm prices, which ensure farmers of a minimum price on particular crops. As long as the equilibrium price of a good or service is above its lower legal limit, or price floor, the free market will not be affected by the limit. However, if the equilibrium price of a good or service falls below the floor, the government-set price will be charged. Since this legally imposed price is higher than the price the free market would have permitted, surpluses begin to appear.

Consider the effect of the minimum wage law as an example. Suppose that the minimum wage is set at $4 per hour. If the supply and demand for a certain type of labor are as shown in Figure 3.15a, the minimum wage will have no impact on the market. The equilibrium wage of $4.50 per hour is greater than the minimum wage, and the number of available workers equals the number demanded.

Now suppose that the government raises the minimum wage from $4 to $5 per hour and that there is no change in supply or demand in this labor market. Since the equilibrium wage rate is $4.50, or less than the minimum wage, the $5 minimum wage will take effect. That is, businesses buying this type of labor must pay $5 per hour rather than $4.50. Figure 3.15b shows the market condition with the new minimum wage rate. At $5 per hour the number of workers demanded falls to 1,000, and the number of willing and able workers rises to 1,200. The price floor has caused a surplus of 200 people unable to obtain a job in this market. Thus, when the free market equilibrium price is below the government-imposed floor, a surplus develops.

In summary, price ceilings, when their effects are felt, keep prices lower than they would otherwise be and result in shortages. Price floors, when their effects are felt, keep prices higher than they would otherwise be and result in surpluses.

Figure 3.15   Effect of a Price Floor on a Market

When the equilibrium price for a resource or a product is above its legal lower limit, the price floor has no effect on the market; but when the equilibrium price is below its floor, the floor takes effect and a surplus develops.

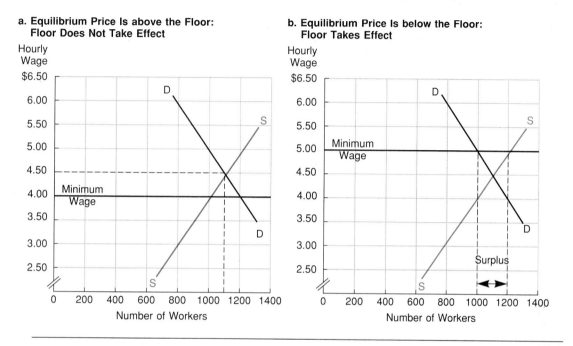

a. Equilibrium Price Is above the Floor: Floor Does Not Take Effect

b. Equilibrium Price Is below the Floor: Floor Takes Effect

It should be noted that the government can also affect markets by influencing the quantities of products, as well as their prices. For example, public utility commissions have the power to limit the number of firms providing residential gas and electric services, the Food and Drug Administration controls the flow of new medications onto the market, and the Small Business Administration can encourage the formation of new companies. Government influence on markets is discussed in detail in Chapter Fourteen.

Price ceilings and price floors benefit some groups and hurt others. Application 3.3, "Rent Control War," describes some problems that have arisen because of ceilings imposed on monthly housing rents. Who gains and who loses from rent control, and what effect does it have on the stock of available housing? Applying these same questions to labor markets, who gains and who loses from the minimum wage law, and what effect does it have on the number of job openings and the supply of available workers?

Application 3.3

Rent Control War

... Cities contend rent control protects poor tenants from escalating rents when housing is in short supply. But study after study indicates that what results is a worsening shortage, a deteriorating rental stock, declining property tax revenues, an immobilized tenantry and warfare between landlords and tenants. The tighter the controls and the longer they are in place, the more pronounced these effects.

New York provides a striking illustration because its controls are among the nation's oldest and strictest. The city has the nation's lowest rental vacancy rate, yet the state ranks last in rental housing starts per capita. Owners abandon some 2,000 dwelling units a month—a loss of nearly a quarter-million units over the past decade. Some estimates put the figure at twice that. ...

Rent controls subsidize all tenants, rich and poor, as long as tenants stay put. People who move a lot benefit least, especially newcomers and the poor. Berkeley's [California] law, for example, was supposed to aid university students; now many students no longer can find housing in Berkeley. Since the city adopted controls in 1979 it has lost more than 4,000 rentals, a 20 percent decline in its stock. ...

Black markets develop. New tenants pay "key money" to old tenants to sublet at the regulated rent. Or the original tenants sublet at market rents and pocket the difference. New tenants shoulder higher rents to offset the building costs that existing tenants do not pay. "It's horrible," says a woman who moved to New York from Oklahoma. She and her husband paid $4,000 in broker fees and key money the last time they moved. "We'll never leave this apartment as long as we're in New York." She is not alone. Single tenants cling to three-bedroom apartments because they cannot afford to move, while families squeeze into one-bedroom units for the same reason. Newcomers find little available. More than 85 percent of the New Yorkers in rent-controlled apartments have not moved in 15 years. ...

Source: Carolyn Lochhead, "Protracted Rent Control War Takes Toll on Housing Stock," *Insight* magazine (April 13, 1987), pp. 38–40. Reprinted with permission.

Price Elasticity of Demand and Supply

It is obvious by now that the quantity demanded of a good or service is inversely related to its price and that the quantity supplied is directly related to its price. But there is one more important aspect of the behavior of both buyers and sellers to be considered—how much will the quantity demanded and the quantity supplied change as the price changes? In other words, when the price of an item increases, will a consumer respond weakly, demanding just a little less of the item, or strongly, demanding much less? Will a seller respond weakly or strongly to a change in the price of the good or service being sold? **Price elasticity** refers to the strength of the response to a price change, and applies to both buyers and sellers. Price changes on some items, such as water and other utilities and prescription drugs, typically bring about weak responses in consumers. Price changes on other items, such as vacation tours and designer clothing, typically bring about strong responses.

Understanding elasticity can be very important to a business. Suppose an ice cream shop sells an average of 100 milkshakes per week at a price of

Price elasticity
A measure of the strength of a buyer's or seller's response to a price change.

$2.00 each. As a result, its weekly revenue from the sale of milkshakes averages $200 (100 × $2.00). Now suppose that the owner decides to increase sales by cutting the price of milkshakes from $2.00 to $1.75. At the new lower price consumers will want to buy more milkshakes, but how many more? Suppose the consumer response to the price cut results in an increase in the sale of shakes to 110 per week. With this new price and quantity combination, the average weekly revenue from the sale of milkshakes falls to $192.50 (110 × $1.75). In other words, although the quantity of milkshakes demanded goes up after the price cut, the response is so weak that revenue falls from $200 to $192.50. A different decision might have been made if the owner had known how little the quantity demanded was going to increase after lowering the price. If the response to the price decrease is strong — for example, if consumers buy 140 milkshakes at $1.75 each — weekly revenue will increase from $200 to $245 (140 × $1.75). With a strong response, the increase in quantity demanded is large enough to raise revenue. In other words, elasticity of demand, or the consumer's responsiveness to a price change, is an important factor influencing a business's revenue from sales.

If buyers or sellers are sensitive to a price change — that is, if their response is strong — their demand or supply is said to be **price elastic**. If buyers or sellers are not sensitive to a price change — that is, if their response is weak — their demand or supply is said to be **price inelastic**.

Measuring Price Elasticity

The degree to which demand or supply is price elastic or inelastic can be measured by calculating an **elasticity coefficient** from the formula

$$\frac{|\% \text{ change in } Q|}{|\% \text{ change in } P|},$$

where Q represents the quantity demanded or supplied of a product, and P represents the product's price. The vertical lines on each side of the numerator and denominator indicate that we are interested in the "absolute values" of the percentage changes in quantity and price. That is, we need to know the *size* of each change but not its direction. Whether the change in price or quantity is up or down, or has a plus or minus sign in front of it, is not important in calculating elasticity: all changes are treated as though they are preceded by a plus sign.[9]

When demand or supply is price elastic, a given percentage change in price leads to a *greater* percentage change in quantity demanded or quantity supplied: using the formula, the *elasticity coefficient is greater than one.* When

Price elastic

A strong response to a price change; occurs when the percentage change in the quantity demanded or supplied is greater than the percentage change in price.

Price inelastic

A weak response to a price change; occurs when the percentage change in the quantity demanded or supplied is less than the percentage change in price.

Elasticity coefficient

The absolute value of the percentage change in quantity demanded or supplied divided by the absolute value of the percentage change in price; greater or less than one when demand or supply is price elastic or inelastic, respectively.

[9] For example, if one item increases by 2 percent and another falls by 2 percent, the *direction* of the first change is +2 percent and the direction of the second is −2 percent, but the *size*, or absolute value, of each change is simply 2 percent.

demand or supply is price inelastic, a given percentage change in price leads to a *smaller* percentage change in quantity demanded or quantity supplied: the *elasticity coefficient is less than one.*[10] For example, if the quantity demanded of a particular style of shoe falls by 20 percent after its price rises by 10 percent, demand is price elastic because the percentage change in quantity demanded is greater than the percentage change in price. Specifically, when the elasticity coefficient is calculated,

$$\frac{|\% \text{ change in } Q|}{|\% \text{ change in } P|} = \frac{20\%}{10\%} = 2,$$

the number is greater than 1, indicating that demand is price elastic. If the quantity demanded of the shoes decreases by 8 percent following a 10 percent price increase, demand is price inelastic because the percentage change in quantity demanded is less than the percentage change in price, and the elasticity coefficient,

$$\frac{|\% \text{ change in } Q|}{|\% \text{ change in } P|} = \frac{8\%}{10\%} = 0.8,$$

is less than 1.

Applying the concept of price elasticity to supply, a 12 percent decrease in quantity supplied following an 8 percent decrease in price results in an elasticity coefficient of 12%/8% = 1.5, indicating that supply is price elastic, or that sellers are responding strongly to the price change. A 6 percent increase in quantity supplied following an 18 percent increase in price means supply is inelastic, or that sellers are responding weakly, as shown by the elasticity coefficient of 6%/18% = 0.33.

The percentage change in quantity and the percentage change in price used to calculate elasticity are determined by dividing the change in quantity by the original, or base, quantity and the change in price by the original, or base, price, or

$$\% \text{ change in } Q = \frac{\text{change in } Q}{\text{base } Q},$$

and

$$\% \text{ change in } P = \frac{\text{change in } P}{\text{base } P}.$$

[10] The elasticity coefficient is greater than one when demand or supply is price elastic because, in this case, the numerator in the formula is larger than the denominator. The elasticity coefficient is less than one when demand or supply is price inelastic because the numerator in the formula is smaller than the denominator.

(Remember, we are still interested in the size, and not the direction, of change.)[11]

For example, suppose that a seller supplies 300 units of a product at a price of $50 each, and 390 units when the price rises to $75, as shown in this supply schedule:

Price	Quantity Supplied
$50	300
75	390

The percentage change in quantity supplied is equal to the change in quantity of 90 units divided by the original quantity of 300 units, or $90/300 = 30\%$. The percentage change in price equals the change in price of $25 divided by the original price of $50, or $\$25/\$50 = 50\%$. From this, elasticity can be calculated in the usual way by dividing the percentage change in quantity supplied by the percentage change in price: $30\%/50\% = 0.6$. The following equation summarizes these calculations:

$$\text{elasticity} = \frac{|\% \text{ change in } Q|}{|\% \text{ change in } P|} = \frac{|\text{ change in } Q/\text{base } Q|}{|\text{ change in } P/\text{base } P|},$$

or

$$0.6 = \frac{30\%}{50\%} = \frac{90/300}{\$25/\$50}.$$

Can you prove that the price elasticity of demand for a product would be 1.2 if the quantity demanded fell from 500 to 200 units following a price increase from $20 to $30?

Finally, a given percentage change in price could result in an equal percentage change in quantity demanded or quantity supplied. For exam-

---

[11] Price elasticity can also be calculated by using a "midpoint," or average, formula. This formula measures the percentage change in quantity and in price by dividing the change in quantity and price by the average quantity and price, rather than a base quantity and price as is done here. That is:

$$\% \text{ change in } Q = \frac{\text{change in } Q}{\text{average } Q},$$

and

$$\% \text{ change in } P = \frac{\text{change in } P}{\text{average } P}.$$

Average Q is found by adding both the quantity before and after the price change and dividing by 2, or $(Q_{old} + Q_{new})/2$. Average P is found by adding both the old and new price and dividing by 2, or $(P_{old} + P_{new})/2$.

Table 3.5	The Measurement of Elasticity

When the absolute value of the percentage change in quantity is greater than, less than, or equal to the absolute value of the percentage change in price, demand or supply is elastic, inelastic, or unitary elastic, respectively.

When Demand or Supply Is:	The Elasticity Coefficient Is:
Elastic	$\dfrac{\|\% \text{ change in } Q\|}{\|\% \text{ change in } P\|} = \dfrac{\|(\text{change in } Q/\text{base } Q)\|}{\|(\text{change in } P/\text{base } P)\|} > 1$
Inelastic	$\dfrac{\|\% \text{ change in } Q\|}{\|\% \text{ change in } P\|} = \dfrac{\|(\text{change in } Q/\text{base } Q)\|}{\|(\text{change in } P/\text{base } P)\|} < 1$
Unitary Elastic	$\dfrac{\|\% \text{ change in } Q\|}{\|\% \text{ change in } P\|} = \dfrac{\|(\text{change in } Q/\text{base } Q)\|}{\|(\text{change in } P/\text{base } P)\|} = 1$

Unitary price elastic

The percentage change in quantity demanded or supplied equals the percentage change in price; elasticity coefficient equals one.

ple, a 4 percent change in price could lead to a 4 percent change in quantity demanded or supplied. When this occurs, the elasticity coefficient is equal to one, and demand or supply is **unitary price elastic.** Table 3.5 summarizes the measurement of elasticity using the elasticity coefficient.

Causes of Price Elasticity

Price Elasticity of Demand   What causes the demand for a good or service to be relatively price elastic or inelastic? The first consideration is the type of good or service demanded; that is, whether it is a luxury or a necessity. Generally, the demand for luxuries is more sensitive to price changes (more price elastic) than the demand for necessities. It would be difficult for a person to cut back on a life-saving treatment or medication because the price rose too much. On the other hand, people have cut back substantially on vacation plans when travel prices have increased.

A second factor influencing the price elasticity of demand for a good or service is the availability of substitute products, or the ability of consumers to switch to other goods or services as a product's price goes up. If the price of movie theater tickets increases, people can switch to other forms of entertainment or spend their time working out or taking walks. But if the price of a basic food such as milk goes up, users have limited alternatives. Demand is more price elastic for a good or service with many substitutes, and demand is more price inelastic for a good or service with few substitutes.

A third factor influencing the price elasticity of demand for a good or service is the portion of one's income that the purchase of the item requires. If you are making $19,000 a year, and the price of birthday candles doubles, it will probably have little effect on your demand for birthday candles. If, however, college tuition were to double, you might find yourself looking for an alternative to a college education. The greater the portion of income devoted to a good or service, the stronger the reaction will be to price changes for that good or service.

Price Elasticity of Supply   A seller's degree of responsiveness to a price change is determined primarily by time. The more time a seller has to adjust production and react to a price change, the greater will be the seller's sensitivity to price, or the more price elastic will be the response. For example, suppose that a particular style of coat becomes very popular and buyers bid its price up. The manufacturers who make that coat are at first able to supply only as many coats as the inventory they have on hand allows. Thus, their immediate response to this increase in price is a very limited change in quantity: supply is price inelastic. Given a little more time, the manufacturers can produce more coats and further increase the quantity supplied. Given even more time, other sellers may see the popularity of the coat and move into the market, with the result that many more coats are supplied in response to the higher price.

How good are you at recognizing buyers' and sellers' sensitivities to price changes, nonprice factors influencing demand and supply, elasticity, and other concepts discussed in this chapter? Test your skill by analyzing the articles excerpted in Application 3.4, "Supply and Demand in Practice."

Summary

The concepts of demand and supply are important for understanding the operation of a market economy. Demand refers to a buyer's plans to purchase different amounts of a product at different prices in a given period of time, when all nonprice factors are held constant. The relationship between a product's prices and the different amounts of the product that a buyer plans to purchase at each of those prices is shown in a demand schedule. Prices and quantities in a demand schedule are graphically illustrated by a downward-sloping demand curve. In both demand schedules and demand curves, higher prices are associated with smaller quantities demanded and lower prices with larger quantities demanded. This inverse relationship between price and quantity demanded is called the Law of Demand, and is based on limited incomes and the availability of substitute products. The movement along a demand curve from one price-quantity point to another as a result of a change in a product's price is referred to as a change in quantity demanded.

A supply schedule shows the different amounts of a product that a seller would offer in the market at different prices in a given time period, when all nonprice factors are held constant. Graphically, a supply schedule is represented by an upward-sloping supply curve. The supply schedule and supply curve behave as they do because of the Law of Supply, which states that there is a direct relationship between price and quantity supplied. The

Supply and Demand in Practice

Much of the information on demand, supply, and prices comes from newspaper articles. And very often, buried in those articles are concepts that you have studied in this chapter. How many of the concepts from this chapter can you find in the articles excerpted below? We found the Laws of Demand and Supply, changes in supply, changes in demand, changes in equilibrium price, specific nonprice determinants of demand and supply, determinants of elasticity of demand and supply, percentage changes in quantity demanded and in price, shortages, and a price floor that doesn't take effect.

Chilled O.J.: Sticker Shock

Sticker shock is what orange juice producers have been calling the reaction of shoppers who recoil at prices resulting from a devastating freeze just after Christmas.

The effect on the pocketbook has been compounded as consumer preference has shifted from cheaper frozen concentrate to more expensive ready-to-drink chilled juice. . . . Chilled juice now accounts for 57.7 percent of sales in the $3 billion orange juice industry.

"It represents a total reversal of consumer buying habits," said [the senior vice president for sales for Tropicana].

Today the typical supermarket devotes a vast amount of space in the dairy case to as many as a dozen different kinds of chilled orange juice, both national brands and private label. Some brands are sold in the produce department.

"Chilled juice," said [the Tropicana vice president], "has reached a point in acceptability that people will buy it no matter what because it has become a household staple."

The Nursing Shortage

There seems to be every indication that there is a national nursing shortage. While nursing shortages tend to be cyclical, the current problem may be more long term.

Some structural changes in medical care have increased the demand for nurses: more home health care, community clinics, rising incomes, increased availability of health insurance, and an aging population.

On the supply side, however, there has been a decline. Women, the traditional sex of nurses, simply have many more options available to them today. Many more are seeking business careers, or, if interested in health care, medical school. Enrollments in nursing programs have declined, and the pool of possible younger candidates is falling.

In the past, nursing shortages have produced considerable wage increases: particularly in the early 1970s and early 1980s. However, this shortage may exist for some time since the nonprice factors influencing supply and demand appear to be moving in a direction that reinforces the shortage.

Why Won't Gasoline Prices Drop?

Crude oil prices are 20 percent lower than they were at this time last year, but the price of gasoline at the pump has not dropped.

The main reason is a bottleneck at the nation's refineries, which are producing all the gasoline they can. Because the oil companies have been unable to produce any extra gasoline and demand has remained more or less constant, gasoline prices are not falling, and refinery profits are soaring.

Law of Supply is based on sellers' abilities to cover costs and earn a profit. The movement along a supply curve from one price-quantity point to another caused by a change in the product's price is called a change in quantity supplied.

The price that equalizes buyers' and sellers' plans, and toward which a market automatically moves, is called the equilibrium price. This price

In other industries, a long-term shortage of production capacity would induce companies to build new plants to make more of their product. But no new refineries are on the drawing boards because of public opposition and strict rules on new pollution sources.

Average Home Price: $937,000

The sun first peeks over the Continental Divide just after 6 on New Year's Day, and particularly at this hour, it seems there could be no more beautiful place on earth than the Roaring Fork Valley — red-tinged clay, bright white snow and a pure blue in the sky that only high altitudes can produce. Below, the narrow streets of Aspen, Colo., are empty, yielding no signs of the previous night's parties. . . .

Sleeping soundly under goose-down Duvets in multimillion-dollar ranches and $2,000-a-night hotel suites is the biggest concentration of rich and famous people in perhaps the world. They gathered here, in this small town in the Rocky Mountains, to witness the end of the 80's.

The rich and famous make their most concentrated ascendance between Christmas and New Year's, when the population of the normally peaceful end-of-the-valley triples, and the roar of private jets breaks the stillness with regularity. . . .

Over all, such intermittent invasions take up just a few weeks each year, but their effect — on both the world's opinion of the place and the town's own state of mind — lasts year long. . . .

[R]eal-estate prices have doubled in the last three years. Affordable housing is virtually nonexistent. (Last year [1989], single-family homes in the United States cost on average $111,755; in Aspen, $937,000.) Traffic jams snarl the two-lane highway that leads into town. Air pollution is increasing.

Minimum wage is about $8 an hour, yet "help wanted" ads are plentiful.

Hard Hit by High Air Fares

Rising air fares are putting the squeeze on two industries that rely heavily on air travelers — car-rental companies and hotels. . . .

[Air fares] rose 20% overall in March [1989] from a year earlier, a record increase.

That increase has led to a 4% drop in domestic air travel this year. For airlines, the mix of higher fares and lower traffic has been just right — profits are booming. But the $8 billion-a-year car-rental industry has been hit hard. Seven out of 10 car-rental customers come from airports. . . .

The impact of higher air fares on hotels, a $50 billion-a-year industry, has been uneven. Hotel chains with many roadside properties have been doing well, since many people are now taking trips by car. . . .

But most chains with many airport and resort properties are off to a slow year. "Everything is a bit flat," says [a Sheraton executive] where about 60% of all guests arrive by airline.

Source: Excerpted from Florence Fabricant, "Chilled Orange Juice: Demand and Prices Continue to Grow," *The New York Times*, April 25, 1990, pp. B1, 8. Copyright ©1990 by The New York Times Company. Excerpted by permission; Timothy Tregarthen, "Critical Conditions: Supply of Nurses Wearing Thin," *The Margin*, October 1987, pp. 12–13; Excerpted from Matthew L. Wald, "Prices for Gasoline Fail to Reflect Drop in Cost of Crude Oil," *The New York Times*, July 2, 1990, p. A1, 10. Copyright ©1990 by The New York Times Company. Excerpted by permission; Excerpted from Jon Bowermaster, "Aspen: The Call of the Wild," *The New York Times Magazine*, January 21, 1990, pp. 16–21, 28, 42–43. Copyright ©1990 by The New York Times Company. Excerpted by permission; Excerpted from Jonathan Dahl, "Car-Rental Firms and Hotels Hit Hard by High Air Fares," *The Wall Street Journal*, May 16, 1989, p. B1. Excerpted by permission of The Wall Street Journal, ©Dow Jones & Company, Inc., 1989. All Rights Reserved Worldwide.

is shown by the intersection of a product's market demand and supply curves. If the actual price of a product is above its equilibrium price, there will be a surplus of the product on the market, and forces will go into motion to bring the price down to its equilibrium level. If the price of a product is below its equilibrium level, there will be a shortage, and forces will go to work to bring the price up to its equilibrium level.

In addition to a product's price, nonprice factors also influence buyers and sellers. Changes in these nonprice factors lead to shifts in demand and supply curves. An increase in demand or supply means that buyers are demanding or sellers are supplying more of a product than before at each price, and the demand or supply curve shifts to the right. When less of a product than before is demanded or supplied at each price, there is a decrease in demand or supply, and the demand or supply curve shifts to the left. Since the equilibrium price and quantity of a product are shown by the intersection of its demand and supply curves, increases or decreases in demand and/or supply cause the product's equilibrium price and quantity to change. It is important to understand the difference between changes in demand and supply, and changes in quantity demanded and quantity supplied.

If the government sets a price ceiling for a good or service, and the free market equilibrium price is above the government-set price, a shortage will develop. If the government sets a price floor for a good or service, and the free market equilibrium price is below the government-set price, a surplus will develop.

Price elasticity measures the sensitivities of buyers and sellers to changes in the price of a product. Demand or supply is price elastic when the quantity demanded or supplied changes by a greater percentage than the price changes, or when the elasticity coefficient is greater than one. Demand or supply is price inelastic when the quantity demanded or supplied changes by a smaller percentage than the price changes, or when the elasticity coefficient is less than one. Unitary price elasticity occurs when the percentage change in quantity demanded or supplied equals the percentage change in price, or when the elasticity coefficient equals one. Elasticity of demand is affected by whether the product is a luxury or a necessity, by the availability of substitutes, and by the price of the product relative to the buyer's income. Time is the major determinant of a product's price elasticity of supply.

Key Terms and Concepts

Demand

Demand schedule

Law of Demand

Demand curve

Supply

Supply schedule

Law of Supply

Supply curve

Market

Market demand and supply

Shortage

Surplus

Equilibrium price and equilibrium quantity

Change in quantity demanded

Change in quantity supplied

Nonprice factors influencing demand

Nonprice factors influencing supply

Change in demand

Increase (decrease) in demand

Change in supply

Increase (decrease) in supply

Change in quantity demanded and quantity supplied versus change in demand and supply

Price ceiling (upper price limit)

Price floor (lower price limit)

Price elasticity

Price elastic

Price inelastic

Elasticity coefficient

Unitary price elastic

Review Questions

1. Why do limited incomes and the availability of substitutes cause less of a product to be demanded as its price goes up? Why does the desire to earn a profit cause more of a product to be supplied as its price goes up?

2. How do surpluses and shortages cause the actual price in a market to fall if it is above the equilibrium price, or rise if it is below the equilibrium price?

3. Explain how each of the following would cause demand or supply to shift and how the equilibrium price and quantity for the good or service in question would change.
   a. An increase in the number of suppliers in the home insulation market
   b. Expectations by automobile buyers that prices on next year's models will increase substantially
   c. An increase in the popularity of a certain clothing maker's product
   d. A wage increase paid to a hospital's employees
   e. A cost-reducing invention that is adopted by the producers of a high-technology product

4. Distinguish between a change in quantity demanded or quantity supplied, and a change in demand or supply. What causes each type of change, and how is each represented graphically?

5. Plot the demand and supply schedules below on the graph that follows, and answer questions a through e.
   a. What is the equilibrium price and equilibrium quantity?
   b. How much of a shortage or surplus would occur at $2.50?
   c. How much of a shortage or surplus would occur at $7.50?
   d. What would happen if the government established a price floor of $8.75 on this item?
   e. What would happen if the government established a price ceiling of $8.75 on this item?

Price per Item	Quantity Demanded	Quantity Supplied
$ 1.25	150	0
2.50	140	50
3.75	125	60
5.00	105	70
6.25	80	80
7.50	50	90
8.75	10	100
10.00	0	110

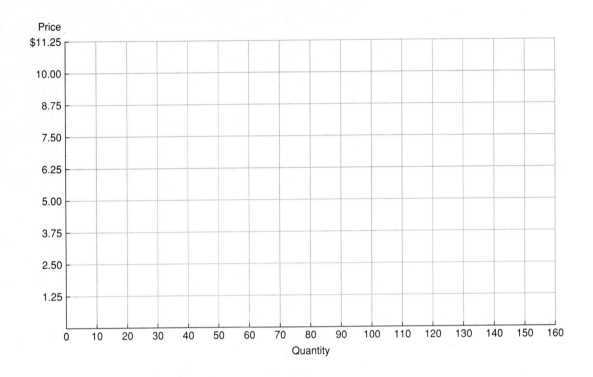

6. Calculate the price elasticity coefficient for demand or supply for each of
    the following.
    a. The number of 16-ounce bottles of a soft drink demanded increases by 30
        percent after its price decreases by 40 percent.
    b. The quantity of available apartment units increases by 8 percent follow-
        ing a 6 percent increase in rents.
    c. The number of chicken dinners demanded at a restaurant increases from
        60 to 80 per week when the price falls from $5.00 to $4.50.
    d. 10,000 exercise bicycles were supplied each month at a price of $200, and
        14,000 are supplied each month since the price increased to $250.
    e. The number of videotaped movies demanded each weekend from a
        rental store falls from 500 to 400 following an increase in the rental
        charge from $2.00 to $2.40.

Discussion Questions

1. People view political upheavals in foreign countries, local and national elec-
    tions in the United States, and environmental and other developments as im-
    portant because of the effects these events may have on their lives. The
    operations of markets, however, may go relatively unnoticed because their ef-
    fects are less obvious or dramatic. How does the operation of markets affect
    your everyday life? If prices were not set in markets how would they be
    determined? Would that affect your life differently?

2. There are more people in the baby boom generation (the generation born after World War II) than there are in the generations preceding or following it. What do you think happens in the markets for college education, luxury-sized automobiles, and the services of a stock broker as the baby boom generation grows older? What other types of markets might be significantly affected by this group in the 1990s?

3. Minimum wage laws keep many workers' hourly wages above what they would be if there were no such laws. Do minimum wage laws help or hurt college students looking for summer work?

4. If a government-imposed price ceiling or floor helps some people but hurts others, what factors do you think the government should consider before deciding on such a policy? (You might consider interest rate ceilings and agricultural price supports in answering this question.)

5. How does price elasticity of demand determine whether a seller's revenues will increase or decrease following an increase in the price of its product? If you were a seller concerned with your revenue position, would you want the demand for your product to be price elastic or inelastic if you were raising your price? Why? What if you were lowering your price? Why?

6. Give some examples of goods and services where a consumer's response to a price change might typically be elastic, and where it might typically be inelastic.

Critical Thinking Case 3

Illegal Drug Markets

Critical Thinking Skills	Define a real world problem in terms of specific analytical tools Determine the arguments supporting different sides of an issue Support a point of view by using specific analytical tools
Economics Concepts	Supply and demand Market equilibrium Externalities

Evidence indicates that the use of addictive, recreational drugs is on the increase in the United States as well as in other parts of the world. A report issued by the State Department notes that the global production of opium poppies, coca, marijuana, and hashish soared in 1989. The worldwide production of cocaine alone grew from about 150,000 tons in 1985 to approximately 225,000 tons in 1989.[a]

In the United States, the markets for drugs operate like markets described in this chapter. There are buyers with downward-sloping demand curves and fairly inelastic responses to price changes, and there are sellers whose motivation for profit causes them to offer more for sale as the price increases. These markets have equilibrium prices toward which they tend to move, and equilibriums change with increases and decreases in supply and demand. For example, sampling, which addicts people to a drug, will increase the demand for that drug and tends to raise its equilibrium price and the quantity sold on the market.

Even though these markets for recreational drugs operate to satisfy demand and provide a profit for sellers, in the United States they have been declared illegal. This illegality occurs largely because drugs impose costs on people who do not participate in these markets either as buyers or sellers, or because these drug markets create "negative externalities." That is, the actions of buyers and sellers in these markets extend beyond the markets to harm those who are not participating in the activities. For example, many people have been victims of crimes or live in fear of crimes by addicted persons, and society has had to bear substantial medical costs for children born to cocaine users.

Society has been searching for ways to curtail this market activity. Over the years, programs, such as "Just Say No," have been developed to decrease demand, and others, such as increased law enforcement, to decrease supply. These programs have not been very successful and the media frequently allude to U.S. losses in the drug war. In an attempt to deal with the drug problem and these losses, some people are advocating the legalization of drugs. The argument for legalization is based on a lessening of the negative externalities caused by addicts who commit crimes to support a habit.

What should the United States do?

Questions

1. What is the fundamental problem (or problems) created for society by the demand for and supply of addictive, recreational drugs?

2. List the problems created by declaring drugs illegal and the problems that would be created by legalizing drugs. Identify the problems on each list that create negative externalities. Which list of problems is the worst? Why?

3. State in terms of their effect on supply and demand some of the policies available in the United States for dealing with the drug problem.

4. Use your tools of supply and demand to make a recommendation about how to deal with the drug issue. Give good arguments to support your recommendations.

[a]Elaine Sciolino, "World Drug Crop Up Sharply in 1989 Despite U.S. Effort," *The New York Times,* March 2, 1990, pp. A1, A2.

Suggested Readings

Douglas R. Bohi and Michael A. Toman, "Understanding Nonrenewable Resource Supply Behavior," *Science,* **February 25, 1983, pp. 927–932.**
Discusses problems in applying economic models of supply to nonrenewable resources such as oil and natural gas.

George J. Church, "Thinking the Unthinkable," *Time,* **May 30, 1988, pp. 12–19.**
Discusses the drug problem in the United States and some arguments for and against legalizing the markets for many recreational drugs.

Robert Lindsey, "Adoption Market: Big Demand, Tight Supply," *The New York Times,* **April 5, 1987, pp. 1, 15.**
Discusses the shortage of adoptable children and problems created by the response to this shortage.

"The Margin's (almost) Sure-Fire Guide to Supply and Demand," *The Margin,* **September/October, 1988, pp. 42–43.**
Provides a humorous, uncomplicated guide to understanding the basics of supply and demand.

Jon Sargent, "Labor Shortages: Menace or Mirage?" *Occupational Outlook Quarterly,* **Winter 1988, pp. 27–33.**
Discusses types of labor shortages, strategies in dealing with them, the relationship between future shortages and education, and the outlook for the 1990s.

Louis Uchitelle, "A Bidding War for Professors Who Know Wall Street Ways," *The New York Times,* **August 1, 1989, pp. A1, A27.**
Explains how supply and demand conditions are affecting the salaries of finance professors.

J. Karl Wise, "Elasticity of Demand for Veterinary Services," *Journal of the American Veterinary Medical Association,* **August 15, 1980, p. 363.**
Application of the principle of price elasticity of demand to the pricing of veterinary services.

Richard Woodbury, "Gushing with Enthusiasm," *Time,* **August 27, 1990, pp. 46–57.**
Discusses obstacles to increasing the supply of domestic oil in the United States.

Part Two

The Macroeconomy

Chapter Four

Goals and Problems of the Macroeconomy: Employment, Prices, and Production

Job availability for people in the labor force is a major goal of the macroeconomy.

Source: © Gabe Palmer/
The Stock Market.

Chapter Objectives

1. To introduce the three fundamental areas on which macroeconomics focuses: employment, prices, and production.

2. To define unemployment and explain its consequences.

3. To identify different types of unemployment and to introduce measures and statistics on employment and unemployment.

4. To discuss discouraged workers, regional differences in unemployment, and the types of jobs held by the employed.

5. To discuss full employment.

6. To define inflation and explain its consequences.

7. To identify the causes of inflationary pressure and to introduce measures and statistics on inflation.

8. To define deflation and disinflation.

9. To define full production and economic growth and to introduce GNP, the primary measure of production.

10. To define productivity and discuss changes in U.S. productivity over the years.

11. To highlight the policy problem that occurs in pursuing the goals of full employment, full production, and price stability simultaneously.

Macroeconomics

The study of the operation of the economy as a whole.

This chapter begins the section of the text devoted to **macroeconomics,** which is the study of the economy as a whole. Macroeconomics includes such topics as aggregate (total) employment and production, unemployment, inflation, economic growth, money, and government stabilization policies. (Microeconomics, which focuses on decision making by individual units in the economy, is covered in Part Three of the text.) The study of macroeconomics will give you an understanding of how the household, business, and government sectors of the economy interrelate and how that interrelationship causes the system to operate, creates problems, and helps in the solving of those problems. However, before beginning the analysis, it is important to become familiar with some basic terms and concepts involving employment, production, and prices, the three areas around which macroeconomics revolves. These three areas can be viewed as either the major problems of the macroeconomy when considered as unemployment, falling production, and inflation, or as the major goals of the macroeconomy when considered as full employment, full production and economic growth, and stable prices. These problems and goals will be explored in this chapter.

In the United States, full employment, full production and economic growth, and stable prices have been regarded as such important economic goals that, as noted in Chapter Two, Congress enacted the Employment Act of 1946 to permit the government to have a hand in creating an economic environment that would lead to the achievement of these goals. This legislation states that:

> *The Congress hereby declares that it is the continuing policy and responsibility of the Federal Government to use all practicable means consistent with its needs and obligations and other essential considerations of national policy . . . to coordinate and utilize all its plans, functions, and resources for the purpose of creating and maintaining . . . conditions under which there will be afforded useful employment opportunities, including self-employment, for those able, willing, and seeking to work,* **and to promote maximum employment, production, and purchasing power.** *(emphasis added)*[1]

Through this Act the government is not ensuring that these goals will be achieved, but rather that the government will aid in providing an environment that will lead to their achievement. This is a good example of the distinction between a planned economy and mixed capitalism.

Unemployment and Full Employment

A primary objective of economies on the macroeconomic level is employment for all available factors of production. Stated another way, the intention is to minimize unemployment. **Unemployment** means that a resource available for production is not being used. Machines, raw materials, warehouses, trucks, and so forth can all be unemployed. Most often, however, the concern over unemployment focuses on people who would like to be working but are not. This concern results from the more obvious consequences of unemployment among people.

The most dramatic siege of unemployment the United States has ever witnessed occurred in the Great Depression of the 1930s. From 1932 through 1935 the unemployment rate stayed at 20 percent or more, and in 1933 it reached almost 25 percent of the civilian labor force: roughly one out of every four people who wanted to work could not.[2]

Unemployment

A resource available for production is not being used.

---

[1] *United States Statutes at Large, 1946,* Vol. 60, Pt. 1, *Public Laws and Reorganization Plans* (Washington, D.C.: U.S. Government Printing Office, 1947), p. 23.

[2] U.S. Bureau of the Census, *Historical Statistics of the United States, Colonial Times to 1957* (Washington, D.C.: U.S. Government Printing Office, 1960), Series D 46–47, p. 73.

Table 4.1

Potential Output, Actual Output, and Lost Output
from Unemployment (Billions of 1982 Dollars)

Because of unemployment, goods and services that might have been produced
are lost to society, and the scarcity problem is intensified.

Year	Potential Output	Actual Output	Lost Output
1980	$3,308.4	$3,187.1	$121.3
1981	3,400.9	3,248.8	152.1
1982	3,440.0	3,166.0	274.0
1983	3,544.8	3,279.1	265.7
1984	3,659.0	3,501.4	157.6
1985	3,779.2	3,618.7	160.5
1986	3,881.4	3,717.9	163.5
1987	3,957.0	3,845.3	111.7
1988	4,082.1	4,016.9	65.2
1989	4,176.0	4,117.7	58.3
1990	4,237.5[a]	4,155.8[a]	81.7

[a]Preliminary figure.

Source: Potential Output is from the Federal Reserve Bank of St. Louis. Based on R. H. Rasche and J. A. Tatom, "Energy Resources and Potential GNP," Federal Reserve Bank of St. Louis, *Review*, June 1977, pp. 10–24; and J. A. Tatom, "Potential Output and the Recent Productivity Decline," Federal Reserve Bank of St. Louis, *Review*, January 1982, pp. 3–16. Actual Output is from U.S., *Economic Report of the President* (Washington, D.C.: U.S. Government Printing Office, 1991), p. 288.

Consequences of Unemployment

Why is there so much concern about unemployment, especially among workers? Unemployment has several undesirable consequences, including an economic loss for all of society, and individual hardship for the unemployed.

Economic Loss for Society   Recall that economics is the study of how people use scarce resources to satisfy unlimited material wants and needs. If more resources are available and put into use, a greater number of wants and needs can be satisfied. If some resources are unemployed, some wants and needs that might have been satisfied will go unsatisfied. Thus, unemployment intensifies the scarcity problem, and the loss to society is the goods and services it might have enjoyed.

How serious is the loss in goods and services resulting from unemployment? One way of answering this question is to compare what was actually produced with what the economy could have produced if all willing and available resources were used. This is shown for the years 1980 through 1990 in Table 4.1. The column titled "Potential Output" indicates the value of the goods and services that could have been produced with resources fully employed. The column titled "Actual Output" shows the total value of the goods and services that were actually produced. The difference between what might have been produced and what actually was produced is shown in the column titled "Lost Output."[3] For example, in 1986, $163.5 billion more goods and services could have been produced if the economy's resources had been fully employed. Put another way, if the unemployment problem had been eliminated in 1986, the economy would have come $163.5 billion closer that year to lessening the scarcity problem.

Individual Hardships   In addition to its effects on society, unemployment can cause private hardships for people who would like to be working but are not. Unemployment intensifies an individual's personal struggle with scarcity. As a period of unemployment lengthens, people might be forced to alter spending habits and thus their lifestyles. And if the loss of income due to unemployment reaches the point where finances are exhausted, dramatic changes such as moving to cheaper housing or liquidating some assets might be necessary.

In addition to the financial dimension, a person's self-esteem and relationships with others may suffer from unemployment. How many times can a person be told that his or her services are not needed before frustration and self-doubt begin to set in? Do families who face the prospect of having to leave their friends and relocate, or of going without things they need, really grow closer in dealing with their problems, or is this simply a romantic vision? A number of studies have dealt with the psychological and physiological costs of unemployment. Problems such as depression, suicide, increasing mental hospitalization rates, ulcers, and even the common cold can be aggravated by being out of work. Application 4.1, "The National Psyche," is concerned with some of the psychological problems that surfaced in late 1990 when the economy fell into a slump.

How serious could the hardships of unemployment become? William Manchester, in *The Glory and the Dream*, gives the following description of what unemployment was like for some in the Great Depression.

The smartly dressed young lawyer who always left home at the same time each morning may have been off to sell cheap neckties, magazines, vacuum cleaners, pressure cookers, or Two-in-One shoe polish door-to-door in a remote neighborhood. He may have changed his clothes and gone to another part of the city to beg. Or he may have been one of the millions who looked for work day after day, year after year, watching his children grow thinner and fighting despair in the night. There were certain skills developed by men who spent their days

---

[3] The difference between potential output and actual output is generally referred to as the GNP gap. The expression GNP (gross national product) is introduced later in this chapter.

Application 4.1

The National Psyche

[As unemployment increases, there is a kind of recessionary psychology that surfaces.] As people change their behavior in the face of layoffs, cutbacks or a sudden drop in net worth, more and more Americans find themselves clinically depressed.

This year [1990] the symptoms are most apparent in those parts of the country—New England, the mid-Atlantic states, parts of the Midwest—that have suffered the greatest economic decline. In the suburbs of Detroit, where sagging auto sales have fanned recession fears, psychiatric referrals from a local counseling service are up nearly 20% over the past six months. Business is also booming at the Massachusetts Psychological Association referral service, where out-of-work lawyers and former bond salesmen seek help in coping with stress, anxiety disorders and panic attacks. Drugstores in the region report brisk sales in Tagamet (for ulcers), Prozac (depression) and Halcion (insomnia).

During the Great Depression of the 1930s, people jumped out of windows, joined left-wing movements or sought escape through watching Fred Astaire movies. In the 1970s, they squabbled in gas lines and drifted into the low-level despondency that Jimmy Carter called "our national malaise. . . ."

As always, some people drown their troubles in alcohol. Others turn to chocolate bars, ice-cream cones or platters of rich food. In the words of [a Columbia University psychiatrist], "When things are lousy anyway, who cares about cholesterol?" Many individuals become violent and abusive, usually to those closest at hand. At the House of Ruth, a Washington shelter for battered women, [the deputy director] reports that the men who are doing the hitting are talking more and more about the economic pressures they feel. . . .

Psychologists say economic losses are no different from other kinds of losses. . . . People who have lost their jobs experience anger, denial and a need to grieve, just as they would if they had lost a loved one. This is especially true of the solid, stable employee who has worked in one place for many years. "That person has a mental contract," [says a management psychologist]. "Even though no one told him that he would be taken care of, that's what he expected."

The emotional effects can spill over to all parts of a person's life. In time of crisis says [the Columbia University psychiatrist] someone who tends toward pessimism will not worry about just the economy but will also fret about getting sick. [And one University of Nebraska observer] warns that there may be psychological fallout for the family. "The tensions come out at home," she says. "A five-year-old may not understand why there won't be a big Christmas."

Source: Philip Elmer-Dewitt, "Is the Country in a Depression?" *Time*, December 3, 1990, pp. 112, C1.

in the streets. You learned to pay for a nickel cup of coffee, to ask for another cup of hot water free, and, by mixing the hot water with the ketchup on the counter, to make a kind of tomato soup. In winter you stuffed newspapers under your shirt to ward off the cold; if you knew you would be standing for hours outside an employment office, you wrapped burlap bags around your legs and tied them in place. Shoes were a special problem. Pasteboard could be used for inner soles, and some favored cotton in the heels to absorb the pounding of the concrete. But if a shoe was really gone, nothing worked. The pavement destroyed the cardboard and then the patch of sock next to it, snow leaked in and accum-

ulated around your toes, and shoe nails stabbed your heels until you learned to walk with a particular gait.[4]

Fortunately, the effects of unemployment are less severe today than during the Great Depression. Since the 1930s the government has instituted some forms of income supplements for those without a job. While the payments do not completely replace lost income, they do soften the impact of unemployment. Unemployment compensation and food stamps are two examples of this government aid.

Types of Unemployment

With unemployment leading to losses for society and hardships for those out of work, it is obvious why such a high priority is given to alleviating it. But before a problem can be remedied, its cause must be known. Unfortunately, there is no single cause of unemployment. Three main sources of the problem are (1) friction in the labor market, (2) cyclical or periodic changes in the demand for goods and services, and (3) changes in the structure of the economy. These three sources form a framework for defining different types of unemployment. Thus, economists speak of frictional unemployment, cyclical unemployment, and structural unemployment.

Frictional Unemployment   Some people who are looking for employment have voluntarily quit a job to search for another one. Others are entering the job market for the first time or after a period of not looking for work. Will these job seekers obtain immediate employment by making a phone call or filling out an application? The answer is probably not. These people will likely experience a period of unemployment between leaving an old job and beginning a new one, or between entering the labor market and finding work. During this time the job seeker will be collecting references and credentials, following up leads, and interviewing with prospective employers.

This failure to make a quick and smooth transition from an old to a new job, or from entering the labor market to employment, can be thought of as "friction" in the labor market. Thus, the **frictionally unemployed** are those who are voluntarily out of work and searching for a job.

Frictional unemployment
Occurs when people are voluntarily out of work and in the process of seeking a new job.

In a mobile economy such as that of the United States, there are always people voluntarily unemployed. They may have quit a job because they were disgruntled with it, they may want to relocate or change their occupation, or they may have some other reason. Thus, there are always workers voluntarily in the process of seeking employment, or there is always some frictional unemployment. Because of this, when we say that the economy is

---

[4]*The Glory and the Dream: A Narrative History of America 1932–1972,* by William Manchester. Copyright © 1973, 1974 by William Manchester. Pages 34–35. By permission of Little, Brown and Company.

at full employment we do *not* mean that 100 percent of the labor force is working. Rather, **full employment** means that everyone in the labor force, except the frictionally unemployed, is working.

Full employment

Occurs when only those voluntarily out of work are unemployed, or the unemployment rate includes only frictional unemployment.

Cyclical Unemployment   Market economies such as that of the United States do not produce goods and services at a constant rate over time. Rather, the economy goes through wavelike movements, or upswings and downswings in production, called business cycles. Periodically, the economy falls into a downswing, or a recession, during which decreases in production and employment occur. When the demand for a good or service decreases in a recession, workers producing that good or service may be involuntarily laid off. This type of unemployment is termed **cyclical unemployment** because it is the result of a recession, or a downswing in the business cycle.

Cyclical unemployment

Involuntary unemployment that results from a downswing in a business cycle, or a recession.

Cyclical unemployment is a matter of serious concern because, unlike frictional unemployment, it is involuntary and continues until the economy breaks out of the recession. This could be a matter of a few months and involve a small number of workers, or it could be a period of several years and extend to millions of families. In 1980 recessionary pressures led to a short period of cyclical unemployment, whereas during late 1981 and 1982 a lengthier period of cyclical unemployment occurred.

Some industries are more sensitive than others to changes in general economic conditions, and workers in these industries are particularly vulnerable to cyclical unemployment. When a recession is impending, the purchase of consumer durable goods, such as automobiles, and business capital goods, such as heavy machinery, may be postponed, causing sales to decline. Workers producing these types of products may then be laid off. Auto workers, steel workers, and construction workers, among others, are especially susceptible to cyclical unemployment.

Workers who are young and lacking in seniority are also vulnerable to cyclical unemployment. When a downswing occurs, the young are usually among the first workers to be laid off; and when the economy improves, they are usually among the last to be rehired.

Structural unemployment

Involuntary unemployment that results when a worker's job is no longer part of the production structure of the economy.

Structural Unemployment   Like cyclical unemployment, **structural unemployment** is involuntary. It occurs when a worker loses a job because that occupation is no longer a part of the structure of the economy. The good or service the worker produced is either no longer demanded or is now made in a manner that has eliminated that particular job. Unlike cyclical unemployment, structural unemployment offers no prospect for rehire in the future.

Structural unemployment results from technological changes in the economy, changes in the types of goods and services people demand, corporate streamlining of management positions as firms merge or reorganize, and the loss of entire domestic industries due to competition from foreign-produced items. For example, the smooth operation of an office used to depend on large numbers of workers to type, file, keep books, and so on. Today, office work has become highly mechanized; with word processors and computer systems, fewer workers are needed to accomplish these tasks. As a result, the services of many typists, bookkeepers, and file clerks are no longer needed. Other examples of structural unemployment include coal miners, typesetters, and many factory workers who are being replaced by sophisticated equipment, and middle-level managers whose positions are eliminated as companies reorganize or seek to become more efficient. One area that has been greatly affected by structural unemployment is the music industry: musicians are being replaced by electronic equipment. For example, disc jockeys are an increasingly popular alternative to live music at parties and weddings, and many musicians accompany themselves using preprogrammed drum and other instrumental tracks.

The structurally unemployed face the choice of finding new occupations or of going without work. Locating new work or learning a new skill is not always a simple matter. A person who is structurally unemployed might possess no other salable skill, might find it difficult to learn a different trade, or might not be able to absorb the financial burden of additional schooling. Also, finding work might require relocating to a new community. Structural unemployment imposes a particular hardship on the older worker who might be too close to retirement to want to retrain, or might find that employers prefer younger workers who will accept a lower salary and have the potential for longer service with the employer.

In recent years, technological advancements in production processes have caused structural changes in the U.S. economy and have eliminated many types of blue-collar, assembly-line jobs. The era of "high tech" and robotics is changing the nature of job requirements in U.S. industry. There is even some concern that the "middle class" is disappearing as semi-skilled jobs are eliminated, leaving a work force of highly skilled and unskilled workers. Retraining workers may become increasingly important to the U.S. economy.

Measures and Statistics on Employment and Unemployment

Labor force

All persons 16 years of age and older who are working or actively seeking work.

When we speak of the labor force, the employed, and the unemployed, whom do we include and how do we arrive at the numbers we use? The **labor force** is defined as all persons 16 years of age and older who are working or actively seeking work. Thus, if an individual is capable of performing innumerable jobs, but is not working nor interested in seeking a job, then that individual is not included in the labor force. It is the desire for employment, not the capability, that determines whether a person is or is not in the labor force.

Table 4.2 presents some frequently used statistics on the labor force. Columns 2 and 3 of Table 4.2 give, respectively, the number of people in the noninstitutional civilian population who are eligible for the labor force, and the number actually in the labor force for selected years. It is important to

Table 4.2   The Labor Force, the Participation Rate, and Unemployment

There are many statistics collected on labor in the United States. Some of the most important relate to the population eligible for the labor force, the labor force, the participation rate, and the unemployment rate.

1 Year	2 Noninstitutional Civilian Population Eligible for the Labor Force[a]	3 Civilian Labor Force	4 Participation Rate	5 Unemployment	6 Unemployment Rate
1929	—	49,180,000	—	1,550,000	3.2%
1933	—	51,590,000	—	12,830,000	24.9
1940	99,840,000	55,640,000	55.7%	8,120,000	14.6
1945	94,090,000	53,860,000	57.2	1,040,000	1.9
1950	104,995,000	62,208,000	59.2	3,288,000	5.3
1955	109,683,000	65,023,000	59.3	2,852,000	4.4
1960	117,245,000	69,628,000	59.4	3,852,000	5.5
1965	126,513,000	74,455,000	58.9	3,366,000	4.5
1970	137,085,000	82,771,000	60.4	4,093,000	4.9
1975	153,153,000	93,775,000	61.2	7,929,000	8.5
1976	156,150,000	96,158,000	61.6	7,406,000	7.7
1977	159,033,000	99,009,000	62.3	6,991,000	7.1
1978	161,910,000	102,251,000	63.2	6,202,000	6.1
1979	164,863,000	104,962,000	63.7	6,137,000	5.8
1980	167,745,000	106,940,000	63.8	7,637,000	7.1
1981	170,130,000	108,670,000	63.9	8,273,000	7.6
1982	172,271,000	110,204,000	64.0	10,678,000	9.7
1983	174,215,000	111,550,000	64.0	10,717,000	9.6
1984	176,383,000	113,544,000	64.4	8,539,000	7.5
1985	178,206,000	115,461,000	64.8	8,312,000	7.2
1986	180,587,000	117,834,000	65.3	8,237,000	7.0
1987	182,753,000	119,865,000	65.6	7,425,000	6.2
1988	184,613,000	121,669,000	65.9	6,701,000	5.5
1989	186,393,000	123,869,000	66.5	6,528,000	5.3
1990	188,049,000	124,787,000	66.4	6,874,000	5.5

[a]For years prior to 1947, the noninstitutional civilian population eligible for the labor force and the civilian labor force included persons 14 years of age and older. Since 1947, the measures include persons 16 years of age and older.

Source: U.S., *Economic Report of the President* (Washington, D.C.: U.S. Government Printing Office, 1991), p. 322.

Table 4.3

Participation Rates for the Civilian Labor Force
and Several Subgroups for Selected Years

Participation rates differ for subgroups in the labor force. Changes in
participation rates affect the composition of the labor force over time.

Group[a]	1965	1970	1975	1980	1985	1990
Overall	58.9%	60.4%	61.2%	63.8%	64.8%	66.4%
Males	80.7	79.7	77.9	77.4	76.3	76.1
Females	39.3	43.3	46.3	51.5	54.5	57.5
Teenagers (16-19 years old)	45.7	49.9	54.0	56.7	54.5	53.7

[a]Includes persons 16 years of age and older in the civilian population.

Source: U.S., *Economic Report of the President* (Washington, D.C.: U.S. Government Printing Office, 1991), p. 327.

Participation rate

The percentage of some specified group that is in the labor force.

appreciate how many millions of people are employed or actively seeking work each year. For example, in 1990 almost 125 million people were in the labor force.

Participation rates for the noninstitutional civilian labor force are shown in column 4 of Table 4.2. The term **participation rate** refers to the percentage of some group that is in the labor force. The group being studied may be the entire noninstitutional civilian population, women, persons in different age groups or of different ethnic backgrounds, and so on. For example, according to Table 4.2, in 1990, 66.4 percent of the noninstitutional civilian population 16 years of age and older was in the civilian labor force. That is, approximately 124.8 million people out of a population group of approximately 188 million were employed or seeking work.

Table 4.3 lists the overall participation rate and the rates for some subgroups within the labor force for selected years. It shows, for instance, that in 1990, 57.5 percent of all women 16 years of age and older were working or actively seeking work. Participation rates are important because, when examined over time, they aid in identifying changes in the composition of the labor force. For example, Table 4.3 shows that the overall labor force participation rate has increased and that much of this growth was over the last two decades due to the increased participation of women and, to a lesser extent, teenagers. At the same time it shows that there has been a drop in the participation rate for men. What do you think are some of the reasons for these changes? Why are a larger percentage of women and teenagers and a smaller percentage of men employed or actively seeking work?

Unemployment rate

The percentage of the labor force that is unemployed and actively seeking work.

Returning to Table 4.2, columns 5 and 6 give some statistics on the unemployed in the labor force. Column 5 shows the number of unemployed persons in the labor force, and column 6 gives the **unemployment rate,** which is the percentage of the civilian labor force that is unemployed and

Table 4.4   Unemployment Rates for All Workers and Various
Labor Force Subgroups for Selected Years

Over the years, some subgroups in the labor force, such as teenagers, have faced
more severe unemployment problems than other subgroups.

Group[a]	1970	1975	1980	1985	1990
All workers	4.9%	8.5%	7.1%	7.2%	5.5%
Male	4.4	7.9	6.9	7.0	5.6
Female	5.9	9.3	7.4	7.4	5.4
White	4.5	7.8	6.3	6.2	4.7
Black	—	14.8	14.3	15.1	11.3
Married men, spouse present	2.6	5.1	4.2	4.3	3.4
Women who maintain families	5.4	10.0	9.2	10.4	8.2
Teenagers (16–19 years old)	15.3	19.9	17.8	18.6	15.5
Male high school dropouts	4.0	10.5	8.2	11.2	11.2[b]
Men with 4 or more years of college	1.1	2.2	1.7	2.4	2.5[b]

[a]Includes persons 16 years of age or older in the civilian labor force.

[b]Rates given are for 1987, a closely comparable year.

Source: U.S., *Economic Report of the President* (Washington, D.C.: U.S. Government Printing Office, 1991),
p. 330. Data for male high school dropouts and men with 4 or more years of college are from U.S. Bureau of the Census, *Statistical Abstract of the United States: 1990,* 110th ed. (Washington, D.C.: U.S. Government Printing Office, 1990), p. 397.

actively seeking work. For example, the unemployment rate of 5.5 percent
in 1990 reflects the fact that 6,874,000 persons in a labor force of 124,787,000
were unemployed and actively seeking work. Since the current labor force
is approximately 125 million persons, a 1 percent rate of unemployment
translates into approximately 1.25 million persons out of work. A 7 percent
rate of unemployment represents about 8.7 million persons unemployed.

The unemployment rate is calculated on a monthly and annual basis by
the U.S. Department of Labor, Bureau of Labor Statistics, and is publicly
announced through the media. Many people have a misconception about
the method used to calculate this rate. They do not realize that the government uses a random-survey technique, not information from state employment offices, to determine the number of workers unemployed, and
that persons are counted as employed if they work just one hour a week in
a paid position. A discussion of this data collection method is found in
Application 4.2, "Determining the Unemployment Rate."

Along with the overall rate of unemployment, rates are also calculated for
various subgroups within the labor force. Table 4.4 lists unemployment rates
for selected labor market subgroups during several different years. Some
interesting observations can be made from this table. For one, in any given

Application 4.2

Determining the Unemployment Rate

The monthly Current Population Survey (CPS) of the U.S. Bureau of the Census uses a stratified probability sample of living quarters representative of the civilian noninstitutional population of the United States. About 60,000 households are interviewed each month. . . . The first interview for each household is carried out in person when possible, while a greater proportion of later interviews are by telephone. The respondent in the household is asked questions about all members of the household.

Among other questions (concerning age, education, marital and veterans status, and so forth), the respondent is asked a series of questions concerning the major activities of each person in the household who was 16 years of age or older during the previous week. . . . The respondent's answers are used to place the individuals in one of three mutually exclusive and exhaustive categories: employed, unemployed, or out of the labor force. The respondents are not asked directly to place the respective household members in these categories, however. Rather, specific questions are asked about labor force activities during recent weeks and the reasons for them. . . .

The answers to these questions determine each eligible household member's labor force status: people are counted as *employed* if during the past week they worked at least 1 hour as paid employees or in their own business, profession or farm, or for at least 15 hours as unpaid workers in a family-operated enterprise, or if they had jobs or businesses from which they were temporarily absent because of illness, bad weather, vacation, labor-management dispute, or various personal reasons. Each employed person is counted only once, no matter how many jobs they might have worked at during the week. Individuals are classified as *unemployed* only if they meet *all* the following conditions: they did not work at all during the survey week, and were looking for work (had made specific efforts to find work within the preceding 4-week period) or were on layoff, and were available for work during the reference period (except for temporary illness). All civilians 16 years of age and older who are not classified as employed or unemployed are defined as being *not in the labor force*.

Source: Richard J. McDonald, "The 'Underground Economy' and BLS Statistical Data," *Monthly Labor Review*, January 1984, p. 8.

year there is a disparity in the unemployment rates of the various subgroups. For example, in 1990 the unemployment rate for married men was 3.4 percent, compared to 15.5 percent for teenagers and 5.6 percent for all men. Next, notice that some groups within the labor force have traditionally experienced unemployment rates that are higher than the overall unemployment rate for all workers, and other groups have experienced unemployment rates lower than the overall rate. This can be seen in Table 4.4 by comparing the unemployment rates for any labor market subgroup with the rates for all workers over several years. For example, the data show a better employment experience for married men in the labor market than for all workers taken as a group, but not for women who maintain families. Notice also that men with four or more years of college have fared better than all workers, while male high school dropouts and teenagers have fared poorly. Statistics such as these have led some policy makers to question whether government programs to alleviate unemployment should be directed toward the unemployed generally or toward specific groups within the labor force such as teenagers.

Problems with Employment Statistics   Several important problems and issues must be considered when using the unemployment rate to evaluate the employment situation in the United States. Three factors in particular merit special attention when assessing the employment picture: discouraged workers; regional differences in unemployment; and the types of jobs held by the employed.

Discouraged workers

Persons who drop out of the labor force because they have been unsuccessful in finding a job for a long period of time.

The expression **discouraged workers** applies to persons who have searched unsuccessfully for a job for such a long period of time that they lose hope of obtaining employment, give up the job search, and drop out of the labor force. When a person actively looks for employment—repeatedly filling out applications, making phone calls, and going on interviews—but is continually rejected, he or she may eventually become disheartened and simply give up the effort. Because the unemployment rate measures only those who are unemployed and actively seeking work, discouraged workers are excluded from the statistic and are not counted as unemployed. Thus, by excluding discouraged workers, the unemployment rate understates the true level of unemployment in the economy.

There is debate over how much the unemployment rate would increase if discouraged workers were included. Also, the number of discouraged workers changes with economic conditions: it is higher when the economy is in a downswing and the prospects for employment are dim than when the economy is closer to full employment and finding work is easier.

Another issue to consider in assessing unemployment conditions is that the overall unemployment rate is a national figure that does not disclose the degree to which some regions of the country are experiencing serious problems with unemployment while others are not. In recent years, there has been an increased focus on evaluating regional employment conditions because unemployment appears to be uneven throughout the United States. The diversity of industries upon which various states and regions depend for their employment means that changes in a particular industry can have an unfavorable impact on employment in one area but not another. For example, the recession that began in late 1990 was particularly difficult for the Northeast and California. The shrinkage of the financial services industry, cuts in defense spending, and real estate problems hurt states on the east and west coasts. Massachusetts, which had a relatively low unemployment rate compared to other states during the mid-1980s because of its dependence on high technology, had one of the highest state unemployment rates in early 1991.[5]

[5] David Wessel, "California, Northeast Hit Hard by Slump," *The Wall Street Journal*, March 22, 1991, p. A2.

One other issue of growing concern is that a low unemployment rate provides no information about the types of jobs held by the employed. Specifically, a low unemployment rate may mask two problems. First, it does not indicate how many people who are classified as employed are working part-time but would like to hold a full-time job. Recall from Application 4.2, "Determining the Unemployment Rate," that a person needs to work just one hour a week as a paid employee to be classified as employed. As a result, people who want full-time employment, but accept part-time positions rather than be unemployed, are counted as employed. Involuntary part-time employment was the fastest growing employment arrangement during the 1980s: it increased four times as fast as full-time or voluntary part-time work.[6] With increasing costs of health insurance, pensions, and other fringe benefits for full-time employees, it is often more profitable for a business to increase its reliance on part-time employees.

A low unemployment rate also does not indicate how many people are in low-paying positions, or how many have valuable skills and accept unskilled jobs rather than be unemployed. For example, a college graduate with a major in accounting who works as a retail clerk because of an inability to obtain an accounting position is classified as employed. Some studies have indicated that there has been increased growth in low-paying positions in general, and in the service sector in particular, where the average pay is low.[7]

The Goal of Full Employment

As stated earlier, full employment is a major macroeconomic goal. However, full employment does *not* mean that 100 percent of the labor force is working. It means that only those who are voluntarily out of work are unemployed.

How do we determine when full employment occurs? How much unemployment can the economy have and still be at full employment? What is the unemployment rate beyond which genuine concern is warranted? There are no absolute answers to these questions. Economists, statisticians, and government policy makers have not been able to agree about the percentage of the labor force that is frictionally unemployed. In practice it is difficult to draw the line between those who are voluntarily and involuntarily without work, or between those who are and are not looking in earnest for a new position. Moreover, the percentage that is generally considered to represent full employment appears to change over time. In the 1950s, a 3 percent rate of unemployment was generally considered to represent full employment. During the 1960s we began to associate full employment with a 4 percent rate, and by the 1970s many believed it was

---

[6]Sar A. Levitan and Elizabeth A. Conway, "Part-timers: Living on Half-rations," *Challenge,* May-June 1988, p. 11.

[7]Lance Compa, "Jobs, But of What Value?" *St. Louis Post-Dispatch,* April 6, 1987, p. 3B.

5 percent. For example, in determining the potential output for the economy from 1975 through 1979, the Council of Economic Advisors benchmarked the unemployment rate at 5.1 percent.[8] During the 1980s some extended the full employment rate of unemployment to 6 percent.

In addition to the disagreement concerning the unemployment rate that represents full employment, some economists believe that achieving the **natural rate of unemployment,** a different measure than full employment, should be the goal of the macroeconomy. The natural rate of unemployment includes the frictionally and the structurally unemployed, or is the rate at which there is no cyclical unemployment. Since it includes the structurally unemployed, the natural rate is higher than the full employment rate and easier to reach. The goal of achieving the natural rate of unemployment has become popular with some policy makers because cyclical unemployment, unlike structural unemployment, is an economic problem that can be affected by macroeconomic stabilization policies.

Notice that while some economists targeted a 6 percent rate of unemployment as full employment in the 1980s, Table 4.2 indicates that the unemployment rates for 1988, 1989, and 1990 were below that level. In fact, the unemployment rate fell to a low of 5.1 percent in March of 1989. Two questions arise from this information: why did economists push the full employment rate up over the years, and why did it fall in the late 1980s?

The unemployment rate that represents full employment was pushed up over the years for several reasons. First, the increased rate may have been caused in part by changes in the composition of the labor force. As shown in Table 4.3, the participation rates for women and teenagers increased over the last few decades, while that for men fell. And as shown in Table 4.4, women—until 1990—and teenagers typically experienced higher unemployment rates than men did. Thus, the increased labor force attachment of women and teenagers, with their traditionally higher rates of unemployment, may have contributed to an increase in the unemployment rate associated with full employment.

A second reason for increasing the unemployment rate that represents full employment may be the availability of unemployment compensation from the government to those who have lost their jobs. Some studies have indicated that larger payments and longer periods of eligibility for payment increase a tendency to remain out of work. Thus, although a person may be technically unemployed, that person's situation might be more voluntary than it would have been if there were no unemployment compensation payments.

After four decades of a gradual increase in the full employment rate of unemployment, no universally accepted explanation has been given for the drop in the unemployment rate below the generally accepted full employ-

Natural rate of unemployment
The unemployment rate that results if cyclical unemployment is eliminated.

---

[8] The 5.1 percent full employment rate for 1975 through 1979 is from U.S., *Economic Report of the President* (Washington, D.C.: U.S Government Printing Office, 1980), p. 90.

ment level in the late 1980s and 1990. However, several factors could have contributed to this phenomenon: the growth in part-time employment, increasing numbers of low-wage service-sector jobs, an unusually long upswing in the economy, substantial spending from borrowing, and the absence of serious inflation and resulting policies (which will be explained in Chapters Six and Eight) that slow the economy.

Because of the disagreement as to the unemployment rate that represents full employment, it is difficult to make policy recommendations or to assess the seriousness of an unemployment problem. If the full employment rate is, say, 5 percent, and the actual rate of unemployment is 6 percent, then approximately 1.25 million workers are involuntarily without a job. If the full employment rate is 6 percent and the actual rate is also 6 percent, then those unemployed are voluntarily so, and no serious problem exists.

Inflation and Stable Prices

Inflation

An increase in the general level of prices.

Another primary macroeconomic concern in market economies is the maintenance of stable prices, or the control of inflation. Like unemployment, inflation can have severe consequences. **Inflation** is an increase in the general level of prices. It does not mean that prices are high, but rather that they are increasing. For example, assume that over the past two years the price of a particular combination of consumer goods in Country A has been stable at $100. Assume that in Country B the price of that same combination of consumer goods has gone up from $10 to $30 over the last two years. Country B, not Country A, faces a problem with inflation. Inflation refers to price movements, not price levels.

With inflation, the price of every good and service does not need to increase because inflation refers to an increase in the *general level* of prices. An inflation rate of 7 percent does not mean that all prices are increasing by 7 percent; it means that, on the average, prices are going up by that amount. Also, the mere existence of an increase in the general level of prices is not necessarily a matter of concern in an economy. An inflation rate of 2 to 3 percent per year would not present a policy problem. However, when prices increase by a larger percentage, such as 8 to 10 percent or more per year, inflation is a serious issue.

How serious can inflation become? In January 1922, nearly 290,000 Russian rubles were necessary to buy what one ruble would have purchased in 1913. Also in January 1922, 48 German paper marks were worth one German gold mark. By July of that year the ratio was 160 paper marks to one gold mark, and by November 1923 it took over one trillion paper marks to equal one gold mark.[9] More recently, some Latin American countries have

[9]Shephard B. Clough, Thomas Moodie, and Carol Moodie, eds., *Economic History of Europe: Twentieth Century* (New York: Harper and Row, Publishers, Inc., 1968), pp. 111, 124.

experienced unusually high inflation rates. For example, the annual inflation rates in Peru and Argentina in 1989 were over 2,900 and 3,700 percent respectively, and Nicaragua's 1988 annual rate of inflation was more than 33,600 percent.[10] A country undergoing extremely rapid price increases such as these is said to be experiencing **hyperinflation.**

Hyperinflation
Extremely rapid increases in the general level of prices.

Consequences of Inflation

When the general level of prices in an economy increases, especially at an unacceptable rate, several problems emerge. Inflation intensifies the scarcity problem when income does not rise as quickly as prices; it penalizes some groups such as savers receiving low interest rates; it changes the value of assets; and inflation can be politically and socially destabilizing.

Inflation and Income   As noted earlier, unemployment intensifies the scarcity problem by reducing or even terminating the income of some people. Inflation also reduces income – not in the same way as unemployment – but by reducing the purchasing power of money. When inflation sets in, a given amount of **money,** or **nominal, income** – income stated in terms of current dollars – buys fewer goods and services. Expressed differently, **real income,** or income measured in terms of the goods and services that a particular amount of money income can purchase, falls. Consequently, the scarcity problem for households and individuals is aggravated when money incomes do not rise as rapidly as prices.

Money (nominal) income
Income stated in terms of current dollars.

Real income
Income measured in terms of the goods and services that can be purchased with a particular amount of money income.

The impact of inflation on real income depends in part on which prices are moving up rapidly and which are not. If the prices of luxuries or products with many substitutes are increasing rapidly, the impact of inflation can be reduced by altering or curtailing purchases. For example, if the prices of new automobiles are increasing, consumers can purchase used cars, maintain and repair their currently owned cars, or use public transportation. If prices of necessities or goods and services with few substitutes are increasing quickly, the effects of inflation on real income might be more pronounced. For example, if increases in the prices of food and heating fuels were particularly acute, consumers would be limited in their abilities to adjust their spending patterns. As more income went to food and heat, consumers would need to reduce their savings or consumption of other goods and services.

How much must money income increase in the face of inflation to sustain the same purchasing power, or real income, from year to year? The answer is suggested in Figure 4.1. Notice from this figure that to maintain the same purchasing power, or real income, with inflation, money income must rise to compensate for both price increases and increases in taxes. For example, according to Figure 4.1, a person with a taxable income of $25,000 in 1970

---

[10] Economic Commission for Latin America and the Caribbean, *Preliminary Overview of the Economy of Latin America and the Caribbean: 1989* (Santiago, Chile: United Nations, 1989), p. 20.

would have been able to purchase $16,096 worth of goods and services after taxes and Social Security contributions. In order to buy the same amount of goods and services in 1990, this person would have needed $79,500. Part of this increase was due to the extra $38,124 necessary to keep up with the rising prices on goods and services, and part was due to this individual's tax bill of $21,356 resulting from the larger money income. Traditionally, the federal personal income tax in the United States has been structured so that rising money income places individuals in progressively higher tax brackets. However, during the 1980s many changes in the federal income tax occurred: overall rates were dropped, the number of tax brackets was greatly reduced, and since 1989 the brackets have been adjusted annually to compensate for inflation. Notice in Figure 4.1 that the total federal income tax paid by an individual earning a $79,500 taxable income in 1990 is less than the amount paid on a $59,300 income in 1980.

There are some groups in society whose money incomes typically do not keep up with inflation. People living on a fixed income, such as pensioners, are one such group. If the size of a person's pension check remains unchanged and prices keep rising, the purchasing power of that check keeps getting smaller. Over time, with a severe bout of inflation, a pensioner's standard of living may decline significantly.

Those who work under contract may also be hurt by inflation if their contracted wage increases are less than the inflation rate. For example, the teachers in a school district might sign a contract that provides for an annual wage increase of 5 percent over the next three years, and then encounter inflation rates that range between 8 and 12 percent annually over the life of the contract. These teachers will clearly experience a decline in their real standard of living. To avoid this situation, many contracts provide for a **cost of living adjustment (COLA),** which is an automatic wage increase when prices go up.

Cost of living adjustment (COLA)
An arrangement whereby an individual's wages automatically increase with inflation.

Interest rate
The price of money; determines the return to savers and lenders of money, and the cost to borrowers.

Inflation and the Interest Rate   The price of money is expressed as an **interest rate.** An interest rate determines the return received by savers of money and individuals and institutions that make loans, and the cost to borrowers of money for the use of funds.

Those who save may be penalized by inflation if the interest rate they receive is less than the rate of inflation. Take the case of a woman who planned to retire in early 1991 and put $10,000 in the bank in 1967, where it earned 5 percent annual interest. By the time she retired and withdrew her money, that $10,000 had grown to $32,250.98. Was this a good investment? How much better off was she in 1991 with her additional $22,250.98? Between the time she put her money in the bank and the time of her retirement, prices had been going up. What could be purchased for $10,000 in 1967 cost $39,131.74 at the end of 1990.[11] The original $10,000 plus the

[11] Based on Table 4.7.

Figure 4.1   The Purchasing Power of Income

A single individual who made a $25,000 taxable income in 1970 would have
needed a taxable income of $34,800 in 1975, $59,300 in 1980, $70,300 in 1985, and
$79,500 in 1990 to maintain the same standard of living reached in 1970, or to
purchase the same amount of goods and services. This increase was needed to
cover inflation and taxes.

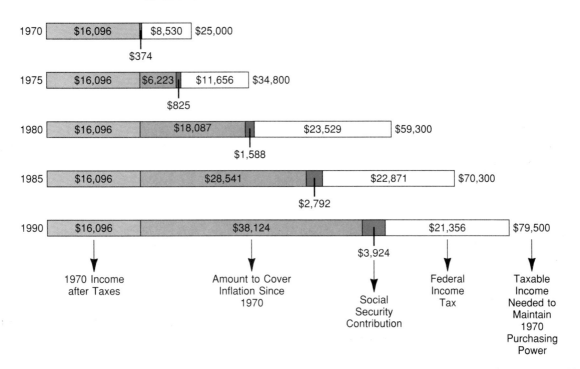

Source: *Federal Tax Guide Reports*, January 1970, pp. 3, 10; February 1976, pp. 3, 10; October 1980, pp. 25, 36; and November 1985, pp. 25, 36.
1040 Forms and Instructions for 1990, pp. 24, 53. U.S., *Economic Report of the President* (Washington, D.C.: U.S. Government Printing Office,
1991), p. 351.

$22,250.98 in interest that our retiree had in 1991 bought less than the
original $10,000 would have bought in 1967. Plus, the retiree's purchasing
power was further reduced because she had to pay income tax on the
interest. Thus, those who save their money can be hurt by inflation if the
after-tax interest they earn on their savings does not keep up with the
inflation rate.

Those who make loans may also be hurt by inflation if the interest rate
they charge is less than the rate of inflation, and if the terms of the loans are
fixed and cannot be altered to allow interest rate increases. This type of
problem often emerges when a lender makes a long-term loan commitment.
In the 1970s and early 1980s, many banks and savings and loans were caught

with long-term, fixed-rate home mortgages[12] carrying interest rates as low as 6 to 8 percent. These interest rates were far below annual inflation rates and the rates charged for new loans. Both the low interest rates and the long terms of the loans were costly to these financial institutions. As a result of this experience, many home mortgages are currently made with variable rates and flexible terms.

Real rate of interest

The nominal, or stated, rate of interest minus the inflation rate; a nominal interest rate adjusted for inflation.

In evaluating how inflation affects savers and borrowers, the real rate of interest must be considered. The **real rate of interest** is the nominal, or stated, interest rate minus the inflation rate. For example, if the nominal interest rate on a certificate of deposit is 6 percent and the inflation rate is 8 percent, the real rate of interest earned by the certificate holder is −2 percent. In this case, the saver is hurt by inflation. If the inflation rate is 3 percent during the term of a 6 percent certificate of deposit, the real rate of interest is 3 percent. In this case, the saver has made positive gains by saving.

Inflation and Wealth   Income and wealth are two different measures of economic well-being. Income represents a flow of funds, or earnings, from selling factors of production; **wealth** is a measure of the stock, or value, of one's tangible assets, or a measure of what one owns. It includes items such as stocks, bonds, real estate, cash, precious metals and stones, and fine art. A person could have a substantial income and little wealth, or great wealth (a large number of valuable assets) and a small income.

Wealth

A measure of the value of tangible assets; includes items such as real estate and corporate securities.

During inflation, the value of many assets tends to increase as prices rise. Thus, the wealthy become wealthier. Consider real estate. A home purchased in 1970 for $30,000 might well be worth $150,000 by the early 1990s largely as a result of inflation.

While inflation benefits the holders of wealth, it penalizes those wishing to acquire assets. Again, consider real estate. As prices rapidly increase, those wishing to purchase a home find it more and more difficult to do so. In this sense, young adults pay a higher penalty than others for inflation as it becomes more difficult for them to accumulate assets.

Social and Political Consequences of Inflation   Finally, in addition to its economic consequences, inflation may have social and political implications as well. Inflation-related issues often form planks in election campaign platforms: incumbents may argue for a return to office to continue their successful fight against increasing prices, and the opposition may argue that it is time for new solutions to old problems.

If prolonged or severe enough, inflation might lead not only to changes in leadership, but to changes in social and political institutions as well. The eminent British economist John Maynard Keynes wrote, "There is no subtler, no surer means of overturning the existing basis of society than to

---

[12] A fixed rate means that the interest rate does not change during the loan repayment period. A long-term loan means that the borrower has a considerable period of time for repayment, perhaps as much as 30 years.

Table 4.5   Winners and Losers from Inflation

Not everyone is affected in the same way by inflation: for some it creates opportunities and for others it creates problems.

Winners	Losers
Individuals whose incomes rise with, or faster than, the rate of inflation.	Individuals on fixed incomes and individuals working under labor contracts or other arrangements where wage increases are below the inflation rate.
Borrowers who are paying back loans at an interest rate less than the inflation rate.	Savers and lenders of money earning interest rates below the inflation rate.
Owners of assets that increase in value as the general level of prices increases.	Individuals wanting to acquire assets that are rapidly increasing in price.
Individuals gaining political power because of popular support for their position on inflation.	Politicians losing popular support because of their inability to control inflation.

debauch the currency."[13] The rise of Adolf Hitler and Nazism can be traced in part to the discontent and social disruption caused by the German hyperinflation of the early 1920s.

Table 4.5 summarizes who gains and who loses from inflation.

Causes of Inflationary Pressure

Since inflation means an upward movement in the general level of prices, and since prices result from the interaction of buyers' demand and sellers' supply decisions, a logical way of classifying the causes of inflation is according to whether they originate from the buyers' or the sellers' side of the market. Inflation originating from upward pressure on prices from the buyers' side of the market is termed demand-pull inflation. Inflation originating from upward pressure from the sellers' side of the market is called cost-push inflation.

When buyers' demands to purchase goods and services outstrip sellers' abilities to supply them, prices are forced up on what is available, and **demand-pull inflation** occurs. When demand subsides, so does the pressure on prices.

Demand-pull inflation has a tendency to occur when the economy is close to or at full employment. At full employment the economy is operating at full capacity and producing the maximum amount of goods and services

Demand-pull inflation

Caused by pressure on prices originating from the buyers' side of the market; tends to occur when buyers' demands (or spending) are greater than the abilities of sellers to supply goods and services.

[13] John Maynard Keynes, *The Economic Consequences of the Peace* (New York: Harcourt, Brace and Howe, 1920), p. 236.

possible. Production cannot be readily expanded. At the same time, with all but the frictionally unemployed working and earning income, consumer demand for goods and services is high. Also, because consumer demand is high, businesses may find it profitable to expand and invest in new buildings and machinery. This demand, or spending pressure, by both households and businesses, coupled with peak production, sets off demand-pull inflation.

Demand-pull inflation is also related to the amount of money in the economy. The ability of households and businesses to spend depends in part on the amount of money available for spending. If the supply of money in the economy increases at a faster rate than the increase in production, there may be upward pressure on prices. Also, if the economy is at full employment and more money is put into the hands of businesses and consumers, the result will be inflationary. Thus, too much money in the economy and in the hands of businesses and consumers can contribute to demand-pull inflation. On the other hand, controlling the money supply places curbs on the ability to spend, and thus on demand-pull inflation.

When price increases are caused by pressures from the sellers' side of the market, **cost-push inflation** occurs. With this type of inflation, increases in sellers' costs are translated into higher prices for goods and services. That is, when sellers pay higher prices for an input into a production process, the increased costs to the sellers may be wholly or partially passed on to buyers in the form of higher prices. Anything that represents a cost to a business is a potential source of price increases, and, if significant enough, of cost-push inflation. This means that upward pressure on prices could come from increased costs of labor, raw materials, fuels, machinery, borrowing, and so on. Attempts to increase profit by raising prices can also be a source of cost-push inflation. Certainly, the increased cost of energy contributed to cost-push inflation in the 1970s and early 1980s. For example, a barrel of crude oil that sold for $3.18 in 1970 increased to $31.77 by 1981.[14] More recently, concern has been voiced about the increasing cost of health insurance for employees and its potential effect on inflation.

Cost-push inflation can be the result of bargaining power by resource owners, poor productivity, limited availability of resources, or chance events that reduce the supply of an important factor of production. For example, a severe drought or too much rain could reduce the harvest of a crop, or political and social unrest overseas could lead to a reduction in the availability of a resource important to production in the United States. In both of these cases the supply of the resource decreases, causing its price to go up, thereby contributing to inflationary pressure.

Cost-push inflation will also more likely result when cost increases push up the product prices of large firms that play an important role in the economy, such as automobile producers, or push up the product prices of

Cost-push inflation
Caused by pressure on prices originating from the sellers' side of the market, particularly from increases in costs of production.

---

[14] U.S. Bureau of the Census, *Statistical Abstract of the United States: 1990*, 110th ed., (Washington, D.C.: U.S. Government Printing Office, 1990), p. 692.

a significant number of firms. For example, increases in the cost of energy had an impact on virtually every seller, big or small, in the economy.

Inflation need not come solely from the buyers' side or solely from the sellers' side of the market; it could come simultaneously from both sides. Consider the potential effect of a recently negotiated wage contract for a large union. On the one hand, these workers are consumers, so the contract puts more spending power in the hands of buyers, making it a potential source of demand-pull inflation. On the other hand, the contracted wages will increase labor costs, creating the potential for cost-push inflation. It is also easy to see from this example how inflation could spiral: rising prices could cause resource owners to seek higher incomes, which in turn could cause businesses to raise their prices to pay the higher incomes.

The influence of expectations of future economic conditions on both demand-pull and cost-push inflation is important. On the demand-pull side, buyers' fears of higher prices in the future may lead them to increase their current purchases as they attempt to obtain desired goods and services before the expected higher prices become reality. At full employment, this increased demand will put additional pressure on an economy already operating at its productive capacity and will result in a rise in prices. On the sellers' side, firms' expectations of increasing costs for their inputs might cause them to raise prices in anticipation of those higher costs. Thus, a curious situation results in which the expectation of rising prices could aggravate inflation.

Measures of Inflation

The three most widely used measures of price changes, or indicators of inflation, are the consumer price index (CPI), the producer price index (PPI),[15] and the GNP deflator. The **consumer price index** measures changes in the prices of goods and services that households typically purchase: shelter, utilities, food, clothing, and so forth. The **producer price index** measures changes in the prices of goods that businesses buy, either for further processing or for sale to a consumer. This includes, for example, farm and textile products, metals, machinery, and chemicals. The **GNP deflator** is a composite index that refers to price changes for the entire economy, regardless of whether the goods and services measured go to businesses, households, or the government. Before these indexes are examined further, it is helpful to understand what a price index is and how it is calculated and interpreted.

A **price index** is a measure of price changes using a percentage scale. A price index can be based on the prices of a single item or a selected group of items, called a market basket. For example, in calculating the consumer price index, approximately 400 items such as rent, electricity, and automo-

Consumer price index (CPI)

Measures changes in the prices of goods and services that consumers typically purchase, such as food, shelter, clothing, and medical care.

Producer price index (PPI)

Measures changes in the prices of goods that businesses buy either for further processing or for sale to a consumer.

GNP deflator

A composite price index that measures price changes for the entire economy, regardless of whether the goods and services measured go to households, businesses, or the government.

Price index

Measures changes in the price of an item or a group of items using a percentage scale.

---

[15] The producer price index was previously termed the wholesale price index.

Table 4.6

A Price Index

The annual dollar outlays over time for a market basket of goods and services are converted to a percentage scale called a price index. Year 2 is the base year in this index.

Year	Dollar Outlay for Market Basket	Price Index
1	$475	95.0
2	500	100.0
3	550	110.0
4	600	120.0
5	625	125.0
6	650	130.0
7	750	150.0
8	775	155.0

biles are included. Since a market basket includes a range of goods and services, it provides a more comprehensive measure of inflationary pressure than a single item would.[16]

Table 4.6 shows how a price index is calculated. The column headed "Dollar Outlay for Market Basket" gives the expenditure required to purchase the same items in years 1 through 8. Notice that this expenditure increases with each year: the same goods and services that cost $475 in year 1 cost $600 in year 4.

Actual dollar outlays for the market basket are converted to a percentage scale, the price index, which is shown in the right-hand column of Table 4.6. Because it uses percentages, the index provides an easy method for comparing and evaluating price changes. To create an index, a **base year** is selected to serve as the year against which all other years' prices are compared. The base year is given the number 100.0, or 100 percent, in the index. In Table 4.6, year 2 is the base year.

The index numbers for the other years represent, in percentages, how many more or fewer dollars than base year dollars are needed to buy the same items. For example, in year 3, $550 are needed to buy what $500 bought

Base year

The year against which prices in other years are compared in a price index; given the index number 100.0.

[16] The items used in the consumer price index market basket are weighted to reflect the spending habits of the average consumer. Periodically, the weights are altered to indicate changes in these spending habits. For example, CPI weights have been modified to indicate that consumers are now spending more on services and less on goods. Weights have also been adjusted to account for increases in spending on meals away from home and legal fees, and decreases in spending on fuel, cars, and red meat.

in the base year. Put differently, one needs the base $500 plus $50, or 10 percent more dollars, to buy the same goods and services. The index number of 110.0 for year 3 reflects that prices have gone up by 10 percent from year 2 to year 3. In year 4, an additional $100, or 20 percent more dollars than in the base year, are needed to buy the market basket; hence, the index reads 120.0, or 120 percent. Prices have gone up by 20 percent between year 2 and year 4.

In year 1 the same goods and services were $25 less than in the base year. Since $25 is 5 percent of the base year's outlay, this represents a 5 percent reduction in price. The index number for year 1 is 95.0, meaning that only 95 percent of the dollars used in the base year were needed in year 1. In summary, indexes permit us to measure changes in prices between a base year and various other years.[17]

The Consumer Price Index   Table 4.7 presents, for selected years, the overall consumer price index and separate indexes for various categories of goods and services in the consumer price index, such as rent, medical care, and fuel oil and other household fuel commodities. In this table the base year is derived from the average of the prices over three years: 1982, 1983, and 1984. That is, by adding the numbers in any of the columns in Table 4.7 for the years 1982 through 1984, and then dividing by three, you arrive at 100.0, or 100 percent.[18]

Some interesting observations can be made from this table. Under the column headed "All Items," notice the changes in the overall consumer price index for the 7-year intervals between 1976 and the middle of the base period, and between the base period and 1990. What could be purchased for $100 on average in the base period cost $56.90, or $43.10 less, in 1976. What could be purchased for $100 in the base period cost $130.70, or $30.70 more in 1990. Notice also that it cost just $38.80 in 1970 to purchase what $100 bought in the base period.

Also observe in Table 4.7 that some goods and services increased in price by less than the overall index and some by more. For example, the cost of apparel and upkeep grew by less than the overall price index between the base period and 1990 (124.1 for apparel as compared to 130.7 overall), but the

---

[17] The equation for calculating an index number for a given year is

$$\frac{\text{dollar outlay for a given year}}{\text{dollar outlay for the base year}} \times 100 = \text{price index number for a given year.}$$

Applying this equation to year 7 in Table 4.6, we have

$$\frac{\$750}{\$500} \times 100 = 150.0.$$

[18] For example, adding the numbers in the "All Items" column of Table 4.7 for 1982, 1983, and 1984 yields $96.5 + 99.6 + 103.9 = 300.0$. Dividing by 3 gives 100.0, or 100 percent.

Table 4.7

Consumer Price Index: All Items and Various Categories
for Selected Years (1982–84 = 100.0)

The consumer price index measures changes in the prices of goods and services
that consumers typically purchase. Increases in prices for some components
within the index, such as medical care, have been greater than the increase in the
overall index.

Year	All Items	Food	Rent, Residential	Fuel Oil and Other Household Fuel Commodities	Apparel and Upkeep	Medical Care
1960	29.6	30.0	38.7	13.8	45.7	22.3
1965	31.5	32.2	40.9	14.6	47.8	25.2
1970	38.8	39.2	46.5	17.0	59.2	34.0
1971	40.5	40.4	48.7	18.2	61.1	36.1
1972	41.8	42.1	50.4	18.3	62.3	37.3
1973	44.4	48.2	52.5	21.1	64.6	38.8
1974	49.3	55.1	55.2	33.2	69.4	42.4
1975	53.8	59.8	58.0	36.4	72.5	47.5
1976	56.9	61.6	61.1	38.8	75.2	52.0
1977	60.6	65.5	64.8	43.9	78.6	57.0
1978	65.2	72.0	69.3	46.2	81.4	61.8
1979	72.6	79.9	74.3	62.4	84.9	67.5
1980	82.4	86.8	80.9	86.1	90.9	74.9
1981	90.9	93.6	87.9	104.6	95.3	82.9
1982	96.5	97.4	94.6	103.4	97.8	92.5
1983	99.6	99.4	100.1	97.2	100.2	100.6
1984	103.9	103.2	105.3	99.4	102.1	106.8
1985	107.6	105.6	111.8	95.9	105.0	113.5
1986	109.6	109.0	118.3	77.6	105.9	122.0
1987	113.6	113.5	123.1	77.9	110.6	130.1
1988	118.3	118.2	127.8	78.1	115.4	138.6
1989	124.0	125.1	132.8	81.7	118.6	149.3
1990	130.7	132.4	138.4	99.3	124.1	162.8

Source: U.S., *Economic Report of the President* (Washington, D.C.: U.S. Government Printing Office, 1991), pp. 351, 352.

cost of medical care grew by more than the overall index between the base
period and 1990 (162.8 as compared to 130.7).

    Finally, observe the column headed "Fuel Oil and Other Household Fuel
Commodities." The price changes in this column provide a basis for understanding the energy crisis of the 1970s and 1980s. Notice that fuel costing $17

Figure 4.2 Annual Percentage Changes in the Overall CPI and the Energy Component

The United States experienced serious inflation problems in 1974 and 1975, and the late 1970s and early 1980s, that coincided with increases in the cost of energy.

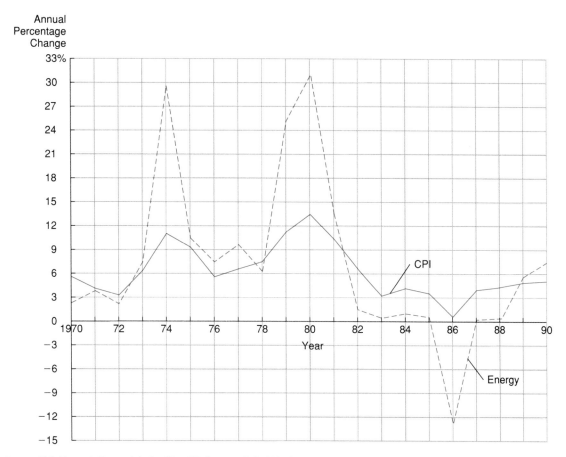

Source: U.S., *Economic Report of the President* (Washington, D.C.: U.S. Government Printing Office, 1991), pp. 355, 356.

in 1970 more than doubled in price by 1975 to $36.40, increased to $86.10 by 1980, reached its peak at $104.60 in 1981, and then dropped in price during most of the 1980s.

Since a price index compares price changes between a given year and a base year, rather than year by year, annual percentage changes in prices, or inflation rates, are not always obvious. As a result, Table 4.7 may mask the inflationary problems the United States faced in the 1970s and early 1980s. Figure 4.2 traces the *annual* percentage change in the CPI from 1970 through

1990 as well as the *annual* percentage change in the energy component of the CPI.[19] This figure illustrates that inflation was particularly serious in 1974 and 1975, and from 1979 through 1981. The figure also indicates a correlation between changes in energy prices and changes in the CPI: high inflation rates coincided with large increases in energy prices. Notice also the relationship in the late 1980s between the low rates of inflation and negligible energy price increases.

Changes in the consumer price index are calculated monthly and announced to the public. Because they show monthly changes, the numbers are usually small. These monthly changes must be "compounded" to arrive at an annual figure for comparison. That is, if a 1.1 percent monthly change in the prices of all items were to persist throughout the year, it would lead to an annual inflation rate of 14.0 percent.[20]

The Producer Price Index   The producer price index (PPI), which measures changes in the prices that businesses pay for materials they consume and for goods they buy for further sale, is given in Table 4.8. Observe that the base year is 1982. The overall producer price index is shown in the column headed "All Commodities," and the remaining columns give price changes for some categories within the producer price index. Notice again the increase and then decrease in energy prices over the years.

Just as with the consumer price index, the producer price index is calculated monthly and announced publicly. The producer price index has an important connection to the consumer price index and is therefore watched carefully. Changes in the prices that businesses pay now contribute to changes in the prices that consumers pay later. Consequently, changes in the producer price index may lead to future changes in the consumer price index.

---

[19]To determine an annual percentage change in prices between two consecutive years, A and B, in a price index, use the following equation:

$$\frac{\text{year B index number} - \text{year A index number}}{\text{year A index number}} \times 100 = \text{percentage change.}$$

For example, using the numbers in the "All Items" column in Table 4.7, the price change from 1980 (year A) to 1981 (year B) would be:

$$\frac{90.9 - 82.4}{82.4} \times 100 = 10.3\%.$$

[20]You can arrive at the annual rate of inflation of 14 percent by compounding in the following way. For each month, 1.1 percent is added to the price level. This means that at the end of each month the price level would be 1.011 times the price level at the end of the preceding month (100 percent, or 1.00, for prices at the beginning of the month, plus 1.1 percent, or 0.011, for the addition to the price level during the month). To determine the annual rate of inflation multiply 1.011 × 1.011, find your answer, and multiply this by 1.011. Continue multiplying by 1.011 for a total of eleven times, and it will give you the annual rate. A shorter method is to plug $(1.011)^{12}$ into your calculator and wait for the answer.

Table 4.8   Producer Price Index: All Commodities and Major
                                      Groups for Selected Years (1982 = 100.0)

The producer price index measures changes in the prices of goods that
businesses purchase. As was the case with consumer goods, the prices of some
producers' goods have risen faster than the price of producers' goods in general.

Year	All Commodities	Farm Products	Industrial Commodities	Energy	Metals and Metal Products
1960	31.7	37.7	30.5	13.9	30.6
1965	32.3	39.0	30.9	13.8	32.0
1970	36.9	44.9	35.2	15.3	38.7
1975	58.4	74.0	54.9	35.4	61.5
1976	61.1	73.6	58.4	38.3	65.0
1977	64.9	75.9	62.5	43.6	69.3
1978	69.9	83.0	67.0	46.5	75.3
1979	78.7	92.3	75.7	58.9	86.0
1980	89.8	98.3	88.0	82.8	95.0
1981	98.0	101.1	97.4	100.2	99.6
1982	100.0	100.0	100.0	100.0	100.0
1983	101.3	102.0	101.1	95.9	101.8
1984	103.7	105.5	103.3	94.8	104.8
1985	103.2	100.7	103.7	91.4	104.4
1986	100.2	101.2	100.0	69.8	103.2
1987	102.8	103.7	102.6	70.2	107.1
1988	106.9	110.0	106.3	66.7	118.7

Source: U.S. Bureau of the Census, *Statistical Abstract of the United States: 1990*, 110th ed., (Washington, D.C.: U.S. Government Printing Office, 1990), p. 476.

GNP Deflator   The GNP deflator, the economy's composite index, is calculated and interpreted similarly to the consumer and producer price indexes. The use of this index is discussed later in this chapter.

Importance of Indexes   The consumer price index, the producer price index, and other measures are not studied by academics and government officials out of idle curiosity. Rather, the indexes have an important impact on policy makers' decisions and on the operation of the economy. They directly affect wages of union workers who receive cost-of-living adjustments based on the consumer price index, and they influence the size of many nonunion income payments as well. Some government programs, such as Social Security, base changes in monthly checks on a variation of one

Application 4.3

Coping with Inflation

At 8:30 on a Saturday morning, hundreds of shoppers are poised at the doors of [a giant Brazilian supermarket. When it opens, shoppers rush to load their carts with bags of rice, sugar, and other items.]

[These Brazilians are] "stocking"—investing in large quantities of food staples and household provisions as a defense against double-digit increases each week in the cost of living. Stocking is one of the many ways that people in Brazil and Argentina use to try to cope with inflation of a magnitude that few countries have ever seen—more than 70 percent a month.

Adjusting to such monetary madness is an everyday drama for the 180 million people in South America's two biggest countries as they struggle against personal impoverishment, business failure and national collapse.

Some political analysts see hyper-inflation as a threat to social order and democracy itself in Argentina and Brazil. Last year, as Argentine prices spiraled toward a record monthly rate of 196 percent in July, popular discontent erupted in looting at thousands of food stores, leaving 15 people dead.

With hyper-inflation, money in the pocket is like water on sand. Even seemingly astronomical interest rates paid on savings accounts—up to 28 percent a day in Argentina in late February—often do not keep up with inflation. And as buying power evaporates, people have less and less to save.

[One of the Brazilian shoppers said that] he stopped making deposits in his savings account several months ago and started stocking groceries in the certainty that their value will increase.

Middle-class Brazilians used to beat inflation by making purchases with credit cards. When credit card bills came due up to a month after the purchase, the cost to the consumer was reduced in effect by the amount of monthly inflation.

. . . But in recent months, Brazilian stores have raised prices for credit-card purchases by as much as—or more than—a month's inflation.

[At one store] prices to customers who pay with credit cards are exactly double the prices for those who pay with cash or check. . . . Most restaurants no longer accept credit cards.

Source: William R. Long and James F. Smith, "Coping as Costs Soar Into Chaos," *Los Angeles Times*, March 11, 1990, pp. A1, 14, 15, 17.

of these indexes. Private business contracts may provide for price adjustments based on the producer price index and, in some instances, other payments such as alimony and rent have been tied to one of these indexes.

The inflation rates experienced by some South American countries have been far higher than those we have just examined for the United States. Application 4.3, "Coping with Inflation," shows how people in some of these countries have tried to adjust to such rapid price increases, and how the price increases have led to civil unrest. Notice that these inflation rates have included monthly price increases ranging from 70 to 196 percent, and that savings accounts in Argentina at one point were earning 28 percent interest a day. (A monthly inflation rate of 196 percent that persisted throughout the year would lead to an annual inflation rate of 3,214.2 percent.)

Deflation and Disinflation

Deflation

A sustained decrease in the general level of prices.

Before leaving the discussion of inflation, two important related terms should be examined: deflation and disinflation. **Deflation** occurs when there is a *sustained* decrease in the general level of prices. This does not mean that a few items decrease in price, or that there is a decrease for a short period of time. In the United States, prices have generally increased since the 1930s, and deflation has not occurred. While a sustained decrease in the general level of prices might sound attractive, deflation, like inflation, can create problems for households and businesses. For example, homeowners wishing to move could be forced to sell their houses for less than they paid for them, and businesses could suffer losses if their products' prices dropped to a level that did not cover previously incurred production costs.

Disinflation

A slowing of the inflation rate.

A reduction of the inflation rate is referred to as **disinflation.** Disinflation does not mean that prices are falling; rather it refers to a slowing of the rate of increases in prices. When the Federal Reserve tried to slow inflation in the early 1980s through its monetary policy actions, it was pursuing a policy of disinflation. Tools available for following a policy of disinflation are discussed in Chapters Six and Eight.

Production

Production

The creation of goods and services.

Production refers to the creation of goods and services. The construction of a piano, the filling of a cavity, the shipping of goods from factories to buyers, and the service provided in a grocery store are all productive activities. Since the scarcity of material goods and services is at the root of economics, measuring an economy's production, as well as evaluating its capacity to produce, is extremely important to any discussion of its goals and problems.

Full Production and Economic Growth

Full production

Occurs when an economy is producing at its maximum capacity, or when it is experiencing full employment.

The macroeconomic goal of **full production** is achieved when an economy is producing as much as it possibly can with its available resources, or producing at its maximum capacity. Although the problem of scarcity always exists, full production permits an economy to minimize its impact. The further an economy moves away from full production, the greater the scarcity problem becomes.

Factors of production are required to produce goods and services. Production, therefore, is closely interwoven with employment. When an economy reaches full production, it also reaches full employment; when it moves away from full production and operates below its peak capacity, it experiences unemployment. This relationship was illustrated earlier in the chapter in Table 4.1, which compared the U.S. economy's actual and potential output from 1980 through 1990. With unemployment, an economy's actual output

Figure 4.3   Growth of an Economy's Productive Potential over Time

An economy must produce up to its potential each year, and that potential must grow over the years if the scarcity problem is to be minimized and material well-being is to increase.

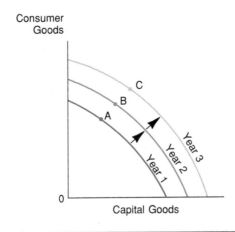

is below its potential, and goods and services that might have been produced are not.

In addition to full production, the third macroeconomic goal includes **economic growth,** which is an increase in the economy's full production, or full employment, level of output over time. In other words, not only is it desirable that the economy's maximum capacity be met, but also that the maximum capacity grows. One of the most important measures of an economy's success is its ability to expand production and not remain stagnant at the same level of output year after year. Economic growth can be achieved by increasing the number of resources available for use in production and through improved technology. For example, in the United States, the increase in the size of the labor force and the utilization of improved computer-based and other production techniques have allowed productive capacity to grow.

The production possibilities curve for capital and consumer goods in Figure 4.3 illustrates the benefits of economic growth.[21] Full production would be reached in the first year by producing at any point, such as A, on the production possibilities curve for year 1. Economic growth would occur when the production possibilities curve shifts to the right, as is done for the second and third years in Figure 4.3. This economy would achieve the third

Economic growth

An increase in an economy's full production output level over time.

---

[21] Remember that capital goods include those goods, such as machinery and equipment, that are used to produce other goods and services, and that consumer goods include those items, such as food, that are not used in further production.

macroeconomic goal of full production and economic growth if it were to produce at a point such as B along the curve for year 2 and C for year 3. Notice that as economic growth occurs, more consumer *and* capital goods can be produced over time. Economic growth is discussed in greater detail in Chapter Nine.

Measures of Production

Gross national product (GNP)

A dollar figure that measures the value of all finished goods and services produced in an economy in one year.

Since production is a basic measure of the material well-being of an economy, the United States, as well as most other countries, calculates on a regular basis how much its economy has produced. **Gross national product,** or **GNP,** is the dollar figure that measures the value of all the finished goods and services produced in an economy in one year. Only finished goods and services, which are goods and services ready for sale to their final users, are counted. Products in a stage of production, or not yet completed, are not measured in GNP. To include an item that is in the process of production and then to include the item again when it is completed would cause a double count, and production would be overstated. Also, GNP is a measure of goods and services produced, not of goods and services sold. Thus, goods involved in second-hand sales are not included since these goods were previously counted in GNP when originally produced.

Money GNP (current GNP)

Measures the value of production in terms of prices at the time of production.

Real GNP (constant GNP)

Money GNP adjusted to eliminate inflation; measures real production.

GNP figures are usually given in two forms: money GNP and real GNP. **Money,** or **current, GNP** is GNP measured according to prices during the year in which the goods and services are produced. It measures the value of current production in terms of current prices. Money GNP, which is also called nominal GNP, is influenced by both changes in production and changes in the prices of what is produced. **Real,** or **constant, GNP** is money GNP adjusted to eliminate inflation. It measures actual (real) production and shows how actual production, not the prices of what is produced, has changed. Real GNP is preferable to money GNP for gauging the state of the economy and for analyzing production conditions. Table 4.9 illustrates why this is so.

Table 4.9 deals with a hypothetical economy that produces only automobiles. The economy's output, given in the column titled "Output of Autos," was at 60 cars in years 1 and 2, 65 cars in year 3, and 55 cars in year 4. In other words, the economy was stagnant from year 1 to year 2, achieved real growth in year 3, and experienced a decline in year 4. During this period, the economy also experienced inflation: the price of autos increased year after year, as shown in the column headed "Price per Auto."

To determine money GNP, or the current dollar value of production, output is multiplied by price for each year. Thus, in year 1, when the 60 cars produced were $8,000 each, money GNP (which is given in the fourth column) was $480,000, and in year 2 when the 60 cars produced were $9,000 each, money GNP was $540,000.

Notice that the price increases caused money GNP to climb each year. These figures would have us believe that production increased from year to

Table 4.9   Determining Money GNP and Real GNP

Money GNP gives a misleading impression of the output performance of an economy over time when the level of prices is changing.

Year	Output of Autos	Price per Auto	Production in Dollar Terms (Money GNP)	Auto Price Index (GNP Deflator)	Production in Real Terms (Real GNP)
1	60	$ 8,000	$480,000	100.0	$480,000
2	60	9,000	540,000	112.5	480,000
3	65	10,000	650,000	125.0	520,000
4	55	12,000	660,000	150.0	440,000

year when, in fact, it did not. Inflation has distorted what actually happened to production. If the true productivity of the economy in Table 4.9 is to be assessed, real levels of production, or real GNP, rather than money GNP, should be examined. To evaluate the economy using the money GNP figures from Table 4.9 would be misleading.

In order to calculate real GNP, it is necessary to have some measure of price changes over the years. In Table 4.9 the prices of the autos over the four years are translated into a price index using year 1 as the base year. This information is given in the column titled "Auto Price Index," or "GNP Deflator." This price index provides the mechanism for converting money GNP to real GNP. (You can double-check these auto price index numbers by using the information on calculating a price index that was just discussed on pages 142–143.)

The equation for determining real GNP is

$$\frac{\text{money GNP for a given year}}{\text{GNP deflator for that year}} \times 100 = \text{real GNP for the given year.}$$

The real GNP, for example, for year 2 in Table 4.9 is calculated by dividing the money GNP of $540,000 by the index number of 112.5, and then multiplying that answer by 100.

It is important to notice in Table 4.9 that real GNP did not change from year 1 to year 2, and that it increased in year 3 and decreased in year 4. Real GNP, not money GNP, reflects the actual annual output for this economy. Money GNP, however, needs to be calculated because it provides the base from which real GNP is determined.

Table 4.10 gives money GNP and real GNP figures for the U.S. economy in selected years. The first noticeable feature of Table 4.10 is the sheer magnitude of the numbers. Money GNP was more than $1 trillion in 1970, and by 1990 it exceeded $5.4 trillion. In 1990, the average daily output of the U.S. economy was over $14.9 billion.

Table 4.10   Money GNP, Real GNP, and the GNP Deflator for Selected Years

Real GNP for a particular year is calculated by dividing that year's money GNP by the GNP deflator, and multiplying that answer by 100.[a]

Year	Money GNP (Billions)	Real GNP (Billions of 1982 Dollars)	GNP Deflator (1982 = 100)
1940	$ 100.4	$ 772.9	13.0
1945	213.4	1,354.8	15.7
1950	288.3	1,203.7	23.9
1955	405.9	1,494.9	27.2
1960	515.3	1,665.3	30.9
1965	705.1	2,087.6	33.8
1970	1,015.5	2,416.2	42.0
1971	1,102.7	2,484.8	44.4
1972	1,212.8	2,608.5	46.5
1973	1,359.3	2,744.1	49.5
1974	1,472.8	2,729.3	54.0
1975	1,598.4	2,695.0	59.3
1976	1,782.8	2,826.7	63.1
1977	1,990.5	2,958.6	67.3
1978	2,249.7	3,115.2	72.2
1979	2,508.2	3,192.4	78.6
1980	2,732.0	3,187.1	85.7
1981	3,052.6	3,248.8	94.0
1982	3,166.0	3,166.0	100.0
1983	3,405.7	3,279.1	103.9
1984	3,772.2	3,501.4	107.7
1985	4,014.9	3,618.7	110.9
1986	4,231.6	3,717.9	113.8
1987	4,515.6	3,845.3	117.4
1988	4,873.7	4,016.9	121.3
1989	5,200.8	4,117.7	126.3
1990[b]	5,463.0	4,155.8	131.5

[a]If you try to check your understanding of the conversion of money GNP to real GNP by applying the conversion formula to the numbers in this table, your real GNP figures will be slightly different than those given here for many of the years. This occurs because, when real GNP was calculated, the government used money GNP numbers carried out to more than one place to the right of the decimal point, not money GNP rounded to one place to the right of the decimal point as appears here. Your real GNP figures will be slightly different because you are working with rounded numbers.

[b]Preliminary figures.

Source: U.S., *Economic Report of the President* (Washington, D.C.: U.S. Government Printing Office, 1991), pp. 286, 288, 290.

Table 4.10 includes the GNP price deflator, the composite price index for the entire economy, which was mentioned earlier in this chapter. The GNP deflator is included in Table 4.10 because it is the price index used for converting money GNP to real GNP. This conversion is made in the same manner as that for the figures in Table 4.9. That is, real GNP for a given year is found by dividing that year's money GNP by that year's GNP deflator, and then multiplying by 100.[22]

Money GNP equals real GNP in the deflator's base year because the index value for that year is 100.0, or 100 percent. Thus, in 1982, the base year in Table 4.10, the money GNP of $3.166 trillion is equal to the real GNP of $3.166 trillion. In years when a dollar buys more than in the base year, the deflator is less than 100.0, and real GNP is greater than money GNP. In Table 4.10, 1970's real GNP of $2.416 trillion is greater than its money GNP of $1.0155 trillion. In years when a dollar buys less than in the base year, the deflator is greater than 100.0, and real GNP is less than money GNP. In 1989, the real GNP of $4.118 trillion is less than the money GNP of $5.201 trillion.

Table 4.10 also illustrates the value of using real GNP rather than money GNP to evaluate economic conditions. This is evident when examining the figures for 1979 through 1982—years in which the economy experienced significant inflation. If one examines money GNP from 1979 through 1982, there are substantial annual increases—in fact, there is more than a half-trillion dollar increase between the money GNPs of 1979 and 1982. These figures could give a false impression of the economy to someone who is not aware of inflation or the meaning of money GNP. The behavior of real GNP from 1979 through 1982 indicates that the economy experienced a decrease in production from 1979 to 1980, an increase in the output of goods and services in 1981, and a fall in output again in 1982. In 1982 the U.S. economy was worse off in real terms than it was in 1979. An increase in money GNP accompanied by a decrease in real GNP also occurred from 1973 to 1975.

The government calculates and publicly announces GNP figures on both a quarterly and an annual basis. Quarterly figures are used to gauge the health of the economy and are usually reported by the media. Concern tends to be generated if little or no growth occurs in GNP from quarter to quarter.

"Test Your Understanding: Calculating Price Indexes and GNP" provides an opportunity to practice calculating and evaluating money and real GNP figures and price indexes.

Does GNP Tell the Whole Story?

GNP does not present a complete picture of production in the U.S. economy. Studies have shown that GNP understates actual output because many goods and services that are produced are never included in the calculation.

---

[22] For example, the 1984 money GNP of $3,772 billion divided by the 1984 GNP deflator of 107.7 is $35.02 billion, which is multiplied by 100 to arrive at the 1984 real GNP of $3,502 billion.

Test Your Understanding

Calculating Price Indexes and GNP[a]

[a]Answers can be found at the end of the book.

The following problems provide an opportunity to calculate price indexes, money GNP, and real GNP.

Money GNP	GNP Deflator	Real GNP
————	————	————
————	————	————
————	————	————
————	————	————
————	————	————
————	————	————

1. Calculate two price indexes for the following market basket. Use year 2 as the base year for one index and record that in column 3 of the table, and use year 4 as the base year for the other index and record that in column 4 of the table.

Year	Price of Market Basket	Price Index	Price Index
1	$176	————	————
2	$220	100.0	————
3	$242	————	————
4	$275	————	100.0
5	$286	————	————
6	$330	————	————

2. Assume that a hypothetical economy produces only water slides for amusement parks, as given in the following table.

Year	Output	Price per Slide
1	500 slides	$10,000
2	550 slides	$11,000
3	500 slides	$12,500
4	450 slides	$13,000
5	600 slides	$15,000
6	600 slides	$15,500

Determine this economy's money GNP, GNP deflator, and real GNP assuming that year 1 is the base year. Record these in the appropriate following columns.

3. Below are money GNP and GNP deflator figures over several years for a hypothetical economy. Calculate real GNP for each of the years given in the table below, record your answers in the appropriate column, and answer the questions following this table.

Year	Money GNP (Billions)	GNP Deflator	Real GNP (Billions)
1985	$ 900.0	90.0	————
1986	1,000.0	100.0	————
1987	1,260.0	105.0	————
1988	1,500.0	120.0	————
1989	1,600.0	128.0	————
1990	1,800.0	150.0	————
1991	2,000.0	160.0	————

a. On the basis of real GNP, how has this economy performed from one year to the next?

b. Generally, for the entire period, how does the picture of the economy's performance using real GNP compare with the picture using money GNP?

For example, many goods and services are not accounted for in GNP because they are not bought and sold in a marketplace. Such nonmarket and unmeasured production includes people repairing their own automobiles, painting their own homes, or volunteering in hospitals and nursing homes. Actions such as these involve the actual production of goods or services and improve the economy's material well-being, but they are not included in GNP because no pay is involved. If someone were paid to perform the same tasks, the dollar value of those tasks would be included in the accounts. For example, if you teach yourself to use Lotus on a computer, it is not included in GNP; but if you pay for a course and an instructor teaches you Lotus, the value of this service is included in GNP.

The classic example of work performed that is not paid for nor included in GNP is the typical range of chores completed by a homemaker—cooking, cleaning, shopping, child care, and so forth. One study estimated that the value of these chores represents between 13 and 30 percent of the value of GNP; that is, GNP would increase by 13 to 30 percent if this work were added.[23] It is important to note, however, that households are purchasing more homemaking services in the market, which means that the value of these services is slowly being added to GNP. Lawn maintenance and child care are two examples of the trend toward purchasing these services outside of the home.

Another type of unmeasured production is work performed for cash and not reported as income to the federal government. Small jobs such as grass cutting and snow removal are included in this category, as well as major productive activities such as moonlighting by plumbers, painters, and housekeepers. Also, services are sometimes swapped, so that production is exchanged for production rather than cash. For example, a dentist might maintain the teeth of a lawyer in return for legal advice. Still another type of unmeasured production involves illegal goods or services such as illegal drugs, prostitution, and much underworld activity.

Underground economy
Productive activities that are not reported for tax purposes and are not included in GNP.

In recent years, the term **underground economy** has been used to refer to productive activities that are not reported for tax purposes and are not included in GNP. While there is concern that these goods and services are not included in GNP, the primary concern about the underground economy is the lost tax revenue.

There is one other important factor related to the calculation of GNP: it does not account for costs that will arise in the future because of current production levels. This is especially true with regard to the environment. GNP fails to measure the impact of production and consumption on the environment, and how that may affect the economy's ability to produce in the future. Currently, there is no accounting for environmental degradation. A high GNP may result in the deterioration of air and water quality,

---

[23] Brooks Albery, "How Much is Housework Worth?" *St. Louis Post-Dispatch,* July 9, 1986, p. B3.

Application 4.4

The Ballad of Joe and Mary

Joe and Mary own a small five acre farm. They work hard to be self-reliant. They grow as much of their food as possible and provide for most of their own needs. Their two children chip in and the family has a rich home life. Their family contributes to the health of their community and the nation. . . but they are not good for the nation's business, because they consume so little.

Joe and Mary realize they can no longer make ends meet. Joe finds a job in the city. He borrows $13,000 to buy a new car and drives 35 miles to work every day. The $13,000 and his yearly gas bill are added to the nation's Gross National Product.

Two years later Mary divorces Joe because she can't handle his bad city moods anymore. The lawyer's $11,000 fee for dividing up the farm and assets is added to the nation's GNP. The people who buy the five acres develop it into townhouses at $200,000 a pop. This results in a spectacular jump in the GNP.

Then, after work one day, Joe and Mary accidentally meet in a pub. They decide to give it another go. They give up their city apartments, sell one of their cars and renovate a barn behind Mary's father's farm. They live frugally, watch their pennies and grow together as a family again. Guess what. The nation's GNP registers a fall and the economists tell us we are worse off.

Source: "The Ballad of Joe and Mary," *Adbusters Quarterly Magazine*, Vol. 1, No. 3, Summer 1990, p. 74. Reprinted with permission.

deforestation, overfishing, toxic soil conditions, and a rapid reduction of nonrenewable natural resources. Application 4.4, "The Ballad of Joe and Mary," presents the point of view that an increasing GNP does not always coincide with a better quality of life.

Productivity

In addition to measuring annual changes in real production, or real GNP, it is also important to the well-being of an economy to evaluate periodically how productively its resources are being used. The basic scarcity problem is affected by the ways in which resources are combined, the efficiency of factor usage, and the types of technology used in production. The concept of assessing the amount of output produced by an economy's resources is called **productivity.**

Productivity

Concept of assessing the amount of output produced by an economy's resources; often measured specifically by output per worker.

A basic measure of productivity is output per worker. This measure takes labor plus the other factors of production into consideration. It does not measure how hard a person works, but rather how much production results from labor and other inputs combined. For example, the output of a laborer on an assembly line at an auto plant is the result of the work performed by that person with the aid of machinery, energy, a factory, and other resources. As equipment becomes more technologically advanced and efficient, a worker becomes more productive. The output of an administrative assistant using a computer is far greater than that of an assistant performing the same tasks by hand.

IMPORTANT!

Table 4.11

Labor Productivity Growth, Business Sector, 1950–1990

The average annual growth in productivity, measured by average output per worker, has been less than 2 percent since 1970.

Years	Average Annual Percentage Change
1950–54	4.22%
1955–59	2.68
1960–64	3.46
1965–69	2.42
1970–74	1.50
1975–79	1.34
1980–84	1.08
1985–90[a]	1.08

[a]Preliminary figure for 1990.

Source: U.S., *Economic Report of the President* (Washington, D.C.: U.S. Government Printing Office, 1991), p. 339.

Table 4.11 gives the average annual percentage change in labor productivity in the U.S. business sector for groups of years from 1950 through 1990. The most important observation from these numbers is that increases in productivity have been declining over the years. For example, the average annual rate of growth in labor productivity in the business sector from 1960 through 1964 was 3.46 percent, but since the middle 1960s this rate has fallen, with average productivity increases of less than 2 percent in the 1970s and 1980s.

The causes of this decline in productivity are not easily identified. It has been suggested that the problem may be due to a decline in the amount of capital used per worker, the diversion of resources to fulfill government regulations, a decline in the effectiveness of education, and the use of corporate funds for mergers and acquisitions rather than for research and development. Some economists have also noted that outmoded and aging capital equipment and technological processes in certain industries may contribute to a decline in productivity.

What are the benefits of increased productivity? The most fundamental benefit comes from improved efficiency in the use of the economy's scarce resources. When productivity per worker is below what it could be, there is an opportunity cost imposed on society in the form of goods and services that could have been provided but are lost because resources were not employed in the most efficient manner. When productivity per worker increases, this opportunity cost diminishes.

More immediate to the goals of economic policy, improved productivity could ease inflationary pressure by allowing firms to meet rising costs through increased output rather than higher prices. Also, if policies to stimulate productivity lead to a general expansion of business activity, another benefit could be improved employment opportunities.

A Policy Problem

In the Employment Act of 1946, the federal government officially committed itself to help create an environment conducive to the attainment of full employment, full production, and price stability. Each of these goals is desirable, but it may be impossible to attain all of them simultaneously.

When the economy reaches full production and full employment, pressures from increased spending power on the buyers' side of the market combine with the inability of the economy to expand its output to cause demand-pull inflation. However, removing upward pressure on prices by curbing buyers' demands could lead to unemployment and less than full production. Policy makers are thus faced with a tradeoff: do they seek full employment and full production accompanied by inflation, or stable prices accompanied by unemployment and less than full production? There are no clear solutions to this tradeoff question. Some prefer full employment and production at the expense of price stability, and others would be willing to endure some unemployment for the sake of controlling inflation. The tradeoff decision is difficult because, either way, some groups in the economy will be hurt.[24]

Summary

The three fundamental problems of the macroeconomy are unemployment, inflation, and falling production. The three fundamental objectives are full employment, stable prices, and full production and economic growth. To help create an environment in which these objectives can be reached, Congress enacted the Employment Act of 1946.

Unemployment is a matter of concern because it leads to an economic loss for society by intensifying the scarcity problem, and to personal hardships for individuals who are out of work. Unemployment can be frictional, cyclical, or structural in nature. Frictional unemployment is voluntary and is primarily due to the time required to locate work. Cyclical and structural unemployment are involuntary. Cyclical unemployment is caused by downswings in the general level of economic activity, and structural unemployment occurs when a particular occupation is no longer in demand.

---

[24] This tradeoff is discussed in greater detail in Chapter Nine.

The labor force includes all persons 16 years of age and older who are employed or actively seeking work. The overall participation rate is the percentage of the civilian noninstitutional population 16 years of age and older that is in the labor force. The overall unemployment rate is the percentage of the labor force that is unemployed and actively seeking work. Unemployment rates and participation rates can also be calculated for subgroups within the labor force and differ from group to group. Discouraged workers, regional differences in unemployment, and the types of jobs individuals hold should be considered when evaluating the nation's employment situation.

Full employment occurs when everyone in the labor force except the frictionally unemployed is working. The unemployment rate associated with full employment is not universally agreed upon and has changed over time. The natural rate of unemployment is the rate when cyclical unemployment is eliminated.

Inflation refers to an increase in the general level of prices. While a small amount of inflation is not a serious problem in an economy, rapid inflation can intensify the scarcity problem for households and businesses. Inflation reduces the purchasing power of money, hurts some groups in society more than others, and may lead to social and political instability. Inflation can be caused by upward pressure on prices coming from the buyers' side of the market, the sellers' side of the market, or both sides of the market. When it originates on the buyers' side of the market, it is termed demand-pull inflation; and when it originates on the sellers' side of the market, it is termed cost-push inflation. Households' and businesses' expectations of future economic conditions can influence demand-pull and cost-push inflation.

Three widely used indicators of inflation are the consumer price index, producer price index, and the GNP deflator. Each index expresses the prices for a collection of goods and services in different years as a percentage of the prices for those same goods and services in a base year. A price index number of 120.0 means that prices in a certain year are 20 percent higher than prices for the same items in the base year.

Deflation occurs when there is a sustained decrease in the general level of prices. Disinflation occurs when there is a slowing of the inflation rate.

An economy's level of production is closely related to its level of employment. Full production is reached when an economy is operating at maximum capacity, or at full employment. A nation's level of material well-being is related to its production, and it experiences economic growth when it increases its full production level of output over time.

The basic measure of production is gross national product (GNP), which is a dollar figure that measures the value of all finished goods and services produced in an economy in one year. Money GNP is the value of output in prices at the time production occurs, and is affected by changes in both output and price levels. Real GNP is money GNP adjusted to eliminate inflation, and changes only as the level of output changes. Real GNP is a better measure of production in an economy than money GNP. Evidence exists that GNP understates actual output, since some production is never included in the calculation.

It is also important to measure the productivity of an economy's resources. This is calculated by determining output per worker, which combines the results of production from labor and other inputs. In the United States, increases in productivity have been declining over the past few decades.

It may be impossible to attain full employment, full production, and price stability at the same time. As the economy approaches full employment, increased spending causes demand-pull inflation. The reduction of spending to dampen demand-pull inflationary pressures can cause employment and production to fall.

Key Terms and Concepts

Macroeconomics	Wealth
Employment Act of 1946	Demand-pull inflation
Unemployment	Cost-push inflation
Frictional unemployment	Consumer price index
Cyclical unemployment	Producer price index
Structural unemployment	GNP deflator
Full employment	Price index
Labor force	Base year
Participation rate	Deflation
Unemployment rate	Disinflation
Discouraged workers	Production
Natural rate of unemployment	Full production
Inflation	Economic growth
Hyperinflation	Gross national product
Money (nominal) income	Money (current) GNP
Real income	Real (constant) GNP
Cost of living adjustment	Underground economy
Interest rate	Productivity
Real rate of interest	

Review Questions

1. Define the three major goals and the three major problems of the macroeconomy. What is the significance of the Employment Act of 1946 with regard to these goals and problems?

2. Identify which of the following individuals would be classified as unemployed, and if they are, the type of unemployment that each is experiencing.

  a. A student who decides at mid-semester to devote the rest of the term to studying and quits her part-time job

  b. A graphic artist who is out of work because a computer now does her job

  c. A waiter who quits his job and is applying for the same type of work in a restaurant where the morale is better

  d. The son of a local farmer who is putting in 20-hour weeks without pay on the farm while waiting for a job at a nearby factory

  e. A travel agent who is laid off because the economy is in a slump and vacation travel is at a minimum

3. Define labor force, unemployment rate, participation rate, full employment, and the natural rate of unemployment. Explain the value of measuring each of these.

4. What is the difference between demand-pull inflation and cost-push inflation? Does the economy experience only one type of inflation at a time, or can these types occur simultaneously? How might inflation tend to spiral?

5. Calculate price index numbers for the following table assuming that year 3 is the base year, and put your results in the last column.

Year	Market Basket Dollar Outlay	Price Index
1	$170	_____
2	$180	_____
3	$200	_____
4	$200	_____
5	$224	_____
6	$250	_____
7	$280	_____

6. What is the difference between deflation and disinflation? Although the United States has not experienced deflation since the 1930s, what problems would result if deflation occurred over the next three years?

7. In each of the following examples, identify whether the person or institution is a loser from inflation, and if so, why.

  a. Kayla borrows $5,000 at an interest rate of 4 percent for her college expenses over 5 years, during which the inflation rate averages 6 percent.

  b. Louis invests $3,000 in securities that pay 5.3 percent annually for ten years, and the inflation rate during that time averages 6.4 percent.

  c. The Lilyton National Bank commits to $4 million in 15-year mortgages at an average mortgage rate of 7.75 percent. The inflation rate averages 8 percent over this 15-year period.

  d. Barney bought a house in 1988 for $100,000 that he now plans to sell for $200,000. During this time the inflation rate has averaged 5 percent.

8. Complete the following table for a hypothetical economy. Determine money GNP, the GNP deflator, and real GNP, assuming that year 1 is the base year.

Year	Real Output	Price per Unit	Money GNP	GNP Deflator	Real GNP
1	100 units	$4.00	_____	_____	_____
2	120 units	$4.40	_____	_____	_____
3	110 units	$5.00	_____	_____	_____
4	110 units	$5.20	_____	_____	_____
5	135 units	$5.20	_____	_____	_____
6	140 units	$5.60	_____	_____	_____

Discussion Questions

1. There is a significant relationship between the data on lost output in the last column of Table 4.1 and the data on the unemployment rate in the last column of Table 4.2. What is this relationship?

2. Suppose that you attend an information session given by two candidates for the U.S. Congress. How do you think a candidate should answer each of your following questions?
   a. Since it may be impossible to have the economy operate at full employment without experiencing inflation, which goal would you choose — stable prices or full employment?
   b. Do you favor using the full employment rate of unemployment or the natural rate of unemployment as a goal?
   c. How would you reduce cyclical and structural unemployment? What policies would you recommend to control inflation?

3. Can you identify someone that you know who is working part-time but would like to be working on a full-time basis, or working in a job that does not allow full utilization of the person's skills? In your opinion, is listing this person as employed a serious flaw in the way unemployment statistics are gathered and reported? What changes, if any, would you make in the method for determining the unemployment rate?

4. Each of the following allows you to integrate this chapter into your everyday life. Choose one from this list to complete.
   a. Interview someone who has been out of work for over a month. Is this person classified as unemployed, and if so, what type of unemployment is this person experiencing? What are the costs of unemployment to this person?
   b. How has inflation affected the tuition you pay at the college you are currently attending? What was the tuition in 1970, 1975, 1980, 1985, and 1990? How have changes in your college's tuition compared to changes in the overall consumer price index?
   c. Compile a list of all of the goods and services that you have produced in the last month that would not be counted in GNP. Why would they not be counted?

5. Why is there so much concern about declining productivity in the United States? In your opinion, what is the major reason for this decline?

6. Create three separate lists showing the groups that are hurt by unemploy-
    ment, inflation, and declining production.

Critical Thinking Case 4

█ Statistics and Decision Making

Critical Thinking Skills | Understand the statistical concepts of population and sampling
Determine whether data support a generalization
Evaluate the reliability of a statistic used to make a judgment

Economic Concepts | Relationship between statistical measures and economic decision making
Factors underlying the calculation of the unemployment rate

"The average age of smokers has risen by 7 percent." "Prices are expected
to increase by 9.9 percent this year." "The unemployment rate has dropped
to 6.4 percent." "Corporate profits rose by 16 percent."[a] We are constantly
bombarded with statistics about economic and noneconomic phenomena.
Statistics are often used because they add precision to statements that might
otherwise be vague and authority to the positions people take. People like
to hear and use statistics.

Statistics often provide the foundation for making a decision. For example, many people have chosen to quit smoking because of statistics on the
health and longevity of smokers and nonsmokers. And, the prediction of a
high unemployment rate—say 10 percent—could induce some households
to save more, cause some businesses to spend less on investment, and lead
to the enactment of certain government stabilization policies.

Too often, though, numbers are accepted without question. We do not
stop to consider where a statistic comes from or how accurately it represents
the statement it supports. Consider an announcement that the unemployment rate in a large metropolitan area has increased from 5.4 percent to 6.2
percent in the last three months. Does this statistic accurately measure this
area's unemployment? In determining the validity of this statistic, we should
consider what data were collected, how they were collected, and how they
were analyzed.

The concepts of population and sampling are important in understanding
what lies behind a statistic. The population defines the group from which the
statistic is to be drawn, or identifies the characteristics of the group that is
to be measured. On learning the unemployment rate for a particular
metropolitan area, many questions concerning the population of that statistic could be asked. For example, does this population have the same
characteristics as the population used to determine the national unemploy-

ment rate? Does it include all suburbs, or does it exclude particular segments of the community?

The sample for the statistic is the group selected from the population for actual measurement. Both the size of the sample and the method of selecting the sample are important because a statistic could misrepresent its population. If your college makes the statement that graduates earn on average $30,000 the first year after receiving their degrees, you might be curious about how many graduates were sampled and how those sampled were selected. This statistic could be based on a response to a questionnaire by only five graduates, all of whom earned high salaries because they had worked for several years before graduating.

Unfortunately, we usually do not have ready access to information on the population and sample from which a statistic is drawn. However, a simple awareness of these concepts reminds us that a statistic is only as good as its population and sample, and that decisions based on faulty statistics can lead to poor results.

Questions

1. The population and sample for deriving the overall unemployment rate in the United States are given in the text of this chapter, although they are not identified as such. What are the population and sample for this statistic?

2. If you could change the current procedures for calculating some key economic statistics, who would you include in the population and sample for measuring the unemployment rate? What would you include when determining the consumer price index?

3. In the next few days, locate the population and sample for three to five publicly issued statistics. These could be on the sports page in your local paper, in a news report, or in this textbook.

4. Assume that it was reported today that "the interest rate on car loans is expected to jump by 5 percentage points." What types of economic decisions might be made as a result of this statement? What serious consequences could occur if this statistic were inaccurate?

[a]The numbers are hypothetical.

Suggested Readings

"Chapter 7: Women in the Labor Force," U.S., *Economic Report of the President* (Washington, D.C.: U.S. Government Printing Office, 1987), pp. 209–226.
A survey of female employment, unemployment, occupational choice, and earnings over the past few decades.

Gary Clayton and Martin Gerhard Giesbrecht, *A Guide to Everyday Economic Statistics* (New York: McGraw-Hill, Inc., 1990).
Examines how statistics about production, employment, prices, and other macroeconomic measures are constructed, and how they can be used.

Elizabeth Corcoran and Paul Wallich, "The Analytical Economist: Tracking the Unemployed," *Scientific American,* August 1989, pp. 63–64.
Discusses interpreting unemployment statistics and understanding their limitations.

John E. Hesson, "The Hidden Psychological Costs of Unemployment," *Intellect,* April 1978, pp. 389–90.
Discusses physical and psychological problems caused by unemployment and cites some important studies in this area.

John P. Hoerr, *And the Wolf Finally Came: The Decline of the American Steel Industry* (Pittsburgh, Penn.: University of Pittsburgh Press, 1988).
Details the decline of the steel industry in the United States and the hardships faced by workers and their families as unemployment in this industry increased.

James Howard Kunstler, "Schuylerville Stands Still," *The New York Times Magazine,* March 25, 1990, pp. 48–60.
A human interest story about a village experiencing economic difficulties after previous prosperity.

Jonathan Levin, "The Economy and the Environment: Revising the National Accounts," *IMF Survey,* June 4, 1990, pp. 161, 168–9.
Discusses how the depletion of some natural resources is covered in GNP and related statistics, and offers proposals for measuring the effects of environmental degradation.

Sar A. Levitan and Elizabeth A. Conway, "Part-timers: Living on Half-rations," *Challenge,* May-June 1988, pp. 9–16.
Surveys statistics and issues concerning part-time workers.

Thomas Mann, "Disorder and Early Sorrow," *Stories of Three Decades,* translated by H. T. Lowe-Porter (New York: Alfred A. Knopf, 1955), pp. 500–528.
Fiction about life in Germany during the hyperinflation of the 1920s.

James Tobin, "High Time to Restore the Employment Act of 1946," *Challenge,* May-June 1986, pp. 4–12.
Discusses reasons for giving high priority to the adoption of federal policies to reach the goals of the Employment Act.

Chapter Five

Foundations of the Macroeconomy

The pattern of a roller coaster with its continuous "ups" and "downs" resembles the expansions and contractions in production and employment in the U.S. macroeconomy.

Source: © 89 ZEFA/London: The Stock Market.

Chapter Objectives

1. To define and explain business cycles.

2. To identify reasons for changes in the level of macroeconomic activity.

3. To understand the relationship between total spending and the levels of aggregate employment and production, and total spending and the level of prices.

4. To examine the spending behavior of households, businesses, government units, and the foreign sector.

5. To establish how the relationship between leakages from the spending stream and injections into the spending stream affects the level of economic activity.

6. To introduce the multiplier effect.

7. To introduce the effect of expectations on output and price levels.

8. To identify the role of total spending in the formation of macroeconomic policies.

9. To provide, in an appendix, an explanation of equilibrium in the macroeconomy.

A market economy continually changes in its level of economic activity; it goes through upswings and downswings, or periods of expansion and contraction, without ever staying at a particular level of output. These fluctuations are obvious from reading newspapers and magazines and listening to news broadcasts that regularly carry stories of the changing pulse of the economy and of impending recessions or recoveries. People are forever forecasting when a downturn or upturn will occur, resulting in a continual flow of predictions of good or bad times ahead.

Two indicators of this constant economic change were discussed in the last chapter. First, in surveying unemployment it was noted that the unemployment rate tends to increase or decrease from year to year. Much of this change comes from cyclical unemployment, which is caused by changes in the general level of economic activity. Second, in the discussion of real GNP, it was shown that production levels tend to change from year to year; in some years growth occurs and in others output declines.

This chapter deals with fluctuations in the level of activity in the macroeconomy. It identifies the pattern of these changes and explains why they occur.

Changes in the Level of Economic Activity

When speaking of changes in the level of macroeconomic activity — upswings and downswings, expansions and contractions — we are generally referring to changes in real GNP. The movement of real GNP from 1973 through 1990 is plotted in Figure 5.1a. This figure indicates that the economy experienced both increases and decreases in its activity level during the 1970s and 1980s. For example, from 1975 through late 1979, real output grew. Then the expansion weakened, and the economy experienced a brief downswing in 1980. Following this contraction, production grew until late 1981, when the economy slipped into a longer downswing, which continued through 1982. Then a strong recovery began, and real GNP grew at an annual rate of 7.0 percent through mid-1984, and, after that, at annual rates of about 2.0 to 4.0 percent until 1989. Production grew very little from 1989 to mid-1990, when the economy fell into a downswing.

One of the primary reasons for concern over changes in real GNP is that changes in the level of real output cause changes in the level of employment. When production increases, more labor is needed and unemployment falls; when production decreases, less labor is needed and unemployment rises. This is shown by comparing the information in Figure 5.1b, which plots unemployment rates for 1973 through 1990, with the real GNP information in Figure 5.1a. Note the inverse relationship between output and unemployment. Observe, for example, that in late 1982, when real GNP was at a low point, the unemployment rate was at a peak, and that when real GNP began to fall in mid-1990, the unemployment rate began to rise. Thus, when a downswing appears imminent, the primary concern is that the macroeconomic problem of unemployment will be aggravated.

Changes in the level of real GNP may also create an inflation problem. Demand-pull inflation has a tendency to occur when real GNP expands to the full-production, full-employment level. However, when real GNP increases, but is well below the full-production level, or when real GNP decreases, price levels may not be affected by the output change. Therefore, while we are cognizant of the full-production, demand-pull inflation problem, we tend to relate the expression "changes in economic activity" to changes in production and employment rather than to changes in prices.

Business Cycles

Business cycles

Recurring periods of growth and decline (or expansion and contraction) in an economy's real output, or real GNP.

While fluctuations in the level of output can adversely affect employment, and perhaps prices, the output changes themselves are somewhat predictable, so their impact can be controlled or at least anticipated. That is, changes in the level of economic activity do not occur randomly or haphazardly. Rather, they occur in wavelike patterns called business cycles.

Business cycles are recurring periods of growth and decline in the real output, or real GNP, of an economy. In a business cycle the level of output

Figure 5.1   Real Gross National Product in 1982 Dollars
and the Unemployment Rate (1973–1990)

A market economy such as that of the United States constantly goes through upswings and downswings in its level of output. There is an inverse relation between the economy's level of output and the rate of unemployment: as ou decreases or increases, unemployment tends to rise or fall.

a. Gross National Product

Trillions of Dollars

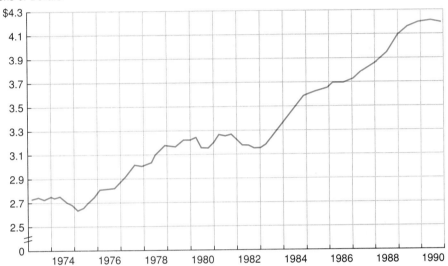

b. Unemployment Rate[a]

Percent

[a]Seasonally adjusted.

Source: The Federal Reserve Bank of St. Louis, *National Economic Trends*, February 27, 1981, pp. 3, 13; February 1988, pp. 3, 13; March 1991, pp. 3, 13.

Figure 5.2   Phases of the Business Cycle

The economy is always in one of the four phases of the business cycle. Activity is either at a peak, in a recession, at a trough, or in a recovery.

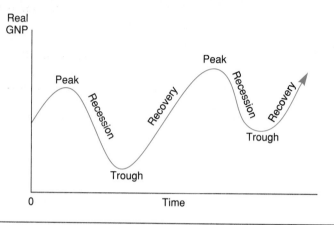

Figure 5.3   Economic Activity (1900–1987)

The length of each phase and the intensity of the change in output differ from cycle to cycle.

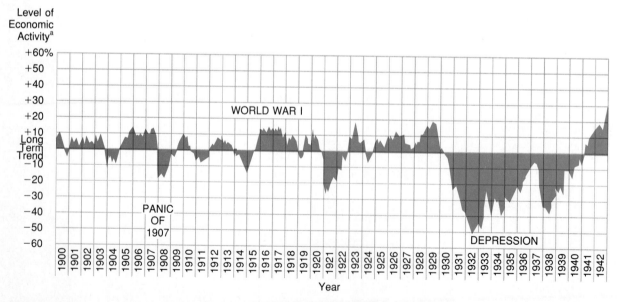

[a]The figure shows the deviation of actual economic activity above or below its long-term trend or average value.

Source: "American Business Activity from 1790 to Today," (Cleveland: AmeriTrust Corporation, January 1988). Reprinted with permission.

increases to a peak from which it ultimately falls. Output then continues to drop to a minimum, where it turns around, rises, and the whole process is repeated again. Figure 5.2 illustrates the wavelike movement of business cycles.

Each cycle is divided into four stages called **phases.** The expansionary phase during which real GNP increases is called the **recovery,** maximum output occurs at the **peak** of the cycle, real GNP falls in the **recession** and reaches its minimum in the **trough.**[1] The economy is always in some phase of a business cycle. It does not remain stationary at a particular level of output until some force causes it to increase or decrease. Instead, the economy is always expanding, contracting, or at a turning point in activity.

The cyclical behavior of real GNP in the U.S. economy can be seen by referring back to Figure 5.1a, which traces the movement of real output from 1973 through 1990. Notice the wavelike pattern of recovery, peak, recession, and trough in this figure.

Figure 5.3 presents a longer view of business cycles in the United States by illustrating output movements from 1900 through 1987. This longer

[1] It should be noted that the terms "recession" and "depression" do not have the same meaning. A recession is a downswing in economic activity, and the Depression was an historical event in the 1930s when the United States and other economies experienced sharp reductions in output and increases in unemployment.

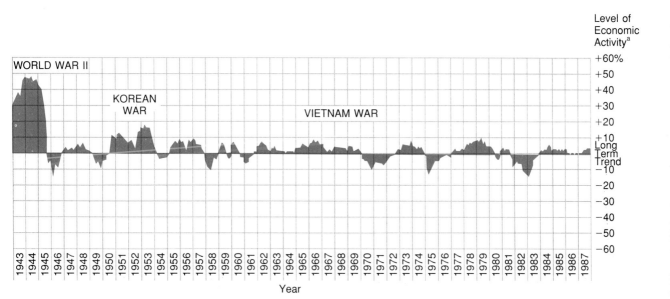

period of time shown in Figure 5.3 more easily illustrates some of the properties of cycles. First, notice that the phases of the business cycles are not of equal length. The recovery of 1959 lasted just a few months, whereas the recovery that began in 1975 lasted until late 1979. Notice also that since the 1940s, periods of expansion have far outweighed periods of recession. This might be due in part to the passage of the Employment Act of 1946, which formalized the government's commitment to providing an environment conducive to full production, full employment, and stable prices; a better understanding of the operation of the economy; and improved information with which to make economic decisions. A second important property of business cycles is that cyclical expansions and contractions are not of equal intensity. For example, the declines in output from 1929 to 1932 and in 1945 were dramatic, whereas the decline in 1970 was not. Every business cycle is unique in the lengths of its phases and the intensity with which output increases or decreases. There is no exact rule for determining the duration and magnitude of cyclical changes.

Perhaps the single most important question to ask about business cycles is what is their cause: what makes the level of economic activity alternately expand and contract? The answer to this question is important since it helps us understand the nature of cyclical movements, and such understanding is necessary for their control.

The cause of economic fluctuations has been pondered for centuries. Over the years some theories have emerged and then disappeared while others have been accepted and refined. In the following section the cause of economic fluctuations is explained in terms of the most popular and generally accepted theory of the day.

Total Spending and the Level of Economic Activity

Total, or aggregate, spending
The total combined spending of all units in the economy (households plus businesses plus government plus foreign) for new goods and services.

The generally accepted theory today is that changes in the level of total spending are the basic cause of expansions and contractions in economic activity. That is, real output responds to changes in total spending. **Total,** or **aggregate, spending** refers to the total spending for all new goods and services by households, businesses, government units, and foreign buyers combined.

Why do changes in spending cause the level of economic activity to change? In a market economy, buyers, through their spending decisions, choose goods and services that are produced by sellers. If buyers do not spend their money on products, sellers will not produce those products for the market. Thus, if total spending were to decrease, output would decrease; if total spending were to increase, output would increase; and if total spending remained unchanged, output would not change.

When the level of spending goes up and sellers increase production, more land, labor, capital, and entrepreneurship are required. This means that

Figure 5.4   Spending and the Level of Economic Activity

Changes in total, or aggregate, spending lead to changes in output, employment, and income.

Recovery or Expansion	Recession or Contraction
Increased Spending	Decreased Spending
↓	↓
Causes	Causes
↓	↓
Larger Output	Smaller Output
↓	↓
Causes	Causes
↓	↓
Increased Employment	Decreased Employment
↓	↓
Causes	Causes
↓	↓
More Income	Less Income

there will be an increase in the employment of resources, which will in turn enlarge incomes. Thus, increased spending leads to economic expansion, or recovery, since it stimulates a growth in output, employment, and income.

When spending falls and sellers reduce their outputs, a cutback occurs in the employment of resources. This cutback in turn leads to a decrease in resource owners' incomes. Thus, a reduction in spending leads to a recession, or contraction in economic activity, because of its dampening effect on output, employment, and income. The relationship between spending, output, employment, and income is summarized in Figure 5.4.

Since aggregate spending is composed of expenditures by households, businesses, the government, and foreign buyers, the spending behavior of each of these sectors will be examined, along with how that behavior affects the level of economic activity.

The Household Sector

In the aggregate, the largest spending group in the economy is households. Households buy far more goods and services than do businesses, government units, and foreign purchasers combined. For example, households purchased about $3.7 trillion of the approximately $5.5 trillion output produced in 1990.[2] Also, over time, household spending increases at a relatively stable pace. Because individuals do not radically alter their ex-

[2] U.S., *Economic Report of the President* (Washington, D.C.: U.S. Government Printing Office, 1991), p. 286. The 1990 figures are preliminary.

Figure 5.5   Real Personal Consumption Expenditures for 1964–1990 (1982 Dollars)

Total spending by households does not fluctuate widely from year to year, and the growth of personal consumption expenditures is relatively stable over time.

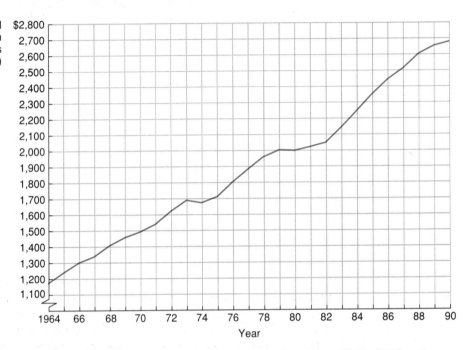

Source: U.S., *Economic Report of the President* (Washington, D.C.: U.S. Government Printing Office, 1991), p. 288. The 1990 figure is preliminary.

Personal consumption expenditures

Household spending on new goods and services.

penditure patterns from year to year, aggregate household spending on new goods and services, which is technically termed **personal consumption expenditures,** tends to fluctuate very little as it grows over time. This is indicated in Figure 5.5, which plots real personal consumption expenditures in 1982 dollars for 1964 through 1990. Since changes in personal consumption expenditures cause changes in the economy's levels of output, employment, and income, it is fortunate that the largest spending group in the economy exhibits stable spending characteristics.

The Household Sector and the Circular Flow of Economic Activity   The majority of spending by the household sector on new goods and services comes from the income earned by households from producing goods and services. The relationship between household earned income and personal consumption expenditures is shown in the circular flow model in Figure 5.6.[3]

[3] The circular flow model was introduced in the discussion of a market economy in Chapter Two.

Figure 5.6

Household Spending, Borrowing, Transfers, Saving, and Taxes

Household spending is influenced mainly by the size of earned income, by transfers and borrowing, which provide injections into the spending stream, and by saving and taxes, which are leakages from the spending stream.

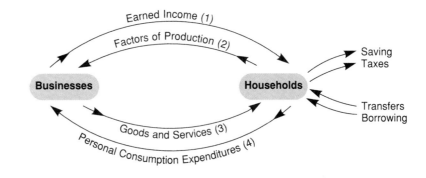

If we ignore the saving, taxes, transfers, and borrowing shown in the figure, and concentrate exclusively on the flows going between businesses and households, it can be seen that the income earned from supplying resources to businesses to produce goods and services (lines 1 and 2) provides households with the spending power to purchase goods and services (lines 3 and 4). Household spending that is based on income earned from producing goods and services is called **income-determined spending.**

If the only spending in the economy were household income-determined spending, and if households always spent all of their incomes, the level of economic activity and the size of the circular flow would never change. That is, a given level of spending would create an equal amount of output and an equal amount of income, all of which would be spent again to create the same amount of output and income. As this pattern repeated itself, the economy's activity level would always stay the same.

Although earned income is the major source of household spending, it is not the only source. As Figure 5.6 illustrates, household spending can also come from borrowing and/or government transfer payments. Borrowing may be done in several different ways, ranging from obtaining a loan from a bank to extending payments on credit card purchases. A **transfer payment** is money from the government for which no direct work is performed in return. Social Security payments, unemployment compensation, and agricultural subsidies are examples of transfer payments.

Personal consumption expenditures that come from household borrowing and transfers are types of **nonincome-determined spending:** they are expenditures that are *not* generated from household earned income. Because these expenditures are based on a source other than earned income, they represent **injections into the spending stream;** that is, they are expenditures

Income-determined spending

Household spending on new goods and services that comes from income earned from producing goods and services.

Transfer payment

Money from the government for which no direct work is performed in return.

Nonincome-determined spending

Spending that is *not* generated from household earned income.

Injections into the spending stream

Spending that comes from a source other than household earned income.

over and above what household earned income alone would allow. *Injections into the spending stream lead to an expansion of output, employment, and income in the economy* as businesses produce more to meet this additional demand.

Figure 5.6 also shows that purchasing goods and services is only one way of disposing of household income. One alternative to consuming is to save income by placing it in a financial institution. **Financial institutions** are organizations such as banks, savings and loan associations, and insurance companies that provide a means for channeling funds that have been saved to borrowers. These institutions also perform other services for buyers, sellers, and holders of money, stocks, bonds, and other financial instruments. Another alternative use of income is to pay personal taxes to the government. Both saving and taxes represent **leakages from the spending stream** since they are income that has been channeled to uses other than consumption. *Leakages from the spending stream cause the levels of output, employment, and income in the economy to shrink* as businesses cut back production in response to the reduced demand.

Since household spending is influenced by the size of earned income and by saving, taxes, borrowing, and transfers, a change in any of these will cause a change in total personal consumption expenditures. For example, fear of a recession could cause households to increase their saving, with a resulting decline in spending; or a decrease in interest rates could lead to an increase in spending by encouraging households to borrow for such items as automobiles and home remodeling. Although earned income, borrowing and transfer injections, and saving and tax leakages all affect household spending and economic activity, the impact of a change in the household sector could be negated by spending changes in the business, government, or foreign sectors. Therefore, before drawing any conclusions about the effect on the economy of changes in household spending behavior, one should examine the other sectors.

The Business Sector

Businesses are major purchasers of goods in markets. Each year they buy billions of dollars worth of new machinery, equipment, replacement parts, buildings, inventories, and the like. Business spending on these types of new goods is called **investment spending.** Like household spending, business investment spending influences output, income, and employment. Also, like household spending from borrowing and transfer payments, investment spending is nonincome-determined spending because it does not originate directly from household earned income.

Unlike household personal consumption expenditures, investment spending tends to fluctuate widely from year to year. Figure 5.7, which plots real gross investment[4] in 1982 dollars for 1964 through 1990, illustrates the

---

Financial institutions

Organizations such as banks, savings and loan associations, and insurance companies that provide a means for channeling saving into borrowing.

Leakages from the spending stream

Uses other than spending for earned income, such as taxes and saving.

Investment spending

Business spending on new goods, such as machinery, equipment, buildings, and inventories; nonincome-determined spending.

---

[4]Gross investment is outright purchases of investment goods plus a depreciation allowance for capital that was used up during the current year.

Figure 5.7   Real Gross Investment for 1964–1990 (1982 Dollars)

Investment spending can fluctuate widely from year to year and is a major cause of changes in economic activity.

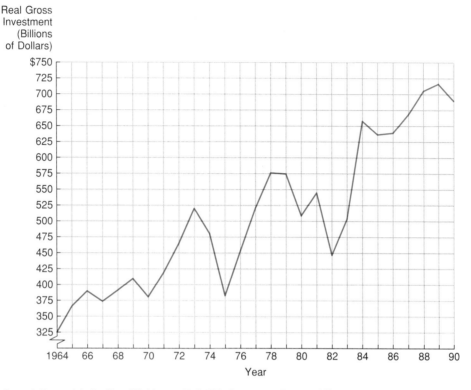

Source: U.S., *Economic Report of the President* (Washington, D.C.: U.S. Government Printing Office, 1991), p. 288. The 1990 figure is preliminary.

fluctuating pattern characteristic of investment spending. *Because of these fluctuations, changes in investment spending are a primary cause of changes in economic activity.* When business spending declines, it can bring about a slowdown or recession; when it increases, it can help pull the economy into a recovery. For example, Figure 5.7 shows a dramatic decline in investment spending in 1974 and 1975, and declines in 1980, 1982, and 1990. During these years the United States experienced recessions and increasing unemployment rates.

Why does business spending fluctuate from year to year? Why does it not exhibit the stability associated with household spending? Primarily, business spending fluctuates because it is influenced by profit expectations. A business will invest in new equipment, a new building, or whatever, because it expects that this investment will increase its profit level. If conditions suggest that a proposed investment expenditure will not be sufficiently profitable, the investment may be postponed or eliminated. Because many investment goods are bought for expansion or replacement purposes, postponement is feasible. It would be easier for a food chain to postpone the replacement of an old but operating refrigeration unit, or for an amusement park to eliminate the construction of a new ride, than it would be for a family to postpone its expenditures on food and utilities.

Profit expectations, and thus investment spending, are related to expectations of future overall levels of economic activity. The fear that a recession is about to occur may encourage a reduction in investment spending as businesses speculate that falling demand and growing inventories of unsold goods will make their operations unprofitable. There was, for example, substantial concern after the stock market crash in October 1987 that businesses would cut back on investment spending in anticipation of a recession. Likewise, expectations of healthy sales and a surge in economic activity can bring about an increase in business spending.

The interest rate that businesses must pay for borrowed funds greatly influences the level of investment spending. If the interest rate is high, businesses may decide that it is to their best advantage to postpone spending because the high cost of borrowing reduces the profitability of the investment. If the interest rate is low, businesses may take advantage of the reduced cost of funds and increase their borrowing for investment purposes. Application 5.1, "Interest Rates and Investment Spending," provides an example of how an investment decision is affected by the interest rate. The importance of the effect of changes in the interest rate on economic activity will be discussed further in Chapter Eight.

When a business invests in machinery, equipment, a building, or other assets, the expense can be staggering. Imagine the price tag on the construction of a large shopping mall or a multistoried building such as the Trump Tower in New York. Where does a business obtain funds for such expenditures? A business is like an individual who buys a house, a car, or another expensive item that is not a part of the normal everyday budget. The individual can make his or her purchase with money that has been saved and/or with money that is borrowed. Businesses face a similar choice—they can use earnings saved from their past operations, which are called **retained earnings,** and/or they can go to outside sources.

Retained earnings

The portion of a business's accumulated profits that has been retained for investment or other purposes.

The Business Sector and the Circular Flow of Economic Activity   Business investment spending and saving are incorporated into the circular flow model in Figure 5.8. Line 1 in the figure illustrates business investment spending, which is an injection into the spending stream because it is nonincome-determined spending. Line 2 represents business saving. Like household saving, business saving is a leakage from the spending stream. Business taxes, shown on line 3 of Figure 5.8, are another leakage from the spending stream. Businesses must pay several types of taxes to the

Application 5.1

Interest Rates and Investment Spending

Suppose that your favorite pizza spot has become so popular that customers must often wait for an hour or longer for a table. The owners, because of this demand, are contemplating refurbishing currently unused space in their facility. They have determined that $100,000 will be needed for this investment and are analyzing the cost of borrowing the money. How will the interest rate that they must pay for these borrowed funds affect their decision to refurbish?

With an annual interest rate of 6 percent, the interest for borrowing $100,000 for one year is $6,000 (6% × $100,000 = $6,000); at 12 percent the interest for borrowing $100,000 for one year is $12,000; and at 18 percent the interest is $18,000. This means that the annual interest cost *alone* will change by $1,000 when the annual interest rate changes by 1 percent. If the restaurant borrows $100,000 for a year at 18 percent rather than at 6 percent, it will cost an additional $12,000. If lenders are charging high interest rates, the owners must

decide whether they want to pay those rates: it will mean a substantial reduction in profit, or perhaps no profit at all.

Assume that the owners of the pizza restaurant would like to borrow the necessary $100,000 and pay it off in equal monthly installments for five years. Also assume that the interest would be recalculated each month to account for the declining balance of the loan as it is paid off.

The following table summarizes the required monthly payment and the total interest paid for a loan of $100,000 that is retired over five years at various interest rates. Notice that the monthly payment for borrowing $100,000 at 18 percent is $2,539.30, and that the monthly payment at 6 percent is $1,933.30 – a difference of $606 *per month*. Notice also the total interest paid over five years. At 6 percent it is $15,998 and at 18 percent it is $52,358. A loan made at 18 percent rather than 6 percent would mean additional forgone profit of $36,360.

Monthly Payments and Total Interest Paid for Retiring a $100,000
Loan Over Five Years at Various Interest Rates[a]

Interest Rate	6%	12%	18%
Monthly Payment	$ 1,933.30	$ 2,224.40	$ 2,539.30
Total Interest Paid	$15,998.00	$33,464.00	$52,358.00

[a]Payments are calculated from amortization tables in Steven C. Lawlor, *Business Mathematics* (San Francisco: Canfield Press, 1976), pp. 216–217.

government: corporate income tax, sales tax, and license fees, to name a few. Because they are injections and leakages, any change in the level of business investment spending, saving, or taxes will cause a change in output, employment, and income.

Figure 5.8 emphasizes that business saving and investment spending are channeled through financial institutions. When a business saves, the company uses a financial institution to hold its deposits or to purchase stocks, bonds, or some other security that allows the savings to earn money until the funds are needed. Investment spending also involves financial institu-

Figure 5.8

Business Investment Spending, Saving, and Taxes

Business investment spending is an injection into the spending stream, and business saving and taxes are leakages from the spending stream.

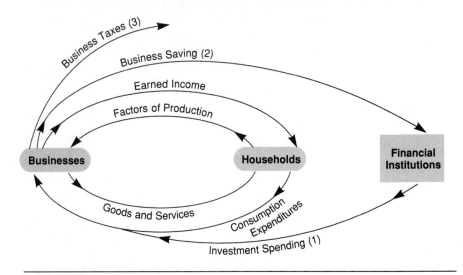

tions because investment is financed from retained earnings, from borrowing, or from issuing new shares of stock. If financed through retained earnings, a business would make its investment by cashing in its savings. If the investment were financed through borrowing, the company would go to a financial institution to make a loan. If new shares of stock were issued, a financial intermediary would also be used.

Saving, Investment, and the Level of Economic Activity   Figure 5.9 modifies the circular flow diagram in Figure 5.8 by removing business taxes and adding household saving and borrowing. This added dimension points out a critical relationship in the operation of the economy: the saving-borrowing and investment relationship, or, as it is more commonly called, the **saving-investment relationship.** Figure 5.9 illustrates that, through the operation of financial institutions, dollars saved by households and businesses—dollars that are leakages from the spending stream—can be borrowed and spent by other households and businesses and thereby returned to the spending stream. In other words, financial institutions are vehicles for changing leakages from the spending stream into injections.

But is every dollar saved put back into the spending stream through investment and household borrowing? Does the amount of saving always equal the amount that businesses invest and households borrow? Because savers have entirely different motives for their actions than do investors and

Saving-investment relationship

The relationship between the amount saved by households and businesses and the amount returned to the spending stream through investment and household borrowing.

Figure 5.9   Saving, Investing, and Borrowing by Households and Businesses

The relationship between saving and investment spending and household borrowing can cause the economy's levels of output, employment, and income to increase, decrease, or remain unchanged.

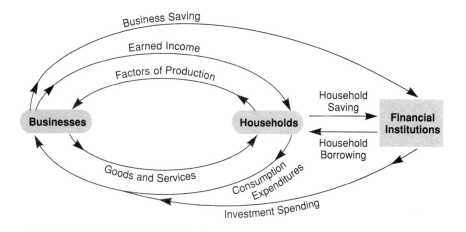

borrowers, it is likely that saving will not equal investment and borrowing.[5] Rather, in this relationship, there are three possible situations: (1) saving equals investment and household borrowing; (2) saving is greater than investment and household borrowing; or (3) saving is less than investment and household borrowing.[6] Let us examine each situation.

If $5 billion is saved, and the entire $5 billion is borrowed and spent, the levels of output, employment, and income will not change. All of the dollars leaked from the spending stream are returned, and no change occurs in the level of aggregate spending. Thus, if saving equals investment and household borrowing, there is no change in output, income, and employment.

If $5 billion is saved, and only $4 billion is borrowed and spent, the economy will contract since $1 billion more has been removed from the spending stream than has been returned. The level of aggregate spending falls by $1 billion, causing a decline in output, employment, and income. Thus, when saving is greater than investment and household borrowing, the economy contracts.

---

[5] Savers are motivated by a desire to have funds available in the future for specific purchases, as a precaution against unknown adversity, or for potential opportunities. Investors and borrowers are motivated by a desire for profit, as in the case of business, or for personal satisfaction, as in the case of an individual borrowing to purchase an automobile or vacation.

[6] We will discuss in Chapter Eight how some financial institutions can lend more than is saved.

If $5 billion is saved, and $6 billion is spent through investment and household borrowing, the economy will expand since a net addition of $1 billion is injected into the spending stream. This increase in spending causes an increase in output, employment, and income. Thus, when investment and household borrowing are greater than saving, the economy expands.

The Government Sector

The third major sector that influences economic activity with its spending patterns is the government sector. Government expenditures occur at the federal, state, and local levels and can be classified into two categories: purchases of goods and services, and transfer payments.

Government spending on such items as new fire trucks, bombers, cement, paper, postal equipment, and the services of government employees is called **government purchases of goods and services.** Like household spending from borrowing and transfers, and business investment spending, government purchases of goods and services is nonincome-determined spending. Government purchases have the same impact on the economy as household and investment spending have. That is, increases in government purchases can increase output, employment, and income; and decreases in government purchases can decrease output, employment, and income. In 1990 government units in the United States purchased about $1.1 trillion worth of goods and services.[7]

Since government spending for goods and services is the second largest component of total spending, it is important to observe the pattern of these purchases over time. Figure 5.10 plots real government purchases of goods and services in 1982 dollars for 1964 through 1990. Like household spending and unlike business spending, government purchases tend to be stable and increasing over time. However, there are some deviations from this pattern. For example, government purchases increased at a more rapid rate in the late 1960s during the Vietnam War and since 1983.

As was pointed out earlier, government transfer payments, such as Social Security and unemployment compensation, are payments from the government to individuals or households who have performed no direct work in return. As was also pointed out, households can use all or part of their transfer payments for personal consumption expenditures. Thus, changing the amount of government transfer payments does not change what is termed government purchases, but it does affect the level of economic activity by changing the amount that households have available to spend. In 1990, $672.1 billion went from government units to households in the form of transfer payments.[8] It will be shown in the next chapter how

Government purchases of goods and services

Government spending on new goods and services; nonincome-determined spending.

---

[7] U.S., *Economic Report of the President*, 1991, p. 287. This figure is preliminary.

[8] U.S., *Economic Report of the President*, 1991, p. 380. This figure is preliminary.

Figure 5.10   Real Government Purchases of Goods and Services for 1964–1990 (1982 Dollars)

The growth in government purchases of goods and services has been relatively stable.

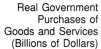

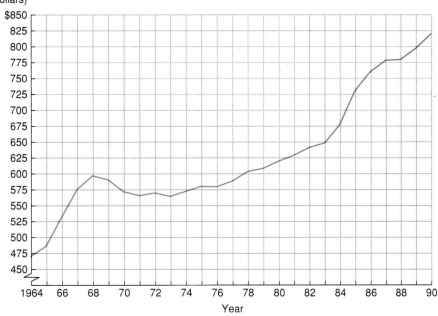

Source: U.S., *Economic Report of the President* (Washington, D.C.: U.S. Government Printing Office, 1991), p. 289. The 1990 figure is preliminary.

Congress can, and has, deliberately altered the size of federal government purchases and transfers to change economic conditions.

The Government Sector and the Circular Flow of Economic Activity   The government sector is added to the circular flow model in Figure 5.11. In this figure, line 1 shows the flow to households of transfer payments, which can be used for consumption spending. Line 2 represents government purchases of goods and services, and lines 3 and 4 illustrate the flow of taxes from households and businesses to government. The circular flow diagram shows clearly that government purchases are a direct injection into the spending stream, transfers provide an injection through households, and taxes are a leakage.

Figure 5.11

The Government Sector and the Circular Flow

Government purchases of goods and services and spending from transfer payments are injections into the spending stream, and taxes paid to government by businesses and households are leakages from the spending stream.

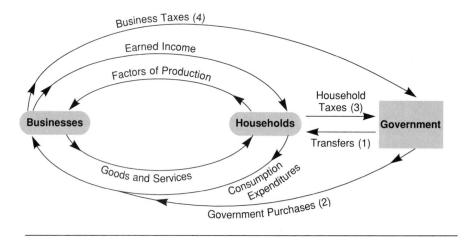

Government Spending, Taxing, and the Level of Economic Activity   Like the saving-investment and household borrowing relationship discussed earlier, the tax–government expenditures relationship is important in the operation of the economy. It is not necessary that the tax–government expenditures relationship be equal. Sometimes (1) the amount put into the spending stream through government purchases and transfers is equal to the amount taken from the spending stream in taxes; (2) the amount put into the spending stream through purchases and transfers is less than the amount withdrawn as taxes; or (3) the amount returned through purchases and transfers is greater than the amount taken from the spending stream as taxes.[9]

[9]We are being careful to compare the amount returned to the *spending stream* through goverment purchases and transfers with the amount taken from the *spending stream* through taxes. This is because not all transfer payments are used to purchase goods and services, and not all taxes are paid with money that would have been spent. When households receive transfer payments, a portion of what they receive from the government may be saved. When households pay taxes, part of that payment comes from money that would have been used for personal consumption expenditures, and part comes from money that would have been saved. For this reason, assessing the impact of government expenditures and taxes becomes somewhat complex. Let us illustrate with the following example.

  Suppose that the government taxes households by $100 billion and uses that money to purchase $100 billion of goods and services. Suppose also that $70 billion of that tax is paid with dollars that households would have used for personal consumption expenditures, and $30 billion is paid with dollars they would have saved. Because of this, the tax of $100 billion reduces household spending by only $70 billion. Thus, the tax of $100 billion and expenditure program

If the government, through taxes, reduces household and business spending by, say, $2 billion, and if all of this $2 billion is used by the government to purchase goods and services or is transferred to households who spend all that they receive, then the flows of leakages and injections perfectly offset each other: all that is taken from the spending stream through taxes is respent through government purchases or transfers. Because aggregate spending does not change, the levels of output, employment, and income do not change either.

If government withdraws $2 billion from the spending stream through taxes and expends only $1.5 billion on purchases and transfer payments, the leakages from spending will be greater than the injections, causing the economy to contract. Because aggregate spending falls, the levels of output, employment, and income also fall.

If government withdraws $2 billion from the spending stream and expends $2.5 billion on purchases and on transfer payments that are all spent, then, on net, its actions will result in an injection of $0.5 billion into the spending stream. Because aggregate spending increases, the levels of output, employment, and income also increase.

In short, if all tax dollars that have been withdrawn from the spending stream are spent by the government or by households, economic activity will stay the same. If these tax dollars are not all spent, output, employment, and income will fall; and if more is spent than collected, the economy will expand.

The Foreign Sector

Transactions between U.S. and foreign buyers and sellers take place in the foreign sector. The sale overseas of corn grown in Illinois, the purchase of a Japanese television set by a family in Texas, and the sale of U.S.–built airplanes to a European government all occur in the foreign sector. As with the other sectors, changes in spending on goods and services in the foreign sector affect the levels of output, employment, and income in the U.S. economy.

Export

A good or service that is sold abroad.

Import

A good or service purchased from abroad.

Goods and services produced in the United States and sold abroad are **exports,** and goods and services produced in foreign countries and sold in the United States are **imports.** The real values in 1982 dollars of U.S. exports

---

of $100 billion enlarges the spending stream by $30 billion and the economy grows. This is because $30 billion that would have been saved by households is now being spent by the government. In this example, if the government wanted the effect of its spending and taxes to be neutral, it would spend $70 billion and tax $100 billion.

This example could be further complicated by assuming that out of the $100 billion in government expenditures, only $50 billion is spent for the purchase of goods and services and that the other $50 billion goes for transfer payments. The $50 billion spent on goods and services goes directly into the spending stream, but part of the $50 billion in transfers could go into savings. If households saved $15 billion and spent $35 billion, then only $85 billion of the government's total expenditures would go into the spending stream.

Figure 5.12

Real U.S. Exports, Imports, and Net Exports of Goods
and Services for 1964–1990 (1982 Dollars)

Real U.S. exports and imports of goods and services have generally increased
from 1964 through the 1980s, and since the early 1980s imports have been
consistently higher than exports.

a. Real U.S. Exports and Imports of Goods and Services

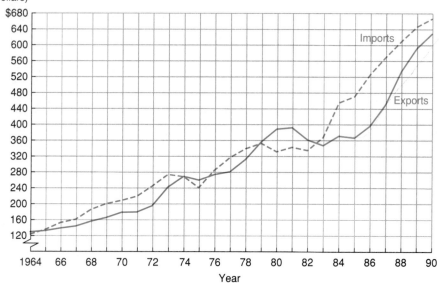

Source: U.S., *Economic Report of the President* (Washington, D.C.: U.S. Government Printing Office, 1991), p. 289. Figures for 1990 are
preliminary.

and imports from 1964 through 1990 are plotted in Figure 5.12a. This figure
illustrates that, although both exports and imports of goods and services
have generally grown over the years, the growth has not been steady. In
addition, in recent years the value of exports has consistently been less than
the value of imports.

The difference between the value of exports and the value of imports
(exports minus imports) is termed **net exports.** If the value of exports is
greater than the value of imports, net exports is greater than zero; if imports
are greater than exports, net exports is negative.

The behavior of real U.S. net exports of goods and services from 1964
through 1990 is plotted in Figure 5.12b. In years where the net export line
is below zero on the graph, the real value of U.S. imports of goods and

Net exports

Exports minus imports; is
positive when exports
exceed imports and
negative when imports
exceed exports.

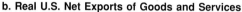

b. Real U.S. Net Exports of Goods and Services

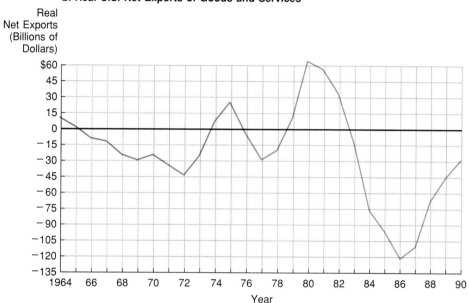

services exceeds the real value of exports. Figure 5.12b shows that negative real net exports have occurred in many years, and that they were exceptionally large in the mid-1980s. As will be noted in Chapter Seventeen, this severe negative net export position posed some serious problems.

The importance of the foreign sector to the macroeconomy has grown in the last few decades. In 1965 U.S. exports of goods and services amounted to 6.1 percent of GNP and imports to 4.7 percent. By 1990 exports and imports had grown to 12.3 and 13.0 percent of GNP, respectively.[10] Trade between the United States and other nations, and international finance are examined in greater detail in Chapters Sixteen and Seventeen.

[10] U.S., *Economic Report of the President*, 1991, pp. 286, 287. The 1990 figures are preliminary.

Figure 5.13   The Foreign Sector and the Circular Flow

Exports of goods and services generate injections into the U.S. economy's
spending stream, and imports cause leakages from the U.S. economy's spending
stream.

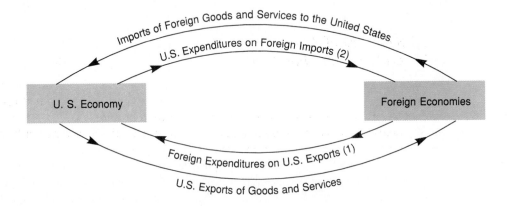

The Foreign Sector and the Circular Flow of Economic Activity   When
buyers in the United States purchase foreign goods and services, their
expenditures cause income, output, and employment to increase in foreign
countries, but not in the United States. Similarly, when foreign businesses,
households, and governments purchase goods and services produced in the
United States, their expenditures cause output, employment, and income in
the United States to increase. Thus, income spent on imports is a leakage
from the spending stream, and sales of U.S. exports produce injections into
the spending stream. Expenditures by foreign buyers on exported U.S.
goods and services are another form of nonincome-determined spending
because they do not originate from U.S. household earned income.

Figure 5.13 illustrates the effect of exports and imports on the U.S.
economy using a variation of the circular flow model. Line 1 represents
injections into the U.S. economy resulting from expenditures by foreign
buyers for exported goods and services. Line 2 illustrates leakages from the
U.S. economy resulting from expenditures by U.S. buyers on imported goods
and services.

As with the other sectors, leakages and injections in the foreign sector are
not necessarily equal. If the value of exports is greater than the value of
imports, or net exports is a positive number, then injections into the
spending stream from the foreign sector exceed leakages, causing aggregate
spending, and thus the levels of output, employment, and income in the
United States to grow. If the value of exports equals the value of imports, or
net exports is zero, then injections equal leakages, and the movement of
goods and services in the foreign sector does not change total spending or,

consequently, the levels of output, employment, and income in the United States. If the value of exports is less than the value of imports, or net exports is a negative number, then foreign sector leakages from the spending stream exceed injections into the spending stream, causing economic activity in the United States to decrease.

Summary of Aggregate Spending, Leakages, and Injections

By now it should be clear that the level of aggregate spending determines the levels of output, employment, and income in the economy. If aggregate spending increases, the economy expands as output, employment, and income increase; if aggregate spending decreases, the economy contracts as output, employment, and income fall. Aggregate spending is determined by adding together the spending of all households, businesses, government units, and foreign buyers in the economy. Of these four groups, business investment spending, because of its size and instability, is a major cause of changes in output, employment, and income.

Certain actions can be taken in each of the four spending sectors to cause leakages from the spending stream. These actions include saving by households and businesses, paying taxes by households and businesses, and importing foreign goods and services. Actions can also be taken in the four sectors to cause injections into the spending stream. These actions include household spending of borrowed dollars and government transfer payments, business investment spending, government purchases of goods and services, and foreign purchases of exported goods and services.

Expansions and contractions in the economy result from the relationship between leakages and injections in total spending. Up to this point in our discussion, we have isolated the expansionary and contractionary impacts of the saving-investment and household borrowing relationship, the tax–government expenditures relationship, and the import-export relationship. To assess the operation of the economy, these relationships must be considered together. For example, while saving could exceed borrowing, causing a contraction, government expenditures could exceed taxes, or exports of goods and services could exceed imports, causing an expansion. Ultimately, what happens to output, employment, and income depends upon the impact of all leakages and injections taken together. If all leakages from the spending stream are equal to all injections, the economy will not change. If leakages are greater than injections, the economy will contract, or fall into a recession. If injections are greater than leakages, the economy will expand into a recovery. These cause-and-effect relationships are summarized in Table 5.1.

Since each component of aggregate spending and each leakage and injection has an impact on total spending and the direction of economic activity, changes in these various elements are watched closely by those

Table 5.1   Leakages, Injections, and Changes in Economic Activity

The economy's levels of output, employment, and income depend on the combined impact of all leakages from and all injections into the spending stream.

The Level of Economic Activity Will

Expand

When all injections into the spending stream exceed all leakages from the spending stream

Remain unchanged

When all injections into the spending stream equal all leakages from the spending stream

Contract

When all injections into the spending stream are less than all leakages from the spending stream

Leakages	Injections
Household saving	Household spending from borrowing
Business saving	Household spending from transfer payments
Household taxes	Business investment spending
Business taxes	Government purchases of goods and services
Import expenditures	Export expenditures

concerned with the state of the economy. For this reason, interest is high in reports from the media about changes in spending behavior, saving levels, borrowing, investment, and such. Application 5.2, "Economic Activity in the Headlines," provides a sample of headlines and stories about the condition of the macroeconomy that appeared in *The Wall Street Journal* during early 1991. Can you identify how the concern expressed in each of these headlines relates to the circular flow model, and how it would affect the overall levels of output, employment, and income?

The effect on the level of economic activity of all leakages and injections considered together is explained in more detail in an appendix at the end of the chapter, where a model for determining the economy's level of output is introduced.

The Multiplier Effect

As was noted earlier, the largest spending group in the economy is households, and most household spending is income-determined spending; that is, it is based on income earned from producing goods and services. We also learned that household purchases through transfers and borrowing, business investment spending, and government and foreign purchases of goods

Application 5.2

Economic Activity in the Headlines

The following is a sample of headlines and excerpts from stories about the economy carried in *The Wall Street Journal* in early 1991.

Durable-Goods Orders Fell 0.7% During January

Orders for big-ticket factory goods fell 0.7% in January, government figures show, indicating that the woes of the manufacturing sector may be leveling off but not offering signs of any rebound. . . .

The report seemed to fit with the view that the economy is still weak, but that the recession isn't worsening significantly. . . .

Consumer Credit Fell Again in January

Consumer credit fell at a 4% annual rate in January, the Federal Reserve reported, marking the second straight monthly decline and clearly signaling that consumers were putting the brakes on spending as the Persian Gulf war began. . . .

"People were worried about unemployment and income declines," [said an economist in banking]. "They were trying to exert a little discipline on their budgets." . . .

Exports Won't Pull U.S. Out of Recession
Foreign Demand Proves Inadequate to Offset Drop on Domestic Side

Exports aren't enough.

For all the well-deserved attention that U.S. exports are getting these days, they weren't enough to keep the U.S. from sliding into recession and they won't be enough to pull it out. . . .

Car Sales Aren't Lifted by Peace

The victory in the Persian Gulf didn't do much for the beleaguered U.S. auto industry in early March.

Sales of North American–made cars and trucks fell 14.4% from weak year-earlier levels, and the annual pace of domestic passenger car sales sagged to a recessionary [level].

Dealers reported there are more customers walking into their showrooms. But doubts over the economy and more conservative lending policies by banks are preventing many of these browsers from buying. . . .

U.S. Consumers' Confidence Rose in Early March

Consumer attitudes improved strikingly during early March, according to preliminary survey results from the University of Michigan's Institute for Social Research. . . .

The sharp rise in consumer confidence could be good news for the sagging U.S. economy, prompting an increase in spending that would help bring an end to the recession. . . .

Orders for U.S. Machine Tools Rose in February

Durable-goods makers regained some appetite for long-term capital spending in February, but they had little hunger to make shorter-term investments, machine-tool orders indicate. . . .

Orders for machine tools, which cut and form metal for a variety of industrial uses, are generally placed a year before the tools are shipped, so the order volume serves as an indicator of manufacturers' middle-term to long-term optimism. . . .

Source: *The Wall Street Journal*, February 27, 1991, p. A2; March 8, 1991, p. A2; March 12, 1991, p. A2; March 14, 1991, p. A2; March 18, 1991, p. A2; March 25, 1991, p. A2.

and services are nonincome-determined spending; that is, they are not based on what households earn. The distinction between income-determined and nonincome-determined spending is important because changes in nonincome-determined spending lead to larger changes in the level of economic activity, or, expressed differently, they are subject to a

Multiplier effect

The change in total output and income generated by a change in nonincome-determined spending is larger than, or a multiple of, the spending change itself.

multiplier effect. That is, because of the multiplier effect, an increase or decrease of, say, $100 million in nonincome-determined expenditures will cause the economy to grow or contract by more than $100 million.

The reason for the multiplier effect is that new dollars introduced into the circular flow through nonincome-determined spending are spent over and over again, thereby creating more and more output, employment, and income. Put another way, when nonincome-determined expenditures are made, they become income to the individuals who own the resources that produce the goods and services purchased. These individuals then use part of that income to buy goods and services from others, who in turn spend part of the income they receive, and so on.

A hypothetical example will illustrate how the multiplier principle works. Suppose a company borrows $100,000 from the local bank to build a garage to house some equipment. When the $100,000 is spent and the garage is built, factors of production are used and are paid $100,000 in income. Thus, this new injection of nonincome-determined investment spending creates $100,000 worth of new output, employment, and income. The households that receive this newly created $100,000 of income from the building of the garage will now use part of it, say, $80,000, for personal consumption expenditures. (The rest will be saved and/or used for taxes.) When this $80,000 is spent, $80,000 in new output, employment, and additional income for other households is created. Thus, so far, the initial investment spending injection of $100,000 has caused an increase in the economy's output and income of $180,000.

The process does not stop here. The households that receive the $80,000 of income will take part of that money, say, $64,000, and spend it on new goods and services, thereby creating $64,000 of additional income for other households, part of which will be spent, and on and on. Thus, the initial injection of $100,000 of new spending continues through the economy in a circular pattern, multiplying output and income along the way. Table 5.2 carries this example of the multiplier process through several rounds. When this example is carried through enough successive rounds to approach a zero increase in the last round, and the output and income created in each round are summed, $500,000 in total output and income results. This means that the initial injection of $100,000 has been multiplied, or magnified, into $500,000 of output and income; there has been a multiplier effect of five times the initial change in spending.

There is an easier way to calculate the multiplier effect than to go through each round of spending, as in Table 5.2. To do so, divide the initial change in nonincome-determined spending by the percentage of the additional income received by households that is *not spent*. For instance, in the preceding example, the households that received $100,000 in income spent $80,000, or 80 percent, and did not spend $20,000, or 20 percent; the households that received $80,000 in income spent $64,000, or 80 percent, and did not spend $16,000, or 20 percent, and so on. Accordingly, in this example, the change in nonincome-determined spending of $100,000 can be divided

Table 5.2				

Effect on Total Output and Income from a
Nonincome-Determined Spending Injection of $100,000

Because of the multiplier effect, an injection of nonincome-determined spending
into the spending stream causes total output and income to increase by more
than the amount of the nonincome-determined spending itself.

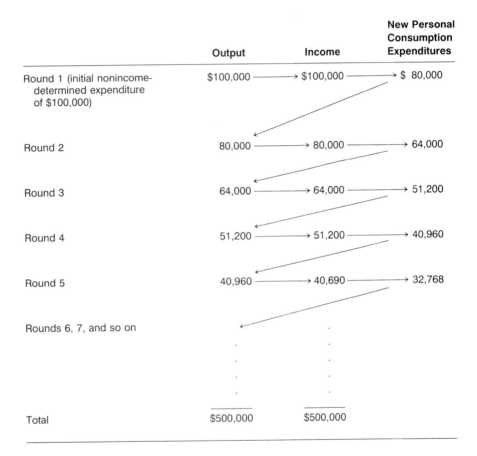

	Output	Income	New Personal Consumption Expenditures
Round 1 (initial nonincome-determined expenditure of $100,000)	$100,000 ⟶	$100,000 ⟶	$ 80,000
Round 2	80,000 ⟶	80,000 ⟶	64,000
Round 3	64,000 ⟶	64,000 ⟶	51,200
Round 4	51,200 ⟶	51,200 ⟶	40,960
Round 5	40,960 ⟶	40,690 ⟶	32,768
Rounds 6, 7, and so on	·	·	
	·	·	
	·	·	
	·	·	
Total	$500,000	$500,000	

by 0.20 (the percentage of additional income not spent in each round) to
result in an answer of $500,000 ($100,000/0.20 = $500,000).[11] In summary, the
multiplier effect can be determined by

$$\frac{\text{change in nonincome-determined spending}}{\text{percentage of additional income not spent}} = \text{total change in output and income.}$$

[11] Be careful when calculating the multiplier effect to always express the percentage of
additional income not spent as a decimal. That is, if 20 percent of additional income is not spent,
then the multiplier effect is determined by dividing the change in nonincome-determined
spending by 0.20, not by 20.

Since the multiplier effect that results from a change in nonincome-determined spending depends upon how much is spent and not spent from each successive round of income and output that is created, the more that is spent, the greater the multiplier effect, and the more that is not spent, the smaller the multiplier effect. If the households in the preceding example had spent only 75 percent and had not spent 25 percent of each successive round of newly created income, the level of economic activity would have grown by $400,000 rather than $500,000 ($100,000/0.25 = $400,000).

The multiplier effect also works in reverse when nonincome-determined expenditures are cut back. A decrease in investment spending of $100,000, by the time it works its way through the economy, will cause the level of economic activity to decline by more than the initial $100,000 decrease.

In summary, changes in nonincome-determined spending such as investment spending, government and foreign purchases, and household expenditures from transfer payments or borrowing will cause changes in the level of economic activity that are a multiple of the initial change in spending. Application 5.3, "Ripples through the Economy," provides three examples of the multiplier effect. The first example deals with a slump experienced in Pittsburgh in the 1980s because of the decline in the steel industry; the second example illustrates the financial reward for attracting conventions to a city; and the third deals with the impact of an auto plant layoff. In reading this application, keep in mind that the multiplier effect applies to both increases and decreases in spending.

A Word about Inflation

When the economy expands or is in the recovery phase of the business cycle, the full production–full employment level of output sets a limit on how far spending can cause production and employment to increase. As a result, if spending continues to grow when the economy is at or close to the full production–full employment level of output, demand-pull inflation will result. We must be careful to understand that it is not always to the benefit of the economy to encourage more spending.

It is possible for inflation to occur when injections into the spending stream are greater than leakages. If the economy is at or near full employment, and investment spending and household borrowing are greater than saving, and/or government expenditures are greater than taxes, and/or exports are greater than imports, then the size of the spending stream could be causing inflation. Either there is too much spending through investment, household borrowing, exporting, and/or government expenditures, or too little saving, importing, and/or taxing.

Expectations
Anticipations of future events; can affect current actions by households and businesses and the likelihood that the future events will occur.

A Word about Expectations

Earlier it was noted that **expectations** of a recession might induce businesses to cut back investment spending in anticipation of a decline in sales.

Application 5.3

Ripples through the Economy

Pittsburgh's Recession Shows Ripples   It's called the ripple-effect theory, and in simple form, it goes like this: A basic industry falters and lays off workers. Suppliers soon succumb and lay off workers too. Next come service firms and more layoffs. Presto, a recession.

The theory works, judging by a visit to the state unemployment claims office in a blue-collar area on this city's South Side. Hundreds of steelworkers who in better times clocked in at Jones & Laughlin Steel Corp.'s big mill just a few blocks away now line up to file for unemployment benefits. . . .

And as the slump in steel continues, out-of-work steelworkers are being joined by thousands of other people formerly employed in steel equipment and repair shops, as well as in restaurants, stores and offices that depend on the steel business. "We're seeing unemployment ripple right through the job market," says John Lester, manager of the South Side unemployment claims office. "With so many steelworkers trying to get by on unemployment checks, local merchants aren't selling and have had to lay off people too." . . .

Meet Market: Convention Ripples   America's need to meet has become one of the hottest growth industries in the country. Last year [1989], the meetings industry turned into a $40 billion operation, up from $17 billion in 1981 and still going strong.

The financial rewards for cities that can nab [conventions] have added a whole new twist to the invitation to "meet me in St. Louie, Louie."

"One meeting can bring $7 million to $8 million to a city's economy," [said an Associations Society public relations director].

Once there, each dollar spent will multiply itself by a factor of 2.5 as it rolls through a city's economy, industry analysts say.

And not only are Americans meeting more, they are meeting in bigger numbers and bigger spaces.

In the last two years, more than 45 cities have built new convention centers, expanded the ones they already have or made plans to grow. . . .

Auto Layoffs Ripple through Economy   Like a pebble dropped in a pool of water, the indefinite layoff of 1,900 workers at Chrysler Corp.'s No. 1 plant in Fenton [Missouri] is expected to cause a ripple effect throughout the area's economy.

The [St. Louis] Regional Commerce and Growth Association estimates that if the Chrysler layoffs were to last a full year, 2,000 additional people would lose their jobs as a result. [It also estimates that] in addition, total spending in the metropolitan area would decrease by $270 million, 35 retail establishments would close, the population would decline by 5,200 and state and local tax revenue would fall by $8 million.

[Fenton's mayor] said a ripple effect would be felt more by merchants and suppliers. "It's going to have an effect metropolitan-wide," he said.

The businesses most likely to feel the effects of the layoffs are small local establishments frequented by autoworkers.

Companies that supply goods and services to the auto plant also will lose business. . . .

Source: Carol Hymowitz, "Pittsburgh's Recession Shows How Layoffs Ripple through Economy," *The Wall Street Journal*, March 16, 1982, p. 31; Kathleen Best, "Meet Market: Convention Cities Reap Big Money," *St. Louis Post-Dispatch*, April 8, 1990, p. B1; Leslie J. Allen, "Layoffs to Ripple through Economy," *St. Louis Post-Dispatch*, November 12, 1989, pp. C1, C7.

Expectations of a recession might also cause households to increase their saving because they fear possible job losses. Such actions prompted by the fear of a recession can actually cause a recession to occur. Fear-induced increases in saving bring about a greater leakage from the spending stream, and a reduction in investment lessens this injection into the spending stream. As saving is increased and investment reduced, the resulting decrease in spending causes output, employment, and income to fall, and the economy slips into a recession.

As also noted, expectations can also cause or worsen inflation. If households and businesses expect prices to be higher, they may try to "beat" the price increases by buying now what they want and need in the future. This surge in spending may serve only to cause or worsen the inflation that is feared.

Expectations of good economic conditions are important to maintaining a healthy economy. Recovery from a recession is more difficult when households and businesses are unwilling to spend because they are pessimistic about the prospects of recovery. Controlling inflation is more difficult if businesses and households believe that prices will continue to go up in the future and that they will be penalized for postponing their expenditures.

Your knowledge of how spending, leakages, injections, the multiplier, the full employment ceiling, and expectations affect the economy can be checked by completing "Test Your Understanding: Changes in Economic Activity."

Total Spending and Macroeconomic Policy

It was noted in Chapter Four that the major objectives of the macroeconomy are full employment, price stability, and full production and economic growth. Chapter Five has shown how changes in the level of spending lead to changes in production and employment, and sometimes to changes in the level of prices. Thus, policies to attain the objectives of the macroeconomy must be based on an understanding of the role of total spending in the economy and how output, employment, and prices can be affected by actions designed to change the level of spending.

There are two major policies for influencing the level of spending to accomplish the objectives of the macroeconomy. In terms of the circular flow model, these policies are designed to regulate the leakages and injections that travel through the government sector and through financial institutions. The first policy focuses on increasing or decreasing the size of the spending stream by changing government taxes and/or expenditures (transfer payments and purchases of goods and services). To increase the level of economic activity, spending is enlarged by lowering taxes and/or increasing government expenditures. The economy is slowed (to counteract demand-pull inflation) by withdrawing spending through increasing taxes and/or reducing government expenditures. This strategy for influencing the economy through government-induced spending changes is called **fiscal policy.** Fiscal policy will be discussed in Chapter Six.

The second policy approach focuses on changing the levels of saving and, especially, borrowing through the economy's financial institutions. The

Fiscal policy

Influencing the levels of aggregate output and employment or prices through changes in federal government purchases, transfer payments, and/or taxes.

Test Your Understanding

Changes in Economic Activity[a]

In the following examples, explain the effect on output and employment that would result from each action taken alone.

1. Businesses in general install new telecommunications systems.

2. Congress increases personal income tax rates by 5 percent.

3. A decrease in mortgage loan rates and a continued strong demand for housing cause a boom in the home construction business.

4. An overseas buyer purchases a large number of personal computers manufactured by a U.S. firm.

5. Newspaper headlines continually carry predictions of a recession in the months to come.

6. Because the economy is at full employment, several companies that issue major credit cards establish successful campaigns to increase the number of cardholders and to encourage more charges by current cardholders.

7. The interest rates for borrowing money increase.

8. Net exports of goods and services changes from a negative to a positive number.

9. Unemployment compensation payments are increased by $15 a week.

10. As prices begin to increase, households, fearing that prices will spiral at an even faster rate since the economy is at full employment, rush into purchases of large ticket items like cars and furniture.

11. Businesses increase their retained earnings and postpone their expansion plans while they wait for better economic times.

12. Political pressure prompts Congress to cut its spending on defense projects.

13. Each U.S. taxpayer receives a tax rebate check when the economy is at full employment.

14. A law is passed limiting the number of new foreign automobiles that can enter the country each year.

15. U.S. citizens in general begin to change their attitudes toward thrift and start to increase their levels of saving.

These last examples relate to the multiplier effect. Determine the direction and size of the change in total output and income that will result from each change in nonincome-determined spending.

16. After several years of drought conditions, farmers in central Illinois spend $50 million on irrigation equipment at a time when households do not spend 25 percent of the additional income they receive.

17. At a time when households are not spending 40 percent of the additional income they receive, the federal government cuts defense expenditures by $35 billion.

18. Developers borrow $60 million and use it for new home construction in a suburb of Cincinnati at a time when households are spending 70 percent of the additional income they receive.

19. Business spending for machinery and equipment falls by $6 billion after predictions of a recession. Households spend only 50 percent of the additional income they receive due to these predictions.

20. (Be careful!) Government transfer payments increase by $100 million at a time when households spend 80 percent of the additional income they receive.

Monetary policy
Influencing the levels of aggregate output and employment or prices through changes in the money supply.

amount of loans that financial institutions can make and the interest rates that are charged on these loans are influenced by actions of the Federal Reserve. The Federal Reserve has the ability to set conditions conducive to borrowing and spending by households and businesses, or to tighten credit conditions and discourage borrowing and spending. These changes in borrowing are related to changes in the money supply. Changing the level of spending by influencing borrowing and the supply of money in the economy is called **monetary policy.** The Federal Reserve, loan making, interest rates, and monetary policy are covered in Chapters Seven and Eight.

There are strong opinions and disagreements about which policies are best for dealing with problems in the macroeconomy. The various points of view on the proper method for reaching objectives or dealing with problems in the macroeconomy and some alternatives to fiscal policy and monetary policy are introduced in Chapter Nine.

In closing this chapter, it should be noted that macroeconomics, with its emphasis on spending and its policy prescription of using spending to change the economy, owes an intellectual debt to the British economist John Maynard Keynes (1883–1946). It was Keynes who focused attention on the role of spending in the economy and, in so doing, revolutionized the discipline. While there are debates over the desirability of depending on taxes and government spending or on changing the supply of money to control the economy, the generally agreed starting point for these diverse views is the work of Keynes.

Summary

Market economies such as that of the United States are constantly experiencing expansions and contractions in their levels of real GNP. These recurring upswings and downswings in production are called business cycles. Business cycles are a matter of concern because they affect not only output, but employment and income as well. Cyclical fluctuations are divided into four phases: recovery, peak, recession, and trough. The length of time in each phase and the intensity of the expansion or contraction differ from cycle to cycle.

Changes in total, or aggregate, spending on new goods and services cause changes in economic activity. An increase in total spending increases output, employment, and income, and the economy grows as long as it has not reached full employment. A decrease in total spending decreases output, employment, and income, and the economy contracts. Total spending is the spending by the household, business, government, and foreign sectors together.

Household spending on new goods and services, or personal consumption expenditures, is fairly stable as it increases from year to year. It also exceeds the combined purchases of businesses, government units, and the foreign sector. The majority of household spending originates from income earned from producing goods and services. Households can also buy goods and services with borrowed funds and transfer payments. Purchases from borrowing and transfer payments are nonincome-determined spending because they do not come from household earned income, and are classified as injections into the spending stream. In addition to buying goods and services, household earned income can be used for saving or paying taxes. Saving and taxes are leakages from the spending stream because they represent income that has been channeled to uses other than consumption.

The purchase of new goods such as machinery and equipment by businesses is called investment spending, and is a form of nonincome-determined spending. Of the major components of total spending, investment is the most unstable and is a major source of fluctuations in the levels of output, employment, and income. Investment spending is influenced by business profit expectations, which in turn are affected by such factors as the expected overall level of economic activity and the interest rate on funds borrowed for investment purposes. When a business invests in new goods, it can finance its expenditures from its own savings, called retained earnings, from borrowed funds, or by issuing new shares of stock. Investment spending is an injection into the spending stream: increases in investment stimulate the level of economic activity, and reductions in investment lead to reductions in output, employment, and income. Business saving and taxes are leakages from the spending stream.

Government can influence the spending stream in three ways: through the purchase of goods and services, transfer payments, and taxes on households and businesses. Government purchases of goods and services are a form of nonincome-determined spending and are direct injections into the spending stream. Transfer payments provide injections, and taxes are a leakage.

Transactions between U.S. and foreign buyers and sellers occur in the foreign sector. Expenditures by U.S. buyers on imported goods and services are leakages from the spending stream. Purchases of exported U.S. goods and services by foreign buyers are injections, as well as nonincome-determined expenditures. In recent years both exports and imports have grown as a percentage of GNP, and imports have exceeded exports.

If all the leakages from the spending stream equal all the injections, the level of economic activity will continue unchanged. If leakages exceed injections, spending decreases, and the level of economic activity falls. If injections are greater than leakages, the spending stream expands, and the level of economic activity grows.

An increase or decrease in nonincome-determined household expenditures, investment spending, government purchases, or foreign spending leads to a multiple increase or decrease in the levels of output, employment, and income. This multiplier effect occurs because dollars introduced into the circular flow are spent over and over again. New spending to buy goods and services becomes income to the owners of the resources used in production, who in turn use that income to buy other goods and services, and so on. The multiplier effect can be calculated by dividing the initial change in nonincome-determined spending by the percentage of additional income received by households that is not spent.

If the economy is operating at or near full employment, increases in spending may lead to demand-pull inflation rather than to increases in output and employment. For this reason, additional total spending is not always desirable and does not always cause the economy to expand.

Expectations can influence total spending and therefore complicate the job of stabilizing the economy. Because of the effect of expectations on spending, fears can cause self-fulfilling prophecies: the fear of a recession can lead to a recession, and the fear of inflation can lead to inflation.

One important avenue for accomplishing the objectives of full production and economic growth, full employment, and stable prices is through increasing or decreasing the level of total spending. Two tools for changing the size of the spending stream to attain these objectives are fiscal policy and monetary policy. Fiscal policy influences total spending through changes in government purchases of goods and services, transfers, and taxes. Monetary policy influences spending through changes in the money supply or lending and borrowing.

Key Terms and Concepts

Business cycles

Recovery, peak, recession, trough

Total, or aggregate, spending

Personal consumption expenditures

Income-determined spending

Transfer payment

Nonincome-determined spending

Injections into the spending stream

Financial institutions

Leakages from the spending stream

Investment spending

Retained earnings

Saving-investment relationship

Government purchases of goods and
  services

Exports

Imports

Net exports

Multiplier effect

Expectations

Fiscal policy

Monetary policy

Review Questions

1. Identify the four phases of a business cycle and describe the changes in economic activity that occur during each phase.

2. What is a recession and what is the basic cause of a recession?

3. What is the difference between income-determined expenditures and nonincome-determined expenditures? What are the different types of nonincome-

determined expenditures? Why are all nonincome-determined expenditures injections into the spending stream?

4.   Changes in the level of economic activity are related to changes in the spending of households, businesses, government units, and buyers in the foreign sector.
   a.   How do personal consumption expenditures, investment spending, government purchases of goods and services, and net exports compare in terms of relative size and stability?
   b.   How are personal consumption expenditures affected by taxes, transfer payments, saving, and borrowing?
   c.   How is investment spending affected by changes in the interest rate?
   d.   Why are government expenditures on goods and services a direct injection into the spending stream, and government expenditures on transfer payments not a direct injection into the spending stream?
   e.   What effects do transactions in the foreign sector have on domestic levels of output, employment, and income?
   f.   Under what circumstances would an increase in total spending lead primarily to an increase in output, and under what circumstances would it lead primarily to an increase in prices?

5.   Identify the various leakages from and injections into the spending stream in a circular flow model of the economy. How does the relationship between leakages and injections cause the level of economic activity to expand, contract, or remain unchanged? What role do financial institutions play in the relationship between leakages and injections?

6.   What is the multiplier effect, and how is it related to nonincome-determined spending and the circular flow of economic activity? What happens to the multiplier effect when the percentage of additional earned income not spent increases? Why does this happen?

7.   In each of the following cases, calculate the change that occurs in the level of economic activity as a result of the multiplier effect.
   a.   Government purchases of goods and services increase by $600 million, and 20 percent of additional income received is not spent.
   b.   Household spending from borrowing declines by $1 billion, and 30 percent of additional income received is not spent.
   c.   Investment spending increases by $800 million, and 75 percent of additional income received is spent.
   d.   Investment spending increases by $2 billion at the same time that U.S. exports decrease by $1.5 billion, and 60 percent of additional income received is spent.

Discussion Questions

1.   Figure 5.1a shows that since 1973 business cycles in the U.S. economy have had long recovery and relatively short recession phases. Why do you think this has happened? Do you think this pattern is typical of what we can expect from the economy in the future?

2. Suppose the economy were in a recession and someone said to you: "If we only had more production, everything would take care of itself." How would you evaluate this statement? Would the act of producing more goods and services by itself be enough to cause the economy to recover?

3. It is said that "a penny saved is a penny earned." Is this true in the macroeconomy?

4. Personal consumption expenditures grow at a relatively constant rate over time, while investment spending fluctuates widely. What reasons might explain why personal consumption expenditures are more stable than investment?

5. Suppose the economy is in a recession and to counteract this recession a congressman sponsors a bill to ban all imports. He says that the bill, if passed into law, would ensure that all the dollars currently leaving the spending stream for imports would instead be spent on domestic products, thereby increasing output, employment, and income, or reversing the recession. Do you agree with this congressman? Do you think that all dollars not spent on foreign goods would automatically be spent on domestic goods? What effect would this law have on foreign demand for domestic goods? Would you vote for this bill if you were in Congress?

6. Expectations play an important role in determining the level of economic activity and how the level of activity will change. What sorts of events might cause people to expect a recession? What sorts of events might cause people to expect inflation? What could be done to make the economy more predictable and help stabilize expectations?

7. The multiplier effect is larger or smaller depending on whether households spend more or less of their additional income. What effect might the expectation of a recession have on the multiplier? What effect might the expectation of inflation have on the multiplier?

8. Fiscal and monetary policies are designed to influence the level of economic activity through their impacts on total spending. Using the circular flow model, identify the leakages and injections each of these policies affects.

Critical Thinking Case 5

Expectations and Results

Critical Thinking Skills | Recognize the fallacy of composition

Economic Concepts | Effects of expectations on economic activity

Economists like to talk about the fallacy of composition: the idea that what is true for an individual is not always true for the group to which the individual belongs. Put another way, a good decision for an individual may adversely affect that person if everyone in the group to which the individual belongs makes the same decision. For example, it may be a good decision for a person to try to drive home immediately after an earthquake. But if everyone in the area attempted to drive home, the group would experience serious traffic jams and no one would arrive at their desired destination.

It is important to understand how this type of fallacious thinking can influence the macroeconomy, particularly with regard to saving, spending, and prices. Saving money is generally regarded as desirable—especially by those who fear that a slowdown in the economy will jeopardize their jobs and incomes. But if everyone saves, spending will be reduced and the economy may slide into the very recession that people are hoping to avoid. At the other extreme, if there is evidence that prices may increase in the future, it is to an individual's benefit to spend his or her money before the prices increase. But if everyone in the economy spends, inflation will result. In short, expectations about economic conditions could lead to individual decisions that hurt the economy because of the fallacy of composition. For this reason, policy makers must be as concerned about people's attitudes as they are about spending, taxes, imports, and other such factors.

On March 12, 1933, President Franklin D. Roosevelt delivered, over the radio, the first of several informal and famous "Fireside Chats." At the time of this speech, the nation was deep in the Depression, the banking system had virtually collapsed, and public confidence in the economy was seriously damaged. Part of that speech is excerpted here.

I want to talk for a few minutes with the people of the United States about banking. . . . I want to tell you what has been done in the last few days, why it was done, and what the next steps are going to be. . . .

What, then, happened during the last few days of February and the first few days of March? Because of undermined confidence on the part of the public, there was a general rush by a large portion of our population to turn bank deposits into currency or gold—a rush so great that the soundest banks could not get enough currency to meet the demand. . . .

By the afternoon of March 3rd scarcely a bank in the country was open to do business. Proclamations temporarily closing them in whole or in part had been issued by the Governors in almost all the States.

It was then that I issued the proclamation providing for the nationwide bank holiday, and this was the first step in the Government's reconstruction of our financial and economic fabric. . . .

It is possible that when the banks resume a very few people who have not recovered from their fear may again begin withdrawals. Let me make it clear that the banks will take care of all needs—and it is my belief that hoarding during the past week has become an exceedingly unfashionable pastime. . . . I can assure you that it is safer to keep your money in a reopened bank than under the mattress. . . .

[T]here is an element in the readjustment of our financial system more important than currency, more important than gold, and that is the confidence of the people. Confidence and courage are the essentials of success in carrying out our plan. You people must have faith; you must not be stampeded by rumors or guesses. Let us unite in banishing fear. We have provided the machinery to restore our financial system; it is up to you to support and make it work.

It is your problem no less than it is mine. Together we cannot fail.[a]

Questions

1. How are expectations and the fallacy of composition related in the bank crisis of late February and early March 1933?

2. What was President Roosevelt trying to accomplish during his first Fireside Chat? What do you think would have been the outcome for policy makers and the economy if he failed?

3. Assume that a major national newspaper carries the headline, "Key Business Leaders Forecast a Deep Recession in the Coming Months." Is this responsible journalism?

[a]S. I. Rosenman, ed., *The Public Papers and Addresses of Franklin D. Roosevelt*, vol. II (New York: Random House, Inc., 1938), pp. 61–66.

Suggested Readings

Robert B. Carson, "Looking over Our Shoulder, I: Origins of the Modern Economy, 1929–1950," *What Economists Know* **(New York: St. Martin's Press, 1990), pp. 51–69.**
A nontechnical survey of economic activity and economic analysis from the crash of 1929, through the Depression and the work of Keynes, to the Employment Act of 1946.

The Federal Reserve Bank of St. Louis, *National Economic Trends* **(published monthly).**
Provides up-to-date data on personal consumption expenditures, investment spending, and government purchases, as well as other production, sales, and price information about the macroeconomy.

Milton Friedman and Anna J. Schwartz, *The Great Contraction* **(Princeton: Princeton University Press, 1965).**
A view of the Great Depression that stresses the role of money-related factors.

John Kenneth Galbraith, *The Great Crash, 1929* **(Boston: Houghton, Mifflin Co., 1961).**
An alternative view of the Great Depression and its causes.

John A. Garraty, "The Big Picture of the Great Depression," *American Heritage,* **August–September 1986, pp. 190–197.**
A multicountry view of the Great Depression and policies to deal with the Depression.

Gottfried Haberler, "Preliminary Remarks," *Prosperity and Depression* **(New York: Atheneum, 1963), pp. 5–13.**
An introduction to business cycle theories. The author identifies different explanations of the business cycle and introduces several methods for classifying the causes of cycles.

Robert L. Heilbroner, "The Heresies of John Maynard Keynes," *The Worldly Philosophers* **(New York: Simon and Schuster, 1967), pp. 225–261.**
A summary of John Maynard Keynes's life, work, and contribution to our understanding of the relationship between saving and investment, and the operation of the macroeconomy.

U.S. Department of Commerce, *Survey of Current Business* **(published monthly).**
Short articles on various aspects of the economy, and statistics on a wide range of topics pertaining to the national economy.

Appendix to Chapter 5

Equilibrium in the Macroeconomy

Equilibrium (in the macroeconomy)

Occurs when the amount of total planned spending on new goods and services equals total output in the economy.

As just explained, the main determinant of the level of economic activity is the level of total spending. When the amount that all households, businesses, government units, and foreign buyers plan to spend on new goods and services is just equal to the total amount of output the economy is producing, the economy is said to be in **equilibrium.** At equilibrium there is no tendency for change in the level of economic activity because the planned spending of all buyers is just sufficient to purchase all of the goods and services that are produced. However, when the amount that households, businesses, government units, and foreign buyers plan to spend on new goods and services differs from the total output being produced, the economy is not in equilibrium, and output, employment, and income will change. If the total planned spending of all buyers is greater than current production, then output, employment, and income will increase, assuming that full employment has not been reached. If the total planned spending is less than current production, then output, employment, and income will fall.

Inventory

Stock of goods on hand; can be intentional or unintentional inventory.

The key to understanding how spending can be more or less than current production is the role played by **inventories.** Most businesses intentionally maintain an inventory of their products. When total spending in the economy is greater than current production, inventories begin to fall, signaling a need to increase output levels. When total spending is less than current production, unintentional inventories begin to accumulate, causing businesses to cut back on production.

Equilibrium, Leakages, and Injections

The most important factor determining whether the economy is at equilibrium, or expanding, or contracting is the relationship between leakages from and injections into the spending stream.

When leakages equal injections, the economy is at equilibrium. For example, suppose an economy produces $2 trillion of goods and services, which results in the creation of $2 trillion in income. Assume that from this $2 trillion income, households spend $1.5 trillion and the rest, $0.5 trillion, is leaked from the spending stream through saving, taxes, and the purchase of imports. Thus, household spending from earned income is $0.5 trillion less than output. In order to keep the production level unchanged at $2 trillion, or to maintain equilibrium in the economy at that level of output, the $0.5

trillion that was leaked must be replaced by an injection back into the spending stream of an equal amount. Business investment spending, government purchases of goods and services, household spending from transfer payments and borrowing, and expenditures on exports must equal $0.5 trillion.

What if the $0.5 trillion that was leaked from the spending stream is not matched by an equal injection back into the stream? What happens if injections amount to only $0.4 trillion, for example? If injections are less than leakages, economic activity will contract. In this case, the spending stream will be reduced to a level $0.1 trillion below output, unintentional inventories will build up, and businesses will respond by cutting back on output and employment.

On the other hand, if injections are greater than leakages, the size of the spending stream will increase to a level greater than output. If $0.5 trillion is leaked, and $0.6 trillion is injected, spending will exceed output by $0.1 trillion, intentional inventories will fall, and businesses will respond by expanding production, assuming that full employment has not yet been reached.

Illustrating the Equilibrium Level of Output

A popular method for illustrating equilibrium in the macroeconomy is presented in Table 5A.1 and Figure 5A.1. Both the table and the figure show the amount of planned total spending and the relationship between leakages and injections that would occur at each level of output produced by a hypothetical economy.

The column in Table 5A.1 titled "Planned Total Spending" represents the total planned expenditures of households, businesses, government units, and foreign buyers at each level of output. For example, all buyers would purchase $2.5 trillion worth of goods and services at an output level of $2.0 trillion, or $3.5 trillion worth of goods and services at an output of $4.0 trillion. Notice that total spending is greater at higher levels of output than at lower levels. This is because personal consumption expenditures, the largest component of total spending, depend mainly on earned income. When output is high, earned income and personal consumption expenditures are high as well, causing more planned total spending than at lower levels of output.[1]

---

[1] Notice that planned spending is $1.5 trillion when the level of output in the economy is zero. What is the source of this $1.5 trillion in spending since there is no output, no earned income, and no personal consumption expenditures based on earned income?

Remember that household spending from transfers and borrowing, investment spending, government purchases, and exports are all nonincome-determined expenditures, which are expenditures *not* generated from income earned producing goods and services. The $1.5 trillion in total spending is the amount of these injections into the spending stream since that is the amount of spending when output and income are zero. Can you explain why there would be no leakages from the spending stream when output is zero?

Table 5A.1   Planned Total Spending and Total Output (Trillions of Dollars)

This macroeconomy is in equilibrium at $3.0 trillion, where the injections into the spending stream are equal to the leakages, and planned total spending is equal to total output.

Total Output	Planned Total Spending	Spending Minus Output	Injections Minus Leakages	Economic Condition
$0.00	$1.50	$ 1.50	$ 1.50	expansion
0.50	1.75	1.25	1.25	expansion
1.00	2.00	1.00	1.00	expansion
1.50	2.25	0.75	0.75	expansion
2.00	2.50	0.50	0.50	expansion
2.50	2.75	0.25	0.25	expansion
3.00	3.00	0.00	0.00	equilibrium
3.50	3.25	−0.25	−0.25	contraction
4.00	3.50	−0.50	−0.50	contraction
4.50	3.75	−0.75	−0.75	contraction
5.00	4.00	−1.00	−1.00	contraction

The columns titled "Spending Minus Output" and "Injections Minus Leakages" show, respectively, the difference between planned spending and output, and between injections into and leakages from the spending stream at each level of output. The values in each of these columns are identical since the difference between total spending and total output is equal to the difference between injections into and leakages from the spending stream at each level of output.

Notice in Table 5A.1 that there is one level of output, $3.0 trillion, where planned spending equals total output. Here the economy is in equilibrium. Equilibrium occurs at this output level of $3.0 trillion because leakages and injections are equal. Notice also that at output levels less than $3.0 trillion, planned spending is greater than output because injections into the spending stream are greater than leakages. As a result of these relationships, the economy will expand toward the equilibrium output level of $3.0 trillion, causing production, employment, and income to grow. This expansion is indicated in the column titled "Economic Condition." For output levels greater than $3.0 trillion, total planned spending is less than output because injections into the spending stream are less than leakages. As a result of these relationships, output, employment, and income will shrink toward the equilibrium level of $3.0 trillion.

In short, given these spending plans, there is one output level—the equilibrium level—toward which the economy will move and from which,

Figure 5A.1

Equilibrium in the Macroeconomy

The macroeconomy is in equilibrium at the output level where the Total Spending line crosses the Spending Equals Output line.

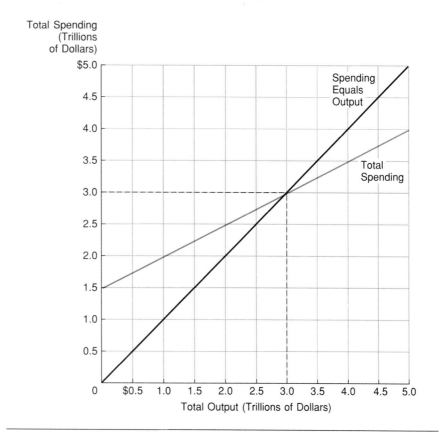

if reached, economic activity will not change.[2] This equilibrium level occurs where planned total spending equals total output, and leakages equal injections.

Figure 5A.1 illustrates the same relationships given in Table 5A.1. Total output is measured along the horizontal axis and total spending along the vertical axis. A 45° line is also plotted on this graph. Every point on this line matches a level of output with exactly the same level of spending. For this reason, the line is named the "Spending Equals Output" line.

---

[2] If nonincome-determined spending changes, the equilibrium may change, causing the level of economic activity to change as well.

The numbers from Table 5A.1 showing planned total spending at each level of output are illustrated by the "Total Spending" line in Figure 5A.1. Notice that the "Total Spending" line crosses the "Spending Equals Output" line at exactly $3.0 trillion of output, which is the equilibrium level in Table 5A.1. At output levels less than equilibrium, the "Total Spending" line is above the "Spending Equals Output" line. Because spending is greater than output, output will increase toward equilibrium. At output levels greater than $3.0 trillion, the "Total Spending" line is below the "Spending Equals Output" line, causing output to fall toward equilibrium.

The difference between the 45° line and the "Total Spending" line at each level of output is equal to the difference between injections and leakages at that output level. When the "Total Spending" line is above the 45° line, injections are greater than leakages; and when it is below, leakages are greater than injections.

Chapter Six

The Role of Government in the Macroeconomy

Federal government tax and spending policies, budget considerations, and level of debt play important roles in the functioning of the macroeconomy.

Chapter Objectives

1. To identify the major types of expenditures and the major sources of revenues of the federal, and state and local governments.

2. To distinguish among progressive, proportional, and regressive taxes.

3. To discuss some of the tax issues and tax reforms of the 1980s and 1990s.

4. To introduce fiscal policy, explain its mechanics, and differentiate between discretionary and automatic fiscal policy.

5. To define a surplus, a balanced, and a deficit budget, and identify the economic impact of each.

6. To explain the relationship between the federal budget and fiscal policy.

7. To discuss some realities of fiscal policy and the budgetary process that can hamper the attainment of fiscal policy objectives.

8. To define the national debt, explain its financing, size, and burden on taxpayers, and introduce crowding out.

This chapter focuses on the role of the government sector in the macroeconomy and on taxes and public expenditures in particular. It is important to understand the operation of the government sector for several reasons. First, the sheer magnitude of taxes and expenditures makes government units extremely important in the functioning of the economy. Not surprisingly, the largest single purchaser of goods and services in the United States is the federal government. A decision made at the federal level to initiate or cancel an irrigation project, defense system, housing or some other program, or to increase or decrease taxes, can have a far-reaching effect on the economy. Similar, if somewhat weaker, effects are felt when state and local governments change their tax and expenditure patterns.

A second reason for understanding the operation of the government sector is that the overall level of economic activity can be influenced through changes in taxes and spending. As shown in the previous chapter, leakages from and injections into the spending stream affect the levels of output, employment, income, and, sometimes, prices in the economy. Taxes paid to the government are leakages, while government spending on goods and services and spending from transfer payments are injections. Thus, by adjusting the balance between taxes and purchases and transfers, government can influence the size of the spending stream and, through that, the levels of output, employment, income, and prices. As noted at the end of the previous chapter, this strategy for modifying the operation of the economy is called fiscal policy.

A third reason for examining the government sector is to gain a foundation to critically evaluate policies affecting taxes and government spending. These policies have received increasing attention by the public in recent years because of serious and persistent federal budget deficits. The size of the national debt, determining which government programs to cut in efforts to control federal spending, tax reform, the Social Security system, and a constitutional amendment requiring a balanced budget have all been topics of serious discussion. In addition, government taxing and spending issues have played an increasingly important role in political platforms and elections.

An overview of government expenditures and taxes begins this chapter. Fiscal policy is then examined to illustrate how taxes and government expenditures can be manipulated in an effort to make the economy expand or contract. Next, the federal government's budget and its relationship to fiscal policy and the overall level of economic activity are explored. And finally, the chapter deals with the national debt and some problems surrounding the debt.

Government Expenditures and Revenues

Government Expenditures

In 1990, all government units together spent over $1.9 trillion, an amount equivalent to about 35 percent of that year's GNP. This $1.9 trillion was used for a variety of disbursements, ranging from the purchase of missiles and the construction of sewage plants to police salaries, welfare checks, and interest payments. Table 6.1 lists the total expenditures of all government units combined, the federal government, and state and local governments for selected years from 1929 through 1990. In addition to the magnitude of government expenditures, notice that, in every year since 1940, federal expenditures have exceeded state and local spending by a wide margin.

There has been growing concern in the United States over increases in government spending and the size of the government sector. Is this concern justified? One method for evaluating the size of government is to measure total government expenditures as a percentage of GNP. This is done in the last column of Table 6.1. A scan down this column indicates that, over the years, government spending has generally (although not systematically from year to year) increased in relation to GNP. For example, it accounted for 9.9 percent of GNP in 1929, 18.4 percent in 1940, 26.6 percent in 1960, and averaged over 34 percent annually in the 1980s.

Government purchases of goods and services

Government spending on new goods and services.

Government expenditures can be classified into several categories. First, some government outlays are for direct **government purchases of goods and services.** As noted in Chapter Five, purchases of goods and services include government expenditures on the services of individuals, and on goods such

Table 6.1

Total, Federal, and State and Local Government Expenditures,
and Total Government Expenditures as a Percentage of GNP,
Selected Years 1929–1990 (Billions of Dollars)

Over the years, government expenditures have increased both in absolute terms
and as a percentage of GNP.

| Year | Expenditures | | | Total Government Expenditures as a Percentage of GNP |
	Total Government[a]	Federal Government	State and Local Government	
1929	$ 10.3	$ 2.7	$ 7.8	9.9%
1933	10.7	4.0	7.2	19.1
1940	18.5	10.0	9.3	18.4
1945	92.9	84.7	9.0	43.5
1950	61.4	41.2	22.5	21.3
1955	98.5	68.6	32.9	24.3
1960	137.3	93.9	49.9	26.6
1965	189.6	125.3	75.5	26.9
1970	317.4	207.8	134.0	31.3
1975	544.9	364.2	235.2	34.1
1976	587.5	393.7	254.9	33.0
1977	635.7	430.1	273.2	31.9
1978	694.8	470.7	301.3	30.9
1979	768.3	521.1	327.7	30.6
1980	889.6	615.1	363.2	32.6
1981	1,006.9	703.3	391.4	33.0
1982	1,111.6	781.2	414.3	35.1
1983	1,189.9	835.9	440.2	34.9
1984	1,277.9	895.6	475.9	33.9
1985	1,402.6	985.6	516.7	34.9
1986	1,491.5	1,034.8	563.5	35.2
1987	1,573.5	1,071.9	604.1	34.8
1988	1,654.2	1,114.2	651.1	33.9
1989	1,772.4	1,187.2	703.5	34.1
1990[b]	1,907.1	1,273.0	764.7	34.9

[a]Total government expenditures have been adjusted to eliminate the duplication of spending from federal grants-in-aid to state and local governments.

[b]Preliminary figures.

Source: U.S., *Economic Report of the President* (Washington, D.C.: U.S. Government Printing Office, 1991), pp. 286, 379.

Public good

A good (or service) provided for all of society; no one is excluded from use of a public good.

Transfer payments

Money from the government for which no direct work is performed in return.

as schools, medical facilities, highways, and paper clips. Many of the purchases government makes are for goods and services that are provided for all members of society—even those who have not paid for their use. When a good or service is provided for everyone and no one can be excluded from its use, it is termed a **public good.** The provision of public goods, such as highways, fire protection, and defense systems, is a widely recognized function of government.

A second category of government expenditures is **transfer payments,** which, as indicated in Chapter Five, are payments from the government for which nothing is received in return. Social Security, veterans' benefits, unemployment compensation, and public assistance programs such as Aid to Families with Dependent Children (AFDC) are all examples of transfer payment programs.

Interest paid for borrowed funds is another type of government expenditure. At times, government units finance some of their activities through borrowing, and the interest on these borrowed funds is an expense that the government unit must meet.[1] Government may also incur expenses from running or contributing to the operation of various public enterprises such as toll roads, airports, and hospitals, or from providing intergovernmental grants. These grants are given primarily by the federal government to state and local governments.

Table 6.2 shows, for selected years from 1965 through 1990, the percentages of federal spending allocated to the various expenditure categories just identified. Notice that significant changes have occurred in the way the federal government has spent its money over this period. In 1970 and prior years, the largest single federal expenditure category was purchases of goods and services, but by 1975 the amount spent on purchases was surpassed by the amount going to transfer payments. Currently, transfer payments is the largest federal government expenditure category. Notice also the increase in the percentage of expenditures for interest payments. Increases in federal government borrowing to finance large amounts of deficit spending have clearly imposed increased interest costs on the government.

The way state and local governments allocate their spending has not changed significantly over the last few decades. Approximately 10 to 20 percent of state and local expenditures goes for transfer payments, and about 80 to 90 percent goes for purchases of goods and services.[2] The largest expenditure is for salaries of police, fire, hospital, school, and other state and local government employees.

Figure 6.1 compares federal government spending and state and local government spending by function: that is, it identifies the purposes for which these funds have been spent. Notice the difference in the functions

---

[1] Borrowing is done at the federal level through various securities issued by the U.S. Treasury, and at the state and local levels with municipal bonds or other instruments.

[2] In most years, state and local government financing and public enterprises have earned their government units money. For this reason they have been excluded here.

Table 6.2   Federal Government Expenditure Categories, Selected Years 1965–1990[a]

The composition of federal spending has changed over the years. Transfer payments is currently the largest expenditure category, and net interest is increasing.

Expenditure Category	Percentage of Total Expenditure[b]					
	1965	1970	1975	1980	1985	1990
Purchases of goods and services	54.5%	50.2%	36.9%	33.9%	35.5%	33.2%
Transfer payments	25.8	28.9	40.4	41.0	38.9	40.3
Grants-in-aid to state and local governments	9.2	11.4	14.4	14.7	10.2	10.2
Net interest paid	6.9	6.8	6.5	8.6	13.3	14.5
Cost of government enterprises	3.6	2.8	1.8	1.8	2.2	1.8
Total	100.0%	100.0%	100.0%	100.0%	100.0%	100.0%

[a]Fiscal years.

[b]Percentages may not add to 100 percent due to rounding.

Source: Figures for 1965 are from U.S., *Economic Report of the President* (Washington, D.C.: U.S. Government Printing Office, 1985), p. 322. Figures for all other years are from U.S., *Economic Report of the President* (Washington, D.C.: U.S. Government Printing Office, 1991), p. 381.

of each type of government unit: the federal government's major spending is for defense and Social Security, whereas the primary purpose of state and local government spending is education.

Government Revenues

The primary source of government revenue is taxes, and legislative bodies have created many different kinds of taxes for people to pay: federal and state income taxes; local wage tax on earnings; sales tax; property tax on a residence; personal property tax; capital gains tax; inheritance and gift taxes; excise taxes on liquor, cigarettes, and the like; and tariffs on imports. People in business also pay certain business taxes and, if the firm is incorporated, corporate income tax.

In addition to taxes, governments receive revenue from other sources. One major source is contributions to social insurance programs — the most familiar being the federal government's Social Security program. Although payment is required from those individuals who participate in the program, the payment is considered to be a contribution to a retirement and welfare fund rather than a tax.

Government revenues have increased substantially over the last few decades. Figure 6.2 gives the annual dollar amounts of total government revenues from 1964 through 1990, as well as revenues of the federal government and state and local governments over these years. Observe from this figure that in 1965 all government units combined received $190.2 billion

Figure 6.1   Federal and State and Local Government Expenditures, by Function

The major federal government expenditures are for defense, Social Security, and interest payments, and the major state and local expenditure is for education.

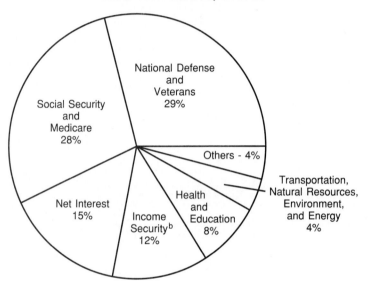

Federal Government Expenditures[a]

[a]Figures are for 1989.
[b]Includes federal employee retirement and disability.
[c]Figures are for 1987.
Source: U.S. Bureau of the Census, *Statistical Abstract of the United States: 1990*, 110th ed. (Washington, D.C.: U.S. Government Printing Office, 1990), pp. 278, 310–311.

in revenue from taxes and other sources, and that by 1990 this amount had increased to more than $1.7 trillion.[3] Notice also that federal revenues are greater than state and local revenues combined.

What kinds of taxes go to which government units? What proportion of revenue comes from taxes and what proportion from other sources? Table 6.3 gives the major sources of federal government revenue, in percentages, for selected years from 1965 through 1989. This table indicates that the principal taxes received by the federal government include individual and corporate income taxes, excise taxes on certain types of goods, estate and gift taxes, and customs duties on foreign goods entering the country. Notice

---

[3]The revenue figures are given in current dollars, not real, or constant, dollars. Consequently, we must remember that much of the increase in revenues is not a real increase but the result of inflation.

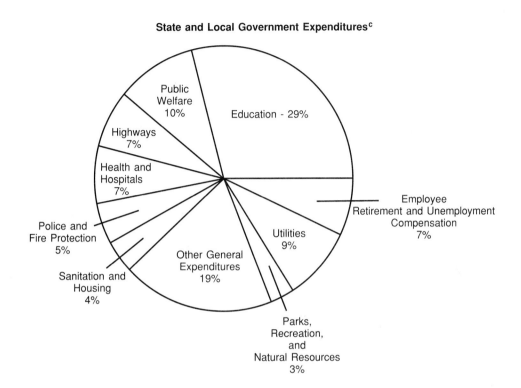

State and Local Government Expenditures^c

Public Welfare 10%

Education - 29%

Highways 7%

Health and Hospitals 7%

Police and Fire Protection 5%

Sanitation and Housing 4%

Other General Expenditures 19%

Utilities 9%

Employee Retirement and Unemployment Compensation 7%

Parks, Recreation, and Natural Resources 3%

from the table that the single most important source of revenue is individual income taxes and that this household contribution to federal revenue has fluctuated relatively little over the years; it has ranged from roughly 42 to 48 percent of total revenue. Over these same years, however, the portion of federal revenue accounted for by corporate income taxes and excise taxes has fallen. Observe also in Table 6.3 that contributions for social insurance have increased substantially: from 19.1 percent of total revenue in 1965 to 37.5 percent in 1989. The growing reliance over the last two decades of the federal government on household income as a source of revenue, particularly through increasing contributions to social insurance, has helped stir public agitation about the size of the tax burden imposed directly on individual households.

State and local government revenues come from a wider variety of sources than do federal revenues. Taxes account for less than 60 percent of

Figure 6.2   Total, Federal, and State and Local Government Revenues, 1964–1990[a]

Generally, over 60 percent of total government revenues goes to the federal government.

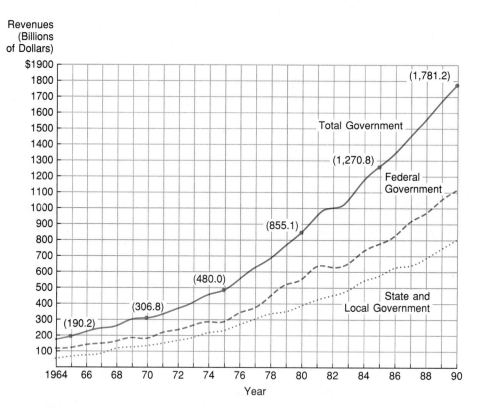

Revenues
(Billions
of Dollars)

[a]The 1990 figures are preliminary.

Source: U.S., *Economic Report of the President* (Washington, D.C.: U.S. Government Printing Office, 1991), p. 379.

state and local revenue. The primary taxes collected by these government units include property, sales, and individual income taxes. Charges and miscellaneous receipts, which include license fees, tuition from public colleges, and some recreation fees, are an important source of revenue, as are federal government funds.

There is a wide disparity in the types of taxes and tax rates (percentages) imposed by different state and local government units. For example, Oregon has a state income tax that ranges between 5 and 9 percent, Pennsylvania has a 2.1 percent flat tax on income, and Texas and Alaska have no state income taxes. Connecticut has a sales tax of 7.5 percent, and Minnesota has an excise tax on cigarettes of 38 cents per pack. In Newark, New Jersey, the

Table 6.3   Sources of Federal Government Revenue, Selected Years 1965–1990[a]

Corporate income taxes and excise taxes have decreased in relative importance over the years as sources of federal government revenue, while social insurance payments have increased in relative importance.

Source	Percentage of Total Revenue Per Year[c]					
	1965	1970	1975	1980	1985	1989[d]
Individual income taxes	41.8%	46.9%	43.9%	47.2%	45.6%	43.6%
Social insurance[b]	19.1	23.0	30.3	30.5	36.1	37.3
Corporation income taxes	21.8	17.0	14.5	12.5	8.4	11.0
Excise taxes	12.5	8.1	5.9	4.7	4.9	3.5
Customs, estate, and gift taxes	3.6	3.1	3.0	2.6	2.5	2.5
Miscellaneous receipts	1.4	1.8	2.4	2.5	2.5	2.1
Total	100.0%	100.0%	100.0%	100.0%	100.0%	100.0%

[a]Fiscal years.

[b]Includes social insurance contributions and taxes.

[c]Percentages may not add to 100 percent due to rounding.

[d]Estimated.

Source: Figures for 1965 are from U.S. Bureau of the Census, *Statistical Abstract of the United States: 1985,* 105th ed. (Washington, D.C.: U.S. Government Printing Office, 1984), p. 307. Figures for 1970–1975 are from *Statistical Abstract of the United States: 1988,* 108th ed., 1987, p. 292. Figures for 1980–1989 are from *Statistical Abstract of the United States: 1990,* 110th ed., 1990, p. 310.

effective tax on residential property is $3.20 per $100, and in Los Angeles, California, it is $0.64 per $100.[4] Some states have or have had unusual revenue sources: for example, a tax on income earned by "persons expounding religious doctrines" in Hawaii, a tax on raw fish in Alaska, and a fee for each parachute jump in New Hampshire.[5]

Progressive, Proportional, and Regressive Taxes

The burden of paying taxes is not the same for all individuals. The proportion of one's income that goes to taxes differs with each specific tax paid and with the level of income. For this reason, taxes can be classified as progressive, proportional, or regressive.

Progressive tax

A tax reflecting a direct relationship between the percentage of income taxed and the size of the income.

With a **progressive tax** the percentage of income taxed increases as income increases, and decreases as income decreases. In other words, there is a direct relationship between the percentage of income taxed and the size

[4]U.S. Bureau of the Census, *Statistical Abstract of the United States: 1990,* 110th ed. (Washington, D.C.: U.S. Government Printing Office, 1990), pp. 287, 288, 298.

[5]"Your Tax Bite is Even Bigger Than You Think," *U.S. News & World Report,* September 11, 1978, p. 78.

of the income. One example of a progressive tax is the federal personal income tax. With increasing increments of income, the federal individual tax rate increases. For example, for 1991, individuals paid 15 percent on income up to $20,350, 28 percent on income between $20,350 and $49,300, and 31 percent on income over $49,300. Some states also have income tax rates with progressive steps.

Proportional tax (flat tax)

A tax equal to the same percentage of income regardless of the size of the income.

With a **proportional tax,** or **flat tax,** the percentage of income taxed is the same for any income, large or small. An example of such a tax would be a city wage tax of, say, 1 percent. An individual earning $10,000 per year would pay 1 percent, or $100, to the city and another individual earning $100,000 would also pay 1 percent, or $1,000. In each case, the same percentage of income is taken as tax.

Regressive tax

A tax reflecting an inverse relationship between the percentage of income taxed and the size of the income.

With a **regressive tax** the percentage of income taxed increases as income decreases, and decreases as income increases. In other words, a regressive tax hits those with low incomes the hardest. Sales taxes and gasoline taxes are two examples of regressive taxes. With a sales tax of 6 percent on food, an annual bill of $4,000 for basic food purchases means that a tax of $240 must be paid. For a family earning a low income, say, $12,000 a year, that $240 tax poses a greater burden than for a family earning a higher income, say, $40,000 a year. The lower income family feels the pinch of the tax more because $240 is 2.0 percent of their income, whereas it is 0.6 percent of the $40,000 income. From the late 1980s until federal personal income tax changes took effect in 1991, the federal personal income tax was regressive: the tax rate decreased at high income levels.[6]

Tax Reform and Issues in the 1980s and 1990s

Since the early 1980s, tax reform has received serious consideration, and many changes have been made in the law. In 1981 Congress passed the Economic Recovery Tax Act, which changed the U.S. tax structure in a number of ways, including a reduction in personal income tax rates and indexation of the federal personal income tax brackets to inflation. Indexation helps to offset "bracket creep," which occurs when taxpayers are pushed into higher tax brackets as their money, or nominal, incomes increase to keep pace with inflation.

Tax Reform Act of 1986

Major legislation that changed federal income tax exemptions, deductions, brackets, and rates.

A major overhaul of the federal income tax system occurred with the **Tax Reform Act of 1986.** This act, when its full impact was felt in 1988, brought important changes in the exemptions and deductions allowed in calculating taxable income. Probably the most significant change, however, was in the number of tax brackets and the rate levels in those brackets. Prior to the 1986 Act, there were 15 tax brackets and the maximum tax rate was 50 percent.

---

[6] In 1990, the tax rate for a single taxpayer dropped from 33 percent to 28 percent for income over $97,620. From U.S. Department of the Treasury, Internal Revenue Service, *Explanation of the Tax Reform Act of 1986 for Individuals,* Publication 920, August 1987, pp. 2–3, and the 1990 Federal Tax Rate Schedule X.

The Tax Reform Act reduced the number of brackets to 4 and the maximum rate to 33 percent.

Some of the changes in the federal personal income tax can be seen in Table 6.4, which provides the tax rate schedules for a single taxpayer for 1980, 1985, and 1990. Notice the reduction in the number of brackets between 1980 and 1990, and the change in the highest marginal, or incremental, rate, which fell from 70 percent to 50 percent to 33 percent during these years. Beginning in 1991, the number of brackets was reduced to 3 and the highest rate fell to 31 percent. That is, for a single taxpayer, income over $49,300 was taxed at 31 percent in 1991.

Modifications such as these are not unique. Tinkering with the federal income tax to accomplish different objectives has a long history in the United States. Application 6.1, "A Chronology of Federal Income Tax Policies," provides highlights of some of the major changes in federal corporate and individual income tax rules since the beginning of this century.

An important tax issue faced by many local and state governments in the 1990s is a declining or changing tax base. A **tax base** is the particular thing on which a tax is levied. For example, the tax base for an income tax is income, and the tax base for a sales tax is the value of the items sold that are subject to the tax. Many large cities in the United States have experienced declines in population and the departure of businesses to other locations, causing local officials to become concerned about an eroding ability to raise adequate revenues through taxes paid by fewer businesses and smaller, generally poorer, populations. On the other hand, many suburban areas have benefited from both property and sales taxes as a result of increases in their populations. For example, from 1980 to 1990 the population of the city of St. Louis fell by over 12 percent while the population of the St. Louis region grew by nearly 3 percent, and the population of St. Charles County, Missouri, part of this region, grew by over 47 percent.[7]

Tax base
The object on which a tax is levied.

Fiscal Policy

The economy's levels of output, employment, and income are influenced by the relationship between the amount that government levies in taxes and the amount that it spends. A change in either taxes or spending may induce an expansion or contraction in the economy. Such changes in government inflows and outflows initiated to accomplish the particular objectives of controlling unemployment or demand-pull inflation are termed **fiscal policy.** This governmental action was warranted by the Employment Act of 1946.

Fiscal policy has evolved largely from the theories of John Maynard Keynes, who focused on the relationship between aggregate spending and the level of economic activity, and suggested that the government could fill

Fiscal policy
Influencing the levels of aggregate output and employment or prices through changes in federal government purchases, transfer payments, and/or taxes.

[7]St. Louis Regional and Commerce Growth Association. Statistics from U.S. Census Bureau.

Table 6.4   Federal Individual Income Tax Rate Schedules
for a Single Taxpayer, 1980, 1985, 1990

From 1980 through 1990 there was a significant decline in the number of brackets
and maximum rates applied to individual incomes for federal tax purposes.

1980

If taxable income is:		The tax is:	
Over—	But not over—		of the amount over—
$ 2,300	$ 3,400	14%	$ 2,300
3,400	4,400	$154 + 16%	3,400
4,400	6,500	314 + 18%	4,400
6,500	8,500	692 + 19%	6,500
8,500	10,800	1,072 + 21%	8,500
10,800	12,900	1,555 + 24%	10,800
12,900	15,000	2,059 + 26%	12,900
15,000	18,200	2,605 + 30%	15,000
18,200	23,500	3,565 + 34%	18,200
23,500	28,800	5,367 + 39%	23,500
28,800	34,100	7,434 + 44%	28,800
34,100	41,500	9,766 + 49%	34,100
41,500	55,300	13,392 + 55%	41,500
55,300	81,800	20,982 + 63%	55,300
81,800	108,300	37,677 + 68%	81,800
108,300	. . . .	55,697 + 70%	108,300

1985

If taxable income is:		The tax is:	
Over—	But not over—		of the amount over—
$ 2,390	$ 3,540	11%	$ 2,390
3,540	4,580	$126.50 + 12%	3,540
4,580	6,760	251.30 + 14%	4,580
6,760	8,850	556.50 + 15%	6,760
8,850	11,240	870.00 + 16%	8,850
11,240	13,430	1,252.40 + 18%	11,240
13,430	15,610	1,646.60 + 20%	13,430
15,610	18,940	2,082.60 + 23%	15,610
18,940	24,460	2,848.50 + 26%	18,940
24,460	29,970	4,283.70 + 30%	24,460
29,970	35,490	5,936.70 + 34%	29,970
35,490	43,190	7,813.50 + 38%	35,490
43,190	57,550	10,739.50 + 42%	43,190
57,550	85,130	16,770.70 + 48%	57,550
85,130	. . . .	30,009.10 + 50%	85,130

1990

If taxable income is:		The tax is:	
Over—	But not over—		of the amount over—
$ 0	$19,450	15%	$ 0
19,450	47,050	$2,917.50 + 28%	19,450
47,050	97,620	10,645.50 + 33%	47,050
97,620	. . . .	27,333.60 + 28%	97,620[a]

[a]Some adjustments to exemptions must be made at this income
level. These will raise the effective tax rate above 28%.

Source: Department of the Treasury, Internal Revenue Service, *1040 Federal Income Tax Forms and Instructions*, 1980, 1985, 1990.

Application 6.1

A Chronology of Federal Income Tax Policies

- **1909** A federal corporate income tax of 1% with a $5,000 exemption is adopted.
- **1913** A federal individual income tax is enacted; applies mainly to a small number of high incomes—the lowest bracket is 1% on taxable income up to $20,000; taxes are paid in quarterly installments in the year following the receipt of the income.
- **World War I Era** The corporate income tax rate is raised to a high of 12% in 1918; the individual rate is raised to 6% on taxable income up to $4,000, and the top bracket rate is raised to 77% on taxable income over $1,000,000.
- **The 1930s** The corporate tax rate changes several times, ranging between 7% and 27%; no significant individual rate changes for most average-size incomes.
- **World War II** The need to raise revenue for the war causes significant increases in tax rates and a lowering of brackets and exemptions. Corporate rates reach as high as 25% on the first $25,000 of profit, 53% on the second $25,000, and 40% on profit over $50,000. Individual income tax rates reach as high as 23% on taxable income up to $2,000, and 94% on taxable income over $200,000.
- **1943** The tax payment system is changed so that individual income taxes are paid when income is earned, rather than in quarterly installments in the following year.
- **1952** The tax on corporate profit over $25,000 is raised to 52% and remains at approximately that level until 1974; however, other changes, such as rules for determining depreciation, occur over this same time period.
- **1964** The first significant cut in individual income taxes since the 1940s occurs; rates are cut on lower income brackets and the highest rate is dropped to 77%.
- **1982** As a result of legislation in 1981, individual income tax rates are significantly lowered; the highest rate drops to 50%.
- **1987** Corporate tax rates, which have continuously declined during the 1980s, are lowered to 15% for the first $50,000 of profit, and 34% on profit over $335,000.
- **1988** A new tax law takes effect that lowers the highest marginal rate on individual income to 33%.
- **1991** The highest marginal rate on individual income becomes 31%.

Source: 1909–1980 from Joseph A. Pechman, *Federal Tax Policy*, 5th ed. (Washington: D.C., The Brookings Institution, 1987).

in a spending gap created by a lack of private spending. His most famous work, *The General Theory of Employment, Interest and Money*, published during the Great Depression, laid a foundation for fiscal policy.[8]

The Mechanics of Fiscal Policy

If you recall the role of aggregate spending in determining the level of economic activity, the circular flow diagram, and the relationship between leakages and injections covered in the previous chapter, the mechanics of fiscal policy should be obvious. Very simply, the manipulation of total

[8]John Maynard Keynes, *The General Theory of Employment, Interest and Money* (New York: Harcourt, Brace and Co., 1936).

spending through taxes and/or government expenditures can expand and contract economic activity.

If the economy is experiencing an objectionably high rate of unemployment due to inadequate demand for goods and services, policy makers can alleviate this condition by actions to increase the level of aggregate spending in the economy. This increased spending could come from (1) increased government purchases of goods and services, and/or (2) increased transfer payments, and/or (3) decreased taxes. Each of these three actions taken separately, or in combination, would raise spending and, consequently, increase the level of economic activity and lower the level of unemployment.

While each of these actions can cause economic activity to grow, the expansionary impact of increasing government purchases by a particular amount is greater than the expansionary impact of increasing transfers or decreasing taxes by the same amount. All of the dollars spent on government purchases are injected directly into the spending stream, whereas increased transfers and decreased taxes provide additional income, part of which will be spent but part of which will be saved.

If the economy is experiencing demand-pull inflation, the correct fiscal policy prescription for lowering the inflation rate is to decrease aggregate spending. Policy makers could seek to remove excess spending from the economy by (1) decreasing government purchases of goods and services, and/or (2) decreasing transfer payments, and/or (3) increasing taxes. Again, a more pronounced decrease in spending results from a decrease in government purchases because some of the reduced transfers and increased taxes would affect saving rather than spending.

It should be noted that because government expenditures and taxes affect nonincome-determined spending, they are subject to a multiplier effect. This means that, for example, if the government injected $50 billion into the spending stream through increased purchases or transfers, or through decreased taxes, the level of economic activity would increase by more than $50 billion. Alternatively, if the government withdrew $50 billion from the spending stream, output, income, and employment would decrease by more than $50 billion.

Discretionary and Automatic Fiscal Policy

Changes in taxes and government expenditures to control unemployment or demand-pull inflation may be either discretionary or automatic.

Discretionary fiscal policy
Deliberate changes in government expenditures and/or taxes to control unemployment or demand-pull inflation.

Congress exercises **discretionary fiscal policy** when it identifies an unemployment or inflation problem, establishes a policy objective concerning that problem, and then deliberately adjusts taxes and/or spending accordingly.[9] Depending upon the situation, Congress could, for example,

[9]While Congress actually carries out the changes in taxes and spending, the president or the executive branch of government may have asked for those changes or given some initial impetus to the program.

institute a tax cut or raise the tax rate, change personal income tax exemptions and/or deductions, grant tax rebates or credits, levy surcharges, initiate or postpone transfer programs, and either initiate or eliminate direct spending projects.

The last few decades have seen several examples of discretionary fiscal policy. The Revenue Act of 1964 lowered both personal and corporate income tax rates. It was passed on the urging of the Kennedy administration, which was concerned with the sluggish state of the economy in the 1950s and sought a more aggressive growth rate in the 1960s. In 1968 a 10 percent surcharge was levied on all individual and corporate income taxes. That is, an additional 10 percent was added to all income tax bills to reduce inflation caused by spending on the Vietnam War. In 1975 a tax cut was passed to counteract the 1974–1975 recession. During the Reagan administration, the Economic Recovery Tax Act of 1981 was passed, which reduced personal income taxes over a three-year period. In the following year, concern over the extent to which government expenditures were outstripping government income spurred passage of the Tax Equity and Fiscal Responsibility Act, which repealed or changed parts of the 1981 act.[10] Further changes in the personal income tax occurred in late 1990 in response to mounting federal budget problems.

Automatic stabilization

Automatic changes in government expenditures and/or taxes that occur as the level of economic activity changes and that help to control unemployment or demand-pull inflation.

The second type of fiscal policy, **automatic stabilization,** occurs when changing economic conditions cause government expenditures and taxes to change automatically in order to combat unemployment or demand-pull inflation. These alterations in government expenditures and taxing, which occur without any deliberate or additional legislative action, automatically stimulate aggregate spending in a recession and dampen aggregate spending when the economy expands. In the face of a severe recession or inflation, however, automatic stabilization alone would not be sufficient to correct the problem.

There are two automatic fiscal policy stabilizers of primary importance: transfer payments, especially unemployment compensation, and the personal income tax. Changes in the federal income tax schedule in recent years, however, have caused the tax stabilizer to become less significant.

To understand how the automatic stabilizers work, consider a recession. During a downswing, when people lose their jobs and their earned incomes are reduced, some important government responses occur automatically. First, some unemployed individuals may become eligible for a number of transfer payments, particularly unemployment compensation. Second, because the federal personal income tax is structured as a progressive tax with three rate steps, some unemployed individuals could experience a decline in the percentage of their income that is taxed, thus resulting in lower tax

---

[10] Wallace C. Peterson, *Income, Employment and Economic Growth,* 4th ed. (New York: W. W. Norton & Co., Inc., 1978), pp. 437–453; Henry J. Aaron, "The Choices Ahead," *Setting National Priorities: The 1984 Budget,* Joseph A. Pechman, ed. (Washington, D.C.: The Brookings Institution, 1983), p. 206.

payments or a tax refund.[11] These government responses to a downswing are automatic and provide additional money, through increased transfer payments and decreased taxes, to households for spending. Without these built-in stabilizers, or automatic responses, household spending would drop more dramatically, and the economy would likely slide into a deeper recession.

When the economy expands, unemployment falls, and incomes rise, the built-in stabilizers automatically remove spending from the economy to dampen demand-pull inflationary tendencies. As more people are employed, the government provides less in transfer payments, and higher incomes push some individuals into higher tax brackets. Without this automatic removal of spending as the economy heats up, particularly toward full employment, inflation could be worse.

Automatic stabilizers soften the impact of cyclical expansions and contractions. Without the help of any deliberate legislative action, they pump spending into the economy during a downswing and decrease aggregate spending during an upswing. However, as previously noted, the impact of automatic stabilization may have been lessened by the Tax Reform Act of 1986. As can be seen from the federal personal income tax schedules in Table 6.4, currently a person must realize a substantial change in income to move to a higher or lower tax rate because the ranges of the tax brackets are so large. For example, in 1990 a 28 percent marginal tax rate applied to income between $19,450 and $47,050 for a single taxpayer, whereas the schedules for 1980 and 1985 show that there used to be 5 tax brackets in this income range. Because of these tax changes, transfer payments may become the most important automatic stabilizer. The role of fiscal policy in economic stabilization is summarized in Table 6.5.

Government Budgets

Each government unit annually prepares a proposed budget, which is a detailed listing of its intended revenues and expenditures by type and amount for the coming year. At the end of the year, after revenues are collected and expenditures are made, an actual budget is compiled. Although the proposed budget presents the government's intentions, the year-end, actual budget is of greater importance because it accounts for that government unit's actual leakages from and injections into the spending

---

[11] The following example helps to clarify this point. Assume that a person was earning a taxable income of $40,000 in 1990, and that an amount sufficient to pay a total federal income tax of $8,679.00 for the year was withheld every month from his pay. If this person lost his job and his 1990 taxable income was reduced by one-half to $20,000, his tax bill would have been only $3,079.00, or less than one-half of the tax on $40,000. This person would have received a tax refund when he filed his 1990 taxes. From Department of the Treasury, Internal Revenue Service, *1040 Forms and Instructions for 1990*, pp. 49, 51.

Table 6.5

Fiscal Policy Summary

Discretionary fiscal policy and automatic stabilization can be used to control unemployment or demand-pull inflation by changing the size of the spending stream.

Problem:	Unemployment	Demand-pull inflation
Remedy:	Increase total spending	Decrease total spending
Fiscal Policy Response:		
Discretionary:	Congress can (a) increase government purchases; (b) increase transfer payments; (c) decrease taxes	Congress can (a) decrease government purchases; (b) decrease transfer payments; (c) increase taxes
Automatic Stabilization:	Automatic increases in some transfer payments (especially unemployment compensation) and decreases in federal personal income taxes	Automatic decreases in some transfer payments and increases in federal personal income taxes
Effect:	Puts more dollars into the spending stream	Withdraws dollars from the spending stream

stream, and summarizes how it influenced the level of economic activity over the past year.

The bottom line of every year-end budget is the dollar figure that results when total expenditures are subtracted from total revenues. This figure indicates whether the government has spent an amount equal to, less than, or greater than its revenues. Put another way, it indicates whether the government that year ran a balanced budget, a surplus budget, or a deficit budget.

Types of Budgets

Balanced budget
A government's total expenditures equal its total revenues.

Surplus budget
A government's revenues are greater than its expenditures.

Deficit budget
A government's expenditures are greater than its revenues.

A **balanced budget** occurs when a government's total expenditures equal its total revenues. A **surplus budget** occurs when a government does not spend all of its revenues, or when the subtraction of total expenditures from total revenues yields a positive dollar amount. A **deficit budget** occurs when a government's total expenditures are greater than total revenues, or when the subtraction of total expenditures from total revenues yields a negative dollar amount. As with an individual who spends more than he or she receives, a government with a deficit budget must either borrow and go into debt, or use its reserve fund (savings) if one exists.

Although all government units prepare annual budgets, the budget of the federal government has the most impact on the macroeconomy. Table 6.6

Table 6.6

Federal Budget Receipts, Outlays, and Surpluses or Deficits
for Fiscal Years, 1940-1990 (Billions of Dollars)

The federal government has operated with a budget deficit for 43 of the 51 years
from 1940 through 1990.

Fiscal Year	Receipts	Outlays	Surplus or Deficit (−)	Fiscal Year	Receipts	Outlays	Surplus or Deficit (−)
1940	$ 6.5	$ 9.5	$ −2.9	1965	$ 116.8	$ 118.2	$ −1.4
1941	8.7	13.7	−4.9	1966	130.8	134.5	−3.7
1942	14.6	35.1	−20.5	1967	148.8	157.5	−8.6
1943	24.0	78.6	−54.6	1968	153.0	178.1	−25.2
1944	43.7	91.3	−47.6	1969	186.9	183.6	3.2
1945	45.2	92.7	−47.6	1970	192.8	195.6	−2.8
1946	39.3	55.2	−15.9	1971	187.1	210.2	−23.0
1947	38.5	34.5	4.0	1972	207.3	230.7	−23.4
1948	41.6	29.8	11.8	1973	230.8	245.7	−14.9
1949	39.4	38.8	0.6	1974	263.2	269.4	−6.1
1950	39.4	42.6	−3.1	1975	279.1	332.3	−53.2
1951	51.6	45.5	6.1	1976	298.1	371.8	−73.7
1952	66.2	67.7	−1.5	1977	355.6	409.2	−53.6
1953	69.6	76.1	−6.5	1978	399.6	458.7	−59.2
1954	69.7	70.9	−1.2	1979	463.3	503.5	−40.2
1955	65.5	68.4	−3.0	1980	517.1	590.9	−73.8
1956	74.6	70.6	3.9	1981	599.3	678.2	−78.9
1957	80.0	76.6	3.4	1982	617.8	745.7	−127.9
1958	79.6	82.4	−2.8	1983	600.6	808.3	−207.8
1959	79.2	92.1	−12.8	1984	666.5	851.8	−185.3
1960	92.5	92.2	0.3	1985	734.1	946.3	−212.3
1961	94.4	97.7	−3.3	1986	769.1	990.3	−221.2
1962	99.7	106.8	−7.1	1987	854.1	1,003.8	−149.7
1963	106.6	111.3	−4.8	1988	909.0	1,064.1	−155.1
1964	112.6	118.5	−5.9	1989	990.7	1,144.1	−153.4
				1990	1,031.3	1,251.7	−220.4

Source: U.S., *Economic Report of the President* (Washington, D.C.: U.S. Government Printing Office, 1991), p. 375.

lists federal government receipts, outlays, and resulting surpluses or deficits
for the years 1940 through 1990. Let us assess this record.

It is obvious from the "Surplus or Deficit" column of Table 6.6 that the
federal government typically operates with a deficit budget. In fact, since
1960 a surplus budget has appeared only once: in 1969. Notice also from
Table 6.6 that wartime is particularly hard on the federal government

budget. World War II and the Vietnam War (especially in 1968) brought relatively high deficits. Finally, observe the significant change in the size of the budget deficits that began in the mid-1970s. Since 1982 the annual deficit has been over $100 billion, and the 1986 deficit of $221.2 billion reached an all-time high.[12] These persistent and high deficits have created substantial problems, which will be discussed later in this chapter.

Balanced Budget and Emergency Deficit Control Act of 1985 (Gramm-Rudman-Hollings Act)
Legislation designed to reduce the federal deficit annually until 1993, when it is to be eliminated.

One result of public concern over rising federal deficits was the passage of the **Balanced Budget and Emergency Deficit Control Act of 1985,** also known as the **Gramm-Rudman-Hollings Act.** This act originally stipulated yearly systematic cuts in the federal deficit until 1991, when the deficit was to be eliminated, but was amended in 1987 to extend this date to 1993. Even though Congress and the president have shown general support for the spirit of this legislation, they have had difficulty making the spending cuts and/or raising the taxes necessary to balance the budget. Congress has maintained the power to waive the deficit-reduction targets—the amounts to be cut each year—and some illusory budget adjustments have occurred. For example, wages to Pentagon workers and some farm price supports were paid in the last few days of fiscal year 1989 rather than when scheduled to be paid in fiscal year 1990. This brought the 1990 budget deficit $4 billion closer to its target.[13]

There is also some concern that the budget deficit figures are misleading because of substantial Social Security trust fund surpluses that reduce the deficit's reported size. Application 6.2, "The Temptations of the Social Security Surplus," explains how Social Security is woven into the federal budget.

The Budget and Fiscal Policy

Government spending and taxing, the budget, and fiscal policy (both discretionary and automatic) are all interrelated. In the analysis of the tax–government expenditure relationship in Chapter Five, it was concluded that if the amount removed from the spending stream through taxes is greater than the amount returned through government expenditures, all other things being equal, the economy will contract. On the other hand, if the amount returned to the spending stream through government expenditures is greater than the amount removed through taxes, all other things being equal, the economy will expand or, if production is at or near full employment, it will inflate.

---

[12] You may want to locate and evaluate the federal budget deficit figures for the years after the publication date of this book. At the writing of this text, the deficit for 1991 was estimated to be $318.1 billion.

[13] John E. Yang, "Fiscal Follies: Ever-Growing Federal Deficits Prove the Gramm-Rudman Budget Law to Be a Failure," *The Wall Street Journal,* October 3, 1989, p. A18.

Application 6.2

The Temptations of the Social Security Surplus

On the periphery of the great political debate over the Federal budget deficit, the Government is collecting $110 million a day for which it has no immediate use. The money is the difference between what the Government collects in Social Security payroll taxes and payments to retirees and disabled workers. The funds will grow for a long time.

The question of what the Government might do with the money, if anything, adds a new dimension to the budget deficit debate. Because the annual surpluses in the Social Security trust fund are part of the Federal budget, on paper at least, and because they are on the plus side of the ledger, they are reducing the minus side—the deficit—by some magnitude. . . .

Projections show the annual surpluses reaching $500 million a day, or close to $200 billion a year, by the start of the next century. Then the surpluses are projected to rise for 15 or 20 years more. Only well into the 21st century do the forecasts show the surpluses fading away, as the baby-boom population retires.

Many politicians and economists now say that they failed to take budgetary and economic implications into account when, worrying about the Social Security system's running out of money in a few months, they overhauled the system [in 1983]. To protect today's youngest Americans from huge tax increases when the baby-boom generation retires, the Government ordered quick step-by-step increases in the Social Security tax rate, leveling off in 1990. . . .

At the moment, the hottest point of debate involves a deceptively simple matter of accounting: whether to continue to include the surpluses in the budget. Faced with the prospect of asking for new taxes to reduce a deficit in the Government's operating budget and to pay for the Vietnam War, President Johnson combined the surplus—then a few billion dollars—into what is called the unified budget to help him win his case against a tax increase. The Federal budget has been unified ever since.

According to the Congressional Budget Office, the projected 1993 budget deficit would double, to more than $200 billion, if the Social Security surplus were not included in a unified budget. . . .

[Some economists think] that the unified budget presents a truer picture of the Government's finances [and could result in a decline in interest rates, reducing] one of the Government's biggest expenditures, the interest on the national debt. This, they point out, could greatly relieve other pressure to reduce the budget deficits with spending cuts and tax increases. . . .

[Other economists] maintain that combining the two accounts diminishes political resolve to cut the operating deficit, risks pork-barrel spending and means that when the trust fund surpluses shrink in the next century from now, the operating budget deficits will emerge again to haunt the economy. . . .

Source: Excerpted from Peter T. Kilborn, "The Temptations of the Social Security Surplus," *The New York Times.* Copyright © 1988 by The New York Times Company. Excerpted by permission. Also see Peter T. Kilborn, "The Temptations of the Social Security Surplus," in *Readings in Introductory Macroeconomics,* 1989–1990 Annual Edition, ed. Peter D. McClelland (New York: McGraw-Hill Publishing, 1990), p. 229.

Since a surplus budget occurs when revenues are greater than outlays, a surplus budget generally causes economic activity to contract.[14] When all tax leakages are not returned to the spending stream because of a surplus

[14] The expression "generally" is used because the ultimate impact of the budget depends upon the types of taxes collected, the percentage of those taxes that would have been saved, the percentage of expenditures that goes directly into purchases of goods and services, the percentage of transfers that is saved, and so forth.

budget, the level of aggregate spending shrinks. Alternatively, if government expenditures are greater than taxes, a deficit budget results. Because it increases the level of aggregate spending by injecting more into the spending stream than it takes out, a deficit budget will expand output, employment, and income or, if the economy is at or near full employment, it will cause demand-pull inflation. A balanced budget, contrary to common belief, does not have a neutral impact on economic activity. In determining the effect of a balanced budget, we must recall that dollars from income that has been taxed by the government would have otherwise been used partly for spending and partly for saving. Thus, when the government spends those tax dollars on goods and services, it is taking some money that would have been saved and is spending it. With this in mind, one can conclude that a balanced budget is slightly expansionary.

How is the budget related to fiscal policy? If the economy has an undesirably high level of unemployment, the recommended discretionary fiscal policy measure is to increase expenditures and/or decrease taxes. This action will push the budget toward a deficit position or increase an existing deficit. Thus, we can generalize that a deficit, or at least a reduction in a surplus, is the budget prescription to fight unemployment. When the economy is experiencing demand-pull inflation, Congress can deliberately decrease aggregate spending by decreasing government expenditures and/or increasing taxes. This action should push the government budget toward a surplus position. We might then conclude that a surplus budget, or at least a reduction in deficit spending, is appropriate for curbing demand-pull inflation.

Automatic fiscal policy also affects the budget. Built-in stabilizers push the government budget toward a deficit in recessionary times as they increase transfers and reduce tax revenues. Automatically, there is a move toward the appropriate budget prescription for correcting a downswing. In periods of expansion, as transfers fall and tax revenues increase, the budget is automatically pushed toward a surplus, which is the proper prescription for correcting demand-pull inflation. In Table 6.6, the sizable budget deficits given for fiscal years 1976 and 1983 were in part caused by automatic stabilizers. The unemployment rate for the civilian labor force reached 10.7 percent during the 1983 fiscal year, the highest level since the Great Depression, causing tax collections to fall and transfers to increase.[15]

As shown in Table 6.6, annual federal budget deficits during the 1980s were consistently high. Since a deficit budget has an expansionary impact on the economy, one could conclude that there was a connection between these budget deficits and the long recovery phase of the business cycle that began in 1983 and continued through the rest of the decade. These deficits,

---

[15] U.S., *Economic Report of the President* (Washington, D.C.: U.S. Government Printing Office, 1984), p. 259. The large deficit of 1983 cannot be attributed solely to the automatic stabilizers. The first of several tax cuts resulting from the Economic Recovery Tax Act passed in 1981 also went into effect during that period.

however, combined with economic expansion, may have caused a complex budgetary situation for the 1990s.

While one of the primary objectives of Congress and the American public is to cut the size of federal deficits, the decrease in spending and/or increase in taxes necessary to accomplish this objective could have a dampening effect on the economy. That is, holding all other factors constant, the economy could slow down in response to deficit trimming.

A complicating factor in the budget reduction scenario is that a slowdown in the economy will trigger the automatic stabilizers to counteract a recession: tax collections should automatically decrease and transfer payments increase. In other words, as discretionary fiscal policy is used to cut the size of the deficits, the automatic stabilizers could work to increase the size of the deficits. The ultimate impact of this complication on the federal budget and the choices that will be made will be interesting to observe as the 1990s unfold.

Full employment budget

The budget position of the federal government if the economy were to reach full employment.

Public policy makers sometimes refer to a **full employment budget,** which gives the budget position of the federal government if the economy were to achieve full employment. That is, it indicates, for a particular year, the amount of revenue the federal government would collect, the amount of expenditures that would be made, and the resulting surplus or deficit that would occur if full employment were reached. Since the automatic stabilizers favor the collection of taxes and a reduction in payments for transfers at full employment, the tendency for a full employment budget is toward a surplus, or at least a reduced deficit, budget. It is important to realize that this type of budget is based on the assumption of full employment, and is not, therefore, directly applicable to most economic conditions.

Fiscal Policy and Budgetary Realities

Does the federal budget always perform according to the proper strategy for fiscal policy control? Is there always an appropriate budget surplus to counteract demand-pull inflation or a budget deficit to reduce unemployment? Are the mechanics of fiscal policy always carried out as smoothly and simply as outlined here? For several reasons, the answer to each of these questions is no.

First, the Employment Act of 1946 does not make the promotion of "maximum employment, production and purchasing power" the sole goal of congressional tax and spending activity. Rather, the act charges ". . . the Federal Government to use all practicable means consistent with its needs and obligations and other essential considerations of national policy. . . ."[16] In short, there may be other objectives that take precedence over the use of

---

[16] *United States Statutes at Large, 1946,* Vol. 60, Pt. 1, *Public Laws and Reorganization Plans* (Washington, D.C.: U.S. Government Printing Office, 1947), p. 23.

taxing and spending to control the level of economic activity. For example, national defense priorities may induce inflationary increases in spending, or a scandal-ridden spending program may be dropped during a period of unemployment.

A second consideration in the reality of fiscal policy and the budgetary process is the emergence of simultaneously high rates of inflation and unemployment, termed **stagflation,** and the effect that stagflation has on attempts to control the economy through appropriate adjustments in taxes and government expenditures. For example, in 1981 prices increased by approximately 9.7 percent and the unemployment rate was 7.6 percent.[17] The U.S. economy was faced with two major problems. In the case of stagflation, appropriate fiscal policy action is difficult to determine and is further complicated when the source of the inflation cannot be easily identified.

A third consideration concerning fiscal policy is the time lag from the onset of an economic problem to its identification and then to the implementation of an appropriate response. For example, with serious unemployment, months may pass before its severity becomes apparent. Then once the problem is recognized, Congress and the administration may present plans and counter-plans, and debate, discuss, and argue over whether to initiate a tax cut, offer tax rebates, or increase spending. In addition, the problem of what to do may be compounded by the question of how much to do: how large should a tax cut or spending increase be? After these decisions are made, more time may be required for implementation of the program. By the time the remedy takes effect, the economy may even have changed so much that the problem no longer exists.

A fourth consideration regarding the reality of fiscal policy and the government budget is the process by which the budget is formed. Many students, especially after reading this far into the chapter, may think that groups of economists and statisticians simply lay out the budget for the year, adjusting spending and taxing to correct predicted economic conditions. On the contrary, development and passage of the federal government budget is a complicated, political, drawn-out process.

The federal budget is first formulated by the executive branch of the government and represents the president's financial priorities for the coming year. At this stage of budget development, fiscal policy may not be considered as much as the maintenance or dismantling of various agency operations and programs. The president's budget is then submitted to Congress, whose members make the final spending decisions through their votes. Congressional review of the president's budget is extensive; it is studied by several committees, and modifications are made by both the House and Senate.

Stagflation

Occurs when an economy is experiencing high rates of both inflation and unemployment.

[17]U.S., *Economic Report of the President* (Washington, D.C.: U.S. Government Printing Office, 1990), pp. 299, 330.

Test Your Understanding

Government's Impact on the Macroeconomy[a]

[a]Answers are found at the end of the book.

Indicate the effect of each of the following actions on the macroeconomy. That is, in each case determine the changes that would result in aggregate output, employment, or prices.

1. The amount that households can deduct from their incomes in calculating their federal personal income taxes increases.

2. Payments to Social Security recipients are increased, but there is an equal decrease in transfer payments to people in other programs.

3. The federal government balances its budget when the economy is at full employment.

4. Congresspersons vote themselves a 20 percent pay increase.

5. A budget surplus occurs as the economy falls into a recession.

6. Taxes on cigarettes and alcohol are raised by 16 percent.

7. The federal government increases taxes with the intention of paying off past deficits within ten years.

8. Across the board cuts are made in defense, highway, and education spending.

9. The economy is at full employment and the Social Security surplus is so large that social insurance taxes are lowered.

10. The federal government runs a deficit budget while the economy is experiencing demand-pull inflation.

As congresspersons consider various aspects of the budget, they may be more responsive to their particular constituencies than to the needs of the macroeconomy. It might be extremely difficult for a representative who wants to be re-elected to place a high priority on controlling demand-pull inflation and thus vote against the funding of a major project that will provide jobs in his or her district. In short, the budget, with all of its economic implications, is part of the political process, and political objectives may take precedence over economic objectives. There is growing interest among economists in **public choice,** which is the study of the economic motives and attitudes of voters and public officials, and how those motives and attitudes affect government decision making. Public choice is discussed more fully in Chapter Eleven.

Public choice

The study of the economic motives and attitudes of voters and public officials, and their effects on government decision making.

Finally, one other problem associated with fiscal policy and the budgetary process is that careless spending may arise because the government can perpetually borrow to cover budget deficits. From time to time, examples of unproductive programs and studies and extravagant expenditures surface that may not have existed without deficit spending.

"Test Your Understanding: Government's Impact on the Macroeconomy" gives you an opportunity to assess how various actions by the federal government influence the economy's output, employment, and price levels.

The National Debt

As pointed out in Table 6.6, there has been a persistent tendency in recent decades for the federal government to run deficit budgets. In order to finance this deficit spending, the government must borrow the necessary funds. As more is borrowed each year, the federal government goes deeper and deeper into debt. A surplus budget, which allows some of this debt to be repaid, occurs infrequently. The accumulated total debt of the federal government is called the **national debt.**

Financing the National Debt

When the federal government needs to raise money to finance its spending, it borrows at the lowest interest rate it can negotiate from anyone who is willing to lend it money. In return for funds, the lender receives a **U.S. Treasury security:** an IOU stating the federal government's promise to make specified interest payments and to repay the loaned funds on a particular date. The time span from issuance to the maturity date determines whether the security is a **U.S. Treasury bill,** which is issued for 13, 26, or 52 weeks; a **U.S. Treasury note,** which matures in 2 to 10 years; or a **U.S. Treasury bond,** which is to be repaid in 10 years or longer.

When it borrows, the government publicly announces the total amount it intends to raise at that time, the repayment date, and the denomination of the security it will be issuing. For example, the Treasury could declare a decision to raise $5 billion over the next week through two-year Treasury notes in minimum or multiple denominations of $5,000. When an announcement such as this is made, potential lenders submit "tenders," which are applications stating both the specific amounts they are willing to lend and the interest rates they will charge the government. Those who submit the tenders charging the lowest interest rates "win" the bid and receive the securities. Small investors, such as a family with a few thousand dollars to lend, can offer funds at the "average rate" that is finally determined and avoid the bidding process. The government announces plans to borrow weekly as well as at other periods throughout the year. Each Tuesday, for example, the government announces the amount it wishes to borrow that week through 13-week and 26-week Treasury bills. These bills, which are issued in a minimum of $10,000 and multiples of $5,000, are the often referred to "T-bills."[18]

Who loans the federal government money or acquires these Treasury securities? The largest portion of the national debt is held by private domestic and foreign investors such as individuals, banks, pension funds,

National debt

The total accumulated debt of the federal government due to deficit spending.

U.S. Treasury security

Issued by the federal government in return for funds lent to it; gives a specified interest rate and repayment date.

U.S. Treasury bill, note, bond

U.S. Treasury securities that mature, respectively, in 13, 26, or 52 weeks; in 2 to 10 years; and in 10 years or longer.

---

[18] Purchasers of Treasury securities do not actually receive a paper certificate. Instead, a receipt is given to the purchaser, and a book-entry is used to record the transaction. Treasury bills are also sold on a discount basis: that is, the bills are sold at a price below their face value, but purchasers are repaid at full face value on the maturity date.

and corporations. The rest of the debt is owned by the Federal Reserve Banks and government agencies and trusts. Perhaps the U.S. Treasury is in debt to you or your family. If you own a U.S. Treasury security, you have provided the federal government with borrowed funds.

Size of the National Debt

By the end of the 1990 fiscal year, the national debt had grown to over $3.2 trillion ($3,200,000,000,000.00), a sum of money that is incomprehensible to most people. Table 6.7 gives, for selected years beginning with 1900, the total national debt in column 1, and the per capita (per person) debt in column 2. Because the debt is linked to the federal budget, those years in which substantial deficit spending occurred were also years during which the national debt increased significantly. Observe the considerable increase in the debt from 1915 to 1920 and from 1940 to 1945 caused largely by deficit spending during World War I and World War II. Notice also the rapid and substantial increases in the debt during the 1980s. The debt reached over $1.0 trillion in 1982, increased to over $2.0 trillion in 1986, and rose to over $3.0 trillion in 1990. Viewed another way, the debt doubled in size over the 25-year period from 1950 to 1975, and grew by almost six times its size over the 15-year period from 1975 to 1990.

The figures in column 2 of Table 6.7, which represent the share of the national debt for every man, woman, and child in the United States, also show startling increases in recent years. To fully pay off the debt in 1990, a family of four would have needed to contribute $49,636 as its share. In 1980 this figure was $15,940 and in 1970, $7,256.[19]

Table 6.7 includes some, though not all, of the years in which the debt was reduced: decreases occurred in 1905, 1925, 1930, and 1950. From your study of fiscal policy, budgets, and economic expansions and contractions, can you comment on the appropriateness of a debt reduction in 1930 in light of the depression that had just gripped the country?

Assessing the Debt

What kinds of burdens does the national debt impose on taxpayers and on future generations? Has the debt become too large? Were the substantial increases in the debt in the 1980s worth it? Should the debt be paid off as soon as possible? These and similar questions typically emerge in discussions — whether academic or political — of the debt. Let us focus on a few critical issues.

---

[19] A word of caution is in order regarding comparisons of the burden of the debt from year to year. As was the case for the figures in the tables showing government revenues and expenditures, the figures in Table 6.7 are in current, not real, dollars, so part of the increase in the dollar value of the debt is due to inflation.

Table 6.7   The National Debt, Selected Years 1900-1990

Over the years the national debt, the burden of the debt per person, and the interest the government pays to finance the debt have all grown.

	Gross Debt		Interest Paid	
	1	2	3	4
Year	Total (Billions of Dollars)	Per Capita (Dollars)	Total (Billions of Dollars)	Percent of Federal Outlays
1900	$ 1.3	$ 17	$ (Z)	7.7%
1905	1.1	14	(Z)	4.3
1910	1.1	12	(Z)	3.1
1915	1.2	12	(Z)	3.0
1920	24.3	228	1.0	15.9
1925	20.5	177	0.9	28.8
1930	16.2	132	0.7	19.2
1935	28.7	226	0.8	12.6
1940	43.0	325	1.0	11.5
1945	258.7	1,849	3.6	3.7
1950	256.1	1,688	5.7	14.5
1955	272.8	1,651	6.4	9.3
1960	284.1	1,572	9.2	10.0
1965	313.8	1,613	11.3	9.6
1970	370.1	1,814	19.3	9.9
1971	397.3	1,921	21.0	10.0
1972	426.4	2,037	21.8	9.4
1973	457.3	2,164	24.2	9.8
1974	474.2	2,223	29.3	10.9
1975	533.2	2,475	32.7	9.8
1976	620.4	2,852	37.1	10.0
1977	698.8	3,170	41.9	10.2
1978	771.5	3,463	48.7	10.6
1979	826.5	3,669	59.8	11.9
1980	907.7	3,985	74.9	12.7
1981	997.9	4,338	95.6	14.1
1982	1,142.0	4,913	117.4	15.7
1983	1,377.2	5,870	128.8	15.9
1984	1,572.3	6,640	153.8	18.1
1985	1,823.1	7,616	178.9	18.9
1986	2,125.3	8,793	187.1	18.9
1987	2,350.3	9,630	195.4	19.5
1988	2,602.3	10,556	214.1	20.1
1989	2,867.5	11,526	—	—
1990	3,206.3	12,409	—	—

(Z) = Less than $50 million.

Source: Figures for 1900–1960 are from U.S. Bureau of the Census, *Statistical Abstract of the United States: 1979*, 100th ed. (Washington, D.C.: U.S. Government Printing Office, 1979), p. 273. Figures for 1965–1988 are from U.S. Bureau of the Census, *Statistical Abstract of the United States: 1990*, 110th ed. (Washington, D.C.: U.S. Government Printing Office, 1990), p. 309. Figures for 1989–90 are from U.S., *Economic Report of the President* (Washington, D.C.: U.S. Government Printing Office, 1991), p. 375. Per capita figure for 1989 is estimated, and for 1990 is from Stanley H. Claud, "Who Deserves the Blame?" *Time*, October 15, 1990, p. 46.

One of the most obvious and significant burdens of the national debt is the interest that must be paid to borrow and maintain a debt of this magnitude. Column 3 of Table 6.7 gives the amount of interest paid annually to sustain these obligations. In 1988, for example, the federal government remitted $214.1 billion in interest to its security holders. To put the interest burden into perspective, column 4 presents the percentage of federal outlays for these payments. Over the years this percentage has edged upward, with dramatic increases in the 1980s. Notice, for example, that in 1988 approximately 20 percent of all funds spent by the federal government were used to meet interest charges. By comparison, in 1988 federal spending for health, education, the environment, and law enforcement combined was less than two-thirds of the net interest paid.[20] Many critics of the federal debt point to the alternative uses, or forgone opportunities, to which those dollars could have been put.

The interest burden of the national debt cumulates as additional debt is incurred each year. Because the debt is not being retired, interest must be paid year after year. The rising burden of the **debt service,** or interest cost of maintaining the debt, will be passed on to future generations who will have to pay the interest on the current debt.

Debt service

The cost of maintaining a debt; generally measured in interest costs.

The question of whether the national debt has become too large is basically a value judgment. At what point, even in the case of one's own finances, do credit obligations become too high? One way to evaluate the size of the debt is to examine it as a percentage of GNP. This is done in Figure 6.3, which gives the debt as a percentage of GNP for the years 1960 through 1990.

Figure 6.3 indicates that the debt as a percentage of GNP generally fell from 1960 to 1974, increased in some years after 1974, and has jumped substantially since 1981. It was 33 percent of GNP in 1981 and increased to 59 percent by 1990. This method of evaluating the size of the debt is analogous to comparing an individual's debt and income. For example, it is obvious that one can comfortably sustain more dollars of debt at an income of $40,000 per year than at an income of $20,000 per year. The problem is whether or not one can sustain a debt that takes a rising percentage of one's income.

Should we pay off the debt? First of all, it would be a huge, probably impossible, burden, even over several years, to raise through taxes and other revenues the amount needed to pay off the debt. (Recall that every person would need to contribute over $12,000.) Second, with repayment of the debt, a significant income redistribution would occur as the average taxpayer became poorer due to the increased tax burden and the holders of government securities became richer with their newly redeemed

[20] U.S. Bureau of the Census, *Statistical Abstract of the United States: 1990,* 110th ed. (Washington, D.C.: U.S. Government Printing Office, 1990), pp. 310–311.

Figure 6.3

National Debt as a Percentage of GNP, 1960–1990[a]

While the national debt is large in dollar terms, it fell as a percentage of GNP through the 1960s and some of the 1970s. The debt has, however, increased significantly as a percentage of GNP in the 1980s.

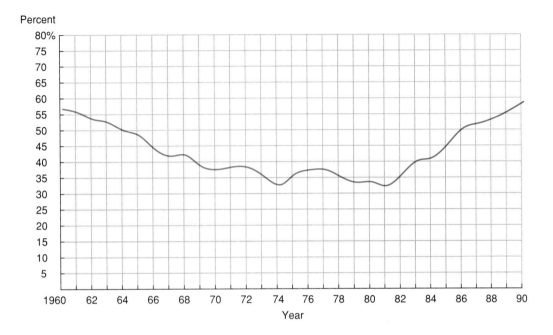

[a]Figures are for fiscal years.

Source: U.S., *Economic Report of the President* (Washington, D.C.: U.S. Government Printing Office, 1991), p. 375.

funds. Also, approximately 13 percent of the debt is external, or foreign-owned.[21] While under normal conditions this is not a serious consideration, in a period of accelerated repayment it would mean a notable outflow of dollars from the United States. Finally, in order to pay off the public debt, a series of surplus budgets would be needed. Recall from earlier in the chapter that a surplus budget has a contractionary impact on the economy. Thus, while the debt was being paid off, economic activity would decline.

[21] From *Monetary Trends,* prepared by the Federal Reserve Bank of St. Louis, March 1991, p. 13. This percentage, which is for September, 1990, fluctuates from year to year.

Crowding Out

One other consideration involving deficit spending and the national debt is the strain that government borrowing puts on funds available for loans. The federal government competes with households and businesses to borrow whatever funds are available for loan making. If government borrowing is sizable, two important effects result in the market for loans. First, because the borrowing and lending of money takes place in a market where the forces of supply and demand determine the interest rate (the price of money), increases in government borrowing increase the demand for loans and cause the interest rate to rise. When the federal government borrows substantial amounts, the impact on interest rates can be significant.

Crowding out

Occurs when borrowing by the federal government reduces borrowing by households and businesses.

A second effect of sizable government borrowing is the **crowding out** of private borrowing. Because households and businesses are interest-rate sensitive, increases in the interest rate cause them to borrow less. The result is that available funds are soaked up by the federal government, which is not interest-rate sensitive in its borrowing, and businesses and households borrow less for capital improvements, plant expansion, homes, automobiles, and such. The major problem that emerges with crowding out is that economic growth may be limited because businesses cannot afford to borrow to buy the machinery and equipment necessary for growth.

Summary

The two main categories of government expenditures are purchases of goods and services and transfer payments. Some of the purchases are for public goods, which are provided for all of society and from which no one can be excluded. Governments receive revenues from taxes and other sources such as contributions for social insurance. The primary source of federal government revenue is the individual income tax. Taxes may be classified according to the relationship between the percentage of income taxed and the size of the income: a progressive tax has a direct relationship, a regressive tax has an inverse relationship, and the percentage stays the same for a proportional tax. Major changes in the federal income tax occurred with the Tax Reform Act of 1986.

Fiscal policy refers to changes in government expenditures and/or taxes for the purpose of influencing the levels of output, employment, or prices in the economy. Fiscal policy can be used to reduce unemployment by injecting more spending into the economy through increased government purchases, increased transfer payments, and/or decreased taxes. Demand-pull inflation is reduced through decreased government purchases, decreased transfer payments, and/or increased taxes.

Fiscal policy is either discretionary or automatic. Discretionary fiscal policy is the deliberate adjustment of government purchases, transfers, and/or taxes by Congress to control unemployment or inflation. Automatic stabilization is the automatic change in some government expenditures, like transfer payments, and some taxes, like the federal personal income tax, that stimulates or dampens aggregate spending as the level of economic activity changes. These changes in spending and taxes help soften the impact of unemployment or inflation automatically.

When a government's outlays are less than its revenues, it is operating with a surplus budget. When its outlays exceed revenues, it is operating with a deficit budget. When its outlays and revenues are equal, it is operating with a balanced budget. Surplus budgets generally cause economic activity to contract, since the government is withdrawing more from the spending stream than it is returning. Deficit and balanced budgets are expansionary, since the government is injecting more into the spending stream than is being taken out as taxes. Thus, a surplus budget would be proper policy for fighting demand-pull inflation, while a deficit budget would be appropriate for fighting unemployment. The full employment budget gives the expenditure, revenue, and surplus or deficit position that would occur in the federal budget if the economy were to reach full employment. In recent times, there has been a tendency to run substantial budget deficits year after year.

Fiscal policy considerations compete with other economic and noneconomic objectives in establishing the federal budget, and the budgetary process is largely political. Also, the effectiveness of fiscal policy may be reduced by the combined presence of high rates of inflation and unemployment and by the time lag from the onset and discovery of a problem to the implementation of a remedy. The government's freedom to persistently run budget deficits can lead to unwise amounts or types of expenditures.

The national debt is the debt owed by the federal government from the financing of its deficit budgets. In raising funds, the government borrows at the lowest interest rates offered from whomever is willing to lend and gives U.S. Treasury securities in return. The absolute size of the public debt has grown substantially over the years, as has the debt in relation to GNP, and the interest the government must pay to carry the debt is a significant amount. In addition, as the federal government increases its borrowing, it crowds out private borrowing.

Key Terms and Concepts

Government purchases of goods and services	Fiscal policy
Public good	Discretionary fiscal policy
Transfer payments	Automatic stabilization
Progressive tax	Balanced budget
Proportional, or flat, tax	Surplus budget
Regressive tax	Deficit budget
Tax Reform Act of 1986	Balanced Budget and Emergency Deficit Control Act of 1985 (Gramm-Rudman-Hollings Act)
Tax base	

Full employment budget

Stagflation

Public choice

National debt

U.S. Treasury security (U.S. Treasury bill, note, bond)

Debt service

Crowding out

Review Questions

1. Identify the federal government's total expenditure amount, its major categories of spending, and its major sources of revenue.

2. Determine whether each of the following taxes is progressive, proportional, or regressive.
    a. A sales tax of 7 percent on clothing
    b. A state income tax with three brackets: 5 percent for income under $20,000, 8 percent for income between $20,000 and $100,000, and 15 percent for income over $100,000
    c. A property tax of $5.85 per $100 of assessed property value
    d. A tax of $3 on room occupancy in all hotels in a city
    e. A tax of 3 percent on all wages earned in a city
    f. A sales tax of 5 percent on utilities
    g. A federal tax of 16 percent on beer and wine

3. Identify the tax base in each of the examples in Question 2.

4. Explain how automatic stabilization stimulates spending in a recession and dampens spending during periods of demand-pull inflation. How does automatic stabilization affect the federal budget?

5. Explain whether the economy will expand, contract, stay the same, or inflate with each of the following fiscal actions.
    a. Congress votes a $75 tax credit to each taxpayer.
    b. Households are taxed an extra 15 percent, and the government does not spend all of these additional tax dollars.
    c. Households are taxed an extra 15 percent, and the government spends the entire amount on purchases of goods and services.
    d. Congress allows many new income tax deductions when the economy is at full employment.
    e. Although Congress intends to balance the budget, a deficit occurs.
    f. At the end of a war, defense expenditures drop dramatically but are replaced by domestic spending programs for health and education.
    g. At the end of a war, defense expenditures drop with no increase in other spending programs.

6. If the U.S. economy fell into a serious recession, what could Congress do to counteract that recession? Specifically, how could it use each of its fiscal policy tools?

7. What effect would each of the following have on a federal budget that is currently balanced? How would the budgetary changes, where they occur, affect the national debt?

a. An increase in the percentage of income taxed in each of the federal personal income tax brackets
b. An increase in government expenditures on pollution control
c. An equal increase in government expenditures and income tax revenues
d. An increase in defense expenditures and a decrease in corporate income tax revenues
e. An increase in Social Security payments by the government matched by a decrease in a subsidy to a particular group in the economy
f. An exemption from federal income tax for interest earned from passbook savings accounts in banks

8. Could the national debt be eliminated over the next ten years? How? What would be the opportunity cost of paying off the debt versus not paying it off?

Discussion Questions

1. Suppose that the legislators in a particular state are choosing between three strategies to raise revenue: (1) imposing a progressive income tax; (2) imposing a sales tax on food; and (3) imposing a 1 percent tax on all earnings within the state. Would it make any difference to residents of the state in the upper, middle, or lower income groups which tax was imposed? Under what circumstances might an individual in the middle income group favor a tax that increases with income over a sales tax on food? Under what circumstances might the same person prefer the sales tax on food? Which of the three strategies do you favor? Why?

2. Give some arguments for and against a federal personal income tax that would be proportional rather than progressive. Who stands to win and who stands to lose from a flat tax?

3. Suppose that government policy makers want to increase spending in the economy by $10 billion and can follow any one of three policies: $10 billion can be put into the spending stream through the purchase of goods and services; transfer payments can be increased to the point where household expenditures would go up by $10 billion; or taxes can be reduced to the point where $10 billion more would be spent by businesses and households. Does it make any difference whether purchases are increased, transfer payments are increased, or taxes are reduced to expand spending by $10 billion? Why might policy makers choose one policy over another?

4. Do you favor a balanced budget amendment to the U.S. Constitution? Why? What are the economic implications of your position?

5. Application 6.2, "The Temptations of the Social Security Surplus," discusses the impact of the recent large Social Security surpluses on the size of the budget deficit. Should we continue to run these surpluses? Should we lower payroll taxes to bring them in line with current Social Security payments? Should we raise payments to current Social Security recipients? Explain your answers.

6. One area of concern regarding the national debt is the burden it might place on future generations. How might a large national debt burden future generations?

7. Assume that you are a congressperson whose district may be awarded a multimillion-dollar rapid transit project. The economy, however, is in the throes of one of the more severe inflationary periods of the decade. How would you vote on the passage of funds for the project? What would you tell your colleagues? Your constituents?

8. Crowding out, where businesses and households are forced out of the market for borrowed funds by federal government borrowing, occurs because businesses and households are sensitive to interest rate changes while the federal government is not. Why is federal borrowing not sensitive to the interest rate? What would be the effect on federal programs if it were sensitive to the interest rate?

Critical Thinking Case 6

The Budget Deficit

Critical Thinking Skills	Locate data
	Formulate a proposal based on data

Economic Concepts	Government expenditures and revenues
	The budget deficit

This case is different from the others because you are asked to locate specific data and to formulate a proposal based on those data.

The budget deficit problem in the United States is serious and most people agree that the habit of running substantial annual deficits needs to be controlled. However, deficit reduction involves difficult choices: spending must be reduced and/or taxes must be increased. No other course will accomplish this.

There are numerous opinions about how to execute deficit reduction. Many think that all the federal government needs to do to solve the problem is tighten up on student loans, slow the rate of increase in military spending, and catch people who cheat on their income taxes. What they do not realize is that Americans have come to expect the federal government to provide superior military, antipoverty, farm, and housing programs, Social Security and Medicare, clean air and water, and much more.

In this case you are to draw up a financial plan for the federal government that would have eliminated last year's budget deficit if the plan had been adopted.[a] That is, you need to generate a list of the spending cuts and/or tax increases that you would have recommended for adoption in order to balance the federal government budget last year. To devise this plan, the following steps need to be taken.

First, locate the size of last year's federal budget deficit. There are many sources of this figure in your college library. (Hint: Check the source notes given in the tables in this chapter.) Second, locate a detailed federal government budget that provides specific figures for spending categories and programs (such as military, farm programs, education, and other classifications of spending), as well as detailed figures on revenue collected from various taxes (such as individual income taxes) and other sources of revenue.

Next, examine the spending and tax figures for last year and determine where you would have recommended spending cuts and/or tax increases to balance the budget. Develop a proposal that contains enough spending cuts and/or tax increases to completely eliminate the deficit. That is, if the deficit was $200 billion, then your proposal must include $200 billion of recommendations.

Once your proposal is completed, one important question remains: If you were in Congress, would you have made the recommendations in this proposal? Why or why not?

---

[a]If this assignment is given before last year's data are generally available to the public, you may need to use spending, revenue, and deficit figures from two years ago to complete this case.

Suggested Readings

Keith M. Carlson, "Federal Fiscal Policy Since the Employment Act of 1946," Federal Reserve Bank of St. Louis, *Review,* December 1987, pp. 14–25.
Summarizes and examines fiscal policy actions since the Employment Act of 1946.

Economic Report of the President, (Washington, D.C.: U.S. Government Printing Office, published annually).
Includes the annual economic report of the president to Congress, the report of the Council of Economic Advisors relating to the state of the economy, and extensive data on the past and current performance of the economy.

Thomas Havrilesky, "Electoral Cycles in Economic Policy," *Challenge,* July–August 1988, pp. 14–21.
Discusses the relationship between politics, elections, and macroeconomic policy.

Joseph A. Pechman, *Federal Tax Policy,* 5th ed. (Washington, D.C.: The Brookings Institution, 1987).
A comprehensive text that covers various types of taxes, tax policy, and tax legislation.

Setting National Priorities (Washington, D.C.: The Brookings Institution, published annually).
Series that evaluates the federal budget and budget-related matters. Begins with the 1971 federal budget.

Lori L. Taylor, "Reduced Defense Purchasing: Anticipating the Impact on State and Industry Employment," Federal Reserve Bank of Dallas, *Economic Review,* November 1990, pp. 17–27.
Analyzes the near-term and long-term effects on states from cuts in defense purchases.

"Changing Course," *U.S. News & World Report,* October 6, 1986, pp. 46–58.
Two special reports devoted to the Tax Reform Act of 1986.

"Tax Reform — At Last," *Business Week,* September 1, 1986, pp. 54–62.

John E. Yang, "Fiscal Follies: Ever-Growing Federal Deficits Prove the Gramm–Rudman Budget Law to Be a Failure," *The Wall Street Journal,* October 3, 1989, p. A18.
Discusses some reasons for the failure of the Gramm–Rudman–Hollings Act.

Chapter Seven

Money, Financial Institutions, and the Federal Reserve

A stable, controlled money supply is essential to a healthy economy.

Source: Stan Fellerman/The Stock Market.

Chapter Objectives

1. To define money and explain the functions of money.

2. To identify the various measures and components of the U.S. money supply and different monetary standards.

3. To introduce the financial institutions that are important for the maintenance and control of the U.S. money supply, and to highlight commercial banks and commercial bank regulation.

4. To explain the role of the Federal Reserve System, its organization, and the functions that Federal Reserve Banks perform.

5. To discuss the recent deregulatory trend in the banking system that has resulted from legislative and structural changes.

6. To identify some of the factors leading to the savings and loan crisis.

Thus far we have explored several topics that in one way or another involve money. For example, the circular flow model is concerned in part with the passing of money between households and businesses; economic activity expands or contracts as the size of the spending stream increases or decreases; and with inflation, the purchasing power of money deteriorates.

Money is the lifeblood of an economy. Without it, modern economies as we know them could not exist. Even though money does not itself produce goods and services as do land, labor, capital, and entrepreneurship, it makes production and distribution of any size possible. In fact, the very idea of the circular flow of economic activity is predicated on the movement of dollars from businesses to households in return for resources, and from households to businesses in return for goods and services. If a nation's monetary system becomes unstable, its impact will be felt throughout the entire economy.

This chapter lays the groundwork in money and financial institutions for Chapter Eight, where the creation and management of money and the effects of changes in the money supply on the economy are studied. First, this chapter defines money, explains why it is important in an economy, identifies what constitutes the money supply of the United States, and discusses monetary standards. The second part of the chapter is devoted to examining the financial institutions central to the operation of the U.S. economy's monetary system, and to studying the Federal Reserve System. An exploration of recent legislative and structural trends in the deregulation of financial institutions, and of the savings and loan crisis, ends this chapter.

Money

The Definition and Functions of Money

Many people believe that money must be made of precious metal or be backed by a tangible asset such as gold or silver. That is, they believe money must have a high intrinsic value or give claim to something of high intrinsic value. This is not true. **Money** is *anything* that is generally acceptable as a medium of exchange.

A **medium of exchange** is something that people are readily willing to accept in payment for purchases of goods, services, and resources because they know it can be easily used for further transactions. For example, in the United States a $10 bill is a medium of exchange; people are willing to take this bill in payment, knowing that it can be used for other purchases. Since a medium of exchange can be anything, possibilities for money include precious metals, stones, beads, coins, cigarettes, pieces of paper, and electronically transferred numbers. The physical form that money takes makes no difference as long as it is the generally accepted means of payment for purchases in an economy. Some unusual types of money that have been used at different times and in different places are listed in Table 7.1.

If anything can serve as money, how is the **value of money** determined? Since money is a medium of exchange, the value of any money—a $10 bill, for example—is measured by the goods, services, and resources that it can purchase, or for which it can be exchanged. Inflation causes the value of money to decline because fewer goods, services, and resources can be purchased with the same amount of money. Serious bouts of inflation can cause a significant deterioration in the value of money.

What would happen if there were no money—no generally accepted means of payment? In the absence of a medium of exchange, a **barter system** would develop. With barter, a direct exchange of goods and services occurs: for example, a student could exchange some camping gear in return for a psychology text. It is virtually impossible to operate an economy with any degree of sophistication on a barter system. Not only must individuals decide what to buy or sell, they must also locate people willing to take what they offer in trade for what they want. A medium of exchange, or money, removes the problems of barter. Wants need not coincide because every person one deals with is willing to accept money in return for goods or services.

While money serves primarily as a medium of exchange, it also performs two additional functions: it is a **measure of value,** and it provides a **method for storing wealth and delaying payments.** Let us consider money as a measure of value first.

Every nation's money can be expressed in terms of a base unit. In the United States the base unit is the dollar, in France the franc, in Germany the mark, and so on. With money defined in terms of a base unit, the value of every resource, good, and service can be expressed either as a fraction or multiple of that unit. For example, when a house is priced at $120,000 and

Money

Anything that is generally acceptable as a medium of exchange.

Medium of exchange

Something that is generally acceptable as payment for goods, services, and resources; the primary function of money.

Value of money

Measured by the goods, services, and resources that money can purchase.

Barter system

A system where goods and services are exchanged for each other rather than for money.

Measure of value

A function of money; the value of every good, service, and resource can be expressed in terms of, or as a fraction or multiple of, an economy's base unit of money.

Method for storing wealth and delaying payments

A function of money; allows for saving, or storing wealth for future use, and permits credit, or delayed payments.

Table 7.1	Different Forms of Money

Anything can serve as money in a society, provided it is generally acceptable as payment for goods, services, and resources.

Form	Location
Cowrie shells	Africa, India, South Seas (perhaps the first money in the world)
Snail shells	Queen Charlotte Islands
Porpoise teeth	Malaita (island in the Solomon Group)
Boar tusks	New Guinea
Red woodpecker scalps	Karok Tribe on the west coast of North America
Feathers	South Seas
Beer	English coal mines in the mid-19th century
Bars of crystal salt	Ethiopia
Round stones with centers removed	Yap
Glass	Ancient Egypt
Wampum (polished beads)	
Animal skins	
Rice	
Sugar	North American settlements and Colonial period
Rum	
Molasses	
Indigo	
Tobacco	
Cowries	
Tortoise shells	Ancient China
Agricultural implements	

Source: Norman Angell, *The Story of Money* (Garden City, N.Y.: Garden City Publishing Co., Inc., 1929), pp. 73–76, 78–80, 82, 84, 85, 88–90.

a new automobile at $12,000, it is understood that the house is worth 120,000 times the base unit and that the automobile is worth 12,000 times the base unit, or one-tenth of the value of the house. In the absence of money as a measure of value, simple comparisons such as these would be difficult. The worth of all resources, goods, and services would have to be determined by comparing each item to each other item. Thus, the ability to express the values of all resources, goods, and services according to a common measure greatly reduces the amount of information needed to make economic decisions.

Money also provides a method for storing wealth. That is, it allows persons to accumulate their wealth or income with the intention of using it in the future. In short, money eases the process of saving. Money also permits the delay of payment for a good or service and thus facilitates lending and borrowing. A lender might be hesitant to provide either money or goods if there were some question as to the future acceptability of the means of payment.

In light of this last function of money, it can be understood how chronic and severe inflation could weaken or even destroy the fabric of an economy. With serious and prolonged periods of price increases, money's ability to serve as a method for accumulating wealth could be impaired. People could become unwilling to save their money if they anticipate that its future purchasing power will be seriously eroded by rising prices. Correspondingly, borrowing for investment or other purposes might be extremely difficult if lenders anticipate that future dollars used for repayment will have a much lower purchasing power. The functions of money as well as some of the types of money described in this section are illustrated in Application 7.1, "Fixed Assets, Or: Why a Loan in Yap Is Hard to Roll Over."

The Money Supply

Every economy has a supply, or quantity, of money that is used to transact exchange. What makes up the money supply of the U.S. economy and how large is this supply? There is disagreement over the answers to these questions, since some define the money supply more broadly than others.

M1

The narrowest definition of the U.S. money supply; includes coins and paper money in circulation, nonbank-issued traveler's checks, most demand deposits at commercial banks, and other checkable deposits.

Table 7.2 lists the components of the U.S. money supply according to its narrowest definition, which is termed **M1.** Included in this definition are coins and paper money in circulation, nonbank-issued traveler's checks, almost all demand deposits (checking accounts) at commercial banks, and other accounts offered by both commercial banks and other depository institutions that have become generally acceptable as a medium of exchange in recent years.[1] These other accounts, which are classified as "other checkable deposits," include NOW (negotiable order of withdrawal) and ATS (automatic transfer service) accounts, credit union share draft accounts, and demand deposits at savings and loans and other thrift institutions.

Token money

Money with a face value greater than the value of the commodity from which it is made.

Components of M1   In the U.S. economy, coins, which are issued by the U.S. Treasury, are **token money:** the value of the metal in the coin is less than the face value of the coin. If this were not the case, coins might disappear from circulation. For example, in the past, when the price of copper increased to a level where a penny contained almost 1¢ worth of copper, pennies became short in supply. Also, in this regard, a "sandwich" was

---

[1] Only coins and paper money *in circulation* are included in the money supply. Although a large amount of both of these items is "warehoused" in bank and Federal Reserve vaults for future use, it is not spendable or acceptable as a medium of exchange, and therefore not counted as money, until it is in the hands of the public. For an explanation of which demand deposits are excluded from the M1 money supply see the source note in Table 7.2.

Application 7.1

Fixed Assets, Or: Why a Loan in Yap Is Hard to Roll Over

YAP, Micronesia — On this tiny South Pacific island, life is easy and the currency is hard.

Elsewhere, the world's troubled monetary system creaks along. . . . But on Yap the currency is as solid as a rock. In fact, it *is* rock. Limestone to be precise.

For nearly 2,000 years the Yapese have used large stone wheels to pay for major purchases, such as land, canoes and permission to marry. Yap is a U.S. trust territory, and the dollar is used in grocery stores and gas stations. But reliance on stone money . . . continues.

Buying property with stones is "much easier than buying it with U.S. dollars," says John Chodad, who recently purchased a building lot with a 30-inch stone wheel. "We don't know the value of the U.S. dollar." Others on this 37-square-mile island 530 miles southwest of Guam use both dollars and stones. Venito Gurtmag, a builder, recently accepted a four-foot-wide stone disk and $8,700 for a house he built in an outlying village.

Stone wheels don't make good pocket money, so for small transactions, Yapese use other forms of currency, such as beer. Beer is proffered as payment for all sorts of odd jobs, including construction. . . .

Besides stone wheels and beer, the Yapese sometimes spend *gaw*, consisting of necklaces of stone beads strung together around a whale's tooth. They also can buy things with *yar*, a currency made from large sea shells. But these are small change.

The people of Yap have been using stone money ever since a Yapese warrior named Anagumang first brought the huge stones over from limestone caverns on neighboring Palau, some 1,500 to 2,000 years ago. Inspired by the moon, he fashioned the stone into large circles. The rest is history.

Yapese lean the stone wheels against their houses or prop up rows of them in village "banks." Most of the stones are 2½ to five feet in diameter, but some are as much as 12 feet across. Each has a hole in the center so it can be slipped onto the trunk of a fallen betel-nut tree and carried. It takes 20 men to lift some wheels.

By custom, the stones are worthless when broken. You never hear people on Yap musing about wanting a piece of the rock. Rather than risk a broken stone — or back — Yapese tend to leave the larger stones where they are and make a mental accounting that the ownership has been transferred. . . .

The worth of stone money doesn't depend on size. Instead, the pieces are valued by how hard it was to get them here. . . .

There are some decided advantages to using massive stones for money. They are immune to black-market trading, for one thing, and they pose formidable obstacles to pickpockets. In addition, there aren't any sterile debates about how to stabilize the Yapese monetary system. With only about 6,600 stone wheels remaining on the island, the money-supply level stays put. "If you have it, you have it," shrugs Andrew Ken, a Yapese monetary thinker.

But stone money has its limits. Linus Ruuamau, the manager of one of the island's few retail stores, won't accept it for general merchandise. And Al Azuma, who manages the local Bank of Hawaii branch, the only conventional financial institution here, isn't interested in limestone deposits or any sort of shell game. So the money, left uninvested, just gathers moss.

But stone money accords well with Yapese traditions. "There are a lot of instances here where you cannot use U.S. money," Mr. Gurtmag says. One is the settling of disputes. Unlike most money, stones sometimes *can* buy happiness, of a sort; if a Yapese wants to settle an argument, he brings his adversary stone money as a token. "The apology is accepted without question," Mr. Chodad says. "If you used dollars, there'd be an argument over whether it was enough."

Source: Art Pine, "Fixed Assets, Or: Why a Loan in Yap Is Hard to Roll Over," *The Wall Street Journal*, March 29, 1984, pp. 1, 23. Reprinted by permission of *The Wall Street Journal*, © Dow Jones & Company, Inc. 1984. All Rights Reserved Worldwide.

Table 7.2   The U.S. Money Supply: M1

M1 is the narrowest definition of the U.S. money supply.

M1
Coins and paper money in circulation
Nonbank-issued traveler's checks
Demand deposits
Other checkable deposits
NOW accounts
ATS accounts
Credit union share draft accounts
Demand deposits at thrift institutions

Source: Notes to Table 1.21, "Money Stock, Liquid Assets, and Debt Measures," *Federal Reserve Bulletin*, August 1990, p. A14.

Federal Reserve Notes

Paper money issued by the Federal Reserve Banks; includes almost all paper money in circulation.

Currency

Coins and paper money.

Demand deposits

Checking account balances kept primarily at commercial banks.

created by inserting cheaper metal in the middle of the dime and quarter in recent decades.

Paper money constitutes a larger share of our money supply than coins, but is only a small fraction of the total when compared to demand deposits and other checkable deposits. Almost all U.S. paper money is **Federal Reserve Notes.** Federal Reserve Banks, which will be discussed shortly, issue and back this paper money. Notice on a paper bill the inscription at the top which states "Federal Reserve Note," and the circle identifying the particular Federal Reserve Bank that issued the note. Coins and paper money constitute **currency.**

Traveler's checks can be purchased from banking organizations, American Express and other companies, and are honored both domestically and in foreign countries. However, only traveler's checks from "nonbank issuers" are categorized separately in M1, since bank-issued traveler's checks are included in the demand deposit component. Nonbank-issued traveler's checks is the smallest component of M1.

The fourth component of the money supply, **demand deposits,** is checking account balances kept primarily at commercial banks. Demand deposits are merely bookkeeping numbers. When a check is deposited or written, numbers are transferred from one set of records or computer entries to another. Since demand deposits are a very large portion of the U.S. money supply, it can be said that much of the money supply is simply numbers in accounts. It is important to realize that checks themselves are not money. They are merely sheets of paper giving a bank the instruction and authority to draw out all or part of a demand deposit account balance so that its owner can use the funds.

Other checkable deposits

Interest-bearing accounts, such as NOW, ATS, and credit union share draft accounts, that are similar to demand deposits and are offered by banks, savings and loans, and other financial institutions.

Other checkable deposits, such as NOW, ATS, and credit union share draft accounts, are similar to demand deposits but offer interest on the funds in these accounts. While some types of these accounts existed in the 1970s, they did not become broadly permitted and accepted until the early 1980s. Banks and other depository institutions such as savings and loans and credit unions provide these accounts. In recent years, interest-bearing checkable deposits have become increasingly popular, and merchants, utility companies, and other payment receivers make little distinction among checks, drafts, withdrawal orders, and such.

Demand deposits and other checkable deposits form the largest and most important components of the money supply for several reasons. First, it is convenient to transact large or complicated payments by check or draft. Imagine the amount of paper money, even using $100 bills, necessary to purchase an automobile. Second, checks, drafts, and similar instruments serve as records of payment, making it unnecessary to receive and retain a receipt for all transactions. Third, these accounts offer an element of safety. If checks or withdrawal orders are stolen or lost, the institutions against which they are drawn can be instructed to stop payment.

Table 7.3 gives the amount of currency, traveler's checks, demand deposits, and other checkable deposits in circulation each December from 1980 through 1990. Demand deposits had been the largest component of the M1 money supply, but began to fall in size in 1987, and by 1990 other checkable deposits was the largest component. The growth in other checkable deposits began in the early 1980s after the Depository Institutions Deregulation and Monetary Control Act of 1980 allowed all depository institutions to offer interest-bearing checkable deposits. Obviously, from Table 7.3, these accounts have been very successful, growing from 6.5 percent of the money supply in 1980 to 35.2 percent in 1990.

Notice the column toward the right-hand side of Table 7.3 that shows the total M1 money supply figure for each year as a percentage of that year's GNP. Every year the total amount spent on new goods and services exceeds the amount of money in circulation. For example, the money supply in 1990 was equal to only 15.4 percent of the total expenditures made on new goods and services over that year. Obviously, so much output can be purchased with so few dollars because of the circular flow of economic activity: the same dollars are spent several times over during the course of the year.

The average turnover of the money supply in relationship to annual GNP is termed the **velocity of money.** In other words, velocity measures the average number of times a dollar is spent during a year as it is used for the purchase of new goods and services. The far right-hand column of Table 7.3 gives the velocity of M1 for the years 1980 through 1990. Notice that while velocity fluctuated somewhat from year to year, it was relatively stable between 6.1 and 6.8 except for the years 1986 and 1987, which deviated from the general trend. It is easy to understand why, generally, velocity does not change radically from year to year when one considers that there is little

Velocity of money

The average number of times the money supply is turned over in a year in relationship to GNP.

Table 7.3

Currency, Traveler's Checks, Demand Deposits, and Other Checkable Deposits (Billions of Dollars)[a]

Demand deposits and other checkable deposits are the largest components of the M1 money supply. Other checkable deposits have grown in importance since 1980.

Year	Currency (Coins and Paper Money)	Traveler's Checks	Demand Deposits	Other Checkable Deposits	Total (M1)	Total (M1) as a Percentage of GNP	Velocity
1980	$118.8	$3.9	$274.7	$ 27.4	$424.8	15.5%	6.5
1981	126.1	4.1	243.6	78.5	452.3	14.8	6.8
1982	136.4	4.1	247.3	104.1	491.9	15.5	6.5
1983	150.5	4.6	251.6	131.2	537.9	15.8	6.3
1984	160.9	4.9	256.9	145.7	567.9	15.1	6.6
1985	173.1	5.5	282.0	180.4	641.0	16.0	6.3
1986	186.2	6.0	319.5	235.0	746.5	17.6	5.7
1987	199.3	6.5	298.6	262.0	766.4	17.0	5.9
1988	214.8	6.9	298.9	283.8	804.5	16.5	6.1
1989	225.3	6.9	291.6	288.4	812.1	15.6	6.4
1990	249.4	7.8	289.4	296.6	843.2	15.4[b]	6.5

[a]Figures are not seasonally adjusted and are given for the month of December.

[b]1990 GNP figure is preliminary.

Source: Table 1.21, "Money Stock, Liquid Assets, and Debt Measures," *Federal Reserve Bulletin*, May 1984, March 1985, March 1988, and March 1991, p. A13. GNP figures for calculation of percentages are from U.S., *Economic Report of the President* (Washington, D.C.: U.S. Government Printing Office, 1991), p. 286.

variation in the monthly frequency with which paychecks are received and major payments are made.

Other Money Supply Measures   As noted earlier, some controversy exists as to what constitutes the nation's money supply. M1, which is the narrowest definition of the money supply, is considered by many to be too narrow. This is especially true in light of the recent creation and growth of new types of accounts, not included in M1, that can be used to transact the purchase of goods and services, or can be readily converted to an account that can be used for payment. For example, suppose a person receives a paycheck for $1,000 and puts $500 into a demand deposit account at a commercial bank, $200 into a savings account at a thrift institution, and $300 into a **money market deposit account (MMDA)** at a commercial bank. According to the definition of M1, only the $500 that went into the checking account at the commercial bank would be considered money. Although the funds in the savings account are easily transferable to a checking account and the funds in the money market deposit account can be spent, they are not counted in M1.

Money market deposit account (MMDA)

An account at a commercial bank or thrift institution that pays interest and allows limited checking privileges.

Table 7.4   Definitions and Sizes of M2, M3, and L

There are several definitions of the money supply, each becoming broader by building on the preceding definition.

M2	M3	L
M1	M2	M3
+ money market deposit accounts	+ time deposits of $100,000 or more	+ commercial paper
+ savings deposits	+ other[a]	+ U.S. savings bonds
+ time deposits of less than $100,000		+ short-term Treasury securities
+ money market mutual funds		+ other[a]
+ other[a]		
M2 = $3.3 trillion[b]	M3 = $4.1 trillion[b]	L = $5.0 trillion[b]

[a]For more specific information on these, see the source given below.

[b]M2 and M3 are for December 1990, and L is for November 1990, not seasonally adjusted.

Source: Notes to Table 1.10, "Reserves, Money Stock, Liquid Assets, and Debt Measures," and Table 1.21, *Federal Reserve Bulletin,* March 1991, pp. A3, A13.

M2

M1 plus savings and small-denomination time deposit accounts, money market deposit accounts, and others.

Other measures of the money supply are M2, M3, and L. The components of each of these measures are given in Table 7.4. Notice that each of these measures builds on a narrower definition. For example, **M2** includes M1 plus money market deposit accounts, savings deposits, certificates of deposit (time deposits) of less than $100,000 and others.

M2 has become an increasingly important measure of the money supply to observe because it includes savings and time deposits that can be easily converted to spendable funds and accounts that allow limited checkable transactions. For example, persons holding funds in a money market deposit account can make a limited number of payments from their account per month by means of a checkable instrument that is not readily distinguishable from a demand deposit check.

Liquidity

Ease of converting an asset to its value in cash or spendable funds.

The money supply measures M3 and L are not watched quite as closely as M1 and M2 because, as can be seen in Table 7.4, some of their components are not very **liquid,** or are not easily convertible to cash or spendable funds. There is also a substantial difference in the sizes of these measures. As pointed out in Table 7.3, M1 was $843.2 billion in 1990, and as indicated in Table 7.4, M2 was $3.3 trillion, M3 was $4.1 trillion, and L was $5.0 trillion in 1990.

Monetary Standards

Whether or not an economy's money supply is backed by something of value depends upon the monetary standard selected by that economy. An economy in which money is backed by something of tangible value is said to be

Commodity monetary standard
Exists when an economy's money is backed by something of tangible value such as gold or silver.

on a **commodity monetary standard.** With this type of standard, the monetary authority has an amount of gold, silver, or other item equal in value to the money. If the money is backed by gold, the economy is on a gold standard; if it is backed by silver, the economy is on a silver standard.

For much of its history the U.S. economy was on a commodity standard. Prior to 1933 the United States had a gold-coin standard, where gold not only backed the money supply, but also freely circulated in the hands of the public. The use of gold pieces as money was common. Then, U.S. citizens were asked to turn their gold in to the government, and in 1934 the United States went on a gold-bullion standard. This meant that gold backed the money supply but was no longer available to the general public. Under this gold-bullion standard, however, foreign holders of dollars were paid in gold. In the years after 1950 more and more international debts were paid in gold, and the U.S. gold supply gradually diminished. This brought about a reduction in the gold backing of the money supply. By 1971 official U.S. gold reserves had decreased to the point where President Richard Nixon thought it advisable to freeze the gold supply. U.S. gold was to be made available to no one, and the dollar was no longer to be converted to gold, not even to settle international transactions.

Paper monetary standard
Exists when money is not backed by anything of tangible value such as gold or silver.

Since 1971 the U.S. economy has been on a **paper monetary standard.** This means that money itself has little or no intrinsic value and that it does not represent a claim to any commodity such as gold or silver. The backing of paper money is the strength of the economy, the willingness of people to accept the money in exchange for goods and services, and faith and trust in the purchasing power of the money.

Is it better or worse for a nation to be on a paper standard rather than a gold, silver, or other commodity standard? It could be argued that there is more faith in a money supply if it is backed by gold or silver. However, history does not bear this out. In the past, panics and monetary crises have occurred even when money was backed by precious metal. In fact, the knowledge that paper money can be converted into gold or silver could make people act more dramatically on their fears than they would if the monetary authority would only redeem paper money for more paper money. It is also true that the amount of gold or silver a nation possesses may have very little to do with its economic needs and potential. Since a nation's money supply is the lifeblood of its economy, it may be more desirable for the amount of money in an economy to be tied to conditions and needs of the economy itself rather than the availability of a commodity like gold or silver. However, an important potential problem with a paper standard is that the administrators of the money supply may have wide latitude in the decisions they make concerning that supply and may not properly manage and control it.

Application 7.2, "Gold! Gold! Gold!," gives some information about U.S.–owned gold and the gold held at the Federal Reserve Bank in New York.

Application 7.2

Gold! Gold! Gold!

The largest known accumulation of gold in the world . . . and about a third of the official monetary gold reserves of the noncommunist nations is stored in the Federal Reserve Bank of New York. . . . Here, in one of the most unusual vaults in the world, about 80 feet below Nassau Street—one of the busiest streets in the Wall Street district—gold belonging to the U.S., foreign nations, central banks and international monetary organizations rests on the bedrock of Manhattan Island. An awesome and impressive chamber nearly half the length of a football field, the gold vault is a popular tourist stop, attracting over 20,000 visitors a year. . . .

Only a very small fraction of the gold in the vault is U.S. owned. More than half of the U.S. gold stock . . . is kept in the bullion depositories at Fort Knox, Kentucky, and West Point, New York. Most of the remainder is kept at the Denver and Philadelphia Mints and the San Francisco Assay Office. . . .

Handling billions of dollars of gold seems like a glamorous job, but it's just plain hard work. Hydraulic lifts and conveyor belts, which can boost bars to ceiling height and bring them down, have partially relieved the physical strain, but lifting, swinging and positioning 27 pounds again and again is arduous. Teams of "gold stackers" work in shifts that allow them frequent rest periods. The job also has its hazards. The stackers wear lightweight, but strong, magnesium shoe covers to protect their feet against accidentally dropped bars. . . .

Storing over $14 billion of gold—not to mention billions of dollars in securities, paper currency and coin—makes extreme security measures mandatory. The total weight of the bullion—about 10,600 tons—makes it virtually impossible to steal, but this is only one deterrent. . . .

The vault's design is a masterpiece of security engineering. The gold vault is actually one floor of a three-story bunker of vaults arranged like strongboxes stacked on top of one another. The massive walls of each vault are made of reinforced structural concrete and are virtually impregnable. . . .

The bank has one of the largest private, uniformed protection forces in the nation. Guards must prove their ability with a revolver each month on the bank's firing range. Although the minimum requirement is a marksman's score, most are qualified as experts. Guards must also be proficient with other "heavier" weapons. The protection force is supplemented by closed-circuit television monitors and by an electronic surveillance system that signals the central guardroom if a vault door is opened or closed. An alarm system alerts guards to seal all security areas and exits from the bank, which can be done very quickly. . . .

A gold bar physically shows its origin and history. Its shape generally indicates whether it was cast in the U.S. or abroad. U.S. bars are usually rectangular bricks, 7 inches long, $3\frac{5}{8}$ inches wide and between $1\frac{5}{8}$ and $1\frac{3}{4}$ inches thick. It is often possible to tell by its shape where a particular U.S. bar was cast—bars cast at the Denver Mint have rounded corners while those cast at the New York or San Francisco Assay Offices have sharp corners. Most bars cast abroad are trapezoidal.

Occasionally, visitors may see bars that are slimmer than usual. These bars, nicknamed "Hershey bars," result when an amount of gold too small to make a full bar is left in the smelter's crucible at the end of the casting process. Since the purity of the gold varies between different pourings, this leftover metal cannot be added to other pourings and must be cast into a separate bar.

Source: Federal Reserve Bank of New York, *Key to the Gold Vault*, revised edition 1989, pp. 2, 4, 6, and 8.

Financial Depository Institutions

Financial depository institutions are important for maintenance and control of the U.S. money supply. These include commercial banks, savings and loan associations, variations on savings and loans such as mutual savings banks, and credit unions. A **financial depository institution** has two basic functions: to accept and maintain deposits, and to make loans. The various types of institutions are distinguished by the kinds of deposits and loans they are permitted to offer, and by the degree of regulation they face.

Financial depository institution

An institution that accepts and maintains deposits, and makes loans; can create and destroy money.

Financial depository institutions are important because they have the ability to create and destroy money. Money is created when loans are made by these institutions and destroyed when loans are repaid. The process through which this is done will be thoroughly explored in the next chapter. For now it is important to know that these institutions, with their special abilities to accept deposits and make loans, are an important vehicle for expanding and contracting the money supply.

Commercial Banks

Commercial bank

An institution that holds and maintains checking accounts (demand deposits) for its customers, makes commercial (business) and other loans, and performs other functions.

The expression "banking" refers to the operations of a particular type of financial organization called a commercial bank. A **commercial bank** is an institution that holds and maintains checking accounts, or demand deposits, for its customers, makes industrial, commercial, and consumer loans, and performs a number of other functions such as the servicing of savings accounts and the sale of traveler's checks. Since the Monetary Control Act of 1980 it has become difficult to distinguish between commercial banks and other financial depository institutions. Prior to that act, the ability to offer checkable deposits and make business loans was held almost exclusively by commercial banks and served as their primary differentiating characteristic.

As seen earlier in Table 7.3, approximately 34 percent of the U.S. money supply (M1) in 1990 was composed of demand deposits, or checking accounts, at commercial banks. This amounted to $289 billion. In addition, commercial banks held some portion of other checkable deposits as well as $1.6 trillion in MMDAs and savings and time deposits.[2] With these figures it is easy to see that commercial banks are the most important of all financial depository institutions.

In the United States there are over 13,000 commercial banks, each organized to be a profit-making corporation. These banks operate by attracting deposits and converting them to loans, securities, and other interest-earning assets for the bank.

Commercial Bank Regulation   Although commercial banks are like other businesses in that they are profit-oriented organizations, they are unlike

[2] Table 1.21, "Money Stock, Liquid Assets, and Debt Measures," *Federal Reserve Bulletin*, March 1991, p. A13.

other businesses in the indispensable role they play in the proper functioning of the monetary system of the U.S. economy. Because these banks maintain a large portion of the money supply, and because their actions can change the actual quantity of money in the economy, it is necessary to ensure that commercial banks be sound and secure, and not abuse their money-creating abilities. To accomplish this aim, a number of agencies, both governmental and quasi-governmental, set standards and regulations for commercial banks.

The regulations imposed upon commercial banks are varied; they differ according to the function of the overseeing agency. Included among these regulations are the amount of backing needed for deposits, the degree of risk permitted in a bank's investments, the amount of money capital needed to begin operations, and the ability of a bank to open branch offices.

Dual banking system
The label given to the U.S. banking system because both the federal and state governments have the right to charter banks.

When a commercial bank is organized, a corporate charter must be obtained before it can function. Because both the federal and state governments have the right to charter banks, the United States has a **dual banking system.** That is, a bank may be chartered by the federal government or by a state government. Thus, the first line of regulation for a commercial bank comes from the government unit from which it obtains its charter. If a bank incorporates under a federal charter, it is subject to regulation by the U.S. Comptroller of the Currency; if it incorporates as a state bank, a state banking agency has supervisory authority.

National bank
A commercial bank incorporated under a federal rather than a state charter.

The second line of regulation comes from the Federal Reserve, an agency that will be discussed shortly. Banks that incorporate with a federal charter, called **national banks,** must belong to the Federal Reserve System. State chartered banks may choose to belong to the system and, on joining, are termed state member banks. In addition to regulating its members, the Federal Reserve imposes some uniform regulations on all commercial banks regardless of whether they belong to the system or not. Since the Monetary Control Act of 1980, Federal Reserve regulatory authority over all banks has expanded, so the distinction between Federal Reserve member and nonmember banks has lessened.

Federal Deposit Insurance Corporation (FDIC)
A government agency established in 1933 to insure deposits in commercial banks up to a specified amount; banks belonging to the Federal Reserve System must join the FDIC.

The third line of regulation comes from the **Federal Deposit Insurance Corporation (FDIC)** , which was established in 1933 and insures deposits in commercial banks up to $100,000.[3] Banks that belong to the Federal Reserve must join the Federal Deposit Insurance Corporation, so that all national and state member banks are insured. State banks that do not belong to the Federal Reserve may affiliate with the Federal Deposit Insurance Corporation. These are termed nonmember state insured banks and constitute the majority of commercial banks. There are relatively few banks that are nonmember noninsured state banks.

---

[3] New insurance coverage rules that took effect in July 1990 specify the amount of coverage by type of deposit account and ownership.

With such a substantial amount of regulation, do banks fail? If they do fail, are they insured? Between 1971 and 1980, 83 banks with deposits totaling $5.4 billion were closed: four of these were noninsured. Between 1981 and 1985, 301 banks with deposits totaling $30.2 billion were closed: two were noninsured. By 1988, 569 more insured banks holding $52.4 billion in deposits were closed. Although the number of closings in recent years does not approach the record number of bank failures in the 1930s — 4,004 in 1933, for example — it is interesting to note the upward movement of closings since the deregulation of financial institutions in 1980 (which will be covered shortly).[4] Most bank failures result from heavy loan losses combined with deposit withdrawal.

Other Financial Depository Institutions

Other financial depository institutions that play an important role in the maintenance of the money supply are savings and loan associations, savings banks, and credit unions. In 1988 there were 2,526 savings and loan associations, 1,113 savings banks, and 13,878 credit unions. While the number of these institutions is larger than commercial banks, their total size is smaller. For example, all savings institutions and credit unions together had $1.8 trillion of assets in 1988, while total commercial bank assets were over $3.1 trillion.[5]

Prior to the banking legislation of the early 1980s, these institutions primarily offered passbook savings accounts and certificates of deposit. Savings and loan associations and mutual savings banks in turn used their deposited funds mainly for mortgage loans, while credit unions made shorter-term loans for such purposes as home improvements and the purchase of durable consumer goods. Regulation of these institutions was under the jurisdiction of a number of agencies such as the Federal Home Loan Bank.

Significant changes were made in the legislation regulating these institutions in the early 1980s in order to permit them to offer a greater variety of deposit accounts, to make different types of loans, and to bring some aspects of their operations under Federal Reserve control. The deregulation of deposits and loans has caused a serious crisis in the savings and loan industry, requiring financial intervention from the government. This crisis will be discussed in the section on deregulation later in this chapter.

---

[4] A bank closing is defined as either a permanent or temporary suspension of operations by order of the bank's supervisory authorities or its directors. The bank closing data are from U.S. Bureau of the Census, *Statistical Abstract of the United States: 1987*, 107th ed. (Washington, D.C.: U.S. Government Printing Office, 1986), p. 483; and *Statistical Abstract: 1990*, 110th ed., 1990, p. 497. The 1933 bank failure figure is from Bruce R. Dalgaard, *Money, Financial Institutions, and Economic Activity* (Glenview, Ill.: Scott, Foresman and Company, 1987), p. 103.

[5] U.S. Bureau of the Census, *Statistical Abstract of the United States: 1990*, 110th ed. (Washington, D.C.: U.S. Government Printing Office, 1990), pp. 494, 500.

Figure   7.1

Functional Structure of the Federal Reserve System

The Federal Reserve System is headed by the Board of Governors, and many system activities are carried out through the Federal Reserve Banks and their branches.

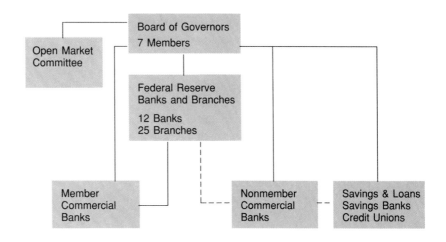

The Federal Reserve System

Federal Reserve System

Coordinates commercial banking operations, regulates some aspects of all depository institutions, and oversees the U.S. money supply.

Created in 1913, the **Federal Reserve** is the system that coordinates commercial banking operations, regulates some aspects of all depository institutions, and oversees the U.S. money supply. Congress created the Federal Reserve System, or the Fed, as it is often called, because money and banking practices had been in disarray. Previous to the creation of the Fed, there had been a lack of central organization, a hodgepodge of state and federal banking legislation, a history of questionable banking practices, and a recurrence of monetary panics.

The authority of the Federal Reserve is considerable. Primary among its responsibilities is the adjustment of the supply of money to meet the needs of the economy. Through its control of the size of the money supply, the Fed has the ability to influence the levels of employment and prices in the economy and to alleviate the problems of unemployment and inflation.

Board of Governors

The seven-member board heading the Federal Reserve System; develops objectives concerning monetary policy and banking and other financial institutional practices; determines appropriate policies to meet those objectives.

Organization of the Federal Reserve System

The Federal Reserve System is organized on both a functional and a geographic basis. Figure 7.1 outlines the important features in the system's functional structure.

At the head of the system is the **Board of Governors,** a group of seven members, each appointed by the president of the United States and confirmed by the Senate for a 14-year term.[6] One member is designated by the president as chairman and serves as the spokesperson for Federal Reserve policy. The Board of Governors assumes duties and responsibilities typical of the head of any organization: it develops objectives consistent with its authority over money and banking practices, and it determines appropriate policies to meet those objectives. The **Open Market Committee,** which includes the Board of Governors among its members, carries out the most important procedure for money supply control: it authorizes the buying and selling of government securities by the Federal Reserve.[7]

Open Market Committee

Oversees the buying and selling of government securities by the Federal Reserve System.

The middle of the Federal Reserve System structure is made up of the 12 **Federal Reserve Banks** and their 25 branches, which are located throughout the country. These are not commercial banks, but instead deal with commercial banks and other financial institutions and perform a variety of functions that will be covered shortly. Each Federal Reserve Bank is an independent corporation with its own board of directors, and all 12 Federal Reserve Banks execute the same functions. The remainder of the Federal Reserve System is made up of member commercial banks that have direct relationships with a Federal Reserve Bank, and nonmember commercial banks, savings and loan associations, savings banks, and credit unions that are influenced by some Federal Reserve policies and may depend on the Fed to perform some services for them.

Federal Reserve Banks

Twelve banks, located in different parts of the country, that deal with commercial banks and other financial institutions.

The Fed is also organized geographically. The United States is divided into 12 Federal Reserve districts, each represented by a Federal Reserve Bank that is responsible for its own branch banks and the member commercial banks in its geographic area. Figure 7.2 illustrates the 12 Federal Reserve districts.

Functions of the Federal Reserve Banks

The Federal Reserve Banks and their branches perform a variety of functions that do not directly involve the typical commercial bank or savings and loan customer. In fact, there is little reason for the average individual or business-person to ever enter a Federal Reserve Bank.

One function of a Federal Reserve Bank is to supervise and examine member banks within its district. For this purpose, each Federal Reserve Bank employs a staff of examiners who periodically check the financial condition and compliance to system regulations of each member bank.

A second function of a Federal Reserve Bank is to maintain reserve accounts for member commercial banks and for nonmember financial de-

---

[6] The original intention of the long, 14-year term was to keep any one president from appointing a majority of the Board of Governors. However, many appointees do not serve for 14 years, causing the original intention of this arrangement to be violated. For example, by the end of President Ronald Reagan's second term, all members of the Board of Governors were his appointees.

[7] The operation of the Open Market Committee will be discussed in detail in Chapter Eight.

Figure 7.2   Federal Reserve Districts

The United States is divided into 12 Federal Reserve Districts, each with its own
Federal Reserve Bank.

LEGEND

—— Boundaries of Federal Reserve Districts   ◉ Federal Reserve Bank Cities

— Boundaries of Federal Reserve Branch   • Federal Reserve Branch Cities
    Territories

✪ Board of Governors of the Federal   Alaska and Hawaii are in District 12.
    Reserve System

Source: *Federal Reserve Bulletin*, November 1990, p. A81.

Reserve account

A deposit in the name of
a financial institution held
at a Federal Reserve Bank
or other designated place.

pository institutions that keep their reserves at the Fed. A **reserve account**
is a deposit in the name of a financial institution that is held at a Federal
Reserve Bank or other designated place. While financial depository institutions must hold a minimum amount on reserve, the actual amount fluctuates
daily and may exceed the minimum. However, because no interest is earned
on these reserves, financial institutions like to keep the balances in their
accounts close to the minimum required.

Third, Federal Reserve Banks provide the means for putting coins and paper money into or out of circulation. Each bank maintains a warehouse of used and newly minted coins and paper money in its vault (with extensive security arrangements). When the public desires to carry more money in the form of coins and paper, as happens, for example, around the Christmas holidays, more checks, drafts, and such are cashed. And as financial institutions require more coins and paper money to convert their customers' deposits to currency, they order what they need from the Fed. When the Fed delivers cash to a financial institution, it is paid for out of that institution's reserve account. When less cash is desired by the public, as happens, for example, after the Christmas season, currency begins to build up at banks, savings and loans, and other depository institutions. These institutions may return their cash to the Fed and receive credit in their reserve accounts. Also, when currency is worn-out, it is retired by the Fed and, in the case of paper money, destroyed.

A fourth function of the Federal Reserve Banks is check clearing. Each day millions of checks are sorted through the Fed's machinery as financial institutions send in checks drawn on other institutions that they have received as deposits. These checks are sorted to be returned to the institutions on which they were drawn. If a check is drawn on a bank or other financial institution within the same Federal Reserve district, the process is simple. However, if the check is drawn on an institution in another Federal Reserve district, it is forwarded to that district for further processing.

Check clearing causes a financial institution's reserve account to fluctuate. When a check that has been deposited at a financial institution is sent to the Fed for clearing, the full amount of that check is credited (added) to that institution's reserve account. When a check drawn on an institution (written by a customer with an account there) goes through the Fed clearing procedure, the full amount of that check is subtracted from that institution's reserve account. Thus, a financial institution's reserve account fluctuates daily, with the size of the fluctuation depending upon the value of checks deposited and written. It is not necessary that all checks go through the Federal Reserve Banks. Other clearing-house arrangements exist, especially where the Federal Reserve Bank is a far distance from financial institutions. Checks that are cleared through facilities other than the Federal Reserve still have the same effect on a financial depository institution's reserve account: *checks deposited increase reserves, and checks written by a bank's customers decrease reserves.*

Finally, the Federal Reserve Banks act as fiscal agents for the U.S. government. In this regard, they perform a variety of chores, such as servicing the checking accounts of the federal government and handling many of the tasks associated with the maintenance of Treasury securities. For example, the Fed conducts the bid auctions for Treasury bills, notes, and bonds, maintains the necessary records for these securities, and prepares the interest payments.

Test Your Understanding

Changes in a Bank's Reserve Account[a]

[a]Answers can be found at the end of the book. All depository institutions in this exercise are hypothetical.

1. The First National Bank of Latrobe starts its day with $899,356 in its reserve account. During the day $125,678 in checks are deposited and cleared, and $137,900 in checks written by the bank's customers are cleared. How much is in First National's reserve account at the end of this day?

2. California One begins its day with $1,566,444 in its reserve account at the Fed. During the day it returns $235,000 to the Fed in currency that has accumulated in its vaults and is not needed to service its customers. What is the bank's reserve account balance after the cash is returned?

3. The MBMB Bank of El Campo has $2,450,221 in its reserve account at the start of the day. During the day, $644,970 in deposited checks and $788,450 in checks written by MBMB's customers are cleared. In addition, $350,000 in currency is delivered to the bank by the Fed. What is the bank's reserve account balance at the end of the day?

4. Westmoreland Bank ends a Wednesday with $4,544,500 in its reserve account. On Thursday its customers deposit $345,660 in checks, and on Friday they deposit $467,845 in checks, both clearing on the day deposited. On Thursday and Friday, $266,890 and $351,115, respectively, in checks written by the bank's customers are cleared. In addition, the Fed picks up $100,000 in currency on Friday from Westmoreland to return to the Fed's vaults. How much does Westmoreland Bank have in its reserve account at the end of business on Friday?

Correspondent banking

An interbank relationship involving deposits and various services.

Many of the functions performed by the Federal Reserve Banks are necessary for the smooth operation of the banking system. However, sometimes banks depend upon each other instead of the Fed for these operational tasks. In this case, banks set up a relationship called **correspondent banking.** Typically, in this arrangement a smaller bank keeps some deposits with a larger bank and receives advice and various services in return.

"Test Your Understanding: Changes in a Bank's Reserve Account" provides an opportunity to explore some of the ways a bank's reserve account changes.

Deregulatory Trends in the Banking System

During the 1980s, after decades of strict government regulatory control over the banking system in the United States, legislative and structural changes occurred causing a movement toward the deregulation of financial institutions. Many of these changes have been so swift that it is difficult to define the roles of various institutions and to fully evaluate the impact of the changes. This movement toward deregulation has allowed a much larger number of financial institutions to perform traditional banking functions, permitted the creation of larger banking organizations, and created some problems in the savings and loan industry.

Legislative Changes

Depository Institutions Deregulation and Monetary Control Act (1980)

Legislation that altered the traditional roles of many financial institutions and increased the control of the Federal Reserve System.

In March 1980 one of the most significant laws pertaining to money and banking in the United States was passed: the **Depository Institutions Deregulation and Monetary Control Act.** This law substantially altered the traditional roles of many financial institutions because it permitted commercial banks, savings and loans, savings banks, and credit unions to perform some nearly identical functions. Prior to this act, there was a clear distinction between commercial banks and the other institutions.

Among other changes, the act permitted all depository institutions to offer interest-bearing checking accounts to individuals and nonprofit organizations. Before this law, commercial banks were the only institutions offering checking accounts. The similarity between commercial banks and other depository institutions was also increased because the act changed the lending abilities of some depository institutions; for example, it authorized federal credit unions to make residential real estate loans, and permitted savings and loan associations to issue credit cards.[8] Provisions were also made to phase out **Regulation Q,** a law that set the maximum amount of interest that could be paid on deposits.

Regulation Q

Determined the maximum interest paid on deposits; phased out by the Monetary Control Act of 1980.

The Monetary Control Act also increased the authority of the Federal Reserve in monetary matters and added a relationship between the Federal Reserve and nonmember depository institutions that had not previously existed. Prior to the act, Federal Reserve activity centered primarily around its member banks. After the act, all depository institutions were able to keep reserves at a Federal Reserve Bank, Federal Reserve control over reserves was broadened, and the services of Federal Reserve Banks (such as check clearing) became available to all member and nonmember institutions for a fee.[9] Other important changes brought about by the Monetary Control Act will be covered in Chapter Eight.

Garn–St. Germain Act (1982)

Act strengthening the deregulatory trend started with the Monetary Control Act of 1980; reinforced similarities among financial depository institutions.

The **Garn–St. Germain Act,** passed by Congress in 1982, strengthened the deregulatory trend started with the Monetary Control Act of 1980. Among its many provisions, this act reinforced the similarity among savings and loans, other thrift institutions, and commercial banks by permitting the

---

[8]"Banking Act Makes Major Changes," *Economic Review,* Federal Reserve Bank of Atlanta, March–April 1980, pp. 4, 5.

[9]Charles R. McNeill (with some discussion by Denise M. Rechter), "The Depository Institutions Deregulation and Monetary Control Act of 1980," *Federal Reserve Bulletin,* June 1980, pp. 445–448.

thrifts to offer new types of accounts and to make commercial loans. This act also enabled some structural changes (which will be discussed shortly) to develop in the system.[10]

Structural Changes

Branch banking

The operation of more than one facility by a bank to perform its functions.

The size of a bank or other financial depository institution depends upon its ability to attract deposits. Two factors are important in this regard: location, and **branch banking**, which is the operation of more than one facility by a bank to perform its functions. A bank located in a city with a significant business base, such as New York, has more potential to become large than a bank located in a small, rural community. Likewise, a bank that can open many branches has more potential to become large than a bank with limited branching ability. Whether a bank can open branches, and where these branches can be established, is determined by state law: there is no uniform federal law regarding branch banking. Some states ban branch banking and allow each bank to operate only one facility, some allow limited branching (such as in the same community or in a contiguous county), and some permit statewide branching. The limitation on branching has kept many banking organizations small.

Some of the key structural changes in financial institutions in more recent years have been the formation and growth of bank holding companies, interstate banking, and nonbank banks. These developments occurred as financial organizations found ways around state branching laws, or successfully lobbied for changes in them.

Bank holding company

A corporation formed for the purpose of owning, or holding, the controlling shares of stock in a bank or banks.

A **bank holding company** is a corporation formed for the purpose of owning, or holding, the controlling shares of stock in a bank or a number of banks. Multibank holding companies provide a means for circumventing branch banking laws by allowing a holding company to own several independent banks and coordinate some of their functions. In 1970 there were 121 bank holding companies, which owned 895 banks and 3,260 branches, and held $93 billion in assets. By 1987 there were 6,503 holding companies, which owned 9,316 banks and 41,362 branches, and held $2.4 trillion in assets.[11]

Interstate banking

The performance of banking services in more than one state by a single organization.

Interstate banking is the performance of banking services in more than one state by a single organization. Prior to the late 1970s, most banks — even those where statewide branching was allowed — were limited to operating facilities within their own state. Since then, changes in federal legislation have permitted interstate operations to finance U.S. exports, acquire failing depository institutions, and open subsidiaries to perform some (but not all)

---

[10] Dalgaard, p. 361; and David S. Kidwell and Richard L. Peterson, *Financial Institutions, Markets, and Money*, 3d ed. (Hinsdale, Ill.: The Dryden Press, 1987), p. 126.

[11] U.S. Bureau of the Census, *Statistical Abstract of the United States: 1990*, 110th ed. (Washington, D.C.: U.S. Government Printing Office, 1990), p. 495.

of the functions of a depository institution. Federal legislation also allows states to change their banking laws to permit some types of interstate operations. In this regard, some states have been entering into reciprocity agreements with contiguous states allowing for the possible development of regional banking.[12] The savings and loan crisis has also increased interstate banking as failed savings and loans are bought by other thrifts and commercial banks. For example, North Carolina National Bank Corporation (NCNB) created NCNB Texas in 1988 which has been purchasing banks and thrifts throughout that state. NCNB also has operations in South Carolina, Georgia, and Florida.[13]

Nonbank bank

A company that can either offer depository accounts or make commercial loans, but cannot do both.

A **nonbank bank** is an organization that can *either* offer depository accounts *or* make commercial loans. Since these are the two distinguishing functions of a commercial bank, a nonbank bank is not permitted to perform both functions. In recent years, major corporations such as Sears, Roebuck and American Express have begun to offer financial services such as credit cards and certificates of deposit that were traditionally performed by banks. The regulation, status, and impact of nonbank banks has become a source of confusion and controversy. Since there are some possible adverse effects that nonbank banks could have on the banking system, legislation has been passed to limit their growth.

Deregulatory Problems

Deregulation has prompted the growth of a complex financial services industry and has caused rapid changes in the performance of traditional banking roles. The biggest problem with deregulation, however, has been in the savings and loan industry, where the failure of a substantial number of institutions and the insolvency of many more have required the federal government to provide a sizable amount of financial assistance to the industry. Some people identify the savings and loan crisis as one of the major concerns facing the United States in the 1990s.

The legislative changes of the early 1980s created several problems that have contributed to the savings and loan situation. First, the phasing out of Regulation Q, which put a cap on interest rates that could be paid on various types of deposit accounts, prompted many savings and loans to offer unprofitably high interest rates on certificates of deposit in order to attract funds. In some cases, especially as this crisis began to unfold, institutions that were already in poor financial condition raised their rates in efforts to bring in additional deposits. This action by weak institutions placed healthy institutions in a predicament: they were faced with having to offer these

[12] Dalgaard, pp. 142–144; and Kidwell and Peterson, pp. 263–265.
[13] Leslie Wayne, "NCNB Texas is No. 1 in Buying Savings Units," *The New York Times*, June 28, 1990, pp. C1, C5.

higher rates in order to stay competitive with other savings and loans and keep their own depositors. As a result, interest rates paid by savings and loans to their depositors were often at unprofitably high levels.

A second factor contributing to this crisis was the types of loans the savings and loans were making. Prior to deregulation, savings and loans concentrated their loan making on home mortgages. With the new legislation, they were now permitted to make many different types of loans. As a result, many S&Ls committed to loans that were risky and resulted in heavy losses. Evidence also exists that some loans were made with little or no collateral, that some were fraudulent (made to family and friends without required backing), and that there were speculative ventures into high risk bonds and real estate. In addition, many of these loans were made in the Southwest, particularly in Texas, at a time when the oil industry was booming. When this regional economy slipped into a recession, some S&Ls were saddled with assets worth much less than the value of the loans. Take the hypothetical case of a developer who borrowed $1,000,000 for a condo project when the economy was healthy. When the condos could not be sold because of the collapse of the oil economy, the developer did what many other borrowers did: defaulted on the loan. This left the S&L from which the money was borrowed as the owner of an asset valued at far less than a million dollars.

Federal Savings and Loan Insurance Corporation (FSLIC)
A federal agency established in 1934 to insure deposits in savings and loan institutions; the FDIC took over many of its functions when the FSLIC was dissolved in 1989.

One other major factor contributed to this situation. Since most deposits were insured by the **FSLIC (Federal Savings and Loan Insurance Corporation)** or a state government agency, much of the risk of poor business decision making was removed for the S&L owners. That is, since the deposits were insured, the S&Ls had little to lose by offering high interest rates and making risky loans.

Congress began to deal with the savings and loan crisis in a substantive way by passing the Financial Institutions Reform, Recovery and Enforcement Act of 1989 (FIRREA). Its major provisions deal with restricting and regulating thrift activities and settling the affairs of closed institutions. The Federal Savings and Loan Insurance Corporation (FSLIC), which did not have enough assets to cover the troubled institutions that it insured, was terminated and many of its powers were given to the FDIC, which had traditionally regulated and insured only commercial banks. The Act also created the **Resolution Trust Corporation (RTC)** to manage the reorganization of troubled savings and loans or close them and dispose of their loans and real estate holdings.

Resolution Trust Corporation (RTC)
The federal agency created to reorganize troubled savings and loans or to deal with their affairs if they have failed and closed.

As of this writing, the savings and loan crisis looms large: a number of S&Ls are in poor financial condition; certain evidence shows that some people are benefitting from the government-structured takeovers and mergers of institutions; political scandals have surfaced; and the government has told taxpayers that it will need hundreds of billions of their dollars to bail out this industry. Application 7.3, "The Steps to the S&L Disaster," summarizes a decade of events that led to this crisis.

Application 7.3

The Steps to the S&L Disaster

The following provides a step-by-step account of events leading to the current savings and loan crisis.

1. Inflation's Toll   In the late 1970's, the Federal Reserve's moves to curb runaway inflation force up interest rates. Savings and loans, set up to provide home mortgages, cannot compete for deposits because they are not permitted to offer higher rates on savings accounts.

2. The Industry Unbound   In 1980, legislation increases deposit insurance to $100,000 for each account and begins to phase out limits on interest rates. In 1982, additional deregulation allows savings institutions to make more risky loans to businesses and real estate developers.

3. The Money Chase   Savings and loans offer higher interest rates to attract deposits. Deposits pour in from individuals and money brokers.

4. Risky Growth   To pay higher rates on deposits, institutions must make more money on their investments. They invest in risky new ventures, particularly construction in the booming Southwest.

5. Gambling and Fraud   The fast-growing savings industry attracts crooks and others looking for a fast buck. They often invest their new pools of cash foolishly or fraudulently. Federal insurance on deposits means taxpayers ultimately pay for losses from poor judgment and fraud. Government supervision is lax.

6. The Southwest Slide   Oil prices plummet, hitting a low of $10 a barrel in 1986. The Southwest, led by Texas, goes into recession.

7. The Wall Street Plunge   The stock market crash in October 1987 marks a weakening of the economy and slows the Wall Street deals that kept many savings and loans afloat.

8. The Bailout   Industry losses mount and many savings and loans become insolvent. The Government is forced to take over more and more failing institutions. With each savings account insured up to $100,000, the Government's losses are the difference between the value of deposits and the often far lower value of insolvent institutions' assets.

9. Tighter Rules   As losses rise sharply, the Government in 1989 reorganizes the agencies that regulate the industry and handle the bailout.

10. The Price Tag   The General Accounting Office estimates that the cost of the bailout, including financing over four decades, could be as high as $500 billion.

Source: David E. Rosenbaum, "A Financial Disaster with Many Culprits," from a special report on The Savings Debacle in *The New York Times*, June 6, 1990, pp. A1, C4. Copyright © 1990 The New York Times Company. Reprinted by permission.

Summary

Money is a medium of exchange, or something generally acceptable as a means of payment for goods, services, and resources. Without money to facilitate transactions, an economy would need to rely on a barter system. Money also serves as a measure of value and as a method for storing wealth and delaying payment. The value of money is measured by the goods, services, and resources it can purchase. Inflation causes the value of money to decline.

There is disagreement as to exactly what constitutes the U.S. money supply. M1, the narrowest definition of the money supply, includes coins and paper money in circulation, nonbank-issued traveler's checks, demand deposits (checking accounts) at commercial banks, and other checkable deposits. Other definitions of the money supply are M2, M3, and L. M2 has become an important measure because it includes M1 plus accounts that have limited checkable features and accounts that are easily convertible to cash.

For any year, the economy's money supply is smaller than the value of goods and services produced, or GNP. The velocity of money measures the average annual turnover of the money supply in relationship to GNP.

When money is backed by a tangible item such as gold or silver, the economy is on a commodity standard. The United States formerly had its money backed by gold but is now on a paper standard, where money is generally backed by people's willingness to accept it and the strength of the economy. There are both advantages and disadvantages to a paper standard.

Financial depository institutions such as commercial banks, savings and loans, and credit unions play a critical role in the economy because they can create and destroy money through their loan-making activities. Commercial banks are the most important of these financial institutions. Agencies such as federal and state banking authorities, the Federal Reserve, and the Federal Deposit Insurance Corporation regulate commercial banks.

The Federal Reserve System coordinates commercial banking operations, regulates other financial depository institutions, and oversees the U.S. money supply. The system, which is organized geographically into 12 districts, is headed by the Board of Governors and carries out its most important procedures for money supply control through the Open Market Committee, which authorizes the Fed's purchase and sale of government securities. The 12 Federal Reserve Banks and their branches provide services to financial institutions rather than directly to the general public. The functions of the Federal Reserve Banks include supervising and examining the operations of member banks in their districts, maintaining reserve accounts, circulating coins and paper money, clearing checks, and acting as fiscal agents for the federal government.

There has been a recent trend toward the deregulation of financial institutions in the United States. The Monetary Control Act of 1980 began legislative changes toward deregulation by allowing savings and loans, savings banks, and credit unions to perform some functions that had been traditionally carried out only by commercial banks. The Garn–St. Germain Act strengthened the Monetary Control Act. Deregulation has also occurred with some structural changes among financial institutions. These include the growth of bank holding companies, the development of interstate banking, and the establishment of nonbank banks. The savings and loan crisis can also be traced to changes brought about by deregulation.

Key Terms and Concepts

Money

Medium of exchange

Value of money

Barter system

Functions of money

Definitions of the money supply

Token money

Federal Reserve Notes

Currency

Demand deposits

Other checkable deposits

Velocity of money

Money market deposit account (MMDA)

Liquidity

Commodity monetary standard

Paper monetary standard

Financial depository institution

Commercial bank

Dual banking system

National bank

Federal Deposit Insurance Corporation (FDIC)

Federal Reserve System

Board of Governors

Open Market Committee

Federal Reserve Banks

Organization of the Federal Reserve System

Reserve account

Correspondent banking

Monetary Control Act of 1980

Regulation Q

Garn–St. Germain Act

Branch banking

Bank holding company

Interstate banking

Nonbank bank

Federal Savings and Loan Insurance Corporation (FSLIC)

Resolution Trust Corporation (RTC)

Review Questions

1. List the basic functions of money and explain how a $20 bill fulfills each of these functions.

2. How much is one dollar worth? What is its value?

3. What are the basic components included in M1 and M2? How do these measures differ? In your opinion, which is a better measure of the money supply?

4. Answer the following questions concerning financial depository institutions.
   a. What distinguishes commercial banks from other financial depository institutions? Why are commercial banks so important?
   b. What characteristics differentiate commercial banks and other financial depository institutions from financial services companies such as nonbank banks and insurance companies?
   c. Give the various classifications of commercial banks and their regulating agencies. Why are commercial banks subject to so much regulation?
   d. What legislation has impacted on the functions of financial depository institutions in the last decade? How has it affected these institutions?

5. What are the functions of the Board of Governors of the Federal Reserve System and the Federal Reserve Banks? How has the Monetary Control Act of 1980 affected the span of control of the Federal Reserve System?

6. The First National Bank of Anytown had $500,000 in its reserve account at the Fed one morning. Later that morning $250,000 in checks that had been deposited at the Bank of Anytown were processed at the Fed, and Anytown ordered $100,000 in currency. Later that day $300,000 worth of checks written by the bank's customers cleared through the Fed. How much did the First National Bank of Anytown have in its reserve account at the Fed at the end of the day?

7. Define each of the following terms and explain how each has affected the banking system in recent years.
   a. Branch banking
   b. Bank holding company
   c. Interstate banking
   d. Nonbank bank

Discussion Questions

1. If demand deposits are a medium of exchange, and if a medium of exchange is generally acceptable as payment for goods and services, why is it sometimes so hard to cash a check?

2. Can you make an argument for returning the U.S. economy to a commodity standard based on gold? More generally, under what circumstances might a commodity standard be preferable to a paper standard?

3. "Regulation of financial depository institutions should be eliminated. These institutions should be free to sell their products like any other business in a free enterprise system. As long as the government continues to insure deposits, regulation is unnecessary." Comment on this statement.

4. Locate the name and a brief biography of each current member of the Board of Governors of the Federal Reserve System.

5. The members of the Board of Governors of the Federal Reserve System are appointed by the president of the United States. Do you think this could create a problem when a president is seeking reelection?

6. What is the branch banking law in your state? What would be the advantages and disadvantages of a federal law that permits interstate banking by all financial depository institutions?

7. Provide an update on the savings and loan crisis since this textbook was written.

Critical Thinking Case 7

■ The S&L Tab

Critical Thinking Skills	Attach meaning to numbers
	Evaluate consequences of alternatives
Economic Concepts	Savings and loan crisis
	Opportunity cost

Some estimates of the cost of the savings and loan bailout range up to $500,000,000,000 — five hundred billion dollars — if interest payments are included. There is something engaging about the number *five hundred billion,* even more so if you put it in perspective.

With $500 billion, the Government could mail a check for $2,000 to every man, woman and child in the United States. If it were in an ecumenical mood and had a global mailing list, it could send $100 to every human being on earth — $10 for every earthling finger. For the same money, the Government could buy approximately 12 million Mercedes, 20 million Volvos, 30 million Mazdas or 100 million Eastern European cars. . . .

It would take a decade to spend $500 billion at $1,585 a second, and if spending at this rate occurred only during business hours, more than 40 years would be required to dispense the sum. Another time analogy is illuminating: A million seconds take approximately 11 days to tick by, whereas a billion seconds require about 32 years. Sixteen thousand years need to pass before 500 billion seconds elapse.

For a more somber equivalence, note that according to UNICEF's 1989 report, millions of children die each year from nothing more serious than measles, tetanus, respiratory infections or diarrhea. These illnesses can be prevented by a $1.50 vaccine, $1 in antibiotics or 10 cents worth of oral rehydration salts.

UNICEF estimates that $2.5 billion (most of it going to staff and administrative costs) would be sufficient to keep these children alive and improve the health of countless others. This amount is 1/200th of $500 billion.

It is this last sort of comparison that truly illustrates the enormity of the savings and loan scandal. There are so many other programs that might have been financed.

The Education Department's annual budget is approximately $25 billion, or 5 percent of $500 billion. Current estimates for next year's [1991] AIDS budget are well under $2 billion, less than four-tenths of 1 percent of $500 billion.

The tendency we have to be mesmerized by "people" stories and bored by "number" stories should be resisted. Ultimately, however, the distinction between the two is specious. We must find better ways to vivify complex issues. The cost of not doing so will be considerably more than $500 billion.

Questions

1. In your opinion, what are the real costs of the savings and loan bailout and who is paying these costs?

2. Should the government have rescued the savings and loan industry? If the government did not come to the assistance of the industry, would the costs be any different, and who would pay them?

Source: John Allen Paulos, "The S&L Tab," *The New York Times,* June 28, 1990, p. A15. Copyright © 1990 by The New York Times Company. Excerpted by permission.

Suggested Readings

Rebel A. Cole, "Thrift Resolution Activity: Historical Overview and Implications," *Financial Industry Studies,* Federal Reserve Bank of Dallas, May 1990, pp. 1–12.
Overview of the handling of problem thrifts between 1980 and 1988. Addresses the costs of various types of settlements.

Federal Reserve Bank of St. Louis, *Monetary Trends* (published monthly).
Contains data and graphs on M1, M2, bank loans, long-term interest rates, and other financial measures.

John Kenneth Galbraith, *Money: Whence It Came, Where It Went* (Boston: Houghton Mifflin Co., 1975).
A critical look at money, banking, monetary policy, and fiscal policy through the years.

John H. Kareken, "Deposit Insurance Reform; or, Deregulation is the Cart, Not the Horse," *Quarterly Review,* Federal Reserve Bank of Minneapolis, Winter 1990, pp. 3–11.
A reprint of an article originally published in 1983. Discusses the problems that could (and eventually did) result from deregulation of financial depository institutions with no change in insurance coverage.

David S. Kidwell and Richard L. Peterson, *Financial Institutions, Markets, and Money,* 4th ed., (Hinsdale, Ill.: The Dryden Press, 1990).
Provides an updated and broad introduction to the operation, structure, institutions, and instruments of the financial system of the United States.

Martin Mayer, "The Banking Story," *American Heritage,* April–May 1984, pp. 26–35.
A brief history of banking in the United States.

Charles R. McNeill (with some discussion by Denise M. Rechter), "The Depository Institutions Deregulation and Monetary Control Act of 1980," *Federal Reserve Bulletin,* June 1980, pp. 444–453.
A comprehensive treatment of this significant banking legislation.

Richard W. Stevenson, "How One Savings Institution Came Apart," from a special report on The Savings Debacle in *The New York Times,* June 12, 1990, pp. A1, C4.
Chronicles the collapse of First Network Savings Bank in 1990.

U.S. Commission on the Role of Gold in the Domestic and International Monetary Systems, "The Past Role of Gold in the U.S. Monetary System," and "Types of Monetary Standards," *Report to the Congress of the Commission on the Role of Gold in the Domestic and International Monetary Systems,* Vol. 1, March 1982, pp. 51–133.
Covers the role of gold in the U.S. economy from 1834 to 1981 and alternative monetary standards.

John R. Walter, "Monetary Aggregates: A User's Guide," *Economic Review,* **Federal Reserve Bank of Richmond, January/February 1989, pp. 20–28.**
Discusses the evolution of the measures of the money supply, the preparation and release of monetary data, how the data are used, and where they can be found.

Chapter Eight

Money Creation, Monetary Theory, and Monetary Policy

Just as a conductor influences the creation of a musical piece, the Federal Reserve influences the creation of money by the way it conducts monetary policy.

Source: Robert Wagoner/The Stock Market.

Chapter Objectives

1. To explain the relationship between the economy's money supply and level of activity.

2. To explain how money is created and destroyed through the loan-making activities of financial depository institutions.

3. To introduce the multiple expansion of money.

4. To explain the role of the interest rate in encouraging or discouraging borrowing from financial depository institutions.

5. To show how interest rates are affected by changes in financial depository institutions' excess reserves.

6. To define monetary policy and explain the major tools for carrying out monetary policy by the Federal Reserve.

7. To show the relationship between government borrowing to cover deficit spending and monetary policy.

8. To evaluate critically monetary policy.

Chapter Seven presented the institutional groundwork in three important areas in the U.S. economy: money, financial depository institutions, and the Federal Reserve System. It was pointed out that the United States is on a paper monetary standard and that control over the size of the money supply is of utmost importance when an economy is on such a standard. Control is a concern because there is a significant relationship between an economy's supply of money and its levels of output, income, employment, and prices: a change in the quantity of money in an economy can lead to a change in its overall level of activity. Because of this, altering a nation's money supply is an important method for trying to attain the macroeconomic objectives of full production and economic growth, full employment, and price stability. This method for accomplishing the macroeconomic goals is called monetary policy and is carried out by the Federal Reserve.

This chapter expands on Chapter Seven by studying the effect of the money supply on the macroeconomy, and the operation of monetary policy. First, a general explanation of how the money supply influences output and prices is presented. Next, the process of increasing or decreasing the supply of money by financial depository institutions is covered. Third, a discussion of how changes in financial depository institutions' abilities to lend affect interest rates, borrowing, and the level of total spending is presented. Finally, the tools of monetary policy are introduced and their use by the

Federal Reserve to alter and control the supply of money to accomplish the macroeconomic objectives is explained.

The Money Supply and the Level of Economic Activity

The primary determinant of the overall level of activity in an economy is the level of total spending by businesses, households, government units, and foreign buyers. The importance of total, or aggregate, spending was the focus of Chapter Five. An increase in total spending leads to an increase in output, income, and employment if the economy is at less than full employment. If the economy is at or near full employment, increased spending leads to an increase in the general level of prices. A decrease in total spending results in a reduction in output, income, and employment, and if the economy is at or near full employment, in a dampening of inflationary pressure.

The ability of households and businesses to spend is related to the amount of money in the economy. More spending is generated when the money supply is increased, and spending falls when the money supply is decreased. Chapter Seven stated that money is created (the money supply is increased) when financial depository institutions such as commercial banks make loans. Because loans are taken out by households to finance the purchase of such things as new homes, automobiles, and appliances, and by businesses to invest in machinery, equipment, and the like, increased loan making results in more spending.[1] Thus, increases in loans by commercial banks and other depository institutions mean a larger money supply and more spending. When loan making falls, the money supply is decreased and spending declines. The relationship between loan making by financial depository institutions, money creation, and the level of spending is explained in detail as the chapter develops.

The Equation of Exchange

The importance of money for total spending and the relationship of the supply of money to the overall level of economic activity are summarized in the **equation of exchange:**

$$MV = PQ.$$

Equation of exchange

$MV = PQ$; illustrates how changes in the supply of money (M) influence the level of prices (P) and/or the total output of goods and services (Q).

On the left-hand side of this equation, M represents the supply of money in the economy and V the velocity of money, which, as explained in Chapter Seven, is the number of times each dollar is spent for new goods and services

---

[1] Banks and other financial depository institutions also make loans to the government when they purchase government securities for their portfolios.

in a year. The larger the supply of money in the economy, the greater is the value of M; the more frequently each dollar is spent per year, the higher is the velocity and the greater is the value of V. On the right-hand side of the equation, P represents the level of prices and Q the actual output of goods and services.

MV, the supply of money multiplied by the number of times it turns over each year, can be viewed as total spending on new goods and services in the economy. PQ, the price level multiplied by the actual output of goods and services, can be interpreted as the dollar value of output produced in the economy, or current GNP. Since the circular flow model tells us that a given level of spending brings forth an output of equal value, we know that MV and PQ are equal.[2] Thus, if the supply of money were $800 billion and velocity were 6, MV (or total spending) would equal $4.8 trillion, as would PQ (the value of the economy's output).

What happens to the level of economic activity when the supply of money changes? The equation of exchange helps answer this question. To keep matters simple, let us assume that the velocity of money does not change. That is, let V be constant in the equation of exchange.[3]

Enlarging the supply of money causes the left-hand side of the equation of exchange (total spending) to increase. Since the two sides must be equal, this means that the right-hand side of the equation (dollar value of output) must also increase by the same amount. If the economy were experiencing unemployment and operating below full production, the increase in the value of output would come primarily in the form of an expansion in production and employment. That is, the increase in the right-hand side of the equation of exchange would come mainly in the Q term. However, if the economy were at or near full employment, production and employment would be at or near their upper limits. If the money supply were to increase under these circumstances, Q in the equation of exchange could go up very little, if at all. In this case, an increase in the supply of money would lead primarily to an increase in the price level, the P term, or to inflation.

A decrease in the supply of money causes a reduction in total expenditures, the left-hand side of the equation of exchange. This, in turn, causes a decrease in the dollar value of output, the right-hand side of the equation. When a decrease in the money supply causes a reduction in total expenditures, it results in a decrease in Q, or employment and income. P, or the price level, usually does not fall because businesses in general respond to decreases in spending by cutting production rather than by lowering prices.

---

[2] Some economists write the equation of exchange as an identity: $MV \equiv PQ$.

[3] In reality, the velocity of money (M1) had been gradually changing upward over the long run until the 1980s, when some downward fluctuations occurred. However, in looking at the effect on the economy of increasing or decreasing the money supply *at any particular moment in time*, the assumption that V is fixed is appropriate. For more on the velocity of money, see Colin D. Campbell, Rosemary G. Campbell, and Edwin G. Dolan, *Money, Banking, and Monetary Policy* (Hinsdale, Ill.: The Dryden Press, 1988), p. 338.

However, if the economy were operating at or near full employment and experiencing inflationary pressure, a decrease in the money supply would dampen some of that pressure by reducing total spending.

In summary, the relationship between total spending and the level of economic activity is influenced by changes in the economy's supply of money. Increasing the money supply facilitates spending and contributes to an expansion of economic activity. Whether this leads to increased production and employment or to inflation depends in large part on how close the economy is to full employment. Decreasing the supply of money inhibits the spending ability of businesses and households and in turn slows the level of economic activity.

Money Creation

Since changes in the supply of money affect the economy's levels of output, employment, and prices, it is important to understand how the money supply is increased and decreased. In Chapter Seven it was noted that financial depository institutions play a critical role in the economy because they can create and destroy money through their loan-making activities. Stated simply, money is created when these institutions make loans, and money is destroyed when those loans are repaid. Although these loan-making institutions include savings and loan associations, savings banks, and credit unions, the primary organizations engaged in money creation and destruction are commercial banks.

The Process of Money Creation

Actual reserves

A financial depository institution's reserve account plus its vault cash.

Every financial depository institution has two assets that it classifies as its **actual reserves:** the institution's reserve account (which was introduced in Chapter Seven) and its vault cash.[4] A commercial bank that belongs to the Federal Reserve System must keep its reserve account at its Federal Reserve Bank. A nonmember institution may choose to keep its reserve account at the Fed or at an approved correspondent institution that will pass it through to the Fed.

Reserve requirement

A specific percentage of deposits that a financial depository institution must keep as actual reserves.

These depository institutions also have a reserve requirement that they must honor. This **reserve requirement** is a specific *percentage of deposits* that must be kept as actual reserves. For example, a reserve requirement of 10 percent on demand deposits means that a bank must have an amount on reserve equal to 10 percent of the value of the demand deposits it is holding. If a bank has $8,000,000 in checking accounts and a 10 percent reserve requirement, it must have at least $800,000 (.10 × $8,000,000) in actual

---

[4] Vault cash is all of the cash in the institution's vault and cash drawers. It does not include anything customers may have in their safe deposit boxes.

Table 8.1

Hometown Bank's Reserve Calculations

A financial depository institution's excess reserves are equal to its actual reserves minus its required reserves.

If Hometown Bank's

Demand deposits = $6,000,000
Reserve requirement = 10 percent, or .10
Actual reserves = $1,000,000,

then Hometown Bank's excess reserves are found by the calculation

Actual reserves = $1,000,000
−Required reserves = $ 600,000 (.10 × $6,000,000)
Excess reserves = $ 400,000.

Required reserves

The amount of actual reserves that a financial depository institution must keep to back its deposits.

Excess reserves

Reserves of a financial depository institution over the amount it is required to maintain in actual reserves; actual reserves minus required reserves.

reserves. The amount of actual reserves that a financial depository institution must keep to back its deposits is called its **required reserves.**

Every day each depository institution must make several calculations pertaining to its deposits and reserves. First, it must compute the value of deposits held in the institution that day. Second, it must calculate its required reserves. And, third, it must determine how much it has in actual reserves. (Remember that Chapter Seven pointed out that a depository institution's reserve account fluctuates daily due to check clearing, and periodically due to currency orders and returns.) In short, the institution must determine what it needs to have and what it actually does have on reserve.

These calculations permit an institution to determine its excess reserves. **Excess reserves** are the institution's actual reserves minus its required reserves, or reserves over and above those that the institution must maintain. Assume that the Hometown Bank, which has a reserve requirement of 10 percent, calculates its demand deposits to be $6,000,000. This means that the bank's required reserves are $600,000 (.10 × $6,000,000). Assume further that Hometown Bank computes its actual reserves to be $1,000,000. Since excess reserves are actual reserves ($1,000,000) minus required reserves ($600,000), Hometown Bank has excess reserves of $400,000. That is, the bank has $400,000 on reserve that it need not keep there. Table 8.1 summarizes these calculations.

Excess reserves are important because they are the foundation for a depository institution's loan-making abilities. Very simply, *a depository institution can make new loans up to the value of its excess reserves.* Why is this so? When a bank, for example, makes a loan to a business or an individual, it usually arranges to give the borrower those funds in either a cashier's check or through a direct deposit into the borrower's checking account. In either case, when the borrower spends these loaned funds and the check for this spending is deposited in another institution and cleared through the check clearing machinery, the lending bank loses reserves. For example, if Hometown Bank loans Joe Smith $20,000 so he can buy a delivery van, it will lose $20,000 in reserves when Joe Smith's check for the van is deposited by the seller in another institution and cleared through the check clearing machinery.[5]

Because an institution loses reserves when a loan is spent, it must be careful to make loans only up to the value of its excess reserves in order to meet reserve requirements. Return to the example of Hometown Bank, which had $1,000,000 in actual reserves, $600,000 in required reserves, and $400,000 in excess reserves. Given these figures, Hometown Bank could make new loans of up to $400,000. If, however, Hometown Bank made loans of over $400,000, say $450,000, its $1,000,000 in actual reserves would drop to $550,000 when the checks written against the loans were cleared. In this case, Hometown Bank would be $50,000 short on its required reserves. It is for this reason that an institution can make new loans only up to an amount equal to its excess reserves.

In making a loan, an institution does *not* take away one customer's money to give to another. Those who hold money at the institution (in demand deposits, negotiable orders of withdrawal, and such) do not have their deposits altered; they retain all of their account balances and are free to spend their money when they so desire. Instead, in making a loan a financial depository institution creates new deposits, or new money; that is, it provides dollars for spending that were not in the economy before the loan was made. If a bank maintains $6 million in demand deposits and makes new loans of $400,000, then the $6 million in demand deposits is still money, but it has been supplemented by the creation of an additional $400,000.

How is money destroyed? When a loan is repaid, money is destroyed. Repayment of a loan withdraws money from the economy by returning it to the lending institution, where it becomes reserves. Until the institution makes another loan based on these reserves, this money has disappeared from the system. Application 8.1 gives some typical questions and answers about reserves and loans.

It should be clear by now that excess reserves form the basis for loan making and thus for changing the money supply. If the supply of money is to be controlled, it can be done through altering the amount of excess reserves in depository institutions. An increase in excess reserves is appropriate to increase the money supply, and a decrease in excess reserves is appropriate to decrease the money supply.

---

[5] The effect on reserves from lending to households, businesses, or the government is the same. When a financial depository institution lends money to the U.S. government by buying a Treasury security, it pays for that security out of its reserve account, causing the reserve account to decrease.

Application 8.1

Questions and Answers about Reserves and Loans

Q: Do all financial depository institutions have the same reserve requirement?

A: There are uniform reserve requirements on all financial depository institutions, although the actual percentage requirement differs by type of account (for example, checkable versus time). These requirements are given in Table 8.4 on page 300.

Q: What happens if an institution does not meet its reserve requirement?

A: First of all, for requirement purposes, depository institutions compute their deposits and reserves over a two-week time period. This permits an institution with a reserve deficiency on one day to correct it within the next few days and still meet its requirement. If an institution has not met its reserve requirement on the average over its given time period, it will usually borrow the needed reserves.

Q: From whom can banks borrow reserves?

A: Banks can borrow reserves from a Federal Reserve Bank or from other banks through the Federal Funds market. In the Federal Funds market, banks lend excess reserves to other banks, usually for a period of one day. Banks borrow in the Federal Funds market to cover reserve deficiencies or to obtain additional reserves with which to make loans.

Q: What is the prime rate, and who determines it?

A: The prime rate is the benchmark interest rate that a commercial bank charges its least risky borrowers for short-term commercial and industrial loans. The prime rate is set by each individual bank but is influenced by general credit conditions. The media typically announce changes in the prime rates of major banks or banks of local interest. Smaller banks frequently follow changes in the prime rate made by major banks.

Q: How much do financial depository institutions keep in vault cash?

A: Financial depository institutions need enough paper money and coins to service their customers who want to cash a check or redeem savings or time deposits in cash. They do not want to keep excessive amounts of vault cash on hand, however, for security reasons. These institutions also consider the amount of cash that is normally deposited daily by their customers in calculating the level of vault cash to maintain.

Source: Colin D. Campbell, Rosemary G. Campbell, and Edwin G. Dolan, *Money, Banking, and Monetary Policy* (Hinsdale, Ill.: The Dryden Press, 1988), pp. 130, 151, 183–184, 254, 291–293.

The Multiple Expansion of Money

Thus far we have dealt with the money-creating ability of a single depository institution. However, to understand the potential impact of changes in reserves on money creation and destruction, all such institutions must be considered together as a system. When the system as a whole is studied, one can observe that changes in excess reserves in the system cause a multiplier effect on the creation and destruction of money. That is, an initial increase in excess reserves in the system will cause the money supply to increase by some multiple of that increase in excess reserves, and an initial decrease in excess reserves in the system will cause the money supply to shrink by some multiple of that decrease. The following example illustrates this principle.

Assume that Hometown Bank experiences a $1,000 increase in excess reserves because of a policy change by the monetary authorities. (Different

Table 8.2

Multiple Expansion of Money (10% Reserve Requirement)

An increase in excess reserves in the system causes the money supply to increase by a multiple of the initial excess reserve change.

	Demand Deposits	Actual Reserves	Required Reserves	Excess Reserves	Loans
Hometown Bank				$1,000.00	$1,000.00
Bank B	$1,000.00	$1,000.00	$100.00	900.00	900.00
Bank C	900.00	900.00	90.00	810.00	810.00
Bank D	810.00	810.00	81.00	729.00	729.00
Bank E	729.00	729.00	72.90	656.10	656.10
Bank F	656.10	656.10	65.61	590.49	590.49
Bank G	590.49	590.49	59.05	531.44	531.44
Bank H	531.44	531.44	53.14	478.30	478.30
Bank I	478.30	478.30	47.83	430.47	430.47
Bank J	430.47	430.47	43.05	387.42	387.42
Bank K	387.42	387.42	38.74	348.68	348.68
Bank L	348.68	348.68	34.87	313.81	313.81
Bank M	313.81	313.81	31.38	282.43	282.43
Bank N	282.43	282.43	28.24	254.19	254.19
Bank O	254.19	254.19	25.42	228.77	228.77
Bank P	228.77	228.77	22.88	205.89	205.89
Bank Q	205.89	205.89	20.59	185.30	185.30
Banks R, S, T . . .	. . .	. . .	. . .	. . .	. . .
Total	$10,000.00				$10,000.00

methods for carrying out these policy changes will be discussed shortly.) These new excess reserves permit Hometown Bank to make a new loan of $1,000, which we will assume goes to a borrower named Mid Jones. This transaction is shown in the top row of Table 8.2. Suppose Mid uses her $1,000 loan to purchase audio equipment and writes out a check in that amount to the seller, who deposits it in the seller's account at Bank B. If Bank B, as well as each other bank in this example, has a reserve requirement of 10 percent, then that $1,000 deposit gives Bank B actual reserves of $1,000, of which $100 are required reserves and $900 are excess reserves (remember—check deposits, when cleared, increase a bank's reserves). On the basis of this check, Bank B can now make a new loan of $900.

Assume that Al Smith borrows $900 from Bank B for a used car. The car dealer takes Al's check for that amount and deposits it in the dealership's account at Bank C, where it brings Bank C $900 in actual reserves, of which $90 are required reserves and $810 are excess reserves. On the basis of this $900 deposit, Bank C can now make a new loan of $810 that will be eventually deposited by someone in Bank D, and on and on. Table 8.2 carries this example through several more rounds, showing how each succeeding bank can make new loans. It is extremely important to realize that none of these loans could have been made without the initial increase in excess reserves at Hometown Bank. It is this initial increase in excess reserves that caused other banks to experience an increase in their excess reserves.[6]

When the full effect of this initial change in excess reserves is carried through the system, all of the new loans can be added together to determine the total amount of money created. From this addition it is apparent that the change in the money supply is some multiple of the initial change in excess reserves. In Table 8.2, a $10,000 increase in the money supply has resulted from an initial $1,000 increase in excess reserves. In this case there has been a **money multiplier** of 10.

Money multiplier

The multiple by which an initial change in excess reserves in the system can change the money supply.

The size of the money multiplier depends upon the reserve requirement. In fact, the money multiplier is the reciprocal of the reserve requirement. (The reciprocal of a fraction is the fraction "flipped over": the reciprocal of 1/3 is 3/1, or 3.) A 10 percent (1/10) reserve requirement means a multiplier of 10/1, or 10; a 25 percent (1/4) requirement means a multiplier of 4; and a 15 percent (3/20) requirement yields a multiplier of 20/3, or 6.67.

The multiplier times the initial change in excess reserves gives the total change that could result in the money supply, or, stated in equation form:

$$\begin{array}{ccc} \text{money} \\ \text{multiplier} \end{array} \times \begin{array}{c} \text{change in} \\ \text{excess reserves} \end{array} = \begin{array}{c} \text{total change in} \\ \text{money supply.} \end{array}$$

An initial increase in the banking system of $8 million in excess reserves with a reserve requirement of 20 percent (multiplier of 5) could generate $40 million of new money, and an $8 million decrease in excess reserves with a 10 percent reserve requirement could decrease the money supply by $80 million. The multiplier can work in either direction: increases or decreases in excess reserves are subject to its effect.[7]

---

[6] The situation would be the same if any of these banks received multiple deposits: that is, if Hometown Bank or Bank B, C, or so on were repeated on the list in Table 8.2.

[7] Another method for calculating the amount by which the money supply could change following an initial change in excess reserves in the system is to divide the initial change in excess reserves by the reserve requirement, or

$$\frac{\text{change in excess reserves}}{\text{reserve requirement}} = \text{total change in money supply.}$$

Thus, if excess reserves increased by $8,000,000 when the reserve requirement was 20 percent (or 0.20), the total change in the money supply could be

$$\frac{\$8,000,000}{0.20} = \$40,000,000.$$

Be careful not to confuse this formula with the multiplier formula in Chapter Five (page 195). The formula given here is used to determine how much the *money supply* could change following an initial change in excess reserves in the depository institutions system. The formula in Chapter Five determines how much *income* and *output* change as a result of an initial change in nonincome-determined spending.

The examples presented here are simplistic versions of the outcome of the money multiplier. In reality, the expansion of the money supply resulting from an increase in reserves can be affected by actions such as converting some portion of the deposits to cash, putting some portion into savings accounts, or having institutions lend less than the maximum amount available. For instance, if the used car dealer in the example in Table 8.2 deposited $600 from Al Smith's $900 purchase in the dealership's checking account, took $100 in cash, and put $200 in a savings bond, the increase in the other banks' excess reserves and loans, and in the money supply, would have been less than the $10,000 shown at the bottom of Table 8.2. In addition, if any of these banks loaned less than the total amount of their excess reserves, the effect on the money supply would also have been smaller than the $10,000 increase shown in Table 8.2.

Excess Reserves, Interest Rates, and the Level of Spending

We know that changes in the money supply are executed through changes in loan making by financial depository institutions. We also know that increases in loan making lead to increases in spending and, ultimately, to increases in output and employment, or to increases in prices if the economy is at or near full employment. Decreases in loan making lead to decreases in spending and decreases in the level of economic activity. This relationship between lending, the money supply, spending, and economic activity is summarized in Table 8.3.

When a business or household takes out a loan with a depository institution, it borrows because it chooses to, not because it has been coerced into doing so by the institution. For this reason, simply having excess reserves available in these institutions does not ensure that money will be created through borrowing. This leads to two important questions. If borrowing is voluntary, how can businesses and households be stimulated to take out loans in situations where an increase in the money supply and spending would help reduce unemployment? And, how can businesses and households be encouraged to borrow less when the money supply should be reduced to dampen inflationary pressure?

Interest rate

The price paid to borrow money; a percentage of the amount borrowed.

The answers are found in the role performed by the **interest rate,** the price paid to borrow money. If $1,000 were borrowed for one year at an annual interest rate of 8 percent, at the end of the year the borrower would have to repay the $1,000 that was loaned plus $80 in interest, or a total of $1,080. If the interest rate were 12 percent, at the end of one year the borrower would have to repay $1,120. Thus, the higher the rate of interest, the greater the price that must be paid to borrow money. Since borrowed money, like any good or service, is subject to the Law of Demand (discussed in Chapter Three), the quantity of funds demanded for borrowing falls as the interest rate rises and rises as the interest rate falls.

Table 8.3

Relationship between Loan Making, the Money Supply, Spending, and the Level of Economic Activity

Changes in loan making lead to changes in spending, which in turn affect the economy's levels of output, employment, and/or prices.

Increases in the Money Supply	Decreases in the Money Supply
Increases in the money supply occur when there are increases in lending by financial depository institutions.	Decreases in the money supply occur when there are reductions in lending by financial depository institutions.
↓	↓
Increased loan making leads to increased spending.	Decreased loan making leads to decreased spending.
↓	↓
Increased spending leads to an increase in output and employment if the economy is at less than full employment and/or an increase in the price level if the economy is near or at full employment.	Decreased spending leads to a decrease in output and employment, and a reduction of inflationary pressure if the economy is near or at full employment.

Businesses are particularly sensitive to the interest rate when making decisions about borrowing for investment spending.[8] The cost of borrowing to finance machinery, equipment, construction, and so forth must be recovered if the investment is to break even, much less earn a profit. As the interest rate goes up, certain investment projects that would have been profitable at lower rates become unprofitable and are dropped from consideration. This in turn leads to a drop in the amount of funds demanded to finance such projects. Households are also sensitive to the interest rate when taking out loans. An increase in the interest rate on mortgages, auto loans, or other consumer loans leads to a decrease in the quantity of borrowed funds demanded by households to purchase homes and other goods.

The Determination of Interest Rates on Loans

How is the interest rate determined for loans made by financial depository institutions? What causes it to change? The interest rate is determined in the same way other prices are determined—through the interaction of demand and supply.

The demand by businesses and households for loans from financial depository institutions is equal to the different amounts that they plan to borrow at different interest rates. A hypothetical demand for loans is given in Figure 8.1 by the demand curve D. As with other demand curves, D in

---

[8] Recall the discussion of this point in Chapter Five on page 180 and in Application 5.1.

Figure 8.1   Determining the Interest Rate for Loans

The interest rate for loans is determined by the demand for and supply of funds for loans.

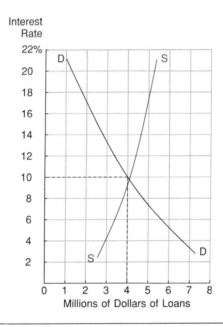

Figure 8.1 slopes downward to indicate an inverse relationship between the amount of planned borrowing and the interest rate.

On the other side of the transaction, the amount of loans that depository institutions are willing to make varies directly with the interest rate. Because a financial depository institution earns its profit from loan making and other sources, it is motivated to use excess reserves in the manner that brings the highest return. If the interest rate it can earn on loans is low, a bank or other depository institution will probably prefer converting some of its excess reserves to higher yielding assets. But when the institution can obtain a high interest rate for loaning funds, it will convert more of its excess reserves to loans. S in Figure 8.1 gives a hypothetical supply curve for loans by depository institutions.

Given D and S in Figure 8.1, the interest rate that emerges is 10 percent, with $4 million in loans resulting. This equilibrium condition occurs because at 10 percent, the amount of funds demanded equals the amount supplied. This equilibrium position can change, however, especially if there is a change in the excess reserves of depository institutions that alters their ability to make loans and shifts the supply curve. For example, if excess

Figure 8.2 Effect of Changes in Excess Reserves on
the Interest Rate and the Quantity of Loans

A decrease in excess reserves in the system will cause interest rates to rise and
the amount of loans granted to fall. An increase in excess reserves will cause
interest rates to fall and the amount of loans granted to rise.

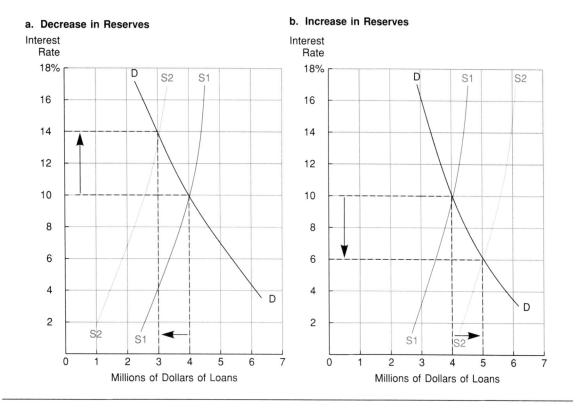

a. Decrease in Reserves

b. Increase in Reserves

reserves are decreased, institutions can make fewer loans, or the supply of
loans decreases. This is shown in Figure 8.2a as a shift in the supply curve
to the left from S1 to S2. As a result of this decrease in reserves, the interest
rate rises to 14 percent in Figure 8.2a, and the quantity of loans made declines
to $3 million. In other words, a decrease in excess reserves causes interest
rates to rise and the amount of loans made to fall.

An increase in excess reserves causes the supply of loans to increase and
the supply curve to shift to the right as shown in Figure 8.2b. When supply
shifts from S1 to S2 in Figure 8.2b, the interest rate falls to 6 percent, and
loans increase to $5 million. Thus, an increase in excess reserves decreases
the interest rate and increases the amount of loans made.

Figure 8.3   Relationship between Excess Reserves, the Interest Rate,
Loan Making, and the Level of Economic Activity

Changes in the level of excess reserves in the system influence institutions'
lending abilities, interest rates, the money supply, total spending, and the
economy's levels of output, employment, and prices.

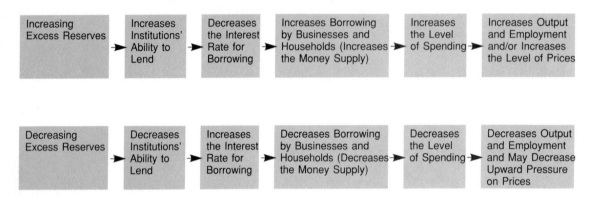

Figure 8.3 extends the relationship between loan making, the money supply, spending, and the level of economic activity summarized in Table 8.3 by including excess reserves and the interest rate.

An additional note of clarification about interest rates is in order. Although we frequently use the expression "the interest rate," in reality no singular interest rate exists. Instead, there are many different types of markets in which money is borrowed and lent: markets for home mortgages, secured corporate loans, student loans, and personal auto loans, for example. The interest rates in these markets differ because of dissimilarities in risk, loan size, length of repayment, and other factors. Therefore, when we refer to a rise in the interest rate because of declining excess reserves, we mean that interest rates *in general* are rising. Likewise, a fall in the interest rate due to increasing excess reserves in the system means that interest rates *in general* are falling.

The Federal Reserve and Monetary Policy

Since changes in loans result from changes in excess reserves, it is obvious that control over the money supply can be exerted through control over excess reserves. Thus, it should come as no surprise that the Federal Reserve, whose responsibility it is to oversee and change the money supply, carries out this charge by altering excess reserves in the banking and depository institutions system. When the Fed acts to deliberately change excess reserves (and, thus, the money supply) to influence the levels of output, employment, and/or prices in the economy, it is engaging in **monetary policy.**

If the economy is experiencing a high rate of unemployment, the appropriate policy action is to stimulate the level of total spending. To accomplish this goal, the Federal Reserve would act to increase excess reserves in the system, which should in turn decrease the interest rate and encourage borrowing. When the money supply is deliberately expanded and loans are more readily available, the Fed is said to be pursuing an **easy money policy.**

If the economy is encountering a problem with demand-pull inflation, the appropriate policy prescription is to reduce spending. In this case the Fed would act to decrease the level of excess reserves in the system, thereby causing the interest rate to rise and borrowing to be dampened. When the money supply is deliberately reduced, the Fed is said to be pursuing a **tight money policy.**

Monetary Policy Tools

The Federal Reserve has three major tools to alter excess reserves in the financial depository institutions system: (1) the reserve requirement, (2) the discount rate, and (3) open market operations.

The Reserve Requirement   If the Federal Reserve wanted to reduce excess reserves to discourage borrowing, it could do so by increasing the reserve requirement. For example, suppose that Hometown Bank has $5 million in demand deposits with a 10 percent reserve requirement: Hometown must keep $500,000 on reserve. If, however, the reserve requirement were raised to 11 percent, Hometown would need to keep $550,000 on reserve to back the $5 million in demand deposits; it would lose $50,000 of its excess reserves. Because the bank would have fewer excess reserves, it would have less loan-making ability, and its reduced loan-making ability would increase the interest rate the bank charges and thus dampen borrowing.

On the other hand, a decrease in the reserve requirement would increase excess reserves in the system, giving institutions the ability to make new loans. This decrease in the reserve requirement would be appropriate to stimulate the economy, whereas an increase in the reserve requirement would be appropriate to fight demand-pull inflation.

Prior to the Monetary Control Act of 1980, reserve requirements differed among the various types of financial institutions and were imposed by different regulatory organizations. For example, a Federal Reserve member commercial bank had a different reserve requirement than a savings and loan. Since the act, all depository institutions[9] must meet the same reserve

---

[9] These include commercial banks, mutual savings banks, savings banks, savings and loan associations, credit unions, agencies and branches of foreign banks, and Edge corporations (bank subsidiaries that conduct some international banking transactions). See Board of Governors of the Federal Reserve System, *Federal Reserve Bulletin*, September 1987, p. A8.

Monetary policy

Changing the money supply to influence the levels of output, employment, and/or prices in the economy.

Easy money policy

A policy by the Federal Reserve to increase excess reserves of depository institutions in an effort to increase spending and reduce unemployment.

Tight money policy

A policy by the Federal Reserve to reduce excess reserves of depository institutions in an effort to reduce spending and inflationary pressure.

Table 8.4

Reserve Requirements[a]

All depository institutions are subject to the same reserve requirements.

Type of Account	Reserve Requirement
Transactions, or checkable, accounts, including demand deposits, credit union share drafts, and others	
Balances of $0–$41.1 million	3%
Balances over $41.1 million	12% (can vary from 8–14%)
Time deposits and savings accounts	No reserve requirement

[a]In effect on December 31, 1990.

Source: Federal Reserve Bank of Chicago, *Leveling the Playing Field*, December 1983, p. 12; and Board of Governors of the Federal Reserve System, *Federal Reserve Bulletin*, March 1991, p. A8.

requirement, although this requirement differs according to the type of deposit. The uniform reserve requirement regulated by the Federal Reserve gives the Fed greater control over the money supply.

Table 8.4 shows the reserve requirements in effect on January 1, 1991. Notice in this table that the only requirement is on transactions, or checkable, accounts, and that this requirement is two-tiered: 3 percent on the first $41.1 million in deposits and 12 percent on deposits over this amount. The level at which the 12 percent requirement takes effect is adjusted each year. Notice also that there are no reserve requirements on savings or time deposits. There was a requirement of 3 percent on one classification of savings and time deposits—those with maturities of less than one and one-half years held by "nonpersons" (corporations, for example)—but it was dropped in December 1990.

The Federal Reserve usually does not radically change reserve requirements in carrying out monetary policy. Either an influx or a removal of an extremely large volume of excess reserves would be a shock to the depository institutions system. An increase of 1 or 2 percent in a reserve requirement on checkable accounts could cause banks and other institutions to have to "find" millions of dollars of reserves to meet that requirement. The removal of the time deposit reserve requirement in December 1990 did not dramatically increase excess reserves in the system since it applied to just one category of time deposits.

The Discount Rate   All financial depository institutions may under certain circumstances borrow from a Federal Reserve Bank.[10] Typically, when an

[10] Prior to the Monetary Control Act of 1980, only member commercial banks could borrow from a Federal Reserve Bank.

institution borrows, its reserve account is increased; and when the institution repays the Fed, its reserves are decreased. Thus, borrowing from the Fed increases the loan-making capabilities of depository institutions.

Discount rate

The interest rate that a Federal Reserve Bank charges a financial depository institution for borrowing reserves.

The interest rate that the Fed charges a depository institution for borrowing reserves is called the **discount rate.**[11] An increase in the discount rate, because it increases the price institutions must pay for reserves, is an attempt by the Federal Reserve to discourage reserve borrowing. A decrease in the discount rate is an attempt to encourage reserve borrowing.

The Federal Reserve does not provide an endless supply of borrowed reserves for depository institutions. It requires the borrowing institution to present a good reason for its loan request, such as an emergency or seasonal problem. Thus, in addition to its control over the actual discount rate, the Federal Reserve can further affect the level of reserves by accepting or refusing institutional loan requests.

Discount rate changes are always announced publicly and serve as an indicator of the intentions of the Fed. For example, an increase in the discount rate signals an attempt to tighten the money supply, with the probable consequence of an increase in the interest rate that depository institutions charge their loan customers. This would be an appropriate policy to fight demand-pull inflationary pressure. A decrease in the discount rate signals an attempt to loosen the money supply, with the probable consequence of a decrease in the interest rate. This measure might be followed when policy makers are concerned with unemployment. Table 8.5 lists the various discount rates charged from 1980 through 1990.

Federal Funds market

The market in which banks borrow reserves from other banks.

As noted in Application 8.1, in addition to borrowing from the Fed, banks can borrow reserves from other banks in the **Federal Funds market.** However, the effect on the system is different when banks borrow reserves from one another rather than from the Fed. When banks borrow from other banks in the Federal Funds market, they are exchanging reserves that are already in the system. When banks borrow from the Fed, new reserves are created in the system.

Open market operations

The buying and selling of securities, primarily U.S. government securities, on the open market by the Federal Reserve.

Open Market Committee

The committee that determines the general policy on Federal Reserve open market operations.

Open Market Operations   The buying and selling of securities, primarily U.S. government securities,[12] on the open market by the Federal Reserve is referred to as **open market operations.** Of the three tools of monetary policy, open market operations is the one used most often for changing excess reserves in the financial depository institutions system. Open market operations are housed in the Federal Reserve Bank of New York and are carried on each business day, thus allowing for immediate alteration of reserves. The **Open Market Committee,** consisting of the Board of Governors and five

---

[11] Be careful to distinguish between the discount rate, which is the interest rate paid by banks to the Fed for borrowing reserves, and the prime rate, which is the interest rate banks charge their best short-term commercial and industrial customers.

[12] Recall that U.S. Treasury securities result from federal government borrowing to finance deficit spending.

Table 8.5 Federal Reserve Bank Discount Rates

Changes in the discount rate encourage and discourage the borrowing of reserves by financial depository institutions from the Federal Reserve, and serve as an indicator of the money supply intentions of the Fed.

Effective Date		Range for All Federal Reserve Banks[a]	Effective Date		Range for All Federal Reserve Banks[a]
1980	Feb. 15	12–13%		Nov. 22	9–9½%
	19	13		26	9
	May 29	12–13		Dec. 14	8½–9
	30	12		17	8½
	June 13	11–12	1984	Apr. 9	8½–9
	16	11		13	9
	July 28	10–11		Nov. 21	8½–9
	29	10		26	8½
	Sept. 26	11		Dec. 24	8
	Nov. 17	12	1985	May 20	7½–8
	Dec. 5	12–13		24	7½
1981	May 5	13–14	1986	Mar. 7	7–7½
	8	14		10	7
	Nov. 2	13–14		April 21	6½–7
	6	13		July 11	6
	Dec. 4	12		Aug. 12	5½–6
1982	July 20	11½–12		22	5½
	23	11½	1987	Sept. 4	5½–6
	Aug. 2	11–11½		11	6
	3	11	1988	Aug. 9	6–6½
	16	10½		11	6½
	27	10–10½	1989	Feb. 24	6½–7
	30	10		27	7
	Oct. 12	9½–10	1990	Dec. 19	6½
	13	9½			

[a]Each individual Federal Reserve Bank determines the discount rate it charges. Generally, the rates of all 12 banks are the same. However, in the event that they are not, the range is given here.

Source: Table 1.14, "Federal Reserve Bank Interest Rates," *Federal Reserve Bulletin*, March 1991, p. A7.

Federal Reserve Bank presidents, determines the general direction of open market policy. Let us examine first the process through which the Fed buys securities.

When the Fed buys securities on the open market, it can do so from banks or from dealers.[13] If a security is purchased by the Federal Reserve from a bank, the Fed takes the security for its own and credits the amount of the security to the selling bank's reserve account. For example, if the Fed wanted to buy government securities and if Hometown Bank were holding $1 million in Treasury notes in its portfolio that it wanted to sell, Hometown could exchange the securities for a $1 million increase in its reserve account.

When the Fed buys securities from a dealer, it pays for them by issuing the dealer a check. The dealer then deposits the check in a depository institution where, when it is cleared, the reserve account of the institution is increased by the amount of the check. A $1 million purchase of securities by the Fed from a dealer will eventually increase reserves in the dealer's depository institution by $1 million. Thus, whether the Fed buys securities from a bank or a dealer, the effect of its buying is an increase in reserves in the system.

When the Fed sells securities, it again trades with banks or dealers. If it sells to a bank, the bank exchanges its reserves for the securities, thus decreasing reserves. For example, if the Fed wants to sell Treasury notes and Hometown Bank wants to buy $2 million worth, Hometown could trade $2 million in its reserve account for these securities.

If the Fed sells to a dealer, the dealer pays for the securities by giving a check to the Fed. When the dealer's check clears, the dealer's depository institution loses reserves. A $2 million sale to a dealer will decrease the reserve account of the dealer's depository institution by $2 million. Thus, when the Fed sells securities, reserves are removed from the system.[14]

It is important to understand that when reserves are increased or decreased because the Fed is buying securities from, or selling them to, banks and dealers on the open market, the Fed is not transferring reserves from one account to another. Rather, the Federal Reserve is either creating new reserves for the system or destroying those that already exist.

Open market operations provide a powerful tool for enacting monetary policy for two reasons. First, changes in reserves can be achieved quickly

---

[13] The Federal Reserve cannot demand that a bank or dealer sell its securities to, or buy them from, the Fed. Rather, if the Fed intends to buy, it must offer a price high enough to induce a bank or dealer to sell. The reverse holds true if the Fed intends to sell. Most of the buying and selling by the Fed is done through dealers. In fact, many banks work through a dealer rather than directly with the Fed.

[14] Securities dealers' banks serve as "pass throughs" for changes in excess reserves since dealers are buying and selling for clients throughout the country. For example, when a dealer in New York sells a security for a client who banks in Texas, ultimately the proceeds from the security sale pass through the dealer's bank to the client's bank in Texas. Thus, the impact of open market operations is felt throughout the banking system and not just at dealers' depository institutions. See "Securities Dealer" in Application 8.2 for more information on the activities of dealers and open market operations.

because operations are carried on every business day. Second, the quantity of reserves can be altered slightly or greatly depending upon whether government securities are bought or sold in small or large quantities.

In summary, the Federal Reserve can increase or decrease depository institutions' excess reserves (and the supply of money) through its open market operations, and/or changes in the reserve requirement, and/or changes in the discount rate. If the Fed were pursuing an expansionary policy to increase excess reserves in the system, it could buy securities from banks and dealers, and/or lower the reserve requirement, and/or lower the discount rate. If the Fed were pursuing a policy to fight demand-pull inflation, it could sell securities, and/or increase the reserve requirement, and/or increase the discount rate to remove excess reserves from the system and shrink the money supply.

"Test Your Understanding: Financial Depository Institution Calculations" provides an opportunity to practice some computations introduced in this chapter that relate to depository institution reserves and lending, and monetary policy tools.

The actions of the Federal Reserve are closely watched because of the impact of policy decisions on interest rates and on economic activity. The public in general has become more aware of monetary terms such as M1 and M2 and of actions such as changes in the discount rate because of the way such matters affect jobs, mortgage rates, automobile loans, and other facets of everyday life. Businesses, particularly those in financial areas, have begun to hire experts to anticipate Federal Reserve moves because changes in the interest rate by even a small percentage can cost them millions of dollars. Application 8.2, "Dealing with the Fed," concerns three professionals whose jobs are affected by the day-to-day operations of the Federal Reserve: a Fed watcher, a securities dealer, and a bank vice-president.

Government Deficits and Monetary Policy

Federal government borrowing has an important effect on the interest rate and the amount of borrowing by households and businesses. As a consequence, there is a potential relationship between government borrowing and monetary policy that needs to be understood.

Recall that the downward-sloping demand curve for loans illustrated in Figures 8.1 and 8.2 came from the demand for loans by households and businesses, which are interest-rate sensitive in their plans to borrow. When the government, which is not interest-rate sensitive, plans to borrow to finance its deficit spending, its demand for borrowing is added to that of households and businesses, thus shifting the demand curve for loanable funds to the right. This is illustrated in Figure 8.4a by a shift in the demand curve for loanable funds from D1, which represents the demand for funds by households and businesses, to D2, which adds government borrowing to that of households and businesses. As a result of government borrowing, the interest rate rises—in this example, from 10 percent to 16 percent—and the

Test Your Understanding

Financial Depository Institution Calculations[a]

[a]Answers can be found at the end of the book. All depository institutions in this exercise are hypothetical.

1. Colorado Savings and Loan, which has a reserve requirement of 10 percent on its deposits, has calculated the following numbers as of the end of business today: total deposits = $1,350,000; reserve account = $375,000; and vault cash = $225,500. Based on this information, determine the following for this S&L.

    Required reserves = _____
    Actual reserves = _____
    Excess reserves = _____

2. How much in new loans can Washington National Bank make if its deposits are $4,500,000, vault cash is $550,500, and reserve account balance is $775,000? Washington's reserve requirement is 8 percent.

    New loans = _____

3. What is the amount that must be borrowed by Goldcoast Savings and Loan to cover its anticipated reserve shortfall if it has a reserve requirement of 12 percent, deposits of $2,750,000, vault cash of $250,000, a reserve account of $325,000, and it has just made a new loan of $250,000 that has not yet cleared?

    New borrowing = _____

4. The Federal Reserve puts $5,000,000 in new excess reserves into the system when the reserve requirement is 8 percent. What is the money multiplier and the maximum amount by which the money supply can increase because of these new reserves?

    Money multiplier = _____
    Money supply increase = _____

5. The Fed decides to raise the reserve requirement from 10 percent to 11 percent. By how much will excess reserves decrease at Lincoln Bank if Lincoln has $3,350,000 in deposits and $575,000 in actual reserves?

    Decrease in excess reserves = _____

6. Continental Iowa Bank has a reserve requirement of 6 percent, deposits of $850,000, vault cash of $125,500, a reserve account of $250,000, and $300,000 in government securities. How much in new excess reserves will be created at Continental Iowa if it sells $200,000 of its government securities to the Fed?

    New excess reserves = _____

quantity of loans made rises—in this example, from $250 million to $300 million. The increase in the interest rate that results from government borrowing discourages business and household borrowing, so that the growth in government borrowing is accompanied by a decrease in private borrowing. This is the **crowding out** problem that was introduced in Chapter Six.[15]

Crowding out

Occurs when borrowing by the federal government increases the interest rate and reduces borrowing by households and businesses.

[15]See page 244.

Application 8.2

Dealing with the Fed

Fed Watcher

David Resler awakens every weekday morning at precisely 5:45, then catches the train or ferry to New York, where he presides over Nomura Securities as chief economist, alias "Fed-watcher."

The first order of business is to update himself on the overseas markets by reaching sources in London and Tokyo. At 8 a.m., he joins 40 others at a daily sales and trade meeting.

Resler, 41, has the floor for the first five minutes, relaying announced economic statistics and projecting any action he expects the Federal Reserve Board to take or new developments that might influence the securities market.

If [he] doesn't have to rush on to a meeting of the equities department or a senior management meeting, he is on the bond department's floor by 8:30 a.m., offering "instant analysis" to traders and salespeople through an intercom system, which is commonly referred to as the squawk box.

By 9:30 a.m., Resler is back at his desk filing a commentary on what he expects the Fed to do within the next several days. If the government releases an economic forecast that day, Resler fields calls from half a dozen or more national news reporters, investigating new twists in the economic data between calls. . . .

A Fed-watcher, says Resler, who was with the Federal Reserve Bank of St. Louis before moving into financial services, has to anticipate the Fed's next policy move as well as analyze the last one.

Securities Dealer

New York—When the Fed light on Richard Kelly's console flashes on it does not signal a chance for a casual chat.

Picking up the phone, he is likely to hear a message something like the following: "We're taking offerings for bills. Regular delivery. Click."

The call is from a Fed staffer at the Open Market Trading Desk of the Federal Reserve Bank of New York advising Mr. Kelly, a dealer at Aubrey G. Lanston & Co., that the Fed is buying Treasury bills—short-term U.S. government securities—for delivery the next day.

"That first call is a quick one," he says. "It takes only about three seconds. They'll usually call back to let us know the time by which they want to receive our offers to sell."

Lanston is one of 36 firms that are primary dealers—firms the traders on the Fed's open market desk will call to announce the intended purchases. All the dealers are reached within the span of a minute to be notified that the Fed is buying bills.

Minutes later, the word will be out in the financial community—world-wide—that "the Fed is in," meaning that the Fed is in the open market to buy securities.

"As soon as we hear from the Fed, we'll call our customers who might have bills they want to sell, and we'll also evaluate our own holdings to see whether we want to make an offer. Then, at the

The rise in the interest rate from government borrowing could be prevented if the Federal Reserve would increase excess reserves in the system by an amount equal to the increase in the demand for funds by the government. Figure 8.4b illustrates a shift in the supply curve for loanable funds to the right, from S1 to S2, by an amount necessary to compensate for the increase in demand. Notice that the increase in supply to S2 keeps the interest rate at the original level of 10 percent. This increase in the money appointed time, we'll call back and make our offers to sell," Mr. Kelly explains. . . .

When Mr. Kelly calls back with an offer of securities already held by Lanston or from Lanston's customers, he will list specific amounts of bills and the "discounts"—percentage reductions from the face values of the bills—at which Lanston or its customers are willing to offer them. The discount determines the price at which the bill is offered—the higher the discount, the lower the price of the bill. . . .

Once the Fed has received bids from the dealers, staffers . . . compare offers. It will take the best offers—those that give the highest discount—for the total quantity of bills the desk is buying that day.

It is typical for the Fed to buy more than a billion dollars worth of bills or bonds on days it is in the market. . . .

Bank Vice-President

According to Mr. [John] Falkenberg [vice-president of United Bank of Denver, the largest bank in the Rocky Mountain region], managing a bank's reserve position is tricky business.

"We need reserves of about $60 million. We keep $10 million of that in the vault, which means we have to have the other $50 million on deposit at the Fed.

"About $1.5 billion flows through our bank every day, so you'd think it would be easy to keep $60 million in reserve. But a sudden outflow of checks can wipe out your reserve position pretty fast."

Mr. Falkenberg's staff meets every morning to assess the bank's reserve position and to discuss likely withdrawals that day. These discussions, and the course of events during the day, determine its policies in lending money and its borrowing in the federal funds market.

"We try to meet our reserve requirement on a continuous basis," Mr. Falkenberg says. "You don't want to get to Tuesday night and find yourself in trouble," referring to the every-other-Wednesday day of reckoning with the Fed.

Like most banks, United rarely goes directly to the Fed for a loan.

"Borrowing at the Fed is a privilege, not a right," observes Mr. Falkenberg. "We only do it about a half-dozen times a year for unusual situations."

Mr. Falkenberg recalls the time a plane carrying checks was delayed by bad weather in Chicago, leaving United short on funds overnight. The bank got an overnight loan from the Fed to cover the shortfall.

"When something like that happens, you don't want the guys at the Fed to be able to say you've been borrowing excessively and to turn you down," he explains. . . .

Source: David S. Kidwell and Richard L. Peterson, *Financial Institutions, Markets, and Money*, 4th ed., (Hinsdale, Ill.: The Dryden Press, 1990), pp. 586–587. Excerpted from Timothy Tregarthen, "Making Money at the Fed," *The Margin*, March 1987, pp. 10–11. Excerpted with permission.

Monetizing the debt
Increasing the money supply by the Federal Reserve to accommodate federal government borrowing and reduce upward pressure on the interest rate.

supply by the Federal Reserve to accommodate federal government borrowing plans and reduce upward pressure on the interest rate is referred to as **monetizing the debt.** By monetizing the debt, the Fed could hold the interest rate at its pre-government borrowing level, and offset the crowding out effect.

Why doesn't the Federal Reserve simply create enough reserves on a regular basis to cover the federal government's demand for funds, thereby

Figure 8.4   Interest Rate and Loan-Making Changes from
                        Government Borrowing and Monetizing the Debt

When excess reserves are increased to keep the interest rate from rising due to
an increase in the demand for funds because of government deficit spending,
a larger quantity of loans is made than would be made if excess reserves were
left unchanged.

**a. Increase in Demand from
Government Deficit Borrowing**

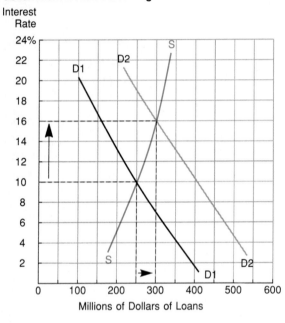

**b. Increase in Demand Met by
an Equal Increase in Supply**

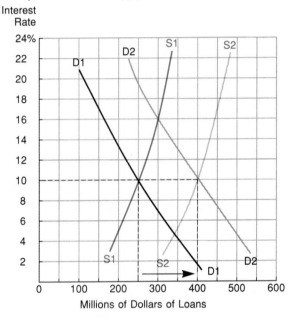

eliminating the upward pressure that government borrowing puts on
interest rates? The Federal Reserve has generally adhered to a philosophy
of controlling the money supply for the benefit of the macroeconomy, rather
than accommodating government deficit spending. If it always increased
reserves to meet government needs, the money supply could increase too
quickly, causing inflation and weakening the value of the dollar. Notice in
Figure 8.4b that when the Fed increases excess reserves to meet increased
government demand for borrowing, a $150 million increase in loans results:
from the original $250 million when demand and supply were at D1 and S1,
to $400 million when demand and supply are at D2 and S2. As illustrated in
Figure 8.4a, were the Fed not to increase excess reserves to accommodate
government borrowing, the quantity of loans would increase by only $50
million.

Advantages and Disadvantages of Monetary Policy

There are several advantages and disadvantages to using monetary policy as a tool for correcting the problems of inflation and unemployment. A primary advantage is the speed with which changes can be implemented. Unlike fiscal policy, which could take months to implement, the first steps toward changing the money supply can be taken the day the decision to do so is made.

A second advantage of using monetary policy is its flexibility with regard to the size of the change to be implemented. Reserves can be increased or decreased in small or large increments.

A third advantage is that monetary policy is largely removed from politics. The members of the Board of Governors, although appointed by a president, are not as subject to political pressure as the members of Congress. This may be partially due to the fact that board members are appointed for lengthy (14-year) terms and are not campaigning for reelection. The Board of Governors' motives in expanding and contracting the money supply are usually economic.

One of the major disadvantages of monetary policy is the loan-making link through which it is carried out. That is, the Fed can increase reserves to stimulate economic activity as much as it wants, but the reserves themselves do not alter the money supply. Before the money supply is increased, someone must be willing to borrow and a bank must be willing to lend. Since the Fed cannot force the loan-making process, it has only indirect control over increasing the money supply.

This loan-making link may reduce the effectiveness of monetary policy in fighting unemployment during a deep and serious recession. If economic conditions are severe, no expansion of reserves or lowering of the interest rate may be enough to induce borrowers to take out loans.

A second problem with monetary policy occurs during inflation. As the Federal Reserve tightens up the money supply and forces the interest rate higher, it raises the price for borrowed money. Businesses that borrow at this high rate may in turn raise prices on their products to compensate. Thus, fighting inflation with monetary policy could worsen it.

Finally, there are those who feel that having the Federal Reserve and monetary policy removed from the political process is a disadvantage. Over the years there have been several proposals to place the Federal Reserve under more congressional control. Proponents of this action do not favor the independence of the Fed and presume that with control it would be more sensitive to public reaction in its policy making.

Before leaving this chapter, two further considerations merit mention. First, recall from Chapter Six that it is possible for unemployment and inflation to occur simultaneously, and that when this happens, there is no clearly appropriate fiscal policy to follow. Likewise, there is no clearly appropriate monetary policy to follow when both problems develop. Application 8.3, "What's the Fed to Do?," illustrates the policy dilemma faced

Application 8.3

What's the Fed to Do?

The Federal Reserve System almost always finds itself in some sort of box. Some people will want the central bank to ease money while others will urge it to tighten up. Usually, the Fed finds a way to work itself out of such trouble. This time, however, it may have waited too long.

Until March [1990], things seemed to be going fairly well. The economy had slowed, but recession forecasts were few. The Shadow Open Market Committee, a group of academic and business economists often critical of the Fed, said at its semiannual meeting, "Monetary policy remains consistent with moderate recovery and declining inflation." That's about as nice a comment as it ever makes about the Fed.

But things soon began to change, and not really for the better. Nearly everyone realized that the 8.2% spurt of the consumer price index in the first quarter, on an annual-rate basis, was a temporary phenomenon, produced by cold-weather increases in food and energy costs. These factors faded in the second quarter, but new price difficulties arose. Labor costs, which had been unusually quiet through the long business expansion, were climbing. Even before the Mideast crisis sent oil prices soaring, analysts were predicting rising inflation the rest of this year. . . .

Ordinarily, the Fed's next move would seem automatic. Inflationary pressures are growing, so the inflation-hating Fed tightens up, right? Not necessarily.

Administration officials for weeks have been reminding the Federal Reserve that it has some responsibility for the health of the economy. The rise in the inflation-adjusted gross national product slowed to an annual rate of 1.2%, and the Mideast oil shock has increased talk of recession. . . .

That leads to the Federal Reserve's current unhappy situation. The central bank can't move against the increased inflationary pressures without, in all probability, triggering a recession. If the Fed, instead, moves significantly to spur the sagging economy, . . . inflation will take off. . . .

What should the Fed do now? If it chooses to ease, the inflationary pressures increase. If it chooses to tighten, the recessionary pressures increase.

Source: Lindley H. Clark, Jr., "It May Be Too Late for the Fed to Ease," *The Wall Street Journal*, August 22, 1990, p. A10.

by the Federal Reserve in late 1990, when the economy was experiencing inflationary pressure while slipping into a recession.

Second, it should be pointed out that there is an economic philosophy called monetarism, and that those who adhere to it are termed monetarists. Generally, monetarists believe that controlling the money supply is the main vehicle for controlling economic activity. Monetarism, Keynesian economics, and other viewpoints on economic policy are discussed in the next chapter.

Summary

A significant relationship exists between an economy's supply of money and its levels of output, employment, and prices. Because of this relationship, one method for accomplishing the macroeconomic goals is altering the money supply.

The effect of money on the level of economic activity can be illustrated by the equation of exchange. This equation shows that, operating through aggregate spending, changes in the supply of money lead to changes in output, employment, and/or prices, depending on how close the economy is to full employment. Generally, if the economy is at less than full employment, increases in the money supply expand output and employment. If the economy is at or near full employment, increases in the money supply cause increases in prices. A decrease in the money supply contracts output and employment and may dampen upward pressure on prices.

Changes in the money supply occur through lending by financial depository institutions: money is created when loans are made and destroyed when they are repaid. The ability of an institution to make loans is limited by the amount of its excess reserves, which is the difference between the institution's actual reserves and its required reserves. Required reserves is the amount of reserves that the institution must hold to back its deposits, and is found by multiplying the reserve requirement by the institution's deposits. If loans were made in an amount greater than the institution's excess reserves, the institution would risk dropping its actual reserves below its required reserves. Lending is not accomplished by transferring funds from one account to another. Rather, loans represent newly created money.

An initial increase or decrease in excess reserves in the system will cause total lending and the money supply to change by a much larger, or a multiple, amount. The money multiplier itself is the reciprocal of the reserve requirement, and the maximum change in the money supply is equal to the multiplier times the initial change in excess reserves.

Because borrowing from financial depository institutions by businesses and households is voluntary, having excess reserves available does not ensure that loans will be made. The stimulus for businesses and households to borrow when increased spending is desired, or to reduce borrowing when spending is excessive, is the interest rate, which is a cost of borrowing money. As the interest rate increases, the amount of borrowing by businesses and households and the amount of total spending based on borrowing decreases. When the interest rate is lowered, the reverse holds true.

The rate of interest on loans made by financial depository institutions is determined by the demand for loans and by the supply of loans available, which is based on excess reserves. Increasing excess reserves increases the supply of loans available, lowers the interest rate, and raises the amount of loans made. Decreasing excess reserves increases the interest rate and reduces the amount of loans made.

Adjusting the money supply to accomplish the macroeconomic goals is a major responsibility of the Federal Reserve. This adjustment is performed through the use of three tools of monetary policy: the reserve requirement, the discount rate, and open market operations. The purpose of each tool is to influence the level of borrowing and spending by causing changes in the excess reserves of financial depository institutions. Monetary policy to stimulate spending calls for lowering the reserve requirement, and/or reducing the discount rate, and/or the Fed's buying securities on the open market. Monetary policy to dampen spending calls for raising the reserve requirement, and/or raising the discount rate, and/or the Fed's selling securities on the open market. Of the three policy tools, open market operations is the most important and the most frequently used.

The Federal Reserve could keep the interest rate stable in the face of large government borrowing to finance deficit spending by increasing excess reserves to accommodate the government's demand for funds. However, such actions on a persistent basis, called monetizing the debt, could weaken the value of the dollar.

The use of monetary policy to correct unemployment or demand-pull inflation has the advantage of flexibility in timing and size. It has the disadvantages, however, of possible ineffectiveness in a severe recession and of the potential to make inflation worse in a tight money situation. The fact that the Federal Reserve is removed from politics is viewed by some as an advantage and by others as a disadvantage.

Key Terms and Concepts

Equation of exchange	Monetary policy
Velocity of money	Easy money policy
Actual reserves	Tight money policy
Reserve requirement	Discount rate
Required reserves	Federal Funds market
Excess reserves	Open market operations
Creation and destruction of money	Open Market Committee
Money multiplier	Crowding out
Interest rate	Monetizing the debt
Prime rate	

Review Questions

1. Assuming that the supply of money in the economy is $750 billion and velocity is 5, answer questions a through d.
    a. What is the dollar value of output produced in the economy?
    b. What would happen to the dollar value of output and the real value of output if $50 billion were added to the money supply when the economy was at full employment?
    c. What would happen to the level of prices and to the level of output produced in the economy if the Fed reduced the supply of money to dampen inflationary pressure when the economy was at full employment?
    d. What would happen to the dollar value of output if people spent money faster (velocity increased) following a reduction in the money supply by the Fed?

 Assume that Hometown Bank has $3,000,000 in demand deposits, a 15 percent reserve requirement, and $520,000 in actual reserves. Based on these figures, what are Hometown Bank's required and excess reserves, and how much in new loans could it make?

3. What is the money multiplier, and how is it related to the reserve requirement? If the Federal Reserve increases excess reserves in the system by $18 million with a reserve requirement of 12 percent, what is the maximum amount by which the money supply can increase as a result of the increased excess reserves?

4. Assume that the reserve requirement is 12.5 percent and that $200,000 is added to Hometown Bank's excess reserves as a result of a change in Federal Reserve policy.
   a. How much in new loans can Hometown Bank make as a result of this increase in excess reserves?
   b. If the entire amount of Hometown Bank's new loans were spent and the funds were deposited in Bank B, by how much could Bank B increase its loan making?
   c. By how much could loan making be increased in the financial depository institutions system as a result of the increase in Hometown Bank's excess reserves?
   d. How much in new loans could have been made in the financial depository institutions system following the initial increase in Hometown Bank's excess reserves if the reserve requirement were 20 percent?

5. Suppose the Federal Reserve is concerned about demand-pull inflationary pressure that is building in the economy.
   a. What would be the appropriate change in excess reserves to counteract this problem?
   b. What would be the appropriate change in the reserve requirement, the discount rate, and open market operations to bring about this change in excess reserves?

6. How would each of the following affect the supply and/or demand for loans, the interest rate, and the actual amount of loans made?
   a. The Federal Reserve sells securities on the open market.
   b. The U.S. government borrows on the open market and the Fed does not monetize the debt.
   c. The U.S. government borrows on the open market and the Fed monetizes the debt.
   d. The Federal Reserve lowers the discount rate.
   e. Private investment spending decreases because of fears of a recession.

7. What would be the effect of each of the following on Uptown Bank's excess reserves and loan-making ability if the bank had $60 million in deposits, a 5 percent reserve requirement, and actual reserves of $4 million?
   a. The Federal Reserve sells $500,000 in government securities to Uptown Bank.
   b. The reserve requirement increases from 5 percent to 6 percent.
   c. The discount rate is increased.
   d. The reserve requirement is lowered from 5 percent to 4 percent and the Federal Reserve buys $1 million in government securities from the bank.

Discussion Questions

1. It is assumed in the equation of exchange that the velocity of money is fixed, or constant. Is this a safe assumption when applied to your own spending habits over the course of a month or a year? What would erratic and unpredictable velocity do to the usefulness of the equation of exchange?

2. In a discussion with a friend you are told that it makes no difference whether the Federal Reserve uses open market operations, the reserve requirement, or the discount rate to change the supply of money, because the impact of each of the policies is exactly the same. Do you agree or disagree with your friend's position?

3. Control by the Federal Reserve over the money supply and over total spending is weakened by the fact that borrowing by businesses and households is voluntary. How might the power of the Federal Reserve over borrowing be strengthened? Is this method consistent with the philosophy of capitalism?

4. Assume that the economy is at full employment and that the federal government needs to borrow $10 billion to finance a deficit budget. Should the Federal Reserve monetize the debt by putting an extra $10 billion in reserves into the system to finance this borrowing? If not, what action should the Fed take?

5. If you were trying to control inflation, would you depend on fiscal or monetary policy? Why? If you were trying to reduce unemployment, would you depend on fiscal or monetary policy? Why?

6. Suppose the economy was experiencing inflationary pressure due to rising food and energy costs at the same time that it was slipping into a recession due to cutbacks in defense spending. As the chairperson of the Board of Governors, how would you balance the attention you give to these two problems and how would you use the tools of monetary policy to deal with this situation? Would it make sense to use monetary policy to solve one of the problems while asking Congress to use fiscal policy to solve the other?

7. Some people have described the chairperson of the Board of Governors of the Federal Reserve as the second most powerful person in the United States. In light of this, what argument could be made for, and what argument could be made against, placing the Federal Reserve under the control of the U.S. Secretary of the Treasury?

Critical Thinking Case 8

■ The Fed during the Great Depression

Critical Thinking Skills | Explore similarities between historical and contemporary events
Identify cause and effect

Economic Concepts | Monetary policy
The Federal Reserve

During the Great Depression of the 1930s, the Federal Reserve took little action in the face of widespread bank failure and a serious decline in the economy. The following deals with some reasons for this inactivity.

It would be hard to find an economic historian of any persuasion who would defend the actions of the Fed during the banking crisis [of the Great Depression]. But there is little consensus on why the Fed remained so passive in the face of an unprecedented collapse of the banking system. In its defense the Federal Reserve Board maintained in its 1932 Annual Report that its use of open-market purchases of bonds (which pump reserves into the banking system) was inhibited by the requirement that Federal Reserve notes be backed by either gold or eligible paper (loans sold by the banks to the Fed). . . . But it is not clear that the Fed made a determined effort to get the rules changed, as it undoubtedly could have. Nor should it be forgotten that in 1931 Fed officials refused to inject reserves for far less technical reasons. In his diary entries during August 1931, Charles S. Hamlin, then a member of the Board, tells us that the Open Market Committee voted 11 to 1 against open-market purchases of $300 million, substituting $120 million instead. The governors of the regional banks, who were still in control of monetary policy, simply could not grasp the extent of the catastrophe, and Governor Meyer of the Federal Reserve Board was even worried about inflation.

Perhaps officials at the Fed were looking at the wrong indicators of monetary policy. If they felt that low interest rates are a certain sign of easy money [the annual interest rate on commercial paper, or short-term business loans, was 2.63 percent in 1931, 2.72 percent in 1932, and 1.67 percent in 1933], then they would have concluded that financial markets were awash with money, and that trying to pump in more could do little good. A power struggle within the Federal Reserve system . . . was also important. In the 1920s the Federal Reserve Bank of New York, under its charismatic president Benjamin Strong, had dominated the system. After Strong's death in 1928 the Federal Reserve Board in Washington tried to assert its authority by resisting pressures from New York. But this power struggle took its toll in the 1930s when the New York Bank pushed for more expansionary monetary policies and the Board in Washington resisted for internal political reasons. Other reasons for the passivity of the Fed have been given, but the important point is that the system, for whatever reasons, failed to stop the greatest banking crisis in American economic history.

Questions

1. What is the significance of knowledge of Federal Reserve actions during the 1930s to the analysis of contemporary monetary policy?

2. In what ways did Federal Reserve policy in the early 1930s likely affect the U.S. economy?

3. What types of historical information (federal budgets, for example) would you want to know before you determined the extent to which monetary policy contributed to the Great Depression?

Source: Gary M. Walton and Hugh Rockoff, *History of the American Economy*, 6th ed., (San Diego, Calif.: Harcourt Brace Jovanovich, Publishers, 1990), pp. 488–490.

Suggested Readings

Michael T. Belongia, "Monetary Policy on the 75th Anniversary of the Federal Reserve System: Summary of a Conference Proceedings," Federal Reserve Bank of St. Louis, *Review*, September/October 1990, pp. 59–65.
Summarizes the papers given by several distinguished economists at a recent conference on monetary policy.

Board of Governors of the Federal Reserve System, *Federal Reserve Bulletin* (Washington, D.C.: Federal Reserve System, published monthly).
Includes articles, statements to Congress, a record of Open Market Committee policy actions, financial and business statistics, and other information.

Andrew Coyne, "The Vote Standard," *National Review*, June 10, 1991, pp. 23–29.
Argues that the Fed should be elected.

Federal Reserve Bank of New York, *Federal Reserve System Public Information Materials* (New York: Federal Reserve Bank of New York, published annually).
A guide to general and specialized information available through the Federal Reserve System.

Milton Friedman, "A Theoretical Framework for Monetary Analysis," *Milton Friedman's Monetary Framework*, R. J. Gordon, ed. (Chicago: The University of Chicago Press, 1974), pp. 1–62, particularly pp. 1–15.
A discussion of different methods of representing the equation of exchange and of factors influencing the demand for and supply of money.

Thomas Kamm, "Brazil's Harsh Attack on Inflation is Risking Deep Economic Slump," *The Wall Street Journal*, May 10, 1990, pp. A1, A14.
Discusses problems faced in the Brazilian economy because of the strong monetary policy being used to counteract hyperinflation.

Cara S. Lown, "Banking and the Economy: What Are the Facts?" Federal Reserve Bank of Dallas, *Economic Review*, September 1990, pp. 1–14.
Explores the relationship between fluctuations in bank lending and economic activity. Considers the importance of bank lending versus security purchases.

Richard D.C. Trainer, *The Basics of Interest Rates* **(New York: Federal Reserve Bank of New York, 1987).**
A short pamphlet on the basics of interest rates: the meaning and effect of interest rates, types of credit markets, the supply and demand of funds, and other topics.

Timothy Tregarthen, "The Fed and the Depression: The Great Conspiracy?" *The Margin,* **September/October 1990, p. 35.**
Discusses a new approach to the role of the Federal Reserve during the Great Depression.

Chapter Nine

Assessing Goals, Tools, and Policies in the Macroeconomy

The road to economic growth, which is one of the macroeconomy's goals, is not always smooth or problem-free.

Source: © Peggy Peattie/
Long Beach Press-Telegram.

Chapter Objectives

1. To discuss economic growth, identify the factors that affect growth, and introduce some costs associated with growth.

2. To explore more fully the tradeoff between employment and price stability.

3. To introduce the Phillips curve and recent U.S. experiences with unemployment and inflation.

4. To discuss wage-price controls, highlight recent U.S. experiences with wage-price controls, and discuss indexing.

5. To survey the classical, Keynesian, monetarist, new classical, and supply-side viewpoints on macroeconomic policy.

6. To present some final thoughts on evaluating macroeconomic policy proposals.

In Chapters Four through Eight the goals of the macroeconomy (full production and economic growth, full employment, and price stability) and fiscal and monetary policies, the main tools for accomplishing those objectives, were introduced. At this point you should be familiar with the relationships between the goals, the measures of the extent to which they are accomplished, and the mechanics of fiscal and monetary policies.

Some fundamental questions and issues regarding these goals and policy instruments should be highlighted to complete your understanding of macroeconomics. For example, up to this point we have not closely examined the growth performance of the U.S. economy. How much has the economy grown over the years, what factors are critical to generating economic growth, and what costs are associated with continual increases in production? In addition, we have learned to think in terms of attaining either full employment or price stability, but not both. Why do we believe that a choice must be made between these two objectives? Is this tradeoff an accurate representation of how the economy actually operates?

Questions and issues also surround the use of fiscal and monetary policies. How well do these policy instruments perform? Are certain types of macroeconomic problems not readily solved by these policies? Do effective alternatives exist, or should there be no intervention in the macroeconomy? What are the different schools of thought on how policy instruments should be used?

Chapter Nine is divided into three sections devoted to these issues. The first section reexamines the goals of the macroeconomy by further exploring various aspects of economic growth and by taking another look at the relationship between levels of unemployment and prices. The Phillips curve, a widely recognized device for illustrating that relationship, is also introduced in this section. The second section evaluates the effectiveness of fiscal and monetary policies in the control of cost-push inflation and discusses two additional tools of economic policy: wage-price controls and indexing. The final section surveys some major macroeconomic schools of thought and policy viewpoints.

Goals of the Macroeconomy: A Further Exploration

Economic Growth

Economic growth

An increase in an economy's full production output level over time.

An economy achieves **economic growth** when it increases its full production level of output over time. As explained in Chapter Four, this requires that an economy produce up to its potential each year, *and* that the potential grow.[1] Expressed in terms of the production possibilities model, economic growth requires that an economy operate on its production possibilities curve, and that the curve shift outward, or to the right, over time. Thus, the process of growth is best understood as a series of small, cumulative advances in full employment output, perhaps in the neighborhood of 2 to 5 percent per year, rather than a few large, dramatic leaps from time to time.

Economic growth is different from the other goals of the macroeconomy. Full employment, price stability, and full production are immediate goals; economic growth is a long-term objective that is accomplished over years. Also, full employment and price stability are typically pursued by fiscal and monetary policy tools that affect aggregate, or total, demand, whereas the attainment of economic growth depends more on policies that work on the supply side of the market.

Although economic growth can be defined as an increase in output over time, it can be more precisely defined as an increase in output per capita, or per person, over time. If output increased over time, but population grew at a faster rate, output per person would decrease; even with more goods and services available, the average person would be worse off. The balance between the growth of an economy's output and its population has been important in the writings of economists from the earliest years of the discipline. For example, one of the nineteenth-century scholars of the classical school of economics, the Reverend Thomas Robert Malthus (1766–1834), theorized in *An Essay on the Principle of Population*, first published in 1798, that any economic growth would lead to a surge in population, so that the laboring class would continually be reduced to living at subsistence. In other words, population increases would always erase the

---

[1] See Chapter Four, pages 149–151.

benefits of increases in production.[2] In the middle of the nineteenth century, this theory earned economics the nickname it carries to this day: the dismal science.

The growth of real per capita GNP in the United States from 1929 to 1990 is illustrated in Figure 9.1. While the figure gives actual, rather than full employment, production, it indicates that real output per person has grown substantially over the years. In 1929, when the U.S. population was 122 million, the economy produced just under $6,000 of real output per person, and by 1989, when the population was 249 million, real output per person had grown to over $16,500. The experience of the U.S. economy denies the Malthusian view of the futility of the growth process. However, it would also be incorrect to say that growth occurs automatically in an economy. The gross domestic product of Nicaragua, for example, fell every year from 1984 through 1989.[3]

Achieving Economic Growth   Economic growth results from increasing the quantity of resources used in the production of goods and services, and/or using existing resources more efficiently. Thus, if government pursues policies to promote economic growth, they should be directed toward increasing the amount and/or efficiency of available resources.

Technically, quantities of all of a country's major resources can be increased. A country's labor force can be expanded by a policy that encourages the immigration of foreign workers or moves back the mandatory retirement age; the Netherlands, Israel, and the United States have claimed farmable land from the sea and desert; and policies such as risk sharing by the government encourage entrepreneurship. However, there are limits on how much or quickly labor, natural resources, or entrepreneurship can be increased. Capital, on the other hand, can be expanded more readily. As a result, policy makers intending to promote economic growth usually direct their attention toward increasing the amount of machines, factories, vehicles, and other capital equipment in the economy. Governments have encouraged businesses to invest in capital in several ways: by changing tax laws to allow investments to be "written off," or depreciated, over a shorter period of time; by following monetary policies to keep interest rates low to facilitate borrowing for these investments; and by participating in the production or financing of the capital itself, to name a few.

Using resources more efficiently leads to economic growth by improving the quality, or productivity, of resources that are available. Probably the most important factor leading to improved resource efficiency is **technological change,** or an increase in knowledge about production and its processes.

Technological change

An increase in knowledge about production and its processes.

[2] Thomas Robert Malthus, *An Essay on the Principle of Population,* Philip Appleman, ed. (New York: W.W. Norton & Co., 1976). Original publication, 1798.

[3] Inter-American Development Bank, *Economic and Social Progress in Latin America* (New York: Inter-American Development Bank, October 1990), p. 154. Distributed by Johns Hopkins University Press.

Figure 9.1   U.S. Economic Growth (Real GNP per Capita in 1982 Dollars)

Real output per person has grown substantially since 1929 in the United States.

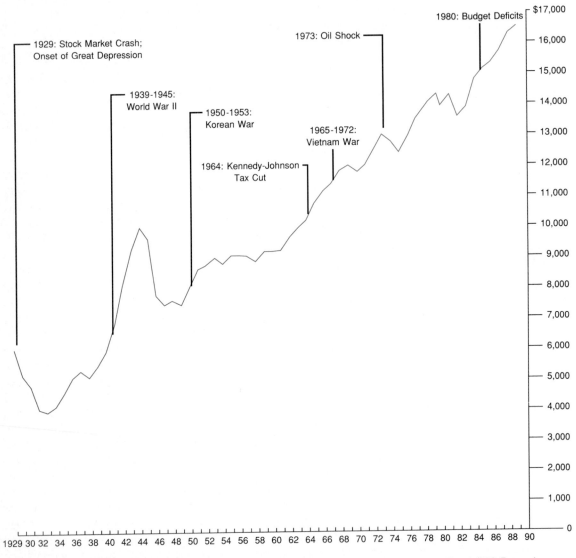

Source: U.S. Department of Commerce, *Survey of Current Business*, July 1990, p. 98. Based on The Conference Board, "U.S. Economic Growth," *Economic Road Maps*, No. 2001–2002, March 1986.

Technological change takes many forms — from rearranging existing processes and equipment to increase output, to designing and developing new and different inputs and processes to produce goods and services. Increasing efficiency through technological change is not limited to capital: improvements in the schooling and on-the-job training of workers strengthen their quality and lead to an increase in output, and better farming and mining methods increase the yield from agricultural and other land resources.

The relative importance of technological change and the increased use of capital for the growth of the U.S. economy were analyzed in a classic study by the Nobel prize–winning economist Robert Solow. Using data from 1909 through 1949, Solow concluded that gross output per worker hour doubled over this period, that technological change accounted for 87.5 percent of this change in output, and that increased use of capital accounted for the remaining 12.5 percent of the change.[4]

Application 9.1, "The 21st Century," considers another noted economist's view of the challenges that will face the United States in the next century as economic activity becomes more global in scope. Two factors are cited by the author as imperatives for economic growth: an improved and updated transportation and communication **infrastructure,** and a skilled, well-educated work force.

Infrastructure

Capital systems such as highways, pipelines, and communications networks.

Finally, if economic growth is to be realized, attention must be paid to maintaining a strong demand for the output from the economy s additional and/or improved resources. If the growth in an economy's productive capability results in the unemployment or underutilization of resources because of insufficient demand for the economy's output, the benefits of the growth effort will be largely nullified. Fiscal and monetary policies, such as those introduced in Chapters Six and Eight, could be used to stimulate demand through tax cuts, increases in government expenditures, and/or increases in the money supply. Demand could also be increased through policies to make the economy's output more competitive in export markets.

Costs of Economic Growth   Some people dispute the idea that attaining a high rate of economic growth is a desirable goal. This viewpoint is based on the argument that future costs are attached to this push for continually increased production. For example, constant annual GNPs in excess of $5 trillion in the United States result in the creation of billions of tons of garbage, including toxic, nonbiodegradable, and nuclear waste. In the years to come, this waste will create problems for society as landfills close, toxic chemicals seep into the soil, waterways are increasingly polluted, and health problems multiply. Some people argue that it may be better to produce a smaller GNP, one perhaps with no growth, and deal properly with the waste

---

[4]Robert M. Solow, "Technical Change and the Aggregate Production Function," *Review of Economics and Statistics,* August 1957, pp. 312–320.

Application 9.1

The 21st Century

[T]here is a growing connection between the amount and kind of investments we make together as a nation and the capacity of America to attract global capital. . . . [T]he skills and insights of a nation's work force, and the quality of its transportation and communication links to the world (its infrastructure), are what make it unique, and uniquely attractive, in the new world economy. Increasingly, educated brainpower—along with roads, airports, computers, and fiber-optic cables connecting it up—determines a nation's standard of living.

To understand why, it's first necessary to grasp what is happening to the global economy. The highest earnings in most worldwide industries are to be found in locations where specialized knowledge is brought to bear on problems whose solutions define new horizons of possibility. Whether the industry is old or new, mature or high-tech, specialized knowledge is accounting for a larger and larger portion of its revenues. The hottest sector of the tool-and-die casting industry, for example, produces precision castings out of aluminum and zinc for computer parts. The leading textile businesses depend on the knowledge needed to produce specially coated and finished fabrics for automobiles, office furniture, rain gear, and wall coverings, among a great many other products. . . .

. . . [T]hey are knowledge-intensive businesses that cannot easily be duplicated by low-cost competitors elsewhere in the world. Worldwide competition continues to compress profits on anything that is uniform, routine, and standard—that is, on anything that can be made, reproduced, or extracted in volume almost anywhere on the globe. . . .

The increasing subordination of financial capital to intellectual capital has confused investors. "Owning" a company no longer means what it once did. Members of the accounting profession . . . have fretted openly about the true worth of enterprises whose value rests in the brains of employees. As intellectual capital continues to displace plant and equipment as the key asset of corporations, shareholders find themselves in an ever more tenuous position, for much of the value of an enterprise can disappear with the departure of key employees. . . .

In the emerging economy of the twenty-first century only one asset is growing more valuable as it is used: the problem-solving, problem-identifying, and strategic-brokering skills of a nation's citizens. Unlike machinery that gradually wears out, raw materials that become depleted, and patents and copyrights that grow obsolete, the skills and insights that come from discovering new linkages between technologies and needs increase with practice.

Source: Excerpted from Robert B. Reich, "The Real Economy," *The Atlantic Monthly*, February 1991, pp. 35–52. Excerpted with permission.

and other problems that could create future costs. Additional problems cited by some who oppose high rates of economic growth include concern over the levels of dissatisfaction that must be created in people's minds about their possessions in order to encourage continual purchases of new goods and services, and the depletion of resources that are not easily regenerated.

The problem of measuring the costs associated with economic growth may arise from using an annual, or yearly, time frame, as is typically done when evaluating growth. That is, what is viewed as an economic contribution over a year could be viewed as detrimental in a longer time frame. The current situation with the world's rain forests provides a good example of this problem. In several countries, economic growth is being achieved by extensively overharvesting the rain forests in order to produce lumber, jobs, and increases in GNP. But viewed in a longer time frame, the future costs to the ecological balance of the entire world from this production could be substantial. The critical thinking case at the end of this chapter, "The Aral Sea," deals with the economic, ecological, and health costs that have resulted from diverting water from the Aral Sea (located in the southern Soviet Union north of Iran) over several decades to produce large amounts of cotton.

Inflation and Unemployment Tradeoff

The relationship between aggregate spending and economic conditions should be clear when dealing with the immediate goals of full employment and stable prices. Changes in the level of total spending cause changes in production, employment, and, under some circumstances, the price level. According to this relationship, increases in aggregate spending cause increases in employment, but only up to a point. At some level of economic activity full employment is reached. As aggregate spending pushes the economy toward full employment, prices begin to rise, and demand-pull inflation occurs. Decreases in aggregate spending, on the other hand, result in decreases in employment. An attempt to alleviate demand-pull inflationary pressure through reduced spending contributes to unemployment.

From this spending, employment, and price scenario, one message is clear: it is difficult for an economy to have both full employment and no inflation. The attainment of one of these goals creates an obstacle to the other. As a result, a choice must be made as to which goal to pursue: full employment with strong upward pressure on prices, or price stability with involuntary unemployment. One method for illustrating this tradeoff is a Phillips curve.

Phillips curve

A curve showing the relationship between an economy's unemployment and inflation rates.

The Phillips Curve The relationship between an economy's unemployment and inflation rates is shown by a **Phillips curve**, such as the one (using hypothetical data) illustrated in Figure 9.2. The Phillips curve in Figure 9.2 slopes downward, illustrating an inverse relationship, or tradeoff, between rates of inflation and rates of unemployment: a low inflation rate is associated with a high unemployment rate, and vice-versa.

How might a Phillips curve for the U.S. economy appear? Data showing the U.S. experience with unemployment and inflation from 1950 through 1990 are presented in Table 9.1. The GNP price deflator is used as the measure of inflation because it is a composite price index, as opposed to the consumer price index, which measures price changes for goods and services purchased by households, or the producer price index, which measures price changes for items that businesses purchase for use in production. Notice in this table that both the inflation and unemployment rates are generally higher in the 1970s and early 1980s than in the 1950s, 1960s, and late 1980s.

Figure 9.2   A Phillips Curve (Hypothetical Data)

A Phillips curve slopes downward, illustrating the inverse relationship between unemployment and inflation rates.

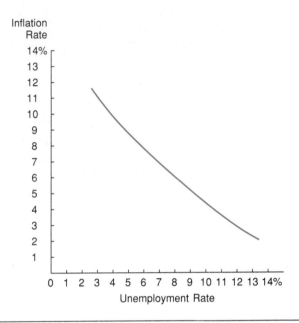

Data from Table 9.1 are plotted in Figure 9.3, where each year's experience with unemployment and inflation is represented by a point on the graph. Observe that the points representing each year shift to the right for the 1970s and early 1980s, and that in several years, particularly 1975, 1980, and 1981, the economy was plagued with unusually high rates of both unemployment and inflation.

One can relate these data to the Phillips curve by observing the inflation-unemployment combinations over the years and fitting representative curves through these points. The experience of the 1950s and 1960s provides a fairly clear-cut Phillips curve relationship. This is shown in Figure 9.3 as PC1. However, if the assumption about a tradeoff between inflation and unemployment is maintained, it is clear that there have been shifts in the Phillips curve since the 1960s. The line PC2 represents the inflation-unemployment tradeoff of the 1970s and early 1980s, and PC3 represents the tradeoff during the mid- and late 1980s. These curves indicate that the tradeoff became much more pronounced during the 1970s and early 1980s, and then weakened during the remainder of the 1980s. For example, using a 6 percent unemployment rate, the inflation rate for PC1 is approximately

Table 9.1   Annual Rates of Unemployment and Inflation in the United States, 1950–1990

Inflation and unemployment rates were generally higher in the 1970s and early 1980s than in the 1950s and 1960s, but fell again in the late 1980s and 1990.

Year	Unemployment Rate[a]	Inflation Rate[b]	Year	Unemployment Rate[a]	Inflation Rate[b]
1950	5.3%	2.0%	1971	5.9%	5.7%
1951	3.3	4.8	1972	5.6	4.7
1952	3.0	1.5	1973	4.9	6.5
1953	2.9	1.6	1974	5.6	9.1
1954	5.5	1.6	1975	8.5	9.8
1955	4.4	3.2	1976	7.7	6.4
1956	4.1	3.4	1977	7.1	6.7
1957	4.3	3.6	1978	6.1	7.3
1958	6.8	2.1	1979	5.8	8.9
1959	5.5	2.4	1980	7.1	9.0
1960	5.5	1.6	1981	7.6	9.7
1961	6.7	1.0	1982	9.7	6.4
1962	5.5	2.2	1983	9.6	3.9
1963	5.7	1.6	1984	7.5	3.7
1964	5.2	1.5	1985	7.2	3.0
1965	4.5	2.7	1986	7.0	2.6
1966	3.8	3.6	1987	6.2	3.2
1967	3.8	2.6	1988	5.5	3.3
1968	3.6	5.0	1989	5.3	4.1
1969	3.5	5.6	1990	5.5	4.1[c]
1970	4.9	5.5			

[a]Percentage of civilian labor force unemployed.

[b]Annual percentage change in the GNP implicit price deflator.

[c]Preliminary figure.

Source: U.S., *Economic Report of the President* (Washington, D.C.: U.S. Government Printing Office, 1991), pp. 291, 322.

1.5 percent, with PC2 the inflation rate is approximately 8.0 percent, and with PC3 the inflation rate is approximately 3.5 percent.

Analyzing the Behavior of the Phillips Curve   Is it valid to assume that the Phillips curve shifts? If so, will it continue to do so? What factors help to explain why these shifts occur? Some of the primary factors causing changes in the Phillips curve include structural changes in the labor force that cause the full-employment rate of unemployment to change, cost-push inflation, and changes in government transfer payment programs.

Figure 9.3

Annual Rates of Unemployment and Inflation in the United States
for 1950–1990 and Representative Phillips Curves

The generally higher unemployment and inflation rates in the 1970s and early
1980s, as compared to the 1950s and 1960s, caused the Phillips curve to shift to
the right from PC1 to PC2, and the drop in these rates in the late 1980s and 1990
caused the curve to shift to the left from PC2 to PC3.

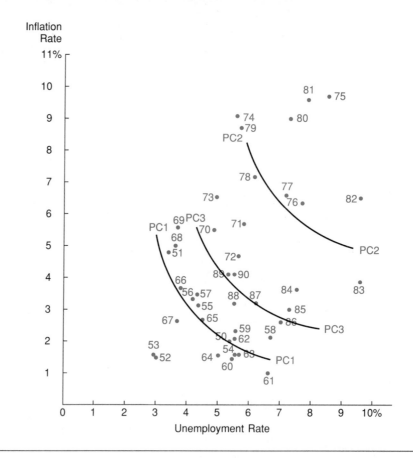

Structural changes in the labor force that cause the rate of unemployment
that represents full employment to change were discussed in Chapter Four,
and may be responsible for some of the shifts in the Phillips curve. In the
1950s and 1960s, full employment was associated with unemployment rates
of 3 and 4 percent. However, increases in the overall labor force participation rate, as well as increases in the participation rates for women and
teenagers—who typically had higher rates of unemployment than men—
pushed the full employment rate of unemployment up. As a result, 5 and 6

percent rates of unemployment were considered to represent full employment in the 1970s and 1980s. This change in the composition of the labor force may be responsible for some of the shift of the Phillips curve from PC1 to PC2 in Figure 9.3.

In the late 1980s and 1990, however, another phenomenon occurred with the labor force: for several years (1988, 1989, 1990), the unemployment rate fell below 6 percent—the rate considered to be full employment. As was noted in Chapter Four, this could have been due to growth in part-time employment, increasing numbers of low wage jobs in the service sector, and other factors. This structural change probably contributed to the shift of the Phillips curve to the left from PC2 to PC3.

A second factor explaining shifts in the Phillips curve is the U.S. experience with cost-push inflation (inflation originating on the sellers' side of the market) and the forces underlying that inflation. In the 1970s and early 1980s the United States was plagued with serious cost-push inflation that was rooted in energy cost increases, particularly oil prices. Since cost-push inflation does not respond to changes in aggregate spending as demand-pull inflation does, it is possible to simultaneously have high unemployment due to a lack of spending *and* cost-push inflation, or **stagflation.** The stagflation experienced in the United States in the late 1970s and early 1980s is reflected in the shift of the Phillips curve in Figure 9.3 from PC1 to PC2.

Stagflation

An economy experiences high rates of both inflation and unemployment.

It is also important to note that decreases in energy prices, particularly in oil prices, held down inflationary pressures in the late 1980s and 1990 and may be partially responsible for the shift in the Phillips curve to the left from PC2 to PC3 in Figure 9.3.[5]

A third factor influencing the Phillips curve is the availability of government transfer payments when people become unemployed. Transfer payments, such as unemployment compensation, allow workers to fill in the income gap created by unemployment. Transfers, however, also allow persons who are unemployed to search for jobs with less intensity than would occur if the transfers were not available. It has been suggested that the amount received in transfer payments and the length of eligibility time affect the unemployment rate and cause the Phillips curve to shift.

In summary, it is quite likely that the Phillips curve shifts. These shifts do not refute the major assumption of a tradeoff between inflation and unemployment, but rather, indicate that the tradeoff occurs at higher or lower rates as economic conditions and the structure of the economy change. Many factors, including changes in labor force participation rates and cost-push inflation, are responsible for these shifts. "Test Your Understanding: Unemployment and Inflation" allows you to draw some Phillips curves from hypothetical data and speculate about the factors causing the Phillips curve to shift.

[5] See pages 133–134 for a discussion of full employment and job structure changes, and pages 144–146 for cost-push inflation and energy price changes.

Test Your Understanding

Unemployment and Inflation[a]

[a]Answers can be found at
the end of the book.

Below are thirteen years of unemployment and inflation data for a hypothetical economy. Answer each of the following questions on the basis of these data.

Year	Inflation Rate	Unemployment Rate
1980	2.0%	8.0%
1981	3.0	6.0
1982	3.5	7.0
1983	4.0	5.0
1984	7.5	4.0
1985	5.0	5.0
1986	6.5	4.5
1987	7.0	2.5
1988	5.5	2.0
1989	4.0	3.0
1990	3.0	2.5
1991	2.0	4.0
1992	2.5	3.5

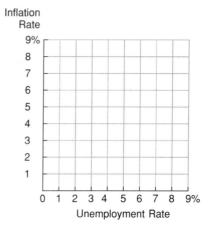

1. Plot the thirteen years of unemployment-inflation data in the accompanying graph and label each year's point, as was done in Figure 9.3.

2. Draw two Phillips curves that you think would accurately summarize the unemployment-inflation experience of this economy from 1980 through 1992. Label the curve for the earlier years PC1 and the curve for the later years PC2.

3. What changes in labor force participation rates could contribute to the shift in the Phillips curve from PC1 to PC2?

4. What changes in cost-push inflationary pressure could contribute to this shift in the Phillips curve?

5. What changes in government policies on transfer payments could contribute to this shift in the Phillips curve?

Controlling the Effects of Inflation

As noted earlier, changes in the level of aggregate spending affect unemployment and demand-pull inflation, but may not affect cost-push inflation. Since both monetary and fiscal policies are directed toward changing aggregate spending, these two major types of policies are not very effective in dealing with inflation of the cost-push variety.

Nothing comparable to monetary and fiscal policies exists for controlling cost-push inflation because the causes of this type of inflation are so varied that they do not lend themselves to correction through any single policy. Cost-push inflation may be the result of long-term forces such as changes in the bargaining power of certain resource suppliers, changes in technology, or scarcities of resources, that cannot be altered by short-term policies. For example, price increases by a few sellers who control a major market, negotiations by a large, powerful union that result in high wages paid through increasing prices, foreign control of an essential resource that is increasing in price, or many other factors could cause cost-push inflation. In none of these cases is there available a fiscal or monetary policy tool that would bring a quick and effective remedy.

One policy instrument that has been used and is sometimes suggested as a remedy for inflation is wage-price controls. These controls provide one possible method for alleviating the symptoms of cost-push inflation.

Wage-Price Controls

Wage-price controls

Mandatory government-imposed restrictions on increases in prices and wages and other incomes.

The expression **wage-price controls** refers to government-imposed restrictions on wage and price increases. It means that price determination through private decision making in the market is overseen by the government. Controls may take the form of a total freeze, where no wages or prices are permitted to rise during a specified period of time, or they may permit wages and prices to rise by a certain percent or gradually through a series of steps. Wage-price controls may apply to all prices, wages, rents, and other income payments, or to just some of these categories. For example, prices and wages, but not profits, could be subject to control.

Wage-price controls are mandatory government restrictions that carry the force of law. When they are violated, punishment such as a fine can result. There have, however, been instances when voluntary wage-price restraints have been requested. In these cases the restrictions are referred to as **wage-price guideposts** or **guidelines** because they are not legally binding like mandatory controls.

Wage-price guideposts

Voluntary wage-price restraints sought by the government.

Controls have been imposed during periods of substantial inflation or when there has been fear of serious future price increases. In most cases there has been a belief that the usual fiscal and monetary policy tools will not adequately alleviate the expected price increases. Wage-price controls have not been used solely for combating cost-push inflationary pressures; they have also been imposed during periods of demand-pull inflation.

It is important to realize that wage-price controls are a stopgap measure. They do not cure inflation; they merely provide a temporary salve and reduce the symptoms. Unless steps are taken to attack the root cause of the inflationary problem while controls are imposed, the inflation will still be there when the controls are lifted.

It is possible to aggravate an inflation problem during the imposition of controls, so that prices may be even higher when controls are removed. For example, increasing government spending far beyond what is collected in taxes during controls builds up spending pressures and will, in all likelihood, cause a serious inflation problem after the controls are removed.

The U.S. Experience with Wage-Price Controls   In recent decades the United States has experienced mandatory wage-price controls on three occasions: during World War II, the Korean War, and the Nixon administration in the early 1970s. Voluntary controls have also been requested several times, the most notable being the Kennedy guideposts of the early 1960s and the Carter standards of the late 1970s.

Wage-price controls were imposed on the U.S. economy in 1942, primarily in response to the pressure from aggregate spending that developed with the World War II effort and substantial wage and price increases prior to 1942.[6] When controls were lifted in 1945 and 1946, a surge of inflation resulted.[7] During the war U.S. citizens accumulated a large amount of potential spending power due to high levels of employment and scarce consumer goods. At the end of the war, this spending power, coupled with significant increases in business investment spending, brought about demand-pull inflationary pressures.

The next experience with mandatory controls occurred during the Korean War, when, following a period of accelerated increases in wages and prices, wage-price controls were adopted and a freeze announced in January 1951.[8] When controls ended in February 1953, no upward surge of prices occurred. The economy had cooled off during this period, and there was no pent-up spending pressure.[9]

The Nixon administration's wage-price control program consisted of four specific parts, or "phases," that were created as inflationary conditions changed from 1971 through 1974. These phases involved wage-price freezes for specified time periods, the creation of a pay board to oversee wage changes, and other activities. In 1974, at the end of this program, the United

[6] The federal government began to run huge budget deficits. For the fiscal year 1940 the budget deficit was $2.9 billion, and for 1941 it was $4.9 billion. But by 1942 this figure had increased to $20.5 billion, and by 1943 to $54.6 billion. Also, hourly wages in manufacturing rose by 30.7 percent, and the wholesale (now called producer) price index increased by 24 percent from January 1941 to October 1942. See Jerry E. Pohlman, *Economics of Wage and Price Controls* (Columbus, Ohio: Grid, Inc., 1972), p. 168, and U.S., *Economic Report of the President* (Washington, D.C.: U.S. Government Printing Office, 1985), p. 318.

[7] In 1946 there was a 15.7 percent increase in the GNP implicit price deflator, and in 1947 a 12.9 percent increase. See Pohlman, p. 169, and *Economic Report of the President,* 1985, p. 237.

[8] The fear of shortages of goods (induced perhaps by the memory of World War II) and of continually rising prices may have been responsible for the buying spurts that caused the precontrol inflationary pressure. See Arthur M. Ross, "Guideline Policy—Where We Are and How We Got There," in George P. Shultz and Robert Z. Aliber, eds. *Guidelines, Informal Controls, and the Market Place* (Chicago: The University of Chicago Press, 1966), p. 118, and U.S., *The Midyear Economic Report of the President* (Washington, D.C.: U.S. Government Printing Office, 1951), p. 42.

[9] See H. Scott Gordon, "The Eisenhower Administration: The Doctrine of Shared Responsibility" in Craufurd D. Goodwin, ed. *Exhortation and Controls: The Search for a Wage-Price Policy 1945–1971* (Washington, D.C.: The Brookings Institution, 1975), p. 110, and Ross, p. 118.

States experienced one of the largest annual price increases in recent times: the GNP implicit price deflator changed by 8.8 percent, the consumer price index by 11 percent, and the producer price index by 15.3 percent.[10] These price increases occurred for a variety of reasons, including world crop failures that pushed up food grain prices, the OPEC cartel's quadrupling of the price of petroleum in 1973, and the expansion of the domestic economy which led to demand-pull inflationary pressures.[11] Interestingly, controls ended at a time when inflationary pressures and price increases were far more serious than they had been when the controls were initiated.

Advantages and Disadvantages of Controls The suggestion to use wage-price controls to alleviate the problem of inflation generally stirs public debate. Some people advocate the use of controls, and others adamantly oppose them. Let us examine some of the strengths and weaknesses of controls.

One of the greatest advantages of a wage-price control program is that it provides an opportunity to arrest the symptoms of inflation while attacking the causes of the problem. For example, if the root cause of the price increases is excess spending, controls can keep prices from rising while other measures, such as a tax increase or a decrease in the money supply, are implemented to reduce demand so that once controls are lifted, the real inflationary problem is resolved. As just noted with the U.S. experience, however, this has not always been the outcome. After both the World War II and the Nixon controls were removed, inflation surged.

A second advantage of controls is the effect that their enactment may have on spending by households and businesses. If households and businesses believe that prices will not continue to rise due to an imposition of controls, they may hold back some of the dollars that they would have otherwise spent trying to "beat" anticipated price increases. This, in itself, could reduce inflationary pressures.

There are several disadvantages to wage-price controls. First, they inhibit the operation of the market system. If wage-price controls do not permit the price of a product to rise to its equilibrium level, a shortage will develop in the market for that product. When shortages occur, illegal, uncontrolled markets, or **black markets**, frequently emerge, where those who purchase goods at the lower, controlled price sell them at a higher price to people who could not otherwise obtain the goods. Thus, wage-price controls may lead to shortages and black markets.

A second disadvantage of controls is that public anticipation of restrictions on price increases could actually encourage both a precontrol and a postcontrol price surge rather than reduce pressure on prices as was

Black market

An illegal market for a good in short supply because of price or other restrictions.

---

[10] *Economic Report of the President*, 1985, pp. 237, 296, 302.

[11] Phillip Cagan, *Persistent Inflation: Historical and Policy Essays* (New York: Columbia University Press, 1979), pp. 180, 185.

indicated earlier. If sellers expect a freeze on the amount by which prices can be increased, they may raise their prices before controls are imposed. Also, unless demand has cooled off, sellers may raise their prices immediately after controls are lifted in order to catch up with what they have lost. And if controls are removed in a period of great uncertainty as to future economic policy, sellers may substantially raise prices out of fear of a reimposition of controls.

Finally, controls may affect the distribution of income if they are applied unequally to the various factor payments. For example, if they are imposed on wages and not on rent, interest, and profit, some factor suppliers may be injured by controls while others are not, and some income redistribution will result.

Indexing

Indexing
Factor, transfer, and/or other payments are automatically increased as prices rise.

A discussion of inflation would not be complete without mention of **indexing,** which refers to automatic increases in factor, transfer, and/or other payments that occur as prices increase, enabling incomes to keep pace with inflation. Indexing is not a policy tool for curing inflation, but is instead a program to reduce the effects of inflation on the buying power of income recipients. Where this program is used, a price index such as the consumer price index is adopted as the basis for measuring inflation, and the payments are then adjusted periodically to reflect the change in the price index. These upward adjustments may be based on the full percentage change in the price index or on some portion of it.

Cost-of-living adjustment (COLA)
An arrangement whereby an individual's wages automatically increase with inflation.

For example, suppose that a union contract contains a **cost-of-living adjustment (COLA)** whereby each worker's pay goes up by an amount equal to the monthly increase in the consumer price index, with a three-month adjustment lag. In this case, if the consumer price index were to go up by 1.5 percent in November, an increase in each worker's pay by that amount would begin with the March paycheck.

As noted in Chapter Four, many income and transfer payments in the United States are adjusted with changes in the various price indexes. These include payments to some union workers as well as Social Security recipients and retired military and federal civil service personnel. In addition, people have negotiated indexed child support payments in divorce settlements.

Some advocate indexing because it permits households to keep pace with price increases and lessens the negative effects of inflation. There is, however, much opposition to indexing, including the argument that it tends to institutionalize an inflationary problem by building it into the structure of an economy: automatically raising income and other payments ensures that buyers will continue to have the spending power needed to exert upward pressure on already increasing prices. Generally, indexation on a macroeconomic level has fallen out of favor in recent years, and countries that used this tool extensively, such as Israel, have moved away from it.

Alternative Macroeconomic Viewpoints and Policies

Over the years, different models have been developed by economists to explain the operation of the macroeconomy, and different policy prescriptions have been advocated to stabilize the economy. For example, fiscal policy is based on a particular view of the economy and is promoted strongly by some economists, while monetary policy is based on another view and is the policy choice of other economists. Alternative viewpoints about the macroeconomy often stem from the different assumptions on which models or policies are formulated. Also, sometimes a viewpoint loses popularity as new data and information provide better explanations of key economic relationships or solutions to problems.

The differences in alternative macroeconomic viewpoints and policy prescriptions can be better understood by examining four major approaches to the macroeconomy: classical economics, Keynesian economics, monetarism, and the new classical school. Supply-side economics, a popular viewpoint during the early 1980s, is also discussed.

Classical Economics

Classical economics
Popularly accepted theory prior to the Great Depression of the 1930s; says the economy will automatically adjust to full employment.

The dominant school of economic thought before the 1930s was **classical economics.** This school, however, was largely rejected during the 1930s because it could not explain the cause of, or offer a successful remedy for, the prolonged and severe unemployment that developed during the Great Depression. The basic premise of the classical school, which dates back to Adam Smith and his book *The Wealth of Nations* in the late eighteenth century, is that a free market economy, when left alone, will automatically operate at full employment. And, since a free market economy always automatically corrects itself to full employment, there is no need for government intervention to rectify its problems. Adam Smith is one of the economists featured in Application 9.2, "The Academic Scribblers."

The classicists arrived at their position about the automatic self-correction to full employment because of several assumptions. First, they assumed that supply creates its own demand in a macroeconomy.[12] In other words, an

---

[12] "Say's Law," named after the French economist Jean Baptiste Say (1767–1832), is the formal statement of the concept that supply creates its own demand. According to James Mill (1773–1836), one of the important popularizers of this position, whatever individuals produce over and above their own needs is done to exchange for goods and services produced by others. People produce in order to acquire the things that they desire, so what they supply and what they demand are equal. And if each person's supply and demand are equal, it follows that supply and demand in the entire economy must be equal. Believing that demand and supply are equal for the entire economy, the classical economists saw surpluses in specific markets that would lead to unemployment as being offset by shortages in other markets. The surpluses would be removed by businesses following their own self-interest and guided by the profit motive. See James Mill, *Elements of Political Economy* (London: Baldwin, Cradock, and Joy, 1826), Chapter IV, Section III, especially pp. 228, 232, 234–235.

Figure 9.4   Aggregate Supply–Aggregate Demand

In the classical model, prices and wages adjust in order to maintain a full
employment level of output.

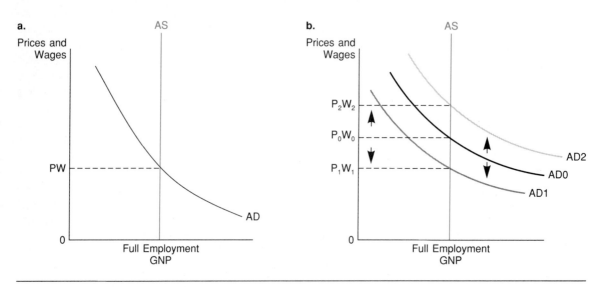

item produced will be bought by someone. As a result, there is no need to
operate at less than full employment and production: the goods and services
that are produced will all be purchased.

A second assumption of classical theory was that wages and prices
increase and decrease to ensure that the economy operates at full employment. This assumption is illustrated in Figure 9.4. The perfectly vertical
aggregate, or total, supply curve (AS) in Figure 9.4a illustrates an economy
producing at the full employment level of GNP, regardless of whether prices
and wages are high or low. The aggregate demand curve (AD) in Figure 9.4a,
which represents the spending plans of households and businesses in the
economy, slopes downward indicating that an inverse relationship exists
between prices and wages, and GNP. When prices fall (which will also bring
wages down in the classical model), households and businesses want to
purchase a greater amount of output, and when prices increase, they want
to purchase less. In Figure 9.4a, aggregate demand and supply are equal at
the full employment level of output with price and wage level PW.

If there is a change in aggregate demand, as illustrated in Figure 9.4b by
the decrease or increase in the aggregate demand curve from AD0 to AD1,
or AD0 to AD2, respectively, there will be a change in prices and wages that
allows the economy to continue to operate at full employment. For example,
if initially in Figure 9.4b, aggregate demand were AD0, aggregate supply
were AS, and the level of prices and wages were P_0W_0, the economy would

be operating at full employment. If aggregate demand were to decrease and the aggregate demand curve shifted to the left to AD1, less would be demanded than supplied at the original price and wage level (P_0W_0), and the economy would experience some temporary unemployment. However, according to the classical assumptions, prices and wages would soon fall to P_1W_1, and the economy would return to full employment. This lower price and wage level would permit full employment at the lower level of demand.

Likewise, if aggregate demand were to increase and the aggregate demand curve shifted to the right from AD0 to AD2 in Figure 9.4b, more would be demanded than could be supplied at the original price and wage level of P_0W_0, and prices and wages would rise to P_2W_2, with the economy continuing to operate at full employment. In the classical model, the adjustment to changes in aggregate demand is through changes in prices and wages, not output. Production will seek the full employment level, regardless of changes in demand.

The classical economists also assumed that savings always equals investment: everything leaked from the spending stream through savings is returned through the investment injection. This equality always occurs, reasoned the classicists, because of the interest rate, which is the mechanism that brings savings and investment into equality. (The tax–government expenditure leakage and injection relationship is irrelevant in the classical model because the classicists did not consider fiscal policy.)

As previously noted, classical economic theory became unpopular in the 1930s when it could not explain the Great Depression and could not offer a policy prescription to solve the unemployment problem. In the 1980s, however, as will be discussed shortly, there was a resurgence of interest in classical theory due, partially, to the popularity of the free market philosophy and the corresponding movement in the United States toward lessening the role of government in the economy.

Keynesian Economics

Keynesian economics

Based on the work of John Maynard Keynes (1883–1946), who focused on the role of aggregate spending in determining the level of macroeconomic activity.

The ideas of the British economist John Maynard Keynes (1883–1946), whose biographical sketch is given in Application 9.2, form the basis for **Keynesian economics.** Keynes's economics was introduced during the 1930s when classical economics was losing popularity.

Keynes revolutionized economic thinking by focusing on the role of aggregate, or total, spending in the economy. His major contribution was to link increases and decreases in production and employment with increases and decreases in spending. Keynes refuted the classical notion of an automatic adjustment to full employment, and reasoned that an economy's output and employment position would improve from less than full employment only if aggregate spending increased. Following from this, Keynes pioneered the idea of using government expenditures and taxes to control the level of economic activity. According to his prescription, the correct policy method for counteracting a recession is to increase aggregate spend-

Application 9.2

The Academic Scribblers

Adam Smith

Adam Smith, considered by many to be the "father" of market economics, or capitalism, was born in 1723 in Scotland. His life came during a time of tremendous change in Britain: the Industrial Revolution brought inventions allowing for more efficient production, factories, a poor working class, the rise of capitalists, and many other economic and social changes.

Smith was a well-known philosopher in his time. At the age of twenty-eight he was offered the Chair of Logic at the University of Glasgow, and later the Chair of Moral Philosophy. *The Theory of Moral Sentiments*, which he published in 1759, gave Smith notoriety as he explored the philosophical question of how man, who is basically motivated by self-interest, considers the moral merits of an action.

Smith's most famous work, *The Wealth of Nations*, was revolutionary for its time since it represented a movement from mercantilist thinking to the idea that individual decision making would best serve a society's interests. In this text Smith focuses on the market mechanism and shows how individual self-interest operating through markets provides the greatest good for society. He also discusses the importance of competition to a market system, and firmly states that government should not intervene in the market mechanism. It is these assertions that strongly connect Smith to classical economics.

No biography of Smith is complete without mention of his absentmindedness; this extended to late night walks in his village in his night clothes, an often quoted tale about Smith. Smith, who lived peacefully with his mother in his later years, died at 67.

John Maynard Keynes

John Maynard Keynes, probably the most influential economist of the twentieth century, was born in 1883 in England. His father, John Neville Keynes, was an economist and logician who taught at Cambridge University. John Maynard was well-educated, but his first interest was in mathematics. Urging by some distinguished professors sent him in the direction of economics.

Keynes led a full and active life intermingling different careers: a brief stint in the civil service, a lectureship in economics at Cambridge, bursar at Kings College, adviser to various London bankers, and a successful personal financier. His interests were also varied: he had close ties to the colorful Bloomsbury set of intellectuals, married a ballerina, financed a theater group, and had an extensive art collection. An observer of Keynes noted that "he would go out of his way to make something flattering out of what a student had said. . . . On the other hand, when a faculty member got up [he] simply cut their heads off."[a]

Although Keynes is well-known for his 1919 book, *The Economic Consequences of the Peace*, which discusses the economics of the Versailles Treaty of World War I, his major work is *The General Theory*

Keynesians
Followers of the ideas of John Maynard Keynes; tend to favor stabilizing the economy through the use of fiscal policy.

ing, which can be accomplished by increasing government expenditures and/or lowering taxes. Thus, fiscal policy, or the manipulation of government taxes and expenditures to improve overall employment or to dampen demand-pull inflationary pressures, is based on the economic thinking of Keynes. Persons who advocate stabilizing the economy through the use of fiscal policy tend to be referred to as **Keynesians.** In other words, Keynesians tend to believe that some government intervention in the macroeconomy is appropriate and necessary.

of *Employment Interest and Money*, published in 1936. This book focuses on Keynes' major contribution—that a market economy's levels of output and employment are the result of the level of aggregate demand. It should be noted that while government interventionist policies are associated with Keynesian economics, Keynes' ideas were rooted in his regard for individualism. The following quote is from *The General Theory*.

But, above all, individualism, if it can be purged of its defects and its abuses, is the best safeguard of personal liberty in the sense that compared with any other system, it greatly widens the field for the exercise of personal choice. It is also the best safeguard of the variety of life, which emerges precisely from this extended field of personal choice, and the loss of which is the greatest of all losses of the homogeneous or totalitarian state.[b]

Milton Friedman

The face and work of Milton Friedman are familiar to many Americans since he writes and lectures in a wide variety of publications and places and has made appearances on television talk shows. Friedman also completed a video series, "Free to Choose," that has been seen on public television and in many classrooms, and his accompanying book, coauthored with his wife Rose, *(Free to Choose: A Personal Statement)* was on *The New York Times* best seller list. In 1976 Milton Friedman received the Nobel Prize in economics.

Friedman was born in 1912 in New York, to hard-working immigrants. Friedman's father died when he was fifteen, placing additional financial burdens on his mother and causing Friedman to need to rely on scholarships to obtain an education. He received his undergraduate degree from Rutgers, went to Chicago for graduate study, and earned his Ph.D. from Columbia University in 1946. Friedman eventually returned to an academic post at the University of Chicago where he remained until 1977.

Milton Friedman's many contributions to economics focus on the importance of money to the operation of the macroeconomy, and he is associated with renewing interest in money and macroeconomic policy. However, he is also known for strongly embracing a free market philosophy and for espousing the view, associated with the Chicago School, that a market economy works best when left alone. In many cases, such as public education, Friedman believes that a competitive market would do a better job and that the government has done more harm than good.

[a]William Breit and Roger L. Ransom, *The Academic Scribblers*, rev. ed. (Hinsdale, Ill.: The Dryden Press, 1982), p. 67. Also see, Harry G. Johnson, "Cambridge in the 1950s," in Elizabeth S. Johnson and Harry G. Johnson, *The Shadow of Keynes* (Chicago: The University Press, 1978), pp. 132–133.
[b]Breit and Ransom, p. 68. Also see, John Maynard Keynes, *The General Theory of Employment Interest and Money* (New York: Harcourt, Brace and World, 1936), p. 380.

Keynesian economics reached its peak of popularity during the 1960s. In the early 1970s, however, it became the target for attack. Some argued that the stagflation of the 1970s could not be explained or remedied in Keynesian terms and that wasteful spending by government and increasing federal government deficits were linked to the Keynesian approach to economic policy. During the 1980s the political mood favored a movement away from government intervention in the economy, causing further attacks on Keynesian economics and a renewed interest in other approaches to macroeconomic policy such as monetarism and classical economics. At the moment there is a debate over whether Keynesian economics is being revitalized. Some policies, such as the tax cuts of the early 1980s, which were pursued as non-Keynesian policies, appear to have produced Keynesian-like results. Regardless of whether one is supportive of the theories of John Maynard Keynes, his ideas given in *The General Theory,* published in 1936, tend to be at the heart of the controversy.

Monetarism

Monetarism

The school of thought that favors stabilizing the economy through controlling the money supply.

Monetarists

Persons who favor the economic policies of monetarism.

The school of thought that emphasizes the importance of money in determining macroeconomic conditions is known as **monetarism,** and those who prefer altering the money supply to stabilize the economy are called **monetarists.** Monetarism, which became a popular economic viewpoint in the 1970s and early 1980s, has challenged Keynesian fiscal policy prescriptions for counteracting inflation and unemployment. Monetarism's most outstanding proponent is Milton Friedman, whose association with the University of Chicago has led some to label followers of his thinking as members of the "Chicago School." Application 9.2 provides some background on Friedman.

Monetarists are inclined to favor free markets and advocate limited government intervention in the macroeconomy. In this sense, they tend to align with the classical school. A typical monetarist would suggest that allowing free markets and maintaining proper control over the money supply is the ideal strategy for reaching full employment or avoiding demand-pull inflation.

Money supply rule

The money supply should increase at a constant annual percentage rate regardless of economic conditions.

There is a debate among monetarists over whether the money supply should be changed to meet problems as they arise, or whether it should increase annually at a constant rate. The constant-rate-of-growth **money supply rule** challenges monetary policy prescriptions to increase or decrease the money supply to counteract unemployment or inflation by arguing that the money supply should be increased by a constant percentage each year regardless of economic conditions in order to achieve a certain level of production and employment without inflation. The constant-rate-of-growth money supply rule is advocated by Milton Friedman. It remains to be seen whether the Federal Reserve will continue to adjust the money supply to meet changing economic conditions, or whether at some point the Board of Governors will follow Friedman's recommendation.

New classical school

Economists who return to the basic classical premise that free markets automatically stabilize themselves and that government intervention in the macroeconomy is not advisable.

The New Classical School

The **new classical school** is a broad term that describes the thinking of some economists who have recently returned to the basic classical premise that a free market economy automatically stabilizes itself and that government intervention in terms of macroeconomic policies is not advisable. Much of

Rational expectations

A proposition that the effects of macroeconomic policies might be distorted or negated by the adjustment of business and household behavior in anticipation of policy makers' strategies.

this advocacy for less influence by government in macroeconomics is based on the rational expectations theory that has developed in recent years.

The basic proposition of **rational expectations** is that the effects of macroeconomic policies are distorted or negated by businesses and households because they anticipate policy makers' strategies and adjust their own behavior accordingly. And, since rational behavior by households and businesses twists the effects of government policies, the macroeconomy would be better off without government intervention. In this sense, the followers of the rational expectations theory align with the classical school.

The rational expectations problem can be illustrated by a simple example. Assume that an instructor has low classroom attendance and decides to improve it by giving periodic unannounced quizzes. If these quizzes are always given on the same day every two weeks, the rational student will be certain to attend class on those days, and the intention of the instructor's policy will be distorted. The only way this policy will work is to give the quizzes randomly.

According to the rational expectations approach, similar problems emerge when government intervenes to influence macroeconomic activity. For example, if businesses and households expect rising interest rates due to the imposition of a restrictive monetary policy measure to curb inflationary pressure, they might react by immediately borrowing and increasing their spending to beat the rise in the interest rate. As a result, this surge in spending distorts the intention of the policy. Supporters of the rational expectations theory believe that the economy would be better off if the policy were not enacted. In its extreme, rational expectations says that government policies to alter the economy may be useless unless they are enacted randomly.

Supply-Side Economics

Supply-side economics

Policies to achieve macroeconomic goals by stimulating the supply side of the market.

An examination of alternative macroeconomic theories would not be complete without some mention of **supply-side economics,** which was born in the late 1970s and popularized by its association with President Ronald Reagan and "Reaganomics." The basic idea behind supply-side economics was to provide an alternative to traditional demand-oriented policies by stimulating the supply, rather than the demand, side of market relationships. Specifically, it proposed the enactment of government policies to stimulate economic activity by creating incentives for individuals and businesses to increase their productive efforts.

The best known supply-side proposal was to lower taxes for businesses and individuals. It was argued that lowering the tax burden on businesses would make investments in plants and other productive resources more profitable, thereby stimulating growth in the economy. Lowering the tax burden on individuals was said to lead to greater savings (which could be channeled through financial institutions to businesses for investment purposes) and increased personal incentives to work. The Economic Recovery

Tax Act of 1981 restructured taxes in a direction generally supportive of supply-side ideas. Supply-side economics also called for government deregulation to increase productivity.

Supply-side proposals had a political as well as an economic dimension. Reduced taxes and regulatory requirements lead not only to potentially greater productivity, but also to a lessened presence of government in private economic decision making. In other words, supply-side proposals would move the economy more toward individual or free market decision making, a popular philosophy in the 1980s.

A Final Word on Macroeconomic Thinking

This completes the section of the book devoted to the goals and instruments of macroeconomic policy. Ideally, a foundation has been established upon which informed judgments can be made about past, present, and future efforts to stabilize the economy.

In assessing various policy proposals it is helpful to keep in mind two facts about economic thinking. First, our understanding of macroeconomic goals and policy instruments must be continually updated and refined as conditions change and knowledge grows. The environment in which goals are pursued and policy tools are employed is continually changing, and new questions and issues are constantly appearing. For example, the age distributions of populations change, international tensions arise and abate, serious worldwide shortages of some resources periodically occur, and new social attitudes evolve over time. These types of developments affect our economic goals and policies. And because of such changes, it is risky to assume that an understanding of the way things operate today will be sufficient to deal with the problems of the future.

Second, in assessing economic policies, keep in mind that the economy is not composed of a set of simple relationships that can be easily manipulated to neatly solve various problems that arise. In learning the role of aggregate spending and the functions of fiscal and monetary policies, one can be misled into thinking that economic woes can be easily cured with a simple increase or decrease in the money supply and/or government spending and taxes. In reality, before any macroeconomic policy is initiated, the many ramifications of that policy action must be considered. For example, in decreasing the money supply to fight demand-pull inflation, one obvious consequence to consider is the rise in unemployment that occurs as spending declines. But other consequences may also ensue, such as adverse pressures on industries sensitive to the interest rate, like the construction and automobile industries. If one of these industries is already undergoing strain from some other problem, a restrictive monetary policy could make matters worse.

Economic conditions in late 1990 and early 1991 provided a good example of the complexity of economic policy making. In the fourth quarter of 1990 the rate of unemployment began to increase as the economy slipped into a recession. The appropriate fiscal policy to counteract this rising unemployment rate would have been to decrease taxes and increase government expenditures, thereby running a larger federal government deficit. But the federal deficit for fiscal 1991 was already estimated at over $300 billion, public concern over the size of the national debt was high, and the United States had just entered into a war against Iraq. The need for an expansionary fiscal policy was not coming at a good time for the federal government. There were also limits on the ability of the Federal Reserve to take appropriate action. The recession called for expansionary monetary policy, and the Fed did lower the discount rate in early 1991. However, there was concern over how low interest rates could fall in order to stimulate the domestic economy without hurting the value of the dollar in foreign exchange markets. In short, responding to the increasing unemployment rate using fiscal policy would have added to the already-large federal deficit and debt, while responding using monetary policy could have put the international position of the dollar at risk.

Application 9.3, "What Is 'Right' Economics?" provides some additional thoughts about the development of economic theories.

Macroeconomics and Microeconomics

In recent years more attention has been given to the importance to the macroeconomy of decisions made by individual units within the household and business sectors, or to microeconomic behavior. The next six chapters are devoted to the operation of individual households and business firms in the microeconomy. The material in these chapters provides an explanation for the behavior of these decision-making units, which obviously is important in its own right, and also sheds additional light on the workings of the macroeconomy.

Summary

Economic growth is an increase in the full employment level of output over time, and is represented by a shift of the production possibilities curve to the right. Growth differs from the other goals of the macroeconomy in that it is longer term and depends more on policies to expand production levels than on fiscal and monetary policies. Total output must grow at a faster rate than population if output per person is to increase. The United States has experienced a significant increase in per capita real output over time.

Economic growth results from an increase in the quantity of resources used and/or an increase in the efficiency with which they are used. Tech-

Application 9.3

What Is "Right" Economics?

Economics is a soft science, meaning that it is not as successful in predicting events as the physical sciences. The success of scientists and engineers in landing a spacecraft on the moon within a thousand yards of the designated landing target is something social scientists can only view with envy. In economics, competing theories can exist side-by-side for decades. Economists cannot perform the controlled laboratory experiments to eliminate decisively one of the contenders. They must wait for time to provide the data for testing propositions and, even then, the historical signals are not unambiguous.

Because economics is not an exact discipline, the human factor assumes importance. There is more room for the individual scholar's own subjective judgment, preconceptions, and biases. Analytic effort is preceded, as one of the important economists of this century, Joseph Schumpeter, once said, "by a preanalytic cognitive act that supplies the raw material for the analytic effort." Since empirical results often fail to prove conclusively the truth or falsity of a theory, the development of economic analysis becomes more personalized. As Arjo Klamer [in his book, *Conversations with Economists*] has written, economists "not only construct models . . . they philosophize, appeal to common sense, and talk about other economists and their work. Economics involves the art of persuasion. . . . This process leaves room for nonrational elements, such as personal commitment and style."

It is possible for two Nobel Prize winners in economics to give a president diametrically opposed advice on a specific problem. In fact, they have done so. One could not blame the layman for wondering who these people are and where they are coming from. . . . In one of his most frequently quoted statements, Keynes wrote that "the ideas of economists and political philosophers, both when they are right and when they are wrong, are more powerful than is commonly understood. Indeed the world is ruled by little else. Practical men, who believe themselves to be quite exempt from any intellectual influences, are usually the slaves of some defunct economist. Madmen in authority, who hear voices in the air, are distilling their frenzy from some academic scribbler of a few years back."

Source: Excerpted from W. Carl Biven, *Who Killed John Maynard Keynes?* (Homewood, Ill.: Richard D. Irwin, Inc., 1989), pp. 2–3. Copyright © 1989, excerpted with permission.

nological change is particularly important in achieving growth. If growth is to be sustained, aggregate demand must be at a level that can absorb the economy's expanded output. Some people question the desirability of economic growth since it may impose future costs to society.

A tradeoff exists between full employment and price stability: as the economy approaches full employment, it encounters demand-pull inflationary pressure, and the control of demand-pull inflation is accomplished at the expense of employment. This tradeoff between the rates of unemployment and inflation is illustrated by the downward-sloping Phillips curve.

Data from the U.S. economy show that from the 1950s and 1960s to the 1970s and early 1980s, the Phillips curve shifted to the right, and then back to the left in the late 1980s and 1990. These shifts in the Phillips curve might be explained by structural changes in the labor force and related labor force statistics, cost-push inflationary pressure, and changes in transfer payments.

Monetary and fiscal policies are not particularly effective for dealing with cost-push inflation. One other policy instrument, wage-price controls, has been used to deal with both demand-pull and cost-push inflation. Wage-price controls are restrictions placed by the government on increases in prices and various income payments such as wages. Such restrictions, which may be mandatory or voluntary, are a stopgap measure to alleviate the symptoms but not the causes of inflation. The United States experienced mandatory wage-price controls during World War II, the Korean War, and the early 1970s.

Controls provide an opportunity to curb the symptoms of inflation while attacking its causes with other policies. They may also ease inflationary pressure by improving businesses' and households' expectations about future price increases. At the same time, however, wage-price controls may lead to shortages and black markets, encourage price surges before and after their imposition, and redistribute income.

Indexing, another policy response to inflation, adjusts income, transfer, and/or other payments to price changes. Its disadvantage of building inflationary pressure into the structure of an economy has caused little use of this tool as a macroeconomic policy in recent years.

There are several alternative viewpoints about the operation of the macroeconomy and the desirability and effectiveness of different macroeconomic policies. Some of these alternatives include the classical school, Keynesian economics, monetarism, the rational expectations approach of the new classical economists, and supply-side economics. The classicists believed that a free market economy always automatically adjusts to full employment and that government intervention is not desirable. Keynesians prefer stabilization of the economy through taxes and government spending, while monetarists favor adjustments in the money supply. Rational expectations, a more recent approach, holds that anticipation of a policy decision distorts its intended impact and, therefore, the economy is better off without government intervention. Supply-side economics, which was popular in the early 1980s, advocated policies such as tax cuts to stimulate the supply, rather than the demand, side of the market.

In evaluating macroeconomic policy proposals, we must continually update our thinking to meet changing conditions. It is also important to realize that the economy is not composed of simple relationships that allow for neat solutions to economic problems. Each policy action has many consequences that must be weighed.

Key Terms and Concepts

Economic growth	Cost-push inflation
Technological change	Stagflation
Infrastructure	Wage-price controls
Phillips curve	Wage-price guideposts

Black market	Monetarism
Indexing	Monetarists
Cost-of-living adjustment (COLA)	Money supply rule
Classical economics	New classical school
Keynesian economics	Rational expectations
Keynesians	Supply-side economics

Review Questions

1. Why is economic growth better measured using real per capita GNP than real GNP? What are some arguments for limiting the objective of economic growth?

2. What are the primary factors responsible for achieving economic growth?

3. Draw curves in the graph below that illustrate how the Phillips curve for the United States has shifted over the past forty years. Why have these shifts occurred?

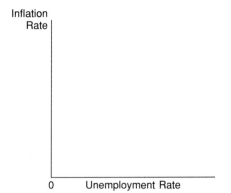

4. What were the unemployment rate and inflation rate in the United States for each year since 1990? Do these numbers generally fall in line with PC3 in Figure 9.3? Comment on your findings.

5. Summarize the U.S. experience with wage-price controls. Are controls an effective policy tool for checking inflation?

6. What is meant by indexing? How does a COLA work? Give some examples of indexing in the United States. What are some arguments for adopting a national policy of indexing, and what are some problems that could result?

7. Fill in the following table by providing, for each listed school of thought, the basic premise with regard to the macroeconomy and the recommended policy to stabilize the economy.

School of Thought	Basic Premise	Macro Policy Action
Classical		
Keynesian		
Monetarism		
Rational Expectations		
Supply-side		

8. Explain why two well-known economists could give conflicting advice on policy proposals to fight unemployment. (You may want to refer to Application 9.3 in answering this question.)

Discussion Questions

1. Economic growth is a goal of the macroeconomy that is accomplished over a long period of time. What are some economic, social, and political reasons that make economic growth important to a nation? How might a population increase contribute to economic growth, and how might it hinder growth?

2. Identify four major technological changes in the twentieth century that have contributed to the significant increase in real per capita output in the United States. Explain how these changes have contributed to that increase in output.

3. When the economy is facing high rates of unemployment and inflation, policy makers must decide which of these problems to curb at the expense of the other. What types of information should policy makers seek before deciding to sacrifice employment for price stability, or price stability for employment?

4. Both demand-pull and cost-push inflation have the same effect on prices. But do these two types of inflation relate in the same way to the level of employment? What policies would you recommend to control inflation if it were of the demand-pull variety? What policy recommendations would you make to limit cost-push inflation?

5. Many people regard wage-price controls as an undesirable policy instrument. Yet, controls are typically given serious consideration in periods of severe inflation. Why do we continue entertaining the use of controls in the absence of their broad support?

6. Would you consider yourself to be Keynesian, classical, monetarist, new classical, or other in your attitude toward macroeconomic policies? On what reasoning is your preference based?

7. What do economists mean by rational expectations? What problems might rational expectations cause for the formulation of economic policy? How might "randomly imposed" government policies affect the economy?

8. Macroeconomic policy proposals are frequently tied to politics. In your opinion, which of the policies that you have studied (Keynesian, monetarist, classical, new classical, and supply-side) is the most politically desirable, and which is the most undesirable? Explain.

Critical Thinking Case 9

The Aral Sea

Critical Thinking Skills | Understanding the relationship between short-term decisions and long-term consequences
Identifying costs and benefits of solutions to problems

Economic Concepts | Economic growth
Costs of economic growth

The Aral Sea in the Soviet Union, one of the world's biggest lakes, is now the scene of one of the world's greatest ecological disasters. In a relentless drive to expand cotton production in the area, water has been diverted from the lake, causing the Aral's level and volume to fall. From 1960 to 1989 the area of the lake declined by 45 percent, its volume declined by 68 percent, and the salinity (saltiness) of the water almost tripled.

The costs of this expansion in cotton production are now enormous. For example, just a few decades ago the sea provided for a prosperous fishing industry. It has now been seven years since a commercial catch has come from the sea, and most of the sea's 24 native fish have disappeared. The deltas around the Aral have also dried up, affecting wildlife and industries dependent on the deltas.

As the sea recedes, the saltbeds become exposed and are carried by dust storms to surrounding areas. It is estimated that 43 million metric tons of salts per year, some of which are toxic to plants, are being carried by storms and deposited on agricultural lands as well as populated areas. It is believed that increased salinity may be responsible for the decline in cotton yields in very recent years.

It appears, however, that the greatest cost associated with the growth of cotton is the damage to the health of the area's population. Pesticides and salt have contaminated the drinking water, and pesticides have been found in mothers' milk. Statistics indicate that in this region over the last fifteen years, the incidence of typhoid fever has increased almost 30 times, and hepatitis, kidney disease, gallstone ailments, and chronic gastritis have markedly increased. Cancer of the esophagus is 50 times the world average and infant mortality is twice the average of the Soviet Union. In one particular section near the sea, a survey found 70 percent of the children ill.

Finally, the costs of the decline in the size of the Aral Sea include more extreme weather conditions. Without the moderating effect of this large body of water, summers have become hotter, winters colder, and growing seasons shorter.

The changes necessary to alleviate the effect of this disaster on human health and the area's ecosystem must be carried out without creating severe problems elsewhere. Proposals for action have been made.

Questions

1. What types of short-term decisions and benefits would explain why the activity in this case — growth in cotton production — continues, despite such disastrous long-term consequences?

2. Identify several proposals that could rectify the ecological problem in the Aral Sea area. What will be the costs of correcting this situation under each proposal? Will the benefits of correcting the situation be worth the costs?

3. How could the costs associated with correcting this environmental problem result in more economic growth in the years to come?

Source: Based on Kenneth D. Frederick, "The Disappearing Aral Sea," Resources for the Future, *Resources,* Winter 1991, no. 102, pp. 11–14.

Suggested Readings

W. Carl Biven, *Who Killed John Maynard Keynes?* **(Homewood, Ill.: Irwin Publishers, 1989).**
Discusses the evolution of economic policy from Keynes through the present time.

William Breit and Roger L. Ransom, *The Academic Scribblers,* **rev. ed. (Hinsdale, Ill.: The Dryden Press, 1982).**
Provides biographies and summaries of the theories of twelve well-known economists, including Keynes and Friedman.

E. Ray Canterbery, *The Making of Economics,* **3d ed. (Belmont, Calif.: Wadsworth Publishing Company, 1987).**
Deals with the development of economics through an examination of the writings of well-known economists in an historical, social, and intellectual setting; includes several chapters on the classical economists, Keynes, and the post-Keynesian era.

Keith Carlson, "On Maintaining a Rising U.S. Standard of Living into the Mid-21st Century," St. Louis Federal Reserve Bank, *Review,* **March/April 1990, pp. 3–16.**
Examines whether the United States can continue to maintain the growth rates achieved from 1948 to 1989 into the 21st century.

E. J. Mishan, "Ch. 1: Growthmania," *Technology & Growth* **(New York: Praeger Publishers, 1971), pp. 3–6.**
Explains how the pursuit of economic growth can reduce well-being.

Peter Passell, "Rebel Economists Add Ecological Cost to Price of Progress," *The New York Times,* **November 17, 1990, pp. B5, B6.**
Reports on the view of some economists that the costs of economic growth are underestimated and that the goal of economic growth should be redefined.

Herbert Stein, "Should Growth Be a Priority of National Policy?" *Challenge,* **March–April 1986, pp. 11–17.**
A summary of various government policies that affect growth, and a discussion of the costs of growth.

Timothy Tregarthen, "Japan: The Rise of the Land of the Rising Sun," *The Margin,* **November/December 1989, pp. 19–21.**
Background on Japan's history and culture that may contribute to its high rates of economic growth.

U.S., "Inflation Control Under the Economic Stabilization Act," *Economic Report of the President* **(Washington, D.C.: U.S. Government Printing Office), 1972, pp. 73–100; 1973, pp. 51–70; 1974, pp. 88–109; 1975, pp. 223–229.**
A detailed, year-by-year explanation and analysis of wage-price controls during the Nixon administration.

Part Three

The Microeconomy

Chapter Ten

Households and Businesses: An Overview

The decisions made by people in households and businesses are the foundation of microeconomics.

Source: © Owen Stayner/ Stayner and Stayner.

Chapter Objectives

1. To provide an overview of some basic characteristics of households and businesses.

2. To introduce the sources and sizes of household income and types of household expenditures.

3. To define the basic objective of economic decision making by individuals.

4. To introduce the balancing process involved in an individual's spending and earning decisions.

5. To identify the legal forms of business, and to discuss business ownership of other businesses.

6. To explain the goal of profit maximization or loss minimization in business decision making, and to explore some questions about the goal of profit maximization.

7. To identify sources of information on households and businesses.

Microeconomics

The study of individual decision-making units and markets within the economy.

This chapter begins the study of microeconomics. Unlike macroeconomics, which is primarily concerned with businesses and households as groups that influence the operation of the total economy, **microeconomics** focuses on individual businesses and households as decision-making units and on their relationships to other businesses and households in markets. Because of this focus, a descriptive overview of businesses and households and their economic objectives is an appropriate starting point for the study of microeconomics.

This chapter is divided into three sections. The first is devoted to households—their characteristics and the objectives household members seek in making their economic decisions. The second part of the chapter deals with businesses—how they are organized, their overall sizes and structures, and their economic objectives. Finally, the third part provides a brief overview of sources of information on households and businesses.

Overview of Households

Characteristics of Households

By 1990 the population of the United States was about 250 million persons: approximately 122 million males and 128 million females. About one-half of this population was under 32 years old, and the great majority lived

Table 10.1   Number and Average Size of U.S. Households in Selected Years

Over the last several decades the number of households has more than doubled, but the average number of persons per household has fallen. This decrease in the average size of households can be explained in part by the growing percentage of households made up of one person.

| | Year | | | | |
Characteristic	1950	1960	1970	1980	1989
Total number of households	43,554,000	52,799,000	63,401,000	80,776,000	92,830,000
Average number of persons per household	3.4	3.3	3.1	2.8	2.6
Percentage of households with one person	9.1%	13.1%	17.1%	22.7%	24.5%

Source: 1950 figures are from U.S. Bureau of the Census, *Statistical Abstract of the United States: 1985,* 105th ed. (Washington, D.C.: U.S. Government Printing Office, 1984), p. 40. 1960–1989 figures are from *Statistical Abstract of the United States: 1990,* 110th ed. (Washington, D.C.: U.S. Government Printing Office, 1990), p. 45.

in urban areas.[1] Almost every one of these persons was part of a household.

A **household** is made up of a person living alone or persons, related or unrelated, living in a group, who occupy a "housing unit" such as a house, apartment, or other separate living quarters.[2] Statistics for households are not the same as statistics for families because the definitions of a household and a family are not the same. Only when two or more related individuals are living in a household is it considered to be a family. Thus, household statistics are more inclusive than family statistics, and will be used where possible in this chapter.

Table 10.1 lists the total number and average size of households in the United States, along with the percentage of single person households for selected years. Although the number of households has more than doubled since 1950, the average size has been steadily falling, and the percentage of households with one person has been rising. Over the last four decades households with two or more persons living together have come to represent a shrinking portion of the total households in the United States. This is obviously due to an increase in the number of unmarried (single, divorced, and widowed) adults establishing households.

Household

A person living alone or a group of related or unrelated persons who occupy a house, apartment, separate group of rooms, or other housing unit.

[1]U.S. Bureau of the Census, *Statistical Abstract of the United States, 1990,* 110th ed. (Washington, D.C.: U.S. Government Printing Office, 1990), pp. 16–17. Some data are projected.

[2]*Statistical Abstract: 1990,* p. 5. Households do not include persons living in group quarters such as jails, military barracks, or college dormitories.

Table 10.2

Sources of Personal Income (Percentage Distribution for Selected Years)

Since 1950, the percentage of income attributable to wages and salaries has remained fairly stable, while interest income and transfer payments have grown, and rent, dividends, and proprietors' income have fallen in relative importance.

Source of Income	Year						
	1950	1960	1970	1975	1980	1985	1990
Earned Income							
Wages, salaries, and other labor income	66.6%	70.4%	70.2%	67.0%	66.8%	65.0%	63.8%
Proprietors' income	17.0	11.7	9.6	9.5	8.0	7.7	8.7
Rental income	3.1	3.5	2.2	1.0	0.3	0.3	0.1
Dividends	3.9	3.2	2.7	2.2	2.3	2.4	2.7
Interest income	3.9	6.2	8.3	9.3	12.0	14.4	14.7
Unearned Income							
Transfer payments	6.7	7.2	10.3	14.7	14.4	14.7	15.0
Personal Contributions for Social Insurance[a]	−1.3	−2.2	−3.3	−3.8	−3.9	−4.5	−4.9
Personal Income[b]	100.0	100.0	100.0	100.0	100.0	100.0	100.0

[a]Contributions for social insurance (Social Security) are subtracted from earned income in calculating personal income.

[b]Columns may not total 100.0 due to rounding.

Source: 1950–1985 figures are from various editions of U.S. Bureau of the Census, *Statistical Abstract of the United States* (Washington, D.C.: U.S. Government Printing Office). 1950 figures are from the 99th ed., p. 447; 1960 from 103d ed., p. 425; 1970–75 from 107th ed., p. 423; 1980–1985 from 110th ed., p. 433. 1990 figures are from U.S., *Economic Report of the President* (Washington, D.C.: U.S. Government Printing Office, 1991), pp. 314–315. 1990 figures are preliminary.

Household Income and Expenditures

In the discussion of a market economy in Chapter Two, the circular flow model illustrated that households perform two basic functions: they sell factors of production to businesses in return for income; and they purchase goods and services from businesses. These two money flows—household income and expenditures—can be examined statistically to obtain a general understanding of the sources and sizes of household income as well as the types of expenditures households make.

Personal income

Household gross, or pretax, income; income households use to pay taxes, spend, and save.

Household Income   Table 10.2 lists the sources of pretax income, or **personal income,** on a percentage basis for selected years. The figures indicate that the sale of resources, particularly labor resources, is the primary source of household income. The figures also show that while wages and salaries have remained relatively stable as a percentage of total income through the

Table 10.3   Percentage of Total Cash Benefit Payments to Various Transfer Programs

Over 50 percent of cash transfer payments in 1970 and 1987 went to recipients of Social Security benefits.

	Year	
Program	**1970**	**1987**
Total[a]	100.0%	100.0%
OASDI[b]	52.2	55.9
Public employee retirement	15.2	20.0
Railroad retirement	2.9	1.8
Veterans' pensions, compensation	9.1	4.0
Unemployment benefits	7.0	4.0
Temporary disability benefits	1.2	0.7
Workers' compensation	3.3	4.8
Public assistance	8.0	4.6
Supplemental security income	—	4.1

[a]Columns may not total 100.0 due to rounding.

[b]Old age, survivors, and disability insurance under the Federal Social Security Act.

Source: U.S. Bureau of the Census, *Statistical Abstract of the United States: 1990*, 110th ed. (Washington, D.C.: U.S. Government Printing Office, 1990), p. 352.

years, other types of earned income have not. Proprietors' income, dividends, and rent have declined in importance, and interest income has increased.

Table 10.2 also illustrates the growing importance of transfer payments in providing income: up from 6.7 percent of total personal income in 1950 to over 14 percent since the middle 1970s.[3] Table 10.3 divides cash transfer payments into various program categories, showing the percentage of total benefits going to each program in 1970 and 1987. The greatest amount of transfer funds in both years went to recipients of Social Security benefits.

How large is the average household income? How much does income differ from household to household due to the sex, age, or education of the head of the household? Table 10.4 gives the average income of all households for March 1988, as well as average income according to selected characteristics of the household head. Although this table shows an average income of $25,986 for all households, there is a significant difference between this average for all households and the average for households in certain subgroups of the population. For example, households headed by a male

[3]Government transfers are payments such as unemployment compensation for which no direct work is performed.

Table 10.4

Average Money Income of Households[a]

The average incomes of households differ according to the sex, age, and education of the household head.

Characteristic	Average Income[b]
All households	$25,986
Households headed by a male	31,534
Households headed by a female	14,600
Households with head aged 25–34 yrs.	26,923
Households with head aged 65 yrs. and over	14,334
Households with head attaining 4 yrs. of high school	25,910
Households with head attaining 4 yrs. of college or more	43,952

[a]Data are for March 1988.

[b]The average used is the median.

Source: U.S. Bureau of the Census, *Statistical Abstract of the United States: 1990*, 110th ed. (Washington, D.C.: U.S. Government Printing Office, 1990) p. 445.

averaged $31,534, while households headed by a female averaged $14,600, or about 46 percent of the average for households headed by a male. Not surprisingly, the average income of households where the head is from 25 to 34 years old, and probably attached to the labor force, is greater than the average income of households where the head is 65 years of age or older, and perhaps retired from the labor force. Notice also from this table that average incomes correlate positively with education: on the average, households headed by a person with four or more years of college earned over $18,000 a year more than households headed by a person with just four years of high school.

Household Expenditures   How do households use their incomes? Basically, income is used for three purposes: spending, saving, and paying taxes. In 1990 each person, on the average, spent 81.1 percent of his or her personal income, saved 3.9 percent, and paid 15.1 percent in personal tax and nontax payments.[4] These figures, however, can be misleading because they are averages. For incomes higher than the average, a greater percentage is taxed and saved, and for incomes lower than the average, a smaller percentage is taxed and saved.

There are several ways to view how households spend their incomes. One popular method is to categorize expenditures according to whether the

[4] U.S., *Economic Report of the President* (Washington, D.C.: U.S. Government Printing Office, 1991), p. 316. Figures are preliminary and percentages do not total 100.0 due to rounding.

Durable good

A good that has a useful lifetime of more than one year.

Nondurable good

A good that has a short useful lifetime.

items purchased are durable goods, nondurable goods, or services. A **durable good** is one that has a useful lifetime of more than one year—an automobile, musical instrument, or furniture, for example—and a **nondurable good** is one with a short span of use—such as food or gasoline. In recent years, the largest portion of household expenditures has gone for services—medical care, for example—followed by nondurable goods and durable goods. In 1990 the average person used 54.2 percent of total expenditures for services, 32.6 percent for nondurable goods, and 13.2 percent for durable goods.[5] The exact proportions spent on these categories have not stayed constant over time; the proportion spent for services has been increasing.

Goals and Decisions of Individuals in Households

It should be apparent by now that the main economic decisions of individuals in households relate to how they earn and how they spend their incomes. These decisions range from major considerations, such as whether to attend college to improve future earnings, to minor daily questions, such as whether to purchase a soda or pretzels from a vending machine. What objective is sought in making these earning and spending decisions?

In making economic decisions, individuals are trying to obtain the most satisfaction possible from their decisions. In other words, they are attempting to **maximize their economic well-being.** Maximizing economic well-being is not the same as acquiring all the goods and services that can possibly be acquired. This course of action would require that an individual spend every waking hour earning income for purchases. After following such a strategy, most people would surely decide that economic satisfaction would be increased with a little more leisure time, even at the expense of some goods and services.

Maximizing economic well-being

Obtaining the greatest possible satisfaction, or return, from an economic decision.

Maximizing economic well-being is a balancing process. It involves weighing the advantages, or benefits, and the disadvantages, or costs, of different courses of action and selecting the one strategy that contributes most to economic satisfaction. This notion of balancing becomes clearer when the maximizing goal is applied to the basic spending and earning decisions.

Maximizing Satisfaction from Consuming Goods and Services   Since incomes are limited, individuals are unable to obtain all of the goods and services they want. This reality is the individual's own version of the basic economic problem: limited resources in comparison to the wants and needs to be satisfied. Because of this basic problem, individuals must choose, within the limits of their incomes, which goods and services and how much of each to acquire.

[5] *Economic Report of the President*, 1991, p. 286. Figures are preliminary.

The actual allocation of dollars for purchases can be done in many different ways. For example, a person might choose dinner in an expensive restaurant instead of enrolling in a recreation program, or might choose several compact discs instead of new clothing. The problem in determining how to spend one's money is that each spending arrangement, or each combination of goods and services purchased, leads to a different level of satisfaction. If an individual is to maximize the satisfaction received from purchasing goods and services, he or she must select that one combination of goods and services that gives more satisfaction than any other combination.

Utility

Satisfaction realized from the consumption of a good or service.

Economists refer to the satisfaction received from consuming a good or service as **utility.** Thus, the goal of the individual in making spending decisions is to pick, within the limits of his or her income, the combination of goods and services that gives maximum total utility. To maximize total utility, an individual must evaluate each good or service that might be purchased by weighing the satisfaction that can be obtained from each unit consumed against the price of the good or service. This decision-making process can be illustrated through some simple examples.

Example 1: Suppose that you are at a movie and would like a box of popcorn and a soft drink. However, a box of popcorn costs $1.50, a soft drink costs $1.50, and you have only $1.50 left. How will this money be spent?

Obviously, it will be spent on whichever of the two items adds the greatest amount of satisfaction. If the popcorn would satisfy you more than the soft drink, the $1.50 will be spent for the popcorn; if the reverse is true, the $1.50 will be spent for the soda. The point is, to maximize satisfaction, your $1.50 will be spent on the item that adds the most for the money to your total utility.

In this example, the choice is easy because, since the prices are the same, all you have to consider is the added satisfaction provided by a box of popcorn compared to a soft drink. But what about the situation where a person is choosing between items with different prices? This is taken up in the second example.

Example 2: Suppose that you have $30 to spend over the weekend and would like to see a movie for $6, dine at the local pizzeria for $15, go to a concert where the tickets are $30 each, buy a videotape for $16, and purchase an $8 paperback book. Obviously, you cannot obtain all of these items for $30. How will you allocate your expenditures?

In making your spending decisions, you must consider the added satisfaction received from each item *in comparison to the dollars spent on that item.* If you use your money to purchase a $30 ticket to the concert, the added satisfaction that you receive from the concert must be at least twice the added satisfaction from the $15 pizza, or five times the added satisfaction from the $6 movie to maximize your utility. If the concert would add only the same satisfaction as a movie or a pizza, you would not be allocating your money in the best manner possible by spending it on the concert. If you spend your $30 to purchase a paperback book, a videotape, and a movie ticket, those items *together* should add as much satisfaction as the concert. If they do not, you have not maximized your utility with this spending arrangement.

A simple rule emerges here: to maximize satisfaction from purchasing goods and services, expenditures must be allocated in a way that *adds the most utility for the purchaser's money.* In deciding between popcorn and soda, you should have spent your $1.50 on the item that gave the greatest satisfaction for the money. In allocating your $30 among the various alternative goods that it could purchase, you should have weighed the added utility received from each item against its price. Maximizing utility is not simply a matter of receiving more satisfaction from one item than another. Rather, it is a matter of receiving more satisfaction for the money. A Porsche or Corvette might give you a great deal of satisfaction—but the price tag is high. You might get more total satisfaction from a less expensive car plus the other goods and services that the lower-priced car allows you to purchase. In making spending decisions, an individual must consider both the utility received from the item and the price of the item.

Can these textbook examples be seen at work in the real world? Do people really use these balancing principles in making purchasing decisions? The answer is yes, they do. The process might not be quite as precise as in the examples presented here, but basically consumers compare the price of an item with the expected addition to satisfaction from acquiring the item. If you have ever walked by a vending machine and noticed a student staring intently at the selections, that student was probably trying to choose the item that would add the most satisfaction for the price. If you were given a free sample of an item, and, on the basis of the sample, decided never to buy it, you applied the additional satisfaction-price test: what the item would add to your total utility was not worth its price. If you left a clothing store with, say, a $30 shirt and a $15 belt, and later returned the belt, you probably discovered that the belt would not give you half the satisfaction received from the shirt. In each of these cases the balancing of satisfactions and prices comes into play. Can you use this balancing process to explain the willingness of the consumers in Application 10.1, "The High-Living Middle Class," to purchase top quality items whenever possible and to scrimp on some things in order to splurge on others?

Maximizing Satisfaction from Earning Income   Why can two people earn the same income on their jobs, and yet one moonlights while the other does not? Obviously, the wants and needs of the two workers must be different. One may contribute to the support of a family while the other may not. One may be saving for a vacation, or paying off a loan, or interested in earning a lot of money because for that person money is a measure of success. The difference between the two workers is that one is moonlighting because, to that worker, the value of the additional income is greater than the additional

Application 10.1

The High-Living Middle Class

Some 3.3 million American households have incomes that enable them to live affluent or rich lives. But far more — 26 million — partake of the good life some of the time, treating themselves to Godiva chocolates, Giorgio Armani cologne, and long weekends in St. Thomas and Jamaica. They are the Joneses of the Eighties, and most have incomes of less than $40,000.

Market researchers at Grey Advertising, a New York agency with billings of $2 billion a year, discovered this new mass of "ultra consumers" while trying to figure out who has been buying so many $380 Burberry raincoats, $250 Louis Vuitton purses, and $200 Mont Blanc fountain pens. There simply aren't enough affluent or near-affluent Americans to account for all the spending on luxury goods.

The ad agency interviewed people across the country between the ages of 21 and 50 with household incomes of more than $25,000 a year, a slice representing about a quarter of the adult population. Of those surveyed, just over half said they bought the top of the line whenever they could afford it. Only 5% of these ultra consumers had incomes above $75,000, Fortune's minimum for an affluent lifestyle.

The vast majority of these folks obviously aren't in the market for Rolls-Royces or complete designer wardrobes. But they do *rent* limos from time to time and are devotees of designer-label accessories like Hermès scarves and Gucci loafers. "This is more an attitude of the mind than the pocketbook," says Barbara Feigin, an executive vice president at Grey.

Wanting it all has long been a hallmark of the middle class. Ultra consumers also want the best. Buying the best is a way to set themselves apart and bolster their self-image. Madison Avenue strives to reinforce that desire. Ads for premium-priced products as varied as Ultress hair coloring and Mitsubishi cars have a cloying sameness: sensual, provocative, and elegant, no matter what's for sale.

Since they cannot afford across-the-board extravagance, most ultra consumers splurge on a few items and scrimp elsewhere. They get by with fewer clothes to afford the Toshiba DX-7 digital VCR with hi-fi sound and do without the new bed so they can sleep between all-cotton sheets. "They don't have all that many wonderful things at once," says Feigin. Small doses of opulence must suffice.

Source: Jaclyn Fierman, "The High-Living Middle Class," FORTUNE, April 13, 1987, p. 27. © 1987 Time Inc. All rights reserved. Reprinted with permission.

effort required to earn it. For the other worker, the extra income is not worth the extra effort.

The moonlighting example illustrates that, as with spending decisions, maximizing satisfaction from earning income is a matter of balancing. On the one hand, there is the additional income from working more hours that can be spent on goods and services. On the other, working extra hours means less time for other activities. A person who spends the same number of hours on a job week after week may not give a great deal of thought to this balancing until the opportunity to earn more income through longer hours of work presents itself. At some point, as more hours are worked, the extra income and the satisfaction it brings may not be enough to justify the dissatisfaction from forgoing other activities as a result of working, and

Application 10.2

Second Thoughts on Having It All

Twice during the past month, colleagues approached 38-year-old Rebecca Murray [not her real name] and volunteered identical assessments of her life: "You are the woman who has everything," they told her. The notion staggered Rebecca. "I have never, ever thought of myself that way," she says. But it's not hard to see what her co-workers had in mind.

For the past eighteen years, Rebecca has been married to the same man—Robert, now 42—and their marriage remains strong. Their five-year-old daughter is pretty and bright. Rebecca works as a records manager for a large financial institution and earns $40,000 a year—with plenty of potential to move up. Robert makes $43,000 a year as the business manager for a publishing house. Free-lance writing brings in another $5,000 a year. He is a novelist, and although his advances have been small so far, that could change with a single success. The Murrays' combined income of nearly $90,000 is . . . a lot of money by nearly any standard. What's more, they pay just $450 a month for a rent-stabilized apartment on a pretty street on the Upper West Side [of New York City]. Among other things, they can afford the $8,500 a year it costs to send their daughter to a private day-care center where the ratio of children to teachers is four to one.

But none of this compensates for what Rebecca feels is missing in her life. "Time," she says, "I don't have enough time for my child, I don't have enough time for myself, and I never have enough time for my husband. He gets whatever I have left at the end of each day, and usually that's nothing. . . . I'm aware that I'm looking at an evening that's not going to be relaxing. Realistically, I'm facing three more hours of work—the child care—and I've already put in a full day at the office."

Rebecca reached her breaking point on a subway during rush hour last summer. "I was standing on this miserable, crowded, hot train," she remembers, "coming from a job that doesn't give me all that much pleasure, to pick up my child, who'd been away from me the whole day, to go home to an apartment so small that my husband and I sleep in the living room on a futon mattress." That night, Rebecca made a decision. "There's such a thing as quality of life," she told her husband, "and this isn't it." . . .

[Note: The couple eventually decided to move to a small town in upstate New York.]

Source: Tony Schwartz, "Second Thoughts on Having It All," *New York* Magazine, July 15, 1985, pp. 32–41. Copyright © 1985 by News America Publishing, Inc. Reprinted with permission of *New York* Magazine.

further overtime is refused. Application 10.2, "Second Thoughts on Having It All," shows how nonmonetary as well as financial costs enter into the balancing process in making income-earning decisions, and how one person decided that her income-earning efforts were not maximizing her economic well-being.

In summary, both spending and earning decisions involve the goal of maximizing economic well-being. The decision maker must weigh the advantages, or benefits, and disadvantages, or costs, of different strategies to choose the one that will come closest to accomplishing that objective. This weighing, or balancing, which is at the heart of the individual decision-making process, is covered in detail in the next chapter.

Table 10.5   The Ten Largest U.S. Industrial Corporations: 1990

The decisions of very large corporations that sell billions of dollars of output and employ hundreds of thousands of people can have a major impact on households, other businesses, governments, and the economy in general.

Rank	Corporation	Sales (Billions of Dollars)
1	General Motors	$126.0
2	Exxon	105.9
3	Ford Motor	98.3
4	International Business Machines	69.0
5	Mobil	58.8
6	General Electric	58.4
7	Philip Morris	44.3
8	Texaco	41.2
9	E. I. DuPont De Nemours	39.8
10	Chevron	39.3

Source: "The Fortune 500 Largest U.S. Industrial Corporations," *Fortune,* April 22, 1991, p. 286.

Overview of Business

Business

An organization established for the purpose of producing and selling goods and services.

A **business** is an organization established for the purpose of producing and selling goods and services. In the United States there are over 17 million legally organized business firms. Many are small operations with annual sales of under $25,000, while others are huge enterprises selling billions of dollars worth of goods and services each year.[6]

Business decisions, especially about output and prices, have a powerful influence on the economy, with the degree of influence depending on the size of the business and the competitive structure of the market in which the business is selling. A very large firm can have a significant impact on employment conditions in the economy in general and in an industry or region specifically. Imagine the consequences of shutting down General Motors, which employed over 760,000 people in 1990, or any of the other firms listed in Table 10.5.[7]

The competitive structure of the market in which a business operates influences the prices that it charges for its products. A company producing items with little or no competition can charge higher prices than those

[6]See Table 10.6.

[7]"The Fortune 500 Largest U.S. Industrial Corporations," *Fortune,* April 22, 1991, p. 322.

charged under more competitive conditions. In fact, a few large firms with a substantial share of a market that accounts for a significant amount of consumer spending could contribute to inflation when they raise prices.

Before the specifics of business decision making are studied, let us examine the legal organizations of business and the current overall structure of American business.

Legal Forms of Business

A business must take on a legal form before it can operate; it may be (1) a proprietorship, (2) a partnership, or (3) a corporation.

Proprietorship   A one-owner business that is typically small—for example, a retailing establishment like an antique or flower shop, or an independent consultant—is called a **proprietorship.** Usually in a proprietorship the owner is the manager and a jack-of-all-trades, performing functions such as those of a bookkeeper, financial analyst, and marketing specialist. For the owner of the business this legal form has the advantage of independence in decision making; the owner is not responsible or answerable to anyone.

A proprietorship, however, poses several problems for its owner: particularly, difficulty in raising money and unlimited liability. The owner of a proprietorship who wants to raise money for expansion, remodeling, or such, can do so only by borrowing from private sources such as family or friends, or from the traditional financial institutions like commercial banks and savings and loan associations, or through certain government programs. Because proprietorships cannot issue stocks and bonds, a large source of money capital cannot be readily tapped by the single-owner business.

A proprietor is also subject to **unlimited liability;** that is, the owner's personal assets are subject to use as payment for business debts. If a creditor cannot be fully paid from the assets of the business, the courts may take the owner's personal property to satisfy such debts.

Partnership   A business that is similar to a proprietorship but has two or more (perhaps hundreds of) owners is a **partnership.** This arrangement permits the pooling of money, experience, and talent. For example, a person who is skilled in cooking and kitchen administration and a person who is adept at business-related matters such as management and finance might form a successful restaurant operation. Unfortunately, the partnership arrangement often leads to dissension between partners, resulting in dissolution of the business.

In a partnership, unless it is legally specified in writing, all partners become general partners. A **general partner** is one who has the burden of unlimited liability, and each partnership must have at least one general partner. If misunderstood, unlimited liability for a partner can be a potential source of problems. In a partnership each general partner is responsible for 100 percent of the business's debts. In case of default, liability is not

Proprietorship
A one-owner business.

Unlimited liability
A business owner's personal assets are subject to use as payment for business debts.

Partnership
The legal organization of a business that is similar to a proprietorship but has two or more owners.

General partner
An owner of a partnership who is subject to unlimited liability.

necessarily divided in half, or in thirds, or other equal amounts. Instead, the debts beyond those covered by the business's assets will be paid through the personal assets of whichever partners possess the means. If one general partner is penniless and the other wealthy, the partner with the assets will pay the debts.

Corporation

A legal entity, owned by stockholders, which can carry on in its own name functions of business normally performed by individuals.

Corporation   An entity created by law, a **corporation** is a "legal person" in that it can sue or be sued, make contracts, pay fines, and carry on other aspects of business normally performed by individuals. The one human characteristic that a corporation does not possess is death: a corporation can continue indefinitely.

To form a corporation, a charter must be obtained from one of the states. The choice of the state for incorporation will probably be based on varying regulations, taxes, and the like. This charter, the acquiring of which involves some cost and red tape, usually contains information such as the corporate name, the corporation's purpose, and the number of shares of stock it is authorized to sell.

As a corporation is established, shares of stock are sold (additional shares may be sold later), and the holders of these shares become the owners of the corporation. One major advantage for the owners of a corporation is limited liability; that is, all of their personal assets are *not* subject to payment for business debts. In case of bankruptcy of a corporation, an owner can lose only the money used to purchase the stock. This sum, however, could be considerable.

Preferred stock

Stock that pays a stated dividend to its holder; preferred stockholders are entitled to their dividends before common stockholders are paid.

Common stock

Stock that pays a dividend dependent upon the profit position of a firm after all other financial obligations have been met.

The owners of a corporation receive profits from the corporation through quarterly dividend checks. The size of the dividend check depends upon the corporation's profitability and the type of stock an owner possesses. Corporations can issue both preferred and common stock. **Preferred stock** remits a stated dividend to its holders, and preferred stockholders are entitled to their dividends before common stockholders are paid. **Common stock** pays a dividend dependent upon the profit position of the firm after creditors and preferred stockholders have been paid. A quarter with healthy sales and sizable profits might yield a high return on common stock, whereas a quarter with no profit will yield no dividend check.[8]

Each share of common stock entitles its owner to one vote. These votes are used to determine some corporate policies and, more importantly, to elect the corporation's board of directors. The board of directors is the governing board of a corporation and makes many major decisions, including the selection of top management of the firm. Top management, in turn, runs the corporation on a day-to-day basis. Figure 10.1 outlines the structure of a corporation.

---

[8] Preferred stock does not guarantee a dividend. If the company has not made enough profit for a return to the preferred stockholders, they will not receive a dividend. However, if the preferred stock is cumulative, the stockholders will receive the return at some future point when profit is made.

Figure 10.1   Structure of a Corporation

The stockholders who own a corporation elect a board of directors that makes major decisions for the corporation and appoints top management to run the corporation.

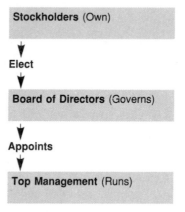

Because each share of common stock carries a vote, control of a corporation centers around those who hold large numbers of shares. These stockholders have the power to elect themselves or their candidates to the board of directors. The number of shares necessary for control depends upon the number of shares outstanding. A few thousand shares in a small corporation might yield control, but a few thousand shares in a company like General Motors might be negligible. "Test Your Understanding: The Price of Stock Shares" discusses how the price of a share of stock is determined by supply and demand, and provides an opportunity to evaluate how changes in supply and demand affect a stock's price.

No discussion of a corporation is complete without some mention of **bonds.** Corporations go into debt and borrow by selling bonds to raise money for building, expansion, and other purposes. Bonds provide a corporation with an avenue other than stocks to tap other corporations, private individuals, and organizations for funds. Corporate bonds are sold in $1,000 denominations and have a specified interest rate and maturity date. A bondholder is a creditor of the company and not an owner.

Bond

A financial instrument through which a corporation can borrow long-term funds.

Numbers and Sizes of Businesses

Table 10.6 gives the number of legally organized businesses in the United States and the size of business receipts (sales) in 1986. Statistics are given for all businesses as a group and for each individual legal form. Observe that according to Table 10.6, in 1986 there were 17,526,000 businesses, with the

Test Your Understanding

The Price of Stock Shares[a]

[a]Answers can be found at the end of the book.

A stock exchange is a facility for trading stocks. Only the stocks of corporations listed on a particular exchange may be traded there. The best-known exchanges are the New York Stock Exchange (NYSE) and the American Stock Exchange (AMEX). Most major newspapers carry the daily market data for companies listed on these two exchanges.

The price at which a share of a corporation's common stock is bought and sold may change daily, or hourly, or by the minute. This is due to changes in buyers' and sellers' plans that affect demand and supply. To illustrate, let us assume that a hypothetical company, the Grand Corporation, is listed on the New York Stock Exchange. We will also assume that the demand and supply for Grand common stock as of the opening of trading today is given in the figure shown here.

The downward-sloping demand curve indicates that as the price per share increases, buyers will decrease the quantity of shares demanded. The upward-sloping supply curve shows that as the price per share increases, sellers will be willing to sell more shares. In this market, the equilibrium price is $18.00 per share, and 3,000 shares are bought and sold.

What could cause this equilibrium price to change? Any factor that increases or decreases the supply and/or demand of Grand stock may do so. For example, suppose that the media carry a rumor that Grand is about to sign a lucrative government contract. This rumor may cause investors to want to purchase Grand stock, increasing its demand (shifting the curve to the right) and causing an increase in equilibrium price.

What would be the effect on demand, supply, and equilibrium price of each of the following?

1. A major pension fund holding a large amount of Grand stock decides to sell its shares.

2. Corporate reports indicate that sales and profits are increasing.

3. Corporate sales and profits are on a slow, constant decline.

4. Returns on alternative investments are increasing.

5. Grand announces a two-for-one split of its stock in which each outstanding share is now worth two shares.

6. The stock market falls by a record amount, signaling a lack of investor confidence in the economy.

7. The Grand Corporation begins a policy of buying back its own stock on the market.

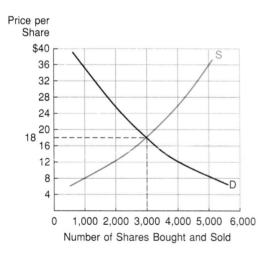

Table 10.6   Number and Receipts of Proprietorships, Partnerships, and Corporations: 1986

Although the vast majority of U.S. firms are organized as proprietorships, they account for a small percentage of business receipts. Most receipts go to corporations.

Business Firms	Number	Number as a Percentage of the Total	Receipts	Receipts as a Percentage of the Total
Total	17,526,000	100.0%	$9.3 trillion	100.0%
Proprietorships[a]	12,394,000	70.7	0.6 trillion	6.5
Partnerships	1,703,000	9.7	0.4 trillion	4.3
Corporations	3,429,000	19.6	8.3 trillion	89.2

[a]Includes only nonfarm businesses.

Source: U.S. Bureau of the Census, *Statistical Abstract of the United States: 1990,* 110th ed. (Washington, D.C.: U.S. Government Printing Office, 1990), p. 521.

vast majority, 12,394,000 (or 70.7 percent), organized as proprietorships. Only 3,429,000 (or 19.6 percent) were corporations. The table also shows, however, that most of the business receipts went to corporations. Of the approximately $9.3 trillion in total sales, corporations accounted for $8.3 trillion (or 89.2 percent). Proprietorships, on the other hand, received only $0.6 trillion (or 6.5 percent) of the total sales. Thus, the vast majority of businesses are proprietorships, which are generally small in size and account for a small percentage of the total sales of the economy. Corporations are fewer in number than proprietorships, but tend to be larger in size and account for most business sales.

Table 10.7 examines the sizes of businesses by classifying firms according to the amount of their annual receipts or sales. The left-hand column gives various size classes of receipts; for example, if a business sold $125,000 in goods and services, it would be included in the $100,000–$499,999 category. The upper portion of the table gives the number of businesses in each category and the dollar value of all receipts acquired by all businesses in each category during 1985. For example, in 1985 there were 1,785,000 businesses that sold between $25,000 and $49,999 in goods and services and whose sales together amounted to $65 billion. The lower portion of the table converts the figures from the upper portion into percentages.

According to the lower portion of Table 10.7, 59.1 percent of all reported businesses sold less than $25,000 in goods and services in 1985. Together these businesses accounted for 0.7 percent of the receipts from all goods and services sold that year. In other words, most business firms are extremely small in size. On the other hand, only 3.7 percent of all businesses sold over $1,000,000 each in goods and services; but these firms together received 87.3

Table 10.7   Number of Businesses and Business Receipts Classified by Size of Receipts: 1985

The majority of business receipts goes to a small percentage of firms. For example, in 1985 only 3.7 percent of all reported business firms were in the category of $1 million and over, but together they accounted for 87.3 percent of total receipts.

Size Class of Receipts	Number of Businesses[a] (Thousands)	Receipts (Billions of Dollars)
Under $25,000	9,997	$ 63
$25,000–$49,999	1,785	65
$50,000–$99,000	1,576	112
$100,000–$499,999	2,451	552
$500,000–$999,999	489	344
$1,000,000 or more	621	7,803
Percentage Distribution		
Under $25,000	59.1%	0.7%
$25,000–$49,999	10.6	0.7
$50,000–$99,999	9.3	1.3
$100,000–$499,999	14.5	6.2
$500,000–$999,999	2.8	3.8
$1,000,000 or more	3.7	87.3

[a]Includes some firms with no receipts; includes only nonfarm proprietorships.

Source: U.S. Bureau of the Census, *Statistical Abstract of the United States: 1990*, 110th ed. (Washington, D.C.: U.S. Government Printing Office, 1990), p. 521.

percent of all receipts in 1985. Both Tables 10.6 and 10.7 confirm that a very small percentage of U.S. businesses is providing the vast majority of what is sold, and that there are far more small U.S. businesses than large ones.

Business Ownership of Business

Owners of corporate stock need not be private individuals. Much stock is owned by funds, such as pension and endowment funds, and by corporations. In fact, in many instances, the controlling shares of stock in one corporation are owned by another corporation. In these cases, the corporation that owns the stock is said to own the other corporation.

It is often not readily apparent that one corporation owns another because both businesses may retain separate identities and operate as distinct entities. For example, you may not be aware that the publisher of this text, The Dryden Press, is a division of Harcourt Brace Jovanovich.

Figure 10.2   The Alltown Bank Holding Company

The purpose of a holding company, such as Alltown Bank Corporation, is to own shares of stock in other companies, such as Hometown Bank and Crosstown Bank.

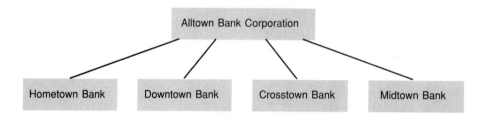

Conglomerate

A corporation that owns other corporations that produce unrelated goods and services.

Vertical integration

A corporation owns other corporations that supply its inputs or distribute its products.

Horizontal integration

A corporation owns other corporations that compete in the same market.

Holding company

A corporation formed for the purpose of owning or holding stock in other corporations.

Merger (acquisition)

The acquiring of one company by another company; can be accomplished by buying a controlling amount of stock.

Sometimes, when one corporation owns another corporation, there is no relationship between the goods or services that the two corporations produce, and the firm is called a **conglomerate.** A manufacturer of toys could own a carburetor company, or an electronic components producer might own a wallpaper firm. American Brands, Inc., for example, owns the American Tobacco Company, The Franklin Life Insurance Company, James B. Beam Distilling Co., Samsonite Corporation, and Foot-Joy, Inc.[9] In other instances, a corporation may own other corporations that are closely related to each other in some way. Pepsico, Inc. owns Pepsi-Cola Company, Frito-Lay, Inc., Pizza Hut, Inc., Taco Bell Corp., and Kentucky Fried Chicken Corporation.[10] When a corporation owns other corporations that supply inputs or distribute products for one another, such as Pepsi Cola and Pizza Hut which are in a supplier-distributor relationship, the firms are said to be **vertically integrated.** When a corporation owns other corporations that compete in the same market, as do Pizza Hut, Taco Bell, and Kentucky Fried Chicken, the firms are said to be **horizontally integrated.** Pepsico has both vertical and horizontal integration.

Sometimes a corporation is formed specifically for the purpose of owning or holding stock in other corporations. This type of company is termed a **holding company.** A holding company produces nothing itself. Figure 10.2 shows a hypothetical example of a bank holding company, Alltown Bank Corporation, which exists only to own controlling shares of stock in Hometown Bank, Downtown Bank, and other banks.

The buying of controlling shares of stock in one corporation by another corporation is referred to as a **merger,** or **acquisition.** Recent years have seen

[9]Moody's Investors Service, *Moody's Industrial Manual: 1990,* vol. 1 (New York: Moody's Investors Service, Inc., 1990), pp. 2556–2557.

[10]*Moody's Industrial Manual: 1990,* vol. 2, p. 4162.

Table 10.8

Annual Number and Value of Completed Acquisitions: 1980–1989

The number and total annual value of acquisitions grew significantly during the 1980s.

Year	Number of Acquisitions	Total Value of Acquisitions (Billions of Dollars)
1980	1,558	$ 32.8
1981	2,328	69.5
1982	2,298	60.7
1983	2,393	52.7
1984	3,175	126.1
1985	3,484	146.0
1986	4,446	205.8
1987	4,015	178.3
1988	4,000	236.4
1989	3,415	231.4

Source: *Mergers and Acquisitions,* March/April 1990, p. 95.

much merger activity, with many of the acquisitions valued in the billions of dollars. For example, Table 10.8 , which summarizes U.S. merger activity over the 1980s, shows that the number of completed acquisitions rose from approximately 1,550 per year in 1980 to over 4,400 in 1986. Notice also the dramatic increase in the total annual value of acquisitions over that period: up from $32.8 billion in 1980 to over $230 billion by the end of the decade. This increase in value is due in part to the increase in the number of mergers and in part to the giant size of some of the acquired firms. Table 10.9 lists the ten largest acquisitions in the 1980s.

There are many reasons why one firm may seek to merge with another: to fill out a product line or move into a new geographic market, to acquire a company with large amounts of cash, or to avoid a hostile takeover from yet another company, to name several. Application 10.3, "Manufacturer Needs Outlets," is about a widely speculated merger between Walt Disney Co. and CBS Inc. What would appear to be the main incentives for these two companies to merge? Mergers and acquisitions are covered in more detail in Chapter Fourteen.

Goals and Decisions of Business Firms

Many decisions must be made over the life of a business firm: whether to organize as a proprietorship, partnership, or corporation; what goods and services to produce, prices to charge, and markets to serve; whether to

Table 10.9   Largest Acquisitions in the 1980s

Billions of dollars were spent in the 1980s for corporate acquisitions.

Acquiring Company	Acquired Company	Value (Billions of Dollars)	Year
Kohlberg Kravis Roberts & Co.	RJR Nabisco Inc.	$24.7	1989
Standard Oil Co. of California	Gulf Corp.	13.3	1984
Philip Morris Cos. Inc.	Kraft Inc.	12.6	1988
Bristol-Myers Co.	Squibb Corp.	12.5	1989
Texaco Inc.	Getty Oil Co.	10.1	1984
Beecham Group PLC	Smithkline Beckman Corp.	8.3	1989
British Petroleum Co. PLC	Standard Oil Co.	7.6	1987
Dow Chemical Co.	Marion Laboratories Inc.	7.1	1989
E. I. duPont de Nemours & Co.	Conoco Inc.	6.9	1981
Campeau Corp.	Federated Department Stores Inc.	6.5	1988

Source: *Mergers and Acquisitions,* March/April 1990, p. 107.

acquire another firm or to be acquired by another firm; and so on. What is a business firm trying to accomplish? What is the ultimate purpose of its decisions? In the study of economics, it is usually assumed that *the fundamental objective of business decision making is to maximize a firm's profit or minimize its loss.* The goal of profit maximization or loss minimization does not mean that a business firm will simply seek to earn a profit and avoid a loss. Rather, the goal says that the firm will operate to earn the largest profit possible or the smallest loss if it cannot earn a profit.

Revenue

Money or income that a company receives from selling its product.

What is profit or loss? When a business sells a product, the money received from its sales is called **revenue.** For example, a firm selling 100,000 units of a product at $10 per unit is earning a revenue of ($10 × 100,000), or $1,000,000. But, in producing its good or service, a firm incurs certain costs such as those for labor, materials, transportation, insurance, and the purchase or rent of a building. These costs must be charged against revenue to determine whether the seller is earning a **profit or loss.** Thus, for a business firm:

Profit or loss

What results when a business subtracts its costs from its revenue.

$$\text{profit or loss} = \text{revenue} - \text{costs.}$$

If revenue is $1,000,000 and costs are $800,000, the firm is earning a profit of $200,000. If revenue is $1,000,000 but costs are $1,500,000, there is a loss of $500,000.

Application 10.3

Manufacturer Needs Outlets

Rumors are rife that the Walt Disney Co. would like to acquire CBS Inc. Whatever the outcome of the reported mating dance, it seems inevitable that CBS will find itself a partner soon.

As one of America's three nationwide television networks, CBS is one of the most powerful delivery systems for news and entertainment. Its potential is enormous. Listen to Shearson Lehman Hutton's canny entertainment analyst, Alan Kassan: "I believe that in the year 2000 we'll have five to seven global television networks. A network is a giant . . . machine for programming that you can distribute in the U.S. and worldwide." In short, any entertainment manufacturer will need a TV network so as to recoup a major part of its costs early on.

That's what makes CBS such an attractive partner for companies that have lots of programming but depend on outsiders for distribution. Companies like Walt Disney. Of such attractions are marriages made. . . .

There are now only three studios of consequence that lack large-scale distribution networks of their own: Disney, Paramount Communications and MCA. There are only three major nationwide networks: Capital Cities' ABC, General Electric's NBC and Laurence Tisch's CBS. For more than a year Wall Street has mixed and matched possible combinations, discarding one and trying another. The one rumor that won't go away is Disney and CBS.

True or not, the rumor has great plausibility. Disney has effected one of the most remarkable turnarounds of the 1980s. . . . But it needs distribution to control its own destiny in the global entertainment business.

CBS, on the other hand, is weak and likely to get weaker. It is well on the way to its third consecutive finish in last place in the prime-time ratings. Its "CBS Evening News" has dropped to second place. . . .

Disney could help improve those ratings. It has strong programming talent in-house. . . .

Source: Excerpted from Subrata N. Chakravarty, "Manufacturer Needs Outlets," *Forbes*, March 5, 1990, p. 42. Excerpted by permission of Forbes magazine. © Forbes Inc., 1990.

Profit goes to those persons who own a firm and bear the risk of its success or failure. Thus, in a proprietorship or partnership, profit goes to the individual owner or owners who organize and operate the business, and in a corporation it goes to the stockholders.

As with economic goals for an individual, profit maximization or loss minimization for a business is a balancing process. A firm weighs or balances the expected revenue and expected costs of each of the operating strategies from which it can choose, and then picks the one strategy that contributes most to its profitability. This balancing of revenues and costs is covered in detail in the next chapter.

Questions about Profit Maximization   The goal of profit maximization or loss minimization is more controversial than the household goal of maximizing economic well-being. One point of controversy is the question of what exactly is meant by profit maximization. Does maximizing mean that a firm seeks the largest profit or smallest loss consistent with maintaining the quality of its product and meeting the needs of its work force? Or does maximizing imply producing a product with minimum regard for quality, working conditions, and wages for the sake of a larger profit? The questions of what is implied by profit maximization and the desirability of the goal are taken up in the critical thinking case at the end of the chapter.

Another controversy centers on the fact that, while economists most often identify profit maximization as the fundamental goal of a firm, sometimes a seller will seek some alternative objective in the short run. For example, a desire to generate large amounts of cash to pay off a debt might cause a business to make its inflow of revenues as large as possible, even if this can be accomplished only at the expense of some profit. Or a company might want to make the greatest possible impact on its market with a new product. Here, rather than maximizing current profit, the firm's goal would be to maximize its share of the market. In these examples, the short-run intentions of maximizing revenue or capturing a large market share need not necessarily be inconsistent with the objective of profit maximization. Rather, they may be a means to improved performance and a larger maximum profit over the long run.

Questions can also be raised about how important the goal of profit maximization is to individuals in the different forms of business. It is easy to see how it might be the most important goal in the operation of sole proprietorships or partnerships, where the owners tend to be involved in the making of business decisions. If an individual has enough interest in profit to form a business firm, and if he or she places a relatively high value on profit, profit maximization may be the best explanation of what motivates that person. It is more difficult to understand profit maximization in a large corporation where the owners who hold stock in the company are typically not directly involved in the decision-making process, and where managers who receive fixed salaries rather than profits run the firm. Management, however, may be motivated by a concern for obtaining maximum profit for several reasons.[11]

First, if the profit performance of a company is unsatisfactory, stockholders could attempt to replace the corporation's directors and management. Second, large institutional investors, such as mutual funds and pension funds, are well-informed about market conditions and business practices, and their presence may make management more conscious of the profit-maximizing objective. Third, the fear of a hostile takeover by another corporation may motivate managers to maximize profit. A decline in the profitability of a corporation may lead to a drop in the price of its stock, making it cheaper and easier for another firm to acquire shares in an effort

---

[11] The following is based on W. L. Baldwin, "The Motives of Managers, Environmental Restraints, and the Theory of Managerial Enterprise," *The Quarterly Journal of Economics,* May 1964, pp. 238–256, especially pp. 251–252.

to gain control. One defense against a takeover is to keep stock prices high by keeping profit high.

Locating Data on Households and Businesses

A person's need to know economic information about households and businesses does not end when a course in economics or business is completed. Sometime in the future you may want to know the cost of living in different parts of the country, the average income of a person with your level of education, or other income- or expenditure-related information. A job offer or a stock tip might also send you searching for information on a particular firm or group of firms. Where can relatively up-to-date information on households and businesses be found?

An excellent source of data on both households and businesses that has been cited frequently in this chapter is the *Statistical Abstract of the United States*. This approximately 1,000-page volume, published annually by the U.S. government, contains hundreds of tables on household-related information, such as income, expenditures, social insurance, employment, and vital statistics. It also contains tables of data on businesses in general as well as on specific business sectors and industries. The *Statistical Abstract* is available in libraries and can be ordered directly from the federal government.

There are several good sources of information on individual corporations. A company's annual report to its stockholders provides current information about its financial performance, products, and other matters. Annual reports are available directly from companies and in many libraries.

Information on a large number of corporations can be found in *Moody's Industrial Manual,* which is published annually and contains financial and descriptive information—such as business histories, plant locations, and products—for industrial corporations listed on the New York, American, and other stock exchanges. Moody's also publishes separate manuals for firms in the utilities, transportation, and banking and financial services sectors of the economy.

Firms listed on the New York, American, and other stock exchanges can also be researched in Standard and Poor's multivolume *Standard Corporation Descriptions.* This reference service, which is published semimonthly, contains information on corporate backgrounds, stock data, capitalization, and earnings and finance.

Finally, information and articles on specific firms, industries, and products from hundreds of financial, trade, and other business-related publications are listed in *Predicasts F&S Index, United States Annual Edition.* The index is published annually with quarterly and monthly updates, and other Predicasts indexes are also available for the rest of the world. Moody's, Standard and Poor's, and Predicasts publications are available in libraries and are fully cited in the suggested readings at the end of this chapter.

Summary

A household is made up of an individual living alone or several persons living in a group. Although the number of households in the United States is increasing, the average number of persons per household is falling, and the percentage of households with one person is increasing. The majority of household income comes from the sale of resources, particularly labor. However, unearned income from government transfer payments has become increasingly important over the years. Of the different types of cash benefit transfer payments, Social Security is the largest.

The average income of all households taken as a group differs from the average income of various subgroups of households. This difference may be related to factors such as the sex, education, or age of the household head.

Household income can be saved, used for paying taxes, or spent, with the vast majority going to purchase goods and services. Purchases of goods can be divided between expenditures on durable and nondurable goods.

The main economic objective of an individual's spending and earning decisions is to maximize his or her economic well-being. Realizing this objective requires weighing alternatives and choosing the course of action that contributes most to economic satisfaction.

The satisfaction from consuming a good or service is called utility. To maximize the total utility from consuming several different goods and services, a purchaser must weigh the additional satisfaction received from consuming a unit of an item against that item's price and compare that with the additional satisfaction and price of other goods and services. If one good costs twice as much as another but adds less than twice as much to total utility (satisfaction), the buyer should limit the purchase of the more expensive good in favor of the cheaper one.

Earning decisions also involve weighing and balancing. In this case, the added satisfaction from more income is weighed against the added dissatisfaction from forgoing alternatives such as leisure time in order to earn that income.

A business is an organization established for the purpose of producing and selling goods and services. A firm may be legally organized as a proprietorship, partnership, or corporation. Each of these legal forms of organization has certain advantages and disadvantages, such as the nature of the owner's liability. Numerically, there are more proprietorships in the U.S. economy than there are partnerships or corporations, but the largest volume of receipts goes to corporations.

Many corporations have a controlling amount of their stock owned by other corporations. When a corporation buys the controlling shares of stock in another corporation, a merger, or acquisition, has taken place. Because two firms are related through ownership is no reason to assume that the goods and services they produce are related in any functional way.

The basic objective of a business firm is to maximize profit or minimize loss. Profit or loss equals revenue minus costs. As is the case with a household, business profit maximizing requires balancing: in this case, the expected revenues and costs from different operating strategies are considered.

Some controversy surrounds the profit-maximizing objective. This includes what is meant by profit maximization, and the extent to which a firm's other short-term goals relate to long-term profit maximization. It is easy to understand why profit maximizing is important to a sole proprietorship or partnership, but there are also reasons for making it an important objective for a corporation.

Several good reference sources that provide up-to-date economic information on households and businesses are available through libraries or directly from the government and individual corporations.

Key Terms and Concepts

Microeconomics	Corporation
Household	Preferred stock
Personal income	Common stock
Durable good	Bond
Nondurable good	Conglomerate
Maximizing economic well-being	Vertical integration
Utility	Horizontal integration
Utility maximization	Holding company
Business	Merger or acquisition
Proprietorship	Revenue
Unlimited liability	Profit and loss
Partnership	Profit maximization
General partner	

Review Questions

1. What are the main sources of household income and the different uses to which household income can be put? How is household income affected by the head of household's age, sex, education, and other factors?

2. Would a person maximize satisfaction by buying a $15 product that adds twice as much satisfaction as a $5 product? Why? Would the person maximize satisfaction by buying the $15 product if the price of the cheaper product rose to $8? Why?

3. If a person is seeking to maximize the satisfaction received from an employment decision, what factors will that person consider to be important in making the decision?

4. An individual maximizes his or her economic well-being by making spending and earning decisions, and a business maximizes its profit by deciding how much of its product to produce and sell. All of these decisions are similar in that they involve a balancing process.
    a. Generally, what is common to the balancing processes in these decisions?
    b. How do these decisions differ in terms of what is balanced?

5. What is the difference between a stock and a bond? Why might it be necessary for a firm to issue bonds in order to acquire another firm?

6. What is the difference between a conglomerate, a horizontally-integrated, and a vertically-integrated corporation? Give some examples of each type of corporation.

7. Where among the references identified in the chapter section titled "Locating Data on Households and Businesses" would you find each of the following?
    a. The corporate president's message to the stockholders of a corporation
    b. The titles and locations of articles on technological change in the computer industry
    c. Data on income of persons living in the Carolinas
    d. A brief history of a company that just offered you a job

Discussion Questions

1. Students who rent apartments close to campuses often say that they have to pay a lot for what they get. How could this fact make it difficult for a student to maximize the satisfaction from consuming goods and services with a limited income? Explain, in terms of the material in this chapter, why students will continue to rent at these high prices.

2. Over the years the percentage of income spent on services in the United States has grown to the point where it outranks the percentages spent on durable goods, such as automobiles, and nondurable goods, such as food. How might this growth in the demand for services be explained by increases in the general standard of living, the movement of homemakers into the labor force, and the aging of the population?

3. Can you explain in economic terms why someone with a so-called sweet tooth might be more than willing to buy an expensive iced fudge cake but would not consider buying a high-quality steak?

4. In his book *The Affluent Society*, John Kenneth Galbraith suggests that the wants we have for some goods may be subject to a "dependence effect."[12] This means that the wants are caused by the goods themselves: if the goods

---

[12] John Kenneth Galbraith, "Ch. XI: The Dependence Effect," *The Affluent Society* (Boston: Houghton Mifflin Co., 1958), pp. 152–160.

did not exist, the wants would not exist. Do you agree or disagree with the idea that wants are subject to a dependence effect? On what do you base your reasoning?

5. Suppose that you are a business organization consultant, and three people come to you, each wanting to start a business. The first person wants to start an engineering firm with her sister, the second a music store, and the third a barge line for moving coal on rivers. Each is seeking your advice on whether to organize as a proprietorship, partnership, or corporation. How would you advise each of them? As a practical matter, does it make any difference which form of organization each person chooses?

6. Suppose a law was passed making it illegal for one firm to acquire another firm without approval of the other firm's management. Who would benefit and who would lose from this law?

7. "Trying to maximize its revenues from sales in order to pay higher salaries to its workers, or trying to maximize its share of the market does not mean that a firm is giving up the objective of maximum profit. Instead, it means that the firm is taking steps now to ensure that it will be able to maximize profit in the future." Do you agree or disagree with this statement? Explain your reasoning.

8. In a proprietorship the owner is often the manager, but in a corporation the owners are often different from the managers. What advantages and disadvantages might there be in having a separation of ownership and management?

Critical Thinking Case 10

▪ Profit Maximization

Critical Thinking Skills	Constructing opposing arguments
	Evaluating tradeoffs
Economic Concept	Profit maximization

In a market system, profit maximization tends to be the force guiding most business decisions and activities. There has always been, however, disagreement about many issues surrounding the profit-maximizing goal. For years people have debated how profit maximization is actually accomplished by businesses, who benefits and who loses from this goal, whether the benefits resulting from profit maximization are worth the costs, and whether businesses should be required to modify their profit-maximizing objectives in order to accommodate some social goals or to reduce some social consequences that arise from this goal.

Here are two brief quotes on the proper role of profit-maximizing behavior that deal with some of the issues listed in the preceding paragraph.

... [P]rofit maximization requires that the business manager think only of the best interest of the shareholders, whereas any responsible manager knows that he must actually consider the interest of all parties who have a stake in the business, of which the shareholders are only one.[a]

... [I]t is precisely the tendency to allow and even to impel the corporations to use their resources for specific ends other than those of a long-run maximization of the return on the capital placed under their control which tends to confer upon them undesirable and socially dangerous powers and ... the fashionable doctrine that their policy should be guided by "social considerations" is likely to produce most undesirable results.[b]

Questions

1. Construct an argument supporting the position that a responsible manager must consider all parties who have an interest in a business—consumers, workers, stockholders, and the general public—when making decisions affecting profit. Construct an argument supporting the position that it would not be desirable to have a manager guided by "social considerations" when making decisions that affect profit.

2. In your opinion, what does profit maximization mean? Are there winners and losers from this goal, or only winners?

3. Must profit-maximizing behavior and social considerations be mutually exclusive? That is, must the attainment of one goal necessarily come at the expense of the other? Why do you hold this position?

[a]R.N. Anthony, "The Trouble with Profit Maximization," *Harvard Business Review,* (November–December 1960), p. 132.

[b] F.A. Hayek, "The Corporation in a Democratic Society: In Whose Interest Ought It and Will It Be Run?" *Management and Corporations 1985,* edited by M. Anshen and G.L. Bach (New York: McGraw-Hill Book Company, Inc., 1960), p. 100.

Suggested Readings

James S. Coleman, *Power and the Structure of Society* **(New York: W. W. Norton & Co., Inc., 1974).**
A critical look at the relationship in society between individuals and corporate actors and how that relationship has changed over time.

Walter R. Fuchs, *How We Live* **(Cambridge, Mass.: Harvard University Press, 1983).**
Explores changes in family life, work, health, and education since World War II from primarily an economic perspective.

John Kenneth Galbraith, "The Uses and Excuses for Affluence," *The New York Times Magazine,* **May 31, 1981, pp. 38–44, 50–52.**
Discusses the enjoyment of wealth and spending and the excuses used to promote and defend the position of the wealthy.

A. R. Gini and T. J. Sullivan, *It Comes with the Territory: An Inquiry Concerning Work and the Person* **(New York: Random House, 1989).**
Presents the thesis that work is a formative process through which people create themselves.

Jonathan P. Hicks, "The Takeover of American Industry," *The New York Times,* **May 28, 1989, section 3, pp. 1, 8.**
Discusses foreign acquisitions of U.S. firms, and some pros and cons about those acquisitions.

George Katona, "Ch. 4: Psychological Economics," *The Mass Consumption Society* **(New York: McGraw-Hill, Inc., 1964), pp. 27–38.**
Introduces the importance of considering psychological factors such as motives and attitudes when studying the economic behavior of households and businesses.

Noble F. McKay, "Mergers' Unwanted Consequences," *Business Forum,* **Winter 1990, pp. 10–12.**
An article on employee reactions to mergers and their effects on a company.

Wesley C. Mitchell, "The Backward Art of Spending Money," *American Economic Review,* **June 1912, pp. 269–281. Reprinted in Wesley C. Mitchell,** *The Backward Art of Spending Money and Other Essays* **(New York: Augustus M. Kelley, Inc., 1950), pp. 3–19.**
A classic and entertaining article on the problems of consumer decision making.

Martin Sikora, "The M&A Bonanza of the '80s . . . And Its Legacy," *Mergers and Acquisitions,* **March/April 1990, pp. 90–94.**
A survey of important features of the merger wave of the 1980s.

The following are the references for researching households and businesses that were described in the text of the chapter.

Moody's Investors Services, *Moody's Industrial Manual* **(New York: Moody's Investors Services, Inc., published annually).**

Predicasts, *Predicasts F&S Index, United States Annual Edition* **(Cleveland: Predicasts, Inc., published annually).**

Standard and Poor's Corporation, *Standard Corporation Descriptions* **(New York: Standard and Poor's Corporation, published semimonthly).**

U.S. Bureau of the Census, *Statistical Abstract of the United States* **(Washington, D.C.: U.S. Government Printing Office, published annually).**

Chapter Eleven

Benefits, Costs, and Maximization

This oil-soaked duck symbolizes the conflict that sometimes exists between maximizing individual interests and minimizing society's interests.

Source: ©1988 Scott Henry/ Marin Independent Journal.

Chapter Objectives

1. To explain the basic process of balancing costs and benefits in economic decision making.

2. To introduce marginal analysis, and to define marginal benefit and marginal cost and explain their relationship to total benefit and total cost.

3. To explain the manner in which individuals measure the costs and benefits of actions they take, and to introduce the Law of Diminishing Marginal Utility.

4. To explain the measurement of business costs, revenues, and profit; and to differentiate between normal and economic profit.

5. To identify the rules for maximizing satisfaction by individuals and maximizing profit by businesses.

6. To introduce the concepts of externalities and social costs and benefits.

7. To examine how individual costs and benefits form the basis of collective, or public, choices.

Chapter Ten indicated that decision makers in households and businesses try to maximize their economic well-being or profit by balancing the benefits and costs of different courses of action in order to choose the one that contributes most to the attainment of their particular goals. In this chapter, the mechanics involved in balancing costs against benefits in order to decide which strategy to follow will be explained, and general rules for maximizing, which can be applied to both businesses and individuals, will be introduced. The mechanics will be illustrated through two examples: the first concerns a decision by an individual on how best to use an evening's time; the second concerns a business trying to maximize its profit. After the weighing of costs and benefits by individuals and businesses has been explored, the chapter will deal with costs and benefits as seen by society as a whole. Finally, the balancing of costs and benefits in making collective, or public, choices will be explained. In going through the discussion of costs, benefits, and maximizing behavior, you will be introduced to marginal analysis, which is the basis of many microeconomic concepts. Marginal analysis will reappear in most of the following chapters.

Cost-benefit analysis
Weighing the costs and benefits of an action in order to maximize the net benefit from the action.

The formal study of the process of balancing costs and benefits, referred to as **cost-benefit analysis,** is helpful in evaluating business investment and production decisions, government decisions concerning spending programs, individual decisions concerning major purchases, and other such decisions. However, the principles of cost-benefit analysis are not limited in their usefulness to evaluating major economic and financial decisions by governments, businesses, and households. The principles can be applied to many more areas of human experience than those dealt with in modern economics. The story of Adam and Eve, and the choice to eat the apple in the Garden of Eden, is a lesson in balancing costs and benefits, as is an expression such as:

'Tis better to have loved and lost
Than never to have loved at all.[1]

All rational decision making, be it economic or noneconomic, is based on the balancing of costs and benefits in order to, in the view of the decision maker, maximize something. This is true for the worker trying to maximize well-being by balancing the costs and benefits of forgoing more income for the sake of leisure, for the child weighing the costs and benefits of lying to a parent, or for the painter deciding whether to move the ladder or stretch to reach the last few inches on a wall.

Balancing Benefits and Costs: The Individual

Defining Benefits and Costs

The goal of decision making is to maximize, or to get the most from a decision. In so doing, an individual, usually subconsciously, uses a type of mathematical process, or applies certain mathematical rules, to weigh the costs and benefits of different courses of action. This process and these rules will be thoroughly discussed shortly. However, before these mechanics are introduced, it is important to understand how an individual measures benefits and costs.

The benefit to a person from any good or service purchased is the amount of satisfaction received from the purchase. This satisfaction was discussed in Chapter Ten and is referred to as utility. In order to understand the behavior of utility, assume that each person has a small register in his or her mind called a "Util-O-Meter." This meter measures total utility by clicking off points according to the amount of satisfaction received from the purchase of each additional unit of a good or service. Satisfaction can be received from actions as well as purchases. Taking a course in photography or running a marathon, for example, may add points to a meter.

Any measurement of satisfaction is highly subjective, as are the numbers registered on a Util-O-Meter for the benefits received from any purchase or

---

[1] Alfred Tennyson, "In Memoriam," *The Poetic and Dramatic Works of Alfred Lord Tennyson,* W. J. Rolfe, ed. (Boston: Houghton Mifflin Co., 1898), p. 170.

action. Because of this, it is extremely difficult for two people to compare the degree of satisfaction received by each from taking the same action, such as eating a pizza. However, an individual can compare the satisfaction from different actions or purchases from which he or she can choose. You, for example, know whether you enjoy a popular recording more, much more, or not as much as Mahler's Seventh Symphony.

An individual usually measures the cost of an item by the dollars paid for it. As discussed in Chapter One, however, a cost can also be measured in terms of the alternative or opportunity forgone to acquire an item or take an action.[2] That is, the cost of something can be measured in terms of its **opportunity cost.** For example, the cost of a $40 textbook could be measured by the dollars required to obtain it, or by the shirt, date, football tickets, or whatever else would have otherwise been purchased.

An opportunity cost is associated with everything one does. The cost of attending a class could be lunch with a friend, finishing a game of racquetball, watching a television program, or working an extra hour at a job. What is your opportunity cost of reading this chapter now?

We can relate opportunity costs to utility, or satisfaction, by measuring the points that would have been added to a Util-O-Meter had another course of action been chosen. For example, if by registering for next term you gave up one hour of jogging, which would have added 125 points to your total utility, then the opportunity cost of registering was 125 points.

Opportunity cost

The cost of acquiring a good or service or taking an action measured in terms of the value of the opportunity or alternative forgone.

Measuring Benefits and Costs

The following example illustrates how individuals measure the benefits and costs of actions and how they apply maximizing rules to their decision making. This example deals with a student who is planning to spend an evening at a concert on campus. The concert features a number of performers and is lengthy and informal: people can come and go as they please. The concert is also free in the sense that there are no dollar costs, but the individual has an opportunity cost in terms of time.

In taking any action, a person attempts to maximize satisfaction. In this case, the individual going to the concert is attempting to maximize the satisfaction from the time spent during the course of the evening. This means that our concertgoer may spend the entire evening at the concert, or may at some point have something else preferable to do and leave the concert. In this example, we will determine whether satisfaction is maximized by attending the entire concert, which lasts for five hours, or by leaving after the first, second, third, or fourth hour.

Measuring Benefits   By attending the concert, our student receives satisfaction, or utility: the concert adds points to the individual's Util-O-Meter.

[2]See pages 6–7.

Table 11.1   Utility Points from Attending a Concert

Total benefit, or utility, is the total satisfaction from consuming a particular amount of a good, service, or activity; marginal benefit, or utility, is the change in total satisfaction from consuming an additional unit of a good, service, or activity.

Number of Hours Attended	Total Benefit (Utility)	Marginal Benefit (Utility)
0	0 points	
1	400 points	400 points
2	700 points	300 points
3	900 points	200 points
4	1,000 points	100 points
5	1,000 points	0 points

Marginal benefit (marginal utility)

The change in total satisfaction from consuming each additional unit of a good, service, or activity.

Total benefit (total utility)

The total amount of satisfaction received from consuming a specified number of units of a good, service, or activity.

Each additional hour spent at the concert adds a certain number of points to total satisfaction. The change in total satisfaction from attending each additional hour is called **marginal benefit** or **marginal utility.** The total satisfaction received by attending the concert for a specified number of hours is called **total benefit** or **total utility.**

Let us assume that our student's Util-O-Meter registers zero before the concert. Let us further assume that by the end of the first hour 400 points of utility have clicked onto the meter. This means that the total benefit, or utility, from spending one hour at the concert is 400 points. At the end of the second hour 700 points are registered on the meter; or we can say that the total benefit from spending two hours at the concert is 700 points. At the end of three hours 900 points are registered; at the end of four hours the total utility received is 1,000 points; and after five hours the meter still registers 1,000 points. This information is given in Table 11.1 in the column labeled "Total Benefit (Utility)."

Marginal benefit, or utility, is the *change* in total benefit that results from attending the concert for each *additional* hour. Since the Util-O-Meter registered zero before the concert and 400 points at the end of one hour, the marginal benefit from the first hour is 400 points. During the first hour 400 points are added to the student's total utility. At the end of the second hour 700 points of total benefit are registered, which means that 300 additional points of utility are added during the second hour (700 points in total utility at the end of the second hour minus 400 points at the end of the first). Thus, the marginal utility or benefit of the second hour is 300 points. During the third hour 200 points of marginal benefit are added (total benefit increases from 700 to 900 points). The marginal benefit of the fourth hour is 100 points;

and the marginal benefit of the fifth hour is zero points, since total benefit does not increase from the end of the fourth to the end of the fifth hour. These measures are given in Table 11.1 in the column labeled "Marginal Benefit (Utility)."

You may have noticed that the marginal benefit points given in Table 11.1 are listed midway between the hours. This is done because marginal values refer to changes in total values, and total values can either increase or decrease. That is, we can refer to the increase in total benefit by going from one to two, or two to three hours at the concert, or we can refer to the decrease in total benefit by going from three to two hours, or two to one. Because the numbers in the table can be read up or down, we list marginal values at midpoints between the hours.

Observe that the marginal benefit points decrease with each additional hour. In this example, the individual really enjoys the first hour of the concert, finds the second hour slightly less satisfactory, and finds each successive hour less enjoyable than the previous one. By the fifth hour no additional satisfaction is received. This result is consistent with a principle in economics called the **Law of Diminishing Marginal Utility,** which states that, as additional units of an item are consumed, *beyond some point* each successive unit of the item consumed will add less to total utility than was added by the unit consumed just before it. In other words, as an individual consumes a good or service, there is some point beyond which he or she enjoys each additional unit of the item less.[3] Food is an excellent example of this principle. If you are eating pizza, tacos, donuts, or anything else, there is some point beyond which each additional piece of pizza or taco or donut gives you less satisfaction than the one before it. Do you generally enjoy the fourth donut as much as the first? Would you enjoy a second bike or stereo as much as the first, and do you find the third hour of a three-hour lecture class as satisfying and stimulating as the second or first hour?

Measuring Costs   In our example of the concertgoer, the student faces costs as well as receiving benefits from attending the concert. These costs are opportunity costs based on forgone activities, such as studying or watching television, that would have also given the student satisfaction, or would have added points to the student's Util-O-Meter. Thus, the costs of the concert can be measured by the number of forgone utility points from alternative opportunities.

Table 11.2 gives the total and marginal costs, measured in forgone satisfaction points, of spending the evening at the concert. **Total cost** is the

Law of Diminishing Marginal Utility

As additional units of an item are consumed, beyond some point each successive unit of the item consumed will add less to total utility than was added by the unit consumed just before it.

Total cost

The cost of a specified number of units of a good, service, or activity produced or consumed.

---

[3] We are not suggesting that the second unit consumed of an item *will* add less satisfaction than the first, or that the third unit *will* add less satisfaction than the second. Rather, as successive units of an item are consumed, *eventually* a point will be reached where each additional unit consumed will add less to total satisfaction than was added by the previous unit. This point may arrive early on, as in the case of our concertgoer, or after the consumption of a large amount of an item.

Table 11.2   Total and Marginal Costs of Attending a Concert

Both the total and marginal costs of an activity, such as attending a concert, can be measured in terms of the utility points that are given up by forgoing an alternative activity.

Hours Attended	Total Cost	Marginal Cost
0	0 points	
		25 points
1	25 points	
		50 points
2	75 points	
		100 points
3	175 points	
		200 points
4	375 points	
		625 points
5	1,000 points	

Marginal cost

The change in total cost from each additional unit of a good, service, or activity produced or consumed.

cost of spending a specified number of hours at the concert. **Marginal cost** is the change in total cost from each additional hour spent at the concert. As before, the marginal measurements are given at the midpoints between the hours.

Our student has many alternatives to attending the concert. Assume that one alternative to attending the concert for one hour is loafing around, an action that would give our concertgoer 25 Util-O-Meter points, thereby making the marginal opportunity cost of the first hour at the concert 25 points. These 25 marginal cost points equal the total cost for attending the concert for one hour, since we are assuming that no previous total cost points have been accumulated.

To attend the second hour of the concert, assume that the student in our example gives up watching a television program that would have yielded 50 additional points of satisfaction, thereby making the marginal cost of the second hour 50 points. When these 50 marginal points are added to the total cost of 25 points for the first hour, the total cost of two hours at the concert becomes 75 points. The marginal cost of the third hour is 100 points of satisfaction which our student would have received from socializing with a friend. When these 100 marginal points are added to the 75 total cost points for two hours spent at the concert, the total cost of three hours at the concert becomes 175 points.

The alternative to the fourth hour at the concert is studying for an economics quiz that must be taken the following morning. The marginal cost of this hour is the 200 points that would be added to total satisfaction by understanding the material for the quiz. These points, when added to the 175 points for three hours, make the total cost of four hours at the concert 375 points. The marginal cost of the fifth hour is 625 points, which is the satisfaction that would be received by completing the typing of a major term

Table 11.3

Benefits and Costs of Attending a Concert

Net benefit is maximized at the point where total benefit exceeds total cost by the greatest amount. Net benefit increases as long as marginal benefit is greater than marginal cost, and decreases when marginal cost is greater than marginal benefit.

Number of Hours Attended	Net Benefit	Total Benefit	Total Cost	Marginal Benefit	Marginal Cost
0	0	0	0		
				400	25
1	375	400	25		
				300	50
2	625	700	75		
				200	100
3	725	900	175		
				100	200
4	625	1,000	375		
				0	625
5	0	1,000	1,000		

paper that is also due the following morning. These 625 marginal cost points bring the total cost of attending the entire five-hour concert to 1,000 points.

Observe that the marginal cost of attending each additional hour of the concert rises with the number of hours attended. The individual first gives up those alternatives that cost the least, and as the evening goes on, the alternatives become more and more expensive.

Maximizing Satisfaction

Thus far we have measured the benefits and costs for a student spending an evening at a concert. Remembering that the goal of any action is to maximize satisfaction, we will now evaluate these benefits and costs to determine the number of hours that the student should spend at the concert to accomplish this objective.

Table 11.3 lists the concertgoer's total and marginal benefits, and total and marginal costs that were given in Tables 11.1 and 11.2. Table 11.3 also includes a measure of the net benefit received from spending a specified number of hours at the concert. Net benefit is what the concertgoer is trying to maximize. Table 11.3 indicates that the net benefit of one hour at the concert is 375 points, the net benefit of two hours is 625 points, and so on.

The net benefit points given in Table 11.3 show that satisfaction from the concert is maximized by attending for three hours. At the end of three hours, 725 net benefit points, the maximum that can be attained, have been realized. Attending the concert for just two hours or staying for four hours will yield less satisfaction than 725 points. To maximize the satisfaction that can be received that evening, the student should attend the concert for three hours.

How is net benefit calculated? The **net benefit** for a specified number of hours at the concert is simply the difference between the total benefit and

Net benefit
That which results when total cost is subtracted from total benefit.

total cost of those hours. For example, as shown in Table 11.3, the total benefit from attending the concert for one hour is 400 points and the total cost is 25 points, leaving a net benefit of 375 points; the total benefit from attending for two hours is 700 points and the total cost is 75 points, leaving a net benefit of 625 points; and so on.

Given total cost and total benefit, one can establish a **net benefit maximizing rule.** This rule states that *maximum net benefit occurs where total benefit exceeds total cost by the greatest amount.* For our student, this occurs at the end of three hours.

A second net benefit maximizing rule deals with marginal cost and marginal benefit. It states that *maximum net benefit occurs where marginal cost equals marginal benefit.* Why is this so? The answer is found by comparing the marginal benefit and marginal cost figures in Table 11.3.

For the first hour of the concert, the marginal benefit is 400 points and the marginal cost is 25 points. If you think of marginal benefit as adding points to a Util-O-Meter, and marginal cost as subtracting points, then 400 points are added and 25 are subtracted during the first hour, leaving a gain in satisfaction, or net benefit, of 375 points. During the second hour, 300 more points, the marginal benefit, are added and 50 points, the marginal cost, are subtracted. The result is a gain of 250 points to be added to the gain from the first hour. Thus, the net benefit after two hours is 625 points (375 points from the first hour plus 250 points from the second hour). During the third hour, 200 marginal benefit points are added and only 100 marginal cost points are subtracted, again adding to the net registered on the Util-O-Meter.

Notice that for each of these three hours, marginal benefit is greater than marginal cost, causing net benefit to increase. But also notice that marginal benefit is shrinking and marginal cost is growing. At some point they will be equal.

During the fourth hour, the marginal benefit is only 100 points, but the marginal cost is 200 points, causing more to be subtracted from total satisfaction than is added. Because of this, net benefit falls. If our individual stayed at the concert for a fourth hour, that fourth hour would cost more satisfaction than it would give. During the fifth hour no points are added, but 625 are subtracted, causing net benefit again to fall.

It can be seen in this example that our individual is increasing satisfaction, or net benefit, by attending the concert as long as more additional utility points are received from the concert than would be received from the alternatives. Once the alternatives become more attractive, it is to the individual's advantage to switch from the concert to something else. It can also be seen that, as was the case using the total cost–total benefit approach, net benefit is maximized by attending the concert for three hours. During the third hour more marginal benefit points are added than marginal cost points are subtracted, but during the fourth hour more marginal cost points are subtracted than marginal benefit points are added. The concertgoer should leave at the end of three hours because at this point marginal cost equals

Net benefit maximizing rules

Net benefit is maximized where total benefit exceeds total cost by the greatest amount, or where marginal benefit equals marginal cost.

marginal benefit. This equality will be easy to see when this relationship is graphed in the next section.

From this we can conclude that as long as marginal benefit is greater than marginal cost, no matter how small the difference, an action should continue because net benefit is increasing. Once marginal cost becomes greater than marginal benefit, net benefit declines because more is subtracted than is added to satisfaction. Maximization occurs at the point where marginal cost equals marginal benefit.

In summary, this example indicates that there are two rules for maximizing net benefit, both yielding the same result. Maximization occurs where total benefit exceeds total cost by the greatest amount or where marginal benefit equals marginal cost.

Would you act as the student in our example did? Most likely you would. Have you ever returned early from a date, concert, or movie because an important test or assignment was due the next morning? You have applied the maximizing rules in countless situations where you, perhaps subconsciously, weighed the marginal cost and marginal benefit of an action. For example, the decision of whether to eat an extra piece of chocolate cake for dessert involves balancing the additional cost of the extra calories against the additional enjoyment from the cake. Other decisions, such as which route to take to work on a snowy day, or whether to buy the study guide accompanying a textbook, or whether to purchase an expensive or cheap pair of jeans, all involve an application of the maximizing rules. What are some of the marginal costs and marginal benefits that might be considered in deciding whether to break the speed limit to arrive at a class on time? Application 11.1, "Anything Worth Doing Is Not Necessarily Worth Doing Well," gives some additional examples of the application of cost-benefit principles.

Graphing Costs, Benefits, and Net Benefit

Our student's total cost and total benefit from attending the concert are shown in the upper graph of Figure 11.1, marginal cost and marginal benefit are depicted in the middle graph, and net benefit is shown in the lower graph. These figures are plotted from the information in Table 11.3. As long as total cost is less than total benefit, there is a positive net benefit. As can be seen in the upper graph of Figure 11.1, net benefit is equal to the vertical distance between total benefit and total cost for any given number of hours spent attending the concert. Thus, maximum net benefit occurs where the vertical distance between total benefit and total cost is the greatest in the upper graph, or at the highest point on the net benefit curve in the lower graph. This occurs at three hours.

Notice also that as long as marginal benefit is greater than marginal cost in the middle graph, net benefit increases in the lower graph, and when marginal cost is greater than marginal benefit, net benefit falls. Net benefit reaches its maximum where marginal cost equals marginal benefit. This

Figure 11.1

Total Cost and Benefit, Marginal Cost and Benefit, and Net Benefit

Graphically, net benefit is equal to the vertical distance between total benefit and total cost, and is at its maximum where total benefit exceeds total cost by the greatest amount. Net benefit is increasing when marginal benefit is greater than marginal cost, at its maximum when marginal benefit equals marginal cost, and decreasing when marginal benefit is less than marginal cost.

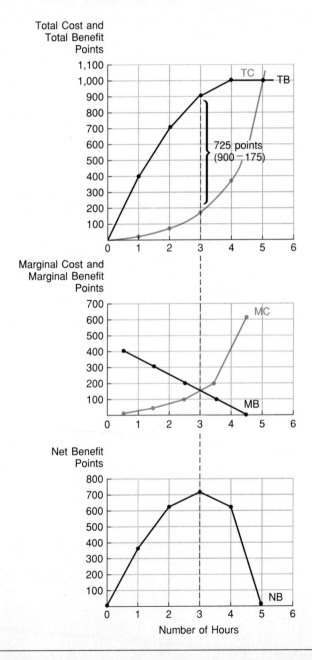

Application 11.1

Anything Worth Doing Is Not Necessarily Worth Doing Well

From early childhood most of us have been taught that "anything worth doing is worth doing well." If we were asked today if we still agree with the statement, many of us would say that we do. It is only natural for a person to prefer a job that has been done well to one that has been done not so well; indeed, such a preference is fully consistent with the basic assumption in economics that more (quality) is preferred to less (quality). It is also easy to see why a person may not like to re-do something that has already been done, particularly if the combined time involved is greater than the time that would have been required to do it right in the first place.

Obviously, people do not behave the way they profess they should. There is probably not a minister around who has not written what he considered at the time to be a poor sermon, and one of the authors recently built a bookcase that was more-or-less thrown together. Wives and husbands have cooked dinners they knew in their hearts were seriously deficient in one respect or another. Students regularly choose to work for a grade of a C (or a GPA far less than 4.0) instead of going all out for an A. This is true even though the A is the preferred grade. How many, do you suppose, of the students who are reading this have written a paper that by their own standards fell far short of a "well done" paper? In fact, can you say at this point that you have read the last few pages "well"?

Admittedly, people do some things well, but the point we wish to emphasize is that they frequently do things less than well, not because they do not want to do better, but because of the *additional* (or *marginal*) cost involved in improving the quality of whatever they are doing. Given the student's ability—which, as a matter of fact, is limited at any point in time—writing a "good" A paper generally requires more effort and time than writing a C paper. If the student spends additional time on the paper, he or she has less time for doing other things—less time to study the subject matter in other courses, in which case he or she may do less

well or even fail. He or she cannot use the time for physical exercise, cannot spend the time in bed, or out on dates. To reiterate, there is usually an additional cost that must be borne for a higher quality paper, and it is because of this cost that he or she may rationally choose to turn in a paper that may "just get by." (Even so, the student may still hope for an A. Can you explain why?) . . .

Quite often one person will admonish another to do a good job. For example, professors may be distressed at the quality of the papers they receive, and may honestly feel that if their students are going to write a paper, they should write a good one. The professors may be even more upset if they find out their students spent the last few days doing very little or having a "good time."

The values the professors and students place on different activities obviously differ. Professors may view the paper as being of greater value than do the students; they may view the "other activities" as being of less value. Consequently, they believe it is in the students' best interests to do better papers. However, since students view the value of the other activities as being higher, they, in effect, view the cost of doing the better paper as being higher. Of course, it is clearly rational for professors to want the students to turn in better papers, but if they had to bear the costs, they might change their minds.

The same line of argument can be used to explain why the preacher's sermon is of low quality even though he or she may have the ability to do better. By writing a better sermon, he or she may have to bear the cost of not seeing the parishioners at the hospital or of giving up something else that is considered valuable. In order to cook a better meal, the homemaker may have to forgo writing letters, discussions with neighbors, or hauling Little Leaguers to practice.

Source: Richard B. McKenzie and Gordon Tullock, *The New World of Economics* (Homewood, Ill.: Richard D. Irwin, Inc., 1978), pp. 27–29. Reprinted by permission of Richard D. Irwin, Inc.

again occurs at three hours. You might also notice that marginal cost and marginal benefit are plotted at the midpoints, just as they were given at the midpoints in the tables.

Balancing Benefits and Costs: The Business

Defining Benefits and Costs

It was shown in Chapter Ten that businesses are similar to individuals in two important ways. First, like individuals, they try to maximize their economic well-being. And second, as with individuals, maximizing by a business requires balancing the costs and benefits of different courses of action to find the one most in its interest.

But a business differs from an individual in that its economic well-being is generally measured in terms of profit rather than utility, or satisfaction. Thus, a business is maximizing its economic well-being when it balances the costs and benefits of operating at different levels of output and chooses the one that maximizes its profit. Since profit is equal to revenue minus costs, the benefits and costs to be balanced are measured in terms of the revenue earned from selling the firm's good or service, and the costs of producing the good or service.

In economics, the costs of producing a firm's good or service fall into two categories: explicit and implicit costs. **Explicit costs** are payments made by a business to acquire its work force, raw materials, machinery, equipment, and so forth. These payments are actual dollar outlays that the firm must provide to outsiders from whom it buys factors of production. Explicit costs are sometimes called accounting costs.

The second cost category is **implicit costs,** which are *not* direct payments to outsiders for factors, but are opportunity costs to the owner(s) of a business that must be recovered in order for production to continue. Implicit costs could include forgone interest from money the owners have invested in the business rather than in securities, rental payments that could have been earned if a building that houses the business were leased to another company, the income the owners could have received by using their talents and efforts in an alternative enterprise, or any other returns that have been given up by the owners.

The proceeds that owners expect to receive to recover their implicit costs are called normal profits. As a result, **normal profit** is the amount of profit owners must receive to keep a business in operation; if this amount is not recovered, the owners will use their money, buildings, labor, and other factors that they have provided for the business in an alternative opportunity.

Since a business will shut down if it does not earn a normal profit, normal profit is considered to be an economic cost of production. Thus,

Explicit costs

Payments that a business makes to outsiders to acquire factors of production such as labor, raw materials, and machinery.

Implicit costs

The opportunity costs to owners of a business of using their factors of production in their own business rather than in an alternative opportunity; must be recovered to keep a business in operation; normal profit.

Normal profit

Profit necessary to recover implicit costs and keep a business in operation; considered to be an economic cost of production.

Economic cost of production

Includes all explicit and implicit costs from producing a good or service.

Excess profit (economic profit)

Profit received beyond normal profit; not considered a cost of production.

the **economic cost of production** is equal to a firm's explicit costs (wages, rent, interest, and other such payments) plus its implicit costs, or normal profit to its owners.

Any profit beyond normal profit is called **excess profit,** or **economic profit.** For example, if an owner were to require $30,000 per year to remain in business, and if actual profit were $42,000, $30,000 of that actual profit would be normal profit and the remaining $12,000 would be economic, or excess, profit. Economic, or excess, profit is not a cost, since the owner would remain with the business if it were not earned. Review question number five at the end of this chapter provides a good opportunity for you to test your understanding of normal and economic profits.

Measuring Revenues and Costs

The fundamental mechanics of profit maximization by a firm are exactly the same as those set out in the example of the student maximizing satisfaction at a concert. The only difference is *what* is being balanced and *what* is being maximized: in this case, revenues and costs from operations are being balanced to maximize profit. Thus, the example we are about to work through introduces no new principles. Rather, it shows how the principles already learned for an individual can be applied to a business.

Measuring Revenues   Suppose a jeweler designs and produces a solid gold, diamond-inlaid pocket watch case. Although this is an exclusive, high-priced item that would sell to very few people, the jeweler knows that the way to sell more is to lower the price. That is, the watch case is subject to the Law of Demand.

The jeweler's problem is to determine how many pocket watch cases to produce and sell in order to maximize profit. The solution to the problem is found by balancing the costs from producing different quantities of the watch case against the benefits, which in this example are the revenues, from different levels of sales. The revenues that the jeweler could earn from selling different quantities of the watch case at different prices are shown in Table 11.4.

The first two columns of the table show different watch case prices and the quantity of watch cases demanded at each of those prices. At a price of $45,000, no watch cases would be demanded. But if the price were lowered to $40,000, one watch case would be demanded; and if the price were $35,000, two watch cases would be demanded; and so on. Thus, the first two columns of Table 11.4 show how the Law of Demand operates with the jeweler's potential buyers.

Total revenue

Revenue received from selling a certain quantity of an item; calculated by multiplying the price of an item by the quantity demanded at that price.

The total revenue column in Table 11.4 shows how much revenue would be earned by the jeweler at each level of demand. **Total revenue** is calculated by multiplying the price of an item by the quantity demanded at that price. For example, two pocket watch cases demanded at $35,000 each would generate $70,000 in total revenue.

Table 11.4   Revenues from Selling Pocket Watch Cases

The total revenue from selling an item, such as a pocket watch case, is calculated by multiplying the price of the item times the quantity demanded at that price. Marginal revenue is the change in total revenue from selling one more unit of an item.

Price	Quantity Demanded	Total Revenue	Marginal Revenue
$45,000	0	$ 0	
			$40,000
40,000	1	40,000	
			30,000
35,000	2	70,000	
			20,000
30,000	3	90,000	
			10,000
25,000	4	100,000	

Marginal revenue

The change in total revenue when one more (or additional) unit of an item is demanded.

The change in total revenue when one more (or additional) unit of output is demanded is termed **marginal revenue.** In Table 11.4 the marginal revenue column gives the change in total revenue with each additional pocket watch case demanded. For example, when the number of watch cases demanded goes from zero to one, total revenue changes from $0 to $40,000, making the marginal revenue from the first case equal to $40,000; when the number of watch cases demanded goes from one to two, total revenue increases from $40,000 to $70,000, making the marginal revenue from the second case equal to $30,000; and so on. As was done with marginal benefits and marginal costs in the previous example, the marginal revenues in Table 11.4 are listed at the midpoints between the quantities demanded.[4] (If you are interested in understanding why marginal revenue is less than price, see footnote four.)

[4] You might have noticed that when the quantity demanded is two, three, or four watch cases, marginal revenue is less than the price of the case. For example, when two cases are demanded at a price of $35,000, only $30,000 is added to total revenue by selling the second case. Why is this so?

If the jeweler only sells one watch case, he or she will earn $40,000 in revenue. However, in order to sell two cases, the jeweler must lower the price to $35,000. This means that the jeweler is going to charge $35,000 to the first buyer as well as the second buyer. Rather than receiving $40,000 from the first buyer, the jeweler will have to give the first buyer a $5,000 discount. Because of this, what is added to total revenue from the sale of the second watch case is not its price. Rather, what is added to total revenue, or the marginal revenue, from the second unit sold is the price of the second unit minus the discount given to the first buyer, or $35,000 − $5,000 = $30,000. Likewise, if the jeweler wishes to sell three cases, the price must be lowered to $30,000. But if the third buyer pays only $30,000, $30,000 must also be charged to each of the other two buyers who would have otherwise paid $35,000. Thus, the marginal revenue from the third unit sold is not equal to the $30,000 price. Instead, the marginal revenue from the third unit sold equals the $30,000 price minus the two $5,000 discounts that were given to the other two buyers, or $30,000 − $10,000 = $20,000. To test your understanding of this principle, see if you can explain why the marginal revenue from the fourth unit is $10,000, while its price is $25,000.

Table 11.5

Costs of Producing Pocket Watch Cases

Total cost is the cost of producing a specified number of units of output, and marginal cost measures the change in total cost from producing each additional unit of output.

Quantity	Total Cost	Marginal Cost
0	$ 0	
		$25,000
1	25,000	
		25,000
2	50,000	
		25,000
3	75,000	
		25,000
4	100,000	

Total cost

Cost of producing a specified number of units of a good, service, or activity.

Marginal cost

The change in total cost when one more (or additional) unit of a good, service, or activity is produced.

Measuring Costs   The jeweler's costs are shown in Table 11.5. To keep matters simple, let us say that these costs, which include implicit costs, or normal profit, come to $25,000 for each pocket watch case.

Table 11.5 shows the jeweler's **total cost,** which is the cost per case times the quantity of cases produced, at various levels of output. At a cost of $25,000 per case, the jeweler's total cost would be zero if no cases were produced ($25,000 × 0), $25,000 if one case were produced ($25,000 × 1), $50,000 if two were produced, and so on. **Marginal cost** measures how much total cost changes as each additional unit of an item is produced. The marginal cost column of Table 11.5 shows the additional cost of producing one more watch case. For example, when the quantity goes from zero to one, total cost goes from $0 to $25,000, making the marginal cost of the first case equal to $25,000. When the quantity changes from one to two, total cost goes from $25,000 to $50,000, and the marginal cost of the second case is again $25,000. As was done with the previous marginal values, the marginal costs in Table 11.5 are listed between the quantities produced.

Maximizing Profit

The number of pocket watch cases that the jeweler should produce and sell to maximize profit can be shown by combining the information from Tables 11.4 and 11.5. This is done in Table 11.6. But before analyzing the numbers in the table, let us review what we should expect to find.

Remember that both the individual at the concert and the jeweler are trying to maximize their net benefit by weighing costs and benefits. The rules for doing so are the same for the concertgoer and the jeweler; the only difference between the two is the actual benefits and costs to be measured and what is being maximized. For the jeweler, benefits are measured in terms of dollar revenues, costs are the costs of production, and net benefit

Table 11.6

Revenues, Costs, and Profit on Pocket Watch Cases

The maximum profit that can be obtained from producing and selling pocket watch cases occurs at two units. At this output level, total revenue exceeds total cost by the greatest amount and marginal revenue equals marginal cost.

Price	Quantity	Profit	Total Revenue	Total Cost	Marginal Revenue	Marginal Cost
$45,000	0	$ 0	$ 0	$ 0		
					$40,000	$25,000
40,000	1	15,000	40,000	25,000		
					30,000	25,000
35,000	2	20,000	70,000	50,000		
					20,000	25,000
30,000	3	15,000	90,000	75,000		
					10,000	25,000
25,000	4	0	100,000	100,000		

Profit or loss

The result when a business subtracts its total cost from its total revenue.

is the profit from selling pocket watch cases. Applying the maximizing rules, we should expect the jeweler's profit to be at a maximum where his or her total revenue exceeds total cost by the greatest amount. We should also expect marginal revenue to equal marginal cost at the output level where profit is at a maximum. Table 11.6 lets us determine whether these expectations are borne out for the jeweler.

The profit column in Table 11.6 shows that a maximum profit of $20,000 occurs at two units of output. How does this relate to total revenue and total cost? **Profit** is derived by subtracting total cost from total revenue at each level of output. For example, if the jeweler were to produce and sell three pocket watch cases, total revenue minus total cost would be $90,000 − $75,000, or $15,000. The largest, or maximum, profit for a business occurs where total revenue exceeds total cost by the greatest amount. This is as expected.

What about the relationship between marginal revenue and marginal cost where profit is maximized? Reading down the last two columns in Table 11.6, it can be seen that from zero to one, and from one to two units of output, marginal revenue is greater than marginal cost: each pocket watch case adds more to total revenue than to total cost, causing profit to increase. This can be verified by noticing that the numbers in the profit column increase as output and sales go from zero to two units.

On the other hand, in Table 11.6 marginal cost is greater than marginal revenue as output goes from two to three, and from three to four units. In this case, the third and fourth units are adding more to total cost than to total revenue, causing profit to fall. This too is confirmed by the figures in the profit column.

Since marginal revenue is greater than marginal cost up to two units of output, and since marginal revenue is less than marginal cost beyond two units of output, marginal revenue and marginal cost must be equal at two

Profit maximizing rules

Profit is maximized at the output level where total revenue exceeds total cost by the greatest amount, or where marginal revenue equals marginal cost.

units. Thus, the two **profit maximizing rules** are satisfied. At an output level of two units, total revenue exceeds total cost by the greatest amount, and marginal revenue equals marginal cost.

Graphing Costs, Revenues, and Profit

The relationships between marginal revenue, marginal cost, and profit, and between total revenue, total cost, and profit that were set out in Table 11.6 are illustrated in Figure 11.2. The bottom graph in Figure 11.2 shows that profit, or net benefit, is at its maximum where two watch cases are produced and sold. The middle graph in Figure 11.2 shows that marginal revenue and marginal cost are equal at exactly two units of output. For smaller output levels, marginal revenue is greater than marginal cost, which causes profit in the lower graph to increase. For output levels larger than two units, marginal revenue is less than marginal cost, causing profit to fall. Finally, in the upper graph in Figure 11.2 the vertical distance by which total revenue exceeds total cost is at its maximum at two units of output, which, of course, is the output level where profit is maximized in the lower graph.

In summary, regardless of whether an individual, business, or government unit is being considered, the net benefit to the decision-making unit from an activity will be maximized if it operates where total benefit exceeds total cost by the greatest amount. This is also where marginal benefit and marginal cost are equal. The main difference between the decision-making units is not that they follow different rules. Rather, the difference is in what is maximized and how costs and benefits are measured. Working through "Test Your Understanding: Maximizing Profit" will allow you to master the maximizing rules.

Private vs. Social Benefits and Costs

In the cases just discussed, any concern over whether, how, or to what extent others might be affected by an individual's or business's decisions was absent. People often choose courses of action after considering only factors that affect them directly, even though sometimes what they do will benefit or impose a cost on others. Because of this, the costs and benefits to individuals and businesses of their actions may differ from the costs and benefits to society of those same actions.

The level of activity that maximizes a particular individual's or business's net benefit may be greater or less than the level that would maximize society's net benefit. This can be illustrated by returning to our earlier example, where the student's net benefit from an evening out was maximized by spending three hours at a concert. Instead of a concert, assume that the same numbers apply to our student filling sandbags to hold back water from a flooding river in a nearby town, and that, as with attending the concert, the student's net benefit from sandbagging would be maximized if

Figure 11.2

Total Revenue and Cost, Marginal Revenue and Cost, and Profit

Graphically, profit is maximized at the output level where the total revenue curve exceeds the total cost curve by the greatest amount, or where the marginal revenue curve crosses the marginal cost curve.

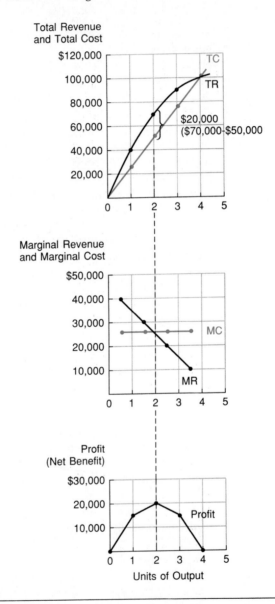

the student quit at the end of three hours. If the effect on society from sandbagging were considered, however, the net benefit of the townspeople would probably be higher if the student stayed and bagged for four or five hours. Or, suppose that the example applied to an evening of drinking and driving by our student. In this case, society's net benefit would be maximized if our student spent less than three hours drinking and driving or even, perhaps, no time at all. In our other example, the jeweler maximized profit by producing and selling two pocket watch cases. However, if some toxic substance were created but not properly disposed of in producing these cases, society might be better off with fewer watch cases and less toxic waste.

The effects that actions have on persons or things that are not primary parties to the actions are called **externalities.** These externalities may be either positive and beneficial to others, or negative and costly to others. For example, getting a vaccination against a contagious disease may benefit not only you, but also those around you who might have otherwise become infected. Keeping your car well maintained benefits you and also all the people who might have been delayed if you broke down on the highway. In both cases your actions have worked to the advantage of others and have created **positive externalities.** On the other hand, a production facility that pollutes the air or water, or individuals who buy alcohol then drive while intoxicated contribute to the detriment of others and create **negative externalities.** Because of pollution, for example, residents of a community might be paying more to clean the environment or on medical care than they would have otherwise. Application 11.2, "Banishing Tobacco," deals with one of the current major controversies involving negative externalities — the costs borne by nonsmokers from those who smoke. In addition to the medical costs cited in this application, can you identify any other negative externalities from smoking?[5]

Maximizing Society's Net Benefit

The positive and negative effects of an action on others must be added to the private benefit-cost calculations of the individual or business to determine how society is affected by the action. The total effect on society of the private benefits and costs plus the externalities of an action are the action's **social benefits** and **social costs.** Thus, we can say:

> private benefits + any positive external effects = social benefits;
> private costs + any negative external effects = social costs; and
> social benefits − social costs = net benefit to society.

The method by which net benefit is calculated for society is exactly the same as that used for businesses and individuals. The only difference is that

Externality

The effect of an action that falls on a person or thing that was not one of the primary parties to the action.

Positive externality

An externality that creates a benefit for others.

Negative externality

An externality that creates a cost for others.

Social benefits and costs

The total effect on society that results from the private benefits, private costs, and externalities of an action.

---

[5]You may also want to review the critical thinking case in Chapter Three, "Illegal Drug Markets," on pages 113 and 114 where externalities from the supply and demand of recreational drugs are considered.

Test Your Understanding

Maximizing Profit[a]

[a]Answers can be found at the end of the book.

Pete Casso has been invited to exhibit two of his works in the annual student art show and sale. Although those who are invited to participate in the show receive a great deal of personal satisfaction, or "psychic income," from having been selected, the show also presents an opportunity for the exhibitors to earn some money. Pete is concerned about making as much money as he can from this sale to help defray tuition costs for next semester. Since he studied economics last year, he realizes the importance of pricing his works of art correctly in order to maximize profit.

Pete has chosen to include a pen-and-ink drawing of a house and a colorful lithograph in the show because both of these items can bring multiple sales. The house drawing will serve as a sample of Pete's custom work in this area. That is, he produces pen-and-ink drawings of individual homes from photographs and, based on the sample, can take orders for these custom drawings. The lithograph that he has chosen can be easily reproduced many times without losing its design and color, so he can sell multiples of this work.

Table 1   Demand, Revenue, and Cost Information for Custom-Drawn Houses

Price per Drawing	Number of Drawings Demanded	Total Revenue	Marginal Revenue	Marginal Cost	Total Cost	Profit
$72	0	_____			_____	_____
66	1	_____	_____	_____	_____	_____
60	2	_____	_____	_____	_____	_____
54	3	_____	_____	_____	_____	_____
48	4	_____	_____	_____	_____	_____
42	5	_____	_____	_____	_____	_____
36	6	_____	_____	_____	_____	_____
30	7	_____	_____	_____	_____	_____
24	8	_____	_____	_____	_____	_____

now we are concerned with social rather than private benefits and costs. Thus, the net benefit to society from an activity is maximized where the total social benefit from the activity exceeds its total social cost by the greatest amount, or where marginal social benefit equals marginal social cost.

How do externalities affect the relationship between private and social net benefits? If an action of an individual or business has no effect on others, there will be no externalities, and the level of activity that maximizes the

Table 1 gives the demand schedule that Pete thinks to be true for custom house drawings. He calculates his cost for each house drawing at $20, which includes his time and materials. Complete Table 1 to determine the price Pete should charge and the number of drawings he should sell to maximize his profit from the drawings. Why is his roommate not correct in advising him to go for volume and charge $24 per drawing?

Table 2 gives the demand schedule for Pete's lithograph. The cost of producing the first lithograph is high—$200—but the marginal cost for each additional print is only $5. Complete this table and indicate the price Pete should charge for his lithograph. What is the maximum profit that he can expect to make from the sale of his lithograph?

Table 2   Demand, Revenue, and Cost Information for Lithographs

Price per Lithograph	Number of Lithographs Demanded	Total Revenue	Marginal Revenue	Marginal Cost	Total Cost	Profit or Loss
$180	0	_____		$200		_____
170	1	_____	_____		$200	_____
160	2	_____	_____	_____	_____	_____
150	3	_____	_____	_____	_____	_____
140	4	_____	_____	_____	_____	_____
130	5	_____	_____	_____	_____	_____
120	6	_____	_____	_____	_____	_____
110	7	_____	_____	_____	_____	_____
100	8	_____	_____	_____	_____	_____
90	9	_____	_____	_____	_____	_____
80	10	_____	_____	_____	_____	_____

individual's or business's net benefit will also maximize the net benefit of society. But where private actions impose costs on others and cause negative externalities, the level of activity that maximizes society's net benefit will be *less* than the level where private net benefit is maximized. For example, if the profit-maximizing output for a business is accompanied by a large amount of air pollution, the cost of which is borne by society, society would be better off if the firm produced a lower level of output and less pollution.

Application 11.2

Banishing Tobacco

"Passive smokers"—who breathe smoky air in the workplace and in public buildings—may accomplish what health professionals have failed to do: curb smoking.

Tobacco causes more death and suffering among adults than any other toxic material in the environment. Increasingly, evidence shows that nonsmokers as well as smokers are at risk. It is now feared that *involuntary* exposure to cigarette smoke causes more cancer deaths than any other pollutant. . . .

Sidestream smoke—which wafts from a smoker's cigarette to an involuntary smoker—puts into the surrounding air 50 times the amount of carcinogens inhaled by the user and has been linked to lung cancer and respiratory disease. The scale of these effects has only recently attracted attention, and much more work is urgently needed to define their total impact.

Passive smoking has been correlated with lung cancer in more than 10 studies. One study in Japan found that wives who did not smoke but who lived with heavy smokers were twice as likely to die of lung cancer as wives of men who did not smoke. Studies in Greece, West Germany, and the United States have yielded similar results. . . .

Passive smoking places unborn children at serious risk. Nicotine, numerous toxic chemicals, and radioactive polonium may all interfere with fetal development, whether the mother smokes or chews tobacco. Furthermore, studies in both industrial and developing countries show that smoking by pregnant women reduces infants' weight at birth by roughly one-tenth. Because birthweight is a key factor in infant mortality, tobacco use seriously endangers infants' lives. . . .

Children with parents who smoke experience much higher rates of respiratory illness, including colds, influenza, bronchitis, asthma, and pneumonia. One British study published almost 10 years ago showed that children under age 1 whose mothers smoke more than one pack a day are twice as likely to get bronchitis and pneumonia. This finding has been repeatedly corroborated. . . .

Source: William U. Chandler, "Banishing Tobacco," *The Futurist*, May–June 1986, pp. 9–15, originally adapted from William U. Chandler, *State of the World 1986*, Worldwatch Institute, © 1986. Reprinted with permission from Worldwatch Institute.

Where an individual's or business's actions benefit others and cause positive externalities, the level of activity that maximizes society's net benefit will be *greater* than the level that maximizes private net benefit. For example, a person might maximize private net benefit by limiting the amount spent on veterinary services for a pet. But, because of infectious diseases and unwanted litters, society would be better off if the pet received a full array of inoculations and was altered.

The relationship between private and social net benefits is shown in Figures 11.3a and 11.3b. Suppose that the private marginal costs and benefits to a business from producing a product are represented by MC and MB in Figure 11.3a.[6] Here private net benefit (in this case, profit) would be maximized where MB = MC, which occurs at the output level shown by

[6]We are using the more general form MB (marginal benefit), rather than MR (marginal revenue), to represent the business's benefit since we are now considering the business's and society's benefits together.

Figure 11.3

Maximizing Social Net Benefit with Negative and Positive Externalities

When the production of a product generates negative externalities, society's net benefit is maximized by cutting back on the output level. When production generates positive externalities, society's net benefit is maximized by increasing the output level.

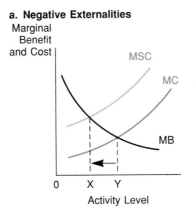

a. Negative Externalities

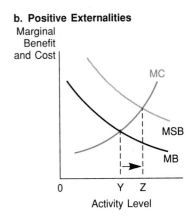

b. Positive Externalities

point Y on the horizontal axis of Figure 11.3a. But also suppose that producing this product imposes costs, or negative externalities (such as air pollution), with no offsetting benefits to other people. From society's point of view, these negative externalities must be added to the private costs to determine social costs, and from that, the best output level for society.

When the negative externalities are added to the private costs, marginal social cost can be calculated and is represented by MSC in Figure 11.3a. From society's perspective, the best level of output is shown by point X on the horizontal axis of Figure 11.3a. At that output, the marginal benefit to society, MB (which is the same as private marginal benefit since the act provides no positive externalities), equals marginal social cost, MSC. In this case, it would be in the interest of society to persuade the business to cut back production from point Y to point X.

The situation where a positive externality results from the production of a product is shown in Figure 11.3b. In this case, private net benefit would be maximized by producing where private marginal benefit, MB, and marginal cost, MC, were equal, or at point Y on the horizontal axis of Figure 11.3b. But suppose that the production of this product benefits society (perhaps by creating jobs in a depressed area) with no offsetting addition to cost, or negative externality. This additional benefit, or positive externality, must be added to the private benefit to determine the output level that would best serve society. These benefits, when added together, result in the marginal social benefit shown by MSB in Figure 11.3b. In this case, where there are benefits but no costs imposed on society, the best position for society would be at output level Z in Figure 11.3b, where MSB = MC. Here it would be in society's interest to have the business increase its level of output from point Y to point Z.

Since too many goods are produced in markets with negative externalities and too few goods are produced in markets with positive externalities when decision making is based only on private benefits and costs, how can society induce individuals and businesses to decrease undesirable and increase desirable activities? Activities that produce negative externalities might be reduced through fines, taxes, outright prohibition, or other penalties. Such methods have been used to control air and water pollution and drunk driving in the United States. To encourage activities that yield positive externalities, government might provide tax breaks, direct grants of money, subsidies, or other inducements. For example, at times local governments have given tax breaks to businesses for locating in their communities, thereby creating new jobs; and the federal government gives various types of financial assistance to students to help complete their educations.

Public Choice

The goal of maximizing economic well-being and the principles of cost-benefit analysis are easily understood in the context of individual and business decision making. In our economic system, however, many important decisions are also made collectively, that is, by a group. Collective decision making occurs primarily through the government sector. As a group we make choices on questions such as how many municipal police cars to purchase, whether to provide more funds for our schools, how much money to allocate to national defense, and whether to permit budget deficits.

How do individuals participate in collective decision making? In the United States, the voting mechanism is the root of collective choice. Individuals elect officials at the federal, state, and local government levels who receive the power and authority to act in behalf of the group. Thus, voting provides the link that transforms individual decision making into collective choice.

Public choice

The study of the economic motives and attitudes of voters and public officials in collective decision making.

The term used to describe the set of economic theories that explains the motives and attitudes of voters and public officials in collective decision making is **public choice.** The basic idea behind public choice is that people try to maximize their own well-being, or operate in their own self-interest, in making collective choices. Thus, the fundamental rules of decision making do not change when a group is involved.

An examination of the voting process helps to illustrate the basics of public choice. Participation in an election involves three considerations for the individual: (1) whether to vote, (2) how much information to seek about candidates and issues, and (3) for whom to vote. Each of these considerations carries costs and benefits.

The act of voting gives individuals varying degrees of satisfaction: if people believe that their votes are important, voting gives them more satisfaction than if they feel that their votes are insignificant. Voting also imposes costs on individuals, especially the opportunity cost of time. Thus, a person's decision about whether or not to vote in an election depends upon his or her marginal benefit and marginal cost of voting. If marginal benefit is greater than marginal cost, a person will vote in an election; if marginal cost is greater than marginal benefit, he or she will not vote. Since voter turnout for a particular election is the result of all of the individual decisions of voters, and since a relatively small percentage of the electorate generally votes, we can conclude that most people believe that it is not in their best interest to participate in collective decision making.

A second consideration in voting involves the amount of information about candidates and issues that a voter possesses when making a decision at the polls. Generally, when individuals make private decisions about spending large sums of money, they attempt to gather as much information as possible. Do you, for example, know someone who is about to purchase a car? That person is probably reading magazines that rate automobiles, taking test drives, and asking current car owners about the advantages and problems of particular models. Many persons will pay the government as much in taxes this year as the cost of a new auto. Are those persons investing as much time and energy in gathering information about the elected representatives to whom they are entrusting their tax dollars as they would if they were using an equivalent sum of money to buy a car? Probably they are not.

Rational ignorance

A person chooses to remain uninformed because the marginal cost of obtaining the information is higher than the marginal benefit from knowing it.

Information seeking about candidates and issues takes time. As a result, the opportunity cost of becoming an informed voter can be high, causing a person to be **rationally ignorant.** That is, a rational voter may perceive that the marginal benefit from becoming better acquainted with a candidate's record and position is less than the marginal cost of enlightenment. Because of this, voters often make choices based on limited information that comes from brief advertisements designed to sell a candidate.

Which candidate does a voter choose? Again, the principles of cost-benefit analysis apply. A voter will select the candidate perceived to bring him or her the greatest net benefit. This decision could be based on the candidate's record, the position of the candidate on an issue important to the voter, or any other consideration.[7]

Special interest group

People who share a common position on a particular issue and actively promote that position.

Public choice theory, with its emphasis on self-interest, helps to explain many of the problems that result from collective decision making. For example, in the collective process, **special interest groups** often cause the will of a minority to be imposed on the majority. Public choice theory explains that members of special interest groups actively promote their

[7] People have been known to vote for candidates about whom they know nothing. A candidate, for example, might receive votes just because his or her name is easy to pronounce or spell.

Application 11.3

Uninsured Drivers Create Wreckage

Growing numbers of uninsured drivers are causing serious accidents, pushing up insurance rates and walking away from the responsibility to reimburse their victims.

As many as 17 million people drive without insurance, industry officials estimate, and these drivers cause one of every eight serious automobile accidents. . . .

"This is an extremely serious situation all around the country," said David N. Levinson, Delaware's Commissioner of Insurance. . . .

Many states . . . require drivers to insure themselves against bodily injury caused by hit-and-run accidents or accidents with motorists who drive illegally without insurance. Thus, in a sense, the conscientious driver is penalized twice: first, his overall premium is higher because of the problem of uninsured drivers; second, he is required to buy the extra coverage specifically against injury caused by the uninsured driver.

The clamor over insurance rates has prompted [several] states to step up enforcement of their mandatory automobile insurance laws in the last 12 months.

But Mr. Levinson and consumer advocates say most of the new enforcement efforts are inadequate, and they blame the insurance industry for blocking more stringent enforcement measures. They complain that the industry is content to collect the total cost of the nation's automobile insurance from a decreasing pool of customers as a way to keep administrative costs down and profits up.

Insurance industry spokesmen acknowledge that companies oppose mandatory auto insurance laws and some stringent enforcement measures proposed by the states, but they contend that the companies are taking the consumer's side in these matters. "The industry does not want to be in the position of saying somebody must buy insurance before he feeds his children," said [the spokeswoman for an insurance trade group].

Industry surveys indicate that most people who do not buy automobile insurance are generally young, unmarried men, who face the highest insurance premiums of any group, and who tend to have low incomes and few assets. It is also the group with the highest rate of accidents. Half the uninsured vehicles are owned by people who are unemployed, employed part time, retired, students or homemakers, according to a 1988 study. . . .

[Legislation in California which would have provided affordable insurance for low incomes, failed last spring. It] would have required insurers to offer a $180 no-frills policy as part of an insurance reform package. The insurance industry and consumer groups supported the bill, but trial lawyers did not. They said the legislation, which was based on a no-fault system that would eliminate most litigation, would have overly restricted people's right to obtain compensation for pain and suffering.

Source: Excerpted from Michael deCourcy Hinds, "Uninsured Drivers Create Other Kinds of Wreckage," *The New York Times,* September 3, 1990, pp. 1, 10. Copyright © 1990 by The New York Times Company. Excerpted by permission.

positions through letters, ads, campaign contributions, and other means because of the benefits they expect to receive. The response to these issues from the rest of the population is weak because of lack of interest or because the opportunity cost of responding is too high. Elected officials are sensitive to the pleas of special interest group members because it is in the officials' best interest.

Application 11.3, "Uninsured Drivers Create Wreckage," provides a good example of many of the concepts covered in this chapter. Can you identify the negative externalities created by uninsured motorists, how individual maximizing choices might lead people not to buy insurance, and the impact of special interest groups on legislation related to mandatory insurance?

Summary

There are general rules for maximizing economic well-being that can be applied to any decision-making unit, be it an individual, business, or society. These rules involve the balancing of costs and benefits from different courses of action in order to select the one that contributes most to economic well-being. The formal study of these rules and the balancing of costs and benefits is called cost-benefit analysis. These rules can be applied to many more areas of human endeavor than those traditionally studied in economics courses.

For an individual, the benefits of an activity can be measured in terms of the satisfaction, or utility, received from the action. Costs can be measured by the opportunity forgone in accomplishing that action.

For a business, benefits are measured by the total revenue received, which is calculated by multiplying the price of an item times the quantity of the item sold. The economic cost of producing a good or service includes explicit costs, which are direct payments to outsiders for factors of production, and implicit costs, which are returns required by the owner(s) to keep the business in operation. Normal profit is what the owner(s) must earn to recover implicit costs. Economic profit is not a cost of production; it is that profit in excess of normal profit.

Total benefit or revenue and total cost are, respectively, the benefit or revenue received and the cost incurred from producing a particular amount of activity or output. Marginal benefit or revenue is the change in total benefit or revenue resulting from each additional unit of an activity performed or output sold. Marginal cost is the change in total cost from producing or adding one more unit of activity or output.

The rules for maximizing economic well-being, or net benefit, are that an activity should be carried out to the point where total benefit exceeds total cost by the greatest amount, or where marginal benefit equals marginal cost. Both rules are satisfied at exactly the same level of activity. The main difference in how these rules are applied to various decision-making units is in what is maximized and how benefits and costs are measured. An individual tries to maximize net satisfaction, and a business tries to maximize profit.

Activities by individuals or businesses may favorably or adversely affect others. These effects are called externalities, and because of externalities, an individual's or business's net benefits from its actions may differ from society's net benefits from those same actions.

Net benefits are calculated for society in the same way they are calculated for individuals and businesses. The only difference is that while the individual or business measures its net benefits in terms of its own private costs and benefits, society measures its net benefits in terms of social costs and social benefits. Social costs are private costs plus any negative external effects. Social benefits are private benefits plus any positive external effects. When negative externalities are present, society's net benefit is maximized at a level of activity lower than that which will maximize private net benefit. When positive externalities are present, society's net benefit is maximized at a level of activity greater than that which will maximize private net benefit.

Public choice deals with the economic theories behind collective decision making, which is carried out through the voting process. How the voting mechanism is used by each individual depends upon that individual's costs and benefits from the acts of voting, information seeking, and candidate selection. Problems that arise from collective decision making, such as the impact of special interest groups, can be explained through the use of cost-benefit analysis.

Key Terms and Concepts

Cost-benefit analysis	Economic cost of production
Opportunity cost	Excess, or economic, profit
Marginal benefit or utility	Total revenue
Total benefit or utility	Marginal revenue
Law of Diminishing Marginal Utility	Profit or loss
Total cost	Externality
Marginal cost	Positive externality
Net benefit	Negative externality
Profit or net benefit maximizing rules	Social benefits and costs
Explicit costs	Public choice
Implicit costs	Rational ignorance
Normal profit	Special interest group

Review Questions

1. In this chapter you have been introduced to marginal benefit, marginal utility, marginal revenue, marginal social benefit, marginal cost, and marginal social cost. What concept is common to all of these terms, and to what specifically does each term refer?

2. Explain why: (1) net benefit is at a maximum when marginal benefit equals marginal cost; (2) net benefit increases when marginal benefit exceeds marginal cost; and (3) net benefit falls when marginal benefit is less than marginal cost.

3. In what respects are the following maximizing decisions similar to each other and in what respects do they differ?

a. The decision by an individual as to how much of an item to consume
b. The decision by a society as to how many resources to devote to law enforcement
c. The decision by a business as to how much of an item to produce and sell
d. The decision by an individual as to how many hours to work

4. The following table gives the utility points received by an individual from each additional hour of exercise per week, as well as the points that each additional hour costs. Using this table, answer questions a through d.

Hours of Exercise	Marginal Benefit	Total Benefit	Marginal Cost	Total Cost	Net Benefit
0		——		——	——
	60		5		
1		——		——	——
	40		10		
2		——		——	——
	30		20		
3		——		——	——
	20		30		
4		——		——	——
	10		40		
5		——		——	——
	0		55		
6		——		——	——

a. Calculate the total benefit and the total cost of exercising for each of the hours in the table.
b. Calculate the net benefit of exercising for each of the hours in the table.
c. How many hours per week should this individual exercise in order to maximize the satisfaction obtained from exercising, and what is the maximum number of net benefit points that can be earned from exercising?
d. Graph total benefit and total cost, marginal benefit and marginal cost, and net benefit on the graphs below. (Remember to plot marginal benefit and marginal cost at the midpoint between the quantities.) Explain how these graphs illustrate the maximizing rules.

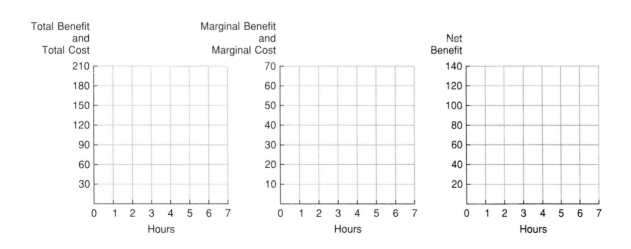

5. Suppose that your aunt has just closed her books from her first year in the retail cookie business and is ecstatic with the profit her accountant says that she has earned. The store grossed $125,000 in sales over the year, and its explicit costs for rent, raw materials, electricity, and the like were $75,000. Your uncle is not quite as elated, but can't figure out exactly why. In discussing the situation with you, he offers the following information. Your aunt and uncle invested $100,000 of their savings, which was earning an 8 percent return, to go into this business. Your aunt gave up her job, which was paying her $32,000 a year, at a local corporation. Your uncle worked every evening and most weekends at the store—giving up the opportunity to take on additional clients or to work overtime. In addition to being tired, he figures that he lost $15,000 in additional income.

    What was your aunt and uncle's economic cost of production? How much normal profit should they have expected to receive? Have they made any economic profit? What kind of advice would you give them?

6. Using the following cost and revenue information, answer questions a through d.

Units of Output	Total Revenue	Marginal Revenue	Total Cost	Marginal Cost
0	$ 0	_____	$ 0	_____
1	50	_____	25	_____
2	90	_____	35	_____
3	120	_____	40	_____
4	140	_____	50	_____
5	150	_____	70	_____
6	150	_____	100	_____
7	140	_____	140	_____
8	120	_____	200	_____

    a. What are the marginal revenue and marginal cost of each unit of output?
    b. At what levels of output is marginal cost greater than marginal revenue, and at what levels is marginal revenue greater than marginal cost?
    c. What is the profit-maximizing level of output?
    d. What is total profit at the profit-maximizing level of output?

7. Use public choice theory to explain
    a. Low voter turnout for the election of a few candidates for minor offices
    b. Voting along party lines instead of judging each candidate's individual merits
    c. A change before an election in an incumbent's position on an issue
    d. Voting according to the recommendations given in a local newspaper
    e. Low voter turnout when the weather is bad

Discussion Questions

1. In each of the following situations, determine what the decision maker might be seeking to maximize and indicate: (1) some factors that should be included in the calculation of costs; and (2) some factors that should be included in the calculation of benefits.
   a. The decision to get a college education
   b. The decision by a shoplifter to steal a coat
   c. The decision by voters to increase property taxes
   d. The decision by a business to market a new product
   e. The decision to adopt a child
   f. The decision to lie
   g. The decision to smoke cigarettes

2. What could be opportunity costs for each of the following actions?
   a. Moving from a smaller home that takes 40 percent of your income to own and maintain, to a larger "home of your dreams" that takes 60 percent of your income
   b. Working overtime during the next two months in the hope of getting a promotion
   c. Deciding to stop seeing someone because you are not right for each other
   d. Cutting back on certain foods to lower your cholesterol level

3. Identify some of the negative externalities associated with living in a city that has a high crime rate.

4. Air pollution is a well-known example of a negative externality. What are some of the costs imposed on society by air pollution? In answering this question be sure to consider possible effects from pollution on health, property values, the maintenance of buildings and other property, and taxes.

5. Since air pollution causes a negative externality, would you back a proposal to eliminate all air pollution? Why?

6. Cost-benefit analysis can be applied to a wide range of economic and noneconomic decisions. Give five examples of noneconomic situations where the cost-benefit analysis developed in this chapter would be useful in arriving at a decision.

7. Although DDT, a pesticide, has been banned in the United States, it is used extensively in many other nations, primarily to curb malaria caused by mosquito bites. In some parts of the world, such as Brazil and India, malaria is a serious health threat. Despite the problems created by extensive use of DDT, many countries find this the least expensive method of attacking malaria and mosquitos. Using cost-benefit analysis, explain why you would favor or disapprove of the continued use of DDT in other countries.

Critical Thinking Case 11

■ Kidneys for Sale?

Critical Thinking Skills	Identifying and evaluating different sides of an issue
Economic Concepts	Private and social benefits and costs
	Externalities

Modern medicine has worked miracles for people who need a new heart or kidney or other organs. Demand for organ transplants has increased sharply. Unfortunately, there are no miracles on the supply side. Thousands of would-be recipients die every year while waiting.

Can anything be done to increase the supply of transplant organs? Some doctors are very quietly talking about compensating donors.

That's right: I'll pay you $5,000 for one of your kidneys. Not enough? How about $20,000? . . .

[It is uncertain] that voluntary donations will ever provide sufficient supply, given advancements in medical science and in organ transplanting. "I can't see why the only persons not to make a legitimate degree of financial advantage from transplantation are the people who give the organs," [says a nephrologist and bioethicist from Canada]. "Everybody else is living by it, including myself."

There are any number of ways to compensate donors or their families. The compensation can come in the form of straight cash, or coverage of burial expenses, or through estate tax breaks or college education benefits for survivors. . . .

In the world's poorer countries, hospitals rarely have the equipment or trained staff to save organs for transplant. Nor can most of these countries afford hemodialysis facilities, thus, in effect, sentencing patients with kidney failure to certain death. In the case of kidney failure, the only real solution in many poor countries is to buy a kidney from a living donor, in a straightforward commercial transaction.

[Consider the case of an Indian fellow whose kidneys failed and who was successfully implanted with a kidney from a 25-year-old garment factory worker with two children. The woman who parted with one of her two kidneys] used her money to buy a piece of land in her home town of Ambattur, just outside Madras, where she plans to build a house one day. Her husband also sold one of his kidneys and used the money to pay off debts and cover his sister's dowry and wedding costs. . . .

Under current U.S. law, a living donor cannot be paid for his or her organ, but can specify who is to receive it. That simply means that most live kidney donors are related to the recipients. Yet doctors will tell you that illegal compensation is sometimes exchanged.

"The fact is that many [living donors] are getting compensated under the table," [says a Dallas doctor]. "Suddenly a [donor] gets a new business, or a new house or a new car, just after he's donated to his nephew or some friend. And medicine has trouble with that, because we don't want to know about it." . . .

Questions

1. Give some arguments for and some against legalizing the sale of human kidneys.

2. Is selling one's own kidney rational? What are the benefits and costs to the seller, and can the sale be justified using cost-benefit principles?

3. What are the social benefits and social costs of allowing individuals to sell their kidneys? How do externalities affect the relationship between the amount of sales that would maximize society's net benefit and the amount that would maximize individuals' net benefits?

4. Is legislation completely banning the voluntary sale of kidneys justifiable on cost-benefit grounds? What special interest groups would likely support this legislation and what groups would likely oppose it?

Source: Excerpted from Ronald Bailey, "Should I Be Allowed to Buy Your Kidney?" *Forbes*, May 28, 1990, pp. 365–368, 370, 372. Excerpted by permission of Forbes magazine. © Forbes Inc., 1990.

Suggested Readings

Natalie Angier, "Human Growth Hormone Reverses Effects of Aging," *The New York Times*, **July 5, 1990, pp. A1, A12.**
Considers some costs and benefits of a growth hormone that has reversed the effects of aging on men.

William J. Broad, "Vast Sums for New Discoveries Pose a Threat to Basic Science," *The New York Times*, **May 27, 1990, pp. 1, 12.**
Presents benefits and costs—particularly opportunity costs—of large scientific projects.

Warren T. Brookes, "The Global Warming Panic," *Forbes*, **December 25, 1989, pp. 97–102.**
Discusses studies supporting and disputing the greenhouse effect, and some costs of lowering the emissions of gases that cause rising temperatures.

James M. Buchanan, "From Private Preferences to Public Philosophy: The Development of Public Choice," *The Economics of Politics* **(London: The Institute of Economic Affairs, 1978), pp. 3–20.**
Discusses the development of public choice theory.

Marilyn Chase, "Solace for U.S. Slobs: Being Fit and Pretty Can Be Bad for You," *The Wall Street Journal*, **July 14, 1986, pp. 1, 10.**
Considers some of the medical costs associated with tanning, false nails, vitamin megadosing, exercising, wearing tight clothing, and other activities in the pursuit of attractiveness.

Ted Gup, "Owl vs. Man," *Time*, **June 25, 1990, pp. 56–65.**
Sets out costs, benefits, externalities, and public choices in the debate over harvesting lumber or saving forests.

Roy Hoopes, "When It's Time to Leave," *Modern Maturity,* August–September 1988, pp. 38–43.
Deals with the debate created by questioning the costs and benefits of limiting access to health care in a person's later years; uses some marginal thinking.

Marshall Jevons, *Murder at the Margin* (Glen Ridge, N.J.: Thomas Horton and Daughters, 1978).
A murder mystery that is solved using economic principles.

Roland N. McKean, "The Nature of Cost-Benefit Analysis," *Microeconomics: Selected Readings,* Edwin Mansfield, ed. (New York: W. W. Norton & Co., Inc., 1979), pp. 509–518.
Sets out and discusses common elements of cost-benefit studies.

G. Tullock and R. B. McKenzie, *The Best of New World of Economics,* 5th ed. (Homewood, Ill.: R. D. Irwin, Inc., 1989).
A cost-benefit approach to marriage, crime, learning, and other topics.

Burton A. Weisbrod, "America's Health-Care Dilemma," *Challenge,* September–October 1985, pp. 30–34.
Discusses increasing costs in medical care due to technological advances that lengthen life, and whether the resulting benefits justify the costs.

Chapter Twelve

Production and the Costs of Production

The cost of producing a particular good or service, such as a house, depends on the inputs and technique chosen to produce it.

Source: © 1989 Jim Gensheimer/San Jose Mercury News.

Chapter Objectives

1. To identify some methods for categorizing productive activity in the U.S. economy.

2. To explain the nature and importance of production methods.

3. To explore the relationship between production methods and technology.

4. To differentiate between production in the short run and production in the long run.

5. To define various types of costs associated with production: fixed, variable, total, average total, and marginal.

6. To explain the behavior of costs as the level of production changes in both the short run and the long run.

This chapter is concerned with production, which is the process of transforming inputs into outputs of goods and services, and with the costs of production. Technically, production is carried out in all sectors of the economy: steel is produced by a business firm, a homemaker produces meals, and the local government's fire department provides fire protection. But while each of these areas of the economy produces goods and services, the vast majority of measured production is by businesses. Consequently, this chapter focuses on the production and the costs of production of business firms.

The first section of the chapter provides an overview of production in the U.S. economy. The second section deals with methods of production and the relationship between those methods and technology. The third section is devoted to classifying and evaluating production and the costs of production in terms of short-run and long-run time frames.

Before embarking on the chapter it should be noted that there is an important connection between a firm's production, its costs of production, and its ability to realize the objective of maximum profit. As was introduced in Chapter Ten, and emphasized in the example of the jeweler in Chapter Eleven, profit is what remains after costs are subtracted from revenue. All other things remaining unchanged, the lower the cost of producing a product, the greater the firm's profit from selling that product.

Overview of Production in the U.S. Economy

In 1990 U.S. business firms produced an output of goods and services valued at about $5.5 trillion.[1] Much of this output, especially that from corporations, was generated by firms that each produce several different types of products. For example, in addition to its beer operations, Anheuser-Busch, through its divisions and subsidiaries, produces wine, bakery goods, other foods, and yeast products; operates transportation and communication services and theme parks for family entertainment; fields a major league baseball team; is in real estate development; and carries out other activities.[2]

With so many businesses producing so many different types of goods and services, gaining an overview of production in the U.S. economy can be a formidable task. To help simplify this task, classification systems have been developed for grouping similar types of goods and services. These systems bring order to an overview of production in the economy by allowing us to categorize production into separate producing sectors and industries.

Producing Sectors and Industries

Sectors
A broad classification system for grouping goods and services, and the firms that produce them.

Producing Sectors   The broadest classification system for grouping goods and services, and the firms that produce them, is producing **sectors.** Table 12.1 identifies the major producing sectors of the economy, along with examples of the productive activities included in each sector and the percentage of private domestic output accounted for by each sector in 1990.

A few points should be noted about Table 12.1. First, in analyzing the table it must be remembered that although we can distinguish different sectors of the economy, those sectors are closely knit in the production and distribution of goods and services. For example, the crops and livestock produced in the agricultural sector become food products in the manufacturing sector. These food products then move from the manufacturers' to households' shelves through the wholesale and retail trade sectors, with the assistance of the transportation sector.

Second, as the economy grows, the relative importance of the different sectors changes. For example, from 1930 through 1988, the position of manufacturing as the dominant producing sector of the economy was unchallenged. But, in 1989 manufacturing was surpassed in size by the services sector. Changes have also occurred in the relative importance of other sectors. From 1930 to the mid-1950s, for example, agriculture, forestry,

[1] U.S., *Economic Report of the President* (Washington, D.C.: U.S. Government Printing Office, 1991), p. 286. 1990 figure is preliminary.

[2] Anheuser-Busch Companies, Inc., *Compact Disclosure USA* (Bethesda, Md.: Disclosure, Inc., June 1990), data base.

Table 12.1

Major Producing Sectors of the Economy

Goods and services produced by businesses can be categorized into the various producing sectors of the economy. Recently, manufacturing has been replaced by services as the largest producing sector.

Sector	Examples of Productive Activities	Percentage of Private Domestic Output in 1990
Agriculture, forestry, and fishing	Crop and livestock production, agricultural services, forestry, fishing, hunting and trapping	2.8%
Mining	Metal, coal and lignite mining, oil and gas extraction	1.1
Construction	Building, highway and heavy construction, general contracting and special trade contracting	6.0
Manufacturing	Production of apparel, food products, fabricated metal products, electronic equipment, transportation equipment and chemical products, petroleum refining, printing and publishing	21.7
Transportation; comunications; electric, gas, and sanitary services	Railroad, water, pipeline and air transportation, trucking and warehousing; radio and television broadcasting, telephone and telegraph; natural gas transmission and distribution, sewer systems, electric services	8.7
Wholesale trade	Wholesale auto supplies, electrical appliances, sporting goods	7.0
Retail trade	Food and general merchandise stores, restaurants, building material and garden supply stores, auto dealers, gasoline stations	10.0
Finance, insurance, and real estate	Banking, commodity and security brokerage, insurance, real estate	17.2
Services	Personal and business services, health, legal and educational services	25.6

Source: Executive Office of the President, Office of Management and Budget, *Standard Industrial Classification Manual, 1987* (Washington, D.C.: U.S. Government Printing Office), pp. 7–8, 40, 43, 45, 55–56, 58, 61, 283–284, 289, 295, 301, 315–317, 319, 321, 328; U.S. Department of Commerce, *Survey of Current Business,* March 1991, p. 15.

and fishing contributed more to total output than did construction. But in the late 1950s, that relationship reversed.[3]

Finally, while dividing productive activities into sectors helps order our thinking about production in the economy, the sectors are broadly defined

[3]U.S. Bureau of the Census, *Historical Statistics of the United States, Colonial Times to 1970, Bicentennial Edition, Part 1* (Washington, D.C.: U.S. Government Printing Office, 1975), p. 239; U.S. Department of Commerce, *Survey of Current Business,* July 1989, p. 78.

Table 12.2

Some Industries in the Manufacturing Sector

Firms producing similar products are grouped into the same industry. A number of industries provide manufactured products.

Industry	Examples of Products Provided by Firms in the Industry
Aircraft	Airplanes, helicopters, hang gliders, blimps
Book printing	Printed and bound books and pamphlets
Carpet and rug	Woven, tufted, and other carpets and rugs made from textiles and other materials
Doll and stuffed toy	Dolls, doll parts and clothing, stuffed toys
Fluid milk	Fluid milk, cream, cottage cheese, and related products
Mobile home	Mobile homes and nonresidential mobile buildings
Motor and generator	Electric motors, generator sets, power generators, motor housings
Pharmaceutical preparation	Tablets, capsules, ointments, and other medicinal products for human and veterinary use
Power-driven hand tool	Power-driven drills, grinders, hammers, and other hand tools
Steel pipe and tube	Seamless steel pipe, boiler tubes, wrought well casings

Source: Executive Office of the President, Office of Management and Budget, *Standard Industrial Classification Manual, 1987* (Washington, D.C.: U.S. Government Printing Office), pp. 71, 90, 111, 127, 138, 175, 207, 222, 236–237, 257.

and include activities that, while related, are not always closely related. For example, frog farming and landscape planning are both included in the agriculture, forestry, and fishing sector.[4] For this reason, it is helpful to classify production into narrower categories than those shown in Table 12.1.

Industry

A group of firms producing similar products.

Industries   A widely used classification system for dividing productive activities into categories smaller than sectors is called industries. An **industry** is a group of firms producing similar products. This similarity results because the firms use similar processes and factors to produce their products, or because buyers view the firms' products as interchangeable, or as substitutes for one another. Examples of industries are the soft drink, greeting card, life insurance, sporting goods, and grocery store industries.

How do industry classifications compare with the sector classifications in Table 12.1? As noted earlier, industries are smaller, or more narrowly defined, than sectors. Table 12.2 illustrates this by listing several manufacturing industries and examples of their products. Although all of the firms in each of these industries manufacture finished products, the products they produce differ significantly from industry to industry.

[4]Executive Office of the President, Office of Management and Budget, *Standard Industrial Classification Manual, 1987* (Washington, D.C.: U.S. Government Printing Office), pp. 29, 34.

Notice that many of the products listed in the different industries in Table 12.2 could be produced by the same firm. Recall, for example, that Anheuser-Busch operates in several unrelated areas, such as beer, real estate, and professional sports.

More specific classifications than industries can be developed for grouping businesses. For example, suppose that you are interested in securing data about firms producing cottage cheese. In this case, information on the fluid milk industry, in which cottage cheese is listed, would be too broad. You would be better served with something narrower than this industry classification. Thus, depending on one's needs, production in the economy can be viewed from many different levels: major producing sectors, industries, narrower parts of industries, or individual firms.

Methods of Production

Production, or the transforming of inputs into outputs, does not occur haphazardly. Rather, it is systematic and occurs according to a plan called a production function.

The Production Function

Production function
Shows the type and amount of output that can be attained from a particular group of inputs when those inputs are combined in a certain way.

A **production function** shows the type and amount of output that can be attained from a particular group of inputs when those inputs are combined in a certain way. Production functions exist for virtually every good and service: for agricultural products, machinery, magazines, chemicals, hamburgers, and everything else that can be produced. For some types of goods and services, such as gasoline or automobiles, production functions can be clearly defined. For other productive activities, such as learning or child rearing, the functions are not as well understood. But in each case, we can think of an output as that which is produced by a set of inputs combined in a particular way.

One common form of a production function that can be used to illustrate the basic features of all production functions is a recipe, such as that shown in Table 12.3. In this production function the output is a chocolate chip cheesecake. The inputs include the ingredients listed at the top of the recipe — cream cheese, chocolate chips, eggs, and so forth — as well as kitchen equipment and the labor provided by the person preparing the cheesecake. The method for combining these inputs is explained in the text of the recipe and involves such operations as mixing and baking. All production functions are concerned with exactly the same types of considerations that underlie this recipe: identifying the type and amount of output, the numbers and types of inputs, and how the inputs are combined.

At any given time there can be more than one method available to a business for producing a particular good or service. A painting contractor might paint the exterior of a house using brushes or spraying equipment. A

Table 12.3   A Production Function

A production function indicates the types and amounts of inputs and how those inputs are combined to produce a particular type and amount of output. A recipe is a simple example of a production function.

Chocolate Chip Cheesecake

---

30 Oreo cookies, crushed into crumbs
6 tablespoons butter, melted
1 12-oz. package mini chocolate chips
1 tablespoon flour
3 8-oz. packages cream cheese
3 eggs
1 teaspoon vanilla
1 14-oz. can sweetened condensed milk
¼ cup heavy cream

Butter 9- or 10-inch springform pan. (Use some of the melted butter.) Mix oreo cookie crumbs and the melted butter. Line springform pan with crumb/butter mixture. Beat cream cheese until fluffy; add eggs and thoroughly beat; beat in vanilla, condensed milk, and heavy cream. Mix flour and chocolate chips and blend into cream cheese mixture. Pour into lined springform pan.

Bake at 325 degrees for approximately 60–70 minutes. Time varies with size of pan.

Note: This cheesecake is better if chilled for a day before it is served.

Labor-intensive production
Production that is strongly dependent on labor inputs.

Capital-intensive production
Production that emphasizes capital inputs.

person might edit a business report with a pencil or by word processing on a computer. Because a business often can choose among several methods to produce an output, it is helpful to differentiate between those methods. One way of doing this is to distinguish between labor-intensive production and capital-intensive production.

Production involving techniques exhibiting a strong dependence on labor as compared to machinery, equipment, and other types of inputs is **labor-intensive production.** The greater the dependence on labor, the more labor-intensive is the production. **Capital-intensive production** involves production techniques that emphasize the use of machinery, equipment, and other capital: the greater the emphasis on capital, the more capital-intensive is the production. A painter using brushes or an editor working with a pencil would be examples of labor-intensive production, while a painter spraying a house or an editor using a computer for word processing would represent more capital-intensive production.

An important consideration affecting the choice between labor-intensive and capital-intensive production methods is the relative availabilities and costs of the different factors of production. Businesses tend toward labor-intensive production techniques where labor is more abundant and relatively cheaper than capital, and toward capital-intensive techniques where labor is relatively more expensive. For example, agricultural production in the United States and Canada is capital-intensive because using a few pieces of capital equipment is cheaper than using a large number of workers. In other parts of the world, where labor is plentiful and inexpensive and machinery is scarce, agricultural production is more labor-intensive.

The ways in which labor and capital are combined and the extent to which production tends to be more labor-intensive or capital-intensive also differ in the various sectors of an economy. For example, distribution of electricity and natural gas depends extensively on capital inputs such as power lines, pipelines, generating stations, and storage facilities. Per-worker expenditures on capital equipment by firms in this sector are high. The construction of a building, on the other hand, requires a great deal of labor, and firms in this sector spend much less on capital inputs per worker. Expressed differently, the distribution of electricity and natural gas is more capital-intensive, while construction is more labor-intensive.

Choosing a Method of Production

Differences in the way capital and labor are combined to produce goods and services are not limited to different sectors of the economy; they are also found in the production techniques used by different firms in the same industry. For example, the management of one retail store might try to control theft by using security personnel, while the management of another store might depend on cameras and other electronic surveillance devices. Or one farmer might use an irrigation system for crop production while another does not.

What causes a firm to choose a particular production technique? Recall that the objective of a firm is to maximize profit, and that profit is what remains after costs are subtracted from revenue. Each production method has a different cost associated with it, and a firm will try to maximize profit by selecting the production method that gives it the desired output at the lowest cost. When a firm produces a good or service in the least-cost manner, **efficient production** and the efficient use of resources occurs. Application 12.1, "PCs Enter the Manufacturing Arena," explains how some firms are turning to more automated techniques involving microcomputers to lower costs.

Efficient method of production

The least-cost method of production.

It is important to understand that the least-cost, or efficient, method of production differs from seller to seller, depending upon the circumstances faced by each seller. It might be less costly for a large retail organization to protect itself from theft by using electronic surveillance devices rather than by paying a staff of security personnel. On the other hand, a smaller, lower traffic retailer may attain a comparable level of protection at the lowest cost by hiring a guard or by rewarding sales personnel who spot shoplifters. A farmer who has poor quality soil may be able to produce average per-acre yields only by incurring the cost of an irrigation system.

The quest for profit also explains why some sellers in an industry continue to use old, outdated production techniques when newer, more efficient techniques are available. Even if a new method of production is more

Application 12.1

PCs Enter the Manufacturing Arena

Armed with a new class of applications designed to address manufacturers' changing needs, a slowly growing number of manufacturing firms are using PCs to cut millions of dollars from their production costs.

Plant managers across the country are attacking the entire spectrum of manufacturing—from process control to planning and scheduling, and from inventory tracking to quality control and cost monitoring.

For some of the companies, PC systems have become powerful competitive weapons, enabling them to lower their prices and provide better service to customers. PCs help trim waste and overhead from production costs, and in turn allow companies to lower their prices. . . .

Microcomputers play two basic roles in manufacturing. The first is as an information processor: gathering, tracking and analyzing data about materials and products in the manufacturing process.

The second category is of direct controller of manufacturing machinery—putting PCs at the control panels.

Currently, information processing is by far the larger of the two roles, comprising about three-quarters of existing microcomputer applications in manufacturing, according to some analysts' estimates.

For many plant managers involved in this area of microcomputing, this boils down to three initials: MRP, or materials-requirements planning. This comprises a family of software designed to opti-

mize production processes by keeping an extremely close watch over inventory and individual stages of production. . . .

One of the most visible effects MRP systems can have on a manufacturing plant's performance is the speed of the production cycle. Shortening the time it takes to turn raw materials into final products can save money for any manufacturing concern. However, it is especially crucial for a "make-to-order" shop, one that only makes products that have been ordered by a customer, as opposed to a "make-to-stock" factory, which steadily churns out its product on the promise of projected sales. . . .

Far less common in manufacturing settings than MRP microcomputer applications is the use of PCs to control factory machinery. These are functions that put PCs at the control switches of production machinery, constantly monitoring the machinery and making minute adjustments.

A few factors are fueling sharp interest in physical-control applications. The availability of powerful yet inexpensive microcomputers that can perform extremely complex functions is one factor. But changes in the manufacturing business are equally important. Manufacturers must be ready to quickly turn out products in a wider variety and with shorter life cycles in the marketplace. . . .

Source: Excerpted from Paul Karon, "PCs Enter the Manufacturing Arena," *PC Week*, April 5, 1988, pp. 40, 44–45. Excerpted with permission from PC Week, copyright © 1988, Ziff Communications Company.

efficient than an existing method, the cost of transferring from the current to the new system could be so high that it would cancel out any cost saving that the new system would offer. For example, many manufacturing companies might not find it profitable to install computer-controlled production systems such as those mentioned in Application 12.1.

Production and Technological Change

In the production of most goods and services, new and presumably better techniques commonly compete with existing methods. For example, new procedures are continually being developed and adopted for the provision of health care services; more advanced types of communication and information systems are being designed and produced; and more efficient manufacturing equipment continues to be constructed. The list of such developments that compete with older systems goes on and on.

Technology

The body of knowledge that exists about production and its processes.

Examples such as these illustrate an important relationship between the methods of production used by businesses and **technology**, which is simply the state of knowledge that society possesses about production at a particular time. Technology refers not only to our knowledge of the design of machinery and equipment, but also to our understanding of such things as the scheduling of production, packaging, personnel relations, and transportation.

The relationship between production and technology is important for two reasons. First, technology restricts the range of production methods from which a business can choose: the choice of methods is limited by what is known at the time about the production of an item. Second, what is known about production at a particular time becomes embodied in the equipment and methods used for production. Therefore, when a business selects equipment for production, it is committing itself to operating on the basis of what was known when the equipment was designed. A factory designed in 1992 embodies the state of knowledge about that type of facility as of 1992.

This last point is important because over a period of time as technology grows, new ideas are developed and appear in more advanced production methods and equipment. Thus, technological change causes existing methods and equipment to become obsolete unless they can somehow be adapted to incorporate newly developed knowledge. Because of this, technological change often causes businesses to abandon older production methods for newer, more efficient techniques in an effort to achieve the goal of maximum profit.

Creative destruction

New technologically advanced machinery and processes cause the disuse and ultimate disappearance of old machinery and methods.

The economist Joseph Schumpeter referred to this process as **creative destruction.** Simply put, creative destruction means that new machinery, production methods, and other fruits of technological change frequently do not exist alongside the old. Rather, the new often replaces the old, causing one area of the economy to grow and prosper, and another to shrink and perhaps ultimately disappear. For example, the introduction of robotics into assembly lines has affected not only the demand for labor, but has also caused some of the formerly used machinery and equipment to become obsolete; and the availability of computerized word processing programs is causing the conventional office typewriter to disappear. Creative destruction can also occur at an international level where an industry in one country is adversely affected by technological advances in that same industry in another country. For example, the U.S. steel industry has been hurt by the development of advanced production techniques for steel in Japan and elsewhere. Application 12.2, ''Recording Enters a New Era, and You Can't Find It on LP,'' gives an account of how technological change is driving the vinyl record off the market. Notice the reference in this reading to the costs

Application 12.2

Recording Enters a New Era, and You Can't Find It on LP

The record, which in its various forms has captured the musical passage of the nation from ragtime to rap, appears to have entered a death spiral. . . .

In 1977, at the height of their popularity, 344 million albums were sold in the United States. By last year [1989] the number had fallen by 90 percent. . . .

For every album sold last year, six compact disks and 13 recorded cassettes were sold. Most record companies have already stopped issuing classical, jazz and country music recordings on vinyl albums, and they are reducing the amount of popular music and rock-and-roll released in album form. . . .

Many record stores have stopped carrying vinyl records because they perceive little demand. And partly because records are less available, consumers are switching to compact disks and cassettes.

Other forces are at work as well. Record stores want to cut their inventory costs and do not like stocking each recording in record, tape and disk. Record companies, not wanting to be caught with obsolete records, are making it more expensive for record stores to return unsold records than to return unsold cassettes or compact disks.

People interested in keeping records alive, like turntable manufacturers, say record companies are promoting compact disks because they can make higher profits from them. The disks sell for as much as $16 at retail, compared with a top price of about $10 for records.

Recording industry officials say production costs of compact disks can be higher than for records. But that is changing as the volume of records declines and the volume of compact disks rises.

Source: Andrew Pollack, "Recording Enters a New Era, and You Can't Find It on LP," *The New York Times,* April 1, 1990, p. 1. Copyright © 1990 by The New York Times Company. Reprinted by permission.

and profits of recording companies and retailers, and to how these are contributing to the disappearance of the long-playing record.

Economic Time, Production, and the Cost of Production

The production technique that a firm chooses is influenced by the time frame in which it views or plans its operations. Generally, a business's production may be regarded as taking place in a short-run or in a long-run period of time. These time periods are not defined in terms of hours, months, or years (the usual manner of measuring time). Rather, they are defined in a more abstract way.

The **short run** is the time frame in which production takes place using some factors that can be varied in amount and some that cannot. Those factors of production that cannot be changed in amount are termed **fixed factors.** Because the amounts of fixed factors cannot be altered as the level of production increases or decreases, their costs do not change, and they must be paid for regardless of whether the firm produces anything or not. Examples of fixed factors might include a building or other production facility, some machinery, and insurance. In essence, the short run is the time

Short run

A production time frame in which some factors of production are fixed and some are variable.

Fixed factors

Factors of production that do not change in amount as the level of production increases or decreases.

period in which fixed factors of production form a boundary within which production takes place.

The **long run** is the time frame in which all factors are regarded as changeable, or variable in amount: there are no fixed factors to limit production. In the long run, a much wider range of production choices is open, since all resources, including buildings and other production facilities, are regarded as alterable.

Suppose that the owners of a restaurant are trying to evaluate the methods and costs of producing meals. If they can alter the number of waiters, tables, and menu selection but not the size of the dining or kitchen area, they are planning in the short run. Those same owners are planning in the long run when they analyze the methods and costs of producing meals as their facilities are expanded, or as they add new restaurants, or, more generally, when they regard their "fixed" facilities as alterable.

This concept of planning in different time frames can be applied to a student's production of a college education. The long run would be a period in which general plans for attaining a degree are formulated and evaluated. In this long-run period, all factors can be altered: the selection of a college, the course of study to be followed, the number of hours to be taken each semester, and the commitment to a part-time job. Once some of these decisions are made and a student is enrolled in particular courses, producing a college education can be viewed in the short run. Each semester could represent a short-run time frame because a student is producing an education within boundaries set by the school attended, the selected course of study, and other factors to which the student is obligated.

In order to make production decisions in either the short run or the long run, a business needs to determine the costs associated with producing various amounts of its output. Because production is planned differently in each time frame, we will examine costs in the short run and long run separately.

Short-Run Costs

In the short run, all factors used in the production of a good or service can be classified as either fixed or variable. Fixed factors, as stated earlier, are those that do not change in amount with a change in the level of production. When a business employs a fixed factor, the cost of that resource is called a **fixed cost.** Thus, the rent or mortgage on a building could be regarded as a fixed cost. Fixed costs must be paid whether the business produces anything or not.

Variable factors are those that increase or decrease in usage as the amount produced increases or decreases. Raw materials, labor, and energy could be regarded as variable factors. **Variable costs** are those costs associated with the use of variable factors. All costs in the short run can be classified as fixed costs or variable costs depending upon whether they refer to the costs of fixed or variable factors.

Long run

A production time frame in which all factors of production are variable in amount.

Fixed cost

The short-run cost of a fixed factor of production.

Variable factors and costs

Factors of production that change in usage as production levels change; variable costs are the costs of using variable factors.

Table 12.4   Monthly Costs of Maintaining Lawns

Total fixed cost does not change as output changes and must be paid even if nothing is produced. Total variable cost is zero when nothing is produced, and both total variable cost and total cost increase as output increases.

Number of Lawns Maintained	Total Fixed Cost (TFC)	Total Variable Cost (TVC)	Total Cost (TC)
0	$400	$ 0	$ 400
1	400	200	600
2	400	225	625
3	400	275	675
4	400	350	750
5	400	475	875
6	400	650	1,050
7	400	895	1,295
8	400	1,220	1,620
9	400	1,670	2,070

A hypothetical example follows in which the short-run costs of operating a lawn maintenance company to service apartment and condominium complexes are calculated and analyzed. The costs given in this example are those for the weekly maintenance of average-size apartment or condominium lawns for one month.

Total Costs   Calculation of the costs of operating this lawn service can begin by adding together all bills that must be paid regardless of the number of lawns maintained: that is, by determining the fixed costs. The fixed costs might include monthly payments on loans for the purchase of mowers and a used truck, and payments for a storage facility, insurance, advertising, and an answering service. Assume that these fixed costs are calculated to be $400 per month.

Total fixed cost

The cost of all fixed factors; total fixed cost does not change as the level of output changes and must be paid even when output is zero.

Table 12.4, which illustrates the costs to the company of maintaining from zero through nine lawns, gives the **total fixed cost** (TFC) for the firm's operations in the second column. Notice that the $400 fixed cost does not change as more or fewer lawns are maintained. Notice also that the $400 per month must be paid even if no lawns are maintained. This is because, regardless of how many lawns are cared for, the fixed factors, and thus the costs of the fixed factors, remain unchanged.

Next, the firm's variable costs must be calculated. Since these are costs that change as the number of lawns maintained changes, variable costs might include expenditures for items such as labor, gasoline, fertilizer and other

Table 12.5   Monthly Total, Average Total, and Marginal Costs of Maintaining Lawns

Average total cost measures the per unit cost at a specific production level, and marginal cost measures the change in total cost from producing an additional unit of output.

Number of Lawns Maintained	Total Cost (TC)	Average Total Cost (ATC)	Marginal Cost (MC)
0	$ 400.00	–	
			$200.00
1	600.00	$600.00	
			25.00
2	625.00	312.50	
			50.00
3	675.00	225.00	
			75.00
4	750.00	187.50	
			125.00
5	875.00	175.00	
			175.00
6	1,050.00	175.00	
			245.00
7	1,295.00	185.00	
			325.00
8	1,620.00	202.50	
			450.00
9	2,070.00	230.00	

Total variable cost

The cost of all variable factors of production; total variable cost increases as the level of output increases, but is zero when output is zero.

Total cost

The cost of acquiring and using all factors of production; total cost is total fixed cost plus total variable cost.

Average total cost

The cost per unit of output produced; total cost divided by the number of units produced.

chemicals, and repair of the truck and mowing equipment. The third column of Table 12.4 gives the company's **total variable cost** (TVC) for maintaining from zero through nine lawns. For example, if this firm were to service four lawns a month, it would face variable costs of $350. Notice that the variable costs are zero if the firm cares for no lawns, that they continually increase as more lawns are maintained, and that they increase significantly when a large number of lawns are maintained. An explanation for this pattern of variable cost increases will be given shortly.

The total cost of maintaining from zero through nine lawns is given in the last column of Table 12.4. The **total cost** (TC) for a particular level of output is all fixed costs plus all variable costs at that level of production. For example, the total cost of maintaining five lawns is $875: $400 in fixed costs plus $475 in variable costs.

Unit Costs   In addition to determining its total costs, a business usually finds it essential to ascertain per unit costs at each level of output. The per unit cost when producing a particular level of output is termed **average total cost** (ATC). Average total cost is found by dividing total cost by the number of units produced.

Table 12.5 gives the total cost of maintaining lawns from Table 12.4 and the average total cost for each individual lawn when a specified number is maintained. For example, the average total cost of servicing each lawn when three are maintained is $225. This is found by dividing the total cost of $675

Table 12.6

Determining Costs for Maintaining Three Lawns a Month

Total cost gives the cost of producing a specified amount of output; average total cost gives the per unit cost; and marginal cost gives the change in total cost of producing one more unit of output.

Total Cost:

$$\text{TFC} + \text{TVC} = \text{TC} \qquad\qquad \text{or} \qquad \$400 + \$275 = \$675$$

Average Total Cost:

$$\frac{\text{TC}}{\text{Number of units of output produced}} = \text{ATC} \qquad \text{or} \qquad \frac{\$675}{3} = \$225$$

Marginal Cost:

$$\frac{\text{Change in TC per additional}}{\text{unit of output}} = \text{MC} \qquad \text{or} \qquad \$675 - \$625 = \$50$$

by three. The average total cost of $185 when seven lawns are maintained is found by dividing the total cost of $1,295 by seven.[5]

Table 12.5 also gives the marginal cost of maintaining lawns. As explained in the previous chapter, **marginal cost** (MC) is the change in total cost from producing one more unit of output—in this case, caring for one more lawn. For example, if no lawns are maintained, the total cost given in Table 12.5 is $400; if one is maintained, total cost increases to $600. Thus, the marginal cost of the first lawn is $200 ($600 − $400). As in the previous chapter, marginal cost is listed midway between the units of output. Table 12.6 summarizes how total cost, average total cost, and marginal cost are calculated and computes these costs for the maintenance of three lawns.

A business could analyze its unit costs in even greater detail. It could, for example, determine its fixed costs per unit (average fixed cost) and variable costs per unit (average variable cost). Although these will not be calculated in this text, can you make these computations at this point?[6]

Marginal cost

The change in total cost when one more (additional) unit of output is produced.

The Pattern of Short-Run Costs

There are patterns to the way total cost, average total cost, and marginal cost behave as production increases in the short run. These patterns can be seen by examining tabular cost figures such as those listed in Tables 12.4 and 12.5. But they can be more easily observed when the short-run costs are graphed.

---

[5] The average total cost of maintaining no lawns is not given since any number divided by zero is undefined.

[6] To help you along, the average fixed cost and average variable cost when five lawns are maintained are $80 and $95, respectively.

Figure 12.1

Total Cost of Maintaining Lawns

Total cost increases slowly when just a few lawns are maintained because few variable factors are needed with the fixed factors. At larger levels of output, total cost increases quickly as more variable factors are needed to compensate for the limitations imposed by the fixed factors.

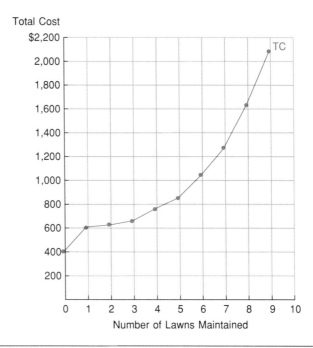

Total Cost Pattern   Figure 12.1 plots the total cost, given in Table 12.5, of maintaining from zero through nine lawns per month. Notice, either from the numbers in Table 12.5 or from the graph in Figure 12.1, that total cost is $400 when output is zero. This, of course, is due to the firm's fixed costs that must be paid regardless of whether production occurs. Notice also that total cost continually increases as more lawns are serviced. Since the fixed cost of maintaining these lawns never changes, this increase is due solely to the change in variable costs.

A closer analysis of total cost shows that in the early stage of production, when few lawns are maintained, total cost increases slowly. But in the latter stage of production, when many lawns are maintained, total cost increases quickly. Why does total cost follow this pattern?

If this company plans to care for just a few lawns, it might manage by hiring one employee (variable factor) to use the truck and mowing equipment (fixed factors). For each lawn maintained, the company would also need to provide other variable factors such as bags for the grass and gasoline for the truck and mowing equipment. However, once labor was hired, the company would not encounter significant increases in the other variable costs to care for each additional lawn if just a few were maintained. Thus, total cost increases slowly for the first few units of output because the increase in variable factors needed to accompany the fixed factors is small.

After a while, maintaining more lawns necessitates more than just an increase in bags and gasoline. Labor costs increase as more workers are needed or as the existing help is paid overtime. As the truck and mowing equipment are used more often, breakdowns occur, causing the cost of repairs to increase. Also, the owner of the firm may expect a higher normal profit in return for the effort and responsibility of increasing production. At some point, these increases in variable costs cause total cost to begin to increase more quickly as production grows.

As production increases to even higher levels, the number of lawns maintained will begin to seriously strain the capabilities of the fixed factors, and variable costs will increase substantially as the firm tries to compensate for the limits of the fixed factors. Perhaps, with the existing mowers and truck, the company might reasonably expect to maintain only six or seven lawns. If it tries to service eight or nine, many variable factors will be needed to fill in for the limitations of the fixed factors. At this point the company may encounter considerably higher variable costs as it rents another truck and more mowers, leases additional storage space, and hires a manager.

In short, total cost increases slowly at first because, with a given amount of fixed factors, few variable factors can increase production significantly. As output levels become larger, total cost increases more rapidly because more variable factors are needed with the fixed factors to increase production. At high levels of production, costs increase very quickly because the fixed factors are approaching the limits of their productivity, and many variable factors are needed to compensate for the fixed factor boundary.

Marginal Cost and Average Total Cost Patterns   Let us next examine the marginal cost (MC) and average total cost (ATC) patterns as production increases. The marginal cost and average total cost data given in Table 12.5 are graphed in Figure 12.2.

Notice that marginal cost, or the change in total cost from maintaining one more lawn, decreases at first and then increases. As with total cost, this drop and rise are due to the behavior of the variable factors as reflected in variable costs. With this in mind, the same reasoning that applies to the explanation of the total cost pattern applies to the explanation of the marginal cost pattern.

To service the first lawn, the marginal cost is $200. If you refer to Table 12.4, you will discover that this equals the change in variable cost associated with maintaining one lawn rather than no lawns. Much of this $200 increase is probably due to the hiring of labor. To maintain a second lawn, the marginal cost is only $25. This decrease in marginal cost occurs because the additional variable factors needed to maintain the second lawn cost the firm

Figure 12.2

Marginal Cost and Average Total Cost of Maintaining Lawns

Both marginal cost and average total cost fall and then rise as production increases. When marginal cost is less than average total cost, it pulls average total cost down; when marginal cost is greater than average total cost, it pulls average total cost up.

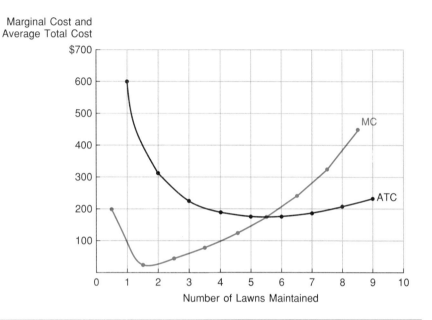

only $25. As explained earlier, at this point there will be only a slight increase in the use of some variable inputs such as gasoline and plastic grass bags.

When a third lawn is maintained, marginal cost begins to rise because of the increase in variable factors needed to increase production. And as more and more lawns are cared for, marginal cost increases more rapidly. This is due to the large amounts of variable factors that are required to compensate for the limits placed on production by the fixed factors.

Return to Figure 12.2 and observe the average total cost curve. Average total cost decreases and then increases with more production. Why is this so?

The cost per unit falls initially because marginal cost is lower than average total cost. When marginal cost is less than average total cost, it pulls average total cost down. When marginal cost becomes greater than average total cost, it pulls average total cost up.[7] Thus, average total cost behaves the way it

---

[7] If average total cost falls when marginal cost is less than average total cost and rises when marginal cost is greater than average total cost, then, as Figure 12.2 shows, marginal cost must cross, or equal, average total cost at minimum average total cost.

does because of the behavior of marginal cost. You encounter this relationship between marginal and average values in determining your average in a course as you take additional exams. If you make a grade on an exam (remember: each additional exam that you take is a marginal exam) that is lower than your average, the marginal exam will pull your average down. If you make a grade higher than your average on a marginal exam, your average will increase. For example, if you have an average of 93 percent in your economics course, and you earn a grade of 70 percent on your next exam, your average will fall. On the other hand, if you earn a grade of 98 percent on your next exam, your average will rise. "Test Your Understanding: Calculating Costs and Averages" provides an opportunity to further explore the average-marginal relationship and to determine short-run costs.

The Law of Diminishing Returns

Law of Diminishing Returns

As additional units of a variable factor are added to a fixed factor, beyond some point the additional product from each additional unit of the variable factor decreases.

Underlying all of these short-run cost patterns is a basic principle termed the **Law of Diminishing Returns.** This law states that as additional units of a variable factor are added to a fixed factor, beyond some point the additional product from each additional unit of the variable factor decreases. This is easily illustrated with an example.

Assume that you own a small restaurant and plan to begin hiring people to prepare and serve meals. The dining room, outfitted with tables and other restaurant furniture, and a fully equipped kitchen are the fixed factors, and the labor used to work in the restaurant is a variable factor.

If one person is hired to work in the restaurant, that person working alone will be able to prepare and serve a certain number of meals per day. If a second person is hired to work, the two persons together can interact, specialize, and work more efficiently. One person can prepare meals and the other can serve them. Together the two will probably more than double the number of meals that can be prepared and served by one person alone. If you hire a third person, work can be further divided, and the number of meals may again significantly increase.

At some point, perhaps after the fourth person is hired, the number of meals that can be prepared and served per day will no longer proportionately increase with additional workers. That is, the number of *additional* meals prepared and served after hiring a fourth worker will not be as great as the number of *additional* meals prepared and served after hiring the third worker. Four workers cannot operate as efficiently as three because the fixed facility is becoming crowded. In other words, the boundary imposed by the fixed factors begins to limit the productivity of the variable factor. When this occurs, and the additional output from hiring an additional worker begins to fall, diminishing returns have set in.

Beyond this point, as more (five, six, seven) people are hired, the *additional* work accomplished by each will further diminish. They will become less efficient, and the fixed factors will more severely limit their full utilization.

Test Your Understanding

Calculating Costs and Averages[a]

[a]Answers can be found at the back of the book.

1. A student's grade in a Civil War history class at a state university is determined by averaging the percentage scores of four examinations. Answer the following questions for a student who earns a grade of 92 percent on the first examination, 84 percent on the second, 85 percent on the third, and 91 percent on the fourth.
   a. The student's average after the first examination is _____ .
   b. The student's average in the course after the second examination will _____ (rise or fall) because the marginal score from the second examination is _____ (higher or lower) than the average after the first exam. The average after the second examination is _____ .
   c. The student's average in the course after the third examination will _____ (rise or fall) because the marginal score from the third exam is _____ (higher or lower) than the average after the second examination. The average after the third examination is _____ .

   d. The student's average in the course after the fourth examination will _____ (rise or fall) because the marginal score from the fourth examination is _____ (higher or lower) than the average from three exams. The average after the fourth examination, or for the course, is _____ .

2. The manager of a college food service has determined that the daily fixed cost of operation is $855. She has also calculated that the total variable cost for preparing 900 meals is $1,170; for preparing 1,800 meals, it is $2,565; and when 2,700 meals are prepared, total variable cost equals $5,328. Given this information, the average total cost per meal when 900 meals are prepared is _____ , average total cost when 1,800 are prepared is _____ , and when 2,700 meals are prepared each costs _____ on the average.

3. Assume that the following table applies to the costs of completing the short-form federal income tax return for senior citizens by a small accounting service. Fill in this table.

Output	Total Fixed Cost	Total Variable Cost	Total Cost	Average Total Cost	Marginal Cost
0	$80	$ 0	$ _____	—	$ _____
1	_____	40	_____	$ _____	
2	_____	60	_____	_____	_____
3	_____	70	_____	_____	_____
4	_____	100	_____	_____	_____
5	_____	150	_____	_____	_____
6	_____	220	_____	_____	_____
7	_____	340	_____	_____	_____
8	_____	520	_____	_____	_____

It would, incidentally, be possible to hire so many restaurant workers that they would get in each other's way, causing the additional output to become negative.[8]

The Law of Diminishing Returns governs all production in the short run. For example, when a student tries to produce sufficient knowledge to pass an exam by studying for an extended and uninterrupted period of time, the Law of Diminishing Returns takes effect. During the first few hours of reading and reviewing, each hour will produce more additional knowledge than the hour before as the material is comprehended. After a while, however, as the student becomes tired and the fixed factor of the mind approaches its limit, diminishing returns take effect, and each additional hour of study is less productive than the one before it. Can you use the Law of Diminishing Returns to explain why it is better to study on a consistent basis for shorter periods of time than it is to cram the night before an exam?

While the Law of Diminishing Returns and the resulting pattern of costs given here are common to all production in the short run, cost figures in the real world, and their graphs, may not be as smooth and clear-cut as our examples. In addition, the point at which diminishing returns sets in differs from product to product. All short-run production can, however, be explained in terms of these patterns: the limitation of the fixed factors, which gives the short run its definition, causes diminishing returns to occur and thus causes marginal, average total, and total costs to rise in the latter stages of production.

Long-Run Costs

The long run has been defined as the time frame in which a business regards all of its factors of production as variable and none as fixed. Thus, calculating the cost of production in the long run means determining the cost of a given level of output if a business can alter the amounts of any and all of its resources. In the long run, production costs are not divided between fixed costs and variable costs because all costs are variable.

Table 12.7 gives the long-run costs of producing from zero through 100,000 units of an item by a hypothetical company. For the sake of simplicity, assume that the product is produced in blocks of 10,000 at a time. The second column of Table 12.7 gives the **long-run total cost** of producing from zero through ten blocks of 10,000 each. Notice that long-run total cost increases as more is produced, and that, since there are no fixed factors or costs, it is zero when nothing is produced.

Long-run total cost can be used to calculate **long-run average total cost,** which is determined in the same manner as short-run average total cost: total cost is divided by the quantity of output produced. In Table 12.7,

Long-run total cost, average total cost, and marginal cost

Total cost, per unit cost, and cost per additional unit of output, respectively; calculated for production when all inputs are variable, or in the long run.

---

[8] This means that a point can be reached where more would be produced if some of the workers would quit.

Table 12.7

Long-Run Total Cost, Average Total Cost, and Marginal Cost

Long-run total cost is the total expenditure for each level of output in the long run. Long-run average total cost measures the per unit cost; and long-run marginal cost measures the cost of producing an additional unit of output in the long run.

Output (Blocks of 10,000)	Long-Run Total Cost (LRTC) (Blocks of 10,000)	Long-Run Average Total Cost (LRATC) (Per Block of 10,000)	Long-Run Marginal Cost (LRMC) (Per Block of 10,000)
0	$ 0	—	
1	400,000	$400,000	$400,000
2	500,000	250,000	100,000
3	600,000	200,000	100,000
4	700,000	175,000	100,000
5	875,000	175,000	175,000
6	1,050,000	175,000	175,000
7	1,400,000	200,000	350,000
8	2,000,000	250,000	600,000
9	2,700,000	300,000	700,000
10	3,500,000	350,000	800,000

long-run average total cost refers to the cost per block of 10,000. **Long-run marginal cost** can also be calculated from long-run total cost. It is found by determining the change in long-run total cost as one more unit is produced. In this case, where the relevant unit is a block of output, long-run marginal cost is the marginal cost of increasing production by a block of 10,000.

Economists typically focus on long-run average total cost in analyzing the pattern of long-run costs. Figure 12.3 plots the long-run average total cost from Table 12.7. In Figure 12.3, long-run average total cost at first decreases as the level of output increases. With an ability to vary production facilities that were fixed in the short run, the company finds that, initially, the cost per unit drops. At some point long-run average total cost reaches a minimum, and, in this example, stays at that level as output continues to grow. But after a while, as production grows even further, the cost per unit of output increases. This decreasing, constant, and increasing cost pattern is typical of long-run average total cost.

Economies of scale

Occur when the increasing size of production in the long run causes the per unit cost of production to fall.

Economies of Scale, Diseconomies of Scale, and Constant Returns to Scale
When long-run average total cost decreases in the initial stages of production, a firm is experiencing **economies of scale.** This means that the larger size (scale) of the operation permits the business to produce each unit of

Figure 12.3   Long-Run Average Total Cost

A typical long-run average total cost curve follows a pattern of decreasing, constant, and increasing per unit costs.

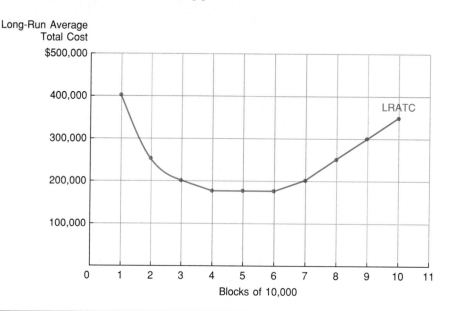

output more cheaply than it could at a smaller size of operation. What causes economies of scale to occur?

As a firm produces a larger output, it is feasible for it to make greater use of highly specialized and efficient inputs that allow it to produce at a lower per unit cost. A large company can employ more assembly-line techniques, more equipment especially suited for performing a narrow range of tasks, more computer systems specifically tailored to its needs, and more specialized personnel. For example, restaurants that are part of a chain are able to utilize a number of these efficient or cost-saving opportunities. Food can be prepared in assembly-line fashion at a central processing plant under the supervision of one highly skilled chef, sent frozen to each restaurant, and heated by unskilled labor for the customer.

Economies of scale also permit individual managers to focus all of their attention on specific subparts of a company's operation. In a smaller business, any one of these subparts might not be important enough to warrant full-time consideration and would compete with other aspects of the operation for a manager's attention. With a person's complete attention directed to a particular task in a business, that person may become more efficient, thereby lowering per unit costs for the company. Finally, as a business becomes larger, it may receive quantity discounts on some resources that it buys and may be able to negotiate lower interest rates on money that it borrows.

Unit cost savings, or efficiency gains, from economies of scale as larger levels of output are produced have been a frequent argument in favor of allowing mergers between competing sellers in the same market. Mergers are covered in more detail in Chapter Fourteen.

Diseconomies of scale

Occur when the increasing size of production in the long run causes the per unit cost of production to rise.

When per unit costs increase in the latter stage of long-run production, a firm is said to be experiencing **diseconomies of scale.** In this case, the size or scale of the operation has become so large that the cost per unit of output increases. Diseconomies of scale generally arise because the large size of a company makes control over its operations difficult. As the organization grows and the chain of command lengthens and becomes more complex, it might be necessary to hire more managers at all levels, thereby increasing the cost of output. With a longer chain of command, authority and responsibility may become overly decentralized and disjointed, causing factors of production to be wasted due to a lack of accountability or poor control. Costs may also be affected by the amount of time required to pass information and commands through such a large organization. Perhaps it is diseconomies of scale that account for inefficiencies in the federal government.

Constant returns to scale

Occur in the range of production levels in which long-run average total cost neither increases nor decreases but is constant.

Between the outputs where economies of scale end and diseconomies of scale begin is a range of production where long-run average total cost neither increases nor decreases. Throughout this range the firm is said to be experiencing **constant returns to scale,** which means that the operation has become so large that it has exhausted all available economies of scale, but not large enough to encounter diseconomies of scale.

Application 12.3, "Gut Instinct," illustrates how a knowledge of economies of scale helped one physician to develop a successful practice. What economies of scale are found in this example? Can you identify any potential diseconomies of scale that would cause long-run average total cost to increase?

Many other real-life examples attest to the existence of decreasing, constant, and increasing long-run average total costs. This does not mean, however, that every company faces a long-run average total cost curve that looks exactly like that in Figure 12.3. Instead, the long-run average total cost of each firm's product differs in the length and strength of its decreasing, constant, and increasing ranges. A company producing automobiles, for example, will have a different shape to its long-run average total cost curve than will a fast food chain producing hamburgers. Figure 12.4 gives the three stages of long-run production costs.

Summary

The greatest portion of measured output in the U.S. economy comes from business firms. Since so many different firms produce different goods and services, categories have been developed for classifying production. Pro-

Application 12.3

Gut Instinct

As a graduate student in health economics at Johns Hopkins University, Mr Ira Rutkow wrote his doctoral thesis on the coming glut of surgeons in the United States. When he later qualified as a surgeon himself, Dr Rutkow's experiences proved that earning a crust was not easy. So he decided to apply some business savvy.

The biggest single market for surgical skills in America is in the repair of hernias, with over 600,000 operations a year. Dr Rutkow and his partner now do only hernia surgery. Helped by some clever marketing, their fortunes have improved dramatically.

This year [1987] Dr Rutkow and partner will make more than $1½m, performing nearly 1,000 hernia operations at an average all-in cost of $1,700 apiece—up from 600 operations in 1986. Such volumes allow economies of scale which enable Dr Rutkow to charge less than many neighbouring hospitals do for similar surgery. He says that, with so much practice, he can perform a better hernia operation than surgeons who only do a few such operations each year.

To keep the patients coming, Dr Rutkow advertises his Hernia Centres heavily both on television and in newspapers near to his five offices in New York and New Jersey. His marketing stroke of genius is a toll-free telephone number: 1-800-HERNIAS.

Some of Dr Rutkow's fellow surgeons frown on such marketing ploys. Those who do are likely to find his latest idea even more distasteful: franchising. Eventually Dr Rutkow would like to see other doctors and surgeons using his business techniques.

One snag is quality control. Doctors cannot be taught surgical technique in the same way as teenagers are trained to cook McDonald's hamburgers or mechanics to install Midas mufflers. Until he finds a way to protect his reputation, his business and (at the same time) his malpractice insurance, Dr Rutkow's franchising plans will have to remain an entrepreneurial pipe-dream.

Source: "Gut Instinct," *The Economist*, September 5, 1987, p. 58. © 1987 *The Economist*, distributed by Special Features. Reprinted with permission.

ducing sectors, one such category, is broad in scope and includes the services, manufacturing, and other sectors. Classifying production into industries is a narrower type of categorization. An industry is a group of firms producing similar products. The similarity is either in the processes used or because buyers regard the products as substitutes.

A production function shows the output that results when a particular group of inputs is combined in a certain way. Firms have a choice of production functions but seek the least-cost, or efficient, method of producing the desired quantity and quality of output in order to maximize profit. The greater the dependence on labor, the more labor-intensive is the production; the greater the dependence on capital, the more capital-intensive is the production.

The development of new productive machinery and techniques is the result of technological change. Technological change can lead to creative

Figure 12.4   The Three Phases of the Long-Run Average Total Cost Curve

The long-run average total cost curve goes through three phases: a decreasing per unit cost phase caused by economies of scale; a phase of constant returns to scale where per unit costs neither increase nor decrease; and a phase where per unit costs increase due to diseconomies of scale.

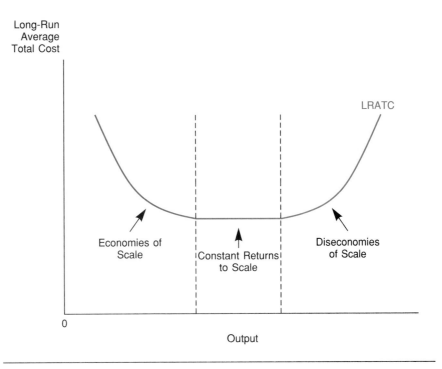

destruction: as new machinery and methods cause others to become obsolete, some areas of an economy grow while some decline.

The choice of a method of production is influenced by the time frame in which a business plans its operations. The short run is a time period in which some factors of production are variable in amount and some are fixed. The capabilities of the fixed factors, because they cannot be changed, serve as a boundary within which production takes place. The long run is a time period in which all factors are regarded as variable.

In the short run, the total cost of producing a certain level of output is found by adding total fixed cost and total variable cost. Total fixed cost is the same regardless of how much is produced; total variable cost increases as production increases. Average total cost is the cost per unit of output at a given level of production and is found by dividing total cost by the number of units of output produced. Marginal cost is the change in total cost resulting from the production of an additional unit of output.

In the short run, total cost increases slowly at low levels of production and rapidly at high levels of production. Average total cost decreases and then increases, as does marginal cost. These patterns are the result of the way in which variable factors increase as production increases. At high levels of production, large amounts of variable factors are needed to compensate for the limits imposed by the fixed factors. Underlying these patterns of short-run costs is the Law of Diminishing Returns, which says that as a variable factor of production is added to fixed factors, beyond some point the additional product from each additional unit of the variable factor will decrease.

Long-run average total cost illustrates the pattern of costs in the long run. The shape of its curve is the result of economies of scale that occur in the early stages of long-run production and cause the cost per unit of output to drop, constant returns to scale where average total cost stays the same, and diseconomies of scale that occur in the late stages of long-run production and cause the cost per unit of output to increase.

Key Terms and Concepts

Production	Total fixed cost
Sectors	Total variable cost
Industry	Total cost
Production function	Average total cost
Labor-intensive production	Marginal cost
Capital-intensive production	Law of Diminishing Returns
Efficient method of production	Patterns of short-run and long-run costs
Technology	
Creative destruction	Long-run total, average total, and marginal costs
Short run	
Long run	Economies and diseconomies of scale
Fixed factors and costs	Constant returns to scale
Variable factors and costs	

Review Questions

1. A friend has just explained that, as far as the costs of operating a business are concerned, short-run costs are the costs that are incurred within the current year and long-run costs are all costs that are incurred for more than one year. As a student of economics, do you agree with your friend's opinion? Why?

2. The short-run average total cost curve and the long-run average total cost curve are similarly shaped. What causes the short-run average total cost curve

to assume its shape? What causes the long-run average total cost curve to assume its shape?

3. When marginal cost is less than average total cost, average total cost decreases. When marginal cost is greater than average total cost, average total cost increases. Why is this so?

4. Why does a firm incur fixed costs over the short run when its output is zero, and why do fixed costs not change as the level of output changes? Why do a firm's short-run total variable costs increase slowly at smaller levels of output and rapidly at larger levels of output?

5. What is the Law of Diminishing Returns and why does it affect short-run but not long-run production? How will the Law of Diminishing Returns affect the productivity of each additional student who is washing cars at a local gas station to raise money for charity? Why does this effect occur?

6. Complete the following table on short-run costs. From the information in the completed table, plot a total cost curve on the left-hand graph below and an average total cost curve and a marginal cost curve on the right-hand graph.

Output	Total Fixed Cost	Total Variable Cost	Total Cost	Average Total Cost	Marginal Cost
0	$ _____	$ _____	$100	—	$ _____
1	_____	_____	150	$ _____	_____
2	_____	_____	180	_____	_____
3	_____	_____	210	_____	_____
4	_____	_____	280	_____	_____
5	_____	_____	400	_____	_____
6	_____	_____	600	_____	_____

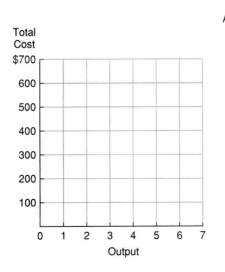

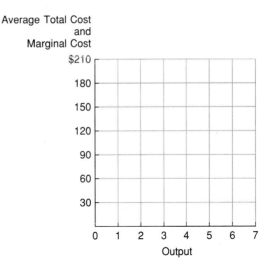

7. Identify the three phases of a long-run average total cost curve. What is the reason for the behavior of long-run average total cost in each phase?

Discussion Questions

1. Can you construct a production function for earning an "A" in this course?
    a. What are the necessary inputs?
    b. How much of each input is required?
    c. How are the inputs combined?

2. Suppose that a particular product is produced in Country A using labor-intensive techniques and in Country B using capital-intensive techniques. What are some possible explanations for the difference in the techniques used in the two countries?

3. Technological change causes creative destruction: because of new technology, one area of an economy may expand while another contracts and perhaps disappears. Give some examples of the process of creative destruction on the national level and on the international level. How is the process carried out in each of your examples?

4. The Law of Diminishing Returns was introduced in this chapter and the Law of Diminishing Marginal Utility was introduced in Chapter Eleven. How are these two laws similar and how are they different? Are there any similarities between a business utilizing additional units of a variable input and an individual consuming additional units of, say, pizza?

5. Indicate whether each of the following is probably a fixed factor or a variable factor in the short run.
    a. Raw materials going into a production process
    b. The steam heat required to keep the pipes in a factory from freezing
    c. Electricity used to run machinery and equipment
    d. The only person in a company who knows the trade secret formula to a highly profitable product

6. It was recently proposed that over 100 towns surrounding the city of St. Louis, Missouri, be consolidated into a few larger towns. What economies of scale affecting fire, police, administrative, and other services might result from the consolidation? What diseconomies of scale might result from the creation of a few large towns in place of many small ones?

7. How might a business's ability to take advantage of economies of scale affect the price it charges for its product, its profitability, and its competitiveness with rival sellers? What concerns could diseconomies of scale create for pricing, profitability, and competitiveness?

Critical Thinking Case 12

■ Good to the Last Condo

Critical Thinking Skills	Identifying criteria used for decision making
	Applying a concept to another context
Economic Concepts	Production functions
	Creative destruction
	Long-run and short-run production

Hoboken, N.J. . . . Once this city was a place where factories outnumbered telephone booths, longshoremen walked to work and people sitting on stoops knew it would rain when they smelled the coffee brewing at the Maxwell House factory on the Hudson River waterfront.

Now most of the factories have been replaced by condominiums and the piers are being razed to make more room for more condos.

And today [June 1990] the conglomerate that owns Maxwell House announced that it would phase out the plant by the spring of 1992. . . .

Today, in the brick factory on Hudson Street and Sinatra Drive, the president of Maxwell House, Raymond G. Viault, told hundreds of workers that Hoboken had lost out to a plant in Jacksonville, Fla., in a competition to see which plant would live and which would die. . . .

At a news conference later, Mr. Viault said Jacksonville had been chosen because labor costs there were about 20 percent lower than in Hoboken, where many workers earn $15 to $20 an hour.

He also said the Florida plant was closer to a can factory that the company owns in Alabama and to the coffee plantations of Central America.

"We are acting to eliminate a costly excess in processing capacity," he said. "We have the excess because people simply aren't drinking as much coffee as they used to." . . .

On the surface the plant here appeared better situated. It is 11 years younger than Jacksonville. It is on 22 acres; Jacksonville has 4. The company has recently invested millions of dollars for upgrading, and Hoboken has 600 workers, as opposed to 400 at Jacksonville.

Recently, the company was offered a substantial package of incentives by the city and the Port Authority of New York and New Jersey, which operates the piers through which the millions of pounds of coffee beans are transported. . . .

The company denied that it had any intention of selling the property or developing it, even though dozens of office and residential buildings have been started along the 18-mile waterfront from the George Washington Bridge to Liberty State Park in Jersey City. The piers a few blocks south of the plant are being torn down for a sprawling complex of apartments, offices and marinas by the Port Authority.

"The value of the property in terms of our own plans is assumed to be zero," said Mr. Viault. He added that the cost of razing the buildings and preparing the land for sale would equal its market value. . . .

Questions

1. What factors appear to underlie this firm's decision to produce coffee in Jacksonville rather than Hoboken?

2. If this firm could choose any technology, do you think it would prefer labor-intensive or capital-intensive production? Why? Why do you think this firm did not make some changes in Hoboken and continue to operate that plant?

3. How can the concept of creative destruction apply to the area around, and economy of, Hoboken?

4. Can you explain why this choice by Maxwell House would be classified by an economist as decision making in the long run?

Source: Excerpted from Anthony DePalma, "Why One Plant Dies, One Survives," *The New York Times*, June 28, 1990, p. C19. Copyright © 1990 by The New York Times Company. Excerpted by permission.

Suggested Readings

Leslie Cookenboo, Jr., "Production and Cost Functions for Oil Pipe Lines," *Price Theory in Action,* eds. Donald S. Watson and Malcolm Getz (Boston: Houghton Mifflin Co., 1981), pp. 110–117. Reprinted from Leslie Cookenboo, Jr., *Crude Oil Pipe-Lines and Competition in the Oil Industry* (Cambridge, Mass.: Harvard University Press, 1955), pp. 13–24, 27–32.
Explains production functions, the behavior of short-run and long-run costs, economies of scale, and other topics relating to oil pipelines.

"Factory of the Future: A Survey," *The Economist,* May 30, 1987.
A series of short articles on computerized production and other changes in manufacturing technology.

John B. Judis, "Mission Impossible," *The New York Times Magazine,* September 25, 1988, pp. 30–33, 50–51, 54.
Examines technology-related and other problems the U.S. Postal Service faces in producing its product.

Edwin Mansfield, "Ch. 2: Technological Change and Productivity Growth," *Technological Change* (New York: W. W. Norton and Co., 1971), pp. 9–38.
Explores the relationship between technological change and production functions, factors influencing the rate of technological change, changes in productivity, measures of technological change, and other subjects.

David F. Noble, "The Wedding of Science to the Useful Arts – I: The Rise of Science-Based Industry," *America by Design* (Oxford: Oxford University Press, 1977), pp. 3–19.
Examines the early growth of science-based industries and the role of technology in the development of industries.

James L. Pappas and Mark Hirschey, "Ch. 7: Cost Analysis," *Fundamentals of Managerial Economics,* 3d ed. (Hinsdale, Ill.: The Dryden Press, 1989), especially pp. 245–286.
A more advanced analysis of many of the cost concepts introduced in this chapter.

David J. Rachman, et al., "The Productivity Paradox," and "The Portable Executive," *Business Week on Business Today* (New York: McGraw-Hill Publishing Co., 1990), pp. 30–38, 88–94. Articles on computerized production and how technology has changed work.

Bill Saporito, "Cutting Costs Without Cutting People," *Fortune,* May 25, 1987, pp. 26–32. Discusses cost reducing strategies that may be more efficient than reducing the size of a firm's work force.

Roger W. Schmenner, "Before You Build a *Big* Factory," *Harvard Business Review,* July–August 1976, pp. 100–104. Points out that economies of scale can be specified more narrowly to refer to economies of volume and/or capacity and/or process technology.

E. F. Schumacher, "Part III, Ch. 2: Social and Economic Problems Calling for the Development of Intermediate Technology," *Small Is Beautiful* (New York: Harper and Row, 1973), pp. 161–179. An argument that the needs of a less developed economy might be best met by not using the most sophisticated, advanced technology available for production.

Chapter Thirteen

Competition and Market Structures

The winner in markets with a great deal of competition is the consumer: prices are lower and goods and services are produced more efficiently.

Source: ©1989 John Gastaldo/The Jersey Journal.

Chapter Objectives

1. To introduce the concept that a firm's pricing and profit behavior are related to the amount of competition it faces in the market.

2. To define what is meant by a market and explain how its boundaries are determined.

3. To give the basic characteristics of the four market structures: pure competition, monopolistic competition, oligopoly, and monopoly.

4. To explain an individual firm's demand curve, pricing behavior, and nonprice competitive behavior for each of the four market structures.

5. To explain how a firm's long-run pricing and profit behavior and the degree of efficiency it achieves are affected by the amount of competition it faces in a market.

6. To develop, in an appendix, the explanation of how a firm determines its profit-maximizing price and output level.

There are over 17 million businesses in the U.S. economy, each behaving differently with respect to the control it has over the prices it charges, the types of nonprice decisions it makes, and its ability to continually earn economic profit (profit beyond what is required to stay in business). Some firms have great control over the prices their products command, while others have little or no control. Some firms spend millions of dollars on advertising, public relations, and other methods of bringing attention to their products; other firms spend nothing. Some firms have the ability to earn economic profit in the long run, while other firms, no matter how well they are managed, have no such prospect.

These differences in pricing and nonprice behavior and in ability to earn economic profit over the long run are influenced by the type and severity of competition that individual firms face from other sellers in a market. All other things being equal, the greater the competition in a market, the less control a firm in that market has over the price its product commands, and the less likely the firm is to earn economic profit on an ongoing basis. The less the competition in a market, the greater the control an individual firm has over the price it receives for its product, and the more likely the firm is to earn economic profit over the long run.

Market structures

A classification system for grouping markets according to the degree and type of competition among sellers.

The degree of competition and the exact form it assumes differ from market to market. However, patterns can be identified that allow us to group sellers into different classes of markets called **market structures.** Economists have adopted four market structures to represent different competitive situations: pure competition, monopolistic competition, oligopoly, and monopoly. These four structures encompass a spectrum of competitive conditions. At one end of the spectrum is pure competition, where the competitive pressure is the strongest, and at the other end is monopoly, where there is no direct competition. In between are monopolistic competition, which is closer to pure competition, and oligopoly, which is closer to monopoly.

In this chapter we will analyze each of the four market structures. Particular attention will be paid to the major characteristics that distinguish each type of market from the others, and to how those characteristics affect a firm's behavior and profit expectations. But before discussing the market structures, it is necessary to distinguish between a market and an industry.

Markets vs. Industries

Industry
A group of firms producing similar products.

Market
Firms are in the same market when they produce similar products and compete for the same buyers.

We know from Chapter Twelve that an **industry** is composed of a group of firms that produce similar products. A **market,** where buyers and sellers come together, is also composed of firms producing similar products. Since sellers in an industry and in a market both offer similar products, can we say that sellers in the same industry are also automatically in the same market? The answer is no. For a group of sellers to be included in the same industry, they need only produce similar products; but to be included in the same market, they must produce similar products, *and* they must compete for the same group of buyers. A motion picture theater in downtown Chicago and one in Manhattan are in the same industry, but because they do not compete for the same buyers they are not in the same market.

The boundaries of a market are determined by geographic and product substitution considerations. The geographic boundary of a market depends upon the size of the area from which buyers are drawn. In this regard, markets may be local, regional, national, or international. An ice cream shop that draws its customers from a particular neighborhood or town competes in a local market, whereas an automobile manufacturer is in an international market because it competes for buyers across national borders. It is interesting to note that as international trade has become more important to the U.S. economy, domestic firms have increasingly found themselves in international markets.

The boundary of a market is also defined by product substitutability; that is, sellers are in the same market if buyers in that market view their products as substitutes. If a tape deck produced by one seller is seen as substitutable for that produced by a second seller, then the tape decks of those two sellers compete in the same market. If a tape deck is seen as substitutable for a compact disc player, a stereo radio, or a video cassette recorder, then all those items are in the same market.

The question of which products and geographic areas are included in a market is important because the size of a market influences the degree of competition that a firm faces: the larger the market, the greater the number of sellers and the greater the competition. However, the definition of a market can be controversial because the boundaries of a particular market are uncertain, and people approaching the market definition question from different perspectives may have different opinions as to what constitutes the geographic and product dimensions of a market. For example, if you ask several friends to define the market that your local movie theater is in, you may receive several varying responses. One person might define the market in a very narrow sense and include only local movie theaters, while another person might regard the relevant market as the market for entertainment, and include all theatrical, sporting, musical, and other such events within 50 miles.

One place where the controversy about the boundaries of a market becomes important is in courts of law hearing cases on alleged violations of the antitrust laws. The antitrust laws, which are designed to protect competition in markets, will be more fully discussed in Chapter Fourteen. For now, however, we can note that one type of antitrust case heard by the courts involves a firm or other organization accused of taking over, or monopolizing, a market. In cases such as this, the definition of the boundaries of the market is of critical importance, since the more broadly the market is defined, the smaller will be the firm's or organization's control, and the easier it will be for the defense to argue that the market has not been monopolized.

One problem that a court hearing an antitrust case faces is that the accused will likely present one definition of its market's boundaries, and the accuser will likely present another. The court must then determine which definition is correct and, partly on that basis, decide on the guilt or innocence of the accused. An example of this type of market definition problem is given in Application 13.1, "Defining the Boundaries of a Market: *The NCAA Case.*" This excerpt from the court record of that case shows some of the considerations that were important to the court in determining which definition of the relevant market to accept when deciding on the legality of National Collegiate Athletic Association control over televising college football games.

The Market Structures

It was noted earlier that the degree of competition that exists in a market influences a business's behavior—the prices it charges, the profit it makes, and the amount of nonprice competition in which it engages. It was also noted that, in order to analyze the effects of competition, economists have created four market models, called market structures, each representative of a different degree of competition: pure competition, monopolistic competition, oligopoly, and monopoly.

Each of these market models has a set of characteristics that differentiates it from the other market models. For example, certain features are associated with a monopoly structure and others with oligopoly. The distinguishing

Application 13.1

Defining the Boundaries
of a Market: *The NCAA Case*

In 1982, a suit brought by the Board of Regents of the University of Oklahoma and the University of Georgia Athletic Association against the National Collegiate Athletic Association over the NCAA's control of the televising of college football games went to trial. In this trial were two definitions of the relevant market: the universities' definition that the market is televising live college football, and the NCAA's definition that the market is all broadcast programming. The court's conclusion and some of its reasoning are given below.

The Court concludes that the relevant market for testing whether the NCAA exercises monopoly power is live college football television. This conclusion is based on the following facts. . . .

. . . The vast majority, some 75%, of intercollegiate football games are played on Saturday afternoon. On Saturdays, college football television is free of competition from the programming which logically is the most substitutable; professional football. . . . The games to be broadcast are quite clearly a perishable item. Once the game is over and the score of the game is made known to college football fans, viewers are not nearly so likely to watch the game on a delayed telecast basis. . . . To suggest that college football competes with the complete spectrum of broadcast programming is to ignore the clear fact that Saturday afternoon is the only time at which this perishable product is uniformly available to the broadcaster.

Another factor supporting this conclusion . . . is that on Saturday afternoons the type of programming against which the NCAA football telecasts compete is qualitatively different from that available at other times of the week. . . . It is generally agreed that the quality of Saturday afternoon television, excepting the sports programming, is lower than that offered during other times of the week. . . .

There are also unique characteristics of the product itself. . . . NCAA football is a unique product because of its history and tradition, the color and pageantry of the event, and the interest of college alumni in the football success of their alma mater. . . .

The defendant's theory that the relevant market is all broadcast programming is untenable. College football simply does not compete with shows such as "M*A*S*H," "Dallas" or "Saturday Night Live." . . . To accept the defendant's theory of relevant market is to say that every type of programming seen on network television competes with every other type of programming. This is simply not so. Programming patterns vary not only by day of the week, but by the time of day. The audiences for different types of programming have extremely diverse demographic characteristics. The types of advertisers who buy commercial time vary greatly depending on the type of programming. . . .

Source: *Board of Regents of the University of Oklahoma* v. *National Collegiate Athletic Association*, 546 F. Supp. 1276 (1982), pp. 1297, 1299.

characteristics of each of the four market models center around three basic areas. The first area concerns the number of sellers in the market. A market may have one seller, thousands of sellers, or some number in between. The second area concerns whether the product sold in the market is identical from seller to seller, or whether each seller offers a differentiated product. If a firm can distinguish its product from those of its competitors through size, color, or any other attribute, then nonprice competition can arise. The third area concerns the ease or difficulty with which firms can enter or leave the market. It may be extremely easy for new firms to begin selling in the market, or it may be virtually impossible. The characteristics that emerge in each of these three areas are important for defining the amount of competition that exists in a market.

The remainder of this chapter is devoted to defining each of the four market structures and analyzing the behavior of firms in each structure. For each structure we will evaluate the control that a business has over the price it charges, the influence and effect of nonprice competition, and whether firms tend to make an economic profit and operate efficiently in the long run.

Pure Competition

Characteristics of Pure Competition

**Purely competitive
markets**

Markets with large
numbers of independent
sellers producing identical
products, and with easy
entry into and exit from
the market.

Barriers to entry

Factors that keep firms
from entering a market;
can be financial, legal,
technical, or other
barriers.

Purely competitive markets are those that have a very large number of sellers acting independently of each other. The outputs produced by these sellers are virtually identical: buyers cannot distinguish the product of one seller from that of another. Entry by business firms into purely competitive markets is easy, as is exit from the market. There are no legal restrictions, fees, impossibly high capital requirements, patents, or other **barriers to entry.**

Although it is difficult to find many cases of pure competition, the markets for agricultural crops such as corn, oats, and wheat have provided classic examples. In each of these markets there are thousands of independent suppliers, and the output of any one supplier is indistinguishable from the output of any other. Entry into these markets is easy because little is required to grow a crop.

The market in which a corporation's common stock is traded may also provide an example of pure competition. With companies such as General Motors, Exxon, and AT&T, millions of shares of stock are held by thousands of owners. Each share of a company's stock is identical to each other share, and it is easy to enter the market to buy and sell.

Behavior of a Firm in Pure Competition

Pure competition is the ideal market structure and that to which other markets are compared. As will be shown, it is particularly ideal from the buyer's point of view because of the pricing, cost, and profit behavior, as well as the efficiency gains, that result from the competition.

Control over Price   One of the most important aspects of the behavior of purely competitive sellers is that no individual firm has any control over the price it receives for its product. Price is determined solely through the market's competitive forces; that is, price is determined by the interaction of *market* supply and *market* demand. The price that a firm charges is a result of the decisions of *all* buyers and *all* sellers in the market.

Figure 13.1   Market Demand and Supply for a Grain Crop

In a purely competitive market, market demand and supply determine the
equilibrium price and quantity of a product.

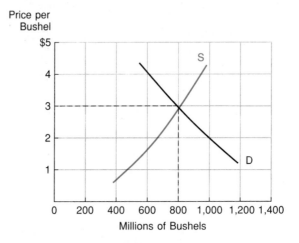

Figure 13.1 illustrates the market for a grain crop and allows us to review
the price-setting process first introduced in Chapter Three. D is the market
demand curve showing the different amounts of grain that all buyers
together plan to purchase at each price. As expected, the curve is downward
sloping, indicating that the lower the price, the greater is the quantity
demanded in the market. S is the upward-sloping market supply curve,
showing that all sellers (grain farmers) together offer more of the product for
sale at a higher price. The actual price that emerges in this market is $3 per
bushel. This is the equilibrium price that equates market demand and
supply.

In this example, an individual purely competitive firm can sell as much
or as little as it wishes at the price of $3 per bushel. It cannot charge more
than $3 and will not charge less than $3. Why is this so?

Due to the large number of independently acting sellers in the market, the
entire production of any one firm represents a "drop in the bucket"
compared with the total available output. A firm that would charge a price
higher than that in the market would sell nothing, because buyers can
choose from thousands of alternative sellers. Also, since one seller's product
is identical to that of all other sellers, it makes no difference with whom a
buyer deals.

It would also be pointless for a single seller to offer output at less than the
market price. A grain farmer would not sell grain at $2, $2.50, or even $2.99
per bushel, knowing that the entire production can be sold at the market
price of $3 per bushel.

Figure 13.2   Demand Curve for the Output of a Purely Competitive Seller

A firm in a purely competitive market can sell as much as it wants at the market price.

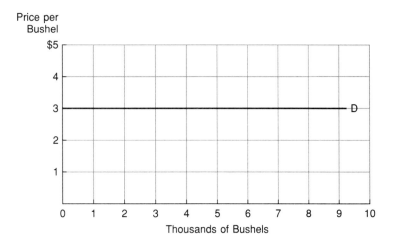

The same pricing behavior exists with regard to common stock. If you own a particular stock and the going price per share is $9.50, you cannot sell your shares for more than $9.50 and have no reason to sell them for less.

Thus, because of large numbers of independent sellers producing identical products, purely competitive suppliers have neither the willingness nor the ability to deviate from the price set in the market.

Demand for an Individual Firm's Product   For any product sold, there is a **market demand curve** such as that shown in Figure 13.1. In addition to the market demand curve, however, each individual firm or seller also has its own demand curve for its product. This represents the amounts of the *firm's* product that buyers are willing to purchase at certain prices. Thus, the **individual firm's demand curve** dictates the price a firm will receive when it chooses an output to sell.

As just stated, in pure competition the price an individual firm receives for its product is set by the forces of supply and demand in the market, and each firm supplies a minute fraction of the market. Since the firm's output is negligible when compared to the total, it can offer as much or as little as it chooses at the market price. Thus, the demand curve for any single purely competitive seller's product is graphed as a straight, horizontal line at the equilibrium market price.

The grain example in Figure 13.1 can be used to illustrate this concept. At an equilibrium price of $3 in the market, the demand curve for a single grain

Market demand curve
The demand curve that results when all buyers in the market are considered together.

Individual firm's demand curve
Shows the amounts of an individual firm's product that buyers are willing to purchase at particular prices.

Figure 13.3   Effect on the Individual Firm of an Increase in Market Demand

An increase in the market demand for a product will increase its equilibrium price and cause the individual firm's demand curve to shift upward.

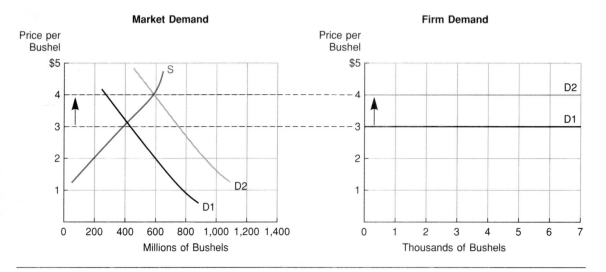

farmer's output would be like that shown in Figure 13.2. At $3 per bushel, buyers are willing to purchase 1,000 bushels, 5,000 bushels, or whatever output the farmer wants to offer. If the farmer were to charge more, say even $3.01, sales would drop to zero. There would also be no incentive to sell for less than $3 per bushel, since that is the price buyers will pay.

There is thus a relationship between the equilibrium market price and the individual firm's demand curve. If the equilibrium price in the market increases or decreases, the individual firm's demand curve will also increase (shift upward) or decrease (shift downward). If, for example, a large number of new buyers enters the market for grain, the market demand curve will shift to the right. As a consequence, the equilibrium price in the market rises, and the individual farmer's demand curve shifts upward. This is shown in Figure 13.3 where the price increases from $3 to $4 after market demand increases from D1 to D2. What would be the effect on an individual firm's demand curve from an increase in market supply?[1]

Much has been written about the plight of the U.S. farmer because of the decline in prices of U.S. agricultural crops during the 1980s. Application 13.2, "World's Grain Output Surges," discusses one reason for the downward shift in farmers' individual demand curves that has resulted in low prices

---

[1] An increase in market supply would cause the market supply curve to shift to the right. The resulting fall in equilibrium price would cause the individual seller's demand curve to shift downward.

Application 13.2

World's Grain Output Surges

. . . Countries around the world are racing toward grain self-sufficiency, impelled by the food-price shocks of the 1970s, the recent African famine and debt burdens that make imports unaffordable. They are irrigating deserts, plowing pasture, and seeding tundra. Many are restricting purchases from abroad while giving their farmers incentives to grow more.

Just 15 years after world leaders warned of a threat of global famine, Saudi Arabia is giving away wheat it can't store. Heavily populated Bangladesh has slashed grain imports, Chinese corn floods the Pacific Rim, and tiny Malawi is trucking maize to its central African neighbors. In frozen Finland, farmers are turning surplus wheat into vodka, mink fodder, and glue.

All this has sent the global grain trade into a tailspin. Volume is down 16% so far in the 1980s. That is a radical change from the 1970s, when a near-doubling in international grain purchases touched off explosive growth in U.S. agriculture, leaving American farmers dependent on foreign markets for one-third of grain sales. . . .

For U.S. farmers and taxpayers, this growing autarky in many nations spells trouble. Since the beginning of the decade annual American grain exports have plunged more than 40%. Corn prices on cash markets in the U.S. are at their lowest levels since 1973, while federal spending on farm programs—which rises as market prices fall—stands at record levels.

Any sharp turnaround in the grain trade is unlikely for years, most economists say. The debt crisis has left many customers, if not broke, at least wary of the kind of heavy borrowing that fueled the 1970s buying binge. The World Bank and other international lenders are pressuring Third World nations to dismantle policies that discourage food production. And the spreading "green revolution" is transforming former wastelands into fecund fields. . . .

The European Community, a major wheat importer just a decade ago, now is the third-largest exporter of the grain. Saudi Arabia, by offering gargantuan subsidies, has literally raised an agriculture out of the sand. Unable to store its surpluses, it donated wheat to Egypt last year.

Turkey has stopped buying corn from the U.S. after increasing its own corn production 66% in the past five years with better hybrids and more fertilizer and pesticides. . . .

. . . China, which as recently as 1983 was a net importer of corn and soybeans, now is the world's third-largest exporter of both crops. . . .

. . . India has so much wheat it is subsidizing exports and arranging sales or barter deals with North Korea, Nicaragua, and Nepal. Still, much of the grain, stored under tarps during the monsoon, simply rots.

Source: Wendy L. Wall, "World's Grain Output Surges as Nations Seek Food Self-Sufficiency," *The Wall Street Journal*, April 6, 1987, pp. 1, 12. Reprinted by permission of *The Wall Street Journal*, © Dow Jones & Company, Inc. 1987. All Rights Reserved Worldwide.

and incomes for farmers. After reading this application, can you describe, using graphs like those in Figure 13.3, the effects that changes in world crop growing patterns have exerted on U.S. markets?

Pricing, Profit, and Loss   The price that a firm in pure competition receives for its product and the cost that it incurs in producing it determine whether that firm operates with a profit or a loss. In the short run, the price-cost relationship could be causing a firm to operate at a loss, to break even, or to make an economic profit. In the long run, a firm that continually receives

Figure 13.4   A Purely Competitive Seller Operating with
                                    an Economic Profit, with a Loss, or Breaking Even

A seller will operate with an economic profit, with a loss, or will break even,
depending upon whether price is greater than, less than, or equal to average
total cost, respectively.

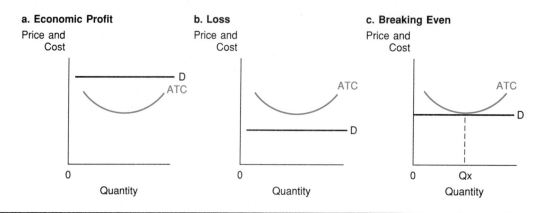

Economic profit, loss,
breaking even

Occurs when price is
greater than average total
cost, less than average
total cost, or equal to
average total cost,
respectively.

prices so low that it cannot cover its costs will eventually go out of business.
(Remember that normal profit is the profit necessary to stay in business and
is included in the cost of production. Economic profit is that profit earned
beyond normal profit.)

It is easy to see the profit or loss position of a firm by graphically
comparing the firm's demand curve and its average total cost curve. The
firm's demand curve gives the price it will receive for each unit of output
sold, and the average total cost (ATC) curve gives the cost for producing each
unit of output. If price is greater than average total cost, an **economic profit**
is earned; if price is less than average total cost, a **loss** occurs; and if price
equals average total cost, the firm is **breaking even.** Figure 13.4 illustrates
these three possible conditions.

Figure 13.4a shows a firm in pure competition that is operating with an
economic profit regardless of the output level chosen by the firm. Profit
results at all output levels because the firm's demand curve is above the
average total cost curve, or price is higher than average total cost.

Figure 13.4b illustrates a firm in pure competition operating with a loss.
This loss occurs because the average total cost curve is above the demand
curve, or average total cost is higher than price, regardless of the level of
output produced. In Figure 13.4c a firm is just breaking even (earning a
normal profit) if it produces and sells Qx units of output because average
total cost is equal to price at that level of output.

The appendix at the end of this chapter explains in greater detail how a firm in pure competition determines its profit-maximizing or loss-minimizing level of output.

Nonprice Competition   A significant behavioral aspect of firms producing in purely competitive markets is a lack of **nonprice competition.** A purely competitive seller makes no expenditures on advertising, public relations, or other efforts to bring its product to a buyer's attention. The reason for this should be obvious. With so many sellers producing identical products, the output of any one producer is indistinguishable from the outputs of all others, and efforts at creating buyer awareness of a particular firm's product would be an exercise in futility.[2]

Nonprice competition

Occurs when firms focus on some feature other than price (for example, quality or a guarantee) in an attempt to attract buyers to their products.

The benefit to consumers from this lack of nonprice competition is that, with no promotional expenditures, firms' costs are lower than they would otherwise be. This in turn means that over the long run, buyers pay less for products than they would if firms engaged in nonprice competition.

Long-Run Costs, Profit, and Efficiency.   One of the most important aspects of pure competition is the long-run behavior of firms in this market structure. *In the long run, purely competitive firms operate at the lowest possible cost, charge the lowest price that they can without going out of business, and earn no economic profit.* All of these conditions are ideal from the consumers' point of view and result from competition among the sellers.

The long-run position of a purely competitive seller is illustrated in Figure 13.5. This figure shows a simple long-run average total cost (LRATC) curve exhibiting economies and diseconomies of scale, and the firm's demand curve. In the long run, an individual seller's position is such that its demand curve just brushes the bottom of its long-run average total cost curve.

A firm operating under the conditions given in Figure 13.5 would sell 4,000 units of output at $3 per unit, or would operate at point A, because any other output level would result in a loss (the long-run average total cost curve would be above the demand curve). Notice that A is the lowest point on the firm's long-run average total cost curve, which means that the firm is producing at the lowest possible cost per unit. Recall from Chapter One that a firm is operating efficiently when its good or service is produced at the lowest cost possible.[3] **Efficient production** is an important goal to be achieved in an economy since the basic problem of economics is scarcity, and efficiency lessens the scarcity problem. Notice also that at point A price equals average total cost, causing the entrepreneur to earn only normal and

Efficient production

A good or service is produced at the lowest cost possible.

[2]It should be mentioned that sometimes trade associations to which firms in an industry or market belong will advertise the product itself: inducements to purchase raisins, beef, and milk are good examples of product — and not firm — advertising.

[3]See page 7. Choosing the efficient method of production was also discussed on pages 425–426 in Chapter Twelve.

Figure 13.5   Long-Run Position of a Purely Competitive Seller

In the long run, a purely competitive seller operates where price equals minimum average total cost, which just allows a normal profit.

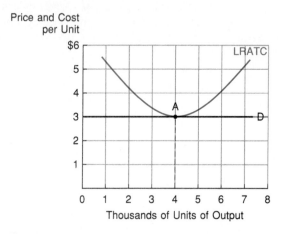

no excess profit. Thus, in the long run in pure competition the cost of production and the price of the product are as low as they can possibly be, firms operate efficiently, and the consumer pays no economic profit. Why does this long-run condition occur in pure competition?

Easy entry into and exit from the market are the basis for the position of the purely competitive firm in the long run. When firms in a purely competitive market earn excess profits, other sellers recognize the opportunity to also earn such profits and, because of easy entry, come into the market. As additional sellers enter the market, the market supply increases, causing the equilibrium market price to fall. As the equilibrium price falls, each individual seller's excess profit begins to disappear. This process of entry and reduction in both the market price and excess profit continues until each seller operates where price equals minimum average total cost, or with just a normal profit.

The mechanics of this process are illustrated in Figure 13.6. With market price P_1 and the individual firm's demand curve D1 (right-hand graph), the firm is making an economic profit because the long-run average total cost curve lies below D1. As other firms, attracted by this economic profit, enter the market, the market supply curve (left-hand graph) increases from S1 to S2, market price falls to P_2, and the individual seller's demand curve falls to D2, which allows no economic profit.

If firms are losing money and experiencing less than normal profits, some sellers will close their operations and leave the market. As sellers leave, the

Figure 13.6

Effect of Entry of Sellers into the Market on
an Individual Firm's Demand and Profit

When individual firms in pure competition make an economic profit, new firms
are attracted to the market in the long run, causing market supply to increase
and equilibrium price to fall. Eventually, the price that each firm receives is equal
to the firm's lowest long-run average total cost.

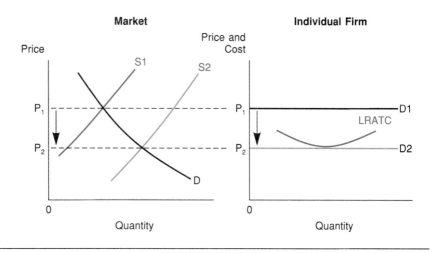

market supply decreases, causing the equilibrium price to increase. As the
price increases, the losses to remaining sellers disappear. This process
continues until, again, price equals minimum average total cost.

Figure 13.7 illustrates the effect on an individual firm of an exodus of other
firms from the market. At market price P_1, the individual firm is operating
at a loss because the cost of producing each unit is greater than the price. As
firms leave the market, the market supply curve shifts to the left, from S1 to
S2, causing market price and the individual firm's demand curve to rise.
When the price rises to P_2, the firm is just breaking even and earning a
normal profit.

Is There Pure Competition?

The extent to which pure competition is found in the real world is questionable. Consider agriculture, which has provided the classic examples of
purely competitive markets because of the large number of economically
independent agricultural sellers. From time to time farmers have organized
into groups to present their grievances about prices, costs, and other
problems to the government. Does political activity such as this influence
market prices? There is also the U.S. Department of Agriculture, which

Figure 13.7   Effect of Exit of Sellers from the Market on
                                   an Individual Firm's Demand and Profit

When individual firms in pure competition operate with a loss, some drop out of
the market in the long run, causing market supply to decrease and equilibrium
price to rise. Price will increase until it equals the minimum long-run average
total cost of the remaining firms.

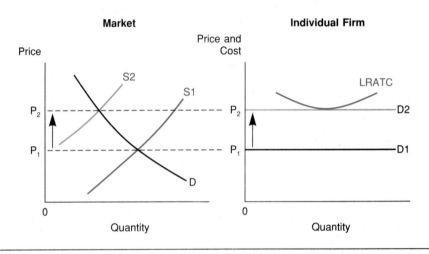

administers various government loan and assistance programs, to consider.
Is a grain market purely competitive if these programs affect market price?
    Further, there is the question of entry into and exit from agricultural
markets. To farm on anything other than a very small scale can require
substantial outlays for land, equipment, and other inputs such as seed and
fertilizer. It is possible that the costs of starting a farm could act as a barrier
to entry into the market. Also, exit from the market may not be easy. A farmer
wanting to use land and equipment for something other than agriculture
might discover that it is not well suited for anything else. Or a farming
couple wanting to leave production completely by selling their land and
equipment or by passing it on to their children might have to alter their plans
after considering the effects of tax laws on the disposal of their property.
    With problems such as these, of what value is the study of pure compe-
tition? Despite issues such as those just raised, the purely competitive model
does help us better understand the behavior of firms in certain markets. It
also provides an ideal against which real-world markets can be judged. In
this regard, pure competition is like human health. There may be no
perfectly healthy person, just as there may be no purely competitive market.
But we cannot understand the meaning of illness or good health without
having the ideal of perfect health for comparison.

Monopolistic Competition

Characteristics of Monopolistic Competition

Monopolistic competition

The market structure characterized by a large number of sellers with differentiated outputs and fairly easy entry into and exit from the market.

Differentiated outputs

The products of competing firms are different and can be recognized as such by buyers.

The market structure closest to pure competition is **monopolistic competition.** Like pure competition, monopolistically competitive markets have large numbers of sellers—not as many as in pure competition, but large numbers nonetheless. Unlike pure competition, the outputs of monopolistically competitive sellers are **differentiated:** buyers can distinguish among the products of different firms. Finally, as is the case in pure competition, entry into and exit from monopolistically competitive markets is fairly easy.

Examples of monopolistically competitive markets may be found where a large number of small retailing establishments such as shoe stores, restaurants, or record shops compete with each other. In these examples each seller's product is somewhat different: location, service, style, guarantees, and such vary from seller to seller. It is also relatively easy to open a small store or restaurant: a building can be rented; there is no need for highly trained or technical personnel; and there are minimal capital equipment requirements.

Another slightly different example of a monopolistically competitive market is the labor market for college graduates in a particular discipline such as communications. Each year a large number of communications majors is graduated from colleges and universities. Each of these graduates is unique in terms of grades, background, experience, selection of courses, and initiative. Entry into this market is relatively easy: the only necessary major expenditure is the cost of a college degree.

Behavior of a Firm in Monopolistic Competition

Because of differences in the characteristics of monopolistically competitive and purely competitive markets, there are differences in the behavior of firms in these structures. Notably, unlike pure competitors, monopolistic competitors have some control over the prices they receive for their products, and they engage in nonprice competition.

Control over Price   With a large number of firms selling identical products, the individual purely competitive firm has no control over the price it receives for its output. In monopolistic competition there is also a large number of sellers, but because the sellers' products are differentiated, buyers do not view the product of one seller as a perfect substitute for the product of another. For this reason, when a monopolistically competitive firm raises its price, it will lose some, but not all, of its sales. Some buyers will continue to purchase the product from the firm at a higher price because they see the firm's product as different from those of its competitors. Thus, product differentiation allows a firm to carve out a little market of its own within the larger market.

Figure 13.8

Demand Curve for the Output of a Monopolistically Competitive Seller

Because of product differentiation, a seller in monopolistic competition will lose some, but not all, of its buyers if it raises its price.

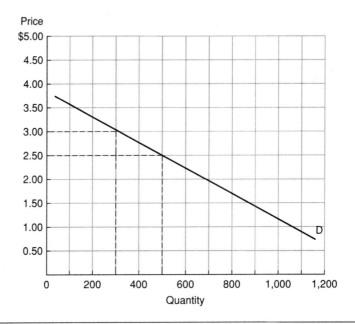

However, even with product differentiation there are limits to the amount of control a monopolistically competitive seller has over price. Since many other firms produce similar products, a firm that raises its price too much risks losing a large share of the market. Some buyers may be willing to pay a little extra for better service or a distinctive style, but if they have to pay a great deal extra, the alternatives become more attractive. For example, you may continue to eat lunch at a favorite restaurant even if it raises its prices somewhat. However, if the price increases become too high, you may seek an alternative luncheon spot.

In short, a firm selling in a monopolistically competitive market has some control over price because of its ability to differentiate its product, but that control is limited by the presence of many other firms producing similar products.

Demand for an Individual Firm's Product   Because of product differentiation, the demand curve faced by an individual monopolistic competitor is downward sloping, like that in Figure 13.8. This demand curve indicates that if the firm raises its price, it will lose some, but not all, of its sales. For example,

Figure 13.9   A Monopolistically Competitive Seller Operating
with an Economic Profit or a Loss

A seller in monopolistic competition earns economic profit when the price of its
product is greater than its average total cost (the demand curve is above the
average total cost curve). It operates with a loss when price is less than average
total cost (the demand curve is below the average total cost curve).

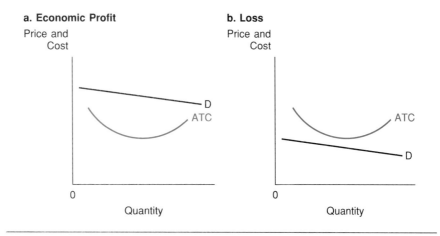

in Figure 13.8, when the seller raises the price from $2.50 to $3 per unit, the
quantity demanded falls from 500 to 300 units, not from 500 units to zero as
would happen if the seller were a pure competitor.[4]

Pricing, Profit, and Loss   As was the case with a firm operating in a purely
competitive market, the profit or loss position of a firm operating in a
monopolistically competitive market can be determined by comparing the
demand curve and average total cost curve for its product. If the average
total cost curve lies below the demand curve, or the cost per unit of output
is less than the price, an economic profit is earned. This is shown in Figure
13.9a. If the average total cost curve is above the demand curve, or the cost
per unit of output is greater than the price, a loss occurs. This is shown in
Figure 13.9b.

Nonprice Competition   Obviously, sellers in monopolistically competitive
markets can compete with one another for buyers by lowering prices. But

[4]Generally, in monopolistic competition the response to a price change is elastic; that is, over
the broadest range of the demand curve, buyers respond strongly to price changes. In Figure
13.8, when the price increases from $2.50 to $3.00, or by 20 percent, the quantity demanded
decreases from 500 to 300 units, or by 40 percent. Since the percentage change in the quantity
demanded is greater than the percentage change in price, the response is characterized as
elastic. Refer to Chapter Three, pages 102–107, to refresh your memory about elasticity.

because their products are differentiated, rivalry through nonprice competition also becomes important.

Nonprice competition includes all forms of rivalry not involving price. A firm competes for customers through its packaging, distribution, service, location, quality, selection, and guarantees. An ice cream parlor, for example, can attract customers because of high quality and a varied selection of flavors, the hours it is open, and access to parking. The importance of nonprice competition can be seen by the amount of advertising and sales promotion directed to that end. Notice how infrequently advertisements in magazines or on television stress price as the selling feature.

Business firms are attracted to nonprice competition for two reasons. First, nonprice competition provides a way for a firm to increase the demand for its product. By increasing buyer acceptance through service, packaging, and other devices, a firm can shift the demand curve for its product to the right—thereby selling more at each price. Second, by highlighting differences and playing down similarities, nonprice competition helps an individual firm make its product appear unique. As this occurs, the seller becomes less sensitive to the presence of rivals. Uniqueness allows a seller to raise prices without losing as many buyers as would otherwise be the case.

Controversy exists over the desirability of nonprice competition. In most instances, nonprice competition increases the cost of doing business, and higher costs can lead to higher prices for buyers. Some people argue that buyers' interests would be better served if rivalry were limited to price competition or if nonprice competition were at least reduced. Others think that nonprice competition can benefit consumers because it provides variety and perhaps more attention to service and quality. After years of buying goods and services, what is your position on this question?

Product differentiation and nonprice competition are important characteristics of many snack food markets. Application 13.3, "In the Chips," illustrates some of the nonprice factors that one company considers in developing new chips for the market. Can you identify some of the costs created for this company because of its product differentiation focus? What benefits result for the consumer?

Long-Run Costs, Profit, and Efficiency   Over the long run, sellers in monopolistically competitive markets earn only normal profits, an attribute shared by firms in purely competitive markets. This occurs because, like purely competitive markets, monopolistically competitive markets are easy to enter and exit. Due to easy entry and exit, the long-run position of a monopolistically competitive seller is like that shown in Figure 13.10. The firm in Figure 13.10 can earn a normal profit by selling 300,000 units of output at $3 each. At any smaller or larger output the long-run average total cost curve is above the demand curve, causing the firm to produce at a loss.

If firms are earning economic, or excess, profit (like the firm shown in Figure 13.9a), new sellers enter the market and take some of the demand away from the existing sellers. This causes the demand curves of these sellers

Figure 13.10

Long-Run Position of a Monopolistically Competitive Seller

Like a purely competitive seller, a monopolistically competitive seller earns no excess profit over the long run; but unlike a purely competitive seller, it operates at a long-run average total cost that is greater than the minimum.

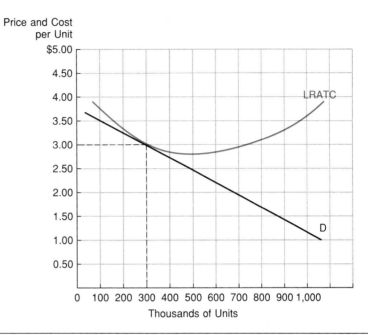

to shift to the left until they reach a position like that shown in Figure 13.10, where economic profit is competed away and only normal profit remains. If firms are sustaining losses (like the firm shown in Figure 13.9b), sellers leave the market, causing the demand curves of the remaining sellers to shift to the right until they reach a position like that shown in Figure 13.10, and the remaining firms operate at a normal profit.

While purely competitive and monopolistically competitive sellers both earn only a normal profit over the long run, the two types of sellers differ in an important way. A firm in a purely competitive market operates at the minimum possible average cost in the long run and is, therefore, efficient, whereas a firm in a monopolistically competitive market does not operate at the least-cost point and is, therefore, not as efficient. For the firm in Figure 13.10, the long-run price and per unit cost are $3. If it were a pure competitor, its price and per unit cost would be $2.75—the minimum point on the long-run average total cost curve. It is impossible for a monopolistic competitor to operate in the long run with price equal to minimum long-run average total cost because of product differentiation, which results in a

Application 13.3

In the Chips

Knowing what consumers crave and tailoring products to fit those needs will be more important to marketers in the 1990s than ever before. . . .

[M]arketers like Frito-Lay are exploring every facet of consumer behavior—from obvious things such as taste preferences, to more subtle psychological desires. In the process, they hope to come up with products that they won't have to beg consumers to buy.

At Frito-Lay, this approach has become something of an obsession. Snack-food research and development costs at the company have about doubled in the past decade—to between $20 million and $30 million a year. At the same time, the company says it is spending proportionately less on advertising than it did in the past. . . .

Inside Frito-Lay's "Potato Chip Pentagon," a boxy, closely guarded building near Dallas, nearly 500 chemists, engineers and psychologists toil. Leaving no consumer preference to guesswork, they use a $40,000 simulated human mouth made of aluminum to measure the jaw power it takes to crunch single chips. By comparing consumer preferences in taste tests with results from the aluminum mouth, researchers calculate that most people prefer a chip that breaks under about four pounds of pressure per square inch. The company tests a few chips from nearly every batch at its 22 factories to make sure that standard is met.

Quality-control engineers measure the thickness of chips to 36/1000ths of an inch for flat chips and 91/1000ths for Ruffles. Consumers have complained about chips that were cut 8/1000ths of an inch too thick or thin, researchers say.

Other engineers test the chemical reactions of single chips on a computer screen that shows "flavor patterns" in eight colors. The printouts [show], for instance, just how much more vinegar an experimental new barbecue flavor could stand before it becomes unpalatable to most people. . . .

. . . "We have to be perfect; after all, no one really *needs* a potato chip," [says Dennis Heard, senior vice president of technology].

But many people *want* them by the bagful—thanks to Mr. Heard. His seasoning department develops 24 new flavor variations a year; they go through more than 6000 consumer taste tests in their quest to develop about six new types of a chip that actually reach the national market each year.

downward-sloping demand curve. This difference gives rise to an important criticism of monopolistic competition: even though price equals long-run average total cost, the cost and price are higher than they would be in pure competition, and some efficiency is sacrificed.

Oligopoly

Oligopoly is further removed from pure competition than is monopolistic competition. In fact, it is so far removed that it makes more sense to discuss how oligopoly and pure competition differ than to discuss what they have in common. While pure competition may be the ideal market structure, oligopoly is the dominant market structure in the U.S. economy. More business is transacted in oligopolistic markets than in any of the three other market structures.

Knowing more about consumers than the consumers themselves know is an important goal at Frito-Lay. . . .

To get in the right mood for creating ads, [executives at the market-research and advertising agency retained by Frito-Lay] prepare a dozen or so videotapes depicting the types of people who they think eat various Frito-Lay snacks. . . .

The videos reflect distinct personality differences among eaters of various snacks. Some examples:

Lay's Potato Chips: Consumers of these flat chips are seen as "affectionate, irresistible, casual and a fun member of the family." . . .

Ruffles Potato Chips: Consumers are depicted as "expressive, aware, confident enough to make a personal statement." . . .

Such personality differences . . . are only a small part of a complex snack-food equation. The basic snack-chip market remains "anyone with a mouth," says [the president of the market-research and advertising agency]. But the impulses behind that hunger for snack food are increasingly diverse. "There's really no national snack-food market anymore," he says.

That's why some of Frito-Lay's 85 kinds of potato chips are sold regionally. For example, vinegar-

flavored chips are sold mainly in the Northeast. Mesquite flavor, a sort of barbecue, is mainly for the Southwest and California. Sour-cream flavor is most popular in the Midwest. . . .

Marketers also have to be more wary these days of health and environmental concerns. . . .

Frito-Lay has . . . made great efforts to avoid using the word "fried." It was once a virtue in potato-chip ad copy — practically synonymous with "crisp" and "crunchy." But don't speak of "frying" around Frito-Lay executives anymore; the word has been stricken from marketing-research papers, brainstorming sessions and consumer interviews. . . .

Frito-Lay also goes to great lengths to make sure its packaging conforms to its consumer insights. For instance, it tested hundreds of shades of blue in focus groups to achieve the right bold, cheerful color on its new Ruffles packages. The bag, trimmed in a gold shade that also received extensive testing, "is a powerful statement about the chip and the person who uses it," says [Frito-Lay's vice president of market research].

Source: Robert Johnson, "In the Chips," *The Wall Street Journal*, March 22, 1991, pp. B1, B2. Reprinted by permission of The Wall Street Journal, © Dow Jones & Company, Inc., 1991. All Rights Reserved Worldwide.

Characteristics of Oligopoly

Oligopolistic markets

Markets dominated by a few large sellers with either differentiated or identical products and where entry by new firms into the market is difficult.

Oligopolistic markets are those dominated by a few large sellers. In some cases the products of oligopolists are differentiated, and in others they are identical. Entry of firms into oligopolistic markets is quite difficult, much more so than entry into purely or monopolistically competitive markets. Barriers to entry include the sheer size of the capital requirement necessary to allow a potential rival to compete equally with established sellers, and the difficulty of taking enough sales away from existing firms to make operating worthwhile.

The retail grocery market is a good example of an oligopoly with differentiated products. In most cities, there are a few large grocery chains; the various chains are differentiated in terms of service, size, diversity of product, location, cleanliness, and other factors; and entry into the market by a new chain is extremely difficult. The market for aluminum ingot

Table 13.1   The International Air Passenger Transportation Market, U.S. Carriers: 1989

International air passenger transportation by U.S. carriers is dominated by a few large competitors and is an example of an oligopoly.

Airline	Percentage of Revenue Passenger Miles
Pan American	22.2%
Northwest	18.6
United	15.0
TWA	14.0
American	10.7
Continental	10.4
Delta	6.9
Eastern	2.0
USAir	0.2
	100.0

Source: Based on L. J. Davis, "And Now, Can Bob Crandall Have It All?" *The New York Times Magazine*, Part 2, September 23, 1990, p. 25. Data source is U.S. Department of Transportation.

provides an example of an undifferentiated oligopoly. There are a few large aluminum firms; ingot is an undifferentiated product; and the cost of entering the market is substantial.

Examples of oligopoly are everywhere. The next time you shop for a car, a computer, or even breakfast cereal, notice how few firms are in these markets. Oligopolies are also found in the markets for baseball gloves, stereo equipment, gasoline, light bulbs, and commercial television broadcasting. Table 13.1 provides an example of a market that is dominated by a few large competitors—international air passenger transportation by U.S. firms. Notice that the four largest carriers account for nearly 70 percent of the market.

Behavior of a Firm in an Oligopolistic Market

Control over Price   With few major sellers, each of the dominant firms in an oligopoly has a large share of the market. A large share allows the firm some control over its price—quite unlike the pure competitor whose output is so small that the firm is at the mercy of the market.

But the existence of few competing sellers introduces an interesting twist to oligopoly that significantly affects a firm's behavior. With so few sellers, the price, output, advertising, and other policy actions of one firm affect the other firms in its market, and may cause these other firms to react. For example, if one automobile company offers a rebate on its cars, it may affect the sales of the other automobile companies in the market. These firms may in turn offer rebates of their own or follow other policies that will be detrimental to the sales of the company that initially offered the rebate. If a pizza chain offers free delivery or two-for-ones, this may reduce the sales of competing companies, which could respond with promotional programs of their own. As a result, in the oligopolistic market structure, sellers are constantly watching and weighing the actions and reactions of their competitors.

Mutual interdependence

Occurs when there are so few sellers in the market that each seller must weigh the actions and reactions of rival sellers in any decision making.

This phenomenon is called **mutual interdependence.** Because of mutual interdependence, sellers must consider not only the effects of their pricing and other policies on buyers, but the effects on their rivals and their rivals' reactions as well. This is the unique aspect of oligopolistic markets. Application 13.4, "Noticing One's Rivals," describes some actions in the markets for pizza, television network advertising, and air transportation that illustrate mutual interdependence among competing sellers.

Price of an Individual Firm's Product   Because mutual interdependence is manifested in different ways, there is no single explanation for oligopoly pricing. Rather, several theories have been developed to accommodate different types of interdependence. Two of the best-known theories are leadership pricing and the kinked demand curve model.

Leadership pricing

One firm in a market sets a price that the other firms in the market then adopt.

With **leadership pricing** one firm in a market sets a price that is then adopted by other sellers. The firm that sets the price is called the price leader, and the firms that respond are the followers. Leadership pricing is not uncommon. Often firms in industries such as aluminum, air transportation, and banking follow suit when a price change is announced by one of their competitors. The price changes by the followers often come within a few days of the leader's announcement.

A seller may emerge as price leader for several reasons. For one, it may be the largest firm in its market, causing rivals to choose to adopt its price rather than attack it head-on and face a possible price war. Or, it may become the price leader because it is more sensitive to changing market conditions than are its rivals. In this case, the rivals respond to the leader's price announcements because that firm acts as a barometer of changing market conditions that will eventually affect other sellers. Banks, for example, experience the same changes in money market conditions, causing a price leadership pattern to emerge with regard to interest rates.

Kinked demand curve

Based on the assumption that rivals will not follow price increases but will follow price decreases; illustrates that as a seller's price rises, the amount of its product demanded decreases substantially, but as its price falls, the amount demanded increases only slightly.

The second theory, the **kinked demand curve** model, is based on the assumption that rivals do not follow a seller's price increases but do follow price decreases. The theory gets its name from the unusual shape of the individual oligopolist's demand curve under this assumption. A kinked demand curve is illustrated in Figure 13.11.

The price currently charged and the corresponding output sold by the firm are shown at the kink, or bend, in the demand curve. For the firm in Figure 13.11, the current price is $3 and sales are 400,000 units. If the firm raises its price above $3, and its rivals do not follow, it stands to lose a large

Application 13.4

Noticing One's Rivals

TWA to Raise U.S. Fares

Trans World Airlines Inc. said Tuesday [August 21, 1990] it would copy the nation's other major carriers and increase domestic fares by 5.3 percent to offset higher fuel costs. . . .

TWA will start charging higher ticket prices on Aug. 30.

The other airlines had planned to raise their fares Aug. 15. But they postponed the increase until today after TWA and Eastern announced they were temporarily reducing prices on many nonrefundable tickets to stimulate fall traffic.

TWA's rivals had not decided Tuesday whether to again delay their increases.

TWA and other airlines decided to raise fares because they were concerned that the sharp increase in fuel prices, coupled with the decline in traffic, would weaken or wipe out profits.

CBS, ABC Adopt NBC Proposal

The three major broadcast networks are closing ranks in the battle over viewer-measurement practices by uniformly adopting a plan to reduce the audience size they guarantee to advertisers.

Yesterday, CBS Inc. and Capital Cities/ABC Inc. announced they will adopt a plan proposed earlier this week by the NBC network. Under the NBC plan, the networks would project audience size for the new TV season, which begins in September, by using an average of audience levels over the last eight years. The networks will make audience-size guarantees to advertisers based on the projections rather than based solely on ratings from A. C. Nielsen Co., as they have in the past.

. . . Because the Nielsen ratings showed an unexplained, steep drop in TV viewership of about 7% earlier this year, the networks had to shell out as much as $200 million in "make goods," or free advertising for sponsors when audience guarantee levels fell below network projections.

To avoid having to pay millions back to advertisers, the three networks have been seeking to change the system by which they guarantee audience size. . . .

The proposal to change the system was suggested earlier this week by No. 1–rated National Broadcasting Co., a unit of General Electric Co. ABC dropped an earlier proposal of its own in favor of the NBC plan, and CBS, which had been mulling over prospects, said late yesterday that the NBC plan "in principle, is acceptable to us."

Pizza Makers Slug It Out

. . . "Consumers today are dollar rich and time poor. They don't want to eat in restaurants," says [an executive of Godfather's Pizza Inc. which] is working on a new ad campaign to reach the couchbound. "It is absolutely essential to our success that we promote, advertise and market *delivery*."

And therein lie the ingredients for what may become 1988's biggest food fight, as the nation's pizza chains slug it out for a bigger slice of the fast-growing takeout and delivery business. . . .

But the takeout and delivery business isn't the only battlefield for the pizza makers. The chains also are warring over price. Deep discounting, led by fast-growing upstart Little Caesars Pizza, spread rapidly last year. And pizza experts say priceslashing, two-for-one offers, and a barrage of coupons will continue to increase in 1988. . . .

Last June, Pizza Hut decided to match Little Caesars with its own two-for-one deals. The other major competitors followed, and each now offers a two-for-one deal at least some of the time. Other kinds of discounts, including newspaper coupons, have soared, too.

Source: Excerpted from Christopher Carey, "TWA To Raise U.S. Fares by 5.3%," *St. Louis Post-Dispatch*, August 22, 1990, p. B1. Copyright 1990, The Pulitzer Publishing Company. Excerpted with permission; Excerpted from Kevin Goldman, "CBS, ABC Adopt NBC Ad Proposal," *The Wall Street Journal*, June 15, 1990, pp. B1, B3. Excerpted by permission of The Wall Street Journal, © Dow Jones & Company, Inc., 1990. All Rights Reserved Worldwide; Excerpted from Joanne Lipman, "Pizza Makers Slug It out for Share of Growing Eat-at-Home Market," *The Wall Street Journal*, January 12, 1988, p. 31. Excerpted by permission of The Wall Street Journal, © Dow Jones & Company, Inc., 1988. All Rights Reserved Worldwide.

Figure 13.11   Kinked Demand Curve for the Output of an Oligopolist

The kinked demand curve of an oligopolist is based on the assumption that the firm's rivals will follow a price decrease but not a price increase.

number of buyers to those other sellers. For example, when it increases its price from $3 to $4, its sales fall by 200,000 units, from 400,000 to 200,000. But notice that when the firm lowers its price from $3 to $2, its sales increase by only 50,000 units, to 450,000. This is because, when a seller's price is lowered, the seller's rivals also cut their prices to avoid losing buyers. With everyone's price lower, some buyers may be attracted to the market, but few existing buyers will be willing to switch to the seller that initiated the price cut.

Thus, the relatively flat portion of the kinked demand curve above the current price shows that a firm increasing its price stands to lose a large number of sales if its rivals do not follow its lead. The steep portion of the curve below the current price illustrates that, with rivals following price cuts, sales increase only slightly. The conclusion to be drawn from this model is that prices are relatively stable in this type of oligopoly market because the fear of rivals' reactions gives little or no incentive to either raise or lower price. In other words, there is not much price competition.

The kinked demand curve model illustrates just one way in which mutual interdependence affects demand in an oligopolistic market. It is valid in cases where firms follow the assumptions of this model and where prices are relatively inflexible.

Nonprice Competition   Nonprice competition in oligopolistic markets differs according to whether the products sold in the market are identical or differentiated. Where rivals produce physically identical products, advertising campaigns that stress an individual seller's product might benefit all sellers in the market, rather than just the individual firm, and would, therefore, be inappropriate. On the other hand, a strong advertising campaign emphasizing an individual seller's product makes sense where sellers' outputs are clearly differentiable on the basis of quality, style, size, or some other characteristic. Automobile ads, for example, usually stress the differentiable characteristics of a particular firm's product.

Nonprice competition is important if a seller faces a situation where price cuts do not lead to large increases in sales. In this case, nonprice competition provides an alternative to price competition. However, sellers must recognize that mutual interdependence also exists with regard to nonprice competition. For example, when one of the fast-food chains introduced salads, the others followed, and most of the airlines decided to give frequent flyer points after one of the airlines created this program.

Long-Run Costs, Profit, and Efficiency   Over the long run, purely competitive and monopolistically competitive sellers earn only normal profit: easy entry allows new firms to come into the market and compete economic profit away. But with oligopoly, entry is not easy. Therefore, oligopolists can continue to earn economic profit over the long run because new sellers cannot readily enter the market.

The ability to earn economic profit over the long run affects the price buyers pay for a product. With pure competition, easy entry ensures that price is equal to cost and is as low as possible. But the ability of an oligopolist to earn economic profit means that the firm's price can be greater than its cost. Thus, over the long run, restricted entry may result in economic profit for the firm and in higher prices for the buyer.

Restricted entry may also allow an oligopolist to operate inefficiently over the long run. The greater the difficulty potential rivals face entering a market, the less the competitive pressure on a firm's demand curve, and the weaker its incentive to operate at lowest average total cost.

Monopoly

Characteristics of Monopoly

Monopoly market
A market with one seller that maintains its position because entry by new sellers is impossible.

Of the four market structures, none is further removed from pure competition than is monopoly. In a **monopolized market** there is only one seller—the monopolist. Since the firm faces no direct competition from other sellers' products, the question of whether or not its product is differentiated is meaningless. The monopolist enjoys its position as sole seller in the market because entry by new sellers is virtually impossible.

Entry into a monopolized market can be blocked for several reasons. First, it may be more efficient to have one seller, rather than several, in a market. This happens when production is accompanied by significant economies of scale that cause long-run average total cost to fall as the seller becomes larger and output expands. In this case, buyers stand to pay less with one large firm producing all of the output at a lower average total cost than they would pay if several firms each produced part of the total supply at a higher average total cost. Thus, if a firm, by servicing the entire market, can take advantage of the cost and price lowering effects of economies of scale, it can keep potential rivals out of the market. Such a situation is called a **natural monopoly** and will be further discussed in Chapter Fourteen.

If a monopoly is a public utility—the only firm providing natural gas, electricity, or some other essential service to a community—entry of new rivals may be blocked by their inability to receive permission to operate from a regulatory authority. For example, a company that wants to provide residential telephone service in a neighborhood cannot do so without obtaining a license from the state commission that regulates utilities.

A monopolist may owe its market power to the ownership of a patent on a product or a process. Any potential rival trying to use the product or process without the monopolist's permission can be sued. For example, Polaroid has regained its position as the sole seller of instant cameras and film in the U.S. market after Kodak was ordered out of the market as a result of a patent-related lawsuit.

A firm may also be a monopolist because it is the sole owner of a factor necessary for production, such as the franchise for a professional sports team in a particular city, or because it has engaged in illegal practices involving prices and contracts that keep potential rivals out of the market. Other examples of monopolies could (depending on how the market is defined) include a company that owns the only pipeline carrying natural gas into a region, the only newspaper in a city, a college bookstore, the firm that has the food concession at an airport or a national park, and a general store near a camping ground.

Related to monopoly is the situation where several sellers formally join together with the intention of acting as if they were a single firm monopoly. The organization they form is called a **cartel,** and its purpose is to obtain more profit and other benefits for its members than they would receive if they competed with one another. Although the best-known example of a cartel is the Organization of Petroleum Exporting Countries (OPEC), other organizations have also been found to carry out cartel-type activities. For example, the court in Application 13.1 called NCAA control over college football a classic cartel. Cartels are illegal in the United States.[5]

Natural monopoly

A market situation where it is more efficient (less costly) to have the entire output of a product come from one large seller rather than from several smaller sellers.

Cartel

An arrangement whereby sellers formally join together in a market to make decisions as a group on matters such as pricing; the behavior of a cartel is like that of a monopoly.

---

[5] Over the years the power of OPEC has diminished due, in part, to two important factors. First, the members of OPEC have had difficulty reaching and maintaining agreements, especially about production levels. As frequently happens in cartels, individual members break the cartel agreement when it is in their own best interest to do so. Second, the power of OPEC has been reduced since the early 1970s by new sources of oil such as the Alaskan pipeline project, alternative supplies of energy such as solar energy, and the development of more fuel efficient automobiles.

For the court's comment on the NCAA as a classic cartel, see *Board of Regents of the University of Oklahoma* v. *National Collegiate Athletic Association,* 546 F. Supp. 1276 (1982), pp. 1300–1301.

Figure 13.12   Demand Curve for the Output of a Monopolist

A monopolist will search its downward-sloping demand curve and choose the one price and output combination that will maximize its profit. The monopolist's demand curve and the market demand curve are the same.

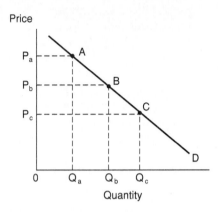

Behavior of a Monopolist

Control over Price   Two important facts about a monopolist's pricing result because it is the only seller in its market. First, all other things being equal, a monopolist has more control over its price than does a firm in any other market structure. There are no direct competitors to take buyers away when a monopolist raises its price. Second, because a monopolist is the only seller in its market, its demand curve *is* the market demand curve: all buyers demanding the product demand it from the monopolist.

Demand for a Monopolist's Product   Since market demand curves are downward sloping, and since the monopolist's demand is identical to the market demand, the monopolist's demand curve is the downward-sloping market demand curve.

Unlike the pure competitor, whose price is determined by the forces of market supply and demand and who must accept the price dictated by the market, a monopolist is a **price searcher** who will assess the costs and revenues from operating at various levels of output, or various points on the demand curve, and select the one price and output combination that maximizes profit. For example, the monopolist facing the demand curve in Figure 13.12 will assess revenues and costs at different levels of output and apply the profit-maximizing rules to find the one price-quantity combination that yields maximum profit. Depending on the behavior of costs, this combination could be shown by point A, B, or C, or any other point on the demand curve in Figure 13.12. The appendix at the end of this chapter

Price searcher

A firm that searches its downward-sloping demand curve to find the price-output combination that maximizes its profit.

illustrates in full detail, using revenue and cost information, how a monopolist chooses the profit-maximizing point on its demand curve.

One of the significant features about pricing in a monopoly market structure is that, since the monopolist's demand and the market demand are the same, the monopolist is establishing the price and output level for the whole market. In other words, one firm makes all of the supply decisions. In addition, once the monopolist chooses a price, there are no direct competitive forces to lower it. The monopolist has no fear of entry by new firms.

Nonprice Competition   Because monopolists face no direct competitors, the nonprice competition in which they engage is slightly different from that typically used by oligopolists or monopolistic competitors. In those market structures nonprice competition is designed primarily to attract buyers to a particular brand of a product. For example, in the passenger car market, nonprice competition encourages buyers toward a Ford, General Motors, Chrysler, or foreign automobile. But with monopoly there are no competing brands; there is simply the product. In this situation, a monopolist's advertising and other nonprice competition may be designed to make people aware of the good or service itself, not the seller. For example, many people are probably more aware of the advertising slogan "A diamond is forever" than they are of De Beers Consolidated Mines, Ltd., the company with which the slogan is associated. While not a total monopolist, De Beers supplies the vast majority of the world's diamonds. If you buy a new diamond, it is very likely to have come from De Beers.

Long-Run Costs, Profit, and Efficiency   The monopolist enjoys its position as sole seller in its market because of impassable entry barriers that keep potential rivals out. Those same barriers allow the monopolist to enjoy economic profit over the long run. Due to barriers to entry, no new rivals can come into the market, force the monopoly firm to lower its price, and compete economic profit away. The monopolist can protect its economic profit as long as its monopoly position can be maintained. Impassable barriers to entry also allow the monopolist to operate inefficiently, or at higher than minimum average cost. The monopolist can produce any output level it chooses regardless of efficiency considerations.

However, even with the monopolist's exclusive position in the market, some restraints on its profit-making ability and ability to operate without regard to efficiency may exist. Although it faces no direct competition in its own market, the monopolist must be concerned with competition from products in other, closely related markets. A natural gas distributor may have no direct competition from other gas distributors, but in some respects, it faces competition from suppliers of other types of energy. For example, a home builder may have the choice of installing gas, electric, oil, or solar heat, and a home owner always has the option of converting from one type of heat to another. Thus, if the gas company's price becomes too far out of line, over the long run as buyers have the opportunity to move into other markets, it could lose business, not to other gas distributors, but to companies supplying alternative forms of energy.

The monopolist is also restrained in its profit-making ability where it is a public utility. In this case, the price it charges is overseen by a public authority or a regulatory commission. Here price is set in such a way that the utility's ability to earn excess profit is limited.

Market Structures, the Consumer, and Efficiency

It is important to review the effects on consumers of buying from sellers in each of the four market structures and the levels of efficiency achieved by firms in these structures. Buyers fare best when facing purely competitive sellers since the market determines the price. Also, in the long run price is equal to average total cost and average total cost is as low as possible. This means that over the long run no economic profit goes to the sellers and consumers get the good or service at the lowest possible price. Since price equals minimum average total cost in the long run, these firms operate efficiently.

In monopolistic competition, price is again equal to average total cost in the long run. But since the demand curve for an individual seller's product is downward sloping, the long-run average total cost of the product is not at its lowest possible level. Thus, even though buyers pay no economic profit to the seller, they do not get the good or service at the minimum possible cost. Since firms do not operate at their lowest average total costs, they are less efficient than purely competitive firms.

In oligopoly and monopoly, the price of a product can remain above its average total cost over the long run; that is, in these market structures the prices buyers pay may regularly include an economic profit to the seller. These market structures may also lack the forces that cause firms to produce efficiently. Because of this and other manifestations of the market power of oligopolists and monopolists, the government has taken steps from time to time to modify their behavior. Some of those measures are taken up in Chapter Fourteen. Table 13.2 summarizes the characteristics and behavior of firms in each of the four market structures.

Summary

A market is composed of firms selling similar products to the same group of buyers. The boundaries of a market are determined by product substitutability and geographic considerations. The degree of competition in a market influences a firm's pricing and nonprice policies as well as its ability

Table 13.2   Characteristics and Behavior of Firms in Each of the Four Market Structures

Consumers fare best when buying in purely competitive markets: sellers have no control over price, and over the long run, average total cost and price are at a minimum and sellers earn no economic profit.

Pure Competition

Characteristics	Results
Very large number of sellers	Price determined by market supply and demand
	No nonprice competition
Identical products	In the long run, price equals minimum ATC and firms
Easy entry and exit	operate efficiently with no economic profit

Monopolistic Competition

Characteristics	Results
Large number of sellers	Firms have limited control over price
Differentiated products	Firms engage in nonprice competition
Fairly easy entry and exit	In the long run, price equals ATC, but not minimum ATC, and firms operate with no economic profit

Oligopoly

Characteristics	Results
Few sellers	Firms have control over price
Mutual interdependence	Firms engage in nonprice competition
Barriers to entry	In the long run, firms can operate with economic profit and not at minimum ATC

Monopoly

Characteristics	Results
One seller	Firm has most control over price
Impassable barriers to entry	In the long run, seller can operate with economic profit and not at minimum ATC

to earn economic profit in the long run. To analyze competition and its effects, markets can be classified into one of four structures: pure competition, monopolistic competition, oligopoly, and monopoly.

Pure competition is characterized by a large number of independent firms producing identical products in a market that is easy to enter and exit. Individual purely competitive firms have no control over price, which is set by the forces of supply and demand in the market. An individual firm's demand curve is a straight, horizontal line at the market price, indicating that it can sell as much as it wishes at that price but nothing at a higher price. Nonprice competition is nonexistent in purely competitive markets since sellers' products are identical.

Due to easy entry and exit, in the long run a purely competitive seller's price is equal to minimum long-run average total cost. This results in efficient production, the lowest possible price that can be charged in the market, and no economic profit for the firm. From the buyer's point of view this makes pure competition the ideal market structure. In the real world, purely competitive markets are difficult to find.

Monopolistic competition is characterized by a large number of sellers producing differentiated products in a market that is fairly easy to enter and exit. Due to product differentiation, individual sellers exercise some control over their prices, resulting in a downward-sloping demand curve for each firm's product. This control, however, is limited by the large number of sellers offering buyers similar products. Nonprice competition through packaging, location, and other methods is important in these markets.

Since entry into and exit from the market is fairly easy, over the long run monopolistic competitors operate where price equals long-run average total cost, resulting in no economic profits. However, these firms do not produce at the lowest point on their long-run average total cost curves, so their prices and costs are higher, and the firms are less efficient, than if they were pure competitors.

Oligopoly is characterized by a few sellers producing identical or differentiated products in a market that is difficult to enter. By virtue of their relatively large size in the market, oligopolists have some control over their prices. But large size also causes the competitive decisions of one firm to affect other firms in its market, giving rise to mutual interdependence among the sellers.

Since mutual interdependence can assume different forms, there are several explanations for oligopoly pricing. Two popular explanations are leadership pricing, which occurs when one firm changes its price and others follow, and the kinked demand curve model, which is based on the assumption that rivals follow price decreases but not price increases. With the entry of potential rivals into the market impeded, oligopolists may be able to charge prices greater than average total cost, earn economic profits over the long run, and not operate efficiently.

Monopoly is characterized by a single seller facing no direct competition in a market that is impossible to enter. All other things being equal, a monopolist has more control over its price than does a firm in any other market structure. Since it is the only seller in its market, the monopolist's demand curve is the market demand curve, and the monopolist chooses the one price and output combination on the demand curve that maximizes its profit. With the entry of new rivals blocked, the monopolist can charge a price greater than its average total cost, earn economic profit over the long run, and not operate efficiently.

Key Terms and Concepts

Market structures

Market vs. industry

Pure competition

Barriers to entry

Market demand curve

Individual firm's demand curve

Economic profit or loss

Breaking even

Nonprice competition

Long-run profit behavior

Efficient production

Monopolistic competition

Identical vs. differentiated outputs

Oligopoly

Mutual interdependence

Leadership pricing

Kinked demand curve

Monopoly

Natural monopoly

Cartel

Price searcher

Review Questions

1. Into which of the four market structures would you place each of the following? Why would you make this classification?
    a. A small grain farm producing wheat on 50 acres
    b. A large grain farm producing wheat on 2,500 acres
    c. A major airline
    d. A college or university
    e. A local water company that faces no direct competition
    f. A small retail shoe store in a large city
    g. A shoe department in a department store in a large city
    h. A college food service
    i. Long-term airport parking

2. How do firms in each of the four market structures differ in terms of their number of rivals, control over price, product differentiation, ability to continually earn economic profit, and efficiency?

3. What is the relationship between price and average total cost when a firm operates with an economic profit, a loss, or breaks even? Illustrate in the graphs provided on the next page, the relationship between an individual firm's demand curve and average total cost curve in each of the following conditions.
    a. A purely competitive firm in the long run
    b. A monopolist earning an economic profit
    c. A purely competitive firm operating with a loss
    d. A monopolistically competitive firm in the long run
    e. A monopolistically competitive firm operating with a loss

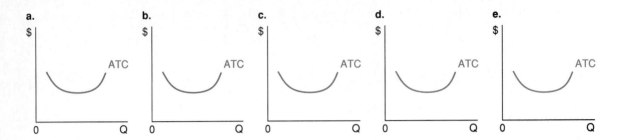

4. Why does a firm in pure competition operate efficiently in the long run while firms in the other three market structures do not? Why is it important to consumers that a firm operate efficiently?

5. Firms in monopoly and oligopoly markets are protected in varying degrees by barriers to entry, and they can earn excess profits in the long run. How do barriers to entry relate to a firm's ability to earn excess profits in the long run?

6. Monopolistically competitive sellers producing differentiated products face downward-sloping demand curves for their products. Pure competitors producing identical products face perfectly horizontal demand curves for their products. Why is a seller's demand curve horizontal or downward sloping depending on whether its product is differentiated or not?

7. Explain what is meant by mutual interdependence and how it relates to the price leadership and the kinked demand curve models.

Discussion Questions

1. Pure competition is said to be the most competitive of all the market structures. If this is true, why is it that no one firm is concerned with what any other firm does in a purely competitive market?

2. The desirability of expenditures for advertising is often debated. What arguments can be made that advertising helps the consumer, and what arguments can be made that advertising hurts the consumer?

3. You have a friend who believes that the automobile industry should be made monopolistically competitive by breaking it into a large number of small firms. Do you agree or disagree with your friend's proposal? Why?

4. A market is defined according to geographic considerations and the extent to which buyers view sellers' products as substitutes. What, in your opinion, would be the substitutes and relevant geographic market for each of the following? Be able to defend your answers.
    a. Beer from a small brewery
    b. A four-door automobile made by a large U.S. manufacturer
    c. A ski resort in the Rocky Mountains
    d. A major state university
    e. Frozen pizza

5. In the United States, people are increasing their purchases from catalogues and through mail orders. Does this growth in catalogue and mail order businesses increase competition for retail stores, or are these firms in a different market? Explain your reasoning.

6. Why are economists so concerned with efficiency? Would the world be a better place to live if all goods and services were produced efficiently and sold in purely competitive markets?

7. Identify a monopoly market in which you sometimes participate as a buyer. Can you determine any negative effects on you as a buyer that would not occur if there were more competition in that market?

Critical Thinking Case 13

Competition Causes Higher Prices

Critical Thinking Skills	Analyzing an anomaly
	Arguing and supporting a position
Economic Concepts	Mutual interdependence
	Natural monopoly and economies of scale

Kalamazoo, Michigan—When the two archrival hospitals here found out that both planned to launch helicopter ambulance services, they flew into action. Borgess Medical Center quickly found a copter, called photographers and was first to get pictures in the local paper.

But Bronson Methodist Hospital struck back, getting its chopper into the air first and proudly proclaiming a nurse aboard every flight.

Borgess retaliated three months later, boasting a *doctor* on every trip. Within a year, each hospital had upgraded to twin-engine choppers—making the announcement the same week. "There are only 90 helicopter ambulances in the whole country," an exasperated executive of Upjohn Co., the city's largest employer, said at the time, "and two of them are here."

Not to mention two heart programs, two maternity wards, two state-of-the-art emergency rooms, and two radiology services. There were even two billboard campaigns. . . .

In most businesses, competition cuts prices. But hospital bills in Kalamazoo, a metropolitan area of 200,000 between Detroit and Chicago, are the second highest in Michigan and among the highest in the nation. In general, hospital costs in two-hospital towns like Kalamazoo are 30% higher than in one-hospital communities, according to a survey by [consultants]. . . .

As a result, Upjohn and other major businesses here have tried hard to get the hospitals to cooperate. But nearly all the efforts have failed. . . .

Bronson and Borgess haven't gotten along since the turn of the century, when a group of doctors left Borgess ... to start their own hospital. Each hospital, of course, has its own version of that.

... [L]ocal businesses just couldn't take it anymore—and not only because of increased costs resulting from duplicated services. Because reimbursements from Medicaid and Medicare don't keep pace with costs, both Borgess and Bronson (as well as hospitals around the country) shift a portion of those costs to their paying customers, effectively charging them extra.

Upjohn and other leading companies, many of which have executives on the boards of both hospitals, began demanding some sort of cooperation. In mid-1987, the chief executives of the two hospitals began merger talks. . . .

... In October 1988, after over a year of courtship, Bronson and Borgess announced intentions to consolidate.

Almost immediately, the romance turned rocky. [Open-heart surgery, the naming of a chief executive, and abortion became sources of dispute.]

... Last October [1989], talks collapsed. And this spring, a new front in the war opened: laser surgery.

Borgess announced in March it intended to triple its annual volume of 500 laser procedures. In April, Bronson, which says it already does 1,500 a year, trumped the plans by performing the region's first laser gallbladder surgery—and trumpeting the feat in newspaper ads.

Questions

1. Unlike the expected relationship between competition and prices, in this case the rivalry between these two hospitals seems to be raising prices. Use economic concepts to explain this anomaly.

2. Indicate how mutual interdependence, natural monopoly, and the relevant market are important in explaining the market behavior and costs of both of these hospitals.

3. Assume that you have been appointed to a citizens' advisory board to make recommendations to lower hospital costs in Kalamazoo. Would you favor merging these two hospitals? Are there other suggestions that you could offer? Fully support your position on the merger argument as well as your other recommendations.

Source: Excerpted from Ron Winslow, "Competitive Anomaly: Consumers Pay More in 2-Hospital Towns," *The Wall Street Journal*, June 6, 1990, pp. A1, A6. Excerpted by permission of The Wall Street Journal, © Dow Jones & Company, Inc., 1990. All Rights Reserved Worldwide.

Suggested Readings

Walter Adams, ed., *The Structure of American Industry,* 8th ed. (New York: The Macmillan Publishing Co., Inc., 1990).
A survey of the operation, structure, history, and other aspects of the auto, computer, beer, motion picture, and other American industries. The book also includes chapters on conglomerate firms and public policy.

Carrie Dolan, "MCA's Yosemite Unit Pays Little, Gains a Lot Running Concessions," *The Wall Street Journal,* March 27, 1990, pp. A1, A6.
Discusses a monopoly at Yosemite National Park and some controversies surrounding the monopoly's role at the park.

John R. Emshwiller and Neil Behrmann, "How De Beers Revived World Diamond Cartel After Zaire's Pullout," *The Wall Street Journal,* July 7, 1983, pp. 1, 12.
A look at the operation of De Beers and the international market for diamonds.

"Marvelous Markets," *The Economist,* October 11, 1986, pp. 84–85.
Gives a brief description of how purely competitive markets work and discusses forces that occur in the real world to prevent the achievement of "perfection."

Thomas G. Moore, "Farm Policy: Justifications, Failures and the Need for Reform"; C. B. Baker, "Changes in Financial Markets and Their Effects on Agriculture"; Geoff Edwards, "U.S. Farm Policy: An Australian Perspective," Federal Reserve Bank of St. Louis, *Review,* October 1987.
Papers from a conference on U.S. agriculture dealing with the conceptual basis of the U.S. farm programs, the relationship between financial markets and agricultural markets, and the international consequences of U.S. farm programs.

Michael E. Porter, "Ch. 1: The Structural Analysis of Industries," *Competitive Strategy: Techniques for Analyzing Industries and Competitors* (New York: The Free Press, 1980), pp. 3–33.
Discusses factors such as barriers to entry and bargaining power of buyers and suppliers that affect competition in an industry.

Virgil Tipton, "Unfare?" *St. Louis Post-Dispatch,* October 24, 1988, pp. 1BP, 3BP; William Stockton, "When Eight Carriers Call the Shots," *The New York Times,* November 20, 1988, section 3, pp. 1, 6.
Two articles on competition in the airline industry and its effects on consumers.

Appendix to Chapter Thirteen

Determining the Profit-Maximizing Price and Output for a Firm

Profit-Maximizing Behavior of a Firm in Pure Competition

Given that a firm in pure competition can sell any output it chooses at the market price, how does it determine what quantity it actually will produce and sell? The objective of decision making by a purely competitive firm is to choose the output level that will maximize profit.

In Chapter Eleven it was shown that a firm will maximize its profit by operating where the additional cost and the additional revenue from the last unit produced and sold are equal. That is, the firm will maximize profit by operating where marginal cost equals marginal revenue. Consider how this rule applies to a purely competitive firm.

Table 13A.1 gives some price, quantity, and revenue information for a purely competitive grain farmer operating in a market where the equilibrium price is $3 per bushel. The first two columns of the table list the demand schedule for the farmer's grain, which shows that regardless of how much is demanded—be it 3, 1,003, or 8,003 bushels—the farmer receives a price of $3 per bushel. Total revenue, given in the third column, is calculated by multiplying price times quantity demanded at each level of output. Total revenue with a demand of three bushels is $9; with 1,003 bushels it is $3 × 1,003 = $3,009; and so on.

Marginal revenue is determined by calculating the change in total revenue as one more unit of a product is demanded. The marginal revenue figures in Table 13A.1 indicate that each time one more bushel of grain is demanded, marginal revenue is $3. No matter how much or how little is produced, the next unit demanded always adds $3 to the farmer's total revenue. Recalling that $3 is the price at which the farmer can sell each bushel of grain, it can be concluded that in pure competition the firm's marginal revenue is equal to its price.

When graphed, marginal revenue is a straight, horizontal line at the equilibrium market price of $3 per bushel. In other words, in pure competition the individual seller's marginal revenue curve is identical to its demand curve. This is shown in Figure 13A.1, which illustrates the demand and marginal revenue data for the grain farmer in Table 13A.1, by the line D = MR.

Table 13A.1   Price, Quantity, and Revenue Information for a Purely Competitive Seller

Because a seller in pure competition receives the same price for its product regardless of the quantity demanded, the seller's marginal revenue is always equal to price.

Price	Quantity Demanded	Total Revenue	Marginal Revenue
$3.00	0	$ 0	
			$3.00
3.00	1	3.00	
			3.00
3.00	2	6.00	
			3.00
3.00	3	9.00	
.	.	.	.
.	.	.	.
$3.00	1,001	$ 3,003.00	
			$3.00
3.00	1,002	3,006.00	
			3.00
3.00	1,003	3,009.00	
.	.	.	.
$3.00	8,001	$24,003.00	
			$3.00
3.00	8,002	24,006.00	
			3.00
3.00	8,003	24,009.00	

The marginal cost for a purely competitive seller behaves like the typical marginal cost curve discussed in Chapter Twelve. Graphically, it is "fish-hook" shaped: as output increases it decreases to a minimum and then increases.

The profit-maximizing output for a firm can be found by examining its marginal cost and marginal revenue curves, as is done in Figure 13A.1. To maximize its profit, a firm should produce where its marginal cost curve intersects its marginal revenue curve. This occurs in Figure 13A.1 at point A. Reading down from point A to the horizontal axis, one can see that the profit-maximizing output is 6,000 bushels of grain. Reading over from point A to the vertical axis, one can see that the profit-maximizing price is $3.

An additional note about profit-maximizing behavior is necessary. Up to this point, the marginal cost equals marginal revenue rule has been presented as a guide to lead the firm to maximum profit. But what if a firm is operating at a loss? What if, at every level of output, its costs are greater than its revenues? Here again the marginal cost equals marginal revenue rule leads to the "best" (where best means least bad) output level.

When a firm is producing at the point where marginal cost equals marginal revenue, it is operating at the strongest net revenue position it can reach. Where revenue is greater than costs, this leads to maximum profit, but where revenue falls short of costs, this leads to minimum loss. Thus, whether the firm is trying to maximize its profit or minimize its loss, the

Figure 13A.1   Profit-Maximizing Output for a Purely Competitive Seller

Graphically, a purely competitive seller's marginal revenue curve is identical to its demand curve, and profit is maximized or loss is minimized by operating at the output level where marginal revenue equals marginal cost.

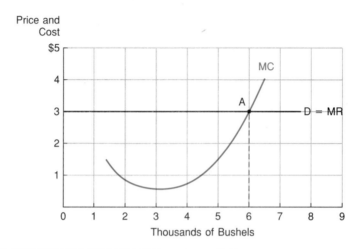

decision-making rule is the same: operate where marginal cost equals marginal revenue.

We can determine whether a firm is maximizing its profit or minimizing its loss by measuring whether the cost of producing each unit of output is less or more than its price at the "best" level of output. Graphically, this is indicated by whether the average total cost curve lies below or above the demand curve at the output level where marginal cost equals marginal revenue.

Figure 13A.2a shows a grain farmer operating with maximum economic profit where marginal cost equals marginal revenue. At the profit-maximizing output of 6,000 bushels, the price is $3 per bushel, and the average total cost is only $2 per bushel. In this case the farmer is earning an economic profit of $1 per bushel, or $6,000 in total economic profit.

Figure 13A.2b shows a grain farmer minimizing a loss by operating where marginal cost equals marginal revenue. At the loss-minimizing output of 6,000 bushels, the cost per bushel is $4 and the price received only $3. The farmer is taking a loss of $1 per bushel, or a total loss of $6,000.

Thus, economic profit is maximized if price is greater than cost per unit, or if the average total cost curve lies below the demand curve, at the output where marginal cost equals marginal revenue. A minimum loss is incurred if cost per unit is greater than price, or if the average total cost curve is above the demand curve, at the output where marginal cost equals marginal revenue.

Figure 13A.2   A Purely Competitive Seller Maximizing Profit or Minimizing Loss

If a purely competitive seller's demand curve is above its average total cost curve, it will maximize profit by operating at the output level where marginal revenue equals marginal cost. If its demand curve is below its average total cost curve, it will minimize its loss by operating at the output level where marginal revenue equals marginal cost.

a. Maximizing Profit

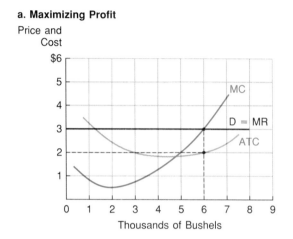

b. Minimizing Loss

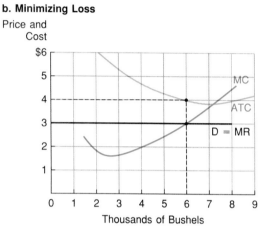

Profit-Maximizing Behavior of a Firm with a Downward-Sloping Demand Curve

If a firm faces a downward-sloping demand curve, such as a firm in the monopoly or monopolistically competitive market structure faces, at what price-output combination, or point on its demand curve, will it choose to operate? If the firm is maximizing profit or minimizing a loss, it will produce the output at which marginal cost equals marginal revenue, and charge the price given by the demand curve at that output.

A firm with a downward-sloping demand curve, where more can be sold only by lowering price, faces demand conditions identical to those given in the example in Chapter Eleven of the jeweler selling pocket watch cases. Table 11.4 showed that with demand behaving in this way, the jeweler's marginal revenue from each additional unit sold was less than its price. Table 11.4 is reproduced in Figure 13A.3.

Since price is shown on the demand curve, and since marginal revenue is less than price whenever price must be lowered to sell more, the marginal revenue curve associated with a downward-sloping demand curve must

Figure 13A.3   Demand and Marginal Revenue from
                                     Selling Pocket Watch Cases (Table 11.4 reprinted)[a]

When price must be lowered to sell a larger quantity, the marginal revenue for
each additional unit demanded is less than price. As a result, the marginal
revenue curve lies below the demand curve.

Price	Quantity Demanded	Total Revenue	Marginal Revenue
$45,000	0	$ 0	
			$40,000
40,000	1	40,000	
			30,000
35,000	2	70,000	
			20,000
30,000	3	90,000	
			10,000
25,000	4	100,000	

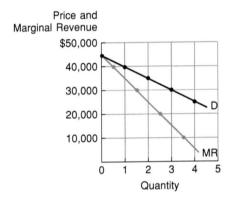

[a]See page 396 for the original table.

also be downward sloping, and must lie below that demand curve. To
illustrate this principle, the demand and marginal revenue curves for the
jeweler selling pocket watch cases are also given in Figure 13A.3. Marginal
revenue, like all marginal measurements, is plotted midway between the
quantities. For example, the marginal revenue of $40,000 for the first unit is
plotted at one-half unit.

The marginal cost curve for a seller with a downward-sloping demand
curve is typically like that for any firm: it decreases to a minimum and then
increases. Figure 13A.4 illustrates representative demand, marginal revenue,
and marginal cost curves for a firm with a downward-sloping demand curve.

To determine the profit-maximizing position for the seller in Figure 13A.4,
the intersection of its marginal cost and marginal revenue curves must be

Figure 13A.4   Profit-Maximizing Output for a Firm with a Downward-Sloping Demand Curve

The rule for maximizing profit is the same for a firm with a downward-sloping demand curve as it is for a firm in pure competition: operate at the output level where marginal revenue equals marginal cost.

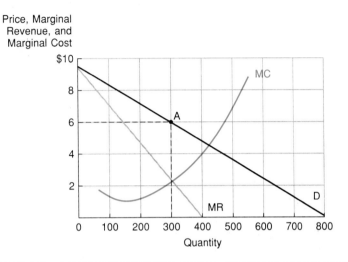

located. To find the profit-maximizing output, one reads from the point where marginal cost equals marginal revenue to the quantity axis. The profit-maximizing output is 300 units. The profit-maximizing price is found by reading up from the intersection where marginal cost equals marginal revenue to the demand curve, and from the demand curve to the vertical axis. For this seller, the profit-maximizing price is $6 per unit. Thus, point A on the demand curve shows the profit-maximizing price and output position for this seller.

As is the case with a purely competitive firm, whether a firm with a downward-sloping demand curve is maximizing economic profit or minimizing a loss depends upon the relationship between price and average total cost at the output level where marginal cost equals marginal revenue. If the average total cost curve lies below the demand curve, economic profit is maximized, and if the average total cost curve lies above the demand curve, the firm is incurring a minimum loss.

Figure 13A.5a shows that at the profit-maximizing price-output level for this firm, an economic profit of $2 per unit is earned. At the output level of 300 units, where marginal revenue equals marginal cost, price is $6 per unit and average total cost is $4. Total economic profit for this seller is $600 ($2 × 300 units).

Figure 13A.5   A Firm with a Downward-Sloping Demand Curve
Maximizing Profit or Minimizing Loss

When the average total cost curve lies below the demand curve at the output where marginal revenue equals marginal cost, the firm is maximizing profit by producing at that output. When the average total cost curve is above the demand curve, the firm is minimizing its loss by producing where marginal revenue equals marginal cost.

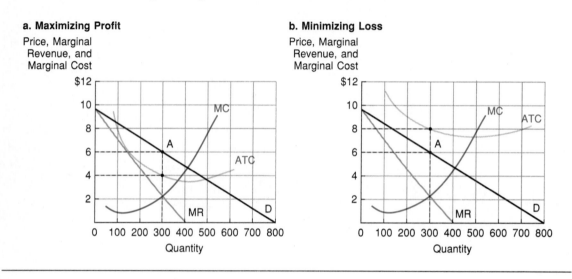

Figure 13A.5b shows the situation where the firm is operating with a loss. At the loss-minimizing level of 300 units, price is $6 and the cost per unit is $8, leaving a per unit loss of $2. The total loss for this firm is $600. "Test Your Understanding: Maximizing Profit and Minimizing Loss" lets you check your skill at identifying the best output level at which a firm can operate and the profit or loss it would earn at that output.

Maximizing Profit and Minimizing Loss[a]

[a]Answers can be found at the back of the book.

1. The table below shows the current market price of corn and various quantities that a purely competitive farmer could sell at that price. Based on this information, complete the table and answer the following questions about this farmer.

a. On the basis of your completed table, draw the demand and marginal revenue curves for this farmer's corn on the graph shown below.

b. To maximize profit or minimize loss, this farmer should sell _____ bushels of corn.

c. At this output the farmer's average total cost is $_____ per bushel, profit/loss is $_____ per bushel, and total profit/loss is $_____ .

d. On the same graph, draw the new demand and marginal revenue curves the farmer would face if the market price were to rise to $3.50 per bushel.

e. At this price, the farmer should sell _____ bushels of corn to maximize profit or minimize loss.

f. At this output, the farmer's average total cost is $_____ per bushel, profit/loss per bushel is $_____ , and total profit/loss is $_____ .

continued

Price	Quantity Demanded (Bushels)	Total Revenue	Marginal Revenue
$2.00	0	$_____	$_____
2.00	1	_____	
2.00	2	_____	
.	.	.	.
.	.	.	.
2.00	1,000	_____	
2.00	1,001	_____	_____
2.00	1,002	_____	_____
.	.	.	.
.	.	.	.
2.00	5,000	_____	
2.00	5,001	_____	_____
2.00	5,002	_____	_____

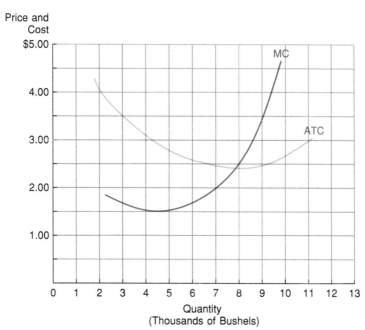

Price and Cost

Quantity
(Thousands of Bushels)

continued

2. Given in the graph below are the demand and cost conditions faced by a pure monopolist. To maximize profit or minimize loss, this firm should produce and sell _____ units of output and charge a price of $_____ per unit. At this level of output the firm's average total cost is $_____ per unit, its profit/loss per unit is $_____ , and its total profit/loss is $_____ .

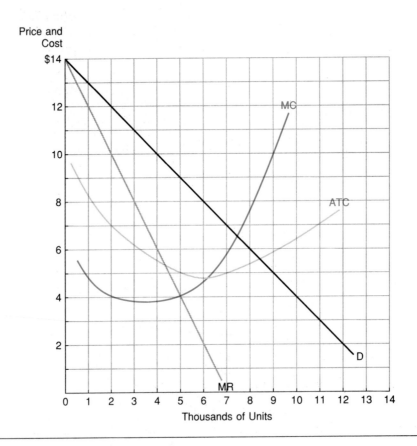

Price and Cost

Thousands of Units

Chapter Fourteen

Government and the Markets

One of the ways in which government intervenes in market activity is by taking companies accused of violating antitrust laws to court.

Source: ©Mug Shots/
The Stock Market.

Chapter Objectives

1. To introduce antitrust enforcement and regulation, the two main forms of government intervention in the operation of markets, and to indicate some reasons why government intervention might be sought.

2. To identify the major federal antitrust statutes, the business practices toward which they are directed, and the penalties they carry.

3. To distinguish among horizontal, vertical, and conglomerate mergers, and to indicate the relative importance of each.

4. To discuss government regulation, identify its forms and organization, and distinguish between industry regulation and social regulation.

5. To explain some justifications for industry regulation and to study price regulation, an important aspect of industry regulation.

6. To introduce the controversy over the effectiveness and desirability of regulation, deregulation, and the implications for antitrust and regulatory policy of the internationalization of economic activity.

Markets and competition play an important role in economic decision making and in determining the well-being of businesses and households. A seller's price, output, promotional decisions, profit, and efficiency are all influenced by the type of market and degree of competition the seller faces.

Economies where decisions are made primarily by individual businesses and households are built on the philosophy that free markets and competition should be at the foundation of economic activity. Although the U.S. economy is based on this philosophy, historically the U.S. government has intervened in the operation of markets in several important ways. For this reason, an understanding of markets requires that we analyze how government influences competition and market forces.

Basically, there are two main forms of government intervention in the operation of market forces in the United States: antitrust enforcement and regulation. Accordingly, this chapter is divided into two sections, the first on antitrust and the second on regulation.

A spectrum of views exists on the appropriate types and amounts of government intervention. Some observers feel that current intervention is too extensive; others feel that it is inadequate. Some hold that government involvement is not achieving its intended results or that it creates an unjustified administrative or financial burden on firms in the private sector;

others are satisfied with its effects and comfortable with the requirements it imposes.

Why would people who basically favor the principle of free markets seek government intervention in the operation of those markets? One reason is a concern that the amount of competition in a particular market is too limited to be effective. For example, government intervention might be sought in cases where the number of firms in a market is so small that there is a question as to whether they genuinely compete with one another, or where a firm's size is so great as to significantly weaken competitive forces. Second, as is the case with many gas, electric, and telephone companies, the argument for government intervention is that the public interest may be better served by a single large, efficient seller, answerable in its operations to a public body, than by several less efficient, smaller sellers competing with one another.

A third reason for seeking government intervention is security. As the economist John Maurice Clark wrote:

> . . . competition has two opposites: which we may call monopoly and security. . . . Nearly everyone favors competition as against monopoly, and nearly everyone wants it limited in the interest of security. And hardly anyone pays much attention to the question where one leaves off and the other begins.[1]

Competition introduces certain risks into private decision making in markets. The desire to reduce these risks may inspire support for some form of government intervention. For example, laws specifying the ground rules as to what types of rivalry are and are not allowed may reduce the risk of failure for smaller or weaker sellers in a market. Laws that create regulated monopolies, such as gas or electric suppliers, increase security for buyers by ensuring a continuous supply of output by these firms at prices that are supervised by a public authority.

Antitrust Enforcement

Antitrust laws
Laws designed to promote the operation of market forces by prohibiting certain practices that reduce competition.

Antitrust enforcement centers on a series of laws designed to promote the operation of market forces by limiting certain practices that reduce competition. Specifically, **antitrust laws** are aimed at two broad categories of practices.

Monopolization and attempts to monopolize
A firm acquires or attempts to acquire a monopoly share of its market through unreasonable means.

The first is **monopolization and attempts to monopolize,** which occurs when a firm, through unreasonable means, acquires or attempts to acquire such a large share of its market that it does not feel strong competitive pressure from its rivals. To appreciate the effect that a firm with a great deal of market power can have on competition, consider the comparison made by economist Walter Adams between rivalry among firms and a poker game where one player has many more funds than the others.

[1]John Maurice Clark, *Alternative to Serfdom* (New York: Alfred A. Knopf, 1948), p. 61.

. . . [I]n a poker game with unlimited stakes, the player who commands dispro-
portionately large funds is likely to emerge victorious. If I have $100 while my
opponents have no more than $5 each, I am likely to win regardless of my
ability, my virtue, or my luck.[2]

Combinations and
conspiracies in
restraint of trade
Practices carried out
jointly by two or more
firms that unreasonably
restrict competition.

The second category of practices toward which antitrust laws are directed
is **combinations and conspiracies in restraint of trade,** which includes acts
carried out jointly by two or more firms that unreasonably limit competition,
such as price fixing and the division of sales territories. These two categories
of practices, monopolization and attempts to monopolize, and combinations
and conspiracies in restraint of trade, will be explained more fully as we
review the major antitrust statutes.

Antitrust enforcement is carried out by both the federal and state governments, with the main responsibility falling on the Department of Justice
and the Federal Trade Commission at the federal level. In addition to federal
and state enforcement, private parties such as business firms can bring
charges that other companies and/or individuals have violated the laws.

Administration of the laws depends heavily on the courts and is carried
out on a case-by-case basis. That is, each violation is treated separately. In
some instances a suit may be dropped because it is judged to have insufficient justification to go to trial, or a pretrial agreement may be reached
where the accused firm promises to discontinue a practice or settles in some
other way. In other instances a trial may be required before the issue is
resolved. Antitrust cases can become very long, costly, and complicated
before they are settled.

In summary, antitrust is concerned with the relationships between firms,
especially rival firms. When a problem arises, the government does not
respond by becoming a participant in the market and overseeing the
behavior of sellers on an ongoing basis. Rather, monopoly and conspiracy
questions are dealt with on a case-by-case basis through the courts.

The Antitrust Laws

Combinations and conspiracies between two or more firms and monopolization and attempts to monopolize by a single firm can occur in several
different ways, and the antitrust laws are designed to deal with these
problems in their various forms. At the federal level, where we will focus our
attention, the antitrust statutes range from laws that are broadly worded to
those that are specific about the practices at which they are aimed. There are
five main federal antitrust laws: the Sherman Act (1890), the Federal Trade
Commission Act (1914), the Clayton Act (1914), the Robinson-Patman Act

---

[2] Estes Kefauver, *In a Few Hands* (New York: Pantheon Books, 1965), p. 196. In this illustration
Professor Adams was referring to a problem that may arise with conglomerate mergers, which
are described later in this section.

(1936), and the Celler-Kefauver Act (1950). The 1936 and 1950 acts both amend the Clayton Act.

The Sherman Act (1890)   The original and most broadly worded federal antitrust statute is the **Sherman Act.** Its first section condemns combinations and conspiracies in restraint of trade without defining what types of policies fall within that category, and reads in part:

> *Every contract, combination in the form of trust or otherwise, or conspiracy, in restraint of trade or commerce among the several States, or with foreign nations, is hereby declared to be illegal.*[3]

The second section attacks monopolization and attempts to monopolize, again without specifying what types of activities are involved. Section Two reads in part:

> *Every person who shall monopolize, or attempt to monopolize, or combine or conspire with any other person or persons, to monopolize any part of the trade or commerce among the several States, or with foreign nations, shall be deemed guilty. . . .*[4]

Combinations and conspiracies condemned by Section One of the Sherman Act are either per se or Rule of Reason violations. **Per se violations** are agreements between firms where proof of the agreement is sufficient to establish guilt: there is no defense for a per se violation. Price fixing and division of sales territories among firms are included in this category. One explanation for the per se rule is that the court's time is a scarce resource, and the likelihood of society benefiting from acts such as price fixing or territorial division is so remote that it would be a waste of time to require a court to listen to a defense for these acts.

Price fixing occurs when sellers take joint action to influence the market pricing mechanism. For example, an understanding between competing sellers as to the prices they will charge their buyers or the price below which they will not sell would be price fixing, as would an agreement on a system for determining who will submit the lowest offer when pricing is done with sealed bids. With price fixing, competition is diminished and sellers act more like monopolists.

Territorial division exists when firms divide a sales area among themselves: one firm concentrating on one geographic location, and other firms concentrating on other locations. For example, territorial division would occur if two national firms agreed that one would sell exclusively east

---

Sherman Act (1890)

Original and most broadly worded federal antitrust statute; condemns combinations and conspiracies in restraint of trade, and monopolization and attempts to monopolize.

Per se violations

Anticompetitive agreements between firms where proof of the agreement is sufficient to establish guilt; include agreements to jointly fix prices and divide sales territories.

Price fixing

Joint action by sellers to influence their product prices; considered to be highly anticompetitive.

Territorial division

Joint action by sellers to divide sales territories among themselves; considered to be highly anticompetitive.

---

[3] *United States Statutes at Large*, Vol. 26 (Washington, D.C.: U.S. Government Printing Office, 1889–1891), p. 209.

[4] *United States Statutes at Large*, Vol. 26 (1889–1891), p. 209.

of the Mississippi River if the other would sell only west of the river. As with price fixing, territorial division diminishes competition.

Rule of Reason violations occur when firms come together in a way that may or may not unreasonably restrain trade. With the Rule of Reason, there is no blanket condemnation of business practices as there is with price fixing and territorial division. Rather, each challenged practice must be examined to see whether *in this particular instance* the restraint is unreasonable.

Activities of industry trade associations and joint ventures fall under the Rule of Reason umbrella. A **trade association** is an organization of firms in a particular industry, such as construction or furniture manufacturing, that performs certain functions that benefit its members. One function that these associations may perform is the collection and distribution of information on the state of the industry. If the reporting includes data on overall industry trends, or general information on supply conditions or buyer behavior, and if it is equally available to all interested parties, the trade association activity may enhance competition by improving the general state of knowledge in the industry. But if the information gives specific details on the terms of each firm's sales and the names of its buyers, or if the information is not equally available to all interested parties, the trade association's information gathering might help to foster a price fixing agreement or division of buyers among sellers, and would therefore be subject to condemnation under Section One of the Sherman Act.

A **joint venture** is a cooperative effort by two or more firms that is limited in scope. The operation of an automobile plant by U.S. and Japanese manufacturers or the drilling of oil in a remote part of the world by several firms acting together would be examples of joint ventures. As with trade association activities, the legality of joint ventures must be judged on a case-by-case basis to determine whether competition has been unreasonably restricted.

Cases involving the Sherman Act Section Two violations of monopolization and attempts to monopolize rest largely on two issues: the specific actions taken by a firm indicating its intent to monopolize its market, and the firm's share of its market. Where the seller's market share is small and it is clearly not a monopolist, an attempt to monopolize may be inferred from actions such as pricing below cost in an attempt to drive rivals out of the market, or from contracts with critical suppliers or distributors that would foreclose their services to the firm's rivals.

For firms with larger market shares, monopolization may be inferred less from what a firm does and more from its relative size in comparison to its rivals. For example, in *United States* v. *Aluminum Company of America*, a leading monopolization case, the court enunciated what has come to be known as the "30-60-90 Rule," which is a rough guide for analyzing Sherman Act monopolization questions: "[a greater than ninety per cent share of the market] is enough to constitute a monopoly; it is doubtful

---

Rule of Reason violations

Violations of the antitrust laws involving actions that are not necessarily anticompetitive; the challenged restraint on competition must be shown to be unreasonable.

Trade association

An organization representing firms in a particular industry that performs certain functions that benefit those firms.

Joint venture

A cooperative effort by two or more firms that is limited in scope.

whether sixty or sixty-four per cent would be enough; and certainly thirty-three per cent is not."[5]

An extremely important aspect of monopolization cases is the definition of the relevant market, which was discussed in Chapter Thirteen. Ordinarily, the more broadly a market is defined in terms of its geographic boundaries and/or number of substitute products, the smaller will be the share of that market taken by any one firm. The more narrowly a market is defined, the larger will be the share taken by the firm. Thus, it may be to the advantage of a firm accused of monopolizing a market to define that market as broadly as possible.

For example, in the Aluminum Company of America case, in which Alcoa was accused of monopolizing the aluminum market, and where the "30-60-90 Rule" was enunciated, there were several possible components to the relevant market: primary domestic ingot, secondary aluminum, imported ingot, and aluminum fabricated by Alcoa. By including or excluding one or more of these components, different definitions of the relevant market could be developed, and each definition resulted in a different market share for Alcoa. As stated by the court:

There are various ways of computing "Alcoa's" control of the aluminum market—as distinct from its production—depending upon what one regards as competing in that market. The judge figured its share—during the years 1929–1938, inclusive—as only about thirty-three percent; to do so he included "secondary," and excluded that part of "Alcoa's" own production which it fabricated and did not therefore sell as ingot. If, on the other hand, "Alcoa's" total production, fabricated and sold, be included, and balanced against the sum of imported "virgin" and "secondary," its share of the market was in the neighborhood of sixty-four per cent for that period. The percentage we have already mentioned—over ninety—results only if we both include all "Alcoa's" production and exclude "secondary." [6]

Application 14.1, "Cases Involving the Sherman Act," gives some details of court cases dealing with price fixing arrangements, territorial divisions, business associations, and monopolizing behavior that were brought under the Sherman Act. The decision of the court in each case is also provided.

The Federal Trade Commission Act (1914)   The Federal Trade Commission (FTC) was created by the **Federal Trade Commission Act** and granted power to ". . . prevent persons, partnerships, or corporations, . . . from using unfair methods of competition in commerce."[7] Included among unfair methods of competition are antitrust violations.

Federal Trade Commission Act (1914)
Created the Federal Trade Commission and empowered it to prevent unfair methods of competition, which include antitrust violations.

[5] *United States* v. *Aluminum Company of America,* 148 F. 2d 416 (1945), p. 424.
[6] *United States* v. *Aluminum Company of America,* 148 F. 2d 416 (1945), p. 424.
[7] *United States Statutes at Large,* Vol. 38, Part 1 (Washington, D.C.: U.S. Government Printing Office, 1915), p. 719.

When the FTC feels that a business is engaged in unfair competition, it can issue a complaint and arrange a hearing to determine whether the practice should be prohibited. If it is found that the practice is unfair competition, the FTC can issue a "cease and desist order" requiring the firm to stop the activity. If a seller fails to follow the order, or if it feels the order is incorrect, either the FTC or the accused can have the order brought before a court for a ruling.[8]

The Clayton Act (1914) Several practices that "...substantially lessen competition or tend to create a monopoly in any line of commerce ..."[9] are the concern of the **Clayton Act.** Unlike the Sherman Act and the Federal Trade Commission Act, which are not specific as to the practices they disallow, the Clayton Act is directed toward several particular activities: exclusionary practices, interlocking directorates, price discrimination, and the acquisition of one firm by another.

Exclusionary practices occur when a seller of a product forecloses its rivals from the market by following policies that make it impossible for the rivals to compete. For example, Company X could agree to sell its product to a buyer only on the condition that it would supply all of the buyer's needs for that type of item. Such an agreement would effectively give Company X a monopoly over the buyer's demand for that product.

Another example of an exclusionary practice is a **tying contract.** This occurs when a buyer can obtain one good from a seller only by purchasing another good as well from the same seller. Suppose that many firms, including Company X, sell good A, but that Company X is the only seller of good B. If Company X "ties" the sale of its brand of good A to good B — that is, it will sell good B only as long as the buyer makes its good A purchases from Company X — it engages in a tying contract. In this way, Company X is using its monopoly of good B to gain monopoly power over good A.

Interlocking directorates occur where the same person sits on the boards of directors of different corporations. For example, an interlock would exist between a manufacturing corporation and a shipping corporation if the same individual served on the boards of directors of both firms. Interlocking directorates are not necessarily anticompetitive, but competition could be injured under certain circumstances. For instance, how might competition be lessened if the same person sat on the boards of directors of two firms producing similar products for the same market? Or how might competition be reduced if an individual sat on the board of a large manufacturing corporation and also on the board of one of several firms competing to sell machinery to that manufacturer?

Clayton Act (1914)
Federal antitrust statute prohibiting specific activities, such as exclusionary practices, that substantially reduce competition or tend to create a monopoly.

Exclusionary practices
Practices through which a seller attempts to prevent its suppliers or buyers from dealing with a competitor.

Tying contract
Contract in which a buyer can obtain one good from a seller only by purchasing another good as well from the same seller.

Interlocking directorates
The same person sits on the boards of directors of different corporations.

---

[8] *United States Statutes at Large,* Vol. 38, Part 1 (1915), pp. 719, 720.
[9] *United States Statutes at Large,* Vol. 38, Part 1 (1915), p. 730.

Application 14.1

Cases Involving the Sherman Act

Price Fixing: *Monsanto Company* v. *Spray-Rite Service Corp.* (1984)

From 1957 to 1968, [Spray-Rite Service Corp.], a wholesale distributor of agricultural chemicals *that engaged in a discount operation* [emphasis added], sold agricultural herbicides manufactured by [Monsanto Co.]. In 1968, [Monsanto] refused to renew [Spray-Rite's] 1-year distributorship term, and thereafter [Spray-Rite] was unable to purchase from other distributors as much of [Monsanto's] products as it desired or as early in the season as it needed them. [Spray-Rite] ultimately brought suit in Federal District Court under § 1 of the Sherman Act, alleging that [Monsanto] and some of its distributors conspired to fix the resale prices of [Monsanto's] products and that [Monsanto] had terminated [Spray-Rite's] distributorship in furtherance of the conspiracy. . . . The District Court instructed the jury that [Monsanto's] conduct was *per se* unlawful if it was in furtherance of a price-fixing conspiracy. . . .

Ruling:

. . . There was sufficient evidence for the jury reasonably to have concluded that [Monsanto] and some of its distributors were parties to an "agreement" or "conspiracy" to maintain resale prices and terminate price cutters. . . .

Territorial Division: *United States* v. *Sealy, Inc.* (1967)

The United States brought this civil action for violation of § 1 of the Sherman Act against [Sealy, Inc.], the owner of the trademarks for Sealy branded mattresses and bedding products which it licensed manufacturers in various parts of the country to produce and sell under a territorial allocation system. Sealy agreed with each licensee not to license anyone else to manufacture or sell in a designated area and the licensee agreed not to manufacture or sell Sealy products outside that area. The Sealy licensees own substantially all [Sealy's] stock and control its day-to-day operations, including the assignment and termination of the exclusive territorial licenses. [Sealy] was charged with conspiring with its licensees to fix the prices at which their retail customers might resell Sealy products and to allocate mutually exclusive territories among the licensees. . . .

Ruling:

. . . The territorial restraints were a part of the unlawful price-fixing and policing activities of Sealy operating as an instrumentality of the licensees and constituted "an aggregation of trade restraints" which was illegal *per se*.

Business Associations: *Los Angeles Memorial Coliseum Commission* v. *National Football League et al.* (1984)

In 1978, the owner of the Los Angeles Rams . . . decided to locate his team in a new stadium . . . in Anaheim, California. That left the Los Angeles Coliseum without a major tenant. Officials of the Coliseum then began to search for a new National Football League occupant. . . .

The L.A. Coliseum ran into a major obstacle in its attempts to convince a team to move. That obstacle was Rule 4.3 of Article IV of the NFL Constitution. In 1978, Rule 4.3 required unanimous approval of all the 28 teams of the League whenever a team . . . seeks to relocate in the home territory of another team. . . . In this case, the L.A. Coliseum was still in the home territory of the Rams.

The Coliseum viewed Rule 4.3 as an unlawful restraint of trade in violation of § 1 of the Sherman Act . . . and brought this action in September of 1978. The district court concluded, however, that no . . . controversy existed because no NFL team had committed to moving to Los Angeles. . . .

The NFL nevertheless saw the Coliseum's suit as a sufficient threat to warrant amending Rule 4.3. . . . to require only three-quarters approval by the members of the League for a move into another team's home territory. . . .

Soon thereafter, Al Davis, managing general partner of the Oakland Raiders franchise, stepped into view. . . .

On March 1, 1980, Al Davis and the Coliseum signed a "memorandum of agreement" outlining the terms of the Raiders' relocation in Los Angeles. At an NFL meeting on March 3, 1980, Davis announced his intentions. . . .

Over Davis' objection that Rule 4.3 is illegal under the antitrust laws, the NFL teams voted on March 10, 1980, 22–0 against the move, with five teams abstaining. . . .

The Los Angeles Memorial Coliseum Commission then renewed its action against the NFL and each member club. . . .

Ruling:

. . . On May 7, 1982, the jury returned a verdict in favor of the Los Angeles Memorial Coliseum Commission and the Oakland Raiders on the antitrust claim. . . .

Monopolizing Behavior: *Aspen Skiing Company* v. *Aspen Highlands Skiing Corporation* (1985)

A ski resort operator filed suit in the United States District Court for the District of Colorado against the operator of three other skiing facilities in the area, alleging that the latter had monopolized the local market for downhill ski services, in violation of § 2 of the Sherman Act . . . by refusing to continue a long-standing marketing arrangement whereby skiers could purchase 6-day tickets usable on a given day at any of the four facilities . . . , and by taking additional actions which made it difficult for the smaller operator to market a multi-area package of its own. The District Court entered judgment on a jury verdict in favor of the smaller operator, after instructing the jury that a firm possessing monopoly power violates § 2 of the Sherman Act if it willfully acquires, maintains, or uses that power by anticompetitive or exclusionary means or for anticompetitive or exclusionary purposes, but does not violate the law by refusing to deal with a competitor if there are valid business reasons for that refusal. . . .

Ruling:

. . . [T]he unanimous view of the eight participating members of the [Supreme Court was] . . . that the actions of the larger operator were properly held to violate § 2 of the Sherman Act since the evidence was sufficient to support a conclusion that they were not taken for legitimate business reasons, but for the purpose of injuring a competitor.

Sources: *Monsanto Co.* v. *Spray-Rite Service Corp.,* 465 U.S. 752 (1984), pp. 752–753; *United States* v. *Sealy, Inc.,* 388 U.S. 350 (1967), p. 350; *Los Angeles Memorial Coliseum Commission* v. *National Football League et al.,* 726 F.2d 1381 (1984), pp. 1384–1386; *Aspen Skiing Co.* v. *Aspen Highlands Skiing Corp.,* 86 L.Ed.2d 467 (1985), pp. 467–468.

In each of the activities addressed by the Clayton Act, as well as those included under its amendments, the practices themselves do not automatically constitute violations of the antitrust laws. They become violations only when the activities tend to significantly reduce competition or create a monopoly.

The Robinson-Patman Act (1936)   Section Two of the Clayton Act is amended by the **Robinson-Patman Act,** which deals with price discrimination. **Price discrimination** occurs when a seller charges different buyers different prices for the same product. For example, if a firm sells you an item at one price, and then sells exactly the same item with exactly the same treatment and service to someone else at a lower price, you are discriminated against in terms of price. The Clayton Act condemns price discrimination when it weakens competition or leads to a monopoly, and the Robinson-Patman Act elaborates further on that condemnation.

Price discrimination can injure competition between a seller and its rivals. Through price discrimination, a seller can lower its price where there is intense competition for potential buyers, while keeping the price unchanged, or even raising it, for remaining customers. If a rival is unable to meet these price cuts, it may lose sales and perhaps be driven from the market.

A buyer's market position can also be injured when, because of discrimination, it must pay a higher price for what it purchases than the price its rival pays. Because of the difference in price, the discriminated-against firm's costs are higher than its rival's costs. This in turn could force the firm to raise its price, or keep its price unchanged but absorb the higher cost through forgone profit, either of which is damaging to its competitive position.

The Robinson-Patman Act attacks outright price discrimination as well as several types of "indirect" price discrimination. The latter includes practices such as granting quantity discounts on terms that only a few large buyers can meet, paying purchasers for services that have not been rendered, and treating buyers unequally in the provision of sales facilities.[10]

The Celler-Kefauver Act (1950)   Section Seven of the Clayton Act is amended by the **Celler-Kefauver Act,** which deals with anticompetitive mergers and acquisitions of firms.

A business can be acquired or merged with another in two ways: by the purchase of a controlling number of shares of stock, or by the outright purchase of assets. Interestingly, the original Clayton Act had a loophole in that it condemned anticompetitive acquisitions through stock purchases but said nothing about the purchase of assets. This loophole was closed by the

---

Robinson-Patman Act (1936)
Federal antitrust statute concerned with anticompetitive price discrimination; amends Section Two of the Clayton Act.

Price discrimination
Different buyers acquire the same product from the same seller with the same treatment and service but pay different prices.

Celler-Kefauver Act (1950)
Federal antitrust statute concerned with anticompetitive mergers and acquisitions of firms; amends Section Seven of the Clayton Act.

---

[10] *United States Statutes at Large,* Vol. 49, Part 1 (Washington, D.C.: U.S. Government Printing Office, 1936), pp. 1526–1527.

Celler-Kefauver Act, which attacks anticompetitive acquisitions either by stock or asset purchase.[11]

There are three main types of mergers or acquisitions, each with its own potentially anticompetitive effects: horizontal, vertical, and conglomerate. A **horizontal merger** occurs where two or more sellers competing in the same market join together. A plumbing contractor who buys out a competitor in the same town, or competing manufacturers serving a national market who combine to form one corporation are examples of horizontal mergers.

If a market contains many firms, and two extremely small sellers merge, the consequence may not be noticeable: a small grain farmer buying a second farm will have no effect on the grain market. But where the acquiring and/or acquired firm has a substantial market share, their joining may have an anticompetitive effect by creating a larger organization with an even greater share of the market. For example, suppose a local area is served by four dairies: one accounting for 40 percent of the total sales, another 30 percent, another 20 percent, and another 10 percent. If the second and third largest sellers were to merge, it would create a single entity controlling 50 percent of the total sales, and would result in a market made up of only two large sellers and one much smaller seller. Because of its potentially adverse effect on the market, this merger could constitute a Celler-Kefauver Act violation.

A **vertical merger** involves the joining of a firm with a supplier or a distributor. A meat packing company that buys a cattle ranch and a furniture manufacturer that purchases retail stores through which to sell its merchandise are examples of vertical acquisitions or mergers.

A vertical merger may be anticompetitive if it forecloses a firm's rivals from key suppliers or distributors. For example, suppose three lumber yards provide building materials to contractors in a particular area. If one of the contractors were to acquire all of the lumber yards, he or she could shut off the local supply of building materials to all rivals and possibly force them out of business. Or a manufacturer of a specialized type of machinery could put its rivals at a competitive disadvantage by acquiring the only firm in an area that distributes and services that type of machinery. If competition is injured, a vertical merger can result in a Celler-Kefauver Act violation.

A **conglomerate merger** occurs when one firm joins with another that is not a competitor, supplier, or distributor. The joining of a steel wire manufacturer and a telephone answering service would be a conglomerate merger, as would be the combining of a publishing company and a chain of retail clothing outlets.

Conglomerate mergers can have anticompetitive effects because of what is known as the "deep pocket." For example, a large, profitable manufacturer of machinery might acquire one of several small competing candy compa-

Horizontal merger
Two or more sellers competing in the same market join together.

Vertical merger
A firm joins with a supplier or distributor.

Conglomerate merger
A firm joins with another firm that is not a competitor, supplier, or distributor.

---

[11] *United States Statutes at Large,* Vol. 38, Part 1 (1915), pp. 731–732; *United States Statutes at Large,* Vol. 64, Part 1 (Washington, D.C.: U.S. Government Printing Office, 1952), pp. 1125–1126.

nies. As a result of the acquisition, the candy firm could receive financial allocations from the manufacturer's "deep pocket" full of money and use these funds for expenditures on such things as advertising, expansion of facilities, and a larger sales staff. On the basis of these funds, the candy company could increase its sales and share of the market at the expense of its rivals who do not have comparable financial resources with which to compete.

Far and away, the largest amount of merger activity has involved conglomeration. From 1948 through 1979, 2,023 large acquisitions occurred in mining and manufacturing. Of these, 1,491, or 73.7 percent, were conglomerate. Horizontal mergers, of which there were 331, were a distant second, followed by vertical mergers, which numbered 201.[12]

Historically, mergers have tended to occur in waves: at times there have been relatively few mergers, and at other times there have been many. For example, from 1935 through 1944, a period that covers the last years of the Depression and most of World War II, fewer than 1,500 acquisitions in mining and manufacturing took place. In contrast, over 12,500 acquisitions in mining and manufacturing occurred during the 1960s, and then the number fell back to less than 7,500 in the 1970s.[13]

In the 1980s, merger activity again became important as the number and relative size of acquisitions increased dramatically. Table 14.1, which is a reprint of Table 10.8, shows the number and value of all acquisitions of $1 million or more from 1980 through 1989. During the 1980s there were over 31,000 mergers, which together totaled over $1.3 trillion in value. One concern to some is the extent to which U.S. companies have been acquired by foreign firms during this recent merger wave. In 1988, for example, 447, or 11.2 percent, of the 4,000 acquisitions were by foreign firms. These acquisitions accounted for nearly 26 percent of the value of all acquisitions in that year.[14]

A striking feature of the 1980s has been the use of leveraged buyouts to finance acquisitions. A **leveraged buyout,** or **LBO,** occurs when an acquisition is financed mainly with borrowed funds and the obligation to pay off those borrowed funds then becomes the responsibility of the newly formed company. One method for borrowing these funds is to issue bonds in the name of the newly formed company. These bonds are regarded as risky investments since they are backed more by the expectation that the firm will do well than by what the owners have put into the business, and are known

Leveraged buyout (LBO)

Acquiring a business mainly with borrowed funds that are to be paid off by the newly formed company.

---

[12] Federal Trade Commission, *Statistical Report on Mergers and Acquisitions 1979,* (Washington, D.C.: U.S. Government Printing Office, 1981), pp. 98, 99, 109. Only acquisitions for which data were publicly available are given. A large acquisition is defined as one where the acquired firm had assets of at least $10 million at the time of the merger.

[13] U.S. Bureau of the Census, *Statistical Abstract of the United States: 1982–83,* 103d ed. (Washington, D.C.: U.S. Government Printing Office, 1982), p. 531.

[14] U.S. Bureau of the Census, *Statistical Abstract of the United States: 1990,* 110th ed. (Washington, D.C.: U.S. Government Printing Office, 1990), p. 534.

Table 14.1   Number and Value of Mergers and Acquisitions in the 1980s[a]

A large number of mergers and acquisitions, some in the billions of dollars, involved U.S. firms in the 1980s.

Year	Number of Acquired Business Concerns	Value of Acquired Business Concerns (Billions of Dollars)
1980	1,558	$ 32.8
1981	2,328	69.5
1982	2,298	60.7
1983	2,393	52.7
1984	3,175	126.1
1985	3,484	146.0
1986	4,446	205.8
1987	4,015	178.3
1988	4,000	236.4
1989	3,415	231.4

[a]Mergers and acquisitions valued at $1 million or more.
Source: *Mergers and Acquisitions*, March/April 1990, p. 95.

Junk bonds

Corporate bonds issued to finance the acquisition of a business and backed mainly by the expectation that the business will succeed; considered to be risky investments.

as **junk bonds.** From 1980 through 1988 there were over 1,900 leveraged buyouts of $1 million or more, and the total value of these buyouts was over $174.5 billion.[15]

Application 14.2, "Cases Involving the Clayton Act and Its Amendments," presents the facts and rulings in court cases pertaining to tying arrangements, price discrimination, and mergers that had antitrust implications under the amended Clayton Act.

Antitrust Penalties   Violation of the antitrust laws can result in one or more of four types of penalties, depending on the offense and who is bringing the suit. The penalties include imprisonment for up to three years, fines of $350,000 per offense for individuals and $10 million per offense for corporations, structural remedies, and triple damages.

Structural remedies involve preventing two or more firms from merging or breaking an offending firm into two or more unrelated units. Preventing firms from merging is appropriate where a proposed merger would violate the antitrust laws. In this situation, competition can be promoted by disallowing the merger and requiring the companies to remain unrelated. Breaking up an offending firm might be used where a single firm has been

[15] *Statistical Abstract: 1990,* 1990, p. 534.

Application 14.2

Cases Involving the Clayton Act and Its Amendments

Tying Arrangements: *International Business Machines Corp.* **v.** *United States* **(1936)**

This is an appeal . . . of a decree of a District Court . . . [enjoining I.B.M.] from leasing its tabulating and other machines upon the condition that the lessees shall use with such machines only tabulating cards manufactured by [I.B.M.], as a violation of § 3 of the Clayton Act. . . .

[I.B.M.'s] machines and those of Remington Rand, Inc., are now the only ones on the market which perform certain mechanical tabulations and computations . . . by the use in them of cards upon which are recorded data. . . .

To insure satisfactory performance by [I.B.M.'s] machines it is necessary that the cards used in them conform to precise specifications as to size and thickness, and that they be free from defects . . . which cause unintended electrical contacts and consequent inaccurate results. The cards manufactured by [I.B.M.] are electrically tested for such defects.

[I.B.M.] leases its machines for a specified rental and period, *upon condition that the lease shall terminate in case any cards not manufactured by [I.B.M.] are used in the leased machine* [emphasis added]. . . .

. . . [I.B.M.'s] contentions are that its leases are lawful [partly because their] purpose and effect are only to preserve to [I.B.M.] the good will of its patrons by preventing the use of unsuitable cards which would interfere with the successful performance of its machines. . . .

. . . [It appears] that others are capable of manufacturing cards suitable for use in [I.B.M.'s] machines. . . .

Ruling:

[I.B.M.] is not prevented from proclaiming the virtues of its own cards or warning against the danger of using, in its machines, cards which do not conform to the necessary specifications, or even from making its leases conditional upon the use of cards which conform to them. . . . [S]uch measures would protect its good will, without the creation of monopoly or resort to the suppression of competition. [Case decided against I.B.M.]

Price Discrimination: *Utah Pie Co.* **v.** *Continental Baking Co. et al.* **(1967)**

This suit . . . by [Utah Pie Co.], a local bakery company in Salt Lake City, against three large companies each of which is a major factor in the frozen pie market in one or more regions of the country, charged . . . violations by each . . . of § 2(a) of the Clayton Act, as amended by the Robinson-Patman Act. The major competitive weapon in the Salt Lake City market was price and for most of the period [Utah Pie], which had the advantage of a local plant, had the lowest prices.

found guilty of monopolizing a market. Here the monopoly could be ended by separating one or more of the company's divisions into independent units.

With triple damages, an injured party can, under certain conditions, collect three times its damages from the offending firm. For example, suppose it was proven in a court suit that over the last three years Company B lost $6 million in profit because of an antitrust violation committed by Company A. On the basis of this, the court could require Company A to pay Company B not $6 million to compensate for the lost profit, but three times $6 million, or $18 million, in damages.

Each [of the other companies] at some time engaged in discriminatory pricing and thereby contributed to a deteriorating price structure during the relevant period. . . . [Pet Milk] sold an economy pie in the Salt Lake City market at a price which was at times lower than that in other markets; and it sold its proprietary label quality pies in Salt Lake City for some months at prices lower than those in California, despite freight charges from its California plant. . . . In June 1961 . . . Continental Baking cut its price in the Utah area to a level well below that applicable elsewhere, and less than its direct cost plus an allocation for overhead. Carnation Co., whose share of the market slipped in 1959, slashed its price in 1960, and for eight months of that year its Salt Lake City price was lower than that in other markets, and that trend continued in 1961. . . .

Ruling:

. . . There was evidence of predatory intent with respect to each of the respondents and there was other evidence upon which the jury could find the requisite injury to competition.

Horizontal Mergers: *United States* v. *Philadelphia National Bank et al.* (1963)

[The Philadelphia National Bank and Girard Trust Corn Exchange Bank] are the second and third largest of the 42 commercial banks in the metro-politan area consisting of Philadelphia and its three contiguous counties, and they have branches throughout that area. [The banks'] boards of directors approved an agreement for their consolidation. . . . After obtaining reports, as required by the Bank Merger Act of 1960, from the Board of Governors of the Federal Reserve System, the Federal Deposit Insurance Corporation and the Attorney General, all of whom advised that the proposed merger would substantially lessen competition in the area, the Comptroller of the Currency approved it. The United States sued to enjoin consummation of the proposed consolidation, on the ground . . . that it would violate § 7 of the Clayton Act.

Ruling:

. . . The proposed consolidation . . . would violate § 7 of the Clayton Act. . . .
. . . The consolidated bank would control such an undue percentage share of the relevant market (at least 30%) and the consolidation would result in such a significant increase in the concentration of commercial banking facilities in the area (33%) that the result would be inherently likely to lessen competition substantially. . . .

Sources: *International Business Machine Corp.* v. *United States*, 298 U.S. 131 (1936), pp. 132–134, 139, 140; *Utah Pie Co.* v. *Continental Baking Co. et al.*, 386 U.S. 685 (1967), pp. 685, 686; *United States* v. *Philadelphia National Bank et al.*, 374 U.S. 321 (1963), pp. 321, 322.

Government Regulation

Government regulation

Government participation, through various agencies and commissions, in business decision making; may be industry regulation or social regulation.

The second major way in which government intervenes in the market process is through regulation. The expression **government regulation** refers to participation by the federal and state governments, through various agencies and commissions, in business decision making. Regulatory activities include the actions of the Securities and Exchange Commission (SEC), Federal Communications Commission (FCC), Interstate Commerce Commission (ICC), state utility commissions, and other such agencies.

In some cases, government regulation involves direct participation in specific aspects of a company's operations. Important decisions concerning such areas as the company's product price, its rate of profit, and the market it serves must be approved by a regulatory commission before they can be carried into practice. In other cases, government regulation involves indirect participation in business operations through setting standards for firms to follow. These standards pertain to matters such as safety, health, and the environment. The Food and Drug Administration (FDA), for example, sets purity and safety standards for food and drugs, and the Environmental Protection Agency (EPA) sets pollution standards.

While the antitrust laws are directed at the relationships between businesses and the degree of competition in specific markets, regulation is concerned with the interests of particular groups in the economy. For example, some regulation is aimed at protection of the consumer, some at labor, and some at the general public.

Government regulation can be divided into two basic types: industry regulation and social regulation. The first type involves regulation of all businesses in a particular industry. In the United States, the railroad, electric power, communications, and some other industries are subject to this type of regulation. Generally, industry regulation is direct: government plays an important role in determining price, profit, and other aspects of the firms' operations.

With social regulation, a regulatory body is created to deal with a particular problem that is common to businesses in many different industries. The commissions with authority over job discrimination (Equal Employment Opportunity Commission), consumer product safety (Consumer Product Safety Commission), and unfair business practices (Federal Trade Commission) are examples of agencies that carry out this type of regulation. Much social regulation is indirect and involves setting standards for businesses to follow.

More than 50 regulatory agencies have been established at the federal level. Table 14.2 lists these in chronological order. Notice that a large number of regulatory agencies was created in the early 1970s. Although historically we associate the Great Depression and the New Deal era with the growth of regulation, the number of federal agencies that originated in the 1970s was nearly double the number created during the 1930s. Notice, in comparison, that virtually no new federal agencies have been established since 1980.

The Structure of Regulation

A particular industry or a specific problem is under federal or state regulation depending upon whether interstate or intrastate commerce is involved. Federal agencies have jurisdiction over interstate commerce. For example, rates on long-distance telephone calls, when they cross state lines, are overseen by the Federal Communications Commission. State commissions regulate where intrastate commerce is involved. The rates charged by utility companies that serve customers within a particular state are under the regulatory jurisdiction of a state public utility commission.

Federal regulatory agencies such as the Occupational Safety and Health Administration (OSHA), the Interstate Commerce Commission (ICC), and others are established by Congress. The legislation authorizing a regulatory agency usually specifies the overall mandate for the regulatory body, the administrative structure of the agency, and other important information pertaining to its operation.

The authority given to a regulatory agency in its enabling legislation is usually stated in general rather than specific terms. For example, the Nuclear Regulatory Commission (NRC), which was established in 1975 and took over the functions of the Atomic Energy Commission, was given the mandate to license and regulate: radioactive waste storage facilities; the construction, operation, and safety of nuclear reactors; the processing, transport, and handling of nuclear materials; and other related matters.[16]

When a regulatory agency is established, it is given the power to carry out the general mandates stated in the enabling legislation. In order to do so, the agency may make detailed rules and regulations that businesses under its jurisdiction must follow. For example, if an agency's mandate is airline safety, it may establish detailed rules regarding air personnel qualifications, airplane inspection, equipment, and such.

An agency also has the power to enforce its own rules and regulations and to punish those that do not comply. In many instances noncompliance results in a fine levied by the agency. Companies that choose to dispute their treatment by an agency may appeal their case to a court of law.

As Table 14.2 illustrates, some regulatory agencies are established as independent bodies governed by commissioners who are appointed to oversee the operations of the agency. Other agencies are created as part of an existing department (such as the Department of Commerce) and are headed by an administrator within that department. For example, the Nuclear Regulatory Commission is an independent body governed by five commissioners appointed by the president of the United States and confirmed by the Senate, whereas the Federal Aviation Administration (FAA) is within the Department of Transportation and is headed by one of its administrators.[17] State public utility commissions, the most important of state regulatory agencies, are usually headed by commissioners who are either elected or appointed by the governor.

[16] *United States Statutes at Large,* Vol. 88, Part 1 (Washington, D.C.: U.S. Government Printing Office, 1974), pp. 1242–1248.

[17] *Directory of Federal Regulatory Agencies,* 2d ed., compiled by Ronald J. Penoyer, Center for the Study of American Business, Formal Publication Number 31 (St. Louis: Washington University, April 1980), pp. 43, 70.

Table 14.2   Chronology of Federal Regulatory Agencies

Regulatory agencies have been formed throughout the history of the economy, with a large number created in the 1930s and 1970s.

Year	Agency	Department Association[a]
1836	Patent and Trademark Office	Department of Commerce
1863	Comptroller of the Currency	Department of the Treasury
1870	Copyright Office	Library of Congress
1887	Interstate Commerce Commission	
1899	Army Corps of Engineers [Regulatory duties from this date; established 1824]	Department of Defense
1903	Antitrust Division	Department of Justice
1913	Federal Reserve System (Board of Governors)	
1914	Federal Trade Commission	
1915	Coast Guard	Department of Transportation
1916	Tariff Commission [Became International Trade Commission in 1975]	
1920	Federal Power Commission [Became Federal Energy Regulatory Commission in 1975]	
1922	Commodity Exchange Authority [Became Commodity Futures Trading Commission in 1974]	Department of Agriculture
1927	Bureau of Customs [Became Customs Service in 1973]	Department of the Treasury
1931	Food and Drug Administration	Department of Health and Human Services
1932	Federal Home Loan Bank Board	
1933	Farm Credit Administration	
1933	Federal Deposit Insurance Corporation	
1934	Federal Communications Commission	
1934	Securities and Exchange Commission	
1935	National Labor Relations Board	
1936	Maritime Administration [Regulatory functions transferred to Federal Maritime Commission in 1961]	Department of Commerce
1937	Agricultural Marketing Service and Other Agencies [Duties transferred to other services in 1972 and 1977]	Department of Agriculture
1938	Civil Aeronautics Authority [Became Civil Aeronautics Board in 1940; abolished in 1984]	
1940	Fish and Wildlife Service [First established as Bureau of Fisheries in 1871]	Department of Interior
1946	Atomic Energy Commission [Functions transferred to Nuclear Regulatory Commission in 1975]	
1951	Renegotiation Board [Abolished in 1979]	
1953	Foreign Agricultural Service	Department of Agriculture
1953	Small Business Administration	
1958	Federal Aviation Agency [Became Federal Aviation Administration in 1967]	Department of Transportation
1961	Agricultural Stabilization and Conservation Service	Department of Agriculture
1963	Labor-Management Services Administration	Department of Labor
1964	Equal Employment Opportunity Commission	

Year	Agency	Department Association[a]
1966	Federal Highway Administration	Department of Transportation
1966	National Transportation Safety Board *[Reestablished as independent agency in 1974]*	Department of Transportation
1966	Federal Railroad Administration	Department of Transportation
1969	Council on Environmental Quality	
1970	Cost Accounting Standards Board *[Abolished in 1980]*	
1970	Environmental Protection Agency	
1970	National Credit Union Administration	
1970	National Highway Traffic Safety Administration	Department of Transportation
1970	Occupational Safety and Health Administration	Department of Labor
1971	Employment Standards Administration	Department of Labor
1971	Occupational Safety and Health Review Commission	
1972	Bureau of Alcohol, Tobacco and Firearms	Department of the Treasury
1972	Consumer Product Safety Commission	
1972	Domestic and International Business Administration *[Became International Trade Administration in 1980; Regulation of Exports under the Export Administration in 1989]*	Department of Commerce
1973	Drug Enforcement Administration	Department of Justice
1973	Federal Energy Administration *[Became Economic Regulatory Administration in 1977, Department of Energy]*	
1973	Mining Enforcement and Safety Administration *[Became Mine Safety and Health Administration in 1977, Department of Labor]*	Department of the Interior
1974	Council on Wage and Price Stability *[Abolished in 1981]*	
1975	Federal Election Commission	
1975	Materials Transportation Bureau	Department of Transportation
1976	Federal Grain Inspection Service	Department of Agriculture
1977	Office of Neighborhoods, Voluntary Associations and Consumer Protection *[Abolished in 1981 and functions transferred to Office of Assistant Secretary of HUD]*	Department of Housing and Urban Development
1977	Office of Surface Mining Reclamation and Enforcement	Department of the Interior
1979	Office of the Federal Inspector of the Alaska Natural Gas Transportation System	Department of Agriculture
1982	Packers and Stockyards Administration *[Previously existed from 1967 to 1978]*	

[a]Not all agencies are associated with a department.

Source: Ronald J. Penoyer, *Directory of Federal Regulatory Agencies—1982 Update,* Center for the Study of American Business, Formal Publica-
tion Number 47 (St. Louis: Washington University, June 1982), pp. 43–48; Paul N. Tramontozzi and Kenneth W. Chilton, *U.S. Regulatory Agencies under Reagan: 1980–1988,* Center for the Study of American Business, OP 64 (St. Louis: Washington University, May 1987), pp. 15–24; Melinda Warren and Kenneth W. Chilton, *Regulation's Rebound: Bush Budget Gives Regulation a Boost,* Center for the Study of American Business, OP 81 (St. Louis: Washington University; May 1990), pp. 15–18, 23, 24.

Industry Regulation

As noted earlier, **industry regulation** applies to firms in certain industries, such as the railroad, communications, and electric power industries. This type of regulation deals with such matters as pricing, entry of new sellers into the market, extension of service by existing sellers, and the quality and conditions of service. In other words, the private decision making ability of a business in a free market does not exist for this type of regulated firm.

In some regulated industries, the firm itself is not free to independently choose or alter the price it charges for its product. Instead, it must seek approval from its regulatory agency to raise or lower its price. For example, telephone companies must obtain government approval before they change their rate structures. Also, in many regulated industries, new firms cannot begin operation unless they receive permission or a license from that industry's regulatory body. Sewage, water, electric, and other utility companies cannot be initiated at will.

Firms already in existence may be required to obtain permission to abandon service or to extend or alter current services. For years the railroads were not permitted to drop unprofitable passenger routes, and an electric company cannot simply cut off service to a university because the company disagrees with the political statements made by some students and professors. These firms may also be subject to a host of other regulations, such as on the quality of the product offered for sale (for example, chemicals permitted in the local water supply) and safety.

Justifications for Industry Regulation   There are two frequently cited explanations as to why certain industries are subject to detailed regulation: the first is economic, and the second is related to the public interest.

The economic justification for regulation is based on efficiency. There are certain production situations where it is more efficient (less costly) to have the entire output in a market come from one large seller rather than from several smaller sellers. In these instances, a **natural monopoly** is said to exist.[18] A good example of a natural monopoly is a gas pipeline company. It would be quite inefficient and complicated to have several such companies shipping natural gas into one area.

Natural monopolies occur because of strong economies of scale in production and distribution. With economies of scale, which were introduced in Chapter Twelve, a seller's long-run unit or average total cost falls as its output grows in size.[19] Economies of scale can result from a firm's ability to spread its expenditures on machinery and equipment over more units of output, or from producing a large enough output to justify replacing inefficient general purpose inputs with highly specialized and efficient equipment and personnel.

---

[18] Natural monopoly was briefly introduced on pages 476–477 of Chapter Thirteen.
[19] See pages 439–441.

Figure 14.1   Economies of Scale and Long-Run Average Total Cost

If, because of economies of scale, the long-run average total cost of production and distribution is lower with one seller in a market than with several, the seller could be classified as a natural monopoly.

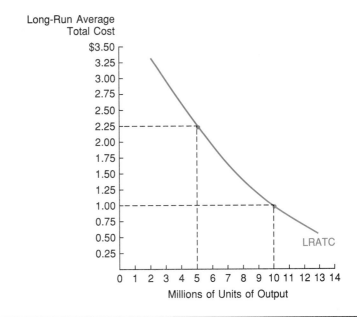

The effect of economies of scale on average cost, and the benefits of a natural monopoly, are illustrated in Figure 14.1, which gives the downward-sloping region of a long-run average total cost (LRATC) curve. This curve indicates that, because of economies of scale, as the level of output increases, the unit or average cost of producing that output falls. This gives rise to the notion of the natural monopoly.

To illustrate, suppose we wanted to produce 10 million units of the output given in Figure 14.1. One method would be to have one firm produce the entire amount at a cost per unit of $1, as indicated in the figure. Another method would be to divide the output between, say, two sellers, with each producing 5 million units at an average cost of $2.25, as also shown in Figure 14.1. Obviously, the total cost of production with one seller ($10 million) is considerably less than with two ($22.5 million). Thus, significant economies of scale can lead to a natural monopoly where it is more efficient to have one seller rather than several in a market.

Significant economies of scale are experienced by firms such as electric power companies. Because of the high cost of plants and equipment (generators, power lines, and so forth), it is extremely inefficient to have several small electric companies duplicate one another's facilities in order to serve the same market. By having one large company that can efficiently use its inputs and spread its costs over a larger output, the cost per kilowatt-hour is considerably less. Can you understand how economies of scale also affect production costs for natural gas, telephone, and water companies?

Unfortunately, natural monopolies create a dilemma for the consumer. On the one hand, because of economies of scale, buyers benefit from lower unit costs when dealing with one seller. But on the other hand, as the only seller in the market, the firm may abuse its monopoly power. The solution to this dilemma is to resort to regulation that allows only one firm in the market, while at the same time placing the firm's operations under detailed scrutiny by a public authority so that it cannot unreasonably exploit its monopoly power.

Natural monopoly may explain regulation in certain areas of the economy where there are advantages to having only one seller in a market. But what about the operation of firms such as motor carriers, communications companies, railroads, and others that produce in industries where there is more than one seller in a market? These instances of regulation may be explained using the second justification: the public interest.

Public interest justification for regulation

A good or service is so important to the public well-being that its production and distribution should be regulated.

According to the **public interest justification**, certain types of businesses provide goods or services so important to the public well-being that the public has a right to be assured of their proper operation. This assurance comes through regulation. Examples of such businesses include radio and television companies whose programming can influence public opinion, and transportation firms such as railroads, motor and water carriers, and airlines, without whose services the nation's commerce would come to a halt.

One of the best-known statements justifying regulation in the public interest is found in *Munn* v. *Illinois,* an 1877 Supreme Court case concerning the regulation of grain elevator operators. Here the Court held that:

> *When . . . one devotes his property to a use in which the public has an interest, he, in effect, grants to the public an interest in that use, and must submit to be controlled by the public for the common good. . . .*[20]

Notice that the public interest justification is not as narrow as the natural monopoly argument in terms of the situations to which it can be applied. The natural monopoly rationale pertains only to markets where it is most efficient to have one seller. The public interest justification applies to any market where it can be argued that the welfare of the public is so affected by the operation of a business that it is desirable to regulate that business. The breadth of this justification was defined in 1934 in one of the most important court decisions on regulation, *Nebbia* v. *New York.* In this case, which dealt with the regulation of milk prices, the Supreme Court stated:

[20] *Munn* v. *Illinois,* 94 U.S. 113 (1877), p. 126.

It is clear that there is no closed class or category of businesses affected with a public interest. . . . [A] state is free to adopt whatever economic policy may reasonably be deemed to promote public welfare, and to enforce that policy by legislation adapted to its purpose. . . . If the laws passed are seen to have a reasonable relation to a proper legislative purpose, and are neither arbitrary nor discriminatory, the requirements of due process are satisfied. . . .[21]

In other words, states are allowed to regulate a broad range of businesses in a number of ways in the name of the public interest, provided certain conditions of fairness are met.

Price Regulation   One important aspect of industry regulation is the public authority's overseeing of the prices, or rates, charged by a regulated company. When a regulated firm, such as a gas or electric company, seeks to raise or lower its rates, the firm presents an argument supporting its request to the appropriate agency or commission, which either approves or denies the request. Figure 14.2 illustrates the steps in the rate approval process for public utilities in the state of Missouri, which are fairly typical of the steps taken in other states. The process begins when a regulated firm files a request for a change in the rates it charges for its product. If, on the basis of data and other documentation submitted with the request, the commission concludes that the request is reasonable, it will grant approval and the rate change can go into effect. If, however, the commission is not convinced that the rate request is appropriate, it will initiate an investigation and hearings before it issues an opinion approving or denying the request.

Cost-plus pricing
Prices are designed to generate enough revenue to cover operating costs plus a fair return to stockholders.

Regulated firms have two concerns in making rate requests: they must cover their costs and, being privately owned, they must earn enough profit to attract and retain stockholders. Because of this, pricing by regulated firms is commonly carried out on a "cost-plus" basis. That is, with **cost-plus pricing** the rates, or prices, buyers pay are designed to generate revenues sufficient to cover the costs of operation plus a fair return to those who invest in the business.

There is one major problem with cost-plus pricing: it does not promote economic efficiency. A regulated firm that is granted permission to collect revenues to cover its costs plus a fair return to its investors may not have as much incentive to keep its costs down as would an unregulated firm competing with other sellers.

Social regulation
Regulation aimed at correcting a problem, such as pollution or job discrimination, found in several industries; not limited to a specific industry.

Social Regulation

Regulation aimed at correcting a situation considered to be problematic, such as pollution, or at protecting a particular group in the economy, such as workers or consumers, is called **social regulation.** Rather than

[21] *Nebbia* v. *New York,* 291 U.S. 502 (1934), pp. 536, 537.

Figure 14.2   The Rate Approval Process

If a rate request is challenged by a regulatory commission, an investigation and hearings may be required before the matter is settled.

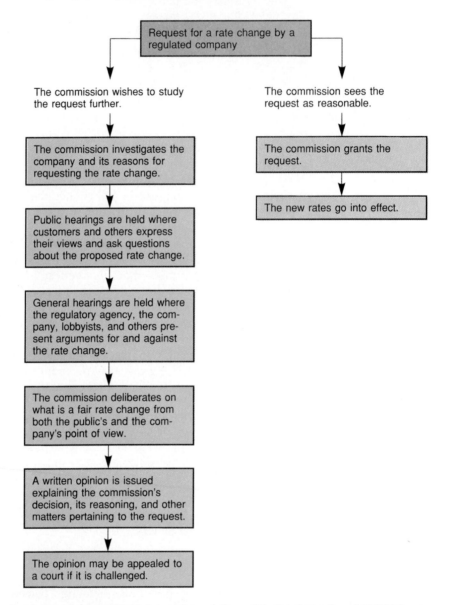

Source: Based on Missouri Public Interest Research Group, "The Rate Setting Game," *MoPIRG Reports,* Vol. 14, No. 2, Spring 1986.

focusing on a single industry, social regulation applies to all firms that are affected by the mandate of the regulatory body, regardless of their industry.

Unlike industry regulation, this type of regulation does not involve direct intervention into a company's price, profit, and other related decisions.[22] Instead, it addresses such matters as the setting and enforcing of standards concerning the characteristics and manufacture of a product, employees' working conditions, and situations created by the firm that could be harmful to the general public. The Occupational Safety and Health Administration (OSHA), which is concerned with worker safety and working conditions, is a good example of an agency dealing with social regulation.

Table 14.3 lists some of the federal agencies responsible for social regulation, and is divided according to the main focal points of this type of regulation: protection of the consumer, the worker, and the environment. A section is also included for energy regulation. Notice that some of the agencies listed in the table affect a broader range of firms and industries than do others. For example, how many industries can you name that might be affected by a ruling of the National Highway Traffic Safety Administration? How does this compare with the number that could be affected by a ruling of the Equal Employment Opportunity Commission?

It is more difficult to summarize what occurs with social regulation than with industry regulation because social regulation is so diverse: for example, consider the differences between the responsibilities of the Consumer Product Safety Commission and the National Labor Relations Board. However, some generalizations can be made about social regulation. First, much more is spent at the federal level on social regulation than on industry regulation. For example, over 80 percent of the expenditures of the major federal regulatory agencies in 1990 went to social regulation. Second, the direction of social regulatory spending has changed over the years. In 1970, 50 percent of all federal regulatory spending went to consumer safety and 15 percent went to the environment. In 1990, 31 percent of regulatory spending went to consumer safety and 37 percent went to the environment.[23]

"Test Your Understanding: Government and Business" lets you practice distinguishing among activities that might call for antitrust enforcement, industry regulation, social regulation, or no government intervention at all.

---

[22] Compliance with social regulation, however, can indirectly affect a company's pricing, costs, and profit.

[23] Melinda Warren and Kenneth W. Chilton, *Regulation's Rebound: Bush Budget Gives Regulation a Boost*, Center for the Study of American Business, OP 81 (St. Louis: Washington University, May 1990), pp. 11, 15–18. 1990 figures are estimates.

Table 14.3   Some Social Regulatory Agencies

The efforts of agencies concerned with social regulation are directed mainly at protecting consumers, workers, and the environment.

Protection of the Consumer

Consumer Product Safety Commission	Federal Aviation Administration
Food and Drug Administration	Federal Highway Administration
Drug Enforcement Administration	Federal Railroad Administration
Federal Grain Inspection Service	Coast Guard
Food Safety and Inspection Service	National Transportation Safety Board
Packers and Stockyards Administration	National Highway Traffic Safety Administration
Bureau of Alcohol, Tobacco and Firearms	

Protection of the Worker

Mine Safety and Health Administration	National Labor Relations Board
Occupational Safety and Health Administration	Employment Standards Administration
Labor-Management Services Administration	Equal Employment Opportunity Commission

Protection of the Environment

Environmental Protection Agency	Army Corps of Engineers
Council on Environmental Quality	Fish and Wildlife Service
Office of Surface Mining Reclamation and Enforcement	

Energy

Nuclear Regulatory Commission	Federal Inspector for the Alaska Natural Gas Pipeline
Economic Regulatory Administration	

Source: Melinda Warren and Kenneth W. Chilton, *Regulation's Rebound: Bush Budget Gives Regulation a Boost*, OP 81 (St. Louis: Washington University, May 1990), pp. 15–17.

Deregulation and the Performance of Regulation

As shown by the Chronology of Federal Regulatory Agencies in Table 14.2, the spectacular growth of regulation in the early and mid-1970s did not carry into the 1980s. Rather, the trend changed as the Carter and Reagan administrations took steps toward **deregulation** of the economy. During the late 1970s and early 1980s, the airline, trucking, natural gas, banking, telephone, and other industries were deregulated, and the number of permanent full-time positions in federal regulatory activities fell from approximately 118,000 in 1980 to just over 101,000 in 1985. From 1985 to the end of the

Deregulation

A reduction in government regulatory control of an industry or activity.

Test Your Understanding

Government and Business[a]

[a]Answers are found at the end of the book.

Below are ten hypothetical situations concerning business practices. Determine in each situation whether the practice would likely:

   a. violate the antitrust laws, and if so, which one,

   b. be subject to industry regulation,

   c. call for social regulation, and if so, by which federal agency, or

   d. call for no government intervention at all.

1. Firms located along major rivers find that the rivers provide an easy method for disposing of liquid wastes from production.

2. The purchaser of a large amount of carpeting that has been specially cut by the seller for installation in an office complex is demanding a refund after he mistakenly ordered the wrong color.

3. The purchaser of a home appliance is injured when properly using the product because it was poorly designed.

4. Two competing manufacturers of a popular consumer product that currently sells for $14 per unit agree that their prices will never fall below $10.

5. After discussing developments in the world grain market, two small farmers agree that now is the time to sell their corn if they want to get the best price.

6. A regional electric company would like to eliminate its service to a small village of 300 people because it is losing money in this market.

7. The theater chain showing 60 percent of the films in a major city wants to acquire the second largest chain that shows 20 percent of the films in the city.

8. A manufacturer charges $30 per unit to buyers who purchase directly from its warehouse, and $35 per unit to buyers who want to pay the additional cost of having the product packaged and shipped to them.

9. A local natural gas distribution company decides to double its charge to residential users in order to increase its profits.

10. A major supermarket chain cuts prices below cost in the Northeast until some of its smaller competitors go out of business.

Reagan administration there were only slight staffing increases each year. Indications are, however, that this trend may not continue under the Bush administration. Real spending by federal regulatory agencies in 1991 was estimated to be the highest on record, and larger staffing increases were scheduled than in previous years.[24]

    Concern over the performance of regulation and its effects on businesses and the economy in general brought about the interest in deregulation. This concern centered largely on the administrative, compliance, and other costs imposed on businesses by regulation. Proponents of deregulation believed

[24]Warren and Chilton, *Regulation's Rebound: Bush Budget Gives Regulation a Boost*, pp. 1, 2.

that in many instances these costs outweighed the benefits to society. Unfortunately, it is more difficult to measure the social benefits of regulation than its costs — many of the benefits are long term and not easy to assess. For example, the benefits of clean air and water may not have an easily measurable dollar value, but the cost to businesses of equipment or disposal methods to reduce pollution can be readily put in dollar terms.

The increasing internationalization of economic activity is another area of regulatory concern. Growing numbers of foreign sellers now compete with domestic firms in U.S. markets, and U.S. buyers and sellers can transact business in foreign markets with ease. As a result, there is an increased awareness of the effects that foreign economic policies have on the U.S. economy and its firms.

Regulatory and antitrust policies are generally national in scope; barring a special international agreement, U.S. policies will not usually affect foreign firms operating in foreign markets. As a result, some believe that U.S. firms are at a disadvantage when competing with foreign firms that face much less regulation at home, or that can coordinate their policies in a way that would violate the antitrust laws if those firms were in the United States. For example, the introduction of new drugs may be slower in the United States than in other countries where pre-introduction testing and other requirements are not as strict as those of the Food and Drug Administration, thus putting U.S. firms at a disadvantage in a global market. On the other hand, it could be argued that vigorous enforcement of the antitrust laws and regulatory standards could make U.S. firms more efficient and competitive and their products of higher quality. In this case, antitrust and regulation could be seen as helping U.S. firms maintain their competitive position against foreign rivals. The questions created by nationally focused antitrust and regulatory policies promise to remain with us as economic activity becomes more internationalized.

Application 14.3, "Consumer Peril from Pesticides," deals with a major current regulatory problem in an international setting — the use of pesticides on imported fruits and vegetables. This application considers some of the problems central to the regulation-deregulation issue: the costs versus the benefits of protecting the U.S. consumer, and differences in the regulatory environments in nations engaged in international trade. After reading this application, do you think internationalization of regulation is a political possibility?

Summary

Despite the free market philosophy underlying the U.S. economy, government intervenes in the operation of markets in two important ways: through antitrust laws and through regulation. This intervention occurs for several reasons: a concern that the level of competition in particular markets is inadequate, a desire to take advantage of efficiencies resulting from large-

Application 14.3

Consumer Peril from Pesticides

As morning mists rise from the foothills of the Sierra Madre, brightly dressed Mixtec Indians shower chemicals over lush fields of tomatoes, cucumbers, eggplants, and green peppers.

Within the next few days, the vegetables—some still coated with pesticides, including a suspected cancer-causing compound—will be harvested and loaded into 500 tractor-trailers that leave here daily for the U.S. Some of the pesticide-laced produce will be spotted by U.S. border inspectors, but the rest will reach tables in American homes.

As food imports to the U.S. rise, so does concern about the safety of Americans' diets. . . .

Pesticides are used on U.S. crops as well as on foreign ones. But detecting chemically tainted food among the imports is tougher than monitoring it domestically. One problem is that pesticide use is poorly regulated in the Third World, where American chemical producers are pushing pesticide sales. In addition, Mexico, a major U.S. food supplier, has a poor safety record handling pesticides. And U.S. border controls are lax.

Food imports, meanwhile, are soaring. Last year, Americans bought a record $24.1 billion of imported food, a 40% rise from 1982, the International Trade Commission estimates. Fruit and vegetable imports led the increase, driven by U.S. consumer demand for fresh produce year round. Fresh fruit imports reached $1.2 billion last year, more than double 1979 levels, according to the commission. . . .

In the last year alone, a number of pesticides banned by U.S. officials as public health threats have been found on imported produce. The compounds are suspected of producing cancer, neurological problems and other ills. More commonly,

the pesticides found on foreign produce are legal but exceed U.S.–approved levels or were sprayed on crops for which the U.S. hasn't approved their use. . . .

Politics compound border problems. Take the example of tainted mangoes, which are still being eaten by U.S. consumers. In 1983, the federal Environmental Protection Agency banned domestic use of the pesticide ethylene dibromide, known as EDB, because of concern that it might cause cancer. But it allowed foreign mango growers to continue using the pesticide until 1985 while they tried to find alternatives. . . .

According to documents filed in a Washington, D.C., federal appeals court, State Department pressure caused the EPA to cancel its planned ban, which would have affected 80% of the mangoes eaten by U.S. consumers. In two letters to the EPA in 1985, State Department officials argued that the ban might be economically harmful to Mexico and Haiti, two major mango-exporting nations, as well as damaging to U.S.–financed mango-growing projects that relied on EDB in Belize and Guatemala. . . .

Meanwhile, U.S. pesticide producers, faced with flat domestic demand, are trying to sell more of their products to foreign growers. "The industry is going to where the crops are being grown," says . . . the president of the National Agricultural Chemicals Association, a trade group.

Source: Barry Meier, "As Food Imports Rise, Consumers Face Peril from Use of Pesticides," *The Wall Street Journal*, March 26, 1987, pp. 1, 25. Reprinted by permission of *The Wall Street Journal*, © Dow Jones & Company, Inc. 1987. All Rights Reserved Worldwide.

scale operations, and a search for security that is not provided by market forces.

Antitrust laws are concerned with the relationships between firms—especially rival firms—and with the level of competition in a market. They are designed to promote market forces by attacking monopolization, attempts to monopolize, and combinations and conspiracies in restraint of trade. This type of government intervention is carried out at the federal and state levels, and depends heavily on the judicial system.

There are five major federal antitrust laws: the Sherman, Federal Trade Commission, Clayton, Robinson-Patman, and Celler-Kefauver Acts. The Sherman Act condemns combinations and conspiracies in restraint of trade, and monopolization. Combinations and conspiracies in restraint of trade may be either per se or Rule of Reason violations. Monopolization cases depend largely on the actions and market share of the firm being challenged.

The Federal Trade Commission Act created the Federal Trade Commission, which, along with the U.S. Department of Justice, carries the primary responsibility for antitrust enforcement for the federal government. The Clayton Act condemns exclusionary practices, interlocking directorates, price discrimination, and horizontal, vertical, and conglomerate mergers, where the effects of these activities are anticompetitive. The price discrimination and merger provisions of the Clayton Act were amended by the Robinson-Patman and Celler-Kefauver Acts, respectively. The penalties facing those found guilty of violating the antitrust laws include imprisonment, fines, structural remedies, and triple damages.

Regulation refers to participation by federal and state government agencies and commissions in business decision making. Unlike antitrust, which is concerned with the relationships between sellers, regulation is aimed at controlling certain industries and problem areas, and at protecting certain groups in the economy. In some instances an agency directly participates in a company's decision making, while in others the regulation is indirect and carried out through methods such as setting standards.

The division of regulatory authority between federal and state agencies depends upon whether the activity overseen is in interstate or intrastate commerce. Federal agencies, some of which are independent and some of which are attached to departments such as the Department of Labor, are created by the laws of Congress. Over the decade of the 1970s there was considerable growth in the number of federal regulatory agencies.

Regulation can be divided into industry and social regulation. Industry regulation involves government participation in pricing, output, profit, and other decisions of firms in certain industries such as the electric, gas, and telephone industries. Social regulation includes such activities as the setting and enforcing of standards and is not limited to firms in any single industry.

Two frequently cited reasons for industry regulation are the existence of a natural monopoly due to economies of scale, and effects on the public interest from the operation of certain businesses. An important aspect of industry regulation is the setting of prices. This is typically done on a cost-plus basis, where prices are designed to generate enough revenue to cover expected costs plus a fair return to investors.

Social regulation focuses mainly on the protection of consumers, workers, and the environment. Interest in deregulation grew during the 1980s due to concern over the costs and benefits of industry and social regulation. The costs and benefits of regulation (and antitrust policy) are also being evaluated in light of the growing internationalization of economic activity.

Key Terms and Concepts

Antitrust laws

Monopolization and attempts to monopolize

Combinations and conspiracies in restraint of trade

Sherman Act

Per se violations

Price fixing and territorial division

Rule of Reason violations

Trade association

Joint venture

Federal Trade Commission Act

Clayton Act

Exclusionary practices

Tying contract

Interlocking directorates

Robinson-Patman Act

Price discrimination

Celler-Kefauver Act

Horizontal, vertical, and conglomerate mergers

Leveraged buyout

Junk bond

Government regulation

Industry regulation

Natural monopoly

Public interest justification for regulation

Cost-plus pricing

Social regulation

Deregulation

Review Questions

1. What do Section One and Section Two of the Sherman Act condemn? What specific acts could be considered violations of Section One? What are the main factors the courts consider when judging whether a firm has committed a Section Two violation?

2. What is the difference between a per se violation of the antitrust laws and a Rule of Reason violation? Why are some business practices considered per se violations while others are not?

3. What activities are prohibited by the Clayton Act, the Robinson-Patman Act, and the Celler-Kefauver Act?

4. In what respects are industry and social regulation similar and in what respects are they different?

5. What is a natural monopoly and how is it related to economies of scale? What sort of dilemma does the combination of efficiency and monopoly power create for the consumer and the policy maker?

6. Explain the difference between the natural monopoly justification for regulation and the public interest justification. Why is the public interest justifica-

tion applicable to a wider range of firms than the natural monopoly justification?

7. What is cost-plus pricing and how might it lead to inefficient performance by a firm?

8. Provide some examples of social regulatory agencies and identify the main groups or areas that each protects.

Discussion Questions

1. Horizontal mergers, vertical mergers, conglomerate mergers, price discrimination, and interlocking directorates may or may not be anticompetitive. For each of these five activities describe a set of circumstances where you think the effect would be anticompetitive and a set of circumstances where it would not be anticompetitive.

2. The antitrust laws are designed to control the growth of monopoly power in specific markets. What are some economic reasons for concern over monopoly power? Are there any noneconomic reasons for wanting to control this power?

3. Antitrust laws reinforce the operation of free markets, while regulation replaces free market forces with an authoritative body. How do you explain that certain economic problems are dealt with by strengthening market forces while others are dealt with by replacing the market mechanism with regulatory authority?

4. Suppose legislation were passed to repeal the major federal antitrust statutes. How do you think such a repeal would affect competition? Would competition between sellers continue much the same as before the repeal? Would there be a blossoming of monopoly power? Would something else occur?

5. Assume that the production of a particular good is accompanied by significant economies of scale. Would you recommend vigorous enforcement of the antitrust laws to ensure that no one firm could monopolize the production of this product, or would you allow a monopoly to form and then subject it to industry regulation? Justify your answer.

6. There is concern about the costs and benefits of regulation. What costs and benefits might be created if the Environmental Protection Agency were abolished? In your opinion would we be better off without the agency than with it? Why?

7. How might people's attitudes on the costs and benefits of regulation explain the dramatic growth of regulation in the 1970s, the move toward deregulation in the 1980s, and a possible increase in regulatory activity in the 1990s?

8. What problems are created for businesses and the economy in general as a result of the administration of regulatory and antitrust policies in an increasingly internationalized environment?

Critical Thinking Case 14

■ College Tuition: Is the Fix On?

Critical Thinking Skills | Distinguishing between essential and incidental facts
Distinguishing facts from opinions and conclusions

Economic Concepts | Anticompetitive behavior
Price fixing
Per se violations

Generations of students have wondered if their colleges are out to get them. Now it appears the U.S. Department of Justice wonders the same thing. Last fall [1989], the department began taking a close [look] at several of the nation's top colleges to see if they're conspiring to fix prices [in violation of the Sherman Act]. . . .

"We are looking at possible violations in three areas: tuition, financial aid and faculty salaries," [an officer of the department] says. . . .

Tuition rates at the eight Ivy League schools are remarkably similar. . . .

The similarity of tuition in itself is not terribly alarming: In a competitive industry one would expect to find little price difference among similar goods. The Justice Department's suspicion, however, is that the Ivy League—and approximately 50 other elite schools—are *not* competitive and that the prices they charge are similar by design.

Colleges typically announce tuition increases for the upcoming year in March or April. Before their final announcements on tuition changes are made, officials at one college often have ample opportunity to obtain information regarding proposed tuition increases at other schools. . . .

Whether the availability of information about other colleges and the similarity of tuition fees at top schools is evidence of direct price setting is what the Justice Department is currently trying to determine.

Another thing the Justice Department will investigate is whether colleges set prices *indirectly* through their procedure for awarding financial aid packages. . . .

Students often apply for admission and financial aid at more than one college. In fact, it's common for students to apply to several top schools, with the hope of getting accepted by at least one. Many top students are accepted by at least two of the top colleges and universities. Therein lies the problem.

Since the 1950s officials from the Ivy League and other elite colleges have participated each spring in a session known among them as a "financial-aid overlap" workshop. The purpose of the meeting . . . is to share financial aid information on common financial-aid applicants. . . .

This practice . . . lies at the heart of the Justice Department's investigation. The exchange by colleges of individual students' financial aid profiles results in the elimination of significant discrepancies in the aid packages the participating schools offer common admittees. Whether the "financial-aid overlap" sessions represent collusion by the colleges to set prices is the Justice Department's big question. . . .

(Postscript: The 1991 meeting of the overlap group was canceled.)

Questions

1. Are charging similar tuitions and holding "financial-aid overlap" sessions sure indications that these colleges and universities have been fixing prices? Why? If you think more information is required to come to a conclusion about whether prices are being fixed, what facts would you want and why?

2. Under a strict interpretation of the per se rule, evidence that schools agreed to fix tuitions and financial aid could itself be enough to establish that they had acted anticompetitively—regardless of their motives—when entering into their agreements. Do you support or oppose the use of per se rules that say, in effect, that a business's behavior is anticompetitive and in violation of the law if a certain set of facts is found to exist?

Source: Excerpted from Suzanne Tregarthen, "College Tuition: Is the Fix On?" *The Margin,* March/April 1990, pp. 17–19. Excerpted with permission.

Suggested Readings

Dan Bertozzi, Jr. and Lee B. Burgunder, *Business, Government, and Public Policy: Concepts and Practices* (Englewoods Cliffs, N.J.: Prentice-Hall, Inc., 1990).
A text on public policy formation, regulation, antitrust, and the future of government-business relations.

William Breit and Kenneth G. Elzinga, *The Antitrust Casebook: Milestones in Economic Regulation* (Hinsdale, Ill.: The Dryden Press, 1989).
Selections from leading court cases on price fixing and market division, mergers, monopolization, and exclusionary practices.

Marian Burros, "New Urgency Fuels Effort to Improve Safety of Food," *The New York Times,* **May 7, 1990, pp. 1, C11.**
A report on the effectiveness of food safety regulation and how it is affected by changes in taste, technology, and other developments.

Andrew Galvin, "The Price of Fixing Prices," *Beverage World,* **January 1990, pp. 24, 26–28, 30, 32, 34.**
Discusses price fixing in the soft drink industry, how the Department of Justice proceeded in its investigations and challenge, and the outcome.

John E. Kwoka, Jr. and Lawrence J. White, eds., *The Antitrust Revolution* (Glenview, Ill.: Scott, Foresman and Company, 1989).
Analyses by leading economists of the issues and positions in various antitrust cases and related matters.

"The Modern Adam Smith," *The Economist,* **July 14, 1990, pp. 11–12.**
An essay on Adam Smith's attitudes toward self-interest, competition, and the role of government as they apply today.

"The Regulatory Process," *Federal Regulatory Directory: 1983–84* **(Washington, D.C.: Congressional Quarterly, Inc., 1983), pp. 1–78.**
A survey of the regulatory process covering reasons for, the history of, approaches to, and the costs and benefits of regulation, as well as other topics.

Chapter Fifteen

Labor Markets, Unions, and the Distribution of Income

The decision to work at a particular job is based on monetary considerations such as wage rate, and on nonmonetary factors such as satisfaction obtained from the job.

Chapter Objectives

1. To understand the reasons for the downward slope of a labor demand curve.

2. To explain, using a basic supply and demand model, how wage rates are determined, and to explain the real world considerations that modify the model.

3. To discuss the types and structure of unions, the process of collective bargaining, and major legislation affecting labor.

4. To examine the distribution of income in the United States and discuss some explanations for that distribution.

5. To define poverty, and to identify the poverty population in the United States and some government programs for alleviating poverty.

In Chapter Thirteen we learned how the prices of goods and services are determined in different types of output, or product, markets. In these markets businesses supply their goods and services to buyers, who may be households, governments, or other businesses.

In order to produce the outputs they intend to sell, firms need land, labor, capital, and entrepreneurship. These factors of production are acquired in resource, or input, markets. In these markets, as in output markets, prices are determined basically by the forces of supply and demand. But unlike output markets, in input markets businesses are the primary buyers.

While there are input markets for land, labor, capital, and entrepreneurship, this chapter focuses on the operation of labor markets. One reason for concentrating on labor markets is that wages, salaries, and other labor income constitute the vast majority of income generated in the U.S. economy. Over the last 25 years, labor income has accounted for about 65 to 70 percent of all income.[1] Labor markets also merit special attention because they are affected by important institutional forces such as unions and laws regulating wages and working conditions.

The first section of this chapter introduces a simple demand and supply model of a labor market, an explanation of the factors determining the demand for and supply of labor, and some complications that modify the simple model. Unions, union membership, and collective bargaining are discussed in the second section. The last section of the chapter presents a

[1] See Table 10.2, page 355.

Figure 15.1

Market for Good B Workers

In a competitive market for labor, there is a downward-sloping demand curve
and an upward-sloping supply curve for workers.

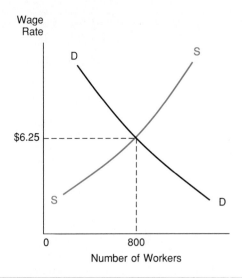

survey of the distribution of income in the United States, some explanations
of why individuals'earnings differ, and an examination of poverty.

Labor Markets

In a market system, as just noted, labor is bought and in the same manner
as goods and services: through the interaction of demand and supply. In the
case of labor, however, businesses are the primary buyers and individuals in
households are the sellers.

Wage

The price of labor.

The price of labor is called its **wage.** If someone works for a wage rate of
$6.72 an hour, this is the price at which that person is willing to sell his or
her labor, and the price at which a buyer is willing to acquire that labor.[2]

Figure 15.1 gives a basic supply and demand model for wage determination, using as an example a competitive market for workers who produce

[2]In reality, workers often receive a fringe benefit package, which includes such features as
health and life insurance, vacation days, and a pension plan, from an employer. These benefits
can be a substantial cost for the employer and an important financial consideration for an
employee. Although this additional compensation package affects labor demand and supply
decisions, we will confine our analysis to money wages for the sake of simplicity. If wages, or
the price of labor, included salary and fringe benefits, our analysis of labor markets in this
chapter would not be affected in any significant way.

an item we will call good B. The vertical axis of the figure is labeled wage rate (price), and the horizontal axis gives the quantity of labor demanded and supplied. In this particular market, the equilibrium wage rate is $6.25 an hour, and the number of workers employed is 800.

According to Figure 15.1, the demand curve for labor is downward sloping and the supply curve of labor is upward sloping: buyers are willing to hire more labor as the wage rate falls, and more labor is offered in the market as the wage rate increases. Why is this so?

The Demand for Labor

Derived demand

The demand for a factor of production depends on the demand for the good or service the factor produces.

The demand for labor, or for any other factor of production, is a **derived demand,** meaning that it is derived from, or depends on, the demand for the good or service the factor produces. Auto workers have jobs because automobiles are demanded; grocery clerks are employed because families buy groceries; and the professors who teach your courses do so only because students enroll in them.

From the point of view of an individual firm, the wage rate that the firm is willing to pay for a unit of labor is based on the dollar value of the labor's productivity — that is, what the worker's product is worth in dollars to the company. An employee whose daily product is valued at $50 will not be paid $75 per day. In fact, the company will not be willing to pay the employee over $50 a day. No firm can afford to hire at a wage rate greater than the employee's dollar contribution to the company. A restaurant that is willing to pay $5 an hour to each of the six waiters it employs, determines this rate based on the value of the waiters' productivity. Baseball players offered in excess of $1,000,000 annually command that amount largely because of their expected financial contributions to their teams. Outstanding players attract fans who purchase tickets to ball games and increase revenues for the clubs.

As seen in Figure 15.1, the typical market demand curve for labor is downward sloping. This demand curve behaves as it does because each individual firm's demand curve for labor is downward sloping: a firm is willing to hire more labor when the wage rate falls and less labor when the wage rate increases.[3] If the amount a firm is willing to pay for labor is based on the dollar value of workers' productivity, then the slope of the demand curve indicates that the dollar value of labor's productivity falls as more labor is hired. Why is this so?

The declining value of productivity and the resulting downward-sloping demand curve for labor occur for two reasons: (1) decreasing marginal productivity as more labor is hired; and (2) the need to lower product price in order to increase the quantity of a good or service demanded.

---

[3] Recall from Chapter Three that market demand curves are found by adding together individual demand curves.

Table 15.1   Total Product and Marginal Physical Product of Labor for a Producer of Good X

As more workers are hired, after some point the Law of Diminishing Returns causes each additional worker's marginal physical product to decline.

Number of Workers	Total Product	Marginal Physical Product
0	0	
		100
1	100	
		80
2	180	
		60
3	240	
		40
4	280	
		20
5	300	
		0
6	300	

Law of Diminishing Returns

As additional units of a variable factor are added to a fixed factor, beyond some point the additional product from each additional unit of the variable factor decreases.

Marginal physical product

The change in total product that results when an additional unit of a variable resource such as labor is utilized.

Labor Demand and Productivity   In discussing the pattern of short-run production costs in Chapter Twelve, the **Law of Diminishing Returns** was introduced. This law says that the extra (marginal) product from adding successive units of a variable resource to a fixed resource diminishes beyond some point. In other words, as more of a variable resource is used, at some point that resource's marginal product falls. This concept applies to labor.[4]

Table 15.1 provides an example of a hypothetical company varying the amount of labor it utilizes to produce good X. The second column of the table shows the total product (TP) that results when a specific number of workers is employed: for example, four workers together produce 280 units of good X. The third column gives **marginal physical product** (MPP), which is the change in total product resulting from the utilization of an additional unit of labor, or, put differently, the additional physical output produced when one more worker is hired. In Table 15.1 the second worker has a marginal physical product of 80 units of good X (total product of 180 $-$ 100), and the fifth worker has a marginal physical product of 20 units (total product of 300 $-$ 280).

The most important point to observe in Table 15.1 is that marginal physical product declines as more workers are used.[5] This decline is significant to the company employing the labor because it shows that, due to the Law of Diminishing Returns, each additional unit of labor utilized produces less than the previous unit and is therefore worth less to the firm. This

[4] For a review of the Law of Diminishing Returns, see Chapter Twelve, pages 436–438.

[5] In this example it is assumed that diminishing returns set in after the first worker. This is not always the case.

Table 15.2   A Good X Producer's Total Product and Price per Unit

A firm facing a downward-sloping demand curve for its product can sell the increased output that results from hiring more workers only if it lowers the price.

Number of Workers	Total Product	Price per Unit
0	0	$6.25
1	100	6.00
2	180	5.75
3	240	5.50
4	280	5.25
5	300	5.00
6	300	5.00

declining marginal productivity is reflected in the downward-sloping demand curve for labor.

Declining marginal productivity can be found in all work situations. Imagine the limited productivity of a baseball team's third, fourth, or fifth catcher. A restaurant will find that at some point the marginal productivity of its waiters declines as more and more are employed, and a high school that hires several assistant principals may find each successive one adding less to total product.

Labor Demand and Product Price   The second reason for the declining value of labor's productivity and the resulting downward-sloping labor demand curve is the price–quantity demanded relationship, or the downward-sloping demand curve, for the good or service the labor is producing. In all market situations except pure competition, firms face downward-sloping demand curves for their products: consumers will increase their purchases of a company's product only if its price falls. This downward-sloping demand curve for the good or service labor produces causes the value of labor's productivity to decrease, since the increased output resulting from hiring more workers can be sold only at lower prices. Thus, additional units of labor are worth less to the company because the product they produce is sold for less.

To illustrate this point, Table 15.2 gives the total product information presented in Table 15.1 for the producer of good X. It also includes a third column listing the prices at which good X can be sold. The price and total product columns reflect the inverse relationship between price and quantity demanded: if the company intends to sell more of its product, it must lower the price. However, lowering the product's price decreases the value of what labor produces.

Table 15.3

A Good X Producer's Total Product, Price, Revenue,
and Marginal Revenue Product

Marginal revenue product is the change in total revenue that results from the
sale of output produced when one more unit of a variable factor such as labor is
utilized.

Number of Workers	Total Product	Price per Unit	Total Revenue	Marginal Revenue Product
0	0	$6.25	$ 0	
				$600
1	100	6.00	600	
				435
2	180	5.75	1,035	
				285
3	240	5.50	1,320	
				150
4	280	5.25	1,470	
				30
5	300	5.00	1,500	
				0
6	300	5.00	1,500	

In short, the demand curve for labor is downward sloping because the
marginal productivity of each additional unit of labor decreases, and because
the value of additional production is diminished by the decline in price
necessary to sell the product. In other words, *the Law of Diminishing Returns
and the Law of Demand combine to determine the value of labor.*

Combining Declining Marginal Productivity and Declining Product Price
The effects of declining marginal productivity and decreasing product price
can be combined to determine what each unit of labor is worth to a company,
or the wage rate a firm is actually willing to pay. This is done in Table 15.3,
which returns to the good X example and adds two columns to those given
in Table 15.2.

The fourth column of Table 15.3 gives the total revenue (TR) received
when various amounts of good X are sold. (Remember: total revenue is price
times quantity.) For example, with a total production of 240 units that can
be sold for $5.50 each, a total revenue of $1,320 (240 × $5.50) is received.

**Marginal
revenue product**
The change in total
revenue that results from
the sale of output
produced when one more
unit of a variable resource
such as labor is utilized.

The last column of Table 15.3 gives **marginal revenue product** (MRP),
which is the change in total revenue that results from the sale of output
produced when one more unit of labor is utilized.[6] When one worker
is hired, 100 units of good X are produced and sold for $6 each, bringing in
$600 for the company. Since the total revenue with no workers is $0, the
marginal revenue product of the first worker is $600. When a second unit of

---

[6]Be careful to distinguish this from marginal revenue, which is the change in total revenue
when one more unit of *output* is sold.

labor is employed, 180 units of output are produced and sold for $5.75 each, creating a total revenue of $1,035. Thus, when the second worker is utilized, the company's total revenue increases from $600 to $1,035, or the second unit of labor brings in an additional $435 in total revenue. $435 is the marginal revenue product of the second worker. For the third unit of labor, the marginal revenue product is $285 because total revenue increases from $1,035 to $1,320. The marginal revenue product of the fourth worker is $150, and of the fifth worker is $30.

Marginal revenue product is important because it determines the firm's demand curve for labor. In the example in Table 15.3, this firm would not be willing to hire any labor if the wage rate were above $600, say, $700. In this case, the wage paid would be greater than the extra revenue created by the production of any worker. The producer would, however, be willing to hire one worker at a wage rate of $600. At $600 the first worker's contribution (marginal revenue product) equals his or her wage rate.

When would the producer of good X consider hiring two units of labor? The wage rate would need to fall to $435, the marginal revenue product of the second worker, before the producer would hire two units of labor. At any wage higher than $435, the second worker's contribution to the firm's revenue would be less than the wage. For three units of labor to be employed, the wage rate would have to fall to $285, the marginal revenue product of the third worker. At any higher wage, the third worker would not contribute enough to the firm's revenue to cover his or her wage. Four workers would be demanded at a wage of $150, and five at $30.

When the wage rates and the amounts of labor the good X producer is willing to hire at each of those rates are plotted in a graph, the firm's **demand curve for labor** results. This is given in Figure 15.2. Notice that the demand curve is equal to the marginal revenue product of labor. "Test Your Understanding: A Small Business Determines Its Demand for Employees" provides an opportunity to derive a labor demand curve.

Demand curve for labor

Downward-sloping curve showing the different amounts of labor demanded at different wage rates; equal to the marginal revenue product of labor.

The Supply of Labor

In a typical labor market there is a direct relationship between the wage rate and the quantity of labor supplied, causing the **supply curve of labor** to slope upward like that given in Figure 15.3. This relationship says that less labor will be attracted to a market at a lower wage rate than at a higher wage rate. In Figure 15.3, for example, 300 people are willing to work in this labor market for $5.00 per hour, but 700 want to work for $8.50 per hour.

In a labor market, money may be only part of the consideration in seeking a particular type of employment. Many important factors other than wage or salary influence the supply of labor available for a job. These nonwage factors include locational preferences, psychological rewards, long-term work objectives, and other considerations.

Location affects the supply of labor in some markets. In a small town with only a few major employers, workers face limited job choices. When earning

Supply curve of labor

Upward-sloping curve showing the different amounts of labor supplied at different wage rates.

Figure 15.2

A Firm's Demand Curve for Good X Workers

A firm's demand curve for labor is based on the marginal revenue product of labor, which declines as additional workers are hired.

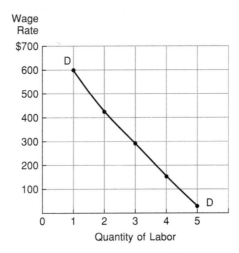

a higher salary means leaving home, family, and friends, many people will choose to work at a lower wage rather than relocate. Likewise, when there are many job opportunities in an area, workers can be more selective and sensitive to wage rates.

Many people seek a position that gives them a "psychic" income; that is, they seek a job that is psychologically rewarding in some way. The psychological reward could be in the form of prestige, self-fulfillment, a sense of accomplishment, or freedom from supervision. Such a reward can induce people to work for a lower wage than would otherwise be the case. A professor of accounting, for example, might prefer to receive a smaller salary from a prestigious university than a higher salary from a large corporation. A free-lance writer might sell material for a paltry sum to a highly recognized magazine because he or she receives a psychic reward from having an article in that particular publication.

The possibility of long-term gains can also influence the supply of labor. A college graduate may take a position with an employer at a lower salary than that offered by other employers because the potential for future advancement is great or because the job will look good on a résumé. Other factors affecting supply include job security; the safety, cleanliness, and working conditions on a job; the degree of skill or formal training required; and the need to obtain a license to work.

It appears that another major job consideration in the 1990s is the ability to balance family obligations and needs with the demands of a career or an

Figure 15.3

Supply Curve of Labor

A typical upward-sloping labor supply curve indicates that a direct relationship exists between wage rates and the quantity of labor supplied in a market.

employer. Child care, recreational time with a partner or children, obligations to elderly parents, and flexibility for family emergencies have become important nonwage considerations in a job market. Application 15.1, "What Do Employees Really Want?" gives excerpts from a panel discussion with people whose employment considerations involved some of these factors.

Changes in Labor Demand and Supply

In any labor market, certain changes can occur that will cause labor demand and/or supply to increase or decrease and the demand and/or supply curves for labor to shift to the right or left. When these changes occur, the equilibrium wage rate and amount of labor hired are affected in the same way that equilibrium price and quantity are affected when demand and/or supply shift in an output market. An increase in the demand for labor, for example, causes the demand curve to shift to the right, resulting in an increase in both the equilibrium wage rate and the number of workers employed. This is illustrated in Figure 15.4, which demonstrates graphically the effect of an increase in the demand for labor from D1 to D2 in a competitive labor market. As demand increases, the equilibrium wage rate rises from W_1 to W_2, and the number of workers employed increases from Q_1 to Q_2.

Test Your Understanding

A Small Business Determines Its Demand for Employees[a]

[a]Answers can be found at the end of the book.

Suppose you plan to start a small business that will label and stuff envelopes for other small businesses, charitable organizations, and political candidates. Since your biggest cost will be for employees to do the actual labeling and stuffing, you are very concerned about determining the hourly wage you would be willing to pay.

Assume that the information given in the following tables is from a study done for a company similar to the one you plan to start. This information serves as the basis for determining the wages you would be willing to pay and how many employees you would be willing to hire at each wage rate.

The total product that can be produced with various numbers of workers is provided in Table 1. Determine the hourly marginal physical product of each worker and answer question 1.

Table 1

Number of Workers	Hourly Total Product	Hourly Marginal Physical Product
0	0	
1	500	_____
2	1000	_____
3	1500	_____
4	1900	_____
5	2200	_____

1. At what number of workers does the Law of Diminishing Returns take effect?_____

Table 2 presents the price that you can receive for stuffing and labeling each quantity of envelopes. That is, if you want to complete 1500 envelopes an hour, you can charge 2.5 cents per envelope completed, but if you want to raise your output to 2200 per hour you will need to lower your price to 2 cents per envelope to sell your services to more buyers.

Table 2

Number of Workers	Hourly Total Product	Charge per Envelope
0	0	$0.0325
1	500	$0.03
2	1000	$0.0275
3	1500	$0.025
4	1900	$0.0225
5	2200	$0.02

Determine the hourly total revenue and the hourly marginal revenue product per worker from the information in Table 2. Put these figures in Table 3 and answer questions 2–4.

Table 3

Number of Workers	Hourly Total Revenue	Hourly Marginal Revenue Product
0	$ _____	
1	_____	_____
2	_____	_____
3	_____	_____
4	_____	_____
5	_____	_____

2. What is the highest hourly wage rate that you would be willing to pay?_____

3. What wage rate would you be willing to pay to hire enough workers to label and stuff 2200 envelopes per hour?_____

4. Suppose you have enough demand for your services to label and stuff 2200 envelopes per hour, but the minimum wage is $4.00 per hour. How many workers would you be willing to hire and how many envelopes would you stuff if you had to pay the minimum wage? _____ workers and _____ envelopes

Based on the figures in Table 3, complete the demand schedule for employees in Table 4 and draw the resulting demand curve for labor in the graph provided.

Table 4

Quantity of Workers Demanded	Wage Rate
1	_____
2	_____
3	_____
4	_____
5	_____

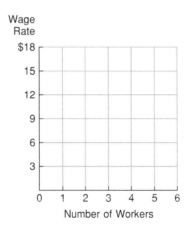

Application 15.1

What Do Employees Really Want?

The following are excerpts from a panel discussion that was part of a work-family conference sponsored by The Conference Board.

David, you said that you left one position because you wanted to spend more time with your daughter. Tell us about that decision.
One Friday over dinner, my wife, after not having had dinner with me Monday through Thursday either that or any other week during that year, said she had married me for me, not for my wallet. We wanted to have a family soon and knew we could not go on that way; we wanted to spend some time together. I also wanted to play an active role in my child's upbringing.

Claire, your four daughters are now ages 13 through 22. Was there ever a time when they were younger that you thought you couldn't do it all?
No, because I never had that option. We needed my income and that was all there was to it. The bottom line was that my children were not going to go without food or without a roof over their heads. The answer I found when my children were younger and I first went back into the workforce was to work nights. It is not fun; you never see your husband and learn to communicate with your older children with letters. We left one another letters on the counter Monday through Friday. I would come home at 1 A.M. and read my Dear Mom letters. . . .

Betty, do you find that [your company's] employees are more willing now to come to management with family difficulties or are people still concerned with how they are perceived?

As the employees see that the company is providing services, this is a sign to them that it is okay to talk about family difficulties. We need supervisors who are able to talk more openly and honestly with employees when they sense problems. It is very important for companies and the individuals who make policy decisions to understand how we as workers feel about companies that are flexible.

I have tried to make it easy for [my employer] to accommodate me. My survival depends on their accommodation . . . .

Claire, what have you seen in terms of elderly family members, needing to take time off, nursing home care, and so on?
At my former job, I worked with a woman who was fired for taking time off to care for a semisenile mother; she was the only person in her mother's life who could take care of her. The attitude was that the mother was an adult and therefore the woman did not need to take care of her personally. That is not a responsible attitude. When you are talking about a production line, you need employees certain hours of the day because you are trying to produce a certain amount of your product. But you can be more flexible about it, and you must understand that no matter what the job is and whether you consider it difficult or not, people who are distracted are not good employees. . . .

Source: Excerpted from "What Do Employees Really Want?", *Across the Board*, July/August 1990, pp. 14–21. Excerpted with permission from The Conference Board.

Changes in Labor Demand   Several factors cause the demand curve for labor to shift to the right or left. Notable among these are changes in the prices of substitute inputs, technology, and changes in the demand for the good or service the labor is producing. Let us consider each of these.

Because of the profit motive, businesses seek the least-cost method of production and are continually assessing the cost and utilization of their inputs. If a good or service can be produced with either labor or machinery, a firm will obviously choose the cheaper alternative. This means that if one

Figure 15.4   Effect of an Increase in Demand in a Labor Market

An increase in the demand for labor causes both the equilibrium wage rate and quantity of workers employed to increase.

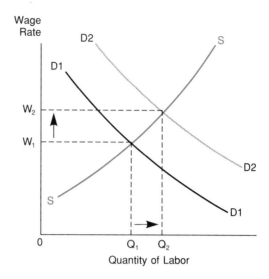

type of input that can be substituted for another becomes less expensive, the demand for the more expensive input will decrease, and its demand curve will shift to the left.

In automobile production, many tasks, such as welding, can be performed by labor or by robots. If auto assembly plants are primarily using labor and the cost of robots falls, the demand curve for labor will shift to the left as the automobile companies make the switch to the relatively less expensive machinery. There are many other examples: vending machines, self-service freezers, and salad bars decrease the demand for food service personnel; toll booths with coin-deposit machines decrease the demand for persons to collect tolls; and a decrease in day care center fees decreases the demand for nannies.

Technology increases the demand for some types of labor while decreasing the demand for others. The advent of the computer age has generated a demand for people with computer science and information systems degrees. At the same time, computers have decreased the demand for many other types of labor: fewer typists are demanded by employers as word processing capabilities make typists more productive; and the demand for grocery store personnel has fallen since computerized checkout has eliminated the need to hand stamp each grocery item and take inventory manually.

Finally, a change in the demand for the good or service that a type of labor is producing may change the demand for that labor. When the demand for new single-family housing is high, developers and construction companies increase their production, causing the demand curve for construction workers to shift to the right. When the government cuts a major defense program from its budget, such as a particular type of aircraft, production of the good stops, and the demand for workers for this project shifts to the left.

Changes in Labor Supply   A number of factors can cause the supply of workers in a labor market to increase or decrease, and the supply curve to shift to the right or left. These include, among others, changes in economic conditions, demographic trends, expectations, and changes in immigration laws.

When the economy falls into a downswing and workers in industries that are prone to cyclical unemployment are laid off, especially for long periods of time, these workers may enter labor markets for lower-paying unskilled jobs, thus increasing the available supply of labor in markets for restaurant help, retail clerks, and other similar positions. For example, many women in the steel and coal industries in western Pennsylvania and West Virginia who were laid off in the recession of the early 1980s never regained their jobs (due to lack of seniority) and became part of the labor supply in markets offering low-paying sales and service positions.[7] Thus, a state or region that is experiencing healthy economic conditions may find a reduced supply of workers in many of its low-paying labor markets, whereas an area that is depressed may find an increase in the labor supply in these types of markets.

Demographic trends also affect labor supply. For example, as the number of teenagers in the population falls, firms that typically hire from this age group, such as fast-food chains, are faced with a decrease in supply. Also, the trend toward early retirement is causing some people to drop out of labor markets offering only full-time jobs and to move into labor markets where part-time employment is available.

The expectation of future job prospects influences the supply curve in some labor markets. College students, for example, tend to major in subjects that are perceived as providing good employment opportunities. When the number of teaching positions in secondary and elementary schools increases, for example, the supply curve of new teachers shifts to the right as more students major in education, and when investment banking appeared to offer high salaries, the supply curve of students majoring in finance shifted to the right.

Many other factors may also cause labor supply to increase or decrease. For example, changes in immigration laws and the extent to which illegal aliens are returned to their home countries affect several labor markets; and

---

[7]For more information, see Carol Hymowitz, "Layoffs Force Blue-Collar Women Back Into Low-Paying-Job Ghetto," *The Wall Street Journal*, March 6, 1985, p. 35.

the number of positions available in professional schools, such as medical and law schools, influences the supply of labor in those markets.

Changes in Demand and Supply and Changes in Quantity Demanded and Supplied   The distinction made in Chapter Three between a change in demand or supply and a change in quantity demanded or supplied applies to labor demand and supply. A **change in labor demand or supply** refers to a *shift* of the entire demand or supply curve to the right or left as a result of changes in nonwage factors such as the prices of substitute inputs, technology, product demand, economic conditions, and expectations about future job prospects. A **change in the quantity of labor demanded or supplied** occurs only as a result of a change in the wage rate (price) of labor. A change in quantity demanded or supplied is represented by a movement from one wage rate–quantity combination to another *along* a demand or supply curve: the curve itself does not change.

> **Change in labor demand or supply**
> A shift in the demand or supply curve for labor caused by changes in nonwage factors.
>
> **Change in the quantity of labor demanded or supplied**
> A change in the amount of labor demanded or supplied that occurs when the wage rate changes; represented by a movement along the demand or supply curve.

Modifications of the Labor Supply and Demand Model

The labor market model introduced in Figure 15.1 at the beginning of the chapter is a useful starting point for analyzing how wages are determined through the forces of supply and demand. But just as there are imperfections in output markets, there are certain factors at work in real world labor markets that go beyond what is explained in the simple supply and demand model, and have an impact on the determination of wages and the amount of labor employed. Three of these factors—wage rigidities, legal considerations, and unequal bargaining power—merit special consideration.

Wage Rigidities   In a labor market such as that shown in Figure 15.1, a decrease in the demand for labor would shift the demand curve to the left, causing fewer workers to be hired and the equilibrium wage rate to fall. In reality, a decrease in the demand for labor will most likely cause employment to drop, but not money wages. Firms whose sales have fallen usually respond by laying workers off rather than by lowering their wages. On the supply side, contrary to the operation of the simple model, an increase in the number of workers in a market (a shift of the supply curve to the right) will most likely not lower the money wage rate. Thus, money wages tend to adjust upward but not downward to changing labor market conditions.

There are several explanations for why money wages tend not to fall. First, some workers are earning the minimum wage, and by law their employers can pay them no less. Second, an employer may be bound by a labor agreement to pay workers a certain wage below which the employer cannot go. Third, it may be in a worker's best interest to be laid off rather than take a cut in pay. When laid off, a worker may become eligible for unemployment compensation, can use the idle time to secure an alternative

Figure 15.5   The Minimum Wage

Over the years, the minimum wage has been increased many times since its original $0.25.

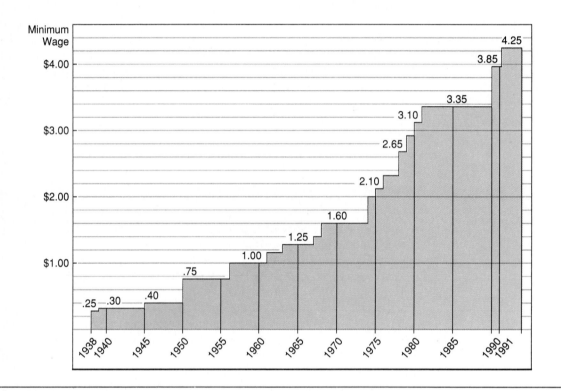

source of income, and will not be acknowledging to an employer that he or she is willing to work for less. Fourth, an employer might believe that better long-term employer-employee relationships can be maintained by laying workers off for a short period of time rather than by asking workers to take a lower wage.

Legal Considerations   Labor markets are affected by legislation that influences wages and the demand for and supply of labor. The most obvious example of legislation affecting wages is the **minimum wage law.** By specifying the minimum hourly earnings a worker can receive, this law can override the operation of a free market by not allowing the wage rate to fall to its equilibrium level. As illustrated in Figure 15.5, the minimum wage

Minimum wage law
Legislation that specifies the lowest hourly earnings that an employer may pay an employee.

Figure 15.6

Effect of a Minimum Wage on a Labor Market

When the equilibrium wage rate in a labor market is lower than the minimum wage, the minimum wage prevails, and a surplus of workers results in that market.

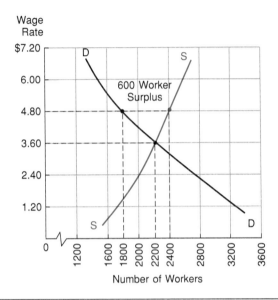

was $0.25 per hour when established in 1933. Through most of the 1980s it was $3.35 per hour, and in 1991 it was raised to $4.25 per hour.

Figure 15.6 shows the influence of the minimum wage law on a labor market. The equilibrium wage rate in Figure 15.6 is $3.60 per hour, and the equilibrium employment is 2,200 workers. If the government establishes a minimum wage above the equilibrium rate, say, $4.80 per hour, employers will want to hire fewer than 2,200 workers—in this case, 1,800 workers. On the supply side, at the minimum wage of $4.80, more than 2,200 workers, in fact, 2,400 workers, will be available. As a result, a surplus of labor will develop in the market; in this case the surplus will be 600 workers (2,400 − 1,800). Many critics of minimum wage legislation point out that it causes unemployment in some labor markets. The graphics in Figure 15.6 suggest this may be so.

Some legislation can change the demand for labor. For example, the minimum wage law may reduce the demand for a certain type of labor if it makes the employment of those workers more costly than the purchase and use of a piece of machinery that performs the same task. Rules, such as those of the Occupational Safety and Health Administration (OSHA) that specify safety and working conditions, may affect employers' costs of using labor and in turn their demand for labor. There are also laws relating to the hiring of specific groups in the labor force, such as women and minorities, that influence labor demand.

The supply of labor is also affected by various laws. Licensing and certification requirements for physicians, beauticians, and others performing personal services have an impact on the supply of labor. Laws limiting the amount persons can earn while on Social Security, laws pertaining to unemployment compensation, and legislation such as child labor laws also affect the supply of labor.

Unequal Bargaining Power   The equilibrium wage rate of $6.25 in the labor market in Figure 15.1 was determined by employers and employees who had equal bargaining power. In many markets this is not the case. In some instances the employer has greater strength than the employees in determining wages, and in others the employees exert more power.

If the bargaining power is on the side of the buyer (the firm), the wage will likely be below that set when both parties are of equal strength. For example, workers living in a town with one major employer may be paid a lower wage rate than they would be paid if there were several firms competing for their services. Also, studies have shown that before baseball players had free agency status, or when team owners had greater control over ball players' mobility, their salaries were farther below their marginal revenue products than after free agency, which gave them greater control over the sale of their own services.[8] In general, the fewer the alternative employers from which workers can choose, the weaker the workers' bargaining power.

If the bargaining strength is on the side of labor suppliers, the wage will likely be above that set when buyers and sellers have equal power. In general, the greater their control over the labor available to a particular employer, the greater the suppliers' ability to raise wages above the competitive level. The primary method used by workers to marshal their strength to raise wages is unionization.

Unions

Union

An organization of workers that bargains in its members' behalf with management on wages, working conditions, fringe benefits, and other work-related issues.

A **union** is an organization of workers that bargains in its members' behalf with management. The main areas of concern for unions in representing their members are wages, working conditions, fringe benefits such as health insurance and pensions, rules relating to seniority, layoffs and firings, and the clarification of tasks to be performed. Unions in the United States are primarily economic in their focus. There is some political activity such as endorsing candidates and presenting a point of view to the government, but

---

[8] See Timothy Tregarthen, "Are Professional Athletes Worth the Price?" *The Margin*, November 1985, pp. 6–8.

by and large, the main emphasis is on bargaining with employers in behalf of a union's membership.

Types of Unions and Union Membership

The fraction of the labor force belonging to unions has not been stable over the years. Union membership as a percentage of nonagricultural employment grew in importance through the 1930s and 1940s, accounted for over 30 percent of nonagricultural employment through much of the 1940s and 1950s, and has fallen in importance since the 1950s, especially during the 1980s. In 1975, 28.9 percent of all nonagricultural employees belonged to unions, but membership fell to 23.2 percent in 1980, and by 1988 only 12.9 percent of all nonagricultural wage and salary workers were union members.[9] The recent erosion in union membership and power could stem from many sources, such as an antiunion political climate strengthened by such actions as the firing of striking air traffic controllers early in the Reagan administration, the growth in the relative importance of service sector jobs, a decrease in the number of blue-collar manufacturing workers, and a negative public image of unions and labor leaders. Labor leaders have been making a concerted effort to reverse this trend.

Labor unions fall into two categories: craft unions and industrial unions. **Craft unions** restrict their membership to workers who possess specific skills, such as bricklayers or plumbers. Thus, for example, bricklayers on a particular construction job would be represented by one union and plumbers on the same job by another.

A craft union may require that its members complete an apprenticeship program or meet some other entrance requirement. By setting such conditions on the practice of the occupation it represents, the union has some control over the supply of workers, and may thus be better able to keep its members' wages and fringe benefits above what they would be if there were open competition for jobs. This can be seen in a simple supply and demand model for wage determination, which indicates that any action that restricts supply (shifts the supply curve to the left) results in a higher wage rate. This is shown in Figure 15.7, where a decrease in the supply of labor from S1 to S2 leads to an increase in the wage rate from W_1 to W_2. Notice also another important result: this action lessens employment, in this case reducing it from Q_1 to Q_2.

An **industrial union**, rather than limiting itself to workers with a single skill, seeks to represent all of the workers in a specific industry. For example, workers performing different jobs in the automobile industry may be

Craft union
A union that represents workers with a specific skill or craft.

Industrial union
A union that represents all workers in a specific industry regardless of the type of job performed.

[9] Figures for 1930–1945 are from U.S. Bureau of the Census, *Historical Statistics of the United States, Colonial Times to 1957* (Washington, D.C.: U.S. Government Printing Office, 1960), p. 98. Figures for the 1950s are from *Statistical Abstract of the United States: 1984*, 1983, p. 439. Figures for 1975–1980 are from *Statistical Abstract of the United States: 1988*, 1987, pp. 401, 402. Figures for 1988 are from *Statistical Abstract of the United States: 1990*, 1990, p. 419.

Figure   15.7

Restricting Supply in a Labor Market

By limiting the supply of labor, which is shown by a shift of the supply curve to the left from S1 to S2, a craft union can obtain higher wages for its members than they would earn if entrance into the occupation were not restricted.

represented by the United Auto Workers, communications workers performing different tasks may be represented by a single union, and so may service employees. Thus, when it comes to membership, craft unions are narrower in their focus than industrial unions.

A union, whether craft or industrial, is typically headed by a national or international organization that operates in behalf of all of the members. Below this headquarters organization are individual "locals" to which the members belong. In some cases, such as musicians, members who work for different employers in a particular area belong to the same local. In other cases, such as auto workers, a local represents members working in a single plant or for a single employer.

Although each union faces its own unique problems in bargaining for wages and working conditions, there are several interests, such as developing educational programs on unionism and supporting or opposing worker-related legislation, that unions have in common. In an effort to further their common interests, labor unions have formed umbrella organizations to which they can belong. The best known of these is the **American Federation of Labor-Congress of Industrial Organizations: the AFL-CIO.**

AFL-CIO

An organization for furthering the common interests of labor unions; does not engage in bargaining with management.

Table 15.4

Ten Largest Unions Affiliated with the AFL-CIO in 1989

Some unions in the United States represent hundreds of thousands of workers.

Union	Paid Memberships
Teamsters	1,161,000
State, County, and Municipal Employees	1,090,000
Food and Commercial Workers	999,000
Automobile, Aerospace and Agriculture (United Automobile Workers)	917,000
Service Employees	762,000
Electrical Workers (International Brotherhood of Electrical Workers)	744,000
Carpenters	613,000
American Federation of Teachers	544,000
Machinists and Aerospace Workers	517,000
Communications Workers	492,000

Source: U.S. Bureau of the Census, *Statistical Abstract of the United States: 1990*, 110th ed. (Washington, D.C.: U.S. Government Printing Office, 1990), p. 418.

The American Federation of Labor dates back to 1886 and was formed with a craft union orientation. The Congress of Industrial Organizations was formed with an industrial union orientation after several unions split from the AFL in the 1930s. In 1955 the two organizations joined to form the AFL-CIO.

Table 15.4 ranks the ten largest unions belonging to the AFL-CIO in 1989. As can be seen, these unions have sizable memberships—some with over one million workers.[10] Not all unions belong to the AFL-CIO. For example, the Teamsters, one of the nation's largest unions, was "independent" for a number of years. The Teamsters, however, recently rejoined the AFL-CIO.

In Application 15.2, "Reinventing Unions," the social and management theorist Peter Drucker reviews the forces contributing to a decline of unionism in the United States and looks at some alternative courses of action unions could follow in light of that decline.

Collective Bargaining and Strikes

In the simple labor market model, wages are set by the interaction of supply and demand. With unions, the process of wage determination is more complicated. Wages are still established by supply and demand in the sense that a union represents the suppliers of labor, and management represents

[10]Some individual union memberships were greater before the decline during the 1980s than those given in Table 15.4. For example, the Automobile Workers had 1.36 million members in 1980. See *Statistical Abstract of the United States: 1984*, 1983, p. 440.

Application 15.2

Reinventing Unions

The labor union might be judged this century's most successful institution. In 1900 it was still outlawed in most countries or barely tolerated. By 1920 it had become respectable. By the end of World War II, 25 years later, it had become dominant. Now the labor union is in tatters and disarray, apparently in irreversible decline. It is losing members fast, and it is losing power even faster. . . .

[In recent years] the labor unions in the United States have lost two-fifths of their members. In the private sector they now enroll a lower proportion of workers . . . than they did before the unionization drives during the late 1930s. . . .

There are several explanations [for the decline of unions]. The labor union certainly has much less to offer. Practically everything it stood for has become law in developed countries: short working hours, overtime pay, paid vacations, retirement pensions, and so on. . . .

There is also . . . the steady deterioration in the quality of union leaders. Before World War II, rising into union leadership was the best opportunity for a young man from a working-class family. Now, ambitious young people go to the university. . . four years later they are management trainees.

Furthermore, the public perception of the labor union has gone down sharply. . . .

The single most important factor in the decline of the labor union is, however, the shift in the center of gravity of the workforce from the blue-collar worker in manufacturing industry to the knowledge worker. Without the industrial workers' unions as its core, there is no labor movement. . . .

The labor union can go in one of three directions. If it does nothing, it may disappear — even in a free, democratic society. Or it may shrink to the point where it becomes irrelevant. . . .

A second choice is to try to maintain itself by dominating the political power structure, having government impose compulsory union membership and such power positions for the union as "codetermination," which gives it a veto over company management. . . .

There is a third choice: that the union rethink its function. The union might reinvent itself as the organ of society — and of the employing institution — concerned with human potential and human achievement, and with optimizing the human resource altogether. . . . The union would work with management on productivity and quality, on keeping the enterprise competitive, and thus maintaining the members' jobs and their incomes.

[The United Automobile Workers has begun to move] toward such a radical redefinition of its policies, behavior, and position. Both General Motors Corporation and Ford Motor Company now have joint management-union committees to reduce union work rules, a main cause of both America's high costs and poor quality, and to boost productivity and quality. . . .

Source: Excerpted from Peter F. Drucker, "Reinventing Unions," *Across the Board*, September 1989, pp. 12, 14. Excerpted with permission from Peter F. Drucker.

a business demanding labor. But now the impersonal forces of the market are replaced by negotiations between union and management representatives seeking to reach an agreement on wages, fringe benefits, and other aspects of a labor contract. This process in which a union negotiates a contract on behalf of its members is referred to as **collective bargaining**.

Collective bargaining
The process through which a union and management negotiate a labor contract.

The objectives bargained for by a union and management in a negotiation are primarily economic: wages, retirement income, payments for health care, and such. But the actual bargaining process itself is largely political. That is, negotiation involves a give-and-take process where each side tries to gain the most of what it seeks while giving up the least. Union representatives go into a negotiation with a list of objectives they want to attain, and management does the same. As the contracting develops, each side may give way on some of its objectives in return for the acceptance of other objectives that are of greater importance. Thus, the terms of a negotiated contract depend in large part on the relative bargaining ability and strength of the participating parties.

If the parties to a negotiation fail to agree on the terms of a contract within a certain amount of time, the union may go on strike against the employer. With a **strike,** union members stop working and ordinarily set up a picket line that other workers may refuse to cross. The purpose of the strike is to bring economic pressure on the employer to return to the bargaining table and draft an agreement more acceptable to the union than the one discussed when the workers walked out.

A strike is not a riskless strategy for a union to follow. For union members, it means managing without a paycheck and taking the risk of possibly losing their jobs. In addition, an employer may hold out against the striking employees by having management or nonunion workers assume the tasks performed by union workers, living off accumulated inventories, or offsetting the loss of revenues by the reduction in labor cost.

Two additional points about strikes should be mentioned. First, employment in related industries can be affected when a striking union shuts down a firm's production. For example, a strike by workers who produce carburetors could cause the shutdown of an automobile assembly plant if carburetors cannot be obtained from another source. Second, in recent years little labor time has been lost due to strikes. In 1988, for example, only 0.02 percent of estimated working time was lost because of strikes.[11]

Collective Bargaining and the Law

Over the years a large body of laws has developed concerning the rights and responsibilities of labor unions in collective bargaining and related matters. Two such laws that have been especially important are the National Labor Relations Act of 1935 and the Labor Management Relations Act, better known as the Taft-Hartley Act, of 1947.

Passed in the depths of the Depression, the **National Labor Relations Act** (also called the **Wagner Act**) strongly supports organized labor, and contributes to unionization in three ways. First, the law specifically gives workers the right to organize and bargain collectively, to choose who will represent them in their collective bargaining, and to carry out "concerted activities" for collective bargaining or other purposes that would advance

Strike

Work stoppage by union members.

National Labor Relations Act (Wagner Act)

Legislation supportive of unionization; permits and strengthens collective bargaining.

---

[11] *Statistical Abstract of the United States: 1990,* 1990, p. 416.

their interests. Second, the law defines certain actions by employers that are considered to be unfair labor practices. For example, it would be unfair for an employer to interfere in the organizing or operation of a labor union, to discriminate against employees on the basis of their membership in a union, or to refuse to enter into contract negotiations with a representative chosen by a majority of the employees. Third, the act created the **National Labor Relations Board (NLRB),** which hears complaints on unfair labor practices, and can order that those practices cease and be remedied where they are found to exist.[12]

National Labor Relations Board (NLRB)

Hears complaints on unfair labor practices and orders remedies where appropriate.

The **Taft-Hartley Act** of 1947 became law in a much different environment than that in which the National Labor Relations Act was passed — 1946 was a particularly troublesome year for work stoppages. This law in part amends the National Labor Relations Act and is generally less supportive of organized labor than the 1935 legislation.

Taft-Hartley Act

The 1947 legislation that contains several provisions limiting union activities.

The Taft-Hartley Act limits union activities in several ways. First, while the National Labor Relations Act gives workers the right to organize or join a union and to bargain collectively, under certain circumstances the Taft-Hartley Act gives workers the right to not join a union or otherwise engage in organized labor activities. One aspect of this right is spelled out in Section 14(b) of the law, which says that union membership cannot be a condition of employment in states that have passed laws to that effect. This is better known as the "right to work" issue, and state laws prohibiting union membership as a condition of employment are called **right to work laws.** With right to work laws, a union's ability to control the supply of labor is diminished, and the union's bargaining strength is weakened.

Right to work laws

State laws prohibiting union membership as a condition of employment.

Second, while the National Labor Relations Act defines unfair labor practices for employers, the Taft-Hartley Act defines similar practices for labor organizations. For example, unions cannot induce employers to discriminate against certain employees, nor can they refuse to negotiate with employers, charge excessive or discriminatory fees to new members, or require employers to pay for services that have not been rendered.

Third, the Taft-Hartley Act allows the president of the United States to impose an 80-day "cooling-off period" during which a particular strike or lockout (when an employer prevents laborers from entering a work site) cannot occur if, in the president's opinion, the work stoppage is a threat to the national interest. If, after 80 days, the situation leading to the strike or lockout is not corrected, the ban is lifted, and the work stoppage can continue.[13]

[12] *United States Statutes at Large,* Vol. 49, Part 1 (Washington, D.C.: U.S. Government Printing Office, 1936), pp. 452–454.

[13] *United States Statutes at Large,* Vol. 61, Part 1 (Washington, D.C.: U.S. Government Printing Office, 1948), pp. 136, 140–142, 151, 155–156.

Table 15.5   Division of Total Income among Households

Income is not distributed evenly among households in the United States. In 1989 the poorest one-fifth of U.S. households received 3.9 percent of total income while the richest one-fifth received 46.7 percent of the total.

	Percentage of Total Income		
Percentage of Households	**1969**	**1979**	**1989**
Lowest 20%	3.7%	3.8%	3.9%
Second 20%	10.5	9.7	9.6
Middle 20%	17.4	16.4	15.9
Fourth 20%	24.7	24.8	24.0
Highest 20%	43.7	45.3	46.7
Total[a]	100.0	100.0	100.0

[a]Columns may not total 100.0 due to rounding.

Source: 1969, 1979 figures from U.S. Bureau of the Census, *Money Income of Families and Persons in the United States: 1979* (Washington, D.C.: U.S. Government Printing Office, 1981), p. 54. 1989 figures from U.S. Bureau of the Census, *Measuring the Effect of Benefits and Taxes on Income and Poverty: 1989* (Washington, D.C.: U.S. Government Printing Office, 1990), p. 5.

The Distribution of Income

Distribution of income
The way in which income is divided among the members of a society.

The **distribution of income** is the way income is divided among the members of society. It reflects the way in which individuals share in the rewards from the production of goods and services.

One of the main questions in evaluating the distribution of income centers on equality. Were the distribution of income to individuals perfectly equal, everyone would receive the same amount: no one would earn more or less than anyone else. But income is obviously not divided equally among the members of society. Some households are better or worse off than others; and at the extremes, some are very rich and others are very poor.

One method for analyzing the distribution of income in the United States is illustrated in Table 15.5. In the first column of the table, households are divided into five groups—each representing 20 percent of all households—according to the amount of income they received. The lowest group represents the 20 percent of all households that received the lowest incomes, and the highest group is the 20 percent of all households that received the largest incomes. The remaining columns of the table give the percentage of total income that went to each of the five groups in 1969, 1979, and 1989.

With an equal distribution of income among households, each of the five groups would have received 20 percent of the total income. However, in each of the years shown in Table 15.5, the lowest 20 percent received less than 4 percent of the total income, while the highest 20 percent of house-holds had claim to over 43 percent.[14]

Obviously, not all members of society fare equally well in the distribution of income: some are more likely to be at the lower or higher ends than others. In Chapter Ten it was noted that, on the average, household heads with certain characteristics tend to earn more than household heads with other characteristics.[15] For example, male household heads typically earn more than female household heads. Other data indicate that households headed by a manager receive more income than households headed by a service worker, households headed by a white person fare better than those headed by a nonwhite person, and households headed by a college graduate fare better than those headed by an individual with less education.[16]

Explanations for the Distribution of Income

Why is income distributed as it is? Why do some households enjoy a large annual income while others do not? There is no single answer to these questions. Some explanations for the distribution of income focus on dif-ferences in the income-earning abilities of individuals, while others focus on factors separate from the individuals themselves. In this section we will look at five of the many explanations for variations in income: differences in productive resources, human capital investments, discrimination, bargain-ing power, and inheritance.

Differences in Productive Resources   One explanation for the distribution of income is based on the simple premise that income depends upon the quality and quantity of the productive resources that individuals possess, and the uses to which those resources are put. When factors of production differ in quality, the outputs from those factors may differ. Because of this, the owners of superior resources stand to earn more money. For example, an outstanding athlete may be more highly paid than teammates with less impressive performances; a highly productive salesperson will earn more on commission than less productive fellow workers; and an acre of farmland in the heart of Illinois should generate more income from the production of soybeans than an acre in the hills of western Pennsylvania.

Variations in income may also be traced to differences in the quantity of resources that individuals possess. All other things being equal, a person owning many productive factors will likely earn a larger income than one

---

[14] Over the years, the distribution of income has not fluctuated significantly, as measured according to the quintile method in Table 15.5. For example, data from 1947 through 1979 indicate that during this period the poorest 20 percent of all households received between 3.1 and 3.9 percent of total income, while the richest 20 percent received between 42.9 and 45.9 percent. See the data sources for Table 15.5.

[15] See pages 356 and 357, especially Table 10.4.

[16] *Statistical Abstract of the United States: 1990*, 1990, p. 448.

possessing few resources. A family that has a highly skilled household head, owns farmland, an apartment complex, and blue-chip stocks will likely have a higher income than a family that receives its only income from the labor of a highly skilled household head.

Differences in the income from productive resources may also be due to the ways in which individuals choose to use their resources. Consider two students from a small town who have each received a marketing degree. If one returns home and goes to work for a small local retailer, while the other chooses to relocate in a large city and take a position with a major department store chain, differences in their incomes may appear because of the different choices they made about using their talents.

Human capital investment

An expenditure made to improve the productivity of a person.

Human Capital Investments   The concept of investment for productivity gains is usually associated with expenditures on machinery, equipment, factories, and technological advances that increase output. In certain respects, people are like machines: their productive capabilities are influenced by what is invested in maintaining and improving themselves. Expenditures for education, training, health care, and other means of self-improvement that affect people's productivity, and therefore their incomes, are called **human capital investments.**

Human capital investments take several different forms. The most obvious is formal education, but training acquired at trade schools and on the job is important, too. Human capital investments also involve less obvious expenditures, such as those for health care. The healthier a worker, the greater his or her ability is to perform tasks effectively and maintain a low absence rate, both of which contribute to higher productivity. In this vein, some companies are encouraging exercise and paying employees to quit smoking or to lose weight. Health care expenditures as a human capital investment are not limited to those incurred while working. The type of health care an individual receives in his or her youth affects productivity and income-earning ability in later years.

The impact on income from investing in oneself is substantial. Not surprisingly, greater investments in education are associated with larger average incomes. Households headed by an individual with less than a high school education earned only $14,142 on the average in 1988, roughly 32 percent of the $45,490 average income for households headed by a person with four or more years of college.[17]

Discrimination

Unequal treatment in a labor market because of an employer's perception of a category to which a worker belongs.

Discrimination   Workers experience **discrimination** when they are treated unequally in a labor market because they are placed in different categories and judged on the basis of the employer's perception of the category to which they belong, rather than on the basis of their skills or productive

---

[17] U.S. Bureau of the Census, Current Population Reports, *Money Income and Poverty Status in the United States: 1988* (Washington, D.C.: U.S. Government Printing Office, 1989), p. 27.

capabilities. In the United States, concern over discrimination centers mainly on the labor market experiences of nonwhite as compared to white workers, female as compared to male workers, and older as compared to prime-age workers. But discrimination can be based on any type of categorical distinction between workers, such as on religious or political preference, or ethnic origin.

Discrimination shows itself in several different ways. It occurs where a worker, because of race, age, sex, or such, receives less pay than others for equal work. It also occurs where a worker, because of race, age, sex, or such, has a smaller or otherwise less desirable selection of employment opportunities from which to choose.

The effects of discrimination on income can also be indirect. For example, unequal access to good housing, medical care, or educational opportunities might lead to smaller or less productive human capital investments, which in turn can result in lower incomes. Affirmative action programs and the Equal Employment Opportunity Commission have been created in the United States in an effort to reduce discrimination and its effects.

Bargaining Power   Income can be raised by bargaining power, which is the ability of a labor supplier to withhold resources from the buyer if the supplier does not receive a satisfactory income. Control over the supply of labor may be exercised by a union bargaining for an entire group of workers or by a single individual who has a unique talent that is in strong demand. Part of this explanation for the distribution of income was covered in the discussion of collective bargaining earlier in this chapter.

Inheritance   Income may also be distributed unequally because of inheritance, which occurs when a person receives income not from his or her own labor, but as the beneficiary of someone else's effort. Typically, this income is from the ownership of inherited capital, real estate, natural resources, or securities.

A Word of Caution   A word of caution is in order regarding these various explanations for the distribution of income. Several of the factors just discussed may simultaneously affect the income pattern for an individual or group of persons in society. For example, the income of a fifty-year-old male might be greater than that of a fifty-year-old female because of sex discrimination. But the variation could also be due to differences in the amount of time spent by each in the labor force or the kinds of human capital investments each made. On the other hand, the types of human capital investments each made may have been influenced by the existence of sex discrimination. In short, any one explanation for the distribution of income does not rule out the remaining explanations and, what is more, the different explanations may be related.

Poverty

In Table 15.5 it was shown that, in 1989, income was distributed in such a way that the lowest 20 percent of all households received only 3.9 percent of the total income, and the next lowest 20 percent received only 9.6 percent. Are these households considered to be the "poor" in our society?

What is meant by "poor"? In general, poverty is based on a person's level of material well-being: the type of housing, clothing, and food that can be afforded, and the ability to acquire medical care, recreation, reading materials, and other goods and services. However, to label a person or household as poor is a value judgment. Each of us has a different concept of poverty. What constitutes being poor to someone living a comfortable existence may be different from the definition of poverty given by an average income earner. One who drives a late-model, expensive automobile may view as poor a person who drives an old, obviously used car. One who drives an old, used auto may view as poor a person who can afford no car at all.

Government Measures of Poverty   In order to calculate an "official" measure of poverty in the United States, the federal government has created a series of income measures called poverty levels. These **poverty levels** are based primarily on family size and indicate the amounts of annual money income that must be received to be considered *not* poor. Any individual or family receiving an income below its designated level is classified as poor and is included in government poverty statistics.

Poverty levels

Government designated levels of income that must be received to be considered *not* poor.

Table 15.6 gives the average annual poverty levels for families and individuals in 1970 and 1989. The table shows that the poverty levels increase as the number of persons in a family increases, and that the measures vary according to whether or not the head of the household is under 65 years of age.

In 1989, 31.5 million persons, or 12.8 percent of the total population, lived in poverty — that is, in households where the money income fell below the poverty levels. Table 15.7 gives some characteristics of this 1989 poverty population. Notice, for example, that many of these 31.5 million people were elderly or children, and that 11.7 million persons, or over 37 percent of the poverty population, lived in families headed by a female. Also, not shown in the table, in poverty-level families, the head of the household worked full-time in 32 percent of the cases in 1989.[18] These facts should dispel the belief that the poor are poor simply because they choose not to work.

Several recent studies have indicated that there is a "feminization of poverty" occurring in the United States: that is, increasingly, the poor are in households headed by women. Two factors may play an important role in this trend. First, the number of female-headed families has in-

[18] U.S. Bureau of the Census, *Measuring the Effect of Benefits and Taxes on Income and Poverty: 1989* (Washington, D.C.: U.S. Government Printing Office, 1990), p. 80.

Table 15.6

Poverty Levels for Families and Individuals

Poverty levels vary according to family size and age of the head of the household, and indicate the annual money income that must be received to be considered *not* poor.

Size of Unit	Income Level[a]	
	1970	1989
1 person	$1,954	$ 6,311
Under 65 years	2,010	6,452
65 years and over	1,861	5,947
2 persons	2,525	8,076
Head of household under 65 years	2,604	8,343
Head of household 65 years and over	2,348	7,501
3 persons	3,099	9,885
4 persons	3,968	12,675
5 persons	4,680	14,990
6 persons	5,260	16,921

[a]1970 and 1989 data are not strictly comparable because of revised procedures.

Source: U.S. Bureau of the Census, *Statistical Abstract of the United States: 1990,* 110th ed. (Washington, D.C.: U.S. Government Printing Office, 1990), p. 423; U.S. Bureau of the Census, *Measuring the Effect of Benefits and Taxes on Income and Poverty: 1989* (Washington, D.C.: U.S. Government Printing Office, 1990), p. 108.

creased due to the rising divorce rate and the increasing number of unmarried women with children. Second, the labor market experience of women is less favorable than that of men. For example, in Chapter Ten, Table 10.4 showed that households headed by a male had an average income of $31,534 in March 1988, whereas households headed by a female had an average income of $14,600.

There has been some disagreement over the definitions of the official poverty levels. Many argue that the levels are too low and do not represent a true measure of poverty. For example, according to Table 15.6, in 1989 the poverty level for a family of four was $12,675—far below the median household income of $28,906.[19] Also, according to the poverty levels in Table 15.6, a family of three persons earning $9,886 in 1989 would not have been "poor" because their income was $1 above the poverty line.

Some people argue that the plight of the poor is overstated because the income levels used to measure poverty do not account for in-kind transfers (the receipt of noncash benefits such as food stamps or medical care) that improve one's standard of living. For example, according to the money

[19]*Measuring the Effect of Benefits and Taxes on Income and Poverty: 1989,* p. 5.

Table 15.7   Some Characteristics of Persons Living below the Poverty Levels

Many of the poor are children, elderly, and persons living in female-headed families. Many are unable to work because of age or disability.

Characteristics	Numbers in 1989
Number of persons living below the poverty levels	31.5 million
Percentage of the total population	12.8%
Number of persons in female-headed families below the poverty levels	11.7 million
Percentage of female-headed families	35.9%
Number of persons in white families below the poverty levels	20.8 million
Percentage of white families	10.0%
Number of persons in black families below the poverty levels	9.3 million
Percentage of black families	30.7%
Number of children under 18 years of age below the poverty levels	12.6 million
Percentage of children under 18 years of age	19.6%
Number of persons 65 years and older below the poverty levels	3.4 million
Percentage of persons 65 years and older	11.4%
Number of families below the poverty levels where the head completed less than 12 years of education	3.3 million
Percentage of families where the head completed less than 12 years of education	22.5%
Number of families below the poverty levels where the head completed 4 or more years of college	0.3 million
Percentage of families where the head completed 4 or more years of college	1.9%

Source: U.S. Bureau of the Census, *Measuring the Effect of Benefits and Taxes on Income and Poverty: 1989* (Washington, D.C.: U.S. Government Printing Office, 1990), pp. 10–12, 38, 46.

income poverty-level approach used in Table 15.6, 12.8 percent of the population was below the poverty levels in 1989. However, if government noncash transfer payments for food and housing (such as food stamps and subsidized rental housing) and medical care were added to people's money incomes, then a smaller percentage of the population would have fallen below the poverty levels.

Government Programs and Poverty   Government outlays to individuals and households in the form of cash transfer payments and in-kind benefits are substantial. These payments and benefits include Social Security, unemployment compensation, housing assistance, food stamps, medical care, vocational rehabilitation, public assistance, job training, and others. Among these, there is no single program aimed specifically and exclusively at persons living below the poverty levels. Rather, each federal and state

Table 15.8

Average Monthly Payments from Various Government Programs

There are many government cash and in-kind benefit programs. Each program has its own eligibility requirements, and the actual amount of the benefit from some programs can differ significantly from state to state.

Government Program	Average Monthly Payment in 1988
Aid to Families with Dependent Children	
Per family	$ 379
Per recipient	130
Old Age Assistance	36
Food Stamps (average monthly value per recipient)	50[a]
Supplemental Security Income	
For the disabled	294
For the aged	188
For the blind	306
Social Security	
Retired workers	537
Disabled workers	530
Children of disabled workers	151
Federal Civil Service Retirement	
Age and service, and disability	1,263
Unemployment Compensation	580[a]

[a]Estimated figure.

Source: U.S. Bureau of the Census, *Statistical Abstract of the United States: 1990,* 110th ed. (Washington, D.C.: U.S. Government Printing Office, 1990), pp. 358, 361, 362, 366, 367.

program has its own eligibility requirements for which a poor person may qualify. For example, a poverty-level retired couple could be eligible for Social Security if they made payments into the system, or a low income could entitle a household to food stamps. One problem with government programs is that some, such as Social Security or unemployment compensation, are closed to the poor who have no regular employment. As a result, some government benefits may not be received by poverty-level families. In addition, in recent years much attention has been focused on the plight of the homeless in the United States. Many of these people receive no government aid because they do not qualify for specific programs, have no address, or do not sign up for benefits.

For those living under the poverty levels, the most likely source of government cash transfers is public aid, which includes programs such as old-age assistance, general assistance, and aid to families with dependent children (AFDC). Table 15.8 lists the average monthly payments for various

Application 15.3

When Welfare Pays the Rent

Can a family of three survive in New York City on $286 a month for rent? The city and state maintain that it can. That is how much they give to the typical welfare family, a single mother with two children, for basic shelter.

But most housing experts say the grants given to the 287,000 families living on welfare in New York City bear little relation to the marketplace. The grants, called shelter allowances, are far below rents for vacant apartments in even the meanest of New York's neighborhoods. Welfare mothers often end up using money earmarked for food and clothing to pay rent, or living doubled- and tripled-up in cramped quarters with friends and relatives. The low level of the grants has also contributed significantly to evictions and, thus, to homelessness, housing experts say. . . .

Numbers tell much of the story. Welfare recipients typically are single mothers with two or three children. A mother with three children receives a $312 monthly shelter allowance. Recipients also get about $200 in food stamps and another check for food, clothing, utilities and other expenses. This second check is $291 a month for a mother with two children and $375 for a mother with three.

Periodic surveys of New York's housing market have shown a growing gap between the welfare housing check and rents, particularly in privately owned buildings, where most of the poor live.

There were virtually no apartments available for less than $400 a month, according to the most recent survey, in 1987. . . .

[W]elfare families who have entered the system recently, and many if not most who have been in it for a while, are squeezed extraordinarily by the cost of housing. [A lawyer for Legal Aid] said poor families often must spend 60 percent to 70 percent of their income on housing. They use food money to help pay the rent, and they fall behind on their electrical bill. Often, they also fall behind on the rent, and many wind up in housing court, facing eviction. "We see people all the time who are about to lose apartments that rent for $400 a month or $450 a month," [he] said. "And they have no reasonable chance of finding another $400 or $450 apartment."

Many families who are evicted find themselves in city shelters and in welfare hotels — often at the cost of $1,500 and $2,000 a month for cramped, decrepit rooms. [Some people] contend that it would be less expensive, and more humane, for government to pay higher rent subsidies to keep welfare families in their homes.

Source: Excerpted from Alan Finder, "When Welfare Pays the Rent," *The New York Times*, June 3, 1990, p. E6. Copyright © 1991 by the New York Times Company. Excerpted by permission.

government programs in 1988. The first few listed are those most likely to be received by someone living in poverty. Notice that the average monthly payment for a family with dependent children was $379, or $130 per recipient. In practice this payment varies from state to state, causing considerable deviation from the average. For example, in Alabama the average family monthly payment in 1988 was $114, while in Alaska it was $599.[20]

The opinion is sometimes heard that people live well on government support payments. Application 15.3, "When Welfare Pays the Rent," provides a different picture of how far various aid programs may actually take

[20] *Statistical Abstract of the United States: 1990*, 1990, p. 368.

their recipients. Notice, incidentally, how the feminization of poverty that was introduced earlier in this section is a factor in this application.

Summary

The prices of land, labor, capital, and entrepreneurship are determined basically by the forces of supply and demand, with businesses as the primary buyers. The demand for labor and all other inputs is derived from the demand for the goods or services that the inputs produce.

A demand curve for labor is downward sloping because of diminishing marginal productivity, and because of the need to lower output prices to increase sales in all but purely competitive markets. The labor demand curve for an individual firm is equal to the marginal revenue product of its labor. A market demand curve for labor is the sum of the labor demand curves of all individual firms in the market, and is also downward sloping.

A market supply curve of labor is upward sloping, indicating a direct relationship between the wage rate and the amount of labor offered in the market. The supply of labor is affected not only by the wage rate, but also by other factors such as psychic income and locational preference.

A change in labor demand or supply is shown by a shift of the demand or supply curve to the right or left, and results from changes in nonwage factors such as the prices of substitute inputs, technology, and future job prospects. A change in the quantity of labor demanded or supplied results from a change in the wage rate.

The simple supply and demand approach to a market for labor can be modified to account for certain real world considerations. Wage rigidities, legislation, and unequal bargaining power influence the determination of wages.

A union is a workers' organization that bargains on its members' behalf with management on such matters as wages, fringe benefits, and working conditions. The number of workers represented by unions has changed over the years, and declined in the last decade. A craft union represents workers who possess a particular skill, while an industrial union represents workers who perform different jobs in a particular industry. Unions are structured around a headquarters organization with locals to which the members belong.

The process through which union contracts are negotiated is called collective bargaining. A strike may occur if the parties to a negotiation fail to reach an agreement on a contract. A strike, designed to bring economic pressure on a business firm, is not without risk to union members.

Two important laws affect collective bargaining: the National Labor Relations Act (Wagner Act) of 1935, and the Labor Management Relations Act (Taft-Hartley Act) of 1947. The National Labor Relations Act is basically supportive of unionism, while the Taft-Hartley Act serves in several ways as a limiting force on unionism.

Income distribution refers to how income is divided among the members of society. In the United States, families with the lowest incomes receive less than a proportional share of the total, while those with the highest incomes receive more than a proportional share. There are many explanations as to why income is distributed as it is. Some of these include: differences in productive resources, human capital investments, discrimination, bargaining power, and inheritance.

The U.S. government has created an official measure of poverty in the United States. The basis for defining poverty is an annual money income level, which varies according to the size of the family. Many of the poor in the United States are old, children, or in a household headed by a woman. Of the government programs providing cash transfers, the most likely to be received by a poverty-level household is public aid.

Key Terms and Concepts

Wage	Craft union
Derived demand	Industrial union
Law of Diminishing Returns	AFL-CIO
Marginal physical product	Collective bargaining
Diminishing marginal productivity	Strike
Marginal revenue product	National Labor Relations Act (Wagner Act)
Demand curve for labor	
Supply curve of labor	National Labor Relations Board
Changes in labor demand or supply	Taft-Hartley Act
Changes in the quantity of labor demanded or supplied	Right to work laws
	Distribution of income
Wage determination	Human capital investment
Minimum wage law	Discrimination
Union	Poverty levels

Review Questions

1. What would be the effect of each of the following on Company X's demand for labor? (Remember the distinction between a change in demand and a change in quantity demanded.)
   a. An increase in the price of Company X's major competitor's product
   b. A decrease in the price of an input that can be substituted for Company X's work force
   c. A decrease in the number of buyers in Company X's product market
   d. A decrease in the price of Company X's product
   e. An increase in the wage paid to Company X's workers

2. Give some examples of how the simple supply and demand model can be modified to account for real world considerations in determining wages.

3. Explain fully why a demand curve for labor is downward sloping. Given the following table, fill in the columns for Total Revenue and Marginal Revenue Product, and then determine this producer's demand curve for labor and illustrate it in the graph below.

Units of Labor	Total Product	Price per Unit	Total Revenue	Marginal Revenue Product
0	0	$13	_____	
1	100	12	_____	_____
2	170	11	_____	_____
3	230	10	_____	_____
4	280	9	_____	_____
5	320	8	_____	_____
6	350	7	_____	_____

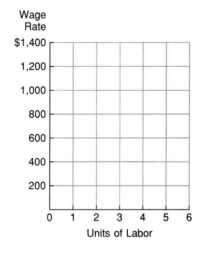

Wage Rate

4. What is the difference between a craft union and an industrial union? How does a craft union keep its members' wages high?

5. What are some major provisions of the National Labor Relations Act and the Taft-Hartley Act and, generally, what is the impact of each act on organized labor in the United States?

6. What is meant by the expression "income distribution"? What are some of the explanations as to why incomes are unequally distributed?

7. What groups in society are most likely to be included among the poor, and why is there controversy over the official definition of the poverty levels?

Discussion Questions

1. Match each occupation with what you think is the correct salary, and explain why you think each match is correct. Salaries are averages for the year given.[a]

Occupation	Average Salary
1. Baseball players in 1987	_____ a. $215,000
2. Football players in 1986–1987	_____ b. $34,000
3. Public elementary school teachers in 1989–1990	_____ c. $410,000
4. Lawyers starting in private industry in 1988	_____ d. $81,000
5. Governor of Missouri in 1986	_____ e. $595,000
6. Corporate chief executives in 1988 (salaries and bonuses)	_____ f. $28,900
7. Major General commanding the 82nd Airborne Division in 1988	_____ g. $70,000
8. Dentists in general practice in 1988	_____ h. $72,500
9. Pediatrician in 1987	_____ i. $88,500

2. Assume that the leaders of the AFL-CIO seek your advice on actions that could be taken to stem the decline of unionism in the United States. What would you suggest to reverse this trend? Do you think that the labor movement will ever return to the status and strength it had during its peak years?

3. Two laws that affect the operation of labor markets are the minimum wage law and the right to work law. Who benefits and who loses from each of these laws?

4. Sometimes a business makes investments in machinery and equipment, and those investments do not pay off — the business does not recover its costs plus something more. Is it possible for an individual to make a human capital investment that does not pay off? In making an informed human capital decision on, say, a college education, what sorts of information would you want to know, and why?

5. You have a friend who argues that poverty is really not a problem in this country because the poor are better off than millions of people in other parts of the world. Evaluate this position.

6. There is much criticism that the poverty levels are not an accurate method for determining who is poor in the United States. Do you think these levels are too high or too low? How would you redefine poverty for statistical purposes?

7. What are the eligibility requirements in your state for a family to receive AFDC (Aid to Families with Dependent Children)? What are the requirements to receive food stamps? What is the monthly AFDC payment? What is the monthly allotment of food stamps? If the qualifications for these two programs are different, explain how and why.

[a]Answers and sources are at the end of this chapter.

Critical Thinking Case 15

■ Tales from the Treadmill

Critical Thinking Skills	Challenging conventional wisdom
	Analyzing the consequences of actions
Economic Concepts	Diminishing marginal productivity
	Labor demand

Among 88 million people with full-time jobs last year, nearly 24 percent—largely executives, professionals, self-employed people, journalists, bureaucrats, and the secretaries and clerks who toil alongside them—spent 49 or more hours a week on the job, according to the Bureau of Labor Statistics. Ten years ago only 18 percent worked so much. . . .

Students of the psyches of hard-toiling workers say that many people thrive on 60- and 70-hour weeks and the fast pace of the electronic workplace. But others find it a sweatshop. One result is a surge in early retirement among men, who have been in the work force longer than most women. In the end, some economists say, it is not even clear that the economy is benefiting from all the frenetic activity.

The government says more workers than ever held both a regular job last year and at least one part-time job—6.2 percent of all working people. The moonlighting among men hasn't changed very much over two decades, but among women, it has soared. . . .

Some managers say that even in a conventional eight-hour day they work much harder, thanks in part to their arsenals of technological gimmickry. They have fax machines, cellular telephones, paging devices, laptop computers that they use on planes and desktop computers that let them send electronic letters, orders and contracts in seconds, across oceans. . . .

People give many reasons for working harder or longer. Most say they must to make ends meet. Some say they also relish the bustle. Some think that if they don't work harder, the competition will. [Others are running] from their own bosses. In the 1980s, hundreds of American companies eliminated whole layers of middle management to cut costs. Those remaining fear they will be next. . . .

Many analysts suspect that the extra work does no more good for the economy than it does for the health. Indeed, they ask, if people are producing more with their labor, why is the economy so sluggish? And why is American productivity—the value of goods and services workers produce—growing so much more slowly than in Asia and Europe?

One explanation might be that many people are just spinning their wheels. Executives hustle from meeting to meeting and make calls to disembodied voices on answering machines because those people, too, are in meetings. [A management consultant] says the average professional worker will spend three years of his life in meetings and two playing telephone tag.

"Working longer and harder is not the same as working smarter," says [another professional in this area].

Questions

1. Thomas Edison is credited with some famous quotes on work, notably, "Genius is one percent inspiration and 99 percent perspiration," and "There is no substitute for hard work."[a] What appear to be the consequences of carrying this philosophy to the extreme? If hard work is not the best way to achieve success, what should replace it?

2. What are the benefits of working a 70-hour week? What are the costs? Would a company, because of the Law of Diminishing Returns, be better off hiring two people for the 70-hour-a-week job?

3. Does this case provide a legitimate reason for the decline in American productivity? Why?

[a]Emily Morison Beck, *Bartlett's Famous Quotations* (Boston: Little, Brown & Co., 1980), p. 661.

Source: Excerpted from Peter T. Kilborn, "Tales from the Digital Treadmill," *The New York Times,* June 3, 1990, section 4, pp. 1, 3. Copyright © 1990 by the New York Times Company. Excerpted by permission.

Suggested Readings

John Steele Gordon, "The Problem of Money and Time," *American Heritage,* May/June 1989, pp. 57–66.
An essay on difficulties in comparing standards of living from the past with those of today.

John Holusha, "Unions Are Expanding Their Role to Survive in the 90's," *The New York Times,* August 19, 1990, Section 3, p. 12; and Michael Massing, "Detroit's Strange Bedfellows," *The New York Times Magazine,* February 7, 1988, pp. 20–27, 52.
Articles dealing with the changing tactics of labor unions to recruit and organize workers and bargain collectively.

Frank Levy, "The Middle Class: Is It Really Vanishing?" *The Brookings Review,* Summer 1987, pp. 17–21.
An article on whether the middle class is shrinking in size, or becoming poorer.

Arthur M. Okun, "Ch. 2: The Labor Market," *Prices and Quantities: A Macroeconomic Analysis* (Washington, D.C.: The Brookings Institution, 1981), pp. 26–80.
Discusses labor market models that explain the downward inflexibility of wages.

Jonathan Rauch, "Kids as Capital," *The Atlantic,* August 1989, pp. 56–60.
Focuses on children as human capital investments, redistributions of income to encourage child rearing, and the importance of children for the future of the economy.

Jeremy Rifkin, "Ch. 12: Time Pyramids and Time Ghettos," *Time Wars* (New York: Simon & Schuster, 1989), pp. 190–197.
Explores the relationship between the distribution of income and people's time orientation.

Harrell R. Rodgers, Jr., *Poor Women, Poor Families* (New York: M.E. Sharpe, Inc., 1986).
Discusses the increase in female-headed households, the increase in poverty among these households, and the role of the welfare system.

Timothy M. Smeeding and Barbara Boyld Torrey, "Poor Children In Rich Countries," *Science,* **November 1988, pp. 873–877.**
Presents research on the poverty rates for children in six industrialized countries and the effectiveness of policies to deal with the problem.

Adam Smith, "Ch. X: Inequalities arising from the Nature of the Employments themselves," *The Wealth of Nations* **(New York: Random House, Modern Library, 1937), pp. 100–110. Original publication, 1776.**
A charming explanation of five factors leading to inequalities in wages among various occupations.

Answers and Sources for Discussion Question 1

Answers: 1. c, 2. a, 3. f, 4. b, 5. d, 6. e, 7. h, 8. g, 9. i. Sources: *The Margin,* November 1987, p. 9; *St. Louis Magazine,* January 1987, p. 19; *The Wall Street Journal,* March 28, 1988, pp. 1, 6, and February 9, 1988, p. 30; U. S. Department of Labor, Bureau of Labor Statistics, *Occupational Outlook Handbook, 1990–91,* April 1990, pp. 99. 133. 140; *Statistical Abstract of the United States, 1990,* p. 103.

Part Four

The International Economy

Chapter Sixteen

International Trade

Many U.S. fast-food companies have successfully established themselves in other countries and contributed to an expansion in international trade.

Source: Ellen Rudolph/
NYT PICTURES.

Chapter Objectives

1. To present an overview of U.S. international trade by highlighting major U.S. exports and imports, and countries with which the United States trades.

2. To explain the principle of comparative advantage.

3. To define free trade and discuss some arguments in its favor.

4. To explain the major tools for restricting trade: tariffs, quotas, and embargoes.

5. To define protectionism and discuss some arguments in its favor.

6. To discuss the U.S. experience with trade policies and some measures for stimulating exports.

7. To examine some key agreements affecting trade among nations.

An introduction to economics would be incomplete without an overview of international economics. As the name suggests, international economics concerns the economic relationships among nations, particularly the movement of goods and services, and financial transactions. Since trading and financial transactions among nations have many dimensions, several topics are included under the heading of international economics. For example, foreign aid, military activity, overseas investments, and the import and export of goods such as oil, wine, grain, and automobiles are all relevant to this area.

Economic activity has become increasingly internationalized in recent years. Consider, for example, how one author describes the conduct of business in the high-fashion apparel industry.

. . . A London department-store buyer of high-fashion apparel orders a line of dresses devised by a New York fashion designer. Within an hour of the order the designer sends via satellite the drawings and specifications for making the dresses to a fiber-optic link in Hong Kong, where they appear on a high-resolution computer monitor, ready for a manufacturing engineer to transform them into prototype garments. The prototypes are then reproduced in a Chinese factory. The designer, the engineer, and the factory supervisor conduct a video teleconference to work out details, and the finished garments arrive in London less than six weeks after the order was placed. . . .[1]

---

[1] Robert B. Reich, "The Real Economy," *The Atlantic,* February 1991, p. 40.

This chapter introduces some of the important topics that relate to the movement of goods and services between nations, or international trade. It begins with an overview of U.S. international trade that describes its growing importance, and identifies the major products that are traded and the United States' most important trading partners. Next, the concept of comparative advantage, a basic theory underlying international trade, is presented. This is followed by a section on one of the great debates in international economics: free trade versus protectionism. Finally, the overall trade policy of the United States, some methods for stimulating exports, and important agreements affecting trade among nations are examined. Chapter Seventeen deals with the financial aspects of international economics.

The trading and financial relationships among nations are important for many reasons. Not only do these relationships affect the domestic economies of various countries, but they have implications for national politics, international relations, and social understanding. For example, an administration might not be reelected to office if its nation's currency performs poorly in foreign exchange markets; dependence on a foreign supplier of a critical resource might affect political relations between two nations; and international understanding might be hurt if it becomes too expensive for a nation's citizens to travel abroad because the value of their money has fallen internationally.

An Overview of U.S. International Trade

International trade
The buying and selling of goods and services among different countries.

An important aspect of international economics is **international trade:** the buying and selling of goods and services among different countries. International trade affects the availability of various goods and services, and the levels of production, employment, and prices in the trading countries. For example, sales in overseas markets can result in the employment of more of a nation's workers and other resources than would be the case if only domestic demand were met. On the other hand, the presence of a strong foreign competitor in a domestic market can lead to a drop in domestic firms' sales, which in turn can foster a reduction in production and employment. Also, the presence of foreign goods in a market increases competition, which in turn influences product prices. And for a country that is dependent on a foreign product, increases in the price of the product can influence that country's inflation rate.

Export
A good or service sold abroad.

Import
A good or service purchased from abroad.

The Size and Composition of U.S. Trade

The importance of international trade to the U.S. economy is illustrated in Table 16.1, which lists data on the **export** and **import** of goods and services for selected years. In the middle columns, titled "Exports" and "Imports,"

Table 16.1   Exports and Imports of Goods and Services (Billions of Dollars)

Both the dollar amounts of exports and imports and exports and imports as a percentage of GNP have increased over the last 40 years.

Year	Gross National Product	Exports	Imports	Exports as a Percentage of GNP	Imports as a Percentage of GNP
1950	$ 288.3	$ 14.5	$ 12.3	5.0%	4.3%
1955	405.9	21.1	18.1	5.2	4.5
1960	515.3	29.9	24.0	5.8	4.7
1965	705.1	42.9	33.2	6.1	4.7
1970	1,015.5	68.9	60.5	6.8	6.0
1975	1,598.4	161.3	130.3	10.1	8.2
1980	2,732.0	351.0	318.9	12.8	11.7
1985	4,014.9	370.9	448.9	9.2	11.2
1986	4,231.6	396.5	493.8	9.4	11.7
1987	4,515.6	449.6	564.3	10.0	12.5
1988	4,873.7	552.0	626.1	11.3	12.8
1989	5,200.8	626.2	672.3	12.0	12.9
1990	5,463.0	670.4	708.4	12.3	13.0

Source: U.S., *Economic Report of the President* (Washington, D.C.: U.S. Government Printing Office, 1991), pp. 286, 287. The figures for 1990 are preliminary.

it can be seen that in recent years U.S. export and import transactions have resulted in the movement of hundreds of billions of dollars in goods and services annually. For example, in 1990 exports and imports amounted to $670.4 billion and $708.4 billion, respectively. Not surprisingly, the data in the middle columns also show that the dollar values of exports and imports have grown over the years.

The last two columns of Table 16.1 list exports and imports of goods and services as percentages of gross national product (GNP) for each of the selected years. Notice that both export and import activities have grown in relative importance when compared to GNP. In 1950 an amount equal to 5.0 percent of GNP was exported, and 4.3 percent of GNP was imported. By 1990 exports were 12.3 percent of GNP, and imports were 13.0 percent of GNP. One can conclude from Table 16.1 that foreign trade has become an increasingly important part of the U.S. economy over the last 40 years.

What types of goods and services does the United States export and import? Table 16.2 gives the distribution of U.S. merchandise exports and imports by broad product group for selected years. A broad product group is composed of several broadly related types of goods. For example, the

Table 16.2　　　　Percentage Distribution of U.S. Exports and Imports by Broad Product Group

Historically, capital goods has been the most important export category, and industrial supplies and materials has been the most important import category.

Product Group	Exports				
	1970	1975	1980	1985	1990
Foods, feeds and beverages	13.8%	18.0%	16.0%	11.2%	9.1%
Industrial supplies and materials	32.5	27.8	31.9	27.9	27.2
Capital goods, except automotive	34.5	34.2	33.5	35.4	39.5
Automotive vehicles and parts	9.1	10.1	7.6	11.5	9.4
Nonfood consumer goods	6.6	6.1	7.3	6.1	11.0
Others	3.5	3.8	3.7	7.9	3.8

Product Group	Imports				
	1970	1975	1980	1985	1990
Foods, feeds and beverages	15.4%	9.8%	7.4%	6.5%	5.4%
Industrial supplies and materials	38.5	51.6	53.0	33.6	29.0
Capital goods, except automotive	10.0	10.4	12.6	18.7	23.5
Automotive vehicles and parts	13.8	12.3	11.2	19.2	17.3
Nonfood consumer goods	18.6	13.5	13.7	19.6	21.3
Others	3.7	2.4	2.1	2.4	3.5

Source: Figures for 1970–1985 are from U.S. Bureau of the Census, *Statistical Abstract of the United States: 1990*, 110th ed. (Washington, D.C.: U.S. Government Printing Office, 1990), p. 790. Figures for 1990 are from U.S. Department of Commerce, *Survey of Current Business*, Vol. 71, No. 3, March 1991, pp. 53–54. The figures for 1990 are preliminary.

foods, feeds and beverages group includes grains, meat products, vegetables, fish, and distilled beverages.[2]

In the upper half of the table it can be seen that the most important class of exports has been capital goods, followed by industrial supplies and materials. The capital goods category includes products ranging from oil drilling and metalworking machinery to hospital equipment and civilian aircraft. Industrial supplies and materials includes such things as iron and steel products, fuels and petroleum products, and building materials.[3]

[2] U.S. Department of Commerce, *Survey of Current Business*, Vol. 71, No. 3, March 1991, p. 53.
[3] *Survey of Current Business*, March 1991, p. 53.

Imports by broad product group are shown in the lower half of Table 16.2. The table indicates that throughout the entire period the most important import group was industrial supplies and materials. More specific significant imports to the United States in recent years have been household appliances (from the nonfood consumer goods group), energy products (from the industrial supplies group), and automobiles.[4] Notice that in 1990 capital goods and industrial supplies and materials were important both as exports and imports. Why do you think this is the case? Does it suggest something about what is traded or with whom we trade?

One important fact that Table 16.2, especially the import section, conveys is that the relative importance of goods and services in international trade changes over time. For example, imports of foods, feeds and beverages have fallen in importance over the years. (In 1965 the dollar value of coffee imported to the United States was higher than the value of imported automobiles and auto parts.) The growth in importance of industrial supplies and materials in the 1970s and early 1980s was due in large part to the increase in the price of imported oil from OPEC, which is included in that category.

The Geographic Distribution of U.S. Trade

The percentage of U.S. merchandise exports to and imports from the continents and selected countries and groups of countries with which the United States traded in 1990 are given in Table 16.3. The majority of U.S. exporting and importing occurred with developed nations in North America, Europe, and Asia.

In terms of specific countries, Canada and Japan are the two most important trading partners of the United States, although Table 16.3 shows that a larger volume of trade is carried on with Europe's Economic Community. The European Community, or EC, is made up of 12 members (Belgium, Denmark, France, Germany, Greece, Ireland, Italy, Luxembourg, Netherlands, Portugal, Spain, and the United Kingdom) that agreed to join into a single market area, or act like a single trading partner, in 1992. In 1990, more was exported to the European Community than to either Canada or Japan, and the European Community surpassed Japan as the leading importer to the United States. Other countries, such as Mexico and Taiwan, are also important trading partners.

Notice from Table 16.3 the relatively small percentage of trade between the United States and Eastern Europe, and that U.S. trade with Taiwan is greater than with Mainland China.

[4] *Survey of Current Business,* March 1991, p. 54.

Table 16.3   Geographic Distribution of U.S. Exports and Imports in 1990

The majority of U.S. trade occurs with developed nations in North America, Europe, and Asia. Canada, Japan, and the European Community are the United States' most important trading partners.

Trade between the United States and	Percentage of U.S. Exports	Percentage of U.S. Imports
North America	28.4%	24.8%
Canada	21.2	18.7
Mexico	7.2	6.1
Latin America and Other Western Hemisphere Countries	13.8	12.9
Brazil	1.3	1.6
Venezuela	0.8	1.9
Europe	29.4	22.4
European Community	24.5	18.3
France	3.5	2.6
Germany	4.7	5.6
Italy	2.0	2.5
United Kingdom	5.8	4.0
Eastern Europe	1.1	0.5
Africa	2.0	3.5
Asia	30.2	42.2
China	1.2	3.1
Japan	12.2	18.0
Republic of Korea	3.6	3.7
Taiwan	2.8	4.7
Australia	2.1	0.9

Source: U.S. Department of Commerce, *Survey of Current Business*, Vol. 71, No. 3, March 1991, pp. 51–52.

Comparative Advantage and International Trade

Scarcity and Specialization

Specialization

Resources used in production are concentrated on a narrow range of tasks or on the production of a limited variety of goods and services.

In the discussion of the definition of economics in Chapter One, it was pointed out that a scarcity of the material things in life forms the basis of the economic problem; that is, there are limited resources to produce goods and services to satisfy unlimited material wants and needs.

One way the scarcity problem can be lessened is through increases in production gained by specialization. **Specialization** occurs when productive resources concentrate on a narrow range of tasks or on the production of a limited variety of goods and services. The concept applies to all factors of production but is most often associated with individuals and locations. For example, a doctor may specialize in cardiovascular surgery; a student may select economics as her major; and northern California is known for its wine production.

Specialization permits greater levels of production than would be attained without it. By concentrating on one type of productive activity, rather than acting like a jack-of-all trades, a factor of production can be used more efficiently—and greater efficiency results in greater output. Specialization, however, depends on the ability to sell what one produces and buy what one needs from someone else, or on the ability to trade. Thus, the availability of appropriate markets and the ability to trade are necessary accompaniments to specialization.

Specialization occurs on an international level when countries concentrate their productive efforts on the goods and services they are best at producing, and trade for the goods and services that are most costly to produce. A country that has a relatively inexpensive labor force might specialize in producing items requiring substantial labor inputs; a country with good agricultural resources might concentrate on growing basic grain crops or on livestock; and a country possessing technologically advanced equipment and production methods might use these to its benefit. When each country concentrates on what it does more efficiently than other countries, international specialization increases total production and permits a lessening of the scarcity problem on a worldwide level.

The Principle of Comparative Advantage

Comparative advantage

One country has a lower opportunity cost of producing a good or service than does another country.

The basic principle behind the proposition that international trade can lessen the scarcity problem by increasing production is called **comparative advantage.** The root of comparative advantage is the concept that if countries produce those goods and services in which they have an advantage in comparison to other countries, and trade for what they are less adept at producing, the world will have more goods and services than it otherwise would. In essence, the principle of comparative advantage is a restatement of the benefits of international specialization.

To have an advantage in comparison to another country means that fewer units of other goods or services are given up to produce one unit of a certain good or service in one country than are given up to produce one unit of the same item in the other country. Put briefly, it means the opportunity cost of production is lower in the country with the comparative advantage.

To illustrate how comparative advantage works, and how it results in overall gains in output, let us examine a hypothetical production and trade relationship between the United States and Japan.

Assume that with 1 unit of resources (where 1 unit is equal to a defined combination of land, labor, capital, and entrepreneurship) the United States can produce either 10 tons of corn or 1 television set. Assume further that

Table 16.4	Production Possibilities from 1 Unit of Resources

The United States and Japan have a choice of production possibilities between corn and television sets when employing 1 unit of resources.

Country	Production Possibilities
United States	10 tons of corn or 1 television set
Japan	1 ton of corn or 10 television sets

with 1 unit of resources Japan can produce either 1 ton of corn or 10 television sets. Table 16.4 illustrates these production possibilities.

The comparative advantage of each country in this example is obvious: the United States has the advantage in corn, and Japan in television sets. How is this determined? Opportunity costs in each country are compared.

The opportunity cost of producing 10 tons of corn in the United States is just 1 television set, while the opportunity cost of producing 10 tons of corn in Japan is 100 television sets. That is, Japan would be required to give up 100 television sets to produce 10 tons of corn, but the United States would need to give up only 1 television set. Clearly, the opportunity cost (measured in forgone television sets) of producing corn in the United States is lower than it is in Japan, giving the United States the comparative advantage in corn. The opportunity cost of producing 1 television set in the United States is 10 tons of corn, whereas in Japan producing 1 television set would mean giving up only one-tenth of a ton of corn. Clearly, the opportunity cost of producing a television set is lower in Japan, giving Japan the comparative advantage in television sets.

Earlier it was stated that the world would be better off in terms of the amounts of goods and services produced if comparative advantage and trade were exercised. Let us continue the corn and television example to illustrate this point. Assume now that the United States has 2 units of resources to employ, and uses 1 unit for the production of corn and 1 unit for the production of television sets. In this case, the United States will produce 10 tons of corn and 1 television set. Assume further that Japan also has 2 units of resources to employ and also uses 1 unit for the production of corn and 1 unit for television sets. In this case Japan will produce 1 ton of corn and 10 television sets. With resources employed in this manner, total production of these items by these two countries is 11 tons of corn and 11 television sets. This is shown in Table 16.5.

Now assume that Japan and the United States each decides to devote its productive resources to the good in which it has the comparative advantage and to engage in international trade. The United States will rely on Japan to provide one of its favorite sources of information and recreation, and Japan will defer to the United States for some necessary foodstuffs. The United States will now devote its 2 units of resources to the production of

Table 16.5

Production from 2 Units of Resources per Country without Specialization

When the United States and Japan both produce corn and television sets with 2 units of resources each, 11 tons of corn and 11 television sets can be produced.

Item	Amount of Production
Corn	10 tons (U.S.) + 1 ton (Japan) = 11 tons total production
Television sets	1 TV (U.S.) + 10 TVs (Japan) = 11 TVs total production

corn, producing 20 tons of corn instead of 10 tons of corn and 1 television set. With Japan's 2 units of resources, it will now produce 20 television sets instead of 10 television sets and 1 ton of corn. Table 16.6 summarizes the resulting production when each country exercises its comparative advantage.

The increased total production registered in Table 16.6 (as compared to the numbers in Table 16.5) demonstrates the benefits of specialization and trade. Without international specialization, a total of 11 tons of corn and 11 television sets could be produced by both countries together. With production based on comparative advantage, Japan and the United States can together produce a total of 20 tons of corn and 20 television sets using the same amount of resources. Clearly, the scarcity problem can be lessened through the exercise of comparative advantage and trade.

Does the principle of comparative advantage work in the real world? How closely is it followed? In order to exercise comparative advantage fully and reap its benefits, an environment of free trade is necessary. **Free trade** exists when goods and services can be bought and sold by anyone in any country with no restrictions. Everyone is free to choose with whom he or she deals, regardless of location, and there are no barriers to trade. Import taxes are not imposed to raise prices artificially and discourage purchases, and limits are not set on the amounts that can be bought and sold. This free flow of trade permits specialization to work to its fullest. You can check your grasp of the material in this section by answering the questions in "Test Your Understanding: Comparative Advantage."

Free trade
Goods and services can be exported and imported by anyone in any country with no restrictions.

Table 16.6

Production from 2 Units of Resources per Country with Specialization

When countries devote their resources to the production of goods in which they have a comparative advantage, the total production of these goods increases.

Item	Amount of Production
Corn	20 tons (U.S.) + 0 tons (Japan) = 20 tons total production
Television sets	0 TVs (U.S.) + 20 TVs (Japan) = 20 TVs total production

Test Your Understanding

Comparative Advantage[a]

[a]Answers can be found at the end of the book.

Assume that Canada can produce 8 tons of wheat or 4 tons of soybeans with one unit of resources, and that Brazil can produce 4 tons of wheat or 8 tons of soybeans with one unit of resources.

a. The opportunity cost to Canada of producing one ton of wheat is _____ tons of soybeans, and the opportunity cost to Brazil of producing one ton of wheat is _____ tons of soybeans. The country with the comparative advantage in wheat is _____ .

b. The opportunity cost to Canada of producing one ton of soybeans is _____ tons of wheat, and the opportunity cost to Brazil of producing one ton of soybeans is _____ tons of wheat. The country with the comparative advantage in soybeans is _____ .

c. If Canada and Brazil each has two units of resources, and each uses one for the production of wheat and the other for the production of soybeans, together they will produce _____ tons of wheat and _____ tons of soybeans.

d. If each country uses its two units of resources to produce the crop in which it has the comparative advantage, Canada will produce _____ tons of _____ and Brazil will produce _____ tons of _____ .

e. If, for political or other reasons, each country uses its two units of resources to produce the crop in which it does *not* have the comparative advantage, together they will produce _____ tons of wheat and _____ tons of soybeans.

Assume that Mexico can produce 500 lamps or 100 gallons of gasoline with one unit of resources, and that Venezuela can produce 25 lamps or 100 gallons of gasoline with one unit of resources.

a. The opportunity cost to Mexico of producing one lamp is _____ gallons of gasoline, and the opportunity cost to Venezuela of producing one lamp is _____ gallons of gasoline. The country with the comparative advantage in lamps is _____ .

b. The opportunity cost to Mexico of producing one gallon of gasoline is _____ lamps, and the opportunity cost to Venezuela of producing one gallon of gasoline is _____ lamps. The country with the comparative advantage in gasoline is _____ .

c. If Mexico and Venezuela each has two units of resources, and each uses one for the production of lamps and the other for the production of gasoline, together they will produce _____ lamps and _____ gallons of gasoline.

d. If each country uses its two units of resources to produce the item in which it has the comparative advantage, Mexico will produce _____ (of) _____ and Venezuela will produce _____ (of) _____ .

e. If, for political or other reasons, each country uses its two units of resources to produce the item in which it does *not* have the comparative advantage, together they will produce _____ lamps and _____ gallons of gasoline.

Free Trade vs. Protectionism

In practice, international trade is carried out in a restricted manner. Policies that impede the international flow of goods and services are often imposed by different trading nations. Such policies, despite the fact that they may reduce a country's ability to fully exploit its various comparative advantages, are generally justified on the grounds that they are perceived to be in the best interest of the nation that is imposing them.

Protectionism

The philosophy that it is in the best interest of a country to restrict importing and/or exporting.

The philosophy that it is in a country's best interest to restrict free trade is known as **protectionism.** According to the protectionist viewpoint, unrestricted importing and/or exporting may lead to certain economic and noneconomic consequences injurious to the economy as a whole, to certain subgroups within the economy such as workers in particular industries, and/or to national security. Because of these potentially adverse effects, protectionists argue that restrictions should be imposed on international trade.

Protectionist policies can be employed to varying degrees. One nation may have detailed regulations as to what, how, and with whom trade is conducted, while the import and export activity of another nation may be subject to loose restrictions. Also, a nation may alter the degree to which it relies on protectionist policies as economic and noneconomic conditions change.

The merits of free trade versus the merits of protectionism have been a source of debate for literally hundreds of years. Application 16.1, "Gloria Flunks the Professor," presents excerpts from one author's view of such a debate, and illustrates how a person's position can be colored by both philosophical commitment and personal interests. In light of this debate over free trade and protectionism, it is useful to know some arguments on both sides of the issue in order to better form your own opinions. But before introducing the cases for free trade and for protectionism, let us examine the different types of trade restricting policies that a country may employ.

Trade Restricting Policies

Three basic policies have traditionally been used to restrict trade: tariffs, quotas, and embargoes. In addition to these, some countries have developed more subtle measures to discourage trade, such as setting up very high product standards that must be met or an overwhelming number of bureaucratic steps that must be taken in order to import a product.

Tariff

A tax on an import.

A **tariff** is a tax placed on an import. Tariffs have the effect of raising import prices to domestic buyers, thereby making foreign goods less attractive to them. This reduces the quantities of imports demanded and makes it easier for domestic producers to sell their own products.

Examples of tariffs on goods entering the United States are illustrated in Table 16.7. The columns to the right classify nations into three categories

Application 16.1

Gloria Flunks the Professor

It's not easy to be an economist these days. It used to be enough to have a theory with a good, positive name: like Free Trade. Now people actually expect you to understand the real world. . . .

Take last night. I'm having a quiet drink with Professor Dyzmil. He teaches economics at our local university. In sails Larry . . . [who] announces that he just bought a new Honda—top of the line, all the extras. People around the bar mutter, "Wow," "Great," and so forth. Gloria [the bartender] just keeps pouring drinks.

Finally she says: "I think it's a shame to buy a foreign car when there's so much unemployment in our own auto industry."

"Hey," says Larry, "What am I supposed to buy? . . . Anyway, one car isn't going to make all that much difference to Detroit."

"I know," Gloria sighs, "but it seems like somebody ought to be doing something to protect our people from all these imports."

"Protect *our* people? *Your* people maybe," says Larry. "I think it's awfully nationalistic to worry about protecting American autoworkers. My lifestyle is international. Whoever makes the most interesting, least expensive product gets my business." . . .

. . . ["Besides, p]rotectionism is bad for the economy. Isn't that right, professor?"

"Absolutely," says Dyzmil, solemnly. "Quotas and tariffs and other devices to keep out foreign goods raise domestic prices. As a result, the consumer pays more."

"So what?" says Gloria. "Wouldn't it be worth it if it saved jobs here? . . ."

Seems like a good point, but the professor isn't impressed. "Very superficial analysis," he says sternly. "The real problem is that protecting U.S. industries will make them less competitive. Having to compete with foreign goods keeps you on your toes, makes you more conscious of quality and price, more responsive to the needs of the customer. Protectionism makes an industry lazy and inefficient." . . .

"By that logic," muses Gloria, "the answer to Japanese imports is to open up our markets to even more imports so our industries will be more efficient. That doesn't make sense."

"It's true that the U.S. is pretty much of an open market," says the professor. "What we need to do is to get other countries to open their economies to free trade."

"Like?"

"Like Japan," the professor replies. "Japan is notoriously protectionist. They have an intricate system of rules and regulations and quotas that keep foreign goods out." . . .

"But if free trade makes a country more competitive and protectionism makes a country less competitive . . ."

"Yes," he nods encouragingly.

"And the Japanese markets are protected and ours are open. . . . Then how come the Japanese are so competitive and we're so uncompetitive?"

for tariff purposes. The column headed "General" is for nations whose products are not imported under any preferential tariff treatment. Countries such as England, France, and Japan fall into this category. The column headed "Special" is for nations whose products are imported at reduced tariff rates, and the rates differ with each country. The rates shown here are for products imported from Canada. Special tariff rates exist as a result of various pieces of trade legislation. For example, developing countries such as Brazil, Mexico, and Egypt can import many products tariff-free. Finally,

"Well ... uh ... ," stammers Dyzmil, "it's very complicated. For one thing, there are cultural differences. ... [T]he Japanese work together better. They work more as a unit, as a community. ... "

"Doesn't sound bad," says Gloria. "Maybe we ought to try some of that here."

"No, my dear," Dyzmil says, shaking his head. "Americans don't like to do things collectively. We thrive on the excitement of competition between individuals."

"Real exciting to be out of work," says Gloria, dryly. "A lot of people *aren't* exactly thriving."

"Not to worry," the professor says. "Our old industries are adjusting. And free trade is helping. ... Old jobs have to die, Gloria. Just like old people. It's a law of economic nature. Jobs will open up in new industries."

"But aren't imports also taking over the new industries? VCRs are the hottest new item around. I read somewhere that the Japanese made 27 million last year and we made zero."

"Not to worry," Dyzmil assures her. "Even if they do take our manufacturing, Americans excel at services."

"Like laundry?"

"No. Like banking, advertising, computer software."

"But it stands to reason that Japanese businesses will use *Japanese* banks and advertising agencies. So as they expand their industry, they'll expand their services too. If they make the computers, won't they eventually make the software?" ... "Anyway," she continues, "how many laid off autoworkers are going to get a job in a bank or advertising?" ...

I can see that the professor is getting annoyed at having to defend free trade. ... After all, in the hierarchy of economic principles, free trade ranks above the law of gravity.

"Look, Gloria," says the exasperated scholar, "there are plenty of other places Americans can work. In bars and restaurants, for example. Granted, the jobs pay less." ...

"OK," says Gloria suddenly. "You've convinced me, but I don't think you've gone far enough with your free trade idea."

"How's that?"

"Why not extend free trade to economics professors? Maybe the reason that the Japanese economy is better is because Japanese *economists* are better. So if we got rid of tenure in our universities, we might import some Japanese economists who could show us how to create more jobs by working together."

"My dear Gloria," says the stunned professor, ... "if America exported its economists, who would be left to defend free trade?"

Source: Jeff Faux, "Gloria Flunks the Professor," *Mother Jones,* October 1985, pp. 50–51. Reprinted with permission.

the column headed "Communist Countries" is for nations such as the USSR, Albania, Bulgaria, and North Korea.[5]

Notice that tariffs can be expressed in dollar terms, as a percentage of the value of the imported product, or as both, and that they differ according to the three country categories given in Table 16.7. Communist countries pay

[5] U.S. International Trade Commission, *Harmonized Tariff Schedule of the United States (1990)* (Washington, D.C.: U.S. Government Printing Office, November 1989), pp. 1–4.

Table 16.7 Tariffs for Selected Goods (1990)

Tariffs, which raise the prices of imported goods to domestic buyers, can be expressed in dollar terms, as a percentage of the value of the imported good, or as both a dollar amount and a percentage.

	Tariff		
Item	**General**	**Special**	**Communist Countries**
Men's wool suits	$0.772 per kilo + 20.0% of value	$0.617 per kilo + 16.0% of value	$0.772 per kilo + 54.5% of value
Women's and girls' ski-suits of manmade fiber	30.0% of value	24.0% of value	72.0% of value
Ski boots	6.0% of value	4.8% of value	35.0% of value
Shampoos	4.9% of value	3.9% of value	75.0% of value
Cheddar cheese	16.0% of value	12.8% of value	35.0% of value
Artificial fire logs	2.5% of value	Free	20.0% of value
Map globes	5.3% of value	Free	35.0% of value
Grand pianos	5.3% of value	4.2% of value	40.0% of value
Motor fuel	$0.525 per barrel	$0.315 per barrel	$1.05 per barrel
Nuclear reactors	6.5% of value	3.9% of value	45.0% of value

Source: U.S. International Trade Commission, *Harmonized Tariff Schedule of the United States (1990)*, (Washington, D.C.: U.S. Government Printing Office, November 1989), pp. I 4–7, V 27–4, VI 33–4, IX 44–3, X 49–3, XI 61–10, XI 61–41, XII 64–4, XVI 84–3, XVIII 92–2.

Quota

A restriction on the quantity of an item that can be imported into a country.

the highest tariffs, while countries that receive special treatment pay the lowest or, in some cases, no tariff at all.

Quotas are restrictions on the quantities of various goods that can be imported into a country. For example, a country may impose a quota allowing only 10 million bushels of wheat to be imported over a one-year period. Once that amount is reached, no more wheat can flow into the country for the remainder of the year. Thus, a quota, like a tariff, restricts the ability of foreign goods to compete with domestic production. Examples of quota restrictions are found in Table 16.8, which lists limits on the amounts of certain textile products that can be imported to the United States from Taiwan.

In practice, there are two types of quota restrictions importers to the United States might face—absolute quotas and tariff-rate quotas. Absolute quotas, such as those given in Table 16.8, limit the amount of a good entering the country over a certain period of time. Tariff-rate quotas place no restrictions on how much of a good enters the country, but limit the amount that can be imported at a lowered tariff.

Embargo

A ban on trade in a particular commodity with another country.

An **embargo** is an outright refusal to trade in a particular commodity with another nation. For example, in late 1990 the United States and other United Nations member countries imposed embargoes on imports to Iraq following

Table 16.8   Limits on Textile Imports from Taiwan (Effective January 1, 1991)

Absolute quotas limit the amounts of specific goods that can be imported into the United States over a defined period of time, such as one year.

Commodity	Limit (in dozens)
Men's and boys' suits of 36% or more wool or related material	39,404
Womens' and girls' suits of 36% or more wool or related material	56,119
Men's and boys' cotton shirts	1,111,110
Women's and girls' cotton blouses and shirts	326,625
Cotton sweaters	99,910

Source: U.S. International Trade Commission, *Harmonized Tariff Schedule of the United States (1990)*, (Washington, D.C.: U.S. Government Printing Office, November 1989), pp. XI 61–32, XI 62–10, XI 62–21, XI 62–36, XI 62–38; U.S. Customs Service, *Status Report on Current Import Quotas (Restraint Levels)*, December 5, 1990, p. 67.

its invasion of Kuwait. These embargoes were imposed for noneconomic reasons — to sanction Iraq in an effort to prompt its withdrawal from Kuwait without resorting to military force. Obviously, this embargo policy did not fully accomplish its intended objectives.

Free Trade Arguments

Arguments favoring unrestricted international trade center on the ability of free trade to increase economic efficiency, to increase the availability of goods and services and decrease their prices, and to provide a source of competition.

Trade, Specialization, and Efficiency   Free trade permits the markets in which goods and services are bought and sold to expand, and the possibility of additional sales from expanded markets makes it feasible for resources to specialize in narrower ranges of tasks. In turn, this specialization allows resources to be used more efficiently than would otherwise be the case.

By using resources more efficiently, more goods and services can be produced, lessening the scarcity problem. This was illustrated earlier in the explanation of the principle of comparative advantage. Recall the corn and television set example given in Table 16.5 and Table 16.6.

Increased Availability of Goods and Lower Prices   A second argument in favor of free trade is that, in the absence of trade restrictions, consumers will pay lower prices and have larger quantities of goods from which to choose. Tariffs have the effect of raising prices; thus, their absence benefits the consumer by making foreign goods available at lower prices. The removal of quotas has the obvious effect of increasing the amounts of goods available for sale.

Trade and Competition   A third argument for free trade is that it increases competition in a market, with resulting benefits to consumers. Recall from Chapter Thirteen that consumers fare better when there are more, rather than fewer, sellers in a market. As the number of sellers increases, the ability of an individual firm to exercise monopoly power over price and output diminishes, and price moves more toward cost. Thus, with foreign producers in a market, domestic sellers are in less of a position to extract monopoly profits.

Notice that in each of the three arguments just presented for free trade, the major beneficiary is the consumer. In the protectionist arguments, this is not the case.

Protectionist Arguments

The main thrust of the protectionist arguments is that, for either economic or noneconomic reasons, it is in the best interest of a nation to place restrictions on the international flow of goods and services. The major protectionist arguments include protection of infant industries and domestic employment and output, diversification, and national security.

Infant industry
An industry in an early stage of its development.

Protection of Infant Industries   As the name suggests, an **infant industry** is an industry in an early stage of its development. Technological break-throughs in areas such as electronics or fuels, the availability of previously unknown or inaccessible resources, or the opening of new regions where production can take place, can spawn industries new to an economy. In the formative stage, or infancy, of an industry, strong competitive pressures from established foreign sellers of rival products may limit or even destroy any prospect for growth. When this occurs, protectionists may argue that government should impose trade restrictions to allow the newly forming domestic industry to establish itself and grow in a protected environment.

For example, due to the construction of a new dam that provides electric power and allows water navigation by large vessels, it may be feasible for a small nation to begin developing a domestic steel industry. However, there are many countries, such as the United States, Japan, and Germany, that also produce steel and whose products could compete in the developing indus-try's domestic market. In such a situation, a proponent of protectionism for the sake of infant industries would likely suggest that tariffs or quotas be imposed on foreign steel to allow the young industry to develop a domestic market for its products.

Protection of Domestic Employment and Output   According to this pro-tectionist argument, both foreign and domestic goods compete for domestic consumers' dollars. When consumer demand is not strong enough to support both foreign and domestic producers, the sale of one more unit of an imported good may come at the expense of its domestically produced counterpart. In other words, the availability of foreign goods may lead to lower domestic output and higher domestic unemployment than would otherwise be the case.

An obvious solution to the problem from the protectionist point of view is to impose trade restrictions that would make it more difficult, or impossible, for foreign goods to compete in domestic markets. Such a policy, it is argued, would help to increase employment and output at home. Support for this argument frequently comes from both manufacturers and unions in specific industries facing strong foreign competition, such as the U.S. automobile industry.

Diversification   The protectionist argument for diversification is a variation on the theme of not putting all of your eggs in one basket. According to this position, there are risks inherent in developing a significant dependency on foreign-produced goods because changes in the prices or availabilities of those goods can lead to economic disruptions at home. A striking example of this problem is the domestic energy crisis that followed changes in the price and availability of OPEC oil in the 1970s.

The protectionist argument is that situations like this could be averted, or at least their impacts reduced, by not specializing to the point where a country develops critical dependencies on foreign products. Rather, domestic production should be diversified so that there are feasible alternatives to foreign-produced goods. Such a strategy would reduce the potential for outside sources to disrupt the economy. Accordingly, the imposition of tariffs and quotas to stimulate domestic production for the sake of diversification would be justifiable.

National Security   For a variety of reasons, arguments have been put forward to impose tariffs, quotas, and embargoes in the name of national security. These reasons include the need to develop strong domestic defense-related industries, and the need to diversify in anticipation of interruptions of foreign supplies resulting from military or economic aggression or some other type of international hostility.

It is up to you to decide which of these free trade and protectionist arguments has greater merit than the others, and whether you lean more toward free trade or protectionism. Are there any positions with which you strongly disagree? Are there counterarguments to any of the free trade or protectionist arguments listed here?

Application 16.2, "Slim Pickings," describes some problems faced by U.S. food producers trying to enter the European market. Can you identify the problems that have resulted from protectionist policies as opposed to those that have resulted from cultural differences?

Application 16.2

Slim Pickings

London—Shopping at a suburban supermarket here, amid the low-calorie frozen dinners, Sioned Jones sees one brand she's inclined to pass by. "There's more of a stigma attached to Weight Watchers," says the 25-year-old computer programmer. She says buying the product, from America's H.J. Heinz Co., "means you're on a diet."

Losing weight appears to interest Britons and Continental Europeans less than it does Americans. Ms. Jones thinks a name like Healthy Options, a line from Britain's Unilever Group, doesn't carry the same connotation.

But nearby, Edna Macleod ignores both contenders and picks out four packages of Lean Cuisine, made by Nestle S.A. of Switzerland. . . .

Many U.S. food companies are having a harder-than-anticipated struggle to raise their bit-player status in the European Community's integrated market. . . .

While hungrily eyeing the Continent's $550 billion food industry, the Americans have underestimated the competitive clout of European food giants, the difficulty of making major acquisitions, and the lingering diversity of 320 million Western Europeans—with their nine languages and distinctive national eating habits.

Though U.S. companies still show much enthusiasm, amplified by the prospect of new markets in Eastern Europe, some of their fears of a discriminatory "Fortress Europe" seem justified. In the food industry, protectionist regulations linger on despite the generally falling trade barriers. Italy, for example, allows only products made from durum wheat—not surprisingly, Italy's predominant type—to be called pasta, even though spaghetti, macaroni and the like can be made from many varieties of wheat.

And, for whatever reason, regulations vary in perplexing ways from one country to another. France won't let Coca-Cola use aspartame [NutraSweet] as an artificial sweetener in Diet Coke. Britain and Ireland let cookie makers add chlorine to their flour in certain products—something no other EC country allows. And Italy has Europe's tightest restrictions on additives in bubblegum—a maximum of 20—while some other European countries allow up to 67 of them.

Quaker Oats Co. ran into protectionism while trying to make Gatorade a pan-European product. After a three-year struggle before the sports drink rang up respectable annual sales of $40 million in Italy (its initial market), the Gatorade launch into France . . . ran afoul of rules about health beverages; the Chicago company had to add extra vitamin B_1.

Source: Excerpted from Joann S. Lublin, "Slim Pickings," *The Wall Street Journal*, May 15, 1990. pp. 1, A20. Excerpted by permission of The Wall Street Journal, © Dow Jones & Company, Inc., 1990. All Rights Reserved Worldwide.

The Real World of International Trade

Most countries do not choose a strict free trade or protectionist philosophy and then adhere only to policies aligned with that philosophy. Instead, these two philosophies are the extremes toward which a country may lean. A country may adopt a comprehensive trade policy based on the principles of free trade or protectionism, or it may adopt more liberal terms of trade with some of its favored trading partners and restrict trade with other countries. Recall from Table 16.7 that the United States gives preferential tariff treatment to goods imported from Canada and imposes higher than average tariffs on goods coming in from communist countries.

A country's policies concerning international trade tend to shift with changing political and economic conditions. The United States, for example, has been altering its trade policies since the early 1800s. During a recession or economic downswing, a country's mood tends to become protectionist, resulting in a greater tendency to raise tariff barriers than would be the case during a period of economic growth. The Smoot-Hawley Tariff, which was passed in 1930 at the beginning of the Great Depression, raised tariff rates to some of the highest levels established by the United States in the twentieth century.

Instead of restricting trade, a country will sometimes adopt policies to promote the export of a domestically produced good. That is, it will not restrict imports but will encourage its own exports. One method for accomplishing this objective is by granting government **trade subsidies** to businesses for the production and export of a particular good. For example, if the United States decided that it wanted to encourage foreign purchases of its domestically produced pianos, it could offer domestic piano manufacturers a subsidy, or payment, for each piano sold abroad. This policy, which might be considered unfair by foreign piano makers, would be useful if the United States wanted to increase its share of the world piano market.

On occasion a country has been accused of **dumping** its products in foreign markets. This occurs when a good is sold in a foreign market below its actual cost or below the price at which it is sold in its own domestic market. Countries pursue this policy to eliminate excess production or to gain a share of a foreign market.

In the interdependent world of foreign trade, a change in a country's trade philosophy, a change in a tariff, quota, embargo, or subsidy, or dumping may cause retaliation by a trading partner. And there is always the danger that changing policies and retaliations will result in a trade war. When a trade war breaks out, the benefits of specialization on an international basis are jeopardized. No one seems to benefit.

Trade Agreements among Nations   Since World War II, world trade has been carried out in a much more liberal environment, thanks to greater international cooperation to reduce tariffs and support organizations that facilitate the trading process. For example, the **International Monetary Fund (IMF)** provides loans and other financial assistance to nations seeking to improve their competitiveness in world trade. Tariff reductions have occurred in large part as a result of the **General Agreement on Tariffs and Trade (GATT),** under which countries held their first round of talks in 1947. Since then, there have been several rounds of negotiations, each leading to lower tariff rates. In addition, in 1988 the United States and Canada entered into a free trade agreement designed to remove tariff and other barriers between the two countries by 1998. A similar agreement was being negotiated between the United States and Mexico in 1991.

Currently, there is great interest in the agreement among the majority of Western European nations to form, in 1992, the single, unified market

Trade subsidy

A government payment to the domestic producer of a good that is exported.

Dumping

Selling a product in a foreign market below cost or below the price of the product in its own domestic market.

International Monetary Fund (IMF)

An international organization that provides loans and other financial assistance to countries.

General Agreement on Tariffs and Trade (GATT)

An international forum for negotiating tariffs.

Table 16.9   The European Community, Its Members, and the United States[a]

The GNP of the EC countries combined is comparable to that of the United States, and the EC population is larger than the U.S. population.

	Population (Millions)	GNP (Billions)	Per Capita GNP
EC	324.8	$4,711	$14,498
Belgium	9.9	147	14,859
Denmark	5.1	104	20,195
France	55.9	933	16,691
West Germany	61.2	1,218	19,907
Greece	10.0	53	5,255
Ireland	3.5	28	7,797
Italy	57.4	810	14,095
Luxembourg	0.4	7	17,838
Netherlands	14.8	226	15,312
Portugal	10.4	39	3,756
Spain	39.1	338	8,645
United Kingdom	57.1	808	14,152
United States	246.3	4,881	19,813

[a]Figures are for 1988.

Source: U.S. Department of State, *Europe 1992: A Business Guide to U.S. Government Resources*, January 1990, p. 3.

European Community (EC)

The single unified market formed by the majority of Western European nations in 1992; a major trading power.

known as the **European Community,** or **EC.** The goal of the EC is to create a trading area within which there are no national barriers to the movement of people, capital, or goods and services. The EC represents a major world trading power—comparable to the United States and Japan. Its population of over 320 million is much larger than that of the United States, and in 1988 the combined gross national product of its twelve members almost equaled that of the United States. Table 16.9 gives the population, GNP, and per capita GNP of the EC, its individual members, and the United States.

The transition to a unified trading community like the EC is not easy: agreements must be reached among the twelve members on a wide range of economic, legal, environmental, and other issues. Application 16.3, "Integrating Europe," describes some of the barriers that must be overcome if there is to be free movement of goods in the EC.

Application 16.3

Integrating Europe

The EC hopes to create a single European market for goods; however, three major types of barriers stand in the way of integrating the 12 separate markets of the EC. All three types of barriers—technical, fiscal, and physical—need to be eliminated before goods can move freely within the EC.

One set of technical barriers comprises health, safety, and environmental standards. Such standards can impede the flow of goods from one country to another. In some cases, these standards reflect varying national preferences for safety and consumer protection. However, many believe that some of the standards were established simply to keep foreign goods out of domestic markets. . . .

Another set of technical barriers relates to the selection process for public contracts. Public contracts represent about 15 percent of the EC's gross domestic product. However, most successful bids for government projects come from firms in the home country. . . .

The second type of barriers to be removed is fiscal barriers, such as differences in tax rates. The value-added tax (VAT), a form of sales tax, provides an example.[1] Broad differences in VAT rates throughout the EC require that individual countries control the movement of goods to prevent consumers and firms from buying goods where VAT rates are low and bringing them into countries where VAT rates are high.

VAT rates vary in several ways from one EC country to another. . . . The United Kingdom, for example, imposes no value-added tax on food or children's clothes. . . . [Italy] imposes a tax of 38 percent on automobiles. . . .

The third type of barriers confronting European nations is physical barriers, namely, border controls. Border controls are perhaps the most visible obstacles to the free movement of goods across borders in the EC. Member countries use border controls to collect VAT taxes, to ensure conformity with varying health and safety regulations, and to regulate products subject to import quotas. . . . In the past, [truck] drivers had to show border officials copies of invoices, forms for import statistics, and reports for tax authorities—sometimes up to 100 separate documents—before entering the country. Consequently, a 750-mile trip from London to Milan, for example, routinely took about 58 hours (excluding crossing the channel), while today [with the adoption of a single document to pass through customs] a similar trip might take only about 36 hours.[2]

[1]A value-added tax is an indirect broad-based consumption tax. It is essentially equivalent to a retail sales tax except in the method of administration. . . .
[2]Kate Bertrand, "Scrambling for 1992," *Business Marketing*, February 1989, p. 54.
Source: Thomas Bennett and Craig S. Hakkio, "Europe 1992: Implications for U.S. Firms," Federal Reserve Bank of Kansas City, *Economic Review*, April 1989, pp. 6–8.

Summary

International economics deals with a variety of topics concerning the economic relationships among countries. International trade, one aspect of this broad area, is concerned with the exporting and importing of goods and services and is important because it affects production, employment, and prices in the trading countries. In the United States, international trade has grown over the years; the value of exports, as well as the value of imports, has been over 12 percent of GNP. The largest classes of U.S. exports and imports are capital goods, and industrial supplies and materials, respectively. Most U.S. trade is with developed countries in Asia, Europe, and North America, particularly Japan, Canada, and the European Community.

Specialization, which occurs when productive resources concentrate on a narrow range of tasks or on the production of a limited variety of goods and services, permits a more efficient use of resources and greater levels of output than would otherwise be the case. Specialization on an international scale is based on the principle of comparative advantage. A country has a comparative advantage when the opportunity cost (measured in forgone items) of producing a good or service is less in that country than in another.

The utilization of comparative advantage and international trade can increase overall production levels and lessen the scarcity problem. For comparative advantage to be exercised fully, an environment of free trade is necessary.

Free trade occurs when there are no restrictions on the flow of international trade. The alternative to free trade is protectionism, which is based on the viewpoint that restricted trade may be in the best interest of a country. Protectionist policies may include tariffs, which are taxes on imports; quotas, which are quantity limits on imports; or embargoes, which are outright refusals to trade a product.

The arguments for free trade center on the production gains that can be obtained from comparative advantage, the increased availability of goods and services for consumers, and the lower prices and other benefits received from more competition in the market.

The protectionist arguments for trade restrictions include the need to protect infant industries and domestic output and employment, to diversify in case of economic disruptions, and to protect national security. The United States has moved toward and away from protectionist policies at different times in its history.

In addition to trade-restricting policies, a nation can seek to increase its foreign sales through the use of subsidies and dumping. International agreements, such as the General Agreement on Tariffs and Trade and the agreements creating the European Community, have a significant effect on world trade.

Key Terms and Concepts

International trade	Tariff
Export	Quota
Import	Embargo
U.S. trading partners	Free trade arguments
Specialization	Protectionist arguments
Comparative advantage	Infant industry
Free trade	Trade subsidy
Protectionism	Dumping

International Monetary Fund (IMF)   European Community (EC)

General Agreement on Tariffs and
  Trade (GATT)

Review Questions

1. Explain how international trade can affect a country's levels of production, employment, and prices.

2. What have been the main categories of exports from and imports to the United States in recent years, and who are the primary trading partners of the United States?

3. "Comparative advantage is the application of specialization on an international level." What is meant by this statement? Define comparative advantage and explain how it lessens the basic scarcity problem of economics.

4. With 1 unit of resources, China could produce either 20 tons of wheat or 60 tons of rice, and Hungary could produce either 40 tons of wheat or 4 tons of rice. Which country has the comparative advantage in wheat? Which country has the advantage in rice? What is China's opportunity cost of 1 ton of wheat and of 1 ton of rice? What is Hungary's opportunity cost of 1 ton of wheat and of 1 ton of rice?

5. Given the information in review question 4, how much wheat and rice would be produced if each country had 2 units of resources and devoted 1 unit to the production of wheat and 1 unit to the production of rice? If each country used both units to produce the item in which it has a comparative advantage, how much wheat and rice would be produced?

6. Differentiate among a tariff, a quota, an embargo, a subsidy, and dumping, and explain how each affects trade.

7. Summarize the arguments for free trade and those for protectionist policies. Who benefits from free trade and who benefits from protectionism?

8. What are the International Monetary Fund (IMF), General Agreement on Tariffs and Trade (GATT), and the European Community (EC)? What is the EC trying to accomplish in 1992 and how will it compare in size to the U.S. economy?

Discussion Questions

1. Over the years, both exports and imports have grown as a percentage of GNP in the United States.
    a. What effect would an increase in exports have on the level of unemployment and the level of prices in the United States if the economy were operating far below full employment?
    b. What effect would an increase in imports have on the level of unemployment and the level of prices in the United States if the economy were operating at full employment?

c. What effect would a U.S. policy of subsidizing exports using funds raised through increased income taxes have on GNP?

d. What effect would dumping a U.S.-produced good in a foreign country have on employment in the United States if that country responded by dumping a good it produces in U.S. markets?

2. If the principle of comparative advantage is true, why can you find both French and California wines or U.S. and Italian shoes in the same wine or shoe store? Would you not expect to find stores selling either French or California wines or U.S. or Italian shoes, depending on which can be produced at a lower cost?

3. International trade must occur in free markets if countries' comparative advantages are to be fully exploited. Why is this so? If the United States produced according to its comparative advantage, in what goods and services do you think it would specialize?

4. The state of tariffs and quotas on foreign cars is a source of continual debate in the United States. What is the current tariff and quota situation on automobiles imported from Japan, Germany, and Sweden? Would you favor increasing or decreasing these tariffs and/or quotas?

5. Some people favor free trade while others favor protectionism. This suggests that some groups gain from free trade while others lose, and that some gain from protectionism while others lose. What is your position on free trade and protectionism, and why do you hold this point of view?

6. Protectionists argue that putting a tariff on a good protects a domestic industry's output and employment. Others argue that the country hurt by the tariff may retaliate by restricting trade from the country imposing the tariff. The end result could be a loss of output and employment in an exporting industry of the country that initiated the tariff action. Comment.

7. Some people think that the 1992 economic unification of nations into the European Community will be a success; others are not sure it will work. What factors seem most important in determining whether the EC will succeed in forming a single, unified market?

Critical Thinking Case 16

■ The Growing Fear of Fortress Europe

Critical Thinking Skills | Identifying central issues
| Comparing similarities and differences in points of view

Economic Concepts | Free trade versus protectionism
| Comparative advantage

There is a magnificently simple vision behind the European Community's plans to remove internal trade barriers in 1992: help the 12-nation community grow faster by encouraging more competition and efficiency.

But companies based outside Europe are starting to get a dark and clouded vision of 1992—they fear that as Europe tears down its internal barriers to form a single, unified market of 320 million people, it might erect higher protective walls to keep competitors out. . . .

The 320 million people in the European Community make it the industrialized world's largest bloc of consumers, so a surge in protectionism in that huge market could seriously hurt American and Japanese companies, not to mention distort world trade. . . .

[F]oreign officials say that the European Commission has the power to make 1992 the beginning of Open Door Europe rather than Fortress Europe. But they recognize that the commission faces intense pressure to set up a thicket of protectionist rules to accompany its internal deregulation.

"At the top of the commission, everyone hews to the free trade line," said [the U.S. Ambassador to the European Community.] "But when you go below the top level of the commission, when you go out to the various member states and talk to business groups and leaders, you hear quite a different tune."

That different tune can be heard loud and clear at the Brussels-based Committee for the European Community Motor Vehicle Industry. The European Commission has insisted that France, Italy, Spain and Portugal scrap their quotas on Japanese car imports as part of an effort to remove conflicting domestic regulations.

But the industry group, led by Peugeot, Renault and Fiat, has proposed instead that the national restrictions be replaced with communitywide quotas . . . that would limit Japanese imports to a little less than 1 million of the 10.5 million cars sold each year in Europe, about 100,000 fewer cars than the Japanese are now selling there.

Those quotas are supposed to last two or three years. Japanese officials worry, however, that they would continue indefinitely. The worries increase when they hear some industry executives . . . say quotas should remain until the Japanese do more to "balance" the situation by greatly increasing their purchases of European cars.

[T]he German car makers worry far more than French and Italian ones that European-wide quotas could spur retaliation. What is more, some European countries that do not manufacture cars, like Ireland and Greece, are happy to have unlimited Japanese access to help hold down car prices.

A matter that threatens more immediate retaliation is the battle over growth hormones in meat, which are commonly used in the United States. The European Community has banned imports of such meat, saying it is simply bowing to the desires of health-conscious consumers. Washington insists that the ban is protectionist and it is threatening to retaliate against $100 million in European ham, pet food, tomatoes, and other products on Jan. 1.

Questions

1. What seem to be the central concerns of the Japanese, the French and Italian car makers, the German car makers, and the Irish and Greeks, respectively? How do these concerns explain their different points of view on the desirability of trade restrictions?

2. Of the European countries cited in this case—France, Italy, Germany, Ireland, and Greece—which would side with the American and Japanese points of view and which would disagree? How does the principle of comparative advantage in automobile manufacturing and meat production influence the various points of view?

Source: Excerpted from Steven Greenhouse, "The Growing Fear of Fortress Europe," *The New York Times*, October 2, 1988, pp. 1, 24. Copyright © 1988 by The New York Times Company. Excerpted by permission.

Suggested Readings

M. Frederic Bastiat, "Petition from the Manufacturers of Candles, Wax-lights, Lamps, Chandeliers, Reflectors, Snuffers, Extinguishers; and from the Producers of Tallow, Oil, Resin, Alcohol, and Generally of Everything Used for Lights," *Sophisms of Protectionism* (New York: G. P. Putnam's Sons, 1893), pp. 73–80.
A satirical petition to government that a law be passed to protect candlemakers and others by banning sunlight.

Thomas Bennett and Craig S. Hakkis, "Europe 1992: Implications for U.S. Firms," Federal Reserve Bank of Kansas City, *Economic Review*, April 1989, pp. 3–17.
An article on the goals of Europe 1992, and opportunities and concerns for U.S. businesses.

"Economics Brief: Growth through Trade," *The Economist*, July 4, 1987, pp. 74–75.
Summary of a World Bank study arguing that free trade, rather than protectionism, may be the best method for achieving economic growth.

Bonnie Gelbwasser and Ruth Trask, "Europe Clears the Way for 1992," *WPI Journal*, Winter 1991, pp. 30–36.
Background on Europe 1992 and answers to questions concerning unification.

Linda C. Hunter, "U.S. Trade Protection: Effects on the Industrial and Regional Composition of Employment," Federal Reserve Bank of Dallas, *Economic Review*, January 1990, pp. 1–13.
A study of how different U.S. industries and regions benefit or suffer from trade restrictions protecting domestic producers.

Richard B. McKenzie, "Jobilism, or, is the world really flat?" *Forbes,* **July 13, 1987, pp. 68, 70.**
A critical appraisal of the job protection argument for restricting free trade, and a comparison of job protectionism and mercantilism.

Charles R. Morris, "The Coming Global Boom," *The Atlantic,* **October 1989, pp. 51–64.**
An optimistic view of the role of the United States in the global economy.

Chapter Seventeen

International Finance

Currencies of different countries are bought and sold in foreign exchange markets so that goods, services, and resources can be traded internationally.

© Michael Newler/
The Stock Market

Chapter Objectives

1. To define exchange rates and explain how they are determined under both fixed and flexible exchange rate systems.

2. To introduce foreign exchange markets, and to identify some factors that affect the supply and demand of currencies in foreign exchange markets and cause exchange rates to fluctuate.

3. To identify the major categories into which international financial transactions can be placed, and to understand how the various categories affect each other.

4. To define balance of trade and balance of trade surplus and deficit, and to discuss the annual balance of trade for the United States for the past few decades.

5. To introduce the problems created by large-scale foreign borrowing and the inability of some borrowing nations to meet their obligations.

Chapter Sixteen centered primarily on international trade, or the exporting and importing of goods and services. Many other types of international transactions are also important to an economy, however. These include the buying and selling of foreign stocks, bonds, and other assets; foreign assistance; and private gifts to foreigners. All of these international transactions involve payment flows between countries, making it necessary to have some mechanism for determining the values of foreign currencies and for exchanging domestic money for foreign money. The value of an economy's currency in foreign money markets is especially important because it affects the prices of the country's exports, imports, and foreign investments. For example, the value of the dollar in relation to the yen, pound, and other foreign currencies is so important to U.S. international transactions and to the economy that it is quoted daily in many news broadcasts and in most major newspapers. The first part of this chapter deals with exchanging currencies and determining exchange rates, and describes how foreign exchange markets operate.

The second section of this chapter explains how different types of international financial transactions affect payment flows between countries, and how these transactions are classified in the United States for analysis purposes. A discussion of the balance of trade, an important and often-referred-to transactions classification, is included in this section.

The chapter closes with a discussion of international debt and the current external debt crisis caused by the inability of some countries that have borrowed heavily from foreign lenders to repay their loans. The change in the U.S. international debt position from that of a net creditor to a net debtor nation is also discussed.

Exchanging Currencies

Exchange Rates

U.S. goods and services and U.S. investment opportunities, such as stocks, bonds, and real estate, carry price tags that are expressed in dollars. You can buy a particular car for, say, $15,000, or invest in a piece of real estate for, say, $1,200 per acre. Regardless of whether the individual who directly acquires U.S. goods, services, and assets is from the United States, France, Saudi Arabia, or some other nation, payment for these items is usually made in dollars. Similarly, buyers and investors, regardless of their nationality, typically pay pounds to acquire British goods and yen to acquire Japanese items. Thus, importing from or investing in another country involves converting one's money into the money of the nation with which one is dealing. An auto importer in the United States who has borrowed dollars to buy Japanese cars will need to convert those dollars to yen to transact business with the Japanese auto manufacturer, and an Israeli student with shekels from home will need to convert them to dollars before paying tuition.

Importers and investors need to know how much foreign goods and services or investment opportunities cost in terms of their own money. For example, the U.S. importer of Japanese automobiles must know not only how many yen each car will cost, but also, and perhaps more importantly, how many *dollars* that price represents. In order to determine the dollar cost of a car purchased from Japan, the U.S. importer must know the exchange rate between the U.S. dollar and the Japanese yen.

Exchange rate

The number of units of a nation's money that is equal to one unit of another nation's money.

The **exchange rate** between two nations' monies is the number of units of one nation's money that is equal to one unit of the other nation's money. For example, the exchange rate between the French franc and the dollar might be 10 francs to $1, or 1 franc to $0.10. At this exchange rate, an item selling for 400 francs in Paris could be purchased by a U.S. tourist for the equivalent of $40. If the exchange rate were 5 francs to the dollar, then each franc would be equal in value to $0.20, and the same 400 franc item could be purchased by the tourist for the equivalent of $80.

Exchange rates between the U.S. dollar and several foreign monies are given in Table 17.1. Using the British pound as an example, Table 17.1 shows that on May 14, 1991, 1 pound was worth $1.7435, or 0.5736 pounds could have been exchanged for 1 dollar ($1/1.7435 = 0.5736). Notice that the exchange rate quotations in the table are for one day only. This is because exchange rates between nations' monies are continually changing in response to economic and noneconomic factors. How and why these rates change will be discussed shortly.

Table 17.1

Exchange Rates between the U.S. Dollar and
Selected Foreign Monies (May 14, 1991)

Exchange rates show how much of a nation's money is equal to one unit of
another nation's money.

Nation	Amount of Dollars Equal to One Unit of Foreign Money	Amount of Foreign Money Equal to One Dollar
Austria	$0.08372 = 1 schilling	11.94 schillings = $1.00
Britain	$1.7435 = 1 pound	0.5736 pounds = $1.00
Canada	$0.8688 = 1 dollar	1.1510 dollars = $1.00
France	$0.17366 = 1 franc	5.7583 francs = $1.00
Germany	$0.5893 = 1 mark	1.6970 marks = $1.00
Israel	$0.4332 = 1 shekel	2.3082 shekels = $1.00
Japan	$0.007241 = 1 yen	138.10 yen = $1.00
Mexico	$0.0003333 = 1 peso	3,000.0 pesos = $1.00
Spain	$0.009506 = 1 peseta	105.20 pesetas = $1.00

Source: "Exchange Rates," *The Wall Street Journal*, May 15, 1991, p. C12.

The Determination of Exchange Rates

Fixed Exchange Rates   Prior to late 1971, exchange rates between the dollar
and many other monies were based primarily on gold; that is, the value of
the dollar and other monies was expressed in terms of the amount of gold
one unit of each country's money would command. For example, if 1 dollar
was worth $\frac{1}{35}$ of an ounce of gold, and if 4 West German marks were worth
$\frac{1}{35}$ of an ounce of gold, then the exchange rate between the dollar and the
mark would have been 1 dollar equals 4 marks, or 25 cents equals 1 mark.

Because the values of their monies were based on gold, nations were on
a **fixed exchange rate** system. That is, the exchange rates between their
monies were generally fixed or fluctuated through a very narrow range. The
only way a major change could occur in exchange rates was if one nation
redefined the value of its money in gold: for example, if the United States
were to have declared that 1 dollar would be worth $\frac{1}{40}$ rather than $\frac{1}{35}$ of an
ounce of gold.

When a country declared that its monetary unit would be backed by less
gold than previously, that country devalued its money. **Devaluation** of a
nation's money constituted an important international economic policy tool
because it changed all exchange rates between the devaluing nation's money
and all other monies. This in turn had an effect on international trade,
investments, and other transactions. For example, when the United States
devalued the dollar prior to 1971, it made the U.S. dollar worth less and

Fixed exchange rates

Exchange rates that do
not fluctuate or fluctuate
slightly because the
values of nations' monies
are defined in terms of
gold.

Devaluation

When the amount of gold
backing a nation's
monetary unit is reduced.

Figure 17.1

Demand Curve for French Francs

The demand curve for foreign money is downward sloping, indicating that less of the money is demanded as its price in U.S. dollars increases.

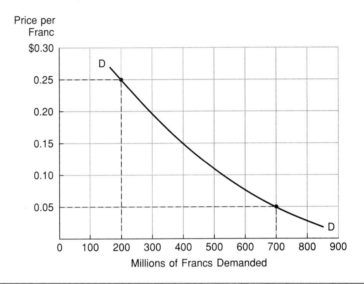

other countries' monies that were backed by gold worth more. It would then take more U.S. money to buy one unit of foreign currency and less foreign money to buy one U.S. dollar. The result was to encourage foreign purchases of U.S. items because U.S. items became cheaper to foreigners, and to discourage purchases of foreign items by those in the United States because foreign items became more expensive.

Flexible (floating) exchange rates

Exchange rates that fluctuate because they are determined by the forces of demand and supply.

Flexible Exchange Rates   Today most economies are on a system of **flexible,** or **floating, exchange rates,** where the rates at which nations' monies exchange are determined by the forces of demand and supply. As demand and supply conditions change, exchange rates change. The process of determining exchange rates under this system can be illustrated with a hypothetical example involving the U.S. dollar and the French franc.

Let us look first at the demand for francs by those with U.S. dollars who want to import French goods or take advantage of French investment opportunities. The demand curve of those importers and investors for French francs is illustrated in Figure 17.1. The horizontal axis indicates the quantity of francs demanded, while the vertical axis shows the price *in U.S. dollars* that must be paid per franc. As expected, the demand curve is downward sloping. At a price of $0.25 per franc in Figure 17.1, 200 million francs are demanded, while at a price of $0.05 per franc, 700 million are demanded.

Figure 17.2   Supply Curve for French Francs

The supply curve for foreign money is upward sloping, indicating that more money is made available as its price in U.S. dollars increases.

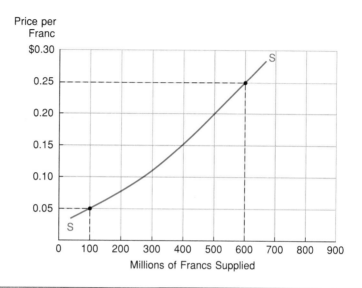

The reason for the inverse relationship between the price and quantity demanded of French francs is that as the dollar price of francs goes up, the prices of French goods and investment opportunities also increase for buyers wishing to convert their dollars to francs. With French goods and investment opportunities becoming more expensive to these buyers, they desire to purchase less of these items, causing the quantity of francs demanded to be lower.

For example, suppose that a particular French automobile has a price tag of 120,000 francs. At an exchange rate of $0.10 = 1 franc, the cost of the car would be $12,000. If the price of francs to U.S. buyers were to rise to $0.20 each, the same 120,000 franc car would cost $24,000. This higher dollar price would cause fewer U.S. buyers to want to purchase this car, which in turn would lower the quantity of francs demanded.

The supply curve for French francs is given in Figure 17.2. This curve shows the amount of francs available at various dollar prices in this currency exchange market. Notice that the supply curve is upward sloping: for example, at a price of $0.05 per franc, 100 million francs would be supplied, and at a price of $0.25 per franc, 600 million francs would be supplied. The supply of francs in this market comes from individuals, corporations, and governments that want to purchase U.S. dollars with francs. For example, a French investor who wants to buy stock listed on the New York Stock Exchange will need to convert francs to dollars in order to complete any

Figure 17.3   Supply of and Demand for French Francs

In a flexible exchange rate system, the exchange rate for a nation's money is determined by the supply of and demand for that money.

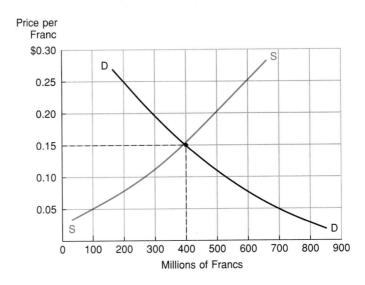

stock transactions. The curve slopes upward because as the dollar price of francs increases, the franc is worth more in terms of the U.S. goods, services, and financial assets that it can purchase, and those holding francs want to convert more of them to dollars.

The rate of exchange between the U.S. dollar and the French franc can now be determined by combining the supply and demand curves just given. This is done in Figure 17.3. Given these supply and demand conditions, the exchange rate that emerges is $0.15 = 1 franc, because this is the price per franc shown at the intersection of the two curves. At this rate, the number of francs supplied to and demanded by buyers who want to convert U.S. dollars to francs is 400 million.

Understanding Foreign Exchange Markets

Foreign exchange market

A market for the trading of two nations' monies.

With a flexible exchange rate system, where the value of a currency is determined by supply and demand, foreign exchange markets are the mechanisms through which the values of different nations' monies are determined and the exchange of these monies is carried out. A **foreign exchange market** is one in which the currencies of two nations are traded: the French franc and the U.S. dollar, the French franc and the British pound, and the Japanese yen and the German mark are traded in three different foreign exchange markets. The process through which foreign exchange markets are made generally involves banks throughout the world that are linked together by sophisticated telecommunications networks. Application 17.1, "Foreign Exchange Markets," provides some detail on the role of banks in these markets.

Since exchange rates are determined by the forces of supply and demand in foreign exchange markets, any factor that causes a change in the supply and/or demand of a nation's currency in one of these markets will cause a change in the currency's exchange rate and amount traded. (Remember from Chapter Three that a change in supply and/or demand causes a change in equilibrium price and quantity.) For example, referring back to Figure 17.3, if the demand for French francs by those with U.S. dollars increases, the demand curve will shift to the right, causing the price of francs as well as the amount exchanged to increase. Can you graphically determine the results of an increase in supply?[1]

When an exchange rate changes, one nation's money becomes worth more in terms of the other, and one becomes worth less in terms of the other. If an increase in the demand for francs raises their price in U.S. dollars, then the franc becomes worth more compared to the dollar, and the dollar becomes worth less compared to the franc. For example, at an exchange rate of $0.10 = 1 franc, $1.00 will buy an item priced at 10 francs. If the exchange rate becomes $0.20 = 1 franc, the dollar is worth less compared to the franc, and it will now take $2.00 to purchase what $1.00 did prior to the change. Expressions that are heard in the media such as "the declining value of the dollar in world trade" refer to the fact that the exchange rate is changing in favor of other nations' currencies and against the U.S. dollar.

It is important to understand some of the major factors that cause supply and demand to change and exchange rates to fluctuate in foreign exchange markets, because a change in the value of a nation's currency in international exchange markets can have serious economic consequences. As exchange rates rise and fall, the international prices of a country's goods and services rise and fall as well. For example, when the value of the dollar drops, foreign-made products become more expensive for U.S. buyers, and goods produced in the United States become cheaper for foreign buyers. In addition, an increase or decrease in the value of a country's money may discourage or encourage foreign ownership of real assets in that country. The decline of the dollar relative to the yen in the mid-1980s encouraged substantial Japanese purchases of U.S. real estate, including the Exxon Building, the Algonquin Hotel, and the Tiffany Building in Manhattan, and the Aladdin Hotel in Las Vegas.[2] In addition, after the stock market crash in October 1987, the value of the stock of many U.S. companies dropped at the same time that the dollar was declining in international exchange markets,

---

[1] The supply curve will shift to the right, causing the price of the money to fall and the amount exchanged to rise.

[2] Louis S. Richman, "The Japanese Buying Binge," *Fortune,* December 7, 1987, pp. 77–94.

Application 17.1

Foreign Exchange Markets

Foreign exchange transactions arising from international trade and investment are frequently large and recurrent. Each day exporters and importers, corporations with international operations, public enterprises in many countries, central banks, international and regional official organizations, and financial institutions of all types receive or disburse a variety of foreign currencies in the course of their activities. For them, foreign exchange is a bank deposit denominated in another currency, rather than a bank note issued by another country. They buy and sell foreign currencies by exchanging one bank deposit for another. . . .

Most commercial banks are equipped to handle foreign exchange transactions for their customers as one of the financial services they provide. But for most U.S. banks currency dealing is not an important activity, and exchange transactions are infrequent. These banks look to correspondents in U.S. money market centers to execute their orders.

A relatively small number of money center banks conduct the bulk of the foreign exchange transactions in the U.S. Virtually all the big New York banks have active currency trading operations. Major banks in Chicago, San Francisco, Los Angeles, Boston, Detroit, Philadelphia, and several other large cities also are active through head office operations as well as affiliates in New York and elsewhere. These facilities complement the extensive trading operations many of the banks maintain in their branches in places such as London, Frankfurt, Zurich, Hong Kong, and Singapore. In addition, and with increasing frequency in recent years, most major foreign banks have established branches or affiliates in New York and other U.S. cities. . . .

All these banks are prepared to buy or sell foreign currency balances for their commercial customers and correspondent banks, as well as for the international banking activities of their own institutions. But in addition many act as *market makers* in one or more currencies. As such, each is prepared to trade at any time with other market-making banks. Together, their trading activities help even out the temporary excesses of supply or demand that inevitably emerge from thousands of individual transactions executed each day. In providing this function, the market maker is almost continuously buying and selling various currencies. . . .

. . . It is in this market where overall supply and demand is consolidated and foreign exchange rates are determined. Of the hundred-plus banking institutions in the U.S. active in foreign exchange, much fewer than 50 would classify themselves as market makers.

Banks throughout the world serve as market makers in foreign exchange. They comprise a global market in the sense that a bank in one country can trade with another bank almost anywhere, provided official regulations permit and a dealing relationship exists. Banks are linked by telecommunications equipment which allows instantaneous communication and puts this "over-the-counter" market as close as the telephone or the telex machine. . . .

Foreign exchange is traded in a 24-hour market. Somewhere in the world banks are buying and selling dollars for, say, German marks at any time during the day. . . .

One implication of a 24-hour currency market is that exchange rates may change at any time. Bank traders must be light sleepers, ready to respond to a telephone call in the middle of the night alerting them to an unusually sharp exchange rate movement on another continent. Many banks permit limited dealing from home by senior traders to contend with just such a circumstance.

Source: Roger M. Kubarych, *Foreign Exchange Markets in the United States,* revised ed. (New York: Federal Reserve Bank of New York, 1983), pp. 7–9.

causing increased purchases of U.S. companies by foreign investors. Recently, Pillsbury was purchased by British, MCA by Japanese, Genentech by Swiss, and Uniroyal-Goodrich by French investors. According to estimates reported in 1990 by Congressional researchers, foreign interests own about 5 percent of all U.S. assets.[3]

Factors Influencing Supply and Demand in Foreign Exchange Markets
Several factors can cause a change in the demand and/or supply of a nation's money in foreign exchange markets. One important factor that causes the demand for foreign currencies to shift is a change in the taste for foreign products: as they become more popular, demand increases, and as they become less popular, demand falls. The demand for foreign-made goods has increased in the United States in recent years. This may be due to real or imagined perceptions of the quality of foreign products, equating status with the ownership of foreign products, or other factors. In addition to consumer products, there has been a strong demand for foreign-produced components for products assembled in the United States.

Figure 17.4a illustrates the impact on exchange rates of an increase in the demand for a nation's currency caused by an increase in the demand for its products. Using the U.S. dollar and the Japanese yen as an example, an increase in the U.S. demand for Japanese products will increase the demand for yen and shift the demand curve to the right from D1 to D2. This causes the price of yen to rise from P_1 to P_2, and the value of the dollar to decline. Can this decline in the value of the dollar be stopped? Simple supply and demand analysis indicates that an increase in the supply of yen could cause the exchange rate to return to its original level. This is shown in Figure 17.4b where the supply curve shifts to the right from S1 to S2 following the shift in demand from D1 to D2. This increase in the supply of yen on the market could occur if there were an increase in the Japanese demand for U.S. products or investment opportunities: a larger quantity of yen would appear on the market because the Japanese would want to purchase dollars to buy U.S. products or invest in U.S. assets.

A second factor that can cause a change in the demand or supply of a nation's currency and its exchange rate is a change in economic conditions in either the demanding or supplying country. For example, consider the effect of inflation on the demand for francs by U.S. importers and investors. If the inflation occurs in the United States, it will make the price tags on French goods relatively lower for U.S. importers and investors, thereby causing the U.S. demand curve for francs to increase, or shift to the right. As a result, the price of francs will rise, as will the number of francs exchanged. If the inflation occurs in France, it will make the cost of French goods relatively higher for U.S. investors and importers, and lead to a decrease, or

[3] Robert Johnson, "More U.S. Companies Are Selling Operations to Foreign Concerns," *The Wall Street Journal,* February 24, 1988, pp. 1, 17; "Who Owns U.S.?" *Time,* December 10, 1990, p. 23.

Figure 17.4   Changes in the Demand for and Supply of a Foreign Currency

An increase in the demand for a nation's money caused by an increase in the demand for that nation's products will raise the price of its money. If an increase in the demand for money is matched by an increase in supply, the exchange rate will remain unchanged.

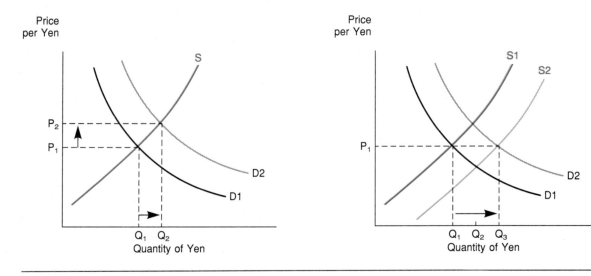

leftward shift, in the demand curve for francs. As a result, the price of francs will fall and so will the amount exchanged. Application 17.2, "What's Hawked at Curbside? Dólares," describes how inflation in Peru has created a strong demand for dollars in that country. Notice also the effective, if somewhat inelegant, foreign exchange markets for dollars and intis that have grown as a result of the inflation.

Real rate of interest

The nominal, or stated, rate of interest minus the inflation rate; the nominal rate adjusted for inflation.

A third factor that influences exchange rates is the **real rate of interest** that can be earned on securities issued by private and government borrowers in different countries. If investment opportunities in another country yield a higher real return than is available domestically, some individuals and corporations with global investment strategies will want to purchase the higher-yielding foreign securities. To do so increases the demand for the currency of the nation with the higher real interest rates, thereby causing a change in its exchange rate. As Application 17.1 pointed out, improved communications technology has allowed many financial markets to become internationalized. The increased buying and selling of financial instruments on a global level in recent years has had an important effect on exchange rate determination.

Fourth, the supply and demand of a nation's money in foreign exchange markets may be influenced by government and central bank policies. For

Application 17.2

What's Hawked at Curbside? Dólares

Lima, Peru — With his white jogging shoes padding on the pavement, [a young man] loped alongside a slowing car and offered the days' special — the United States dollar at 65,000 intis.

"Dólares, dólares," he said. It was a June day, and he was flashing the tools of his trade — a pocket calculator and a stack of bills.

Traffic intersections in many third-world cities offer an ambulatory bazaar of goods ranging from coat hangers to papayas. In Lima, the curbside service offers dollars. . . .

With the inti's value shrinking by 1 percent a day, Peru's economy has spawned a new profession — thousands of so-called cambistas offering instant exchange. . . .

Fueling the constant trading is a fear of holding intis for even an hour longer than needed.

"In the final stage of hyperinflation, people reject the local currency," said an American economist here. He noted that by the time Alan García steps down from Peru's presidency on July 28, prices will have gone up 1 million percent during his five-year tenure.

"By law, the inti is the means of exchange," the economist said. "But people only keep enough intis to cover daily transactions." . . .

Reflecting the new stability of inflationary instability, [one cambista] has started handing regular customers a salmon-pink business card. It is printed with two dollar signs, his street-corner address and his radio paging telephone number.

"I have clients on all these floors," [the cambista] said, waving expansively to high-rise office buildings rising above heavily trafficked José Pardo Avenue. . . .

"The state workers cash their paychecks, and then come straight across the street," he said between making sidewalk trades. "During the week, people exchange what they need for the day — $20 for groceries, $10 for the movies."

No one knows how many dollars flow through the cambistas' hands. The best guess is that they change a large part of the annual $1 billion in drug money that goes through Peru. . . .

People involved in the street practice say that while the dollar is freely convertible here, the street trading is illegal because the cambistas pay no taxes. At the outset of the García Government in July 1985, they say, some arrests were made. But now the practice is tolerated. Street changers say their biggest fear is not the police but holdup men. . . .

Source: James Brooke, "What's Hawked at Curbside? Dólares," *The New York Times,* July 4, 1990, p. 4. Copyright © 1990 by The New York Times Company. Excerpted by permission.

example, in an effort to keep the value of a country's money from falling, a government or central bank might intervene in a foreign exchange market. Government intervention in foreign exchange markets has occurred from time to time, despite the fact that they are considered to be basically free markets.

Changes in exchange rates will also cause buyers and sellers of foreign currencies to enter or leave the market if they regard foreign goods, services, and assets as substitutes for domestic items. For example, when the value of the dollar falls, foreign travel becomes more expensive, causing some U.S. tourists to postpone trips abroad and perhaps to travel domestically until the dollar regains some strength. This decline in foreign travel causes the demand curves for some types of foreign currencies to shift to the left until

Test Your Understanding

Changes in Exchange Rates[a]

[a]Answers can be found at the end of the book.

Each of the following hypothetical situations could affect the exchange rate between the U.S. dollar and another country's money. For each situation, indicate how supply or demand and the equilibrium price and quantity in that particular foreign exchange market would change, and whether the U.S. dollar would become worth more or less in that market.

1. A report is issued that certain wines produced in Austria could contain chemicals that are harmful to a person's health. As a result, the U.S. demand for Austrian schillings would _____ , the dollar price of schillings would _____ , the equilibrium quantity of dollars traded for shillings would _____ , and the value of the dollar in relation to the shilling would _____ .

2. Real rates of interest in the United States move above real rates in Britain. As a result, the supply of British pounds to the United States would _____ , the dollar price of pounds would _____ , the equilibrium quantity of pounds traded for dollars would _____ , and the value of the dollar in relation to the pound would _____ .

3. Japan introduces a newly designed sports car that is an immediate hit with U.S. automobile enthusiasts. As a result, the U.S. demand for Japanese yen would _____ , the dollar price of yen would _____ , the equilibrium quantity of dollars traded for yen would _____ , and the value of the dollar in relation to the yen would _____ .

4. The rate of inflation in the United States rises above the rate of inflation in Belgium. As a result, the supply of Belgian francs to the United States would _____ , the dollar price of francs would _____ , the equilibrium quantity of francs traded for dollars would _____ , and the value of the dollar in relation to the Belgian franc would _____ .

5. More U.S. citizens travel to Israel as airlines offer substantial discounts on fares. As a result, the U.S. demand for shekels would _____ , the dollar price of shekels would _____ , the equilibrium quantity of dollars traded for shekels would _____ , and the value of the dollar in relation to the shekel would _____ .

6. Severe political unrest develops in South Africa. As a result, the U.S. demand for South African rands would _____ , the supply of rands to the United States would _____ , the dollar price of rands would _____ , the equilibrium quantity of rands traded for dollars would _____ , and the value of the dollar in relation to the rand would _____ .

tourists travel abroad again. Finally, other factors such as political climates, expectations, trade restrictions, and the like can cause the demand and/or supply curve for a nation's money to shift, and the exchange rate to change. "Test Your Understanding: Changes in Exchange Rates" lets you practice evaluating how changes in economic and noneconomic conditions in two countries would affect exchange rates between their monies.

International Financial Transactions and Balances

As noted at the beginning of this chapter, a wide variety of transactions involve payment flows from one country to another: importing and exporting goods and services, buying and selling foreign financial instruments and real assets, military and foreign assistance, gifts, grants, and travel. Some of these transactions involve major outlays for real estate, production equipment, and corporate stock, while others involve small sums for gifts to relatives back home.

In order to analyze the many and varied types of financial transactions that occur between the United States and other nations, financial movements are grouped into major categories, and statistics are maintained for these groupings. Through the use of these categories, the accounting process for international transactions is simplified, and more importantly, transactions areas that could cause problems for the economy can be more readily identified. The two major transactions categories are the current account and the capital account.

The Current Account and the Capital Account

Current account
A category of international transactions that records figures for imports and exports of merchandise, unilateral transfers, and other foreign dealings.

The **current account** records payments for exports and imports of goods, military transactions, foreign travel and transportation, and other services, as well as income from investments and unilateral transfers (gifts). The major components of the current account and their dollar values for 1989 are shown at the top of Table 17.2. In presenting these figures, dollar payment outflows are indicated by negative numbers and dollar payment inflows by positive numbers. For example, the value of U.S. exports of merchandise (goods) in 1989 is listed as $360.5 billion, a positive number because exports bring payment inflows, while the value of imports of merchandise in 1989 is given as −$475.3 billion, a negative number because dollars flow out when foreign goods are purchased. When merchandise imports are subtracted from exports, a net figure called the **balance of trade** results. In 1989 the balance of trade was −$114.9 billion, indicating that U.S. buyers purchased $114.9 billion more of foreign goods than foreign buyers bought of U.S. goods.[4]

Balance of trade
The figure that results when merchandise imports are subtracted from exports.

The dollar figures for the other current account classifications in Table 17.2 are given as net amounts; that is, unlike merchandise exports and imports, the payment outflows have already been subtracted from the inflows and are not given separately. For example, on net services and investment

---

[4]Be careful to notice that the term balance of trade is different from the term net exports, which was discussed in Chapter Five. The balance of trade is calculated on the basis of exports and imports of goods, whereas net exports is calculated on the basis of exports and imports of both goods and services. Notice that net exports of goods and services is given as a separate component in Table 17.2.

Table 17.2

U.S. International Transactions

The current account records payments flows for goods, services, gifts, and the like; the capital account records payments for financial and real assets; and the official reserve account records government intervention in international payments.

Type of Transaction		Amount in 1989 (Billions of Dollars)
Current Account		
Balance of trade		−$ 114.9
Exports of merchandise	$ 360.5	
Imports of merchandise	−475.3	
Plus: Net services and investment income		19.6
Equals: Net export of goods and services	−95.3	
Plus: Unilateral transfers		−14.7
***Equals*: Current Account Balance**		−$ 110.0
Capital Account		
Net capital outflows	−103.0	
Net capital inflows	205.8	
***Equals*: Capital Account Balance**		102.8
Official Reserve Account		
Change in U.S. official reserve assets and other U.S. government assets	−24.1	
Change in foreign official reserve assets	8.8	
***Equals*: Official Reserve Account**		−15.3
Statistical Discrepancy		22.4
Total		$ 00.0

Source: U.S. Department of Commerce, *Survey of Current Business*, Vol. 71, Number 3, March 1991, pp. 34, 40.

Current account deficit (surplus)

A negative (positive) figure results when all current account transactions are added together.

Capital account

A category of international transactions that records the purchase and sale of financial and real assets between the United States and other nations.

income, more payment inflows than outflows occurred, resulting in a net figure of $19.6 billion.

The balance of trade, net services and investment income, and unilateral transfers are added together to arrive at the current account balance, which was −$110.0 billion in 1989. This figure means that transactions from the current account components caused 110.0 billion more U.S. dollars to flow out for payments than the value of money that flowed in. This is referred to as a **current account deficit**. Had the figure been a positive number, there would have been a **current account surplus**.

The **capital account,** which is listed in the middle of Table 17.2, records payment flows for investment purchases such as stocks, bonds, government securities, and real estate. When corporate financial instruments, government securities, and real estate owned by U.S. entities are purchased by foreigners, there are payment flows to the United States, and the amount recorded in the capital account component titled "Net capital inflows" is a positive number. When U.S. individuals and businesses buy foreign-owned financial or real assets, there are payment flows from the United States, and the amount recorded in the capital account component titled "Net capital outflows" is a negative number.

In Table 17.2, the capital account balance for 1989 is $102.8 billion, a positive number indicating that there was more foreign investment in U.S. assets than U.S. investment in foreign assets during that year. If you recall the preceding analysis of changes in foreign exchange rates, this positive number in the capital account makes sense in light of the large negative current account balance listed in Table 17.2. The large demand by U.S. buyers for imports was not offset by an equal foreign demand for U.S. exports, causing the value of the dollar to drop. As the dollar became cheaper for foreigners to purchase, U.S. financial and real assets became less expensive and more attractive to these buyers.

The Balance of Trade As Table 17.2 indicates, the balance of trade is only one part of the current account balance. It is significant, however, because it involves the largest flow of money, reflects the results of a nation's international trade activity, and is frequently cited in studies and discussions of international transactions. When the value of a country's exports of goods is greater than the value of its imports, a **balance of trade surplus** occurs; when the value of a country's imports of goods is greater than the value of its exports, a **balance of trade deficit** arises.

Balance of trade surplus (deficit)
The value of a country's merchandise exports is greater (less) than the value of its imports.

Figure 17.5 charts the annual balance of trade for the United States from 1950 through 1990. Observe that the United States experienced a trade surplus in each year during the 1950s and 1960s. In the 1970s and 1980s and in 1990, however, sizable trade deficits occurred. Since 1984, the trade deficit has become so large that it is a matter of serious concern for the United States. The deficits of the 1970s can be explained in part by increases in the price of imported oil. Factors such as the popularity of foreign goods like automobiles and home electronic equipment, and strong foreign rivals in markets for U.S. export products have contributed to the significant deficits of recent years.

Balancing International Transactions

Official reserve account
An international payments category that indicates the degree and direction of government and/or central bank intervention in U.S. and foreign currency exchange markets.

There are two additional categories in Table 17.2 that are important. The first is the **official reserve account,** which indicates the degree and direction of U.S. and foreign government (and central bank) intervention in U.S. international payment transactions. According to Table 17.2, in 1989 U.S. government intervention caused a payment outflow from the United States of $24.1 billion. This, combined with foreign government purchases of $8.8

Figure 17.5   U.S. Balance of Trade: 1950–1990

Since the mid-1970s, the United States has run significant balance of trade deficits as the value of merchandise imports has exceeded the value of exports.

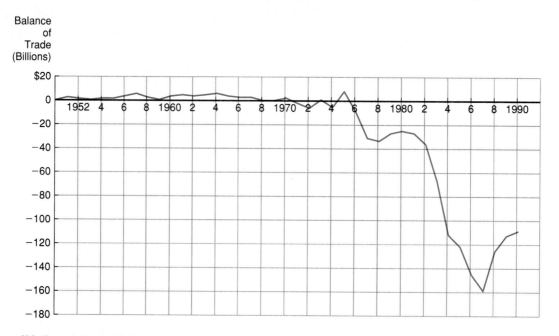

Balance
of
Trade
(Billions)

Source: U.S., *Economic Report of the President* (Washington, D.C.: U.S. Government Printing Office, 1991), p. 402. 1990 figure, which is preliminary, is from U.S. Department of Commerce, *Survey of Current Business*, Vol. 71, Number 3, March 1991, p. 50.

billion worth of U.S. assets, caused a negative outflow of $15.3 billion from the United States.

In recording these payment inflows and outflows, there should be a balance: the dollars used to purchase foreign goods, assets, and the like should be matched by an equal amount of foreign currency flowing into the dollar exchange markets to accommodate those purchases. As a result, the current account balance, the capital account balance, and the official reserve account together should total zero. However, because of the volume of money traded and the diversity of locations and customs in foreign exchange markets, the accounting for these transactions may not be completely accurate. To make payment inflows and outflows equal, the government adds an amount for statistical discrepancies to its accounting process. This is given at the bottom of Table 17.2 and, when added to the balances for the three major transactions categories, results in a zero balance in the very last line.

International Debt

One important type of international financial transaction included in the capital account is loan making. Many governments and businesses, including those in developing nations, borrow from lenders, such as banks and individuals, in other countries to help finance investments and other activities. For example, a U.S. bank could lend money to the government of Brazil, a Saudi Arabian could buy U.S. Treasury bonds, or Canadian and U.S. investors could buy corporate bonds in each others' companies. This type of borrowing is termed **external debt** because it is owed to lenders outside of, or external to, the borrowing country.[5]

External debt
Money owed by borrowers in one country to lenders in other countries.

The External Debt Crisis

The size of the external debt of some borrowing nations has become so large that serious concerns have been raised over their abilities to repay the interest on their loans, much less the loans themselves. In addition, some nations, like Brazil and Mexico, found themselves so overburdened by their external debts in recent years that they suspended payments in hopes of restructuring those debts.

The magnitude of the external debt problem is illustrated in Table 17.3, which ranks several highly indebted developing countries according to the amount each owed to foreign lenders as a percentage of that country's GNP in 1989. Also shown in the table is the size of each country's external debt, measured in U.S. dollars. While Nicaragua's debt as a percentage of GNP is the highest of those listed, the dollar size of its external debt is relatively small. Nicaragua's dilemma is due in part to the fact that, between 1982 and 1989, its GNP shrank at an annual rate of 6 percent. Brazil, on the other hand, has a relatively small external debt when compared to GNP, but in dollar terms it is the most indebted country of any listed in the table. The cost to Brazil of maintaining, or servicing, that $111.3 billion debt in 1989 was $11.6 billion.[6]

The Opportunity Cost of External Debt   The external debt problem has been a serious concern since the early 1980s. In 1980, the total external debt outstanding in developing countries was $639 billion. By 1990, the debt exceeded $1.3 trillion, and serious questions existed as to whether this amount could ever be repaid.[7] There are substantial opportunity costs for

[5] The expression "internal debt" refers to the total amount of debt owed to domestic banks, individuals, businesses, and others.

[6] The World Bank, *World Debt Tables 1990–1991: External Debt of Developing Countries*, Vol. 1 (Washington, D.C.: The World Bank, 1991), p. 19.

[7] *World Debt Tables 1990–1991: External Debt of Developing Countries*, p. 4.

Table 17.3   External Debt of Selected Highly Indebted Developing Countries, 1989

Some countries have an external debt that is greater than their GNPs.

Country	External Debt as a Percentage of GNP	Dollar Size of External Debt (Billions)
Nicaragua	623.7%	$ 9.2
Congo	214.9	4.3
Cote d'Ivorie	182.2	15.4
Egypt	159.0	48.8
Argentina	119.7	64.7
Costa Rica	91.2	4.5
Poland	68.3	43.3
Mexico	51.2	95.6
Brazil	24.1	111.3

Source: The World Bank, *World Debt Tables 1990–1991: External Debt of Developing Countries*, Vol. 1 (Washington, D.C.: The World Bank, 1991), p. 19.

borrowing nations if they seek to repay these loans, and substantial opportunity costs for lending nations if they do not.

In order to honor their financial obligations to foreign lenders, borrowing nations must cut back on spending by their households, businesses, and governments in order to send money to their debt holders. (This is the same situation that a family faces when it falls deeply into debt: it must cut back on current consumption in order to pay lenders.) In developing nations where incomes are low, the harsh austerity measures needed to cut back spending to repay the debt may not be tolerable, or even possible. In addition, payment of a debt of this magnitude would cause the postponement of spending on investment goods, thus hampering future economic growth. In short, the opportunity cost of repayment is substantial: there would be a decline in current spending that would send the economy into a recession, making payments even more difficult, and future economic growth would be sacrificed. To these economic costs can be added the political upheaval that would likely result from such serious economic disruptions. Application 17.3, "Mexico Feels Squeeze of Years of Austerity," describes some of the suffering endured by the Mexican population as that country tried to control its external debt problem.

If these debtor nations declare bankruptcy and default on their loans, the lending institutions that hold these bad debts will face serious difficulties because the amounts of the debts are so large. For example, in a recent year U.S. banks held $23.3 billion of debt for Brazil and $23.5 billion for Mexico—

Application 17.3

Mexico Feels Squeeze
of Years of Austerity

Seven years after the Latin American debt crisis erupted here, Mexico is a country battered by debt-induced austerity, in which the $100 billion owed to foreign creditors is likely to remain the dominant factor in the nation's economic and political life. . . .

Since 1982, the Mexican Government has followed a policy that distinguishes it from Argentina, Brazil and other third-world countries that have often fallen behind on their obligations. Mexico has spent $56 billion more on debt payments than it has received in new assistance, a drain of resources that is equal to 6 percent a year of all the goods and services produced here. . . .

The social cost has been enormous, but the Government has acted nevertheless, not only because the measures are expected to strengthen the long-term health of the country, but also because Mexico's creditors have demanded such actions in return for continued financing. . . .

The austerity that has accompanied the debt problem is hardest on wage earners, who have seen the purchasing power of their salaries decline by half since the start of the decade. That has forced millions of Mexican families to cut back on expenses, even when what were formerly seen as necessities are involved. . . .

According to Government statistics, per-capita consumption of milk has fallen drastically. Many families have started to use soda pop as a substitute for milk because it costs half the price and does not need refrigeration. Since the debt crisis began, soda sales have soared. Now, sales of soda are three times those of milk.

"If Social Security didn't give us milk for the baby, I don't know how we'd make it on a total budget of 46,000 pesos a week," said Mrs. Pacheco, the mother of sons 6 years and 3 months old, referring to a sum equivalent to $18.40. "I'm worried about what is going to happen once my little guy passes the age limit for the free milk program."

A recent United Nations study indicates that more than half of all Mexicans, or more than 42.5 million people, now live below minimum international nutrition standards. . . .

In the area of education, the situation has become nearly as gloomy. After many years of steadily rising enrollments, the total number of children registered in elementary schools has actually dropped since 1985, even though Mexico's population is growing by more than 1.5 million people a year.

According to Government estimates, half of all children are now dropping out of elementary school, in many cases to go to work on behalf of their families, which find they need as many wage earners as possible. . . .

In further efforts to economize, and thereby meet the spending targets set by Mexico's creditors, the Government has cut back on maintenance of existing roads, telephone lines, hospitals, sewer systems and other essential national services.

At the same time, the nation's population has grown from 67 million in 1980 to an estimated 85 million, putting even greater pressures on a national infrastructure that will need years to recuperate even if a solution to the debt problem is found soon. . . .

just two of the many countries that have borrowed from U.S. banks.[8] Defaults of the magnitude that would occur if these or other countries declared nonpayment of their debts could put some U.S. banks into jeopardy and threaten the financial institutional structure of the United States. If the U.S. government were to come to the rescue of these lending institutions, then the opportunity cost of the debt would fall on the U.S. taxpayer.

The International Debt of the United States

Much has been written recently about the change in the position of the United States from a net creditor to a net debtor nation. This means simply that, on net, individuals, businesses, and government units in the United States now owe more to foreign creditors than foreign individuals, businesses, and governments owe to U.S. lenders. Recall from Figure 17.5 that the United States has been running serious trade deficits since 1984. These deficits have caused the current account balance to be negative and the value of the dollar to fall. With a negative current account balance and a declining value of the dollar, it makes sense that the capital account balance, which reflects foreign lending to the United States, should be a positive number. The current situation is that several years of positive U.S. capital account balances have accumulated and put the United States into a net debtor position. Whether this will continue, and what costs it will bring, have yet to be determined.

Summary

In order to translate the prices of foreign goods, services, and investments into a domestic money, an exchange rate is needed. An exchange rate is the number of units of one country's money that is equivalent to one unit of another country's money. In the past, exchange rates were often fixed because they were tied to the value of the gold backing a country's money. When the gold backing was reduced, devaluation occurred.

Today, most exchange rates are flexible and continually changing because they are determined by supply and demand. The demand curve for a country's money by those holding another country's money is downward sloping, and the supply curve for a country's money is upward sloping.

Foreign exchange markets are the mechanisms through which the monies of different nations are traded and exchange rates are determined. When an exchange rate changes, one nation's money becomes worth more in terms of another nation's money, and one becomes worth less. Changes in

---

[8] Roger Cohen, "Brazil Stays Buoyant, Mexico Is Dispirited in the Face of Troubles," *The Wall Street Journal,* March 24, 1987, pp. 1, 14.

exchange rates affect economic conditions through their effects on the prices of exports, imports, and financial and real assets.

Any factor that causes demand and/or supply in a foreign exchange market to change will alter the exchange rate, as well as the amount of money traded. Some important factors affecting the demand for and/or supply of a foreign money include the popularity of imports and exports, economic conditions in either the importing or exporting nation, real interest rates that can be obtained on investments in other countries, and intervention in foreign exchange markets by governments or central banks.

All international transactions that cause payment outflows or inflows are of economic importance. For accounting and analysis purposes, these transactions are placed into different categories, the most important of which are the current account and the capital account.

The current account includes the balance of trade, as well as figures for investment income, unilateral transfers, and the like. When the current account balance is a negative number, more dollars have flowed out than foreign payments have flowed in, and a current account deficit exists. When the current account balance is a positive number, more foreign payments have flowed in than dollars have flowed out, resulting in a current account surplus. In recent years, a substantial balance of trade deficit has contributed to a negative current account balance and caused serious concern in the United States.

The capital account records payment flows for financial and real assets. It has a positive balance when more money flows into the United States for stocks, bonds, real estate, and the like than flows out of the United States for foreign assets. A positive capital account balance may be the result of a negative current account balance. The categorizing of international payments also includes figures for government intervention into U.S. and foreign currency exchange markets, and a measure for statistical discrepancy that allows all payments to balance.

Several nations have accumulated large external debts that may be beyond their abilities to repay. The external debt crisis presents problems for both lending and borrowing countries. Significant opportunity costs exist whether the debt is repaid or not.

Key Terms and Concepts

Exchange rate	Current account
Fixed exchange rates	Current account deficit (surplus)
Devaluation	Balance of trade
Flexible (floating) exchange rates	Balance of trade deficit (surplus)
Foreign exchange market	Capital account
Exchange rate determination	Official reserve account
Real rate of interest	External debt

Review Questions

1. Would the value of the dollar, compared to the Swiss franc, increase or decrease if the exchange rate went from 1.3 francs = $1.00 to 1.2 francs = $1.00? Why?

2. Explain why, under a fixed exchange rate system, devaluation of a nation's currency could increase the demand for that nation's exports and decrease the demand by that nation for imports.

3. Why is the demand curve for a money in a foreign exchange market downward sloping, and why is the supply curve upward sloping?

4. Illustrate graphically how the exchange rate for a money is determined in a flexible exchange rate system, and show how the rate would be affected by an increase and a decrease in demand, and by an increase and a decrease in supply.

5. Into which major transactions category would each of the following be classified? How would each transaction affect payment flows into or out of the United States?
   a. The purchase of U.S. Treasury securities by a Canadian bank
   b. The sale of U.S. grain to the USSR
   c. A gift of cash from a family in Pennsylvania to relatives in Poland
   d. The purchase of a Volvo by a family in Vermont
   e. The purchase of stock in a Swiss company by an economics professor in Chicago

6. What are some major components of the current account category? Give some examples of international transactions that would cause a positive dollar amount to register in the current account and examples that would cause a negative dollar amount to register in the current account.

7. What is an external debt and what opportunity costs does its repayment impose on a highly indebted country?

Discussion Questions

1. Locate a recent listing of foreign exchange rates. (These are given in *The Wall Street Journal* and many other major newspapers.) Compare the recent rates with those given in Table 17.1. Are there any instances in which the rate has changed substantially? If so, give your opinion as to what factors might have caused such a change.

2. Perform the required calculation in each of the following.
   a. How many German marks would have to be converted to dollars for a person in Berlin to purchase a $21,000 U.S. automobile if the exchange rate were 1.5 marks = $1.00?
   b. How many marks would have to be converted to dollars to purchase the $21,000 automobile after the exchange rate changed to 1.2 marks = $1.00?

    c. How many dollars would have to be converted to marks for a person in Los Angeles to purchase a 60,000 mark German automobile if the exchange rate were 1.5 marks = $1.00?

    d. How many dollars would have to be converted to marks to purchase the 60,000 mark automobile after the exchange rate changed to 1.2 marks = $1.00?

3. What would be some advantages and disadvantages of a fixed exchange rate system and of a flexible exchange rate system?

4. Explain how each of the following developments, taken alone, would affect the value of the dollar. Use supply and demand analysis in your answer.

    a. A global image that goods produced in the United States are of inferior quality

    b. A large federal government budget deficit that raises real interest rates in the United States

    c. Intervention by the Federal Reserve in foreign exchange markets that results in dollars moving into those markets

    d. A poor harvest in most of the grain-producing countries of the world except the United States

    e. The expectation of war between several Middle Eastern countries

5. The United States has primarily experienced balance of trade deficits since the early 1970s, and serious deficits since 1984. What could be the short-term and long-term effects if this condition persists? What policy actions would you recommend to reverse this trend?

6. Suppose that a country's officials were trying to decide whether to incur external debt or to borrow from the country's own citizens. What difference would it make to the country whether repayment of the debt was to outsiders or to its own citizens?

7. What problems would arise if a developing country defaulted on its external debt? Who would be hurt? What policies would you recommend to ease the external debt crisis, and what would be the effects of these policies on borrowing countries?

Critical Thinking Case 17

■ Japan's Buying of U.S. Securities

Critical Thinking Skills | Recognizing stereotypes and clichés
| Making informed judgments

Economic Concepts | Capital account transactions
| Exchange rates
| External debt

Tokyo—It's 9:25 on a Friday night, but here at North Chukin Bank, about 50 Japanese men in shirt sleeves are staring into computer terminals, preparing to alter the course of U.S. interest rates.

In five minutes, the monthly employment numbers will be announced in Washington. If the employment figure is too big, the Japanese traders will suspect inflation is on the rise and sell U.S. Treasury bonds. That, multiplied by similar actions in dozens of other trading rooms across the city, could [change] interest rates for the U.S. government, U.S. home buyers and U.S. corporations.

More than ever before, U.S. interest rates are made in Japan. Large financial institutions here have become such huge players in American markets that Wall Street analysts constantly fret over whether "the Japanese" will participate in a coming Treasury auction or whether they will divert their money to Europe.

Some analysts argue this dependence has made American markets more volatile. Single Japanese institutions control huge blocks of money, and can, if they choose, pull out quickly. Such scare scenarios, however, are largely overstated. . . . And a closer look at the recent role of Japanese money in American markets suggests that, if anything, the Japanese have had a stabilizing influence.

For one thing, Japanese investors are by nature conservative and reluctant to make rapid moves. Also, they, as well as other investors, still view the U.S. as a safe investment haven. "The world's mattress is right here in our markets, and I don't see anything on the horizon that will change that," says Treasury Secretary Nicholas Brady.

Moreover, many large Japanese institutions still respond to the wishes of the bureaucrats at the Ministry of Finance. In times of disruption in the U.S. market, such as October 1987 and October 1989, a few judiciously-placed phone calls from the ministry can prove enormously helpful. "Most people in this business are guessing that the Ministry helped the U.S. market on Black Monday [October 19, 1987 when the stock market dropped by the largest amount ever] by requesting insurance funds and trust banks to buy and support the market," says [one observer].

Still, U.S. dependence on Japanese money remains unsettling. Analysts say that a collapse of Japan's staggeringly high land prices, for instance, could force Japanese investors to bring their money home, with devastating effects on the U.S. economy. Similarly, a shattering earthquake in Tokyo, like the one in 1923, would have "a major impact on the U.S.," according to a study by Tokai bank.

"It's kind of scary for the U.S. to depend on Japan for its capital," says Akio Mikuni, president of a bond-rating firm in Tokyo. "It's quite dangerous for U.S. financing."

Questions

1. Many people are concerned about the extent to which foreign interests own U.S. securities. What are some of the popularly expressed concerns about foreign ownership of U.S. securities and to what extent do stereotypes and clichés underlie those concerns? What issues raised in this article should be balanced against each other before making an informed judgment about the desirability of foreign ownership of U.S. securities?

2. How would legislation prohibiting further foreign ownership of U.S. securities affect exchange rates, the value of those securities, payments accounts, and the external debt of the United States? Would you support such legislation? Why?

Source: Alan Murray, "Japan's Buying of U.S. Securities May Add Stability, Not Volatility," *The Wall Street Journal,* June 19, 1990, p. A12. Reprinted by permission of The Wall Street Journal, © Dow Jones & Company, Inc., 1990. All rights reserved worldwide.

Suggested Readings

E. Gerald Corrigan, "Reforming the U.S. Financial System: An International Perspective," Federal Reserve Bank of New York, *Quarterly Review,* Spring 1990, pp. 1–14.
A statement by the New York Federal Reserve Bank president about the U.S. financial system with reference to financial systems in other countries.

John Dornberg, "The Spreading Might of Deutsche Bank," *The New York Times Magazine,* part 2, *The Business World,* September 23, 1990, pp. 28–30, 60–61.
Describes the operation of a large German bank and how it participates in foreign financial markets.

Urban C. Lehner and Alan Murray, "Strained Alliance," *The Wall Street Journal,* June 19, 1990, pp. A1, A12.
An article on controversies surrounding Japanese investment in the United States.

Carolyn Lockhead, "Debtors, Bankers in Woeful Chorus," *Insight Magazine,* August 31, 1987, pp. 8–11.
Chronicles conditions that created the external debt crisis.

Arthur J. Rolnick and Warren E. Weber, *A Case for Fixing Exchange Rates* **(Minneapolis, Minn.: Federal Reserve Bank of Minneapolis, 1989).**
An argument that floating exchange rates have not performed as expected, and that a fixed exchange rate system could work.

Daniel Rosen, *The Basics of Foreign Trade and Exchange* **(New York: Federal Reserve Bank of New York).**
Discusses comparative advantage, foreign exchange trading, changes in exchange rates, and other topics in international trade and finance.

James F. Tucker, *You and Foreign Money* **(Richmond, Va.: Federal Reserve Bank of Richmond, 1990).**
A booklet on foreign currency, exchange rates, international payments, and other topics.

Beth V. Yarbrough and Robert M. Yarbrough, *The World Economy: Trade and Finance* **(Hinsdale, Ill.: The Dryden Press, 1988).**
A textbook that focuses on the theoretical principles basic to international economics.

Glossary

Acquisition (merger) The acquiring of one company by another company; can be accomplished by buying a controlling amount of stock.

Actual reserves A financial depository institution's reserve account plus its vault cash.

AFL-CIO (American Federation of Labor-Congress of Industrial Organizations) An organization for furthering the common interests of labor unions; does not engage in bargaining with management.

Antitrust laws Laws designed to promote the operation of market forces by prohibiting certain practices that reduce competition.

Assumption A condition held to be true, usually in a model; forms the framework within which a theory is explained.

Automatic stabilization Automatic changes in taxes and/or government expenditures that occur as the level of economic activity changes and that help to control unemployment or demand-pull inflation; important automatic stabilizers include some transfer payments, especially unemploy-ment compensation and the personal income tax.

Average total cost The cost per unit of output produced; determined by dividing total cost by the number of units of output produced.

Balanced budget A government's total outlays equal its total revenues.

Balanced Budget and Emergency Deficit Control Act of 1985 Also known as the Gramm-Rudman-Hollings Act; legislation designed to reduce the federal deficit annually until 1993 when it is to be eliminated.

Balance of trade The figure that results when a country's merchandise imports are subtracted from its exports.

Balance of trade deficit The value of a country's merchandise imports is greater than the value of its exports.

Balance of trade surplus The value of a country's merchandise exports is greater than the value of its imports.

Bank holding company A corporation formed for the purpose of owning, or holding, the controlling shares of stock in a bank or banks.

Barriers to entry Factors that keep firms from entering a market; can be financial, legal, technical, or other barriers.

Barter system A system where goods and services are exchanged directly rather than for money; occurs where a medium of exchange does not exist and requires a coincidence of wants.

Base year The year against which prices in other years are compared in a price index; assigned the number 100.0 in a price index.

Basic economic decisions Choices that must be made in every economy; include (1) what goods and services to produce and in what quantities; (2) how to produce these goods and services; and (3) who receives the production.

Black market An illegal market that sometimes emerges when price or quantity restrictions are imposed in a free market.

Board of Governors–Federal Reserve System Seven-member board heading the Federal Reserve System; develops objectives pertaining to monetary policy and banking and other financial institutional practices, and determines the appropriate policies to be followed to meet those objectives.

Bond A financial instrument through which a corporation or a government unit can borrow long-term funds; sold in $1,000 denominations with a specified interest rate and maturity date (date on which the bond is redeemed); a debt instrument.

Branch banking The operation of more than one facility by a bank to perform its functions.

Business An organization established for the purpose of producing and selling goods and services; may be legally organized as a proprietorship, partnership, or corporation.

Business cycles Recurring periods of growth and decline (or expansion and contraction) in an economy's real output, or real GNP.

Capital Man-made items such as machinery and equipment used in the production of goods and services.

Capital account A category of international transactions that records the purchase and sale of financial and real assets between the United States and other nations.

Capital goods Goods, such as machinery and equipment, that are used to produce other goods and services.

Capital-intensive production Production that emphasizes capital inputs.

Capitalism An economic system based on private property and free enterprise; economic decision making occurs in a market environment.

Cartel An arrangement whereby sellers formally join together in a market to make decisions as a group on pricing and such; the behavior of a cartel is like that of a monopoly.

Celler-Kefauver Act (1950) Federal antitrust statute concerned with anticompetitive mergers and acquisitions of firms; amends Section Seven of the Clayton Act.

Change in demand A change in the demand schedule for a product, or a shift in the product's demand curve; caused by a change in a nonprice influence on demand.

Change in labor demand or supply A shift in the demand or supply curve for labor caused by changes in nonwage factors.

Change in quantity demanded A change in the amount of a product demanded that is caused by a change in its price; represented by a movement along a demand curve from one price-quantity point to another.

Change in quantity supplied A change in the amount of a product supplied that is caused by a change in its price; represented by a movement along a supply curve from one price-quantity point to another.

Change in supply A change in the supply schedule for a product, or a shift in the product's supply curve; caused by a change in a nonprice influence on supply.

Change in the quantity of labor demanded or supplied A change in the amount of labor demanded or supplied that occurs when the wage rate changes; represented by a movement along the demand or supply curve.

Charter The legal document that creates a corporation.

Circular flow model A diagram showing the real and money flows between households and businesses, and the relationships between households and businesses in output, or product, markets and input, or resource, markets.

Classical economics Popularly accepted theory prior to the Great Depression of the 1930s; says the economy will automatically operate at full employment.

Clayton Act (1914) Federal antitrust statute prohibiting specific activities, such as exclusionary practices, that substantially reduce competition or create a monopoly.

Collective bargaining The process through which a union and management negotiate a labor contract.

Combinations and conspiracies in restraint of trade Practices carried out jointly by two or more firms that unreasonably restrict competition.

Command (planned) economy Decisions are made by command rather than by individual businesses and households.

Commercial bank An institution that holds and maintains checking accounts, or demand deposits, for its customers, makes commercial (business) and other loans, and performs other functions.

Commodity monetary standard Exists when an economy's money is backed by something of tangible value such as gold or silver.

Common stock Stock that pays a dividend dependent upon the profit position of a firm after all other financial obligations have been met.

Comparative advantage One country has a lower opportunity cost of producing a good or service than does another country.

Conglomerate A corporation that owns other corporations that produce unrelated goods and services.

Conglomerate merger A firm joins with another firm that is not a competitor, supplier, or distributor.

Constant GNP Real GNP; GNP with the effect of inflation removed from the figures; measures real production.

Constant returns to scale A range of production levels in the long run through which long-run average total cost neither increases nor decreases but is constant.

Consumer goods Goods, such as food and household furniture, that are produced for final buyers.

Consumer price index (CPI) Measures changes in the prices of goods and services that consumers typically purchase, such as food, shelter, clothing, and medical care.

Corporation A legal entity owned by stockholders that can carry on in its own name some functions of business normally performed by individuals.

Correspondent banking An interbank relationship involving deposits and various services.

Cost-benefit analysis The formal study of the process of balancing costs and benefits.

Cost-of-living adjustment (COLA) An arrangement whereby an individual's wages automatically increase with inflation.

Cost-plus pricing Prices are designed to generate enough revenue to cover operating costs plus a fair return to stockholders.

Cost-push inflation Caused by pressure originating from the sellers' side of the market, particularly from increases in costs of production.

Craft union A labor union that represents workers with a specific skill or craft.

Creative destruction New, technologically advanced machinery and processes cause the disuse and ultimate disappearance of old machinery and methods.

Crowding out When borrowing by the federal government increases the interest rate and reduces borrowing by households and businesses.

Currency Coins and paper money.

Current account The category of international transactions that records figures for imports and exports of merchandise, unilateral transfers, and other foreign dealings.

Current account deficit (surplus) A negative (positive) figure results when all current account transactions are added together.

Current GNP Money GNP; measures the value of production in terms of prices at the time of production.

Cyclical unemployment Involuntary unemployment that results from a downswing in the business cycle, or a recession.

Debt service The cost of maintaining a debt; generally measured in interest costs.

Decrease in demand A change in a nonprice influence on demand causes less of a product to be demanded at each price; the demand curve shifts to the left.

Decrease in supply A change in a nonprice influence on supply causes less of a product to be supplied at each price; the supply curve shifts to the left.

Deficit budget A government's expenditures are greater than its revenues; has an expansionary or inflationary impact on the economy and is appropriate for controlling unemployment.

Deflation A sustained decrease in the general level of prices.

Demand A buyer's plan giving the amounts of a product that would be purchased at different prices in a defined time period when all nonprice factors are held constant.

Demand curve A line on a graph that illustrates a demand schedule; slopes downward because of the inverse relationship between price and quantity demanded.

Demand curve for labor Downward-sloping curve showing the different amounts of labor demanded at different wage rates; equal to the marginal revenue product of labor.

Demand deposits Checking account balances kept primarily at commercial banks.

Demand-pull inflation Caused by pressure on prices originating from the buyers' side of the market; tends to occur when buyers' demands (or spending) are greater than the abilities of sellers to supply goods and services.

Demand schedule A list of the amounts of a product that a buyer would purchase at different prices in a defined time period when all nonprice factors are held constant.

Depository Institutions Deregulation and Monetary Control Act (1980) Legislation that altered the traditional roles of many financial institutions by permitting different types of depository institutions to perform nearly identical functions; increased the control of the Federal Reserve System over nonmember depository institutions.

Deregulation Establishing policies to lessen the amount of government regulatory control of an industry or activity.

Derived demand The demand for a factor of production depends on, or is derived from, the demand for the good or service the factor produces.

Devaluation When the amount of gold backing a nation's monetary unit is reduced; associated with a fixed exchange rate system.

Differentiated outputs The products of competing firms are different and can be recognized as such by buyers.

Direct relationship Occurs when two variables move in the same direction: when one increases, so does the other; graphs as an upward-sloping line.

Discount rate The interest rate that a Federal Reserve Bank charges a financial depository institution for borrowing reserves.

Discouraged workers Persons who drop out of the labor force because they have been unsuccessful in finding a job for a long period of time.

Discretionary fiscal policy
Deliberate changes in taxes and/or government expenditures to control unemployment or demand-pull inflation.

Discrimination Unequal treatment in a labor market because of an employer's perception of a category to which a worker belongs.

Diseconomies of scale Occur when the increasing size of production in the long run causes the per unit cost of production to rise.

Disinflation A slowdown in the rate of inflation.

Distribution of income The way in which income is divided among the members of a society.

Dual banking system The label given to the U.S. banking system because both the federal and state governments have the right to charter banks.

Dumping Selling a product in a foreign market below cost or below the price of the product in its own domestic market.

Durable good A good that has a useful lifetime of over one year.

Easy money policy A policy by the Federal Reserve to increase excess reserves of depository institutions in an effort to increase spending and reduce unemployment; carried out primarily through Fed purchases of government securities in the open market and/or a reduction in the reserve requirement and/or a reduction in the discount rate.

Econometrics The use of statistical techniques to test and describe the relationships between economic variables.

Economic cost of production Includes all explicit and implicit costs from producing a good or service; includes a normal profit.

Economic growth An increase in an economy's full production, or full employment, output level over time.

Economic policy An action taken to change an economic condition.

Economic profit, loss, breaking even Occurs when price is greater than average total cost, less than average total cost, or equal to average total cost, respectively.

Economics The study of how scarce, or limited, resources are used to satisfy unlimited material wants and needs.

Economic system The way in which an economy is organized to deal with scarcity; defined by the method chosen to make the basic economic choices.

Economic theory A formal explanation of the relationships between economic variables.

Economies of scale Occur when the increasing size of production in the long run causes the per unit cost of production to fall, or each unit of output to be produced more cheaply.

Efficiency Producing the largest possible output of a desired quality with a given set of resources; producing a good or service at its lowest possible cost.

Efficient method of production The least-cost method of production.

Elasticity coefficient The absolute value of the percentage change in quantity demanded or supplied divided by the absolute value of the percentage change in price; demand or supply is price elastic when the coefficient is greater than one, price inelastic when the coefficient is less than one, and unitary price elastic when the coefficient equals one.

Embargo A ban on trade in a particular commodity with another country.

Employment Act of 1946
Legislation giving the federal government the right and responsibility to provide an environment for the achievement of full employment, full production, and stable prices.

Entrepreneurship The function of organizing resources for production and taking the risk of success or failure in a productive enterprise.

Equation of exchange $MV = PQ$; illustrates how changes in the supply of money (M) influence the level of prices (P) and/or the output of goods and services (Q).

Equilibrium (in the macroeconomy) Occurs when the amount of total planned spending on new goods and services equals total output in the economy.

Equilibrium price The price at which demand equals supply in a market; shown by the intersection of the demand and supply curves in a graph; the price toward which a free market automatically moves. At the equilibrium price there are no shortages or surpluses.

Equilibrium quantity The quantity at which demand equals supply in a market; shown by the intersection of the demand and supply curves in a graph; the quantity toward which a free market automatically moves.

Equity Justice or fairness in the distribution of goods and services.

European Community (EC) The single unified market formed by the majority of Western European nations in 1992; a major trading power.

Excess, or economic, profit Profit received beyond normal profit; not considered an economic cost of production.

Excess reserves Actual reserves of a financial depository institution over the amount it is required to maintain; actual reserves minus required reserves.

Exchange rate The number of units of a nation's money that is equal to one unit of another nation's money.

Exclusionary practices Practices whereby a seller attempts to prevent its suppliers or buyers from dealing with a competitor.

Expectations Anticipations of future economic activity; expectations of a recession can prompt households and businesses to take actions that cause a recession, and expectations of inflation can prompt actions that cause inflation.

Explicit costs Payments that a business makes to outsiders to acquire factors of production such as labor, raw materials, and machinery.

Exports Goods and services that are produced in one country and sold to someone in another country.

External debt Money owed by borrowers in one country to lenders in other countries.

Externality The effect of an action that falls on a person or thing that was not one of the primary parties to the action; the effect may benefit (create a positive externality) or cost (create a negative externality) the affected person or thing.

Factors of production (resources) Persons and things used to produce goods and services; limited in nature; categorized as labor, capital, land, and entrepreneurship.

Federal Deposit Insurance Corporation (FDIC) A government agency established in 1933 to insure deposits in

commercial banks up to a specified amount.

Federal Funds market The market in which banks borrow reserves from other banks; interest rate charged is called the federal funds rate.

Federal Reserve Banks Twelve banks, located in different parts of the country, that deal with commercial banks and other financial depository institutions. Each bank supervises and examines Federal Reserve System member banks, maintains and services reserve accounts, puts coins and paper money into circulation, clears checks, and serves as a fiscal agent for the U.S. government. Each bank is an independent corporation with its own board of directors.

Federal Reserve Notes Paper money issued by the Federal Reserve Banks; includes almost all paper money in circulation.

Federal Reserve System Created in 1913, coordinates commercial banking operations, regulates some aspects of all depository institutions, and oversees the U.S. money supply; organized on both a geographic and functional basis.

Federal Savings and Loan Insurance Corporation (FSLIC) A federal agency established in 1934 to insure deposits in savings and loan institutions; the FDIC took over many of its functions when the FSLIC was dissolved in 1989.

Federal Trade Commission Act (1914) Created the Federal Trade Commission and empowered it to prevent unfair methods of competition, which include antitrust violations.

Financial depository institutions Organizations, such as banks or savings and loans, that exist primarily to accept and maintain deposit accounts and to make

loans; money is created through the loan making of these institutions that serve as the vehicle for expanding and contracting the money supply.

Financial institutions Organizations such as banks, savings and loans, and insurance companies, that provide a means for channeling saving into borrowing.

Fiscal policy Changing federal taxes and/or government expenditures to control unemployment or demand-pull inflation; may be discretionary or automatic.

Fixed cost The cost of a fixed factor of production; applies only to the short run.

Fixed exchange rates Exchange rates that do not fluctuate or fluctuate very little because the values of nations' monies are defined in terms of gold, especially for the purpose of exchanging foreign currencies.

Fixed factors Factors of production that do not change in amount as the level of production increases or decreases; as long as some factors of production are fixed, a business operates in a short-run time frame.

Flat tax A proportional tax; a tax equal to the same percentage of income regardless of the size of the income.

Flexible (floating) exchange rates Exchange rates that fluctuate because they are determined by the forces of demand and supply.

Foreign exchange market A market for the trading, or exchange, of two nations' monies.

Free enterprise The right of a business to make its own decisions and to operate with a profit motive.

Free trade Goods and services can be exported and imported by anyone in any country with no restrictions.

Frictional unemployment Occurs when people are voluntarily out of work and in the process of seeking a new job.

Full employment In an overall sense, it refers to a condition where all available factors of production are employed. As pertains to the labor force, it occurs when only those voluntarily out of work are unemployed, or the unemployment rate drops to a level that includes only frictional unemployment; currently full employment occurs when approximately 94–95% of the labor force is employed.

Full employment budget The budget position of the federal government if the economy were to reach full employment.

Full production Occurs when an economy is producing at its maximum capacity, or when it is experiencing full employment.

Functions of money Money serves as a medium of exchange, measure of value, and method for storing wealth and delaying payments.

Garn–St. Germain Act (1982) Act strengthening the deregulatory trend started with the Monetary Control Act of 1980; reinforced similarities among financial depository institutions.

General Agreement on Tariffs and Trade (GATT) An international forum for negotiating tariffs.

General partner An owner of a partnership who is subject to unlimited liability; every partnership must have at least one general partner.

Glasnost A policy of openness allowing greater freedoms in the USSR.

GNP deflator A composite price index that measures price changes for the entire economy; includes goods and services purchased by households, businesses, and the government.

GNP gap The difference between actual GNP and the GNP that could be produced with full employment.

Government expenditures Dollar outlays by government units; includes purchases of goods and services, transfer payments, interest on money borrowed, expenses incurred in operating public enterprises, and intergovernmental grants.

Government purchases of goods and services Government spending for new goods and services; nonincome-determined spending.

Government regulation Government participation, through various agencies and commissions, in business decision making; may be industry regulation or social regulation.

Gramm-Rudman-Hollings Act of 1985 The Balanced Budget and Emergency Deficit Control Act of 1985, which is legislation designed to reduce the federal deficit annually until 1993 when it is to be eliminated.

Graph An illustration showing the relationship between two variables that are measured on the vertical and horizontal axes.

Gross national product (GNP) A dollar figure that measures the value of all finished goods and services produced in an economy in one year.

Holding company A corporation formed for the purpose of owning or holding stock in other corporations.

Horizontal integration A corporation owns other corporations that compete in the same market.

Horizontal merger Two or more sellers competing in the same market join together.

Household A person living alone or a group of related or unrelated persons who occupy a house, apartment, separate group of rooms, or other such housing unit; along with businesses and government, households are one of the basic decision-making units in the economy.

Human capital investment An expenditure made to improve the productivity of a person; examples include expenditures on education, training, and health care.

Hyperinflation Extremely rapid increases in the general level of prices.

Implicit costs Payments that a business must make to its owner(s) to cover the costs of an owner's factors that could be used in alternative production opportunities; must be paid if the business is to remain in operation; normal profit.

Imports Goods and services sold in one country that are produced in another country.

Income-determined spending Household spending on new goods and services that comes from income earned from producing goods and services.

Increase in demand A change in a nonprice influence on demand causes more of a product to be demanded at each price; the demand curve shifts to the right.

Increase in supply A change in a nonprice influence on supply causes more of a product to be supplied at each price; the supply curve shifts to the right.

Indexing Factor, transfer, and/or other payments are automatically increased as prices rise.

Individual firm's demand curve Shows the amounts of an individual firm's product that buyers are willing to purchase at particular prices.

Industrial Revolution A time period during which an economy becomes industrialized; characterized by social and technological changes such as the growth and development of factories.

Industrial union A labor union that represents all workers in a specific industry regardless of the type of job performed.

Industry A group of firms producing similar products.

Industry regulation Regulation affecting several aspects of the operations of firms in a particular industry; influences pricing, entry of new sellers, conditions of service, and so on.

Infant industry An industry in an early stage of its development.

Inflation An increase in the general level of prices.

Infrastructure Capital systems such as highways, pipelines, and communications networks.

Injections into the spending stream Spending that comes from a source other than household earned income; includes household spending from borrowing and transfer payments, business investment spending, government purchases of goods and services, and export expenditures.

Input markets (resource markets) Markets in which the factors of production are bought and sold; households are sellers and businesses are buyers.

Interest Income return to the owners of capital.

Interest rate The price of money; determines the return to savers and lenders of money, and the cost to borrowers; a percentage of the amount saved or borrowed.

Interlocking directorates The same person sits on the boards of directors of different corporations.

International Monetary Fund (IMF) An international organization that provides loans and other financial assistance to countries.

International trade The buying and selling of goods and services among different countries.

Interstate banking The performance of banking services in more than one state by a single organization.

Inventory Stock of goods on hand; can be intentional or unintentional inventory.

Inverse relationship Two variables move in opposite directions: when one increases, the other decreases; graphs as a downward-sloping line.

Investment spending Business spending on new goods such as machinery, equipment, and buildings; influenced by the expected rate of profit and other factors such as the interest rate; nonincome-determined spending. Because of its fluctuations, it is a primary cause of changes in economic activity.

Invisible hand doctrine Adam Smith's concept that producers acting in their own self-interest will provide buyers with what they want, and thus advance the interests of society.

Joint venture A cooperative effort by two or more firms that is limited in scope.

Junk bonds Corporate bonds issued to finance the acquisition of a business and backed mainly by the expectation that the business will succeed; considered to be risky investments.

Keynes, John Maynard (1883–1946) British economist who focused on the role of aggregate spending in determining economic activity; his most famous work was *The General Theory of Employment, Interest and Money,* published in 1936.

Keynesian economics Based on the work of John Maynard Keynes, who focused on the role of aggregate spending in determining the level of macroeconomic activity; replaced classical economic theory as the dominant macroeconomic theory; basis of much current macroeconomic theory.

Keynesians Advocates of the work of John Maynard Keynes; generally believe in stabilizing the economy through the use of fiscal policy.

Kinked demand curve An oligopoly pricing model based on the assumption that rival firms will not follow price increases but will follow price decreases; illustrates that as a seller's price rises the amount of its product demanded decreases substantially, but as its price falls the amount demanded increases only slightly.

L The broadest definition of the money supply; includes M3 plus commercial paper, U.S. savings bonds, short-term Treasury securities, and other items.

Labor All physical and mental human effort used to produce goods and services.

Labor force All persons 16 years of age and older who are working or actively seeking work.

Labor-intensive production Production that is strongly dependent on labor inputs.

Laissez-faire capitalism Capitalism with little or no government interference.

Land Productive inputs that originate in nature, such as coal and fertile soil.

Law of Demand There is an inverse relationship between the price of a product and the quantity demanded: when price increases, quantity demanded falls, and when price decreases, quantity demanded increases.

Law of Diminishing Marginal Utility As additional units of an item are consumed, beyond some point each successive unit of the item consumed will add less to total utility than was added by the unit consumed just before it.

Law of Diminishing Returns As additional units of a variable factor are added to a fixed factor, beyond some point the additional product from each additional unit of the variable factor decreases.

Law of Supply There is a direct relationship between the price of a product and the quantity supplied: when price increases or decreases, quantity supplied increases or decreases, respectively.

Leadership pricing One firm in a market charges a price that the other firms in the market then adopt.

Leakages from the spending stream Uses for earned income other than spending on domestically produced goods and services, such as taxes, saving, and import expenditures.

Least-cost (efficient) method of production The method of production that allows a good or service to be produced at the lowest cost.

Leveraged buyout (LBO) A business acquired mainly with borrowed funds that are to be paid off by the newly formed company.

Liquidity Ease of converting an asset to its value in cash or readily spendable funds.

Lockout An employer prevents laborers from entering a work site.

Long run A production time frame in which all factors of production are regarded as variable.

Long-run total cost, average total cost, and marginal cost Total cost, per unit cost, and cost per additional unit of output calculated for production in the long run.

Lower price limit A price floor; a government-set minimum price that must be charged for a particular good or service; if the equilibrium price is below the lower price limit, a surplus will develop.

M1 The narrowest definition of the U.S. money supply; includes coins and paper money in circulation, nonbank-issued traveler's checks, most demand deposits at commercial banks, and other checkable deposits.

M2 Definition of the money supply that includes M1 plus money market deposit accounts, savings deposits, time deposits of less than $100,000, money market mutual funds, and other items.

M3 Definition of the money supply that includes M2 plus time deposits of $100,000 and more, and other items.

Macroeconomics The study of the operation of the economy as a whole.

Marginal benefit The change in total satisfaction from consuming each additional unit of a good, service, or activity.

Marginal cost The change in total cost from each additional unit of a good, service, or activity produced.

Marginal physical product The change in total product that

results when an additional unit of labor or other variable resource is utilized.

Marginal revenue The change in total revenue when one more, or additional, unit of an item is demanded.

Marginal revenue product The change in total revenue that results from the sale of output produced when one more unit of labor or other variable resource is utilized.

Marginal utility The change in total satisfaction, or total utility, from consuming each additional unit of a good, service, or activity.

Market A place or situation in which the buyers and sellers of a product interact for the purpose of exchange; firms are in the same market when they produce similar products and compete for the same group of buyers.

Market clearing price The equilibrium price in a market; the price at which supply equals demand and there are no shortages or surpluses.

Market demand The demand in a market for a particular good or service; is composed of all of the individual demands for the product.

Market demand curve The demand curve that results when all buyers in the market are considered together.

Market economy The basic economic decisions are made by the interaction of individual buyers and sellers in a market through the language of price.

Market failure A market system generates a problem or cannot achieve a goal set by society.

Market socialism A socialistic economic system in which some goods and services are allocated through markets, and others are allocated by planners.

Market structures A classification system for grouping markets according to the degree of competition among sellers; the four market structures are pure competition, monopolistic competition, oligopoly, and monopoly.

Market supply The supply of a particular good or service in a market; is found by adding together all individual supply curves or schedules.

Marxian economic theory Based on the work of Karl Marx (1818–1883), who argued that recessions are a symptom of a fundamental flaw in capitalism because the quest for profit by capitalists forces workers out of jobs as they are replaced by machines.

Maximizing rules Used by households and businesses to maximize satisfaction and profit; net benefit or profit is maximized by operating where total benefit or revenue exceeds total cost by the greatest amount, or where marginal benefit or revenue equals marginal cost.

Measure of value A function of money; the value of every good, service, and resource can be expressed in terms of, or as a fraction or multiple of, an economy's basic unit of money.

Medium of exchange The general acceptability of something as payment for goods, services, and resources; the primary function of money.

Mercantilism An economic system or philosophy in which the interests of the nation are of greatest importance; individual interests are subservient to those of the nation.

Merger (acquisition) The acquiring of one company by another company; can be accomplished by buying a controlling amount of stock.

Method for storing wealth and delaying payments The function of money that allows for saving, or storing wealth for future use, and permits credit, or delayed payments.

Microeconomics The study of individual decision-making units and markets within the economy.

Minimum wage law Legislation that specifies the lowest hourly earnings that an employer may pay an employee.

Mixed capitalism An economic system with the basic features of capitalism but with some degree of government intervention in economic decision making.

Mixed economy The basic economic decisions are made through a combination of market and centralized decision making.

Model The setting within which an economic theory is presented.

Monetarism The school of thought that favors stabilizing the economy through controlling the money supply.

Monetarists Advocates of the economic policies of monetarism.

Monetary Control Act of 1980 The Depository Institutions Deregulation and Monetary Control Act; legislation that altered the traditional roles of many financial institutions by permitting different types of depository institutions to perform nearly identical functions; increased the control of the Federal Reserve System over nonmember depository institutions.

Monetary policy Influencing the levels of aggregate output and employment or prices through changes in the money supply; carried out by the Federal Reserve through open market operations, changes in the reserve requirement, and changes in the discount rate.

Monetizing the debt A policy carried out by the Federal Reserve of increasing the money supply to accommodate federal government borrowing; reduces upward pressure on the interest rate.

Money Anything that is generally acceptable as a medium of exchange, or means of payment for goods, services, and resources.

Money GNP (current GNP) Measures the annual value of the production of new goods and services in prices at the time of production.

Money market deposit account (MMDA) An account at a commercial bank or thrift institution that pays interest and allows limited checking privileges.

Money (nominal) income Income stated in terms of current dollars.

Money multiplier The multiple by which an initial change in excess reserves in the depository institutions system can change the money supply; is the reciprocal of the reserve requirement.

Money supply rule The money supply should increase at a constant annual percentage rate regardless of economic conditions.

Monopolistic competition The market structure characterized by a large number of sellers with differentiated outputs and fairly easy entry into and exit from the market.

Monopolization and attempts to monopolize A firm acquires or attempts to acquire a monopoly share of its market through unreasonable means.

Monopoly market A market with one seller that maintains its position because entry by new sellers is impossible.

Multiplier effect The change in total output and income generated by a change in nonincome-determined spending is larger than, or a multiple of, the spending change itself.

Mutual interdependence Occurs when there are so few sellers in the market that each seller must weigh the actions and reactions of rival sellers in any decision making; associated with oligopoly markets.

National bank A commercial bank incorporated under a federal rather than a state charter; a national bank must belong to the Federal Reserve System.

National debt The total accumulated debt of the federal government due to deficit spending.

National Labor Relations Act (Wagner Act) Legislation, passed in 1935, supportive of unionization; permitted and strengthened collective bargaining, defined unfair labor practices, and set up the NLRB.

National Labor Relations Board (NLRB) Hears complaints on unfair labor practices and orders remedies when appropriate; created by the National Labor Relations Act in 1935.

Natural monopoly A market situation where economies of scale make it more efficient (less costly) to have the entire output of a product come from one large seller rather than several smaller sellers.

Natural rate of unemployment The unemployment rate that would result if cyclical unemployment were eliminated.

Negative externality A cost from an action that falls on a person or thing that was not one of the primary parties to the action.

Net benefit That which results when total cost is subtracted from total benefit.

Net benefit maximizing rules Net benefit is maximized where total benefit exceeds total cost by the greatest amount, or where marginal benefit equals marginal cost.

Net exports Exports minus imports; can be a positive or negative number.

New classical school A return to the basic classical premise that free markets automatically stabilize themselves and that government intervention in the macroeconomy is not advisable.

New Deal A series of programs and legislative reforms instituted during the administration of Franklin D. Roosevelt in the Great Depression of the 1930s.

Nonbank bank A company that can either offer depository accounts or make commercial loans, but cannot do both.

Nondurable good A good that has a short useful lifetime.

Nonincome-determined spending Spending that does not come from household earned income; includes household spending from transfer payments and borrowing, business investment spending, government purchases of goods and services, and export expenditures.

Nonprice competition Firms focus on some feature other than price (for example, quality or a guarantee) in an attempt to attract buyers to their products.

Nonprice factors influencing demand Factors other than price, such as income, taste, and expectations, that help to formulate the demand for a product.

Nonprice factors influencing supply Factors other than price, such as the cost of production and the number of sellers, that help to formulate the supply of a product.

Normal profit The profit necessary to recover implicit costs and to keep a business in operation; considered to be an economic cost of production.

Official reserve account An international payments category that indicates the degree and direction of government and/or central bank intervention in U.S. and foreign currency exchange markets.

Oligopolistic markets Markets dominated by a few large sellers with either differentiated or identical products and where entry by new firms into the market is difficult.

Open Market Committee Determines general policy on the buying and selling of securities by the Federal Reserve System on the open market.

Open market operations The buying and selling of securities, primarily U.S. government securities, on the open market by the Federal Reserve; method most often used by the Fed to change financial depository institutions' excess reserves.

Opportunity cost The cost of acquiring a good or service or taking an action measured in terms of the value of the opportunity or alternative forgone.

Other checkable deposits Interest-bearing accounts, such as NOW and credit union share draft accounts, that are similar to demand deposits and are offered by banks, savings and loans, and other financial institutions.

Output markets (product markets) Markets in which businesses are sellers and households are buyers; consumer goods and services are exchanged.

Paper monetary standard Exists when money is not backed by anything of tangible value such as gold or silver; is backed by confidence in the money and a willingness to accept the money in exchange for goods, services, and resources.

Participation rate The percentage of some specified group that is in the labor force.

Partnership The legal organization of a business that is similar to a proprietorship but has two or more owners.

Peak The phase of the business cycle during which real GNP reaches its maximum.

Perestroika A program of economic reforms to lead the USSR to greater dependence on markets and individual initiative.

Per se violations Anticompetitive agreements between firms where proof of the agreement is sufficient to establish guilt; include agreements to jointly fix prices and divide sales territories.

Personal consumption expenditures Household spending on new goods and services.

Personal income Household gross, or pretax, income; income households use to pay taxes, spend, and save.

Personal taxes Taxes paid by households.

Phases of a business cycle Four stages through which every business cycle goes: recovery, peak, recession, and trough; accordingly, real GNP expands, reaches a maximum, declines, and reaches a minimum.

Phillips curve A curve showing the relationship between an economy's unemployment and inflation rates.

Planned (command) economy The basic economic decisions are made by planners rather than by private individuals and businesses.

Planning failure Centralized planning creates a problem for a society or fails to achieve a society's goals.

Positive externality A benefit from an action that falls on a person or thing that was not one of the primary parties to the action.

Poverty levels Government-designated levels of income that must be received to be considered *not* poor.

Preferred stock Stock that pays a stated dividend to its holders; preferred stockholders are entitled to their dividends before common stockholders are paid.

Price ceiling A government-set maximum price that can be charged for a particular good or service; if the equilibrium price is above the price ceiling, a shortage will develop.

Price discrimination Different buyers acquire the same product from the same seller with the same treatment and service, but pay different prices.

Price elastic A strong response to a price change; occurs when the percentage change in the quantity demanded or supplied is greater than the percentage change in price.

Price elasticity A measure of the strength of a buyer's or seller's response to a price change; a weak response is termed inelastic and a strong response is elastic.

Price fixing Joint action by sellers to influence their product prices; considered to be highly anticompetitive.

Price floor A government-set minimum price that can be charged for a particular good or service; if the equilibrium price is below the price floor, a surplus will develop.

Price index Measures changes in the prices of an item or a group of items using a percentage scale; all figures are compared to a base year that is designated by a value of 100.0 on the price index.

Price inelastic A weak response to a price change; occurs when the percentage change in the quantity demanded or supplied is less than the percentage change in price.

Price searcher A firm that searches its downward-sloping demand curve to find the price-output combination that maximizes its profit or minimizes its loss.

Price system A market system; one in which buyers and sellers communicate their intentions through prices in markets.

Prime rate Interest rate that a commercial bank charges its least risky borrowers for short-term commercial and industrial loans.

Producer price index (PPI) Measures changes in the prices of goods that businesses buy for further processing or for sale to consumers; formerly termed the wholesale price index.

Production The process of creating goods and services.

Production function Shows the type and amount of output that can be produced from certain types and amounts of inputs and a particular production process.

Production possibilities table or curve An illustration of the various amounts of two goods that an economy can produce with full employment and fixed resources and technology.

Productivity Concept of assessing the amount of output produced by an economy's resources; often measured in terms of output per worker.

Product markets (output markets) Markets in which businesses are sellers and households are buyers; consumer goods and services are exchanged.

Profit maximizing rules Profit is maximized at the output level where total revenue exceeds total cost by the greatest amount, or where marginal revenue equals marginal cost.

Profit or loss What results when a business subtracts its total cost from its total revenue; the income return for performing the entrepreneurial function.

Progressive tax There is a direct relationship between the percentage of income taxed and the size of the income.

Property rights Rights to possess and dispose of goods, services, and resources; in capitalism these rights are privately held by individuals.

Proportional tax One that taxes the same percentage from any income regardless of size.

Proprietorship A one-owner business; owner is subject to unlimited liability.

Protectionism The philosophy that it is in the best interest of a country to restrict importing and/or exporting.

Public choice The study of the economic motives and attitudes of voters and public officials, and their effects on collective or government decision making.

Public good A good (or service) provided for all of society; no one is excluded from use of a public good.

Public interest justification for regulation A good or service is so important to the public well-being that its production and distribution should be regulated.

Purely competitive markets Markets with large numbers of independent sellers producing identical products, and with easy entry into and exit from the market.

Quota A restriction on the quantity of an item that can be imported into a country.

Rational expectations A proposition that the effects of macroeconomic policies might be distorted or negated by the adjustment of business and household behavior in anticipation of policy makers' strategies.

Rational ignorance Choosing to remain uninformed because the marginal cost of obtaining the information is higher than the marginal benefit from knowing it.

Real GNP (constant GNP) Current GNP adjusted for inflation; measures real production.

Real income Income measured in terms of the goods and services that can be purchased with a particular amount of money income.

Real rate of interest The nominal, or stated, rate of interest minus the inflation rate; a nominal interest rate adjusted for inflation.

Recession The phase of the business cycle during which real output falls; in general terms it is a period in which an economy's production is falling and unemployment is rising; sometimes used to refer to the condition of an economy when real GNP has fallen for two successive quarters.

Recovery The phase of the business cycle during which real GNP is increasing.

Regressive tax There is an inverse relationship between the percentage of income taxed and the size of the income. A sales tax is a regressive tax.

Regulation Q Determined the maximum interest paid on deposits; phased out during the 1980s.

Rent Income return to the owners of land resources.

Required reserves The amount of actual reserves that a financial depository institution must keep to back its deposits.

Reserve account A deposit in the name of a financial institution that is held at a Federal Reserve Bank or other designated place.

Reserve requirement A specified percentage of deposits that a financial depository institution must keep as actual reserves.

Resolution Trust Company (RTC) The federal agency created to reorganize troubled savings and loans or to deal with their affairs if they have failed and closed.

Resource markets (input markets) Markets in which factors of production are bought and sold; households are sellers and businesses are buyers.

Resources (factors of production) Persons and things used to produce goods and services; limited in availability; categorized as labor, capital, land, and entrepreneurship.

Retained earnings Business savings; the portion of a business's profit that has been retained for investment or other purposes.

Revenue Money that a company receives from selling its product.

Right to work laws State laws prohibiting union membership as a condition of employment.

Robinson-Patman Act (1936) Federal antitrust statute concerned with anticompetitive price discrimination; amends Section Two of the Clayton Act.

Rule of Reason violations Violations of the antitrust laws involving types of agreements between firms that are not necessarily anticompetitive; the challenged restraint on competition must be shown to be unreasonable.

Saving-investment relationship The relationship between the amount saved by households and businesses and the amount returned to the spending stream through investment and household borrowing.

Scarcity The result of not enough material goods and services to satisfy the wants and needs of all individuals, house-holds, businesses, and societies; root of the study of economics.

Sectors A broad classification system for grouping similar types of goods and services and the firms that produce them.

Sherman Act (1890) Original and most broadly worded federal antitrust statute; condemns combinations and conspiracies in restraint of trade, and monopolization and attempts to monopolize.

Shortage Occurs in a market when the quantity demanded is greater than the quantity supplied, or at a price below the product's equilibrium price.

Short run A production time frame in which some factors of production are fixed and some are variable.

Smith, Adam (1723–1790) A Scottish philosopher who wrote *The Wealth of Nations,* 1776, which extolled the benefits of an economic system based on individual decision making; considered to be the most important early spokesman for capitalism.

Social benefits and costs The total effect on society that results from the private benefits, private costs, and externalities of an action.

Socialism An economic system in which many of the factors of production are collectively owned and there is an attempt to equalize the distribution of income.

Social regulation Regulation aimed at correcting a problem found in several industries, such as pollution or job discrimina-tion; not limited to a specific industry.

Special interest group People who share a common position on a particular issue and actively promote that position.

Specialization Resources used in production are concentrated on a narrow range of tasks or on the production of a limited variety of goods and services.

Stagflation Occurs when an economy is experiencing high rates of both inflation and unemployment.

Strike Work stoppage by union members.

Structural unemployment Involuntary unemployment that results when a worker's job is no longer part of the production structure of the economy.

Supply A seller's plan giving the amounts of a product that would be offered for sale at different prices in a defined time period when all nonprice factors are held constant.

Supply curve A line on a graph that illustrates a supply schedule; slopes upward because of the direct relationship between price and quantity supplied.

Supply curve of labor Upward-sloping curve showing the different amounts of labor supplied at different wage rates.

Supply schedule A list of the amounts of a product that a seller would offer for sale at different prices in a defined time period when all nonprice factors are held constant.

Supply-side economics Policies to stimulate the supply side of the market; proposals center on the use of tax policy and regulatory reform to stimulate business investment activity and productivity; popular in the 1980s.

Surplus Occurs in a market when the quantity demanded is less than the quantity supplied, or when the product's price is above the equilibrium price.

Surplus budget A government's revenues are greater than its expenditures; has a contractionary effect on economic activity and is appropriate for controlling demand-pull inflation.

Taft-Hartley Act The 1947 legislation that contains several provisions that limit union activities.

Tariff A tax on an import.

Tax base The object on which a tax is levied; could be income, property, purchases, and the like.

Tax Reform Act of 1986 Major legislation that changed federal income tax exemptions, deductions, brackets, and rates.

Technological change An increase in knowledge about production and its processes.

Technology The body of knowledge that exists about production and its processes.

Territorial division Joint action by sellers to divide sales territories among themselves; considered to be highly anticompetitive.

Tight money policy A policy by the Federal Reserve to reduce excess reserves of depository institutions in an effort to reduce spending and inflationary pressure; carried out primarily through the sale of government securities in the open market by the Fed and/or an increase in the reserve requirement and/or an increase in the discount rate.

Token money Money with a face value greater than the value of the commodity from which it is made.

Total benefit (total utility) The total amount of satisfaction received from consuming a specified number of units of a good, service, or activity.

Total cost Cost of producing a specified number of units of a good, service, or activity.

Total fixed cost The cost of all fixed factors of production; total fixed cost does not change as the level of output changes and must be paid even when output is zero; associated with the short run.

Total revenue Revenue received from selling a certain quantity of an item; calculated by multiplying the price of an item times the quantity demanded at that price.

Total, or aggregate, spending The total combined spending of all units in the economy (households plus businesses plus government plus foreign) for new goods and services; changes in aggregate spending cause changes in aggregate output, employment, and income, and sometimes in the price level.

Total utility The total amount of satisfaction received from consuming a specified number of units of a good, service, or activity.

Total variable cost The cost of all variable factors of production; total variable cost increases as the level of output increases, but is zero when output is zero.

Trade association An organization representing firms in a particular industry that performs certain functions that benefit those firms.

Tradeoff Giving up one thing for something else.

Trade subsidy A government payment to the domestic producer of a good that is exported.

Transfer payment Money from the government for which no direct work is performed in return; examples include Social Security and unemployment compensation.

Trough The phase of the business cycle in which real GNP reaches its minimum after falling during a recession.

Tying contract Contract whereby a buyer can obtain one good from a seller only by purchasing another good as well from the same seller.

Underground economy Productive activities that are not reported for tax purposes and are not included in GNP.

Unemployment A resource available for production is not being used.

Unemployment rate The percentage of the labor force that is unemployed and actively seeking work; can also refer to the percentage of a group in the labor force that is unemployed.

Union An organization of workers that bargains in its members' behalf with management on wages, working conditions, fringe benefits, and other work-related issues.

Unitary price elastic The percentage change in quantity demanded or supplied equals the percentage change in price; elasticity coefficient equals one.

Unlimited liability A business owner's personal assets are subject to use as payment for the business's debts.

Upper price limit A ceiling price; a government-set maximum price that can be charged for a

particular good or service; if the equilibrium price is above the upper price limit, a shortage will develop.

U.S. Treasury bill A U.S. Treasury security that matures in 13, 26, or 52 weeks.

U.S. Treasury bond A U.S. Treasury security that matures in 10 years or longer.

U.S. Treasury note A U.S. Treasury security that matures in 2 to 10 years.

U.S. Treasury security A financial instrument issued by the federal government when it borrows money; states the federal government's promise to make specified interest payments and to repay the loaned funds on a particular date.

Usury law Establishes the maximum rate of interest (an interest ceiling) that can be charged on a particular type of loan.

Utility Satisfaction realized from consuming a good or service; the goal of individual economic decision making is to maximize total utility.

Value judgment The relative importance one assigns to various actions or alternatives.

Value of money Measured by the goods, services, and resources that money can purchase.

Variable factors (and costs) Factors of production that increase and decrease in amount as production increases and decreases; variable costs are the costs of using variable factors.

Velocity of money The average number of times the money supply is turned over in a year in relationship to GNP; GNP divided by the money supply.

Vertical integration A corporation owns other

corporations that supply it inputs or distribute its products.

Vertical merger A firm joins with a supplier or distributor.

Wage Income return to labor; price of labor.

Wage-price controls Mandatory government-imposed restrictions on increases in prices, wages, and other incomes.

Wage-price guideposts Voluntary wage-price restraints sought by the government; also called guidelines.

Wealth A measure of the value of tangible assets; includes items such as real estate and corporate securities.

Answers to
Test Your Understanding Quizzes

Chapter One

The economy's production possibilities curve is shown by the solid line in the figure accompanying these answers.

1. 12 million units of capital goods (opportunity cost of going from 20 to 30 million units of consumer goods); 10 million units of consumer goods (opportunity cost of going from 40 to 45 million units of capital goods).

2. Point A should be somewhat to the left of the production possibilities curve, and point B should be further to the left than point A.

3. The location of point C is subjective and will differ with each student. Point C will be closer to the horizontal axis if capital goods are more important, and closer to the vertical axis if consumer goods are more important.

4. If only consumer goods were produced, no machinery or equipment would be produced to replace what is currently being used, and future production would be adversely affected. If only capital goods were produced, there would be nothing to sustain people currently.

5. The production possibilities curve would shift to the right as illustrated by the dashed line in the accompanying figure.

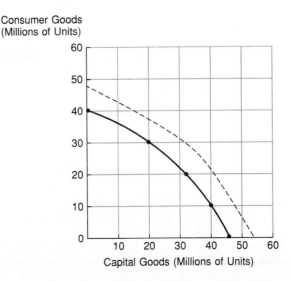

Chapter Two

1. a. pure market

    b. pure planned

    c. mixed

    d. pure market

    e. pure planned

    f. mixed

2. a. There is a flow of money from households to businesses and a flow of goods and services from businesses to households. The decision to save more and spend less will reduce the money flow and the goods and services flow.

    b. There is a flow of factors of production from households to businesses and a flow of income from businesses to households. The actions to reduce the flows on the bottom half will reduce the flows on the top half.

    c. Spending less causes a decrease in the money flow from households to businesses, followed by decreases in goods and services, factors of production, and income flows, respectively.

Chapter Three

1. d; supply curve shifts to the left; increase; decrease

2. a; demand curve shifts to the right; increase; increase

3. d; supply curve shifts to the left; increase; decrease

4. e; no shifts; none; none

5. b; demand curve shifts to the left; decrease; decrease

6. a; demand curve shifts to the right; increase; increase

7. c; supply curve shifts to the right; decrease; increase

8. b; demand curve shifts to the left; decrease; decrease

9. a; demand curve shifts to the right; increase; increase

10. e; no shifts; none; none

11. b; demand curve shifts to the left; decrease; decrease

12. c; supply curve shifts to the right; decrease; increase

13. e; no shifts; none; none

14. c; supply curve shifts to the right; decrease; increase

Chapter Four

1.

Price Index	Price Index
80.0	64.0
100.0	80.0
110.0	88.0
125.0	100.0
130.0	104.0
150.0	120.0

2.

Money GNP	GNP Deflator	Real GNP
$5,000,000	100.0	$5,000,000
6,050,000	110.0	5,500,000
6,250,000	125.0	5,000,000
5,850,000	130.0	4,500,000
9,000,000	150.0	6,000,000
9,300,000	155.0	6,000,000

3. Real GNP 1985: $1,000; 1986: $1,000; 1987: $1,200; 1988: $1,250; 1989: $1,250; 1990: $1,200; 1991: $1,250

   a. The economy's output did not grow from 1985 to 1986, grew from 1986 through 1988, did not grow in 1989, decreased in 1990, and grew again in 1991.

   b. Unlike the impression given by money GNP, the economy's real GNP, or output, did not grow every year, and in 1990 it actually declined. Also, the overall growth rate in output from 1985 through 1991 was not nearly as great as money GNP would lead one to believe.

Chapter Five

From each action taken alone, output and employment would change as follows.

1. increase
2. decrease
3. increase
4. increase

5. decrease

6. no change (demand-pull inflation would result)

7. decrease

8. increase

9. increase

10. no change (demand-pull inflation would result)

11. decrease

12. decrease

13. no change (demand-pull inflation would result)

14. increase

15. decrease

From each of these actions, total output and income would change as follows.

16. increase by $200 million

17. decrease by $87.5 billion

18. increase by $200 million

19. decrease by $12 billion

20. increase by $400 million (80 percent of $100 million transfer payment = $80 million in spending; $80 million divided by 0.20 = $400 million)

Chapter Six

1. output and employment increase

2. no effect on output and employment

3. price levels increase

4. output and employment increase

5. output and employment decrease

6. output and employment decrease

7. output and employment decrease

8. output and employment decrease

9. price levels increase

10. price levels increase

Chapter Seven

1. $887,134

2. $1,801,444

3. $1,956,741

4. $4,840,000

Chapter Eight

1. required reserves = $135,000; actual reserves = $600,500; excess reserves = $465,500

2. new loans = $965,500

3. new borrowing = $5,000

4. money multiplier = 12.5;
   money supply increase = $62,500,000

5. decrease in excess reserves = $33,500

6. new excess reserves = $200,000

Chapter Nine

1 and 2.

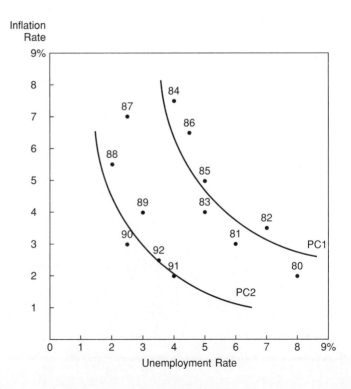

3. Labor force participation rates of groups that have relatively high rates of unemployment, perhaps teenagers, decline, and participation rates for groups that have low unemployment rates increase. These changes could cause the overall rate of unemployment associated with any rate of inflation to fall.

4. Cost-push inflationary pressure decreases. With less pressure on prices coming from the sellers' side of the market, any rate of unemployment would be associated with a lower rate of inflation.

5. Government becomes less generous in its transfer payment policies. With less transfer income, any rate of inflation would be associated with a lower rate of unemployment.

Chapter Ten

1. increase in supply causing equilibrium price to fall

2. increase in demand and a possible decrease in supply causing equilibrium price to rise

3. decrease in demand and a possible increase in supply causing equilibrium price to fall

4. decrease in demand and increase in supply causing equilibrium price to fall

5. increase in supply causing equilibrium price to fall

6. decrease in demand and increase in supply causing equilibrium price to fall

7. increase in demand causing equilibrium price to rise

Chapter Eleven

According to Table 1, which is completed below, Pete should charge $48 and complete 4 drawings to maximize his profit from the drawings. In going for volume, as suggested by his roommate, his total profit would be $80 less than that received from producing and selling 4 drawings.

Table 1   Custom-Drawn Houses

Price per Drawing	Number of Drawings Demanded	Total Revenue	Marginal Revenue	Marginal Cost	Total Cost	Profit
$72	0	$ 0			$ 0	$ 0
			$66	$20		
66	1	66			20	46
			54	20		
60	2	120			40	80
			42	20		
54	3	162			60	102
			30	20		
48	4	192			80	112
			18	20		
42	5	210			100	110
			6	20		
36	6	216			120	96
			−6	20		
30	7	210			140	70
			−18	20		
24	8	192			160	32

As for the lithographs, Pete should charge $90 each and sell 9, earning a total profit of $570. This is indicated in Table 2, which is completed below.

Table 2   Lithographs

Price per Lithograph	Number of Lithographs Demanded	Total Revenue	Marginal Revenue	Marginal Cost	Total Cost	Profit or Loss
$180	0	$ 0			$ 0	$ 0
			$170	$200		
170	1	170			200	−30
			150	5		
160	2	320			205	115
			130	5		
150	3	450			210	240
			110	5		
140	4	560			215	345
			90	5		
130	5	650			220	430
			70	5		
120	6	720			225	495
			50	5		
110	7	770			230	540
			30	5		
100	8	800			235	565
			10	5		
90	9	810			240	570
			−10	5		
80	10	800			245	555

Chapter Twelve

1. a.   92%

    b.   fall, lower, 88%

    c.   fall, lower, 87%

    d.   rise, higher, 88%

2. $2.25; $1.90; $2.29

3.

Output	TFC	TVC	TC	ATC	MC
0	$80	$ 0	$ 80	—	
					$ 40
1	80	40	120	$120	
					20
2	80	60	140	70	
					10
3	80	70	150	50	
					30
4	80	100	180	45	
					50
5	80	150	230	46	
					70
6	80	220	300	50	
					120
7	80	340	420	60	
					180
8	80	520	600	75	

Chapter Thirteen

1. The total revenue values in the table are: $0, $2, $4, $2,000, $2,002, $2,004, $10,000, $10,002, $10,004. All marginal revenue values are $2.00.

   b. 7,000 bushels

   c. $2.50; loss $0.50; loss $3,500

   e. 9,000 bushels

   f. $2.50; profit $1.00; profit $9,000

Figure A

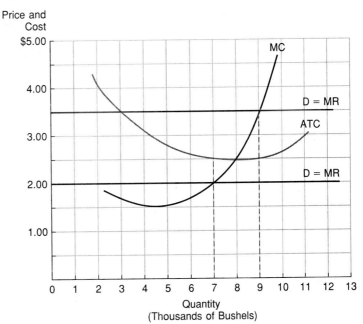

Price and Cost

Quantity
(Thousands of Bushels)

2. 5,000 units; $9.00; $5.00; profit $4.00; profit $20,000

Figure B

Price and
Cost

Chapter Fourteen

1. social regulation—Environmental Protection Agency

2. no government intervention

3. social regulation—Consumer Product Safety Commission

4. antitrust enforcement—Sherman Act Section 1 price fixing violation

5. no government intervention—the sellers are pure competitors responding to the price rather than fixing it

6. industry regulation

7. antitrust enforcement—Celler-Kefauver Act

8. no government intervention

9. industry regulation

10. antitrust enforcement—Sherman Act Section 2 monopolization violation

Chapter Fifteen

In Table 1, marginal physical product is 500, 500, 500, 400, 300.

1. the fourth worker

In Table 3, total revenue is $0, $15, $27.50, $37.50, $42.75, $44. Marginal revenue product is $15, $12.50, $10, $5.25, $1.25.

2. $15.00 per hour

3. $1.25 per hour

4. 4 workers, 1,900 envelopes

In Table 4, the quantity of workers demanded with each wage rate is 1—$15; 2—$12.50; 3—$10; 4—$5.25; 5—$1.25. These numbers are used to plot the demand curve in the figure.

Chapter Sixteen

1. a. ½, 2, Canada

   b. 2, ½, Brazil

   c. 12, 12

   d. 16 of wheat, 16 of soybeans

   e. 8, 8

2. a. ⅕, 4, Mexico

   b. 5, ¼, Venezuela

   c. 525, 200

   d. 1,000 lamps, 200 gallons of gasoline

   e. 50, 200

Chapter Seventeen

1. decrease, decrease, decrease, increase

2. increase, decrease, increase, increase

3. increase, increase, increase, decrease

4. decrease, increase, decrease, decrease

5. increase, increase, increase, decrease

6. decrease, increase, decrease, decrease or increase depending on whether the effect of the change in demand was greater or less than the effect of the change in supply, increase

Index

Definitions of terms appear on page numbers in bold type.